Mesoamerican Figurines

UNIVERSITY PRESS OF FLORIDA

Florida A&M University, Tallahassee
Florida Atlantic University, Boca Raton
Florida Gulf Coast University, Ft. Myers
Florida International University, Miami
Florida State University, Tallahassee
New College of Florida, Sarasota
University of Central Florida, Orlando
University of Florida, Gainesville
University of North Florida, Jacksonville
University of South Florida, Tampa
University of West Florida, Pensacola

Mesoamerican Figurines

Small-Scale Indices of Large-Scale Social Phenomena

EDITED BY
CHRISTINA T. HALPERIN, KATHERINE A. FAUST,
RHONDA TAUBE, AND AURORE GIGUET

University Press of Florida
Gainesville/Tallahassee/Tampa/Boca Raton
Pensacola/Orlando/Miami/Jacksonville/Ft. Myers/Sarasota

Copyright 2009 by Christina T. Halperin, Katherine A. Faust, Rhonda Taube, and Aurore Giguet

Printed in the United States of America. This book is printed on Glatfelter Natures Book, a paper certified under the standards of the Forestry Stewardship Council (FSC). It is a recycled stock that contains 30 percent post-consumer waste and is acid-free. All rights reserved

16 15 14 13 12 11   6 5 4 3 2 1

First cloth printing, 2009
First paperback printing, 2011

Library of Congress Cataloging-in-Publication Data
Mesoamerican figurines : small-scale indices of large-scale social phenomena / edited by Christina T. Halperin . . . [et al.].
p. cm.
Includes bibliographical references and index.
ISBN 978-0-8130-3330-3 (cloth)
ISBN 978-0-8130-3687-8 (paper)

1. Indian pottery—Mexico. 2. Indian pottery—Central America. 3. Maya pottery. 4. Pottery figures—Mexico. 5. Pottery figures—Central America. 6. Indians of Mexico—Antiquities. 7. Indians of Central America—Antiquities. 8. Mayas—Antiquities. I. Halperin, Christina T.
F1219.3.P8M47 2009
972.004'97—dc22   2008054949

The University Press of Florida is the scholarly publishing agency for the State University System of Florida, comprising Florida A&M University, Florida Atlantic University, Florida Gulf Coast University, Florida International University, Florida State University, New College of Florida, University of Central Florida, University of Florida, University of North Florida, University of South Florida, and University of West Florida.

University Press of Florida
15 Northwest 15th Street
Gainesville, FL 32611-2079
http://www.upf.com

Contents

Part IV. Embodiment

Part V. State and Household Relations

Part VI. Discussion

Figures

Tables

Preface

AURORE GIGUET

This comprehensive volume breaks new ground by bringing together, for the first time, an important body of figurine data sets from several time periods throughout Mesoamerica. The study of figurines has been frequently overlooked even though they are found in considerable numbers throughout Mesoamerica. As a result, the field lacks both generalizing commentary on the state of figurine research and accessible sources for engaging with and comparing these small figural objects.

To expand and encourage Mesoamerican figurine research, two symposia were independently organized in 2006. Christina Halperin, Katherine Faust, and Rhonda Taube organized a symposium entitled "Mesoamerican Iconography and Symbols in Action: Small-Scale Figurines as Large-Scale Social Phenomena" for the 71st Annual Meeting of the Society for American Archaeology (SAA) in San Juan, Puerto Rico. Mannetta Braunstein and Aurore Giguet organized the first annual Braunstein Symposium, held at the Marjorie Barrick Museum at the University of Nevada, Las Vegas, entitled "Figurines of Ancient Mesoamerica: Power and Guidance." This publication includes fully developed versions of many of the presentations from the two symposia. Some of the participants (Joyce and R. Taube) presented at both the Braunstein and SAA venues. In addition, two papers by scholars (Marcus; McCafferty and McCafferty) who had expressed interest in participating in the SAA symposium but were unable to present were added to the volume. Together, they provide complementary, well-rounded perspectives on Mesoamerican figurine research. Our hope is that future and current researchers will be stimulated to expand their interests and reexamine figurines as significant components in the lifeways of ancient and contemporary peoples.

The editors would like to thank the contributors, particularly Karl Taube, who suggested the merging of the symposia papers into one comprehensive publication. We would also like to thank Michael C. and Mannetta Braunstein, who make the Braunstein Symposia possible; Mannetta's love for Mesoamerican figurines and continued support will help bring figurine research to the forefront. We thank Eli Bortz, Michele Fiyak-Burkley, and the University Press of Florida staff for their guidance and support of the volume. Christina Halperin and Katherine Faust would also like to thank Tom Patterson and Wendy Ashmore, whose diligent commentaries, advice, and kindness are indispensable.

Approaching Mesoamerican Figurines

KATHERINE A. FAUST AND CHRISTINA T. HALPERIN

Mesoamerican figurines have allured archaeologists, art historians, and aficionados, as well as the general public, since their first appearance in excavated contexts, publications, museum exhibits, and private collections. One of the most striking aspects of figurines is their iconic quality, in which images of humans, supernaturals, and animals are depicted in the round and in small-scale form. As the volume title suggests, figurines include but go beyond such iconic referencing by serving as indices for the social processes of the ancient peoples who produced and used them. They contribute to our understandings of ancient Mesoamerican political economies, the production of gendered ideologies, ritual and religion, and mechanisms of social practice and change. These social roles speak to a growing scholarly discourse that underscores the significance of "bottom-up" and heterarchical models as a complement to "top-down" models typical of those used to interpret prestige goods and large-scale monumental art.

Despite their analytical potential and a long history of appeal, figurines remain underrepresented in academic research. While they are often depicted on the covers of books, these small-scale objects are rarely the principal foci therein. In fact, the present compilation of texts represents the first attempt to situate Mesoamerican figurines at the forefront of political, social, economic, and religious analyses within an edited volume. This oversight is all the more striking given that figurines are among the most abundant classes of artifacts known in this culture area. That the ancient people of Mesoamerica produced figurines of clay, stone, and other media by the millions testifies to their important status within the social and cosmological worlds of their producers.

This volume underscores the centrality of figurines to Mesoamerican peoples. It brings together figurine research from multiple temporal periods and regions throughout this vast culture area. Spatial and chronological foci include Preclassic period figurines from the Basin of Mexico, Oaxaca,

Chiapas, Veracruz, Tabasco, and Morelos, Mexico; Classic and Terminal Classic period figurines from the Maya area and the Ulúa Valley, Honduras; Postclassic period figurines from Santa Isabel, Nicaragua, the Basin of Mexico and the northeastern Gulf Coast, Mexico; and contemporary figurines made by Nahuatl speakers of northern Veracruz, Mexico. The aim of the volume is not to provide a regional study of all Mesoamerican figurine traditions but rather to present some recent case studies that highlight different approaches and theoretical frameworks. These range from functional analyses, stylistic and distributional comparisons, and semiotic investigations to theories of embodiment, cultural aesthetics, gender, social practice, and mass media. Together the chapters reflect an increasing emphasis on holistic analysis, which considers how multiple avenues of inquiry can productively merge to arrive at a better vantage point of the past. As Jeffrey Blomster (2002: 171) has stated, "Attempts to apply only one interpretation to figurines as an artifact class homogenize the wide variety of objects classified etically by archaeologists as 'figures' and neglect the multivalent emic meanings dependent on the specific audience, temporal, and spatial context." Thus, it is our hope that the volume not only serves as a resource for inquiring about Mesoamerican figurines but also draws attention to the diversity of ways in which one can go about making such inquiries.

In order to situate the following chapters, we provide a brief background on Mesoamerican figurine studies. We begin this exploration by discussing human responses to and preoccupations with figurative representations, which help explain the contradiction of why figurines have been such a source of fascination while also remaining peripheral to scholarly research. We then review some of the major approaches that scholars have taken in investigating figurines. While these trends can be categorized in a number of different ways (for example, Lesure 2002; Thomas 2002), we look specifically at the construction of typologies and culture histories, iconographic interpretations, functional approaches, the investigation of political-economies, and analyses incorporating agency, practice, and dialectics. Finally, we briefly comment on how the authors contributing to this volume use figurine data to broaden our understanding of how Mesoamerican societies expressed, maintained, resisted, and changed their social worlds.

Figural Representations: Engagement and Reflexivity

Regardless of the methodological approach adopted in figurine analysis, we simultaneously harbor a philosophical vision of the world that is based on disciplinary and personal histories. Our intent in the following discussion is to explore some of the affective features that Mesoamerican figurines harness on structural, historically contingent, personal, and popular levels. Scale and aesthetic content represent two key emotive factors. Responses to these traits are significant not only to the people who produced and used figurines in the past but also to the investigators who study them.

Scale

As human beings, we understand and relate to figurines through cognitive assessments of their physical attributes. Small-scale three-dimensional objects invoke different psychological and behavioral responses than do monumental ones (Bailey 2005). Monuments, architecture, and other materials larger than the human form guide sight lines, direct bodily movements, and formalize practice (Joyce and Hendon 2000; Moore 1996; Sanders 1990). While these large forms orchestrate movement, the diminutive quality of figurines has a reverse effect in which they can be manipulated by people. As predominantly palm-sized objects, figurines are easy to move, hang, arrange, place, and cache. We need only point to Joyce Marcus's (1998) well-known depiction of a Zapotec woman engaged with her figurines to recognize the intimate types of interaction cued by these pieces (see figure 2.1, this volume). Furthermore, small-scale objects are uniquely suited to trigger memory because of the personal engagement that they require and because they literally invade the space of the human body (Bailey 2005: 33–34). A person's contact with a figurine may infuse the small object with some essential part of the individual simply by having been within such personal space. In this case, figurines can embody personal powers, histories, accomplishments, and losses.

While we suggest that differences in the perception of small- and large-scale objects were significant in the past, scale clearly also matters to contemporary scholars. Throughout the history of Mesoamerican archaeology, the attention received by monumentality is unrivaled. Prints by Frederic Catherwood continue to exemplify the fascination with Mesoamerican monuments and civic and ceremonial architecture today, as they did during the era of their production. Similarly, the mobilization of labor required by Olmec rulers to orchestrate and commission monumental stone portraits has been one of the most popular examples linking sheer mass with political influence (Coe 1968; Cyphers Guillén 1996; Porter 1989; Reilly 1996). While large sculptures are discussed in numerous investigations of the Olmec, the study of small, clay figurines is more infrequent (see Cheetham

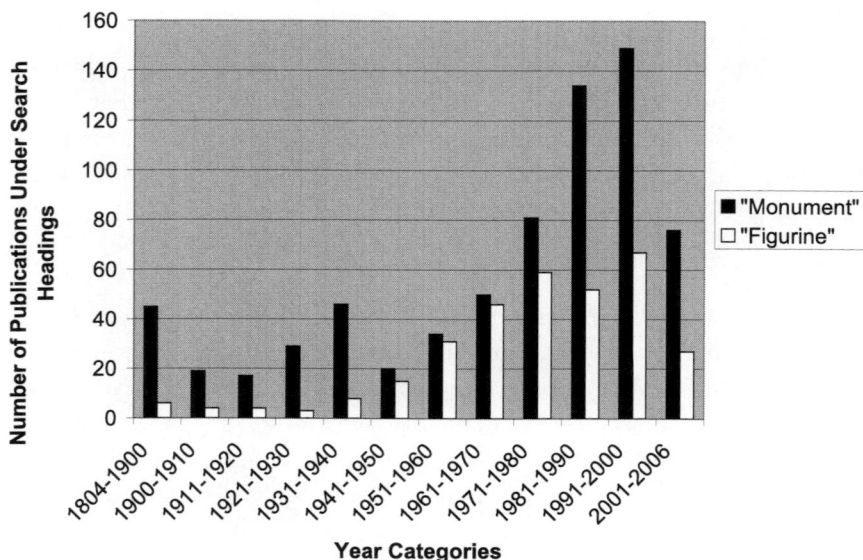

Figure 1.1. Graph of the number of Mesoamerican "monument" and "figurine" publications through time. Data are derived from the Bibliografía Mesoamericana of the Foundation for the Advancement of Mesoamerican Studies, Inc. (FAMSI), on July 7, 2006. This search engine was chosen over others because it had a disproportionately larger number of hits for Mesoamerican "Monument" and "Figurine" categories. It includes Spanish- and English-language book, article, and chapter publications in addition to master's and Ph.D. dissertation theses.

and Follensbee chapters in this volume). This phenomenon is apparent throughout Mesoamerica. In a comparison of the number of studies featuring Mesoamerican figurines and monuments published throughout the last century, research on monuments has clearly taken precedence (figure 1.1). This tendency to focus on the monumental to the exclusion of the small-scale echoes the tendency to focus on the elite at the expense of the common.

Figurines have been construed to index commoners, women, children, or complementary and diffuse power structures (Arroyo 2004; Brumfiel 1996; Cyphers Guillén 1988, 1998; Lesure 1997, 2002; Marcus 1998). Scholarly attention to these topics and frameworks has developed only recently in the history of archeology (Ardren and Hutson 2006; Baxter 2005; Conkey and Gero 1997; Conkey and Spector 1984; Ehrenreich et al. 1995; Gero and Conkey 1991; Lohse and Valdez 2004; Plunket 2002; Schwartz and Falconer 1994). These emphases, however, have as much to do with figurine iconography, production, context, and meaning as they do with scale. Furthermore, dichotomies of elite and commoner, hierarchical and heterarchical power, and male and female may be misleading. In some cases, figurines were also used by the elite, played a role in legitimizing hierarchical relations, were produced by skilled artisans using exotic materials and labor-intensive techniques, and possessed overlapping styles or imagery seen on large-scale media. In many ways, their abilities to address both sides of these dichotomies is what makes them so compelling.

Aesthetic and Scientific Interpretations

The tensions between different aesthetic traditions or between aesthetic and scientific interpretations also help explain why scholars emphasize or ignore figurines (or which particular figurines) in their research. The concept of the aesthetic, in its original formulation, speaks not to art "but to the whole region of human perception and sensation" (Eagleton 1991: 13). Yet in the Eurocentric understanding of the aesthetic, the concept has merged with the ahistorical, atemporal notion of fine art, which assumes universality in response to expressive culture.

The attraction of the aesthetic and artistic content of figurines is apparent in the way they have been depicted and described in scholarly work for over a century, in museum exhibitions and catalogs, and on the market. These tendencies underscore the application of Western aesthetic notions to figurines, whereby they are in some capacity envisioned as works of art. Even when ancient figurines are not considered as art for art's sake but as non-Western, tribal, or folk art, figurines are consistently accorded higher value when they demonstrate characteristics that align with Western sentiments regarding beauty, style, skill, sophistication, and even portraiture and exoticism. The "finer" the figurine, the more likely it is to be highlighted in museum exhibits and as the foci of publications. Figurines do not necessarily manifest the same style, form, or content in comparison to other Mesoamerican media, both large and small. Thus, researchers may separate and discount figurines in favor of other Mesoamerican categories of media and aesthetic expressions.

While archaeologists, anthropologists, and art historians have been affected by their own cultural conceptions regarding aesthetic values, they have also confronted these biases and made attempts to avoid conflating such biases into their analyses. At the same time, we do not maintain that the intent is to altogether ignore the capacity that figurines have in touching emotional chords, for it was the very aesthetic quality, whatever that may have been, that lent figurines their command in the first place—their ability to "work" properly in ancient societies. As do all objects of material and expressive culture, Mesoamerican figurines embody locally shared and understood aesthetic content. They visually reflect and produce the internal logic and cultural norms shared among members of a society by compressing and distilling larger ideological constructs into artifacts. In this sense, these small objects embody the politicized concerns inherent in the somatic and sensational elements of life.

Given the complexities of assessing aesthetic content in figurines, however, this affective aspect can also be completely disregarded. Some emphases on figurine manufacturing techniques, political economies, functions, and typologies may not address figurine aesthetics at all. These analyses are often considered more objective and scientific. While the characteristics of figurines speak to both scientific and humanistic inquiries (Houston et al. 2006; R. Joyce 2000; Lesure 1997, 1999), they are often slotted into one realm of analysis over the other. Thus, by addressing only the scientific or only the humanistic side of figurines, a comprehensive examination of the past is impeded. Use of the term *significant finds* is warranted as an indication of the tallies of numbers, emergent patterns, and the comparisons made, as well as of the recognition of less-tangible affective and aesthetic attributes (Bailey 2005).

Historical Review and Thematic Approaches

Typologies and Culture Histories

An early foundational approach to the study of Mesoamerican figurines was the focus on stylistic and technological traits to establish the placement of these artifacts within cultural historical frameworks (Butler 1935; Cook de Leonard 1971; Ekholm 1944; Kroeber 1925; Noguera 1954, 1975; Piña Chan 1971; Vaillant 1930, 1931, 1935a, 1935b). Many figurine typologies took the form of binomial classification schemes similar to those used in ceramic vessel analysis. They included technological (for example, molded versus modeled), stylistic, and iconographic elements. These studies typified a concern over chronology and the establishment of cultural boundaries during the early half of the twentieth century (Willey and Sabloff 1993). While the establishment of time-space references was a key concern in the creation of these typologies, they simultaneously provided a framework for data analysis that fit into theoretical models of social-cultural evolution in which human stages of development were indicated by material culture from early village societies to more complex social arrangements (Patterson 2003: 63–72). Many of the typologies formulated in the 1930s and 1940s continue to be used today, although elements may be elaborated, revised, and extended on the basis of new data or research questions (for example, Barbour 1975, 1998; Charlton 2001; Goldstein 1979, 1980; Rands and Rands 1965; Róman and Jaffer 1997; Trejo 1993).

Cultural typologies have also allowed archaeologists to discuss possible migrations, trade, and cultural influence through distributional analysis of figurine traits across space (see, for example, Blomster 2002; Cheetham, this volume; Goldstein 1994; Stocker 1983). While most figurine studies continue to situate their data within these broad references to culture area and time period, more finely tuned analyses of trait distributions may also illuminate social interactions at the level of intracultural region, site, and intrasite (Schlosser 1978; Willey 1972, 1978).

Iconographic and Interpretative Approaches

Another common approach to the investigation of figurines is the iconographic or interpretive approach, whereby scholars attempt to understand the symbolism and meaning embedded in salient iconographic motifs and styles of depiction. Mesoamerican figurines have much to offer in this domain because they portray a wide range of different peoples, animals, supernatural figures, activities, and social arrangements that are often underrepresented in textual references and other iconographic artifacts.

Late Preclassic West Mexican figurines, for instance, are among the few examples of iconographic media to depict humans within their architectural settlements and landscapes (Butterwick 1998; Townsend 1998; von Winning 1969). They reference social hierarchies and living arrangements that have been tested archaeologically through excavations of settlements and shaft tombs (Weigand and Beekman 1998). Archaeologists similarly face challenges in their attempts to investigate the nature of the ballgame in ancient Mesoamerica. Ballcourts at the Formative period site of Tlapacoya in the Basin of Mexico, for example, have not been recovered archaeologically, but the recovery of Formative period ballplayer figurines from the site suggests that the game was played there (Niederberger 2000: 179). These and other figurines help shed light on who played the game, what equipment the players wore, and ephemeral movements made by players (Day 1998; Ekholm 1991; Schele and Miller 1986).

In many cases, clay figurines stand in stark contrast to the iconography depicted on monuments, painted murals, prestige wares, and even figurines made of precious materials (such as jade and marine shell). Ceramic figurines may depict common peoples engaged in everyday activities, such as those from Lubaantun, Belize (Cohodas 2002; R. Joyce 1993; T. Joyce 1933; Wears 1977). They often include higher frequencies and more diverse representations of women. As such, they have provided important data sets for gendered approaches to the past (Brumfiel 1996; Cyphers Guillén 1998; R. Joyce 1993, 2000; Lesure 1997; Marcus 1998; Serra Puche 2001). Beyond the scope of Mesoamerica, Old World scholars have also drawn heavily on figurines in their discussions of prehistoric gender relations, identities, and religion (Bailey 1994; Beck 2000; Conkey and Tringham 1995; Goodison and Morris 1998; Hamilton 1996; Ikawa-Smith 2002; Meskell 1995; Talalay 1994). Many of these discussions have been couched as challenges to unitary conceptions of a Mother Goddess complex among Upper Paleolithic and Neolithic peoples as invoked by Marija Gimbutas (1982, 1989) and others.

In addition to including complex representations of anthropomorphic forms, many Mesoamerican figurine data sets simultaneously include numerous species of animals, unusual supernatural characters, and figures that represent transformative stages between animals, humans, and supernatural beings (Furst 1973; Schöndube 1998; Taube 1989). Yet there are comparatively few studies that engage with these perplexing figures as the foci of inquiry. Our focus on figurative representations of the human body simultaneously reflects a Western bias toward the value of anthropomorphism, that is, the priority of humans and deities of human form above other manifestations in the natural environment. The overlap apparent in many of these categories is in opposition to the rather strict classifications that typify Western thought and may conversely point to a historically contingent, Mesoamerican worldview regarding what it means to be human (Houston and Stuart 1989; R. Joyce 2003; Meskell and Joyce 2003).

Functional Approaches

The focus on figurine function stems, in part, from functionalist notions in anthropology whereby all behavioral patterns are thought to possess some level of cultural utility. A behaviorist focus in archaeology became more popular in the 1960s and 1980s alongside emphases on processualism and the New Archaeology (Brumfiel 1992; Cowgill 1993; Patterson 2003: 72–79). Functional approaches, however, have been consistently embedded in figurine analyses since some of the earliest studies and continue to be important modes of inquiry today alongside typological, iconographic, and other emphases. In 1880, for example, Miguel Orozco y Berra (1880: 359) argued that at Teotihuacan, clay figurines had been used in mortuary rituals, as indicated by the recovery of figurine heads from burials. Mary Butler (1935: 641) noted the possible use of Maya figurines as whistles in religious ceremonies, as amulets to be worn, as offerings, or as household gods, while Frans Blom suggested that Formative period animal whistles from Uaxactun, Guatemala, had been used for hunting, because the whistles' notes mimicked the call of the animal represented (Ricketson 1937: 217).

More recently, analysts have gone to greater lengths to incorporate ethnographic and ethnohistoric analogies into studies that emphasize archaeological contexts, figurine form (including iconographic, technological, and musical attributes), and figurine alteration (use patterns, wear, breakage, and so forth) as a means of assessing how these objects were used in the past (Heyden 1996; Lee 1969; Marcus 1996, 1998; Prufer et al. 2003; Ruscheinsky 2003; von Winning 1991). Although some studies have focused on single-function explanations or choosing between sacred or secular roles, greater attention to both ethnographic analogies and multiple lines of evidence reveal a more textured and socially complex understanding of figurine uses. This variability is supported, in part, by changes in figurine attributes, contexts, and imagery over time and space. Even a single figurine may have had multiple purposes or social meanings depending on its context of use and personal history. Likewise, archaeological and art historical research of Old World figurines have also moved from dichotomous (for example, dolls/toys versus ritual objects) and single-function explanations to appreciate the nuances in the prehistoric roles played by figurines (Bailey 2005; Biehl 2006; Conkey and Tringham 1998; Ucko 1968, 1996). Perhaps some of the puzzlement over figurine use lies in their polyvalent capacity and the difficulty in critically focusing on multiple variables. Functional approaches are clearly intertwined with other types of analyses (Lesure 2002), and many studies combine these concerns with other goals (for example, Charlton 2001; Mountjoy 1991; Rands and Rands 1965).

Political Economies

Mesoamerican archaeologists have also examined figurines in light of the production, exchange, and consumption systems of which they were a part. Investigations of figurine exchange were implicitly embedded within early typological approaches because cultural diffusion, one of the processes responsible for the creation of archaeological "types," required the exchange of ideas and material goods, such as figurines. These typological investigations, however, tended to focus on interregional and intercultural exchange relations and ignored productive systems and relations as well as the political implications of such exchange networks.

Compared to functional and iconographic approaches, attention to figurines as elements within political-economic systems has emerged more recently (Bishop et al. 2000; Charlton 1994; Charlton et al. 1991; Douglas 2002; Feinman 1999; Feinman and Nicholas 2000; Goldstein 1979; Ivic de Monterroso 2001; Lopiparo 2003; Olson 2007; Schortman and Urban 1994; Sears et al. 2004; Smith 2003). For example, chemical analysis of figurine pastes is relatively rare compared with that of ceramic vessels (see Bishop et al. 2000; Goldstein 1979; Halperin 2007; Sears et al. 2004). Nonetheless, the focus on political economies has become possible as archaeological attention to household-based and large-scale regional studies has increased in the past few decades (Ashmore and Wilk 1988; Blanton et al. 1993; Sanders et al. 1979; Wilk and Rathje 1982).

In some cases, research on figurines in conjunction with other crafts has helped us reevaluate our understandings of ancient Mesoamerican economies. At the Classic period site of Ejutla in the Valley of Oaxaca, for example, Gary Feinman and Linda Nicholas (Feinman 1999; Feinman and Nicholas 2000), following their discovery of high-intensity production of figurines, ceramics, and shell ornaments from a household context, have argued that common, nonroyal households could have engaged in "multicrafting" on a full-time basis. This finding challenges the long-held assumption that ancient household craft production could only have been a part-time activity that accompanied agriculture. A similar phenomenon has been detected at the Postclassic Aztec city of Otumba, where archaeologists have found evidence for large-scale, household-based production of figurines and other crafts concentrated in a single neighborhood or *barrio* of the city (Charlton 1994; Charlton et al. 1991).

Some scholars have taken the study of figurine economies one step further by incorporating imagery, meaning, and function into their analyses. One attempt to incorporate social meaning into a more materialist-based analysis is reflected in Richard Lesure's (1999) study of Formative period figurines from Paso de la Amada. In examining the possible meanings behind the different figurines and assessing productive labor inputs, he argues that developments in figurine manufacture and changes in figurine representations set the stage for the representational appropriation of figurines by chiefs, a move that legitimized chiefly authority.

Agency, Practice, and Dialectics

In the past decade of figurine studies, greater attention has been placed both on the agency of those who produced and used figurines and on the social meaning and significance of these objects. Central to this emphasis is the notion that culture emerges and is embodied in a dialectical interplay of agency and structure (Giddens 1984) habitual behavior and conscious action (Bourdieu 1977), mind and material (Hall 1966), and the historical contexts "given" to a person (or persons) and a person's making of history (Marx [1852] 1963). The premise is that artifacts (more specifically, figurines) not only reflect culture but also, because they possess and are imbued with cultural meaning, play a role in shaping the thoughts, behaviors, and customs of people. Thus, humans actively shape their material and cultural surroundings, and their material and cultural surroundings shape them.

Some Mesoamerican scholars, for example, have suggested that figurine styles and symbolism communicate ideologies of dominance or resistance. Elizabeth Brumfiel (1996) has argued that Aztec women in hinterland areas of the Aztec empire resisted gender ideologies of the Aztec state. She suggests that the changing patterns of figurine frequencies and the distinctions in style between official and popular imagery signify a degree of "ideological reformulation" by hinterland peoples. Despite political subordination, the agency of hinterland peoples was apparent in their rejection of state-based ideologies and continued use of alternative or opposing figurine symbols during Aztec rule.

Embodied approaches to figurines are another way in which researchers have dealt recently with the dialectical interplay of mind and material (Houston et al. 2006; R. Joyce 1998, 2005). People understand, create, and legitimate their experiences through the medium and manipulation of the physical body. In turn, images of the body and the manner in which the body is aesthetically treated can be viewed as an index for sociopolitical, religious, and ideological experience. Rosemary Joyce (1993, 1998, 2000), for example, regards bodily representations, including figurines, as sources of reflection and inscription of gendered practices. Bodily practices of everyday experience were made permanent in materialized representations. At the same time, these inscriptions influenced and naturalized social understandings and experience of the body. These and other approaches have been incorporated into and taken to new levels in the chapters in this volume.

Outline of the Volume

This volume is organized into six thematic sections: (1) context and practice, (2) social identities, (3) cultural aesthetics, (4) embodiment, (5) state and household relations, and (6) discussion.

The contributions in the first section emphasize the importance of contextual data for understanding human behaviors and the social experiences surrounding figurines. The perennial lack of contextualizing information is highlighted by Joyce Marcus in chapter 2 as one of the largest challenges facing scholars interested in behavioral analyses of Mesoamerican figurines. Drawing on data from Formative through Classic period sites in the Valley of Oaxaca, the Basin of Mexico, Morelos, and Tabasco, she examines rare archaeological examples of both stone and ceramic figurines, which were buried in situ in arranged scenes. While she promotes a methodology that is geared toward the recovery of intact figurine assemblages, Marcus simultaneously cautions that even these rare and highly prized instances do not ensure straightforward interpretations. One of the many kinds of information difficult to assess from figurines is the meaning that arises as a result of prolonged human-object interactions. This issue is addressed in chapter 3 by Jeanne Lopiparo and Julia A. Hendon, who explore issues of production, use, and social meaning by comparing figurine-whistles excavated from Classic to Terminal Classic period sites in the lower Ulúa Valley, Honduras, with evidence from contemporary habitation sites. They argue that meaning derives not only from iconographic symbols or formal properties of figurines and whistles but also from the ways in which these items become active participants in various household-related practices that contributed to the renewal of social identities and relations.

The section on social identities highlights the efficacy of examining figurines to understand how ancient social identities were expressed and negotiated. Billie J. A. Follensbee's study (chapter 4) of sexed, gendered, and age-related traits of Formative period Gulf Coast figurines compares ceramic figurines with small and large stone figures. Her inclusion of the underanalyzed ceramic figurines allows for a richer interpretation of the social identities depicted in the stone figures and broadens our understandings of the different social categories present in both media. In chapter 5,

Jeffrey P. Blomster diachronically examines the social identity of figurines from the Formative site of Etlatongo, Oaxaca. In emphasizing a flexible assignment of gender that may not have been strongly tied to biological traits, he argues that social identities became more rigidly structured later in the Early Formative period as social inequalities became more prominent. David Cheetham's comparative study (chapter 6) of Olmec-style figurines from Cantón Corralito, Chiapas, and San Lorenzo, Veracruz, represents a possible incidence of long-distance Olmec colonization. He finds that despite distance and a long history of continuous production, figurines made at Cantón Corralito were extremely similar to those of San Lorenzo and that a rigid set of figurine meanings and practices was integral to Olmec identity even beyond the geographical Olmec heartland.

The chapters pertaining to cultural aesthetics demonstrate some of the ways in which information relevant to identity, religious beliefs, and social ideals is communicated in images of the aesthetic body. In chapter 7, Geoffrey G. McCafferty and Sharisse D. McCafferty challenge the etic view expressed in ethnohistorical documents that migrations of Oto-Manguean- and Nahuatl-speaking groups accounted for Mexican ethnicity at the Early Postclassic site of Santa Isabel, Nicaragua. They consider a combination of adornments, skeletal remains, polychrome pottery, and anthropomorphic figurines to compare Mesoamerican ideals of the culturally aesthetic self with preceding styles from the Greater Nicoyan region. In chapter 8, Katherine A. Faust similarly combines iconographic and ethnohistorical data in her comparative analysis of Postclassic Huastec figurines, vessels, and sculptures. She argues that motifs adorning these examples of anthropomorphic art reference pan-Mesoamerican religious and ideological concepts pertaining to creation, fire drilling, and ritual blood sacrifice. As portrayals of actual tattoos or scarifications, symbols of sacrifice memorialize an aesthetic ideal of penitence on the Huastec body. In contrast, Rhonda Taube and Karl Taube (chapter 9) find that themes conveyed in Classic period Maya figurines are often distinct from those appearing in monumental art. They argue that figurines, unlike the monumental art, depict aged and repulsive beings who lampoon inappropriate and amoral behavior. As probable mementos of public performances and material reminders of social lessons, these small-scale scenes reflect Maya attitudes about appropriate social comportment and idealized beauty.

The contributions in the section entitled "Embodiment" underscore the inseparability of physical and spiritual aspects of human beings in Mesoamerican thought. Alan R. Sandstrom's study (chapter 10) examines the tradition of ritually cut paper figures among the contemporary Nahuatl speakers of northern Veracruz, Mexico. Consistently anthropomorphic in form, ephemeral figurines embody the spiritual essence of people, plants, animals, natural phenomena, and the environment. As the sole ethnographic chapter in the volume, it provides a crucial perspective on the ways in which images of the body link spiritual, social, and physical worlds. In chapter 11, Elizabeth M. Brumfiel and Lisa Overholtzer examine embodiment from another perspective. They emphasize the role of sensory experiences to help interpret the functions and meanings of widely distinct figurine types from Postclassic Xaltocan in the Basin of Mexico. In addition, they point to the significance of the representational body in not only prescribing social ideals within a given society but also conceptualizing those outside society, such as presocial beings or peoples from an earlier era.

The final section, on state and household relations, provides examples of how figurines address conflicting ideologies between those of the state and its subjects. Cecelia F. Klein and Naoli Victoria Lona's (chapter 12) iconographic analysis of Aztec ceramic and copal figurines reevaluates the interpretations of ceramic figurines as deities and emphasizes their significance for curing and protection. Klein and Victoria Lona's comparison of ceramic and copal figurines provides a rare glimpse into two contrasting figurine traditions: the former centered on local ideologies and needs of common peoples and the latter centered on the official state religion of the Aztec empire. Christina T. Halperin (chapter 13) also examines state and household relations in her archaeological study of Late Classic period Maya figurines. She argues that figurines represented a type of mass media in that molded versions could easily transmit images across a polity or region. In the case of the archaeological site of Motul de San José, she finds a widespread distribution of ruler images that took political discourses of the state beyond the main public plazas and into the homes of everyday peoples.

The concluding chapter, by Rosemary A. Joyce (chapter 14), brings together the various different approaches of figurine studies by discussing how the different chapters articulate with one another and with the future of figurine research as a whole. Together, the compilation of chapters draws attention not only to the significance of figurines in understanding past social processes but also to the diversity of perspectives that can be used to accomplish such aims. In this sense, it helps bridge traditional disciplinary constraints and brings out the multivocal and multidimensional characteristics inherent in the data sets. We hope that the volume will stimulate future discourse between figurine analyses and other research foci as well as provoke additional volumes that tackle the role of these small, but socially potent, figural objects.

Acknowledgments

We would like to thank Wendy Ashmore, Chelsea Blackmore, Reiko Ishihara, and Joel Palka for their constructive comments on this chapter. All errors are our own. We would also like to thank Wendy Ashmore, Tom Patterson, and Karl Taube for their kind advice and support of this edited volume project and related research endeavors.

References Cited

Ardren, Traci, and Scott R. Hutson, eds. 2006. *The Social Experience of Childhood in Ancient Mesoamerica*. University Press of Colorado, Boulder.

Arroyo, Barbara. 2004. Of Salt and Water: Ancient Commoners on the Pacific Coast of Guatemala. In *Ancient Maya Commoners*, ed. J. C. Lohse and J. F. Valdez, 73–95. University of Texas Press, Austin.

Ashmore, Wendy, and Richard R. Wilk. 1988. Household and Community in the Mesoamerican Past. In *Household and Community in the Mesoamerican Past*, ed. R. R. Wilk and W. Ashmore, 1–28. University of New Mexico Press, Albuquerque.

Bailey, Douglass W. 1994. Reading Prehistoric Figurines as Individuals. *World Archaeology* 25 (3): 321–31.

———. 2005. *Prehistoric Figurines: Representation and Corporeality in the Neolithic*. Routledge, London.

Barbour, Warren D. T. 1975. The Figurines and Figurine Chronology of Ancient Teotihuacán, Mexico. Ph.D. diss., Department of Anthropology, University of Rochester, Rochester, N.Y.

———. 1998. Figurine Chronology of Teotihuacán, Mexico. In *Los ritmos de cambio en Teotihuacán: Reflexiones y discusiones de su cronología*, ed. R. Brambilla and R. Cabrera, 243–54. Instituto Nacional de Antropología e Historia, Mexico City.

Baxter, Jane Eva, ed. 2005. *Children in Action: Perspective on the Archaeology of Childhood*. Archaeological Papers of the American Anthropological Association. Washington, D.C.

Beck, Margaret. 2000. Female Figurines in the European Upper Paleolithic: Politics and Bias in Archaeological Interpretation. In *Reading the Body: Representation and Remains in the Archaeological Record*, ed. A. E. Rautman, 202–14. University of Pennsylvania Press, Philadelphia.

Biehl, Peter. 2006. Figurines in Action: Methods and Theories of Figurine Research. In *A Future for Archaeology: The Past in the Present*, ed. R. Layton, S. Shennan, and P. Stone, 195–215. University College London Press, London.

Bishop, Ronald, Guzman Roberto Ruiz, and William J. Folan. 2000. Figurines and Musical Instruments of Calakmul, Campeche, Mexico: Their Chemical Classification. *Los Investigadores de la Cultura Maya* 7 (2): 322–28.

Blanton, Richard E., Stephen A. Kowalewski, Gary M. Feinman, and Laura M. Finsten. 1993. *Ancient Mesoamerica: A Comparison of Change in Three Regions.* Cambridge University Press, Cambridge.

Blomster, Jeffrey P. 2002. What and Where Is Olmec Style? Regional Perspectives on Hollow Figurines in Early Formative Mesoamerica. *Ancient Mesoamerica* 13: 171–95.

Bourdieu, Pierre. 1977. *Outline of a Theory of Practice.* Cambridge University Press, Cambridge.

Brumfiel, Elizabeth M. 1992. Breaking and Entering the Ecosystem—Gender, Class, and Faction Steal the Show. *American Anthropologist* 94 (3): 551–67.

———. 1996. Figurines and the Aztec State: Testing the Effectiveness of Ideological Domination. In *Gender and Archaeology,* ed. R. P. Wright, 143–66. University of Pennsylvania Press, Philadelphia.

Butler, Mary. 1935. A Study of Maya Mould-Made Figurines. *American Anthropologist* 37: 636–72.

Butterwick, Kristi Martens. 1998. Days of the Dead: Ritual Consumption and Ancestor Worship in an Ancient West Mexican Society. Ph.D. diss., Department of Anthropology, University of Colorado, Boulder.

Charlton, Cynthia Otis. 1994. Plebeians and Patricians: Contrasting Patterns of Production and Distribution in the Aztec Figurine and Lapidary Industries. In *Economies and Polities in the Aztec Realm,* ed. M. G. Hodge and M. E. Smith, 195–220. Institute for Mesoamerican Studies, State University of New York, Albany.

———. 2001. Hollow Rattle Figurines of the Otumba Area, Mexico. In *The New World Figurine Project,* vol. 2, ed. T. Stocker and C. O. Charlton, 25–54. Research Press at Brigham Young University, Provo, Utah.

Charlton, Thomas H., Deborah L. Nicholas, and Cynthia Otis Charlton. 1991. Aztec Craft Production and Specialization. *World Archaeology* 23 (1): 98–114.

Coe, Michael D. 1968. San Lorenzo and Olmec Civilization. In *Dumbarton Oaks Conference on the Olmec,* ed. E. P. Benson, 41–71. Dumbarton Oaks, Washington, D.C.

Cohodas, Marvin. 2002. Multiplicity and Discourse in Maya Gender Relations. In *Ancient Maya Gender Identity and Relations,* ed. L. S. Gustafson and A. M. Trevelyan, 11–54. Bergin and Garvey, Westport, Conn.

Conkey, Margaret W., and Joan M. Gero. 1997. Programme to Practice: Gender and Feminism in Archaeology. *Annual Review of Anthropology* 26: 411–37.

Conkey, Margaret W., and Janet D. Spector. 1984. Archaeology and the Study of Gender. *Advances in Archaeological Method and Theory* 7: 1–38.

Conkey, Margaret W., and Ruth E. Tringham. 1995. Archaeology and the Goddess: Exploring the Contours of Feminist Archaeology. In *Feminisms in the Academy,* ed. D. C. Stanton and A. J. Stewart, 199–247. University of Michigan Press, Ann Arbor.

———. 1998. Rethinking Figurines: A Critical View from Archaeology of Gimbutas, the "Goddess" and Popular Culture. In *Ancient Goddesses: The Myths and the Evidence,* ed. L. Goodison and C. Morris, 22–45. University of Wisconsin Press, Madison.

Cook de Leonard, Carmen. 1971. Minor Arts of the Classic Period in Central Mexico. In *Handbook of Middle American Indians, Archaeology of Northern Mesoamerica, Part I*, ed. G. F. Ekholm and I. Bernal, 179–205. University of Texas Press, Austin.

Cowgill, George L. 1993. Distinguished Lecture in Archaeology: Beyond Criticizing New Archaeology. *American Anthropologist* 95(3): 551–73.

Cyphers Guillén, Ann. 1988. Las Figurillas C8 de Chalcatzingo, Morelos. In *Ensayos de alfarería prehispánica e histórica de Mesoamérica: Homenaje a Eduardo Noguera Auza*, ed. M. C. S. Puche and C. N. Cáceres, 85–95. Universidad Nacional Autónoma de México, Mexico City.

———. 1996. Reconstructing Olmec Life at San Lorenzo. In *Olmec Art of Ancient Mexico*, ed. E. P. Benson and B. de la Fuente, 61–71. National Gallery of Art, Washington, D.C.

———. 1998. Women, Rituals, and Social Dynamics at Ancient Chalcatzingo. In *Reader in Gender Archaeology*, ed. K. Hays-Gilpin and D. S. Whitley, 269–89. Routledge, London.

Day, Jane Stevenson. 1998. The West Mexican Ballgame. In *Ancient West Mexico: Art and Archaeology of the Unknown Past*, ed. R. F. Townsend, 151–68. Thames and Hudson, New York.

Douglas, John G. 2002. *Hinterland Households: Rural Agrarian Household Diversity in Northwestern Honduras*. University Press of Colorado, Boulder.

Eagleton, Terry. 1991. *The Ideology of the Aesthetic*. Blackwell, Oxford, U.K.

Ehrenreich, Robert M., Carole M. Crumley, and Janet E. Levy, eds. 1995. *Heterarchy and the Analysis of Complex Societies*. American Anthropological Association, Arlington, Va.

Ekholm, Gordon F. 1944. *Excavations at Tampico and Panuco in the Huasteca, Mexico*. American Museum of Natural History, New York.

Ekholm, Susanna M. 1991. Ceramic Figurines and the Mesoamerican Ballgame. In *The Mesoamerican Ballgame*, ed. V. L. Scarborough and D. R. Wilcox, 241–49. University of Arizona Press, Tucson.

Feinman, Gary M. 1999. Rethinking Our Assumptions: Economic Specialization at the Household Scale in Ancient Ejutla, Oaxaca, Mexico. In *Pottery and People: A Dynamic Interaction*, ed. J. M. Skibo and G. M. Feinman, 81–98. University of Utah Press, Salt Lake City.

Feinman, Gary M., and Linda M. Nicholas. 2000. High-Intensity Household-Scale Production in Ancient Mesoamerica: A Perspective from Ejutla, Oaxaca. In *Cultural Evolution: Contemporary Viewpoints*, ed. G. M. Feinman and L. Manzanilla, 119–42. Kluwer Academic/Plenum, New York.

Furst, Peter T. 1973. West Mexican Art: Sacred or Secular? In *The Iconography of Middle American Sculpture*, 98–134. Metropolitan Museum of Art, New York.

Gero, Joan M., and Margaret W. Conkey, eds. 1991. *Engendering Archaeology: Women and Prehistory*. Blackwell, Oxford, U.K.

Giddens, Anthony. 1984. *The Constitution of Society: Outline of the Theory of Structuration*. University of California Press, Berkeley.

Gimbutas, Marija. 1982. *The Goddesses and Gods of Old Europe.* University of California Press, Berkeley.

———. 1989. *The Language of the Goddess.* Harper and Row, San Francisco.

Goldstein, Marilyn M. 1979. Maya Figurines from Campeche, Mexico: Classification on the Basis of Clay Chemistry, Style and Iconography. Ph.D. diss., Department of Anthropology, Columbia University, New York.

———. 1980. Relationships between the Figurines of Jaina and Palenque. In *The Third Palenque Round Table, 1978, Part 2,* ed. M. G. Robertson, 91–98. University of Texas Press, Austin.

———. 1994. Late Classic Maya-Veracruz Figurines: A Consideration of the Significance of Some Traits Rejected in the Cultural Exchange. In *Seventh Palenque Round Table, 1989,* ed. M. G. Robertson and V. M. Fields, 169–75. University of Texas Press, Austin.

Goodison, Lucy, and Christine Morris, eds. 1998. *Ancient Goddesses: The Myths and the Evidence.* University of Wisconsin Press, Madison.

Hall, Edward T. 1966. *The Hidden Dimension.* Anchor/Doubleday, Garden City, N.Y.

Halperin, Christina T. 2007. Materiality, Bodies, and Practice: The Political Economy of Late Classic Figurines from Motul de San José, Petén, Guatemala. Ph.D. diss., Department of Anthropology, University of California, Riverside.

Hamilton, Naomi. 1996. The Personal Is Political. *Cambridge Archaeological Journal* 6 (2): 282–85.

Heyden, Doris. 1996. La posible interpretación de figurillas arqueológicas en baro y piedra según las fuentes históricas. In *Los arqueólogos frente a las fuentes,* ed. R. Brambila Paz and J. Monjarás-Ruiz, 129–46. Instituto Nacional de Antropología e Historia, Mexico City.

Houston, Stephen, and David Stuart. 1989. The Way Glyph: Evidence for "Co-essences" among the Classic Maya. *Research Reports on Ancient Maya Writing* 30: 1–16.

Houston, Stephen, David Stuart, and Karl Taube. 2006. *The Memory of Bones: Body, Being, and Experience among the Classic Maya.* University of Texas Press, Austin.

Ikawa-Smith, Fumiko. 2002. Gender in Japanese Prehistory. In *In Pursuit of Gender: Worldwide Archaeological Approaches,* ed. S. M. Nelson and M. Rosen-Ayalon, 323–54. AltaMira Press, Walnut Creek, Calif.

Ivic de Monterroso, Matilde. 2001. Resultados de los análisis de las figurillas de Piedras Negras. Paper presented at the XV Annual Simposio de Investicaciónes Arqueológicas, Museo Nacional de Arqueología y Etnología, Guatemala City.

Joyce, Rosemary A. 1993. Women's Work: Images of Production and Reproduction in Pre-Hispanic Southern Central America. *Current Anthropology* 34 (3): 255–74.

———. 1998. Performing the Body in Pre-Hispanic Central America. *RES* 33: 147–65.

———. 2000. *Gender and Power in Prehispanic Mesoamerica.* University of Texas Press, Austin.

———. 2003. Making Something of Herself: Embodiment in Life and Death at Playa de los Muertos, Honduras. *Cambridge Archaeological Journal* 13 (2): 248–61.

———. 2005. Archaeology of the Body. *Annual Review of Anthropology* 34: 139–58.

Joyce, Rosemary A., and Julia A. Hendon. 2000. Heterarchy, History, and Material Reality: "Communities" in Late Classic Honduras. In *The Archaeology of Communities: A New World Perspective*, ed. M. A. Canuto and J. Yaeger, 143–59. Routledge, London.

Joyce, T. A. 1933. The Pottery-Whistle Figurines of Lubaantun. *Journal of the Royal Anthropological Institute of Great Britain and Ireland* 63: xv–xxv.

Kroeber, Alfred Louis. 1925. *Archaic Culture Horizons in the Valley of Mexico.* University of California, Berkeley.

Lee, Thomas A. 1969. *The Artifacts of Chiapa de Corzo, Chiapas, Mexico.* Papers of the New World Archaeological Foundation 26. Brigham Young University, Provo, Utah.

Lesure, Richard G. 1997. Figurines and Social Identities in Early Sedentary Societies of Coastal Chiapas, Mexico, 1550–800 BC. In *Women in Prehistory: North America and Mesoamerica*, ed. C. Claassen and R. A. Joyce, 227–48. University of Pennsylvania Press, Philadelphia.

———. 1999. Figurines as Representations and Products at Paso de la Amada, Mexico. *Cambridge Archaeological Journal* 9 (2): 209–20.

———. 2002. The Goddess Diffracted: Thinking about the Figurines of Early Villages. *Current Anthropology* 43 (4): 587–610.

Lohse, Jon C., and Fred Valdez, eds. 2004. *Ancient Maya Commoners.* University of Texas Press, Austin.

Lopiparo, Jeanne Lynn. 2003. Household Ceramic Production and the Crafting of Society in the Terminal Classic Ulúa Valley, Honduras. Ph.D. diss., Department of Anthropology, University of California, Berkeley.

Marcus, Joyce. 1996. The Importance of Context in Interpreting Figurines. *Cambridge Archaeological Journal* 6 (2): 285–91.

———. 1998. *Women's Ritual in Formative Oaxaca: Figurine-Making, Divination, Death and the Ancestors.* Memoir 33. Museum of Anthropology, University of Michigan, Ann Arbor.

Marx, Karl. [1852] 1963. *The Eighteenth Brumaire of Louis Bonaparte.* International Publishers, New York.

Meskell, Lynn. 1995. Goddesses, Gimbutas and "New Age" Archaeology. *Antiquity* 69: 74–86.

Meskell, Lynn, and Rosemary A. Joyce. 2003. *Embodied Lives: Figuring Ancient Maya and Egyptian Experience.* Routledge, London.

Moore, Jerry D. 1996. *Architecture and Power in the Ancient Andes: The Archaeology of Public Buildings.* Cambridge University Press, Cambridge.

Mountjoy, Joseph B. 1991. The Analysis of Preclassic Figurines Excavated from the Site of La Pintada in the Central Coastal Plain of Jalisco, Mexico. In *The New World Figurine Project*, vol. 1, ed. T. Stocker, 85–97. Research Press at Brigham Young University, Provo, Utah.

Niederberger, Christine. 2000. Ranked Societies, Iconographic Complexity, and Economic Wealth in the Basin of Mexico toward 1200 BC. In *Olmec Art and Iconogra-*

phy, ed. J. E. Clark and M. E. Pye, 169–91. Studies in the History of Art 58. National Gallery of Art, Washington, D.C.

Noguera, Eduardo. 1954. *La cerámica arqueológica de Cholula*. Editorial Guarania, Mexico City.

———. 1975. *La cerámica arqueológica de Mesoamérica*. Instituto de Investigaciones Antropológicas, Universidad Nacional Autónoma de México, Mexico City.

Olson, Jan. 2007. A Socioeconomic Interpretation of Figurine Assemblages from Late Postclassic Morelos, Mexico. In *Commoner Ritual and Ideology in Ancient Mesoamerica*, ed. N. Gonlin and J. C. Lohse, 251–79. University Press of Colorado, Boulder.

Orozco y Berra, Manuel. 1880. *Historia antigua y de la conquista de México*, vol. 2. G. A. Esteva, Mexico City.

Patterson, Thomas C. 2003. *Marx's Ghost: Conversations with Archaeologists*. Berg, Oxford, U.K.

Piña Chan, Román. 1971. Preclassic or Formative Pottery and Minor Arts of the Valley of Mexico. In *Handbook of Middle American Indians, Archaeology of Northern Mesoamerica, Part I*, ed. G. F. Ekholm and I. Bernal, 157–78. University of Texas Press, Austin.

Plunket, Patricia, ed. 2002. *Domestic Ritual in Ancient Mesoamerica*. Monograph 46. Cotsen Institute of Archaeology, University of California, Los Angeles.

Porter, James B. 1989. Olmec Colossal Heads as Recarved Thrones: "Mutilation," Revolution and Recarving. *RES* 17–18: 23–29.

Prufer, Keith M., Phil Wanyerka, and Monica Shah. 2003. Wooden Figurines, Scepters, and Religious Specialists in Pre-Columbian Maya Society. *Ancient Mesoamerica* 14: 219–36.

Rands, Robert L., and Barbara C. Rands. 1965. Pottery Figurines of the Maya Lowlands. In *The Handbook of Middle American Indians*, ed. R. Wauchope, 535–60. Middle American Research Institute, Tulane University, New Orleans.

Reilly, F. Kent, III. 1996. Art, Ritual, and Rulership in the Olmec World. In *The Olmec World: Ritual and Rulership*, ed. E. P. Benson, 27–45. Art Museum, Princeton University, Princeton, N.J.

Ricketson, Edith Bayles. 1937. *Uaxactun, Guatemala, Group E, 1926–1931, Part II, The Artifacts*. Carnegie Institution of Washington Publication 477, Washington, D.C.

Róman, Padilla, and Araceli Jaffer. 1997. Las figurillas preclásicas de Temamatla, Estado de México. In *Homenaje a la doctora Beatriz Barba de Piña Chán*, ed. A. G. Díaz, V. B. Olivares, M. d. C. L. García, and F. R. Castro, 157–75. Instituto Nacional de Antropología e Historia, Mexico City.

Ruscheinsky, Lynn Marie. 2003. The Social Reproduction of Gender Identity through the Production and Reception of Lowland Maya Figurines. Ph.D. diss., Department of Art History and Visual Art Theory, University of British Columbia, Vancouver.

Sanders, Donald. 1990. Behavioral Conventions and Archaeology: Methods for the Analysis of Ancient Architecture. In *Domestic Architecture and the Use of Space*, ed. S. Kent, 43–72. Cambridge University Press, Cambridge.

Sanders, William T., Jeffrey Parsons, and Robert S. Santley. 1979. *The Basin of Mexico: Ecological Processes in the Evolution of a Civilization.* Academic Press, New York.

Schele, Linda, and Mary E. Miller. 1986. *The Blood of Kings: Dynastic Ritual in Maya Art.* Kimbell Art Museum, Fort Worth, Texas; George Braziller, New York.

Schlosser, Ann L. 1978. Ceramic Maya Lowland Figurine Development with Special Reference to Piedras Negras, Guatemala. Ph.D. diss., Department of Anthropology, Southern Illinois University, Carbondale.

Schöndube, Otto. 1998. Natural Resources and Human Settlements in Ancient West Mexico. In *Ancient West Mexico: Art and Archaeology of the Unknown Past,* ed. R. F. Townsend, 205–16. Thames and Hudson, New York.

Schortman, Edward M., and Patricia A. Urban. 1994. Living on the Edge: Core/Periphery Relations in Ancient Southeastern Mesoamerica. *Current Anthropology* 35 (4): 401–3.

Schwartz, Glenn M., and Steven E. Falconer, eds. 1994. *Archaeological Views from the Countryside: Village Communities in Early Complex Societies.* Smithsonian Institution Press, Washington, D.C.

Sears, Erin L., Ronald L. Bishop, and M. James Blackman. 2004. Las figurillas de Cancuen: El surgimiento de una perspectiva regional. Paper presented at the XVIII Simposio de Investigaciones Arqueológicas en Guatemala, Guatemala City.

Serra Puche, Mari Carmen. 2001. The Concept of Feminine Places in Mesoamerica: The Case of Xochitecatl, Tlaxcala, Mexico. In *Gender in Pre-Hispanic America,* ed. C. F. Klein and J. Quilter, 255–84. Dumbarton Oaks, Washington, D.C.

Smith, Michael E. 2003. Economic Change in Morelos Households. In *The Postclassic Mesoamerican World,* ed. M. E. Smith and F. F. Berdan, 249–58. University of Utah Press, Salt Lake City.

Stocker, Terrence L. 1983. Figurines from Tula, Hidalgo, Mexico. Ph.D. thesis, Department of Anthropology, University of Illinois, Urbana.

Talalay, Lauren E. 1994. A Feminist Boomerang: The Great Goddess of Greek Prehistory. *Gender and History* 6: 165–83.

Taube, Karl A. 1989. Ritual Humor in Classic Maya Religion. In *Word and Image in Maya Culture: Explorations in Language, Writing and Representation,* ed. W. F. Hanks and D. S. Rice, 351–82. University of Utah Press, Salt Lake City.

Thomas, Julian. 2002. Comments to "The Goddess Diffracted: Thinking about the Figurines of Early Villages." *Current Anthropology* 43 (4): 605–6.

Townsend, Richard F. 1998. Before Gods, Before Kings. In *Ancient West Mexico: Art and Archaeology of the Unknown Past,* ed. R. F. Townsend, 107–35. Thames and Hudson, Chicago.

Trejo, Silvia. 1993. Escultura Huaxteca en Barro. In *Practicas agricolas y medicina tradicional: Art y sociedad,* vol. 2, ed. J. R. Mercado and G. Alcala, 171–86. Centro de Investigaciones y Estudios Superiores en Antropología Social, Mexico City.

Ucko, Peter J. 1968. *Anthropomorphic Figurines of Predynastic Egypt and Neolithic Crete with Comparative Material from the Prehistoric Near East and Mainland Greece.* Royal Anthropological Institute Occasional Paper 24. Szmidla, London.

———. 1996. Mother, Are You There? *Cambridge Archaeological Journal* 6 (2): 300–307.

Vaillant, George C. 1930. *Excavations at Zacatenco.* Anthropological Papers of the American Museum of Natural History 32, part 1. New York.

———. 1931. *Excavations at Ticoman.* American Museum of Natural History, New York.

———. 1935a. *Early Cultures of the Valley of Mexico: Results of the Stratigraphical Project of the American Museum of Natural History in the Valley of Mexico.* American Museum of Natural History, New York.

———. 1935b. *Excavations at El Arbolillo.* Anthropological Papers of the American Museum of Natural History 35, part 2. New York.

von Winning, Hasso. 1969. Ceramic House Models and Figurine Groups from Nayarit. In *Proceedings of the International Congress of Americanists,* 129–32. Stuttgart and Munich.

———. 1991. Articulated Figurines from Teotihuacán and Central Veracruz—A Reanalysis. In *The New World Figurine Project,* vol. 1, ed. T. Stocker, 63–83. Research Press, Provo, Utah.

Wears, Priscilla. 1977. *A Typological Study of Some Mayan Figurines from Lubaantun, Belize.* Master's thesis, University of Bradford, Bradford, U.K.

Weigand, Phil C., and Christopher S. Beekman. 1998. The Teuchitlan Tradition: Rise of a Statelike Society. In *Ancient West Mexico: Art and Archaeology of the Unknown Past,* ed. R. F. Townsend, 35–52. Thames and Hudson, New York.

Wilk, Richard R., and William L. Rathje. 1982. Household Archaeology. *American Behavioral Scientist* 25 (6): 617–39.

Willey, Gordon R. 1972. *The Artifacts of Altar de Sacrificios.* Papers of the Peabody Museum of Archaeology and Ethnology 64. Harvard University, Cambridge, Mass.

———. 1978. Artifacts. In *Excavations at Seibal, Department of Peten, Guatemala,* ed. G. R. Willey, 1–189. Peabody Museum of Archaeology and Ethnology, Harvard University, Cambridge, Mass.

Willey, Gordon R., and Jeremy A. Sabloff. 1993. *A History of American Archaeology.* 3rd ed. W. H. Freeman, New York.

Part I

Context and Practice

2

Rethinking Figurines

JOYCE MARCUS

Figurines fascinate us—images of fellow humans small enough to be held in our hands, seemingly encouraging us to look into their faces, making us believe that we can read the minds of their makers even though thousands of years separate our culture from theirs. Their shared humanity entices us into thinking that figurines should be easy to interpret. The scores of publications on them, however, indicate that figurines continue to intrigue and confound us, particularly those scholars who seek a single universal interpretation. Our evidence suggests that figurines played diverse roles in different parts of the world (Bailey 1994, 1995; Bolger 1996; Cook 1992; Cory 1956, 1961; Cyphers Guillén 1988, 1990, 1993; Fewkes 1923; Garfinkel 2003; McDermott 1996; McIntosh and McIntosh 1979; Morss 1954; Renaud 1929; Renfrew 1969; Sánchez de la Barquera Arroyo 1996; Ucko 1962).

Earlier generations of scholars tended to study figurines as isolated art objects, attaching each to its own piece of plywood in a display case, describing and studying them divorced from their former social context. Today's scholars would argue that more attention should be paid to context and to an entire sequence of behaviors, from the way the original clay was selected by figurine makers to how the figurines were fired, arranged, stored, reused, broken, and discarded. Unfortunately, most archaeologists recover figurines only at the end of that behavioral chain, when they are merely broken and discarded fragments.

Occasionally, with luck or with extensive horizontal exposure, archaeologists recover entire scenes of arranged figurines. Owing to preservation problems, however, even these fortunate discoveries include only stone or pottery figurines, although many figurines in Mesoamerica are known to have been made of wood, paper, copal, or rubber (see, for example, Broda 1971, 2001; Guilliem Arroyo et al. 1998; López Luján 1994; Sahagún 1950; Sandstrom 1991). In fact, some ethnohistoric sources reveal that the Aztecs made miniature figures out of *tzoalli*, a dough made from amaranth. These dough figures could wear bark-paper clothing that was removed and burned as an offering; they could be "sacrificed" by having their heads lopped off; they could be eaten by ritual participants;[1] or they could be arranged in scenes (Broda 1971: figs. 12, 14; Sahagún 1950: 21–22). Many of these perishable figurines seem to have been "stand-ins," or substitutes, for living humans, deceased ancestors, animals, or anthropomorphized mountains.

Thus although my focus in this chapter is on figurines made of nonperishable materials, I realize that a much wider range of raw materials would have been used during pre-Columbian times. I glimpse this in those fortunate instances when perishable figures have been preserved, for example, at a waterlogged site such as El Manatí (Ortiz and Rodríguez 1996, 1999) or in the offering boxes at Tlatelolco and Tenochtitlan (Guilliem Arroyo et al. 1998; López Luján 1994). Such rare finds remind us how much information we are missing.

Formal versus Functional Analyses

The vast majority of figurine studies are formal, focusing on the attributes of each specimen to create types and subtypes. Although such studies are very useful, helping us to create chronologies and compare figurines from different sites, they do not require data on context; context, however, is what helps us the most when we move to the question of figurine function.

Deliberately arranged figurine scenes help us understand function because they constitute primary contexts. A focus on such scenes seems particularly appropriate at this time, when anthropology as a whole shows renewed interest in four topics—ritual performance, social relations, gender, and ancestors (Balzer 1996; Butler 1997; Cox 1998; Gable 1996; Garfinkel 2003; Kendall 1985; Plunket and Uruñuela 2002; Renfrew and Zubrow 1994; Weiss and Haber 1999).

The wonderful thing about scenes is that they were created by prehistoric people, not by the investigator (Plunket 2002). Such scenes hold the potential for transmitting more information than do isolated specimens (Drucker et al. 1959; Ortiz and Rodríguez 1996, 1999).

Before looking at some scenes, I offer four cautionary statements. First, the sample of figurine scenes is very small, and second, they are widely separated in time and space. Third, as mentioned above, many figurines are undoubtedly missing from our sample because they were made of perishable materials such as wood, dough, paper, copal, rubber, or cloth. Fourth, other key perishable components, including clothing, string, ribbons, feathers, and so forth, may have disappeared from figurine scenes. These missing materials may have supplied valuable data on gender, status, office, or role.

Bearing in mind some of these inherent limitations and preservation problems, let us proceed.

Whole Figurines in Primary Contexts

In the case of Mesoamerica's smaller figurines, one major obstacle to interpretation is the scarcity of primary contexts. Stray figurine heads and limbs, swept into rubbish pits or dumped onto middens, usually provide us only with material for speculation. Occasionally, however, extensive excavation at an archaeological site can provide insights even in the case of fragments. In the Formative Valley of Oaxaca, for example, we have found hundreds of small, handmade figurine parts in residences and their dooryards but not in the small public buildings we regard as men's houses (Flannery and Marcus 2005; Marcus 1999). Our conclusion is that these small figurines were used by women in household ritual, providing a venue for the spirit of recently deceased ancestors who continued to play a role in the lives of their descendants (figure 2.1).

Figure 2.1. To communicate with her ancestors, this woman has created a figurine scene that provides a venue for the spirits of recent ancestors (drawing by John Klausmeyer).

Some of our most prized opportunities for interpretation come from those rare occasions when figurines (or larger pottery figures) are found whole and in primary contexts such as caches and burials (Marcus 1996, 1998). Some deliberately arranged scenes in caches seem to be snapshots frozen in time, commemorating events such as elite funerals or sacrificial rites. In other scenes, the figurines appear to be stand-ins for human counterparts. Still other scenes seem both to sanctify a location and to allow ongoing communication with ancestors and past culture heroes (Marcus 1978, 1996).

In the case of temple and pyramid dedications at Teotihuacán, stone statuettes and anthropomorphic obsidian figures served as stand-ins or substitutes for human sacrificial victims, and some of these, as in Offering 4 at La Venta, were placed in a standing position (Sugiyama and Cabrera Castro 2004: fig. 5; Sugiyama et al. 2004: 21, fig. 33; Sugiyama and López Luján 2006: 45). When the ancient Zapotec of Oaxaca placed pottery sculptures inside tombs or in their antechambers, those figures facilitated communication between ascending and descending generations, both reassuring the ancestors that they were remembered and allowing their elite descendants to claim genealogical continuity (Marcus 2006: 230). As we will see, the Zapotec invested considerable energy in all aspects of ancestor ritual, constructing tombs even before building the palaces that went with them and incorporating offering boxes into the floors of temples at the time of construction (Marcus and Flannery 1994). Scenes made with pottery sculptures were important in both cases. For the Zapotec, the royal tomb was considered a key part of the living household; the "house of the dead" was immediately below the residence of the living, and connecting the two was a stairway that led from the patio of the residential unit to the tomb below (see Caso 1938, 1942; Flannery 1983; Miller 1995).

Small Figurines in Caches Associated with Public Buildings

Some caches of small figurines seem to have been buried as a group to preserve their arrangement as a scene. An example would be Feature 63 of San José Mogote, Oaxaca (discussed later in this chapter). Other caches seem to have been offerings left in public areas during a dedicatory ritual of some kind. Perhaps the best-known cache of this type is Offering 4 at La Venta.

Offering 4, found in front of the Northeast Platform in Complex A at La Venta, consisted of sixteen stone (mostly jadeite) figurines and six tongue-depressor-like jade celts, all "arranged in such a way that they represented a scene" (Drucker et al. 1959: 152). The celts and figurines were still standing upright in the soil and "the feet and lower legs of the figures and the polls of the celts were buried about 1½ inches into the reddish-brown sand to hold them upright" (Drucker et al. 1959: 154). Following its arrangement, the whole scene was covered with white sand (figure 2.2). After some interval of time, a small hole was made, perhaps indicating that someone needed to inspect the figurine scene one last time. After that inspection, the hole was refilled, not to be seen again until archaeologists uncovered the scene approximately 2,500 years later. Thus, the scene's intended audience probably included only those who witnessed it being arranged in the ground and the sacred Earth who received it (Marcus 1989: 173).

Drucker and colleagues (1959: 155–56) offered a range of interpretations for Offering 4 but seemed to favor two possibilities: that it showed a series of individuals reviewing a line of sacrificial victims as they passed by or that it showed religious specialists performing a ritual. The excavators concluded, "We suggest that it [the scene] offers some very interesting clues as to the way in which at least some of the Mesoamerican figurines may have been used."

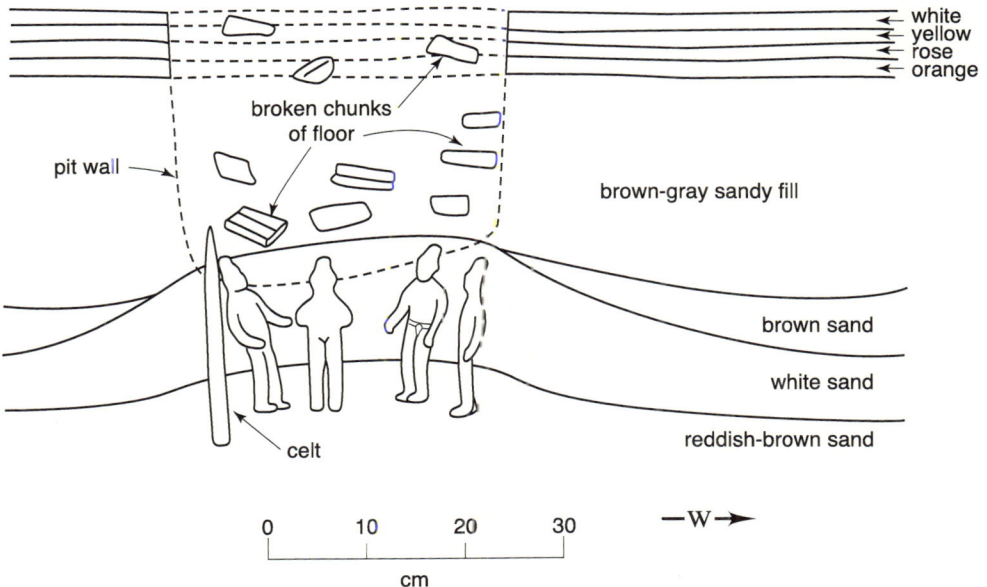

Figure 2.2. Cross section of Offering 4 at La Venta, showing the figurine scene set in reddish brown sand, with white sand fill, and the inspection pit that cut through a series of floors (white, yellow, rose, orange) (redrawn from Drucker et al. 1959: fig. 39).

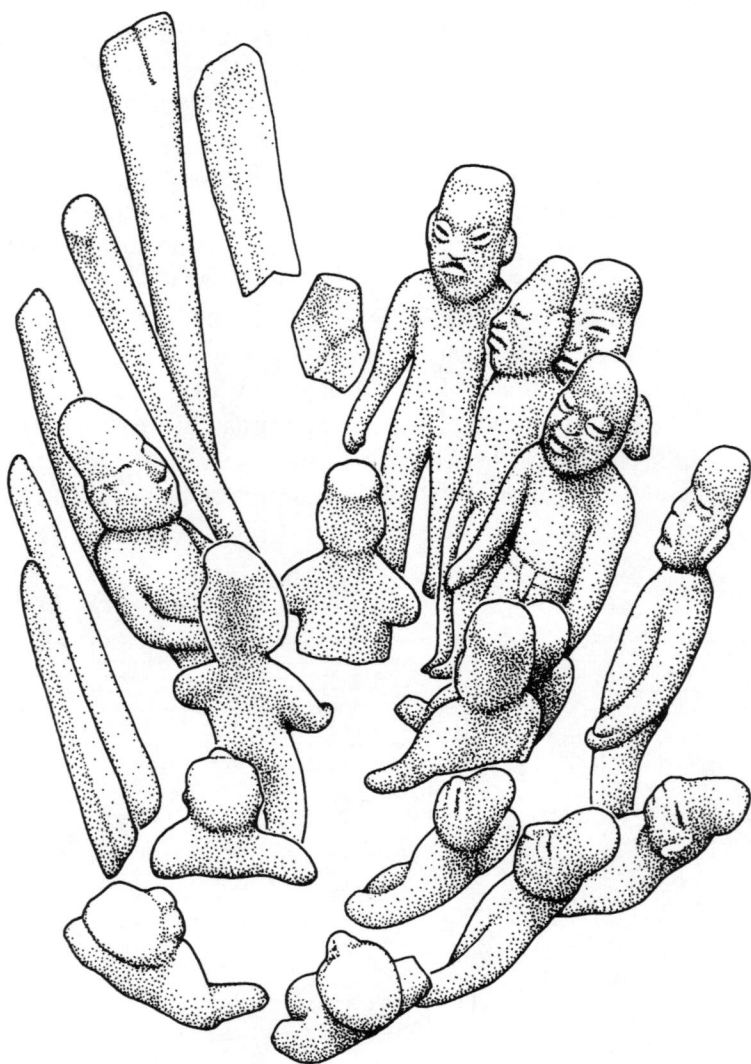

Figure 2.3. Reconstruction of the figurine scene in Offering 4 at La Venta; the celts (on the left) average 25 centimeters in height (redrawn and adapted from Drucker et al. 1959: fig. 38).

Several facts about Offering 4 are noteworthy (figure 2.3): all the figurines are of stone; all appear to be males (most have a breechclout); all are standing; all are similar in size; and all appear to have deliberate cranial deformation. If cranial deformation was a sign of high rank at La Venta, this scene may have included only elite individuals, and these individuals may have been further differentiated from each other, since some show evidence of dental mutilation while others do not. In various regions of Mesoamerica, dental mutilation, like cranial deformation, was a sign of high rank; however, unlike cranial deformation, which had to be applied to infants, tooth filing was done later in life, after all the permanent teeth had erupted.

In Offering 4, one figurine stands out from the others not only because many of the other figures seem to be gazing at it but also because it is made of a different stone (it is sandstone instead of the jadeite or nephrite used for the other fifteen). The sandstone figurine has his back against a row of six standing celts. This row of celts is reminiscent of the wall of basalt columns that delimits the court above the offering. Thus, the arrangement of the figurines in Offering 4 may correspond to the positions that real individuals assumed in the court above while witnessing an historic event. This offering could then be seen as a permanent record of the event. What is unclear is whether the sandstone figure was being honored or prepared for an unpleasant sacrifice.

From Small Figurines to Medium-sized Ceramic Sculptures

Sometime during the Monte Albán Ic period (300–100 BC), the Formative chiefdoms of the Valley of Oaxaca were consolidated into a Zapotec state centered at Monte Albán (Spencer and Redmond 2001, 2003, 2004, 2006). The small, handmade pottery figurines of the Formative period gradually disappeared, but ritual scenes continued to be made with medium-sized ceramic sculptures and effigy funerary urns (Caso and Bernal 1952; Marcus 1998:313; Saville 1899). Examples of such scenes can be found both at Monte Albán, the Zapotec capital, and at secondary administrative centers such as San José Mogote and Xoxocotlan.

Structure 35, San José Mogote, Valley of Oaxaca, Mexico

Structure 35 was a colonnaded two-room temple of the Monte Albán II period. Charcoal from the burning of incense dated this temple to 1930 ± 40 BP or circa AD 20 (Marcus and Flannery 2004: 18259–61). Offerings were found in stone masonry boxes below the floor of the temple, where they had presumably been left during "rituals of sanctification" (Rappaport 1971,

Figure 2.4. Jade figures found in situ in Feature 94, an offering box below the floor of a two-room temple (Structure 35) at San José Mogote, Valley of Oaxaca, Mexico; the larger statue is 49 centimeters in height (photo by the author).

1972) that accompanied the dedication of the temple. Of the five offering boxes below the temple floor, the most important seemed to be those below the floor of the inner (and more sacred) room: Features 94, 95, and 96. Features 94 and 95 were below the north half of the inner room. Feature 95 contained no artifacts but may once have contained perishable artifacts.

Feature 94 contained a jade statue, a jade figurine, two jade beads, and several small jade fragments that could have been by-products of jade working, all lying in a deposit of red pigment (figure 2.4). Both the statue and the figurine seem to be male and have perforations in their earlobes, perhaps to receive perishable ornaments. The statue has a hollow on the top of its head, which could have held the base of a perishable headdress; for example, removable headdresses are known from figures in a scene at Monte Albán (see below).

The jade statue and figurine may have been stand-ins for sacrificial victims, and both may have been dressed in elegant though perishable attire, given the perforations in the earlobes and the hollow in the larger figure's head.

Below the south half of the inner room was another offering box, Feature 96, which contained seven ceramic pieces arranged in a scene (figure 2.5). At the center of the scene was a miniature tomb made of adobe bricks. Inside this tomb was a bowl with a small effigy of the type Alfonso Caso called an *acompañante* (Caso 1938; Caso and Bernal 1952). Resting against the

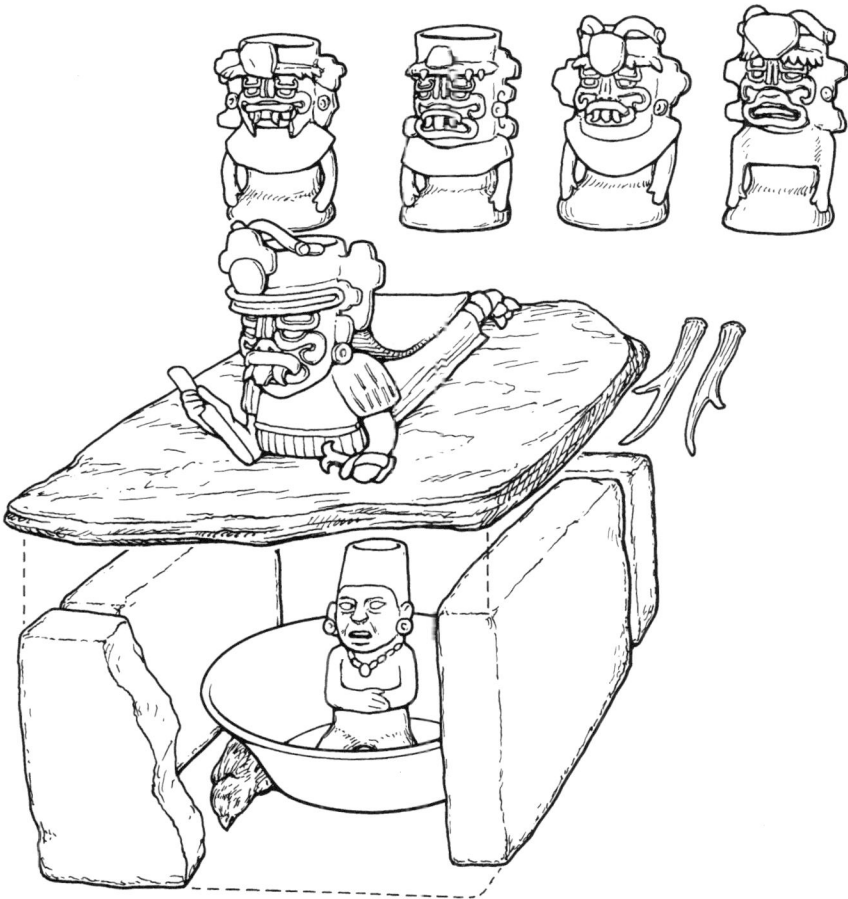

Figure 2.5. Reconstruction of the ritual scene in Feature 96, an offering box below the Structure 35 temple at San José Mogote. The scene includes a miniature tomb with a stone roof. Inside the miniature tomb is a figure kneeling in a bowl and a sacrificed quail. A metamorphosed flying figure lies on the stone roof; nearby were two deer antler drumsticks and four female figures (drawn by John Klausmeyer).

bowl was the skeleton of a sacrificed bobwhite quail. Nearby was a pair of deer antlers of the type used as drumsticks for a turtle-shell drum. Lying on the roof of the miniature tomb was a flying figure wearing a mask, carrying a stick in his right hand, and holding the bifid tongue of a serpent in his left hand.

In some Zapotec dialects, the words for "serpent" and "young maize" are near-homonyms. I therefore suspect that the object in his right hand was a planting stick, that the serpent tongue was a metaphor for newly sprouted maize, and that the figure's association with maize is consistent with his wearing the mask of Lightning (Cociyo). Finally, behind the flying figure were four ceramic effigies, each depicting a woman wearing a Lightning mask. These four women may represent Clouds, Rain, Hail, and Wind, which the Zapotec considered the companions of Lightning (see Cruz 1936, 1946).

This scene may represent the metamorphosis of a deceased lord into a Cloud Person, a flying figure in contact with Lightning. He could represent an ancestor of the man kneeling in the bowl in the miniature tomb or perhaps the partial metamorphosis of that same individual, caught at a stage where his body was still that of a human but his face was that of Lightning.

Cache below a Period IIIa (circa AD 250–500) Temple in Building I at Monte Albán, Mexico

A dedicatory offering placed below the floor of a temple in Building I at Monte Albán contained two dozen greenstone figurines (Caso 1938: 10). Although not arranged in a scene, all were found inside a large urn depicting Lightning. They may have been arranged in a scene at an earlier stage of a temple dedication ritual only to be gathered up afterward and placed in the urn for burial.

Figurines with Burials

Another primary context in which figurines have been found is with burials. Let us consider some Formative examples, followed by examples of the larger ceramic sculptures that replaced them over time.

Tlatilco, Basin of Mexico

Several Early and Middle Formative burials at Tlatilco included deliberate groupings of figurines, some of which included figures that originally may have been standing. Of the 214 burials excavated during the 1969 season at Tlatilco, 37 included clusters of figurines (García Moll et al. 1991).

Burial 27, a girl 17–19 years of age, was accompanied by a cluster of eight female figurines (figure 2.6). Burial 86 (figure 2.7) was a nine-month-old baby buried with fourteen figurines (in this case, we can be sure that the inclusion of the figurines was not due to achievement during the baby's short

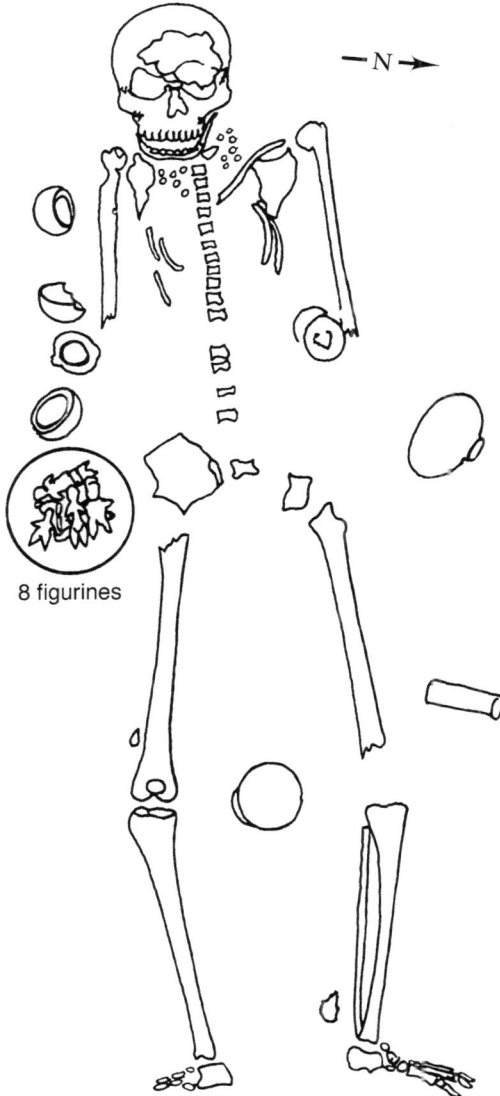

8 figurines

Figure 2.6. This burial of a teenage girl at Tlatilco, Basin of Mexico, contains a cluster of eight female figurines (redrawn from García Moll et al. 1991: 93).

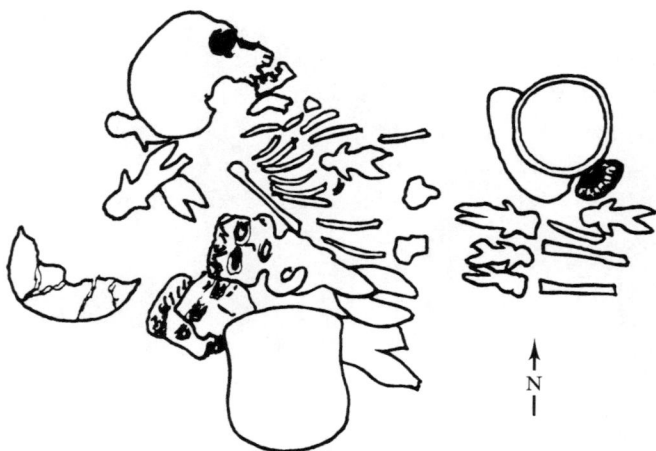

Figure 2.7. This burial of a nine-month-old baby at Tlatilco, Basin of Mexico, included fourteen figurines (redrawn from García Moll et al. 1991: 113).

lifetime). Burial 9, a woman 20–24 years of age, had ten figurines with her. Burial 104, an adult woman, likewise had ten figurines. Burial 144, an adult whose sex could not be determined, had seven figurines. These figurines could represent recent ancestors of the deceased.

Another Tlatilco burial, reported by Miguel Covarrubias (1957), was an adult woman accompanied by twenty figurines (figure 2.8). This was Covarrubias' Burial 60. Four of the twenty figurines were clustered near the woman's left hand, while the remaining sixteen were in a group near her legs. These two clusters of figurines may have originally been placed upright but over time the weight of the soil had caused them to fall; when excavated, many of them appear to have been face down.

Gualupita, Morelos, Mexico

One Middle Formative burial at Gualupita included four figurines, all found under the skull of Skeleton 9 (Vaillant and Vaillant 1934). Two figurines were male, two female. One woman was shown carrying a baby on her back; the other was seated cross-legged. One of the male figurines was a man wearing a loincloth; he was the tallest of the group at 19.5 centimeters. The other male had special attire, indicating that he may have been a ballplayer (Vaillant and Vaillant 1934: fig. 7).

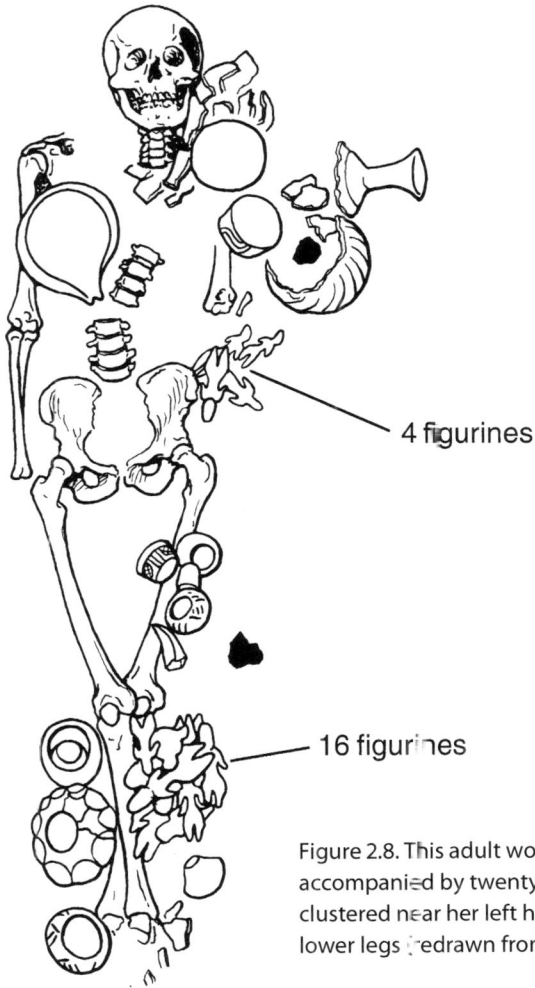

Figure 2.8. This adult woman at Tlatilco was accompanied by twenty figurines—four were clustered near her left hand and sixteen near her lower legs (redrawn from Covarrubias 1957: fig. 5).

Nexpa, Morelos, Mexico

Burial 8 at Nexpa, probably an adult female, was supine and associated with a bracelet of fourteen beads on her left wrist and one complete female figurine (Grove 1974). The placement of this Formative figurine was similar to the one accompanying a Middle Formative burial in the Valley of Oaxaca (Burial 54 at Fábrica San José, Oaxaca; see below). Burial 7 at Nexpa was a secondary burial whose bones were stacked in a neat pile, associated with a tall fluted bottle, two hemispherical bowls, and a figurine that depicts a dancing woman with her arms raised and her skirt swinging (Grove 1974: 26).

Hacienda Blanca, Valley of Oaxaca

Near Hacienda Blanca in the Valley of Oaxaca, one Early Formative burial had four figurines—a male, two females, and one fetus. The fetus was found inside the belly of one of the female figurines. Three of these figurines are shown in figure 2.9 (Marcus 1998: fig. 5.1; Marcus and Flannery 1996:85; Ramírez Urrea 1993).

Tomaltepec, Valley of Oaxaca

Two Early Formative burials at Tomaltepec, Oaxaca, involved young women who had figurines buried with them. Burial 21, a 20–25-year-old woman, was associated with a hollow seated figurine. Burial 35, an adult woman, was buried with two solid figurines (Whalen 1981: 130–31).

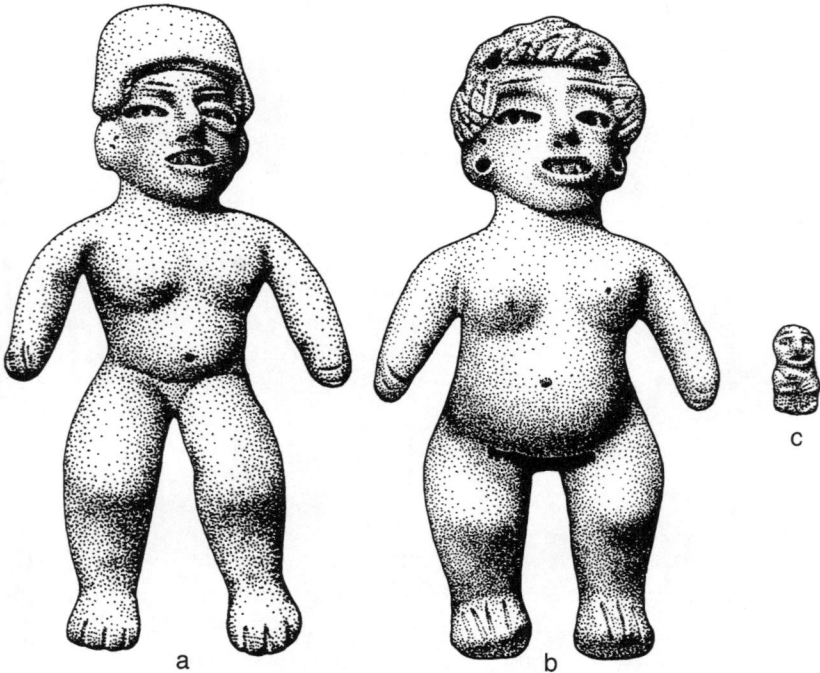

Figure 2.9. An Early Formative man, woman, and fetus (the fetus was found inside the woman's abdomen). These three figurines were found at Hacienda Blanca in the Valley of Oaxaca by Susana Ramírez (redrawn from Marcus 1998: figs. 5.1, 8.1).

Fábrica San José, Valley of Oaxaca

Burial 54 at Fábrica San José was a 15-year-old girl with her skull deformed in tabular oblique fashion. She was associated with one large hollow figurine placed on her right shoulder (Drennan 1976: figs. 84, 89). The position of the figurine in this Middle Formative burial was similar to that in Burial 8 at Nexpa, Morelos.

Later Tombs in the Valley of Oaxaca

In later periods, following the disappearance of small handmade figurines, the Zapotec continued to place ceramic sculptures either in the chamber of an elite tomb or in front of the tomb door. Let us look a few examples.

Monte Albán

After Tomb 103 on the North Platform at Monte Albán had been closed, the Early Classic (AD 250–500) residents living above the tomb laid down a patio floor. Later, they made a pit through the patio floor to arrange more than a dozen figurines in a scene, which was discovered by Martín Bazán in front of the tomb door (figure 2.10). The five large figurines that hold mirrors have removable headdresses (see earlier comments on Feature 94 at San José Mogote). Some of the smaller figurines (in the foreground) seem to be singing or chanting. Both the larger and smaller figurines are ceramic.

Two other items in the same scene, however, were made of stone—the step pyramid and funerary mask. The whole scene has been interpreted as a funeral (Caso 1942: 183, figs. 18, 19; Paddock 1966: 150), in which clay was

Figure 2.10. Figurine scene created and deposited below the patio of Tomb 103 at Monte Albán, Valley of Oaxaca (drawn by K. Clahassey from photographs in Caso 1942: figs. 18, 19; Paddock 1966: fig. 151).

used to model the funeral attendants while stone was reserved for the pyramid and funerary mask, with the stone items interpreted as representing a deceased lord.

Xoxocotlan

Xoxocotlan was an important secondary center just south of Monte Albán during the Classic period. At the turn of the twentieth century, Marshall Saville excavated several important tombs there, including those in Mounds 7 and 9.

The area immediately in front of the tomb doors at Xoxocotlan tended to have scenes of ceramic sculptures or effigy urns. Several of these scenes included urns "placed in series of five in front of the tombs, on the roof, or

Figure 2.11. Five ceramic figures were placed in the façade above the carved lintel of Tomb 3 in Mound 9 at Xoxocotlan, Valley of Oaxaca (redrawn by K. Clahassey from Saville 1899: pl. 22).

fastened into the façade" (Saville 1899: 361). For example, five urns depicting human figures wearing the mask of Lightning were placed above the door and carved lintel of a tomb in Mound 9 (figure 2.11), while a similar group lay on the ground in front of Tomb 1 in Mound 7 (Saville 1899: pl. 22).

These groupings of Lightning figures may have been placed there to serve several functions: (1) to protect or guard the tomb, (2) to mediate the flow of communications between the deceased in the tomb and his or her descendants in the residence above, (3) to honor the deceased ancestors, and (4) to rekindle memories of the ancestors on the anniversaries of their deaths (Marcus 2006: 224–30). Indeed, it may have been on the anniversaries of their deaths that new scenes and offerings were placed at the tomb doors.

Lambityeco

Lambityeco was an important center in the eastern Valley of Oaxaca during Monte Albán IV (AD 700–900). Of particular interest there is Tomb 2, where John Paddock and colleagues (1968) recovered a series of unfired clay figurines that were hastily made with thin sticks used as armature. In fact, perhaps 50 percent of Tomb 2's contents consisted of unfired clay. One of the figurines seems to depict a male with a beard. Other unfired figurines show males and females wearing articles of cloth on their head and body. The excavators suspected that all these unfired clay figures had been made hurriedly by family members to accompany an important person who died unexpectedly (Paddock et al. 1968: fig. 22).

Another interesting discovery at Tomb 2 of Lambityeco was a group of five identical funerary urns, each sporting the face of Lightning, a pattern similar to that noted by Saville at Xoxocotlan during the immediately preceding period. Paddock and colleagues (1968: 3) suggest that all five urns had been made from identical molds and were only partly baked, reinforcing the evidence of haste.

Figurines in Residential Units

In addition to those figurines found in caches or burials, several have been discovered in scenes or as dedicatory offerings with residences.

Feature 63, San José Mogote, Valley of Oaxaca

House 16/17 at San José Mogote, Oaxaca, was a household unit consisting of a residence (House 17) and a lean-to or roofed work space (House 16)

Figure 2.12. This figurine scene (called Feature 63) was found at San José Mogote in the Valley of Oaxaca.

set on an artificial terrace hacked out of sloping bedrock (Flannery and Marcus 2005: 307). This household dated to the late San José phase (940 BC uncalibrated). Below the floor of House 16, in an area that was probably a woman's work space, we discovered four figurines buried in the form of a scene (figure 2.12).

Like Offering 4 at La Venta, Feature 63 seemed to depict only male individuals. Three figurines were lying on their backs with their arms folded across their chests. The central figure had his arms folded in such a way that his wrists crossed; those figurines to either side had their arms lying parallel to each other. This arrangement provides symmetry and confirms that we are dealing with a carefully arranged scene. The fourth figurine of the group appears to have been seated atop the bodies of the three supine figurines in what we consider a position of authority (figure 2.13).

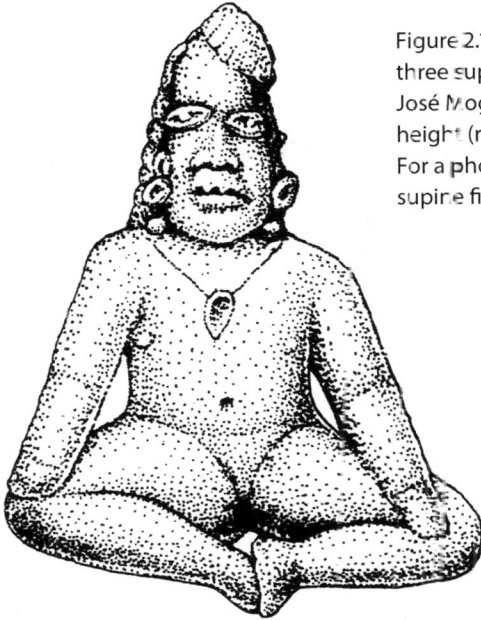

Figure 2.13. This figure, found sitting atop three supine figures in Feature 63 at San José Mogote, measures 6.8 centimeters in height (redrawn from Marcus 1998: fig. 8.15). For a photograph of this figure and the supine figures, see fig. 2.12.

All four figurines in Feature 63 are similar enough to have been made by the same woman. All have conical (possibly deformed) heads, and the teeth that are visible show that they were filed, like those of some figurines in Offering 4 at La Venta. Each Feature 63 figurine wears prominent ear spools with elements dangling from them. Each also wears a pendant on his chest, with those worn by the three supine men being circular in shape. The pendant worn by the seated figure, however, was oval. I suspect that these pendants depict shell ornaments (perhaps *Spondylus* or pearl oyster, which were common at the site), although I cannot rule out the possibility of small magnetite mirrors in mother-of-pearl holders (see, for example, Flannery and Marcus 2005: fig. 23.6d).

We suspect that Feature 63 may represent the burial of a seated individual in a position of authority, laid to rest seated atop three male subordinates buried in positions of obeisance. Although different in scale, such an arrangement reminds us of an actual grave at Coclé, Panama, where a chief was buried in a seated position atop a layer of twenty-one fully extended subordinates or sacrificial victims (Lothrop 1937: fig. 31).

Why was this scene placed below the floor of House 16? Perhaps some member of the household had a male ancestor of high rank who was buried with three subordinates. The burial scene may have been the means by which this family could maintain contact with that ancestor or may have provided him with a venue from which he could witness ongoing events in the residence of his descendants.

House 2, San José Mogote

House 2 at San José Mogote also belonged to the San José phase (900 BC uncalibrated). Like most houses of the phase, it produced abundant figurine fragments. Unlike most houses, however, it also produced a complete figurine, apparently deliberately buried (Flannery and Marcus 2005: fig. 9.14; Marcus 1998: 110).

This figurine, depicting a seated figure with his arms folded across the abdomen, had been placed beneath a wall foundation stone just north of the doorway of the house. I suspect that, by analogy with village societies elsewhere (McIntosh and McIntosh 1979; Marcus 1998: 19), this dedicatory figure had been placed there to serve as a protector or guardian of House 2; he might even represent an ancestor of someone in the household.

This interpretation is reinforced by what we know from the ethnohistory of later Zapotec societies. Like many other Mesoamerican groups, the Zapotec focused much of their religion on communicating with ancestors, both recent and remote (Marcus 1978, 1992). Honoring ancestors during funerals and on the anniversaries of their entombment were key events, which could involve the burning of incense; the letting of one's blood; the sacrifice of animals such as quails, doves, and dogs; the offering of food; and the arranging of scenes of figurines or placement of larger clay sculptures at tomb entrances.

As we have seen, many Zapotec effigy vessels depicted deceased individuals who had either metamorphosed into Lightning or were wearing the masks (or other attributes) of supernatural beings (Caso and Bernal 1952; Marcus 1983). Particularly common are the effigy vessels called "urns," which combine a beaker or cylinder-like vessel with an effigy. What these vessels originally held is not always clear, because owing to poor preservation they are usually empty when found. Some may have contained ritual beverages such as pulque or chocolate. Others, placed in building dedications, might contain jade beads, shells, or obsidian knives (this is evident in Building I at Monte Albán, where one urn contained twenty-four stone figurines).

Were Some Figurines Dressed?

As I argued in an earlier study (Marcus 1998), many Formative Mesoameri-can figurines show more attention to detail in their hairstyles and orna-ments than in their clothing. To be sure, some figurines are shown in skirts, loincloths, sandals, ballplayer's equipment, or even ritual costumes. Many, however, appear to be nude and have no genitalia indicated. This has led some scholars to describe them as "sexless."

I gained some perspective on this phenomenon while working at a site on the desert coast of Peru, where textiles are preserved. There we found many of the complete figurines dressed in miniature clothing (Marcus 1987: figs. 21a, 22d). Their bodies would have been considered "sexless" except for the fact that their clothing clearly indicated their gender. We should thus consider the possibility that many Mesoamerican figurines would have had additional information on their gender, social status, and so forth pro-vided by clothing that has since decomposed (see also Follensbee, this vol-ume). Our Peruvian figurines even had necklaces of seeds strung on cotton thread.

The Future of Figurine Studies in Mesoamerica

The biggest problem facing students of figurines and ceramic sculptures in Mesoamerica is lack of context. So much of our sample consists of frag-ments from midden debris, public building fill, or looters' excavations that a lot of our interpretations are pure speculation. The rituals involving figu-rines had many components—(1) the ritual participant who arranged the figurines; (2) the audience, which could be other humans, supernaturals such as Earth or Lightning, or one's ancestors; (3) a ritual location, such as a house, temple, patio, or tomb; (4) a purpose such as communicating with one's ancestors, re-creating a historic event, or sanctifying a new temple; (5) a span of time; and (6) a series of associated actions such as chanting, sing-ing, dancing, playing music, wearing masks and costumes, burning incense, letting blood, or sacrificing humans and animals. When context is lost, we lose the information provided by these six components, and we are forced to try to reconstruct the past having only the figurines themselves. This is rarely enough.

Our few cases of figurines in primary context become crucial, yet even those cases do not exhaust the possibilities of the ways figurines could have been used. We can see that some figurines were arranged to commemorate important funerals, placed in caches to sanctify temples, and buried during the dedication of houses. Both animals and human figurines could serve as stand-ins during sacrifices. Other figurines could provide the venue to which ancestors could return on special occasions; to make that venue more suitable, some figurines may have been dressed in appropriate clothing and ornaments (for example, the removable headdresses at Monte Albán and removable ear spools at Teotihuacán). Such interchangeable parts would allow some figurines to be used over and over again simply by varying accessories.

There is nothing wrong in presenting a student with a collection of "figurines from Site X" and telling him or her to describe them. In fairness to the student, however, we should explain that such collections lack most of the contextual data necessary to make plausible interpretations. If the student then asks "What can I do to advance figurine studies?" we might answer "When you excavate, please open huge horizontal exposures to increase your chances of finding intact figurines in meaningful contexts." Indeed, recovering many more figurines in meaningful contexts should substantially increase our understanding of their function and meaning.

Notes

1. "They called them Tepicme: [they said they were] like men. Hence they placed masks upon them. And this the *tlamacazque*, the priests of the Tlalocs, did. And when they made these, the common men, those who had made vows, laid offerings before them; they ate, drank, and danced in their presence. And when their feast-day came, they cut up and divided the Tepicme, and they ate them" (Sahagún 1950: 44–45).

References Cited

Bailey, Douglass W. 1994. Reading Prehistoric Figurines as Individuals. *World Archaeology* 25 (3): 321–31.

———. 1995. The Representation of Gender: Homology or Propaganda. *Journal of European Archaeology* 2 (2): 215–28.

Balzer, Marjorie M. 1996. Sacred Genders in Siberia. In *Gender Reversals and Gender Cultures*, ed. S. P. Ramet, 164–82. Routledge, London.

Bolger, Diane. 1996. Figurines, Fertility, and Emergence of Complex Society in Prehistoric Cyprus. *Current Anthropology* 37: 365–72.

Broda, Johanna. 1971. Las fiestas aztecas de los dioses de la lluvia: Una reconstrucción según las fuentes del siglo XVI. *Revista Española de Antropología Americana* 6: 245–327.

———. 2001. Ritos mexicas en los cerros de la cuenca: Los sacrificios de niños. In *La montaña en el paisaje ritual*, ed. J. Broda, S. Iwaniszewski, and I. A. Montero García, 295–317. Conaculta e Instituto Nacional de Antropología e Historia, Mexico City.

Butler, Judith. 1997. Performative Acts and Gender Constitution: An Essay in Phenom-
enology and Feminist Theory. In *Writing on the Body: Female Embodiment and
Feminist Theory*, ed. K. Conboy, N. Medina, and S. Stanbury, 401–17. Columbia
University Press, New York.

Caso, Alfonso. 1938. *Exploraciones en Oaxaca, quinta y sexta temporadas, 1936–1937.*
Instituto Panamericano de Geografía e Historia Publicación 34. Mexico City.

———. 1942. Resumen del informe de las exploraciones en Oaxaca, durante la 7a y 8a
temporadas 1937–1938 y 1938–1939. *Actas del XXVII Internacional Congreso de
Americanistas, 1939*, vol. 2, pp. 159–87. Mexico City.

Caso, Alfonso, and Ignacio Bernal. 1952. *Urnas de Oaxaca.* Memorias del Instituto
Nacional de Antropología e Historia 2. Mexico City.

Cook, Anita. 1992. The Stone Ancestors: Idioms of Imperial Attire and Rank among
Huari Figurines. *Latin American Antiquity* 3 (4): 341–64.

Cory, Hans. 1956. *African Figurines.* Faber and Faber, London.

———. 1961. Sumbwa Birth Figurines. *Journal of the Royal Anthropological Institute of
Great Britain and Ireland* 91 (1): 67–76.

Covarrubias, Miguel. 1957. *Indian Art of Mexico and Central America.* Alfred A.
Knopf, New York.

Cox, James Leland. 1998. *Rational Ancestors: Scientific Rationality and African Indigenous Religions.* Cardiff University Press, Cardiff.

Cruz, Wilfrido C. 1936. Los Binigulazaa. *Neza* [Juchitán, Mexico], vol. 2, no. 11.

———. 1946. *Oaxaca recóndita: Razas, idiomas, costumbres, leyendas y tradiciones del
estado de Oaxaca, Mexico.* Privately published, Oaxaca.

Cyphers Guillén, Ann. 1988. Thematic and Contextual Analyses of Chalcatzingo Figurines. *Mexicon* 10 (5): 98–102.

———. 1990. Figurillas femeninas del preclásico en Chalcatzingo. *Arqueología* 3:
41–48.

———. 1993. Women, Rituals, and Social Dynamics at Ancient Chalcatzingo. *Latin
American Antiquity* 4: 209–24.

Drennan, Robert D. 1976. *Fábrica San José and Middle Formative Society in the Valley of Oaxaca.* Memoir 8. Museum of Anthropology, University of Michigan, Ann
Arbor.

Drucker, Philip, Robert F. Heizer, and Robert J. Squier. 1959. *Excavations at La Venta,
Tabasco, 1955.* Bureau of American Ethnology Bulletin 170. Smithsonian Institution, U.S. Government Printing Office, Washington, D.C.

Fewkes, J. Walter. 1923. Clay Figurines by Navaho Children. *American Anthropologist*
25 (4): 559–63.

Flannery, Kent V. 1983. The Legacy of the Early Urban Period: An Ethnohistoric Approach to Monte Albán's Temples, Residences, and Royal Tombs. In *The Cloud People*, ed. K. V. Flannery and J. Marcus, 132–36. Academic Press, New York.

Flannery, Kent V., and Joyce Marcus. 2005. *Excavations at San José Mogote 1: Household Archaeology.* Memoir 40. Museum of Anthropology, University of Michigan,
Ann Arbor.

Gable, Eric. 1996. Women, Ancestors, and Alterity among the Manjaco of Guinea-
Bissau. *Journal of Religion in Africa* 26 (2): 104–21.

García Moll, Roberto, Daniel Juárez Cossío, Carmen Pijoan Aguade, María Elena Salas Cuesta, and Marcela Salas Cuesta. 1991. *Catálogo de Entierros de San Luis Tlatilco, Mexico,* vol. 4. Instituto Nacional de Antropología e Historia, Mexico City.

Garfinkel, Yosef. 2003. *Dancing at the Dawn of Agriculture.* University of Texas Press, Austin.

Grove, David C. 1974. *San Pablo, Nexpa, and the Early Formative Archaeology of Morelos, Mexico.* Vanderbilt Publications in Anthropology 12. Nashville, Tenn.

Guilliem Arroyo, Salvador, Saturnino Vallejo Zamora, and Ángeles Medina Pérez. 1998. Ofrenda en el Templo Mayor de México-Tlatelolco. *Arqueología* 19: 101–17.

Kendall, Laurel. 1985. *Shamans, Housewives, and Other Restless Spirits: Women in Korean Ritual Life.* University of Hawaii Press, Honolulu.

López Luján, Leonardo. 1994. *The Offerings of the Templo Mayor of Tenochtitlan.* Trans. B. R. Ortiz de Montellano and T. Ortiz de Montellano. University Press of Colorado, Niwot.

Lothrop, Samuel K. 1937. *Coclé, Part I.* Memoir of the Peabody Museum of Archaeology and Ethnology, vol. 7. Harvard University, Cambridge, Mass.

Marcus, Joyce. 1978. Archaeology and Religion: A Comparison of the Zapotec and Maya. *World Archaeology* 10 (2): 172–91.

———. 1983. Zapotec Religion. In *The Cloud People,* ed. K. V. Flannery and J. Marcus, 345–51. Academic Press, San Diego.

———. 1987. *Late Intermediate Occupation at Cerro Azul, Perú: A Preliminary Report.* University of Michigan Museum of Anthropology, Technical Report 20. Ann Arbor.

———. 1989. Zapotec Chiefdoms and the Nature of Formative Religions. In *Regional Perspectives on the Olmec,* ed. R. J. Sharer and D. C. Grove, 148–97. School of American Research, Santa Fe, N.Mex.

———. 1992. *Mesoamerican Writing Systems.* Princeton University Press, Princeton, N.J.

———. 1996. The Importance of Context in Interpreting Figurines. *Cambridge Archaeological Journal* 6: 285–91.

———. 1998. *Women's Ritual in Formative Oaxaca: Figurine-making, Divination, Death and the Ancestors.* Memoir 33. Museum of Anthropology, University of Michigan, Ann Arbor.

———. 1999. Men's and Women's Ritual in Formative Oaxaca. In *Social Patterns in Pre-Classic Mesoamerica,* ed. D. C. Grove and R. A. Joyce, 67–96. Dumbarton Oaks, Washington, D.C.

———. 2006. Identifying Elites and Their Strategies. In *Intermediate Elites in Pre-Columbian States and Empires,* ed. C. M. Elson and R. A. Covey, 212–46. University of Arizona Press, Tucson.

Marcus, Joyce, and Kent V. Flannery. 1994. Ancient Zapotec Ritual and Religion: An Application of the Direct Historical Approach. In *The Ancient Mind,* ed. C. Renfrew and E. B. W. Zubrow, 55–74. Cambridge University Press, Cambridge.

———. 1996. *Zapotec Civilization.* Thames and Hudson, London.

———. 2004. The Coevolution of Ritual and Society: New ^{14}C dates from Ancient Mexico. *Proceedings of the National Academy of Sciences* 101 (52): 18257–61.

McDermott, LeRoy. 1996. Self-Representation in Upper Paleolithic Female Figurines. *Current Anthropology* 37 (2): 227–75.

McIntosh, Roderick J., and Susan Keech McIntosh. 1979. Terracotta Statuettes from Mali. *African Arts* 12 (2): 51–91.

Miller, Arthur G. 1995. *The Painted Tombs of Oaxaca, Mexico: Living with the Dead.* Cambridge University Press, Cambridge.

Morss, Noel. 1954. *Clay Figurines of the American Southwest.* Papers of the Peabody Museum of American Archaeology and Ethnology, vol. 49, part 1, pp. 1–115. Harvard University, Cambridge, Mass.

Ortiz, Ponciano, and María del Carmen Rodríguez. 1996. El Manatí, Veracruz. *Arqueología Mexicana* (special edition entitled "Olmecs"), 38–41. Instituto Nacional de Antropología e Historia, Editorial Raíces, Mexico City.

———. 1999. Los espacios sagrados Olmecas: El Manatí, un caso especial. In *Los Olmecas en Mesoamérica,* ed. J. E. Clark, 68–91. Citibank, Mexico City.

Paddock, John, ed. 1966. *Ancient Oaxaca.* Stanford University Press, Stanford.

Paddock, John, Joseph R. Mogor, and Michael D. Lind. 1968. *Lambityeco Tomb 2: A Preliminary Report.* Boletín de Estudios Oaxaqueños 25. Museo Frissell de Arte Zapoteca, Mitla, Oaxaca.

Plunket, Patricia, ed. 2002. *Domestic Ritual in Ancient Mesoamerica.* Cotsen Institute of Archaeology Monograph 46. University of California, Los Angeles.

Plunket, Patricia, and Gabriela Uruñuela. 2002. Shrines, Ancestors, and the Volcanic Landscape at Tetimpa, Puebla. In *Domestic Ritual in Ancient Mesoamerica,* ed. P. Plunket, 31–42. Cotsen Institute of Archaeology Monograph 46. University of California, Los Angeles.

Ramírez Urrea, Susana. 1993. *Hacienda Blanca: Una aldea a través del tiempo, en el Valle de Etla, Oaxaca.* Tesis de la Escuela de Antropología, Universidad de Guadalajara, Mexico.

Rappaport, Roy A. 1971. Ritual, Sanctity, and Cybernetics. *American Anthropologist* 73 (1): 59–76.

———. 1972. The Sacred in Human Evolution. *Annual Review of Ecology and Systematics* 2: 23–44.

Renaud, A. E. B. 1929. Prehistoric Female Figurines from America and the Old World. *Scientific Monthly* 28: 507–12.

Renfrew, Colin. 1969. The Development and Chronology of the Early Cycladic Figurines. *American Journal of Archaeology* 73 (1): 1–32.

Renfrew, Colin, and Ezra B. W. Zubrow, eds. 1994. *The Ancient Mind.* Cambridge University Press, Cambridge.

Sahagún, Bernardino de. 1950. *Florentine Codex, Book 1—The Gods.* Trans. A. J. O. Anderson and C. E. Dibble. Monographs of the School of American Research 14, Part 2. Santa Fe, N.Mex.

Sánchez de la Barquera Arroyo, Elvia Cristina. 1996. *Figurillas prehispánicas del Valle de Atlixco, Puebla.* Serie Arqueología Instituto de Antropología e Historia, Mexico City.

Sandstrom, Alan R. 1991. *Corn Is Our Blood: Culture and Ethnic Identity in a Contemporary Aztec Indian Village.* University of Oklahoma Press, Norman.

Saville, Marshall H. 1899. Exploration of Zapotecan Tombs in Southern Mexico. *American Anthropologist* 1 (2): 350–62.

Spencer, Charles S., and Elsa M. Redmond. 2001. Multilevel Selection and Political Evolution in the Valley of Oaxaca, 500–100 BC. *Journal of Anthropological Archaeology* 20: 195–229.

———. 2003. Militarism, Resistance, and Early State Development in Oaxaca, Mexico. *Social Evolution and History* 2: 25–70.

———. 2004. Primary State Formation in Mesoamerica. *Annual Review of Anthropology* 33: 173–99.

———. 2006. Resistance Strategies and Early State Formation in Oaxaca, Mexico. In *Intermediate Elites in Pre-Columbian States and Empires,* ed. C. M. Elson and R. A. Covey, 21–43. University of Arizona Press, Tucson.

Sugiyama, Saburo, and Rubén Cabrera Castro. 2004. Voyage to the Center of the Moon Pyramid: Recent Discoveries in Teotihuacan. In *Voyage to the Center of the Moon Pyramid: Recent Discoveries in Teotihuacan,* ed. S. Sugiyama and R. Cabrera Castro, 8–10. Conaculta, Instituto Nacional de Antropología e Historia, Mexico City; Arizona State University, Tempe.

Sugiyama, Saburo, Rubén Cabrera Castro, and Leonardo López Luján. 2004. The Moon Pyramid Burials. In *Voyage to the Center of the Moon Pyramid: Recent Discoveries in Teotihuacan,* ed. S. Sugiyama and R. Cabrera Castro, 20–30. Conaculta, Instituto Nacional de Antropología e Historia, Mexico City; Arizona State University, Tempe.

Sugiyama, Saburo, and Leonardo López Luján. 2006. Sacrificios de consagración en La Pirámide de la Luna, Teotihuacan. In *Sacrificios de consagración en La Pirámide de la Luna,* ed. S. Sugiyama and L. López Luján, 25–52. Conaculta, Instituto Nacional de Antropología e Historia, Mexico City; Arizona State University, Tempe.

Ucko, Peter J. 1962. The Interpretation of Prehistoric Anthropomorphic Figurines. *Journal of the Royal Anthropological Institute of Great Britain and Ireland* 92 (1): 38–54.

Vaillant, Suzannah B., and George C. Vaillant. 1934. *Excavations at Gualupita.* Anthropological Papers of the American Museum of Natural History, vol. 35, part 1, pp. 1–135. New York.

Weiss, Gail, and Honi F. Haber, eds. 1999. *Perspectives on Embodiment.* Routledge, London.

Whalen, Michael E. 1981. *Excavations at Santo Domingo Tomaltepec: Evolution of a Formative Community in the Valley of Oaxaca, Mexico.* Memoir 12. Museum of Anthropology, University of Michigan, Ann Arbor.

3

Honduran Figurines and Whistles
in Social Context

Production, Use, and Meaning in the Ulúa Valley

JEANNE LOPIPARO AND JULIA A. HENDON

Excavations at five Late to Terminal Classic period sites (AD 600–1000) in the lower Ulúa valley in northwestern Honduras have produced a sizeable collection of ceramic figural artifacts, including figurines and whistles, from controlled contexts. Our research draws on secure provenience information to address issues of production, use, and social meaning by comparing evidence from contemporary habitation sites that range in size from large centers to small communities. This evidence suggests multiple production locales, use of figurines and whistles in ritual events at different social scales, and variation in the use and imagery of figurines and whistles among these sites. The presence of these artifacts in structured deposits, including contexts related to the production, consumption, and destruction of the objects, demonstrates that meaning does not exist as some fixed and essential property inherent in the objects themselves but develops from their participation in the social practices and events that contribute to the renewal of social identities and relations. These objects are part of a process of meaning-making that involves people and things in recursive and constituting practices in specific social and spatial contexts. Paraphrasing Daniel Miller (2005), we ask, how do the figurines and whistles that people make help make people?

We have evidence for the production of figurines and whistles, "making" in its most literal sense. We are also interested, however, in how the materiality and meaning of figural artifacts are intimately bound up in the making of identities and social relations across space and through time. The multiple contexts in which these objects are found suggest that they may be fruitfully understood as nonhuman subjects or "actants" (Latour 1991,

1996) with shifting and multivalent roles in meaning-making throughout their life histories. The interaction among humans and nonhumans in the formation of intersubjective relationships draws our attention to the agency of objects (Gell 1998; Gosden 2005; Hoskins 2006; Latour 1999; Miller 2005). Analysis of our multicomponent sites contributes a long-term perspective to approaches in material culture studies that attempt to dissolve the subject/object dichotomy and to focus on "the dialectic of people and things" (Meskell 2004: 7).

Archaeological and Social Contexts

The sites considered in this study include Cerro Palenque (CR-157), CR-80, CR-103, CR-132, and CR-381, which represent a range of sites in the settlement hierarchy of the lower Ulúa valley (figure 3.1). Cerro Palenque is a hilltop settlement that became the valley's largest center during the Late to Terminal Classic transition (circa AD 850), which is marked at the site by massive growth to over five hundred mounds, reorientation of settlement, expansion and relocation of monumental architecture, shifts in the proportions of local and imported resources, and a change in ceramic style indicative of a realignment of social ties with other societies in Honduras and more widely in Mesoamerica (Hendon 2002, 2003b, 2005, 2006a, 2007; Hendon and Lopiparo 2004; Joyce 1985, 1986, 1988, 1991, 1993). The Terminal Classic occupation spreads over a series of ridges and is organized into more than one hundred clusters of structures made up of buildings arranged around a central open area or patio. The occupants of the dwellings in these groups formed a co-residential domestic group or household. In some cases, several of these patio-centered clusters were built in such close proximity as to create a larger social unit made up of several households. Domestic structures are built on small foundation platforms. The buildings have walls made from river cobbles and more perishable materials such as clay and wood (wattle and daub). The Great Plaza, a large space enclosed by monumental architecture, serves as the civic-ceremonial center of the settlement with smaller groupings of monumental architecture located among the patio-centered clusters of dwellings. We consider figurines and whistles found throughout the site but focus our discussion on the extensive horizontal excavations directed by Julia Hendon in a large patio group near the ballcourt at the southern end of the Great Plaza (figure 3.2).

The other four sites discussed here, CR-80, CR-103, CR-132, and CR-381, are located in the central alluvium of the valley (Lopiparo 2003, 2004, 2006,

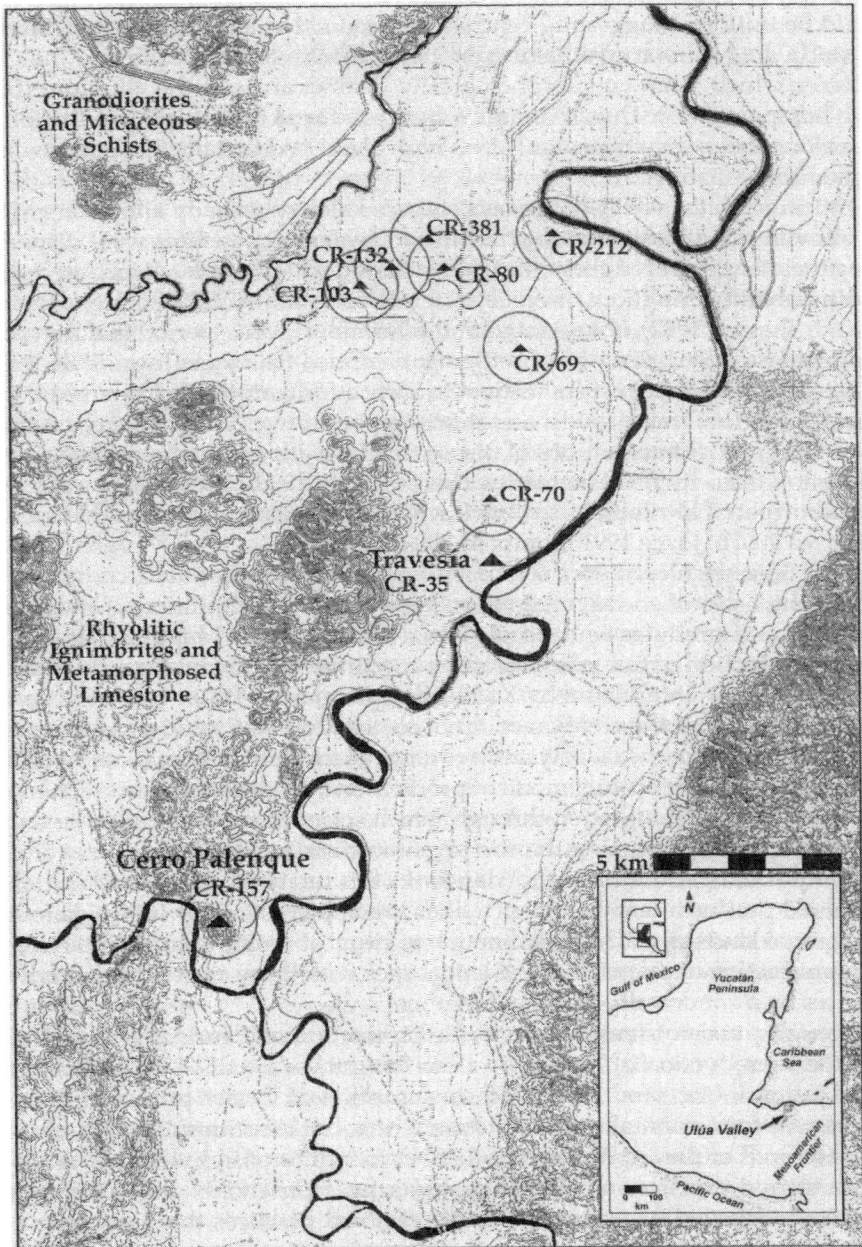

Figure 3.1. The lower Ulúa valley with the hilltop center of Cerro Palenque and the central alluvium sites indicated, as well as other important sites in the region (map by Jeanne Lopiparo).

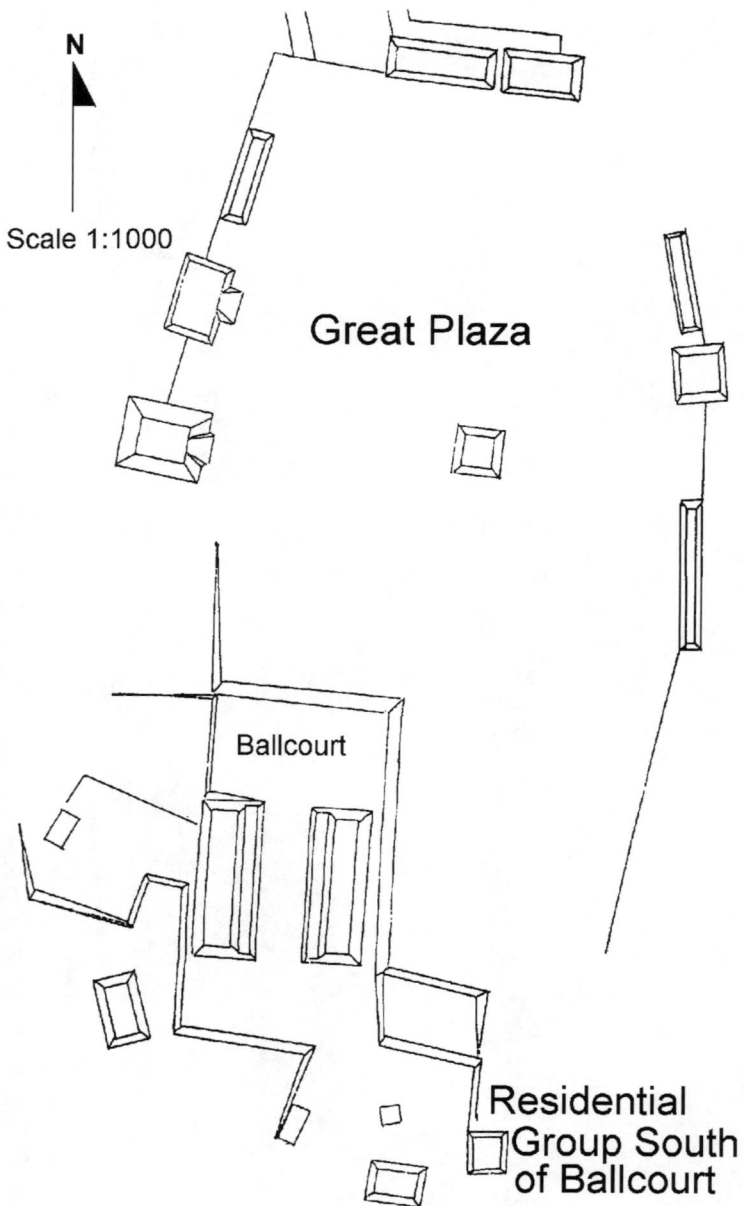

N

Scale 1:1000

Great Plaza

Ballcourt

Residential
Group South
of Ballcourt

Figure 3.2. Map of the central part of Cerro Palenque showing the Great Plaza, the ballcourt, and the residential group to its south (courtesy of Rosemary A. Joyce and the Instituto Hondureño de Antropología e Historia, used by permission).

2007, forthcoming; Lopiparo et al. 2005). These multicomponent domestic sites consist of multiple broad earthen rises, called *lomas,* which were built up over hundreds of years through the intentional destruction, in-filling, and renewal of groups of small wattle-and-daub structures that define a central patio and were sometimes constructed on low, plastered platforms. The frequent renovation of houses was associated with the placement of human burials and marked by elaborate rituals involving the caching of unique artifacts directly beneath the living surfaces of the patio group. While settlement was very dense all along watercourses, lomas occur in distinct clusters ranging in size from small domestic sites with one or two equal-sized lomas to large sites with over ten (Henderson et al. forthcoming; Sheptak 1982), some of which are unusually large or suggestive of specialized use. The sites discussed here encompass that range of variation. CR-80 features an enormous central loma. It is about 200 meters long with an open platform on one end. Like Cerro Palenque, CR-132 has a ballcourt. Both CR-80 and CR-132 have unusually elaborate construction, suggesting that they were the focus of community-wide gatherings in the central alluvium (Lopiparo forthcoming; Joyce et al. forthcoming).

Research at the central alluvium sites and Cerro Palenque has demonstrated that the perishable wattle-and-daub structures at loma sites are analogous to cobble-mound structures in terms of function and the social organization of their inhabitants, with abundant evidence for very similar domestic activities. By extension, the lomas are like patio groups at Cerro Palenque in that they are the living space of a co-residential domestic group. Both lomas and patio groups are unevenly distributed, being found in clusters that we refer to here as household groups (Joyce and Hendon 2000). Household groups are made up of patio groups or lomas that, because of their close proximity, are considered to be the material manifestation of a house society form of organization. These social houses were integrated through the performance and maintenance of a shared set of responsibilities, property, and rights through time (see Gillespie 2000a, 2000b; Hendon 2007; Joyce 2000; Lopiparo 2007). Household groups range from single patio groups with a few structures to clusters of about ten patio groups with as many as thirty to forty structures.

Household groups were the units of small-scale production in the central alluvium and at Cerro Palenque; each has evidence related to the full range of production activities. They participated in community-wide activities and gatherings based on local sociopolitical and economic relations of kinship, exchange, and shared participation in ritual practices, such as ballgames and communal feasting, that might have been associated with calendrical and life-cycle events. While the sites in this study differ in the arrangement and scale of their architectural features, they share several significant functional and organizational characteristics. They were all places where production, consumption, destruction, and renewal of material culture and architecture played an integral role in social practices that reproduced social identities over time. Thus, the differentiation of sites in terms of size or physical scale is not paralleled in any consistent way by centralization in the production or consumption of prestige goods, suggesting that settlements were ranked in different ways on the basis of such diverse measures as wealth, prestige, or size (Henderson et al. forthcoming; Hendon 2002, 2003b; Joyce 1985, 1991; Joyce and Hendon 2000; Joyce et al. forthcoming; Lopiparo 2007, forthcoming; Sheptak 1982).

Production and Distribution of Molded Ceramic Artifacts

The ceramic figural artifacts from the excavated sites that we consider here consist of three-dimensional figures. CR-103, CR-80, and CR-381 produced an especially rich sample of 1,578 figurines (whole and fragmentary) and 440 molds (Lopiparo 2003). The ballcourt residential group at Cerro Palenque yielded 91 figurines or whistle fragments. Most of the figural artifacts from all five sites have hollow heads and bodies that were mold-made (figures 3.3–3.7). The assemblage also includes artifacts that were full-figure, single-chambered whistles and various figural heads attached to multichambered whistle bodies (or ocarinas). The miniature figural masks and beads produced and consumed at CR-381 are an unusual component of the sample.

Many of these figural artifacts and the molds used to create them have a fine orange paste (Tacamiche), which is part of a continuous, valleywide, fine-paste tradition dating back to at least the Late Classic period (Joyce 1985). Although these wares mostly lack temper, very fine inclusions do sometimes occur, suggesting that various clay recipes or sources were used. Archaeological contexts of production and deposition indicate that ceramic production in the valley was dispersed rather than centralized (Hendon and Lopiparo 2004; Lopiparo 2003). Stylistic and physicochemical artifact research using petrography and Instrumental Neutron Activation Analysis provide further confirmation that the molds and mold-made figural artifacts were produced in many different household groups at sites at all levels of the settlement hierarchy, including the sites in this study. Instrumental

Left: Figure 3.3. Raptorial bird forming part of the headdress of a figurine from Cerro Palenque (photo by Julia A. Hendon).

Below: Figure 3.4. Pieces of figurines and molds from CR-381 depicting faces and headdresses (photo by Jeanne Lopiparo).

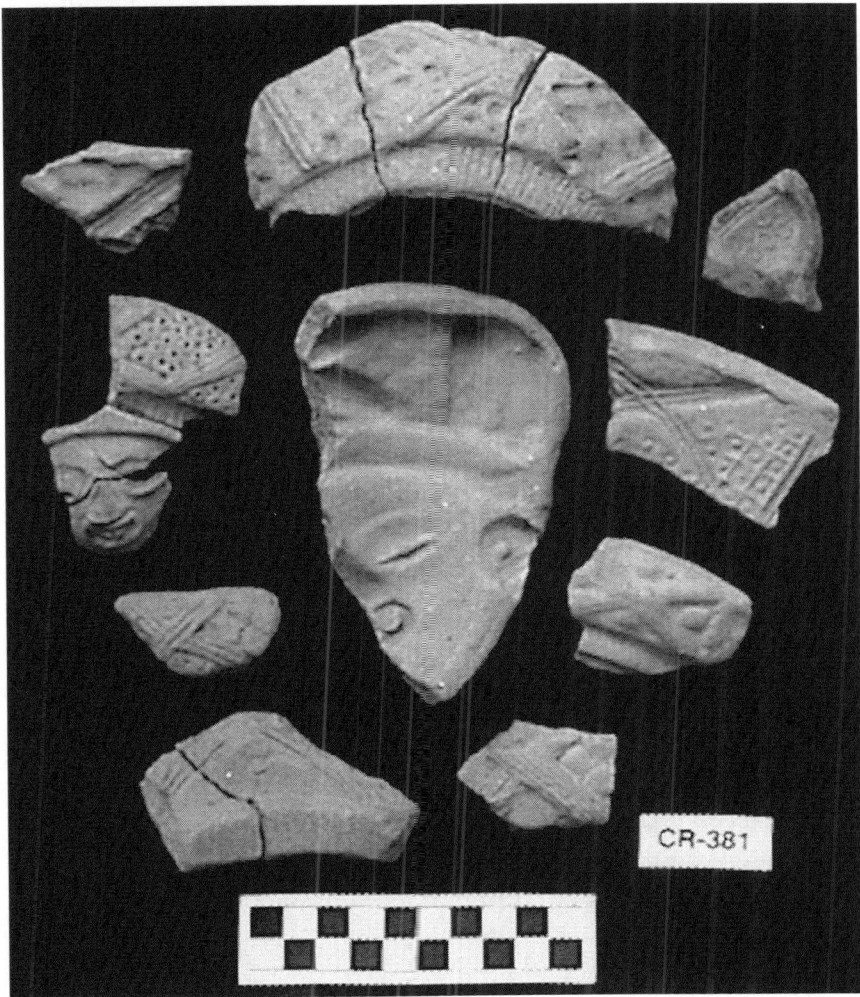

CR-381

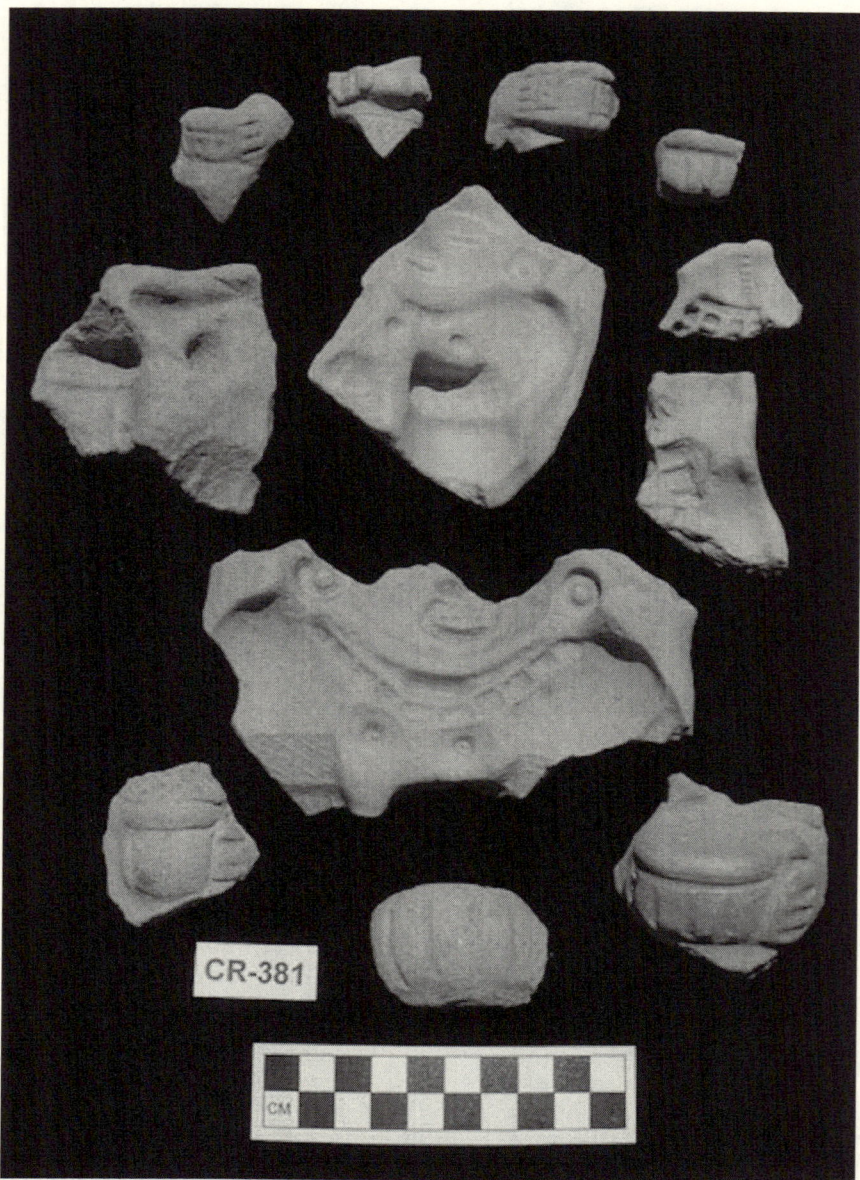

Figure 3.5. Figurines and molds from CR-381 in the shape of a woman carrying a ceramic vessel (photo by Jeanne Lopiparo).

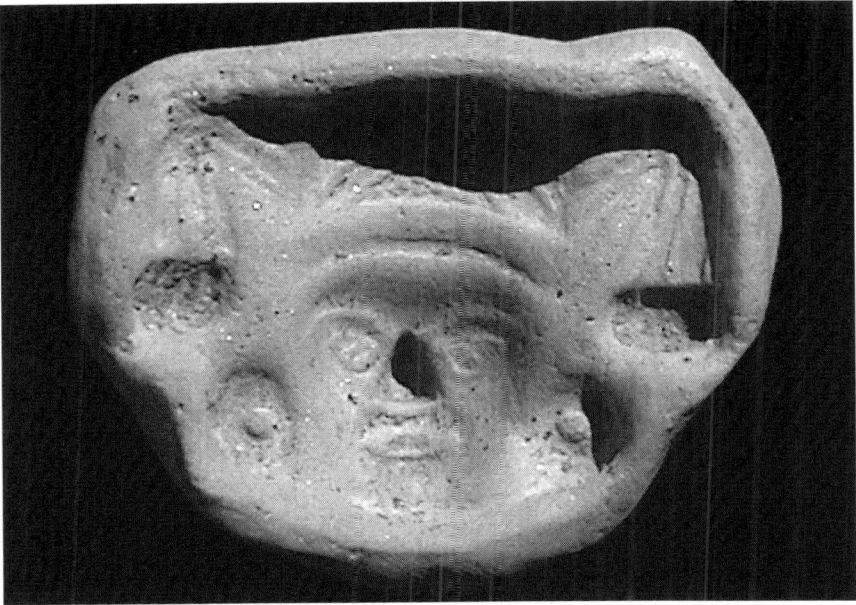

Figure 3.6. Mold designed to create the face of a large figurine (photo by Jeanne Lopiparo).

Figure 3.7. Body of a female dressed in a short cape from Cerro Palenque (photo by Julia A. Hendon).

Neutron Activation Analysis reveals at least three distinct chemical signatures in the study area alone (Lopiparo 2007; Lopiparo et al. 2005; Speakman and Glascock 2003).

People made figurines by pressing clay into molds to form the front part. The backs were usually not as finely finished and appear to be hand-modeled (compare Schortman et al. 1992: 73). The musical instruments may have only one chamber and produce a single tone or may have several chambers with multiple apertures to create a range of sounds. Such instruments are sometimes labeled ocarinas although we prefer to refer to all musical instruments as whistles because not all of our examples are intact enough to permit a determination of how many chambers existed originally. While the figural representations attached to the front of the sound chambers appear to be mold-made, we could not ascertain how the whistle bodies were made. Generic, bulbous whistle bodies and fragments are often found with the head broken off at a seam, indicating that the two parts were modeled separately before being joined. Sometimes the figural heads served as chambers for the whistles, while in other cases the multichambered whistle body functioned independently of the attached figural representation. Some simple whistles appear to be hand-modeled. Producers of the complex, multichambered ones needed to be skilled to create objects that would make the desired range of sounds. Schortman and colleagues (1992: 73) have suggested that the hollow chambers were modeled around smoothed, fired clay spheres, then were cut in half to extract the sphere and were later reattached. At all of the sites, we found a range of smooth, ceramic spheres of varying sizes that are consistent with the range of chamber sizes found in ocarinas, suggesting that this is a plausible explanation (though artifact breakage did not reveal any obvious seams). Another possibility is the use of a perishable material that would have melted or burned off during firing.

Excavations at CR-103, CR-132, and CR-381 revealed evidence of all phases of ceramic production, including multiple firing facilities, clay preparation pits, specialized middens, and large numbers of molds and mold-made artifacts, including many matches (Lopiparo 2003; Lopiparo et al. 2005). In contrast to the multiple production locales in the central alluvium, the full range of features associated with figurine and whistle production at Cerro Palenque has been discovered only in the ballcourt residential group (Hendon 2005, 2006a; Hendon and Lopiparo 2004). This is the largest known patio group from the Terminal Classic occupation of the site and is located next to the ballcourt. Two kilns, and a possible third, have been found here. One was in front of the largest structure that closes off the south side of the courtyard. The other was to one side of this building, in an area behind the western building. Nearby trash pits contain broken molds for the production of figurines or whistles as well as for mold-made, Tacamiche fine-paste vessels, including at least one instance of a match between a figural vessel and a mold fragment. Test pits excavated south of the kilns, into the area outside of the residential group's patio but still on the same raised terrace that supports the group and the ballcourt, suggest the presence of a third kiln or a work area with more production debris.

Based on the excavated assemblage and documented collections of whole artifacts, the variety of representational subject matter does not seem to differ dramatically between figurines and whistles. Both include representations that are zoomorphic, anthropomorphic, neither, or both. As a heuristic convenience, we have followed Gordon Willey (1972, 1978) in calling the "neither or both" examples "supernaturals" (with no implication that they represent specific deities). The overlap in imagery is particularly true for the figural heads because certain body forms are specific to the multichambered whistles for functional reasons. Additionally, naturalistic representations of whole animals (heads and bodies) seem more likely to be musical instruments because they do not occur as often in non-sound-producing figurine forms (though this is difficult to quantify because of the fragmented nature of much of the assemblage).

One of the most striking features of the assemblages of mold-made ceramic artifacts in the valley is the incredible diversity of designs found in both the artifacts and the molds. This diversity and the concomitant difficulty in characterizing it is reflected in the variety of typologies and the large number of categories that have been devised to classify figurines from the Ulúa and neighboring Naco valleys (see, for example, Lopiparo 2003; Schortman et al. 1992: 36–37; Tercero 1996). Despite what we often assume about production processes based on molds, their adoption in the lower Ulúa valley does not seem to have been primarily for mass production. Nor did it result in the use of a limited number of motifs or a simplification of imagery (compare Halperin, this volume). Frustrating as this diversity is from the point of view of typology construction, the variation in artifacts and molds further contributes to our argument for dispersed production and the incorporation of these artifacts into localized practices associated with the assertion and reproduction of social identities discussed in the next section.

Spatial Variation in the Consumption of Figural Artifacts: Social Identity and Rituals of Renewal

Craft producers in the valley created figurines and figural whistles with both unique and shared representations; these artifacts were prominently incorporated into the activities that served as foci for social interactions among members of different social groups (Hendon 2005, 2006a; Joyce 1993; Lopiparo 2003, 2007, forthcoming). Household workshops produced mold-made, figural artifacts that were incorporated into rituals involved in the renewal of houses and the celebration of the life cycle of their inhabitants. Rituals involved the placement of whole, unburned artifacts in the burned, collapsed debris of wattle-and-daub structures and ovens; the caching of whole artifacts beneath the floors of houses and patios; the burial of humans beneath the floors of houses and patios; the disposal of special ceramic artifacts in pits and ovens; the depositing of smashed and burned vessels on the living surface adjacent to a razed structure or beneath the fill of a new occupation surface or new house construction; and the deposition of broken vessels and special artifacts immediately along the front of house platforms.

Both mold and artifact styles that are iconographically unique to certain sites were recovered from ritual contexts associated with the renewal of these multicomponent sites (Lopiparo 2006). Some figurines are unique to or more likely to be found at particular sites. Site-specific artifacts at CR-80, CR-103, and CR-381 occur disproportionately in structured ritual deposits. Of the twenty-two whole or mostly whole heads of anthropomorphic figural artifacts recovered from ritual deposits accompanying construction renewals at central alluvium sites, for example, seven are unique in that they represent the only one of their kind from the excavated assemblage, three are from form classes with multiple examples in the assemblage, and ten are representations of supernaturals that are rare overall, representing less than 10 percent of the assemblage from all contexts. The remaining two are indeterminate. For comparison purposes, we note that the proportion of stylized figural artifacts with common motifs to unusual or unique artifacts in the general diagnostic sample is about one to one. More broadly, structured deposits associated with rituals of renewal contain many more unusual or unique figural representations than do other contexts. However, figurines with the same or similar motifs are found at all of the sites. We see these figurines as one way that the people living at these sites created connections with those from other communities as part of a shared sense of identity.

Despite the variability in the size and settlement density of the sites discussed here, the comparison between contexts of structured deposition at Cerro Palenque and sites in the central alluvium such as CR-80, CR-103, CR-132, and CR-381 is illuminating. Fine-grained, horizontal excavations have demonstrated that structured deposition occurred at all of the sites in association with the construction and renewal of residential group architecture, with extensive evidence at both Cerro Palenque and loma sites of caching behavior below surfaces and of the intentional smashing, breaking, and burning of artifacts in front of platforms. Analysis of ritual contexts from Cerro Palenque suggests that whole figural artifacts and vessels were embedded before new construction, while fragments of "consumed" figural artifacts formed part of repeated ritual practices of renewal in the renovation cycles of houses and, by extension, in the life cycles of their inhabitants. No evidence of human burials has been recovered, although human and animal bones are incorporated in caches and architectural fill between construction episodes (Hendon 2005, 2006a). Although figurines and whistles appear to have been manufactured in only one residential group, they were used by people living throughout the site (Hendon 2003b, 2005, 2006a; Hendon and Lopiparo 2004; Joyce 1985).

Figural artifacts played a role in ritualized action that reinforced social solidarity and differentiation, and in this sense, their use parallels that of the loma sites in the central alluvium. In the ballcourt residential group, one of the main contexts where Hendon (2007) found figurine pieces was in a deposit containing censers, fine-paste serving vessels, and a human bone cache put in place as part of the renovation and rebuilding of the western structure in the group. Another ritualized deposit comes from Group 1, a residential group that is near the Great Plaza, although not as close as the ballcourt residential group (Joyce 1991: 95–96; 1993). Two figurines and one whistle had been placed inside a low platform shrine as part of a ritual cache. Dressed in a skirt and necklace, one of the figurines is a woman who stands with her left arm raised and her hand clasping her hair. Balanced on her head is a jar with two handles that looks like the actual jars used to carry water by the people living in this and other residential groups at the site as part of everyday life. The other figurine takes the form of a man wearing a helmet in the shape of a bird's head and a costume made of feathers. He holds a musical instrument, in this case a conch shell trumpet, again referring to real life activities of the communities of practice based in the residential place.

The Cerro Palenque figurines are generally in pieces, but an emphasis on birds can be identified, suggesting the association of local identities with certain iconography represented in figural artifacts. The cached figurine in Group 1 wears a bird helmet, and Rosemary Joyce (1991: 95) notes that some of the fragmentary figurines from trash deposits also wore bird helmet headdresses. A partial figure from the ballcourt residential group has a headdress that includes feathers. A more striking example also comes from this group. The preserved side of a face has a large bird projecting from the side of the headdress. Shown in profile, the bird looks like a raptor of some kind (figure 3.3). Two other headdress elements that may be identified are a pompon and a long-nosed animal.

At the loma sites, where change is characterized by multiple episodes of resurfacing and rebuilding, caches of whole artifacts are often associated with both the interment of humans and the burial of destroyed structures before the occupation surfaces were filled. In fact, whole, unburned artifacts were sometimes intentionally embedded directly into the burned collapse (Lopiparo 2003). Major episodes of destruction and deposition of fill, followed by resurfacing, are associated with deposits of smashed vessels, figural artifacts, ground-stone fragments, and other special artifacts (Lopiparo 2003). Comparable dense deposits of smashed, whole vessels have been recovered adjacent to platforms in the ballcourt residential group at Cerro Palenque. However, the number of vessels represented is greater at Cerro Palenque than at sites in the central alluvium. If, as Hendon suggests (2003b, 2006a), these deposits represent the remains of periodic celebrations (such as feasting accompanying ballgames), then the much larger scale of the gathering would account for the high concentrations of fine-paste serving vessels recovered from these contexts. Similar gatherings likely took place at small centers in the central alluvium, such as CR-80, but the scale of these events would have been smaller, limited to members of the local community and more immediate environs.

Distinctions can be drawn between Cerro Palenque and sites in the central alluvium in the scale and diversity of production and in the differential use of figural artifacts in structured deposition associated with their consumption or destruction. While at least three of the four household groups in the community in the central alluvium (CR-103, CR-80, and CR-381) have evidence for independent household ceramic industries, only one residential group at Cerro Palenque has similar evidence. In addition, residents of loma sites all seem to have consumed, destroyed, or buried unusual or unique artifacts that are iconic of household identities as part of ritual practices associated with the life cycles of houses and their inhabitants (Lopiparo 2007). This elaboration of household production and consumption among small-scale sites suggests that the diversity of iconography in figural artifacts was "legible" on the local level, serving to establish, renew, and distinguish household identities within their communities. At sites that served as foci of wider gatherings, from small-scale centers such as CR-80 to regional centers such as Cerro Palenque, periodic rituals of consumption focused more on establishing connections, affiliations, and shared social identities among more-diverse social groups. Here the consumption and production of fine-paste serving vessels would have formed an essential part of maintaining alliances and social relationships. Caches of figural artifacts in household groups at Cerro Palenque indicate that residents also participated in rituals of renewal that emphasized the significance of figurines and whistles as active participants in social reproduction and the enchainment of human and nonhuman actors in maintaining social identities through time in the Ulúa Valley.

One elaborate example of such a structured deposit was excavated at CR-103. It was associated with three successive Late to Terminal Classic occupation surfaces in the southeast quadrant of the loma (Lopiparo 2003). These occupation surfaces, labeled Terminal Classic Surface C and Late Classic Surfaces D and E, were associated with the structural collapse of wattle-and-daub houses in the form of large chunks of burned clay with cane impressions. On Surface E, a domed mound of ash and a *bajareque* (a circular oven surrounded by burned clay) were buried in place, as was a human burial aligned with the house walls. The second level of collapse was found on top of the previous structure, indicating that the second structure was built in approximately the same place. The destruction of the structures was marked by ritual deposits that were associated with the living surfaces on which the structures were destroyed. A complex, multilayered deposit found to the south of the collapsed building represents the remains of a series of very elaborate ritualized practices. These deposits included the burial of an animal, probably a feline, on top of the burned sherds of a broken vessel. To its side were large pieces of a metate and mano. On top of the animal burial was another level of burned vessel sherds, including several special ceramic artifacts, such as the whole head of a burned figurine, as well as a pendant of a *"viejo"* and a mold of a wrinkly-faced anthropomorphic figure, both of which fall into the category of supernatural. A decapitated figurine depicting a person holding an offering in his or her hands was found in another ceramic concentration on the Late Classic D surface.

To the south-southwest of the burned structure, Late Classic Surface E also featured a bajareque, as noted above, forming a dense structural collapse of its domed superstructure. Four special ceramic artifacts were embedded in this debris: a pendant/miniature mask of a face with an elaborate wrinkly faced design (which also possibly represents a supernatural), a solid figurine of a standing monkey looking upward, the head of a stylized anthropomorphic figurine, and a whistle in the form of a caiman. To the south of the hearth, the excavators found a whole miniature Tacamiche paste vessel that had been turned over and a dense concentration of burned sherds that seem to be the smashed remains of almost whole vessels.

A mold with a design identical to the caiman whistle was found in the structured deposit associated with Terminal Classic Surface C. Although later in time, the Surface C deposit comes from the same area of the loma, indicating continuity in figural representation. This suggests that certain imagery was associated with particular houses through time. The caiman mold was associated with an unusual stuccoed and painted figural jaguar head and half of a very unusual mold for a large vessel with a mold-impressed squirrel motif.

Conclusions: Figurines as Agents of Social Reproduction

Recognizing that meaning resides in the practices that create contexts for interaction between human and nonhuman agents leads to a different perspective on the significance of whole and broken objects. Fixating on an object as a repository of some stable meaning suggests that its destruction or dissolution destroys the integrity of this meaning (Küchler 1999). Structured deposits such as caches or burials tend to be interpreted differently depending on the physical integrity of the artifacts included. Caching of whole artifacts is often seen as the result of a desire for continuity or remembering, whereas deposits of broken, dispersed, or burned artifacts have more often been viewed as part of a process of termination and, sometimes, as a form of forced forgetting or even a kind of symbolic or literal violence (Mock 1998; see also Inomata and Webb 2003). We argue that an integrated, relational conceptualization of subjects and objects emphasizes the diachronic aspect of these deposits, in which their meanings are both actively constituted by and constitutive of the performative acts of interment and the social practices of remembering and forgetting. Through time, these meanings are produced and reproduced through the relationships among human and nonhuman agents. These relations do not depend on the visibility or intact nature of the object. Hidden knowledge is a critical component in the assertion and enactment of group membership and social distinctions in Mesoamerica (Hendon 2000).

Evidence for structured deposits at sites in the Ulúa Valley that are consistent in their placement and orientation of cached artifacts and human burials confirms that this knowledge was maintained as part of the social memory of residential groups over hundreds of years (Lopiparo 2003, 2007). Shared iconography further underlines these connections. Visible or hidden, these nonhuman actants transform the landscape by demarcating and sacralizing domestic spaces, evoking shared memories, and materializing the mutual knowledge that constitutes an inalienable part of group membership (Hendon 2000). The linking together of humans and nonhumans becomes integral to the production of social identities through time (Chapman 2000). "The dual notions of dedication and termination, while conceptually diametric, . . . should not be seen as opposing acts but, rather, as mutually embedded markers in a cyclical process of birth, death, and rebirth. Such a view of ritual practice and deposition is in fact closely related to current understanding of how the ancient Maya viewed the composition of households and the active role of the deceased as ancestors" (Kunen et al. 2002: 198).

The distinction between dedication and termination rituals becomes blurred by the entangling of humans and nonhumans. The intentional burning, razing, and rebuilding of dwellings in the same place, the interment of caches of special artifacts (including many figurines), and the burial of the dead in patios, platforms, and house floors in Classic period Ulúa Valley sites played a central role in rituals of renewal. The treatment of houses parallels that of their inhabitants, suggesting a conceptual parallel between the human life cycle and the life span of the dwelling. These parallels suggest that processes of dissolution and interment, of death and rebirth are fundamental to social continuity, as house members became house ancestors. These connections are part of processes that were fluid and ongoing. They did not necessarily depend on the wholeness, inviolability, or physical integrity of material objects. It was not always (or even most often) their archiving that produced meaning, but rather their active use and consumption in a variety of practices, some unique and others repeated, some localized and others widespread, for which we have recovered archaeological traces at sites in the Ulúa Valley.

Thus, it seems that meaning derives not solely from an object's form or imagery but also from the social practices in which it interacts with people and other objects. Such practices may include the breaking, burning, burying, or throwing away of objects. We suggest that the destructive use or consumption of figurines did not dissolve the meaning of the object but rather was essential to the role of that object in meaning-making. The act of destructive consumption was a form of renewal even when consumption resulted in an object that is no longer intact or visible. We see evidence for this pattern in other forms of material culture in the Ulúa Valley, most notably in the burning, burial, and rebuilding of perishable architecture and in the smashing and often burning of serving vessels in deposits associated with burials and household renovations in domestic contexts and sometimes associated with gatherings that focused on ballgame events in centers.

An analogy might also be made to other forms of consumption that transform material through processes of burial in the ground (planting), exposure to heat (cooking), or ingestion (eating) for renewed growth. The preparation of fields for planting on the fertile valley bottom might have included burning vegetation, the intentional movement of earth, and taking advantage of the natural process of alluviation by the Ulúa River. In a similar way, the interment or "planting" of the dead in house floors was essential for the renewed growth of the house (Lopiparo 2006, 2007). Iconographic, ethnohistoric, and ethnographic sources from Mesoamerica agree on a common association among seeds/semen/bone and flesh/blood/corn or, more broadly, on what is planted, interred, or renewed and what is consumed, ephemeral, and sustaining (Gillespie 2001, 2002; Joyce 2006; Monaghan 1998, 2001; Stross 2006). The life-cycle practices of "making" human subjects, from pregnancy, birth, and child rearing to rites of passage through adulthood to death and interment, are tied metaphorically to specific, ephemeral production and consumption practices such as planting, sowing, cooking, and weaving that were located within and around houses (Gillespie 2000b; Hendon 2000, 2006b; Vogt 1969). Through the process of production in households, figural objects became nonhuman subjects in ways that are analogous to the formation of the substance of human agents. They are formed from raw materials that were treated like corn, being ground using manos and metates and transformed through water and fire to result in figures modeled into human forms that embodied idealized characteristics of members of social groups.

Archaeologists infer the meaningful practices analogous to those documented in the ethnographic and ethnohistoric literature primarily from such evidence as the placement and interment of intact artifacts, from unusual patterns in the frequencies of serving vessels, or from a high occurrence of certain food remains. Traces of the communal practices of feeding and eating in Mesoamerican domestic contexts, which are so significant in the formation of intersubjective relationships, come most frequently from patterned distribution of deposits that we often characterize as garbage (Brown 2001; Hendon 2003a). In other words, many of the deposits that archaeologists might characterize as garbage seem to have been generated intentionally, in the sense that they exhibit clear patterns not only of consumption and breakage but also of careful placement. This suggests that the dissolution of substance was an active practice rather than a passive result. Thus, intentional placement includes not only caches of whole artifacts but also patterned deposition of broken (and often burned) ceramic figural artifacts and vessels.

Mesoamerican figurines occupy that ambivalent space of "human nonhumans." They have often been interpreted as proxies for or icons of humans to be interred, offered, decapitated, or otherwise subjected to corporal mortification to dedicate, terminate, or supplicate. Such interpretations focus on only one stage of figurines' life history, their "death," and on their occurrence in particular kinds of archaeological contexts, usually caching rituals characterized as dedicatory or termination rituals. However, we also have ample contextual evidence for other social practices involving figural objects that result in much more ambiguous traces in the archaeological record. In fact, because most such objects are not found intact in pristine contexts, we should not dismiss this fragmentary evidence simply as garbage or as decontextualized secondary or tertiary deposits. Rather, these deposits emphasize the importance of understanding how figural artifacts were differentially incorporated in human activities and interactions.

If we look at figurines as nonhuman agents, they too are composed of ephemeral and perdurable substances. Like flesh and bone, there is a part that remains and a part that is consumed (Joyce 2006). And like the bones of the ancestors that are "implanted" beneath floors, and the perishable structures that are burned or consumed as the basis for rebuilding and renewal, these figural artifacts were both implanted or interred in caches and consumed or transformed through fire and dissolution. Both of these processes were fundamental to the reproduction of social groups, as was participation in the practices through which group substance was sustained and renewed.

Acknowledgments

All of the research discussed in this chapter was carried out under agreements with the Instituto Hondureño de Antropología e Historia, whose support and staff assistance is greatly appreciated. Hendon's research at Cerro Palenque has been supported by grants from the Gettysburg College Research and Professional Development Fund and a Presidential Research Fellowship, the H. John Heinz III Fund (Heinz Family Foundation), the National Science Foundation (BCS-0207114), and the Stahl Endowment and Committee on Research of the University of California, Berkeley. Lopiparo's research in the central alluvium has been supported by the Wenner-Gren Foundation (Individual Research Grant #6716, the Lita Osmundsen Fellowship, and the Richard Carley Hunt Postdoctoral Fellowship). Work at CR-132 was supported by the Department of Anthropology, Phi Beta Kappa, and the Center for Latin American and Iberian Studies of Harvard University as part of a regional project directed by John S. Henderson and Rosemary A. Joyce. Instrumental Neutron Activation Analysis was carried out by Robert J. Speakman and Michael D. Glascock of the Missouri University Research Reactor. The analysis was supported by a Stahl Grant from the Archaeological Research Facility, University of California, Berkeley, and was subsidized in part by NSF Grant SBR-0102325 supporting the MURR Archaeometry Lab. The support of these organizations is gratefully acknowledged.

References Cited

Brown, Linda A. 2001. Feasting on the Periphery: The Production of Ritual Feasting and Village Festivals at the Ceren Site, El Salvador. In *Feasts: Archaeological and Ethnographic Perspectives on Food, Politics, and Power,* ed. M. Dietler and B. Hayden, 368–90. Smithsonian Institution Press, Washington, D.C.

Chapman, John. 2000. *Fragmentation in Archaeology: People, Places and Broken Objects in the Prehistory of South Eastern Europe.* Routledge, London.

Gell, Alfred. 1998. *Art and Agency: An Anthropological Theory.* Clarendon Press, Oxford, U.K.

Gillespie, Susan D. 2000a. Beyond Kinship: An Introduction. In *Beyond Kinship: Social and Material Reproduction in House Societies,* ed. R. A. Joyce and S. D. Gillespie, 1–21. University of Pennsylvania Press, Philadelphia.

———. 2000b. Maya "Nested Houses": The Ritual Construction of Place. In *Beyond Kinship: Social and Material Reproduction in House Societies,* ed. R. A. Joyce and S. D. Gillespie, 135–60. University of Pennsylvania Press, Philadelphia.

———. 2001. Personhood, Agency, and Mortuary Ritual: A Case Study from the Ancient Maya. *Journal of Anthropological Archaeology* 20: 73–112.

————. 2002. Body and Soul among the Maya: Keeping the Spirits in Place. In *The Space and Place of Death,* ed. H. Silverman and D. B. Small, 67–78. Archaeological Papers of the American Anthropological Association 11. Arlington, Va.

Gosden, Chris. 2005. What Do Objects Want? *Journal of Archaeological Method and Theory* 12: 193–211.

Henderson, John S., Rosemary A. Joyce, and Russell N. Sheptak. Forthcoming. Travesía and Its Neighbors: From Settlement Patterns to Social Landscapes. In *Another Way of Being Maya: Local Practices and History in the Ulúa Valley, Honduras,* ed. R. A. Joyce and J. S. Henderson.

Hendon, Julia A. 2000. Having and Holding: Storage, Memory, Knowledge, and Social Relations. *American Anthropologist* 102: 42–54.

————. 2002. Social Relations and Collective Identities: Household and Community in Ancient Mesoamerica. In *The Dynamics of Power,* ed. M. O'Donovan, 273–300. Occasional Paper 30. Center for Archaeological Investigations, Southern Illinois University, Carbondale.

————. 2003a. Feasting at Home: Community and House Solidarity among the Maya of Southeastern Mesoamerica. In *The Archaeology and Politics of Food and Feasting in Early States and Empires,* ed. T. L. Bray, 203–33. Kluwer Academic/Plenum, New York.

————. 2003b. Honor, Shame and Reciprocity: Feasting in Southeastern Mesoamerican Complex Societies during the Late to Terminal Classic Period. Paper presented at the 102nd Annual Meeting of the American Anthropological Association, Chicago.

————. 2005. Social Identity and Practice in the Terminal Classic Community of Cerro Palenque, Honduras. Paper presented at the 70th Annual Meeting of the Society for American Archaeology, Salt Lake City, Utah.

————. 2006a. Social Identity and Daily Life in the Terminal Classic: Local Histories and Global Connections in the Ulúa Valley, Honduras. Paper presented at the 52nd International Congress of Americanists, Seville, Spain.

————. 2006b. Textile Production as Craft in Mesoamerica: Time, Labor, and Knowledge. *Journal of Social Archaeology* 10: 354–78.

————. 2007. Memory, Materiality, and Practice: House Societies in Southeastern Mesoamerica. In *The Durable House: House Society Models in Archaeology,* ed. R. A. Beck, 292–316. Occasional Paper 35. Center for Archaeological Investigations, Southern Illinois University, Carbondale.

Hendon, Julia A., and Jeanne Lopiparo. 2004. Investigaciones recientes en Cerro Palenque, Cortés, Honduras. In *Memoria VII Seminario de Antropología de Honduras,* ed. K. Rubén Ávalos, 187–95. Instituto Hondureño de Antropología e Historia, Tegucigalpa.

Hoskins, Janet. 2006. Agency, Biography and Objects. In *Handbook of Material Culture,* ed. C. Tilley, W. Keane, S. Küchler-Fogden, M. Rowlands, and P. Spyer, 74–84. Sage Publications, Thousand Oaks, Calif.

Inomata, Takeshi, and Ronald W. Webb, eds. 2003. *The Archaeology of Settlement Abandonment in Middle America.* University of Utah Press, Salt Lake City.

Joyce, Rosemary A. 1985. Cerro Palenque, Valle de Ulúa, Honduras: Terminal Classic Interaction on the Southern Mesoamerican Periphery. Ph.D. diss., Department of Anthropology, University of Illinois, Urbana. University Microfilms, Ann Arbor, Mich.

———. 1986. Terminal Classic Interaction on the Southeastern Maya Periphery. *American Antiquity* 51: 313–29.

———. 1988. The Ulúa Valley and the Coastal Maya Lowlands: The View from Cerro Palenque. In *The Southeast Classic Maya Zone*, ed. G. R. Willey and E. Boone, 269–95. Dumbarton Oaks, Washington, D.C.

———. 1991. *Cerro Palenque: Power and Identity on the Maya Periphery.* University of Texas Press, Austin.

———. 1993. Women's Work: Images of Production and Reproduction in Pre-Hispanic Southern Central America. *Current Anthropology* 34: 255–73.

———. 2000. Heirlooms and Houses: Materiality and Social Memory. In *Beyond Kinship: Social and Material Reproduction in House Societies*, ed. R. A. Joyce and S. D. Gillespie, 189–212. University of Pennsylvania Press, Philadelphia.

———. 2006. When the Flesh Is Solid but the Person Is Hollow Inside: Formal Variation in Hand-Modeled Figurines from Formative Mesoamerica. Paper presented at the 71st Annual Meeting of the Society for American Archaeology, San Juan, P.R.

Joyce, Rosemary A., and Julia A. Hendon. 2000. Heterarchy, History, and Material Reality: "Communities" in Late Classic Honduras. In *The Archaeology of Communities: A New World Perspective*, ed. M. Canuto and J. Yaeger, 143–59. Routledge, London.

Joyce, Rosemary A., Julia A. Hendon, and Jeanne Lopiparo. Forthcoming. Being in Place: Intersections of Identity and Experience on the Honduran Landscape. In *Archaeologies of Place*, ed. B. Bowser and N. Zedeño. University of Utah Press, Salt Lake City.

Küchler, Susanne. 1999. The Place of Memory. In *The Art of Forgetting*, ed. A. Forty and S. Küchler, 53–72. Berg, Oxford, U.K.

Kunen, Julie L., Mary Jo Galindo, and Erin Chase. 2002. Pits and Bones: Identifying Maya Ritual Behavior in the Archaeological Record. *Ancient Mesoamerica* 13: 197–211.

Latour, Bruno. 1991. Technology Is Society Made Durable. In *A Sociology of Monsters: Essays on Power, Technology, and Domination*, ed. J. Law, 103–31. Routledge, London.

———. 1996. On Interobjectivity. *Mind, Culture, and Activity* 3/4: 228–45.

———. 1999. *Pandora's Hope: Essays on the Reality of Science Studies.* Harvard University Press, Cambridge, Mass.

Lopiparo, Jeanne. 2003. *Household Ceramic Production and the Crafting of Society in the Terminal Classic Ulúa Valley Honduras.* Ph.D. diss., Department of Anthropology, University of California, Berkeley.

———. 2004. La evidencia arqueológica de la producción doméstica de las cerámicas en el Valle del Río Ulúa. In *Memoria VII Seminario de Antropología de Honduras,* ed. K. Rubén Ávalos, 151–60. Instituto Hondureño de Antropología e Historia, Tegucigalpa.

———. 2006. Crafting Children: Materiality, Social Memory, and the Reproduction of Terminal Classic House Societies in the Ulúa Valley, Honduras. In *The Social Experience of Childhood in Ancient Mesoamerica*, ed. T. Ardren and S. Hutson, 133–68. University Press of Colorado, Boulder.

———. 2007. House Societies and Heterarchy in the Terminal Classic Ulúa Valley, Honduras. In *The Durable House: House Society Models in Archaeology*, ed. R. A. Beck, 73–96. Occasional Paper 35. Center for Archaeological Investigations, Southern Illinois University, Carbondale.

———. Forthcoming. Ritual Landscape and the Heterarchical Integration of the Late to Terminal Classic Ulúa Valley. In *Another Way of Being Maya: Local Practices and History in the Ulúa Valley, Honduras*, ed. R. A. Joyce and J. S. Henderson.

Lopiparo, Jeanne, Rosemary A. Joyce, and Julia Hendon. 2005. Terminal Classic Pottery Production in the Ulúa Valley. In *Geographies of Power: Understanding the Nature of Terminal Classic Pottery in the Maya Lowlands*, ed. S. L. López Varela and A. E. Foias, 107–19. BAR International Series 1447. Archaeopress, Oxford, U.K.

Meskell, Lynn. 2004. *Object Worlds in Ancient Egypt: Material Biographies Past and Present*. Berg, Oxford, U.K.

Miller, Daniel. 2005. Materiality: An Introduction. In *Materiality*, ed. D. Miller, 1–50. Duke University Press, Durham, N.C.

Mock, Shirley Boteler, ed. 1998. *The Sowing and the Dawning: Termination, Dedication, and Transformation in the Archaeological and Ethnographic Record of Mesoamerica*. University of New Mexico Press, Albuquerque.

Monaghan, John. 1998. Dedication: Ritual or Production. In *The Sowing and the Dawning: Termination, Dedication, and Transformation in the Archaeological and Ethnographic Record of Mesoamerica*, ed. S. Boteler Mock, 47–52. University of New Mexico Press, Albuquerque.

———. 2001. Physiology, Production, and Gendered Difference: The Evidence from Mixtec and Other Mesoamerican Societies. In *Gender in Pre-Hispanic America*, ed. Cecilia F. Klein, 285–304. Dumbarton Oaks, Washington, D.C.

Schortman, Edward M., Patricia Urban, Kirk Anderson, Katherine Cruz-Uribe, and Ellen Ruble. 1992. *Sociopolitical Hierarchy and Craft Production: The Economic Bases of Elite Power in a Southeast Mesoamerica Polity*, part 3, *The 1992 Season of the Naco Valley Archaeological Project*. Technical report on file at the Instituto Hondureño de Antropología e Historia, Tegucigalpa.

Sheptak, Russell N. 1982. Fotos aéreos y el patrón de asentamiento de la zona central del valle de Sula. *Yaxkin* 5 (2): 89–94.

Speakman, Robert J., and Michael D. Glascock. 2003. *Instrumental Neutron Activation Analysis of Terminal Classic Period Pottery from the Ulúa Valley, Honduras*. Technical report in possession of senior author.

Stross, Brian. 2006. Maize in Word and Image in Southern Mesoamerica. In *Histories of Maize: Multidisciplinary Approaches to the Prehistory, Linguistics, Biogeography,*

Domestication, and Evolution of Maize (Zea mays *L.*), ed. J. E. Staller, R. H. Tykot, and B. F. Benz, 577–98. Elsevier, Amsterdam.

Tercero, Geraldina. 1996. Figurines from the Ulúa Valley, Honduras: A Preliminary Study of Their Distribution and Uses. Master's thesis, Department of Anthropology, Arizona State University, Tempe.

Vogt, Evon Z. 1969. *Zinacantan: A Maya Community in the Highlands of Chiapas.* Belknap Press, Cambridge, Mass.

Willey, Gordon R. 1972. *The Artifacts of Altar de Sacrificios.* Papers of the Peabody Museum of Archaeology and Ethnology, vol. 64, no. 1. Harvard University, Cambridge, Mass.

———. 1978. *Excavations at Seibal, Department of Petén, Guatemala: Artifacts.* Memoirs of the Peabody Museum of Archaeology and Ethnology, vol. 14, no. 1. Harvard University, Cambridge, Mass.

Part II

Social Identities

4

Formative Period Gulf Coast Ceramic Figurines

The Key to Identifying Sex, Gender, and Age Groups in Gulf Coast Olmec Imagery

BILLIE J. A. FOLLENSBEE

While the task of isolating and understanding concepts such as gender, age groups, and sociopolitical structures in the remains of any ancient culture is difficult, studying these concepts in Gulf Coast Olmec material culture is especially problematic. Unlike scholars of later cultures such as the Maya and the Aztec, scholars of Formative period cultures have no ethnographic or ethnohistoric resources, nor do they have extensive pictographic or hieroglyphic texts. Although hieroglyphs are now known to date from well before the Classic period (see, for example, Justeson and Kaufman 1993; Pohl et al. 2002; Rodríguez Martínez et al. 2006), relatively few Formative period glyphs survive, and even for these, their current translations and their viability as true writing systems are not without dispute (see Bruhns and Kelker 2007; Cyphers 2007a, 2007b; Houston 2004; Macri and Stark 1993; Ortíz Ceballos and Rodríguez Martínez 2007; Rodríguez Martínez et al. 2007). Furthermore, because the Gulf Coast Olmec flourished in a tropical rainforest environment with heavily acidic soils, osteological and other perishable remains recovered at these sites are meager (compare Ortíz Ceballos and Rodríguez Martínez 1997; Rodríguez Martínez and Ortíz Ceballos 1994); only the most durable of Gulf Coast material culture survives—that made of stone and ceramic.

Given these limitations, thorough analysis of all available imagery is crucial to proper understanding of these cultures. Many scholars have studied Gulf Coast Olmec stone sculpture in attempts to identify and interpret important iconography. Few, however, have studied the most common form of Olmec sculpture: the small, handmade ceramic figurines. Beyond determinations of typologies, recovery contexts, and probable usage, Gulf Coast ceramic figurines have been, in general, sorely underanalyzed. The iconography of these ubiquitous ancient sculptures has the potential to provide important insights into imagery portrayed in the larger sculpture and ultimately to reveal much about the cultures that produced them.

Identifying Gender in Gulf Coast Olmec Imagery

Previous to my dissertation research (Follensbee 2000),[1] no systematic study of male and female sexed or gendered characteristics in Gulf Coast Olmec imagery had been undertaken, and gender representation was poorly understood in Olmec imagery.[2] In most past analyses, gender determination was made by summary assertion, generally assigned in an inconsistent and arbitrary manner. For example, small jade figurines with fleshy, rounded chests and short skirts (figure 4.1) were nearly always designated as female,

Figure 4.1. La Venta Figure 1, jade figurine of a woman (drawing by the author, after author's photographs and Benson and Fuente 1996: 16).

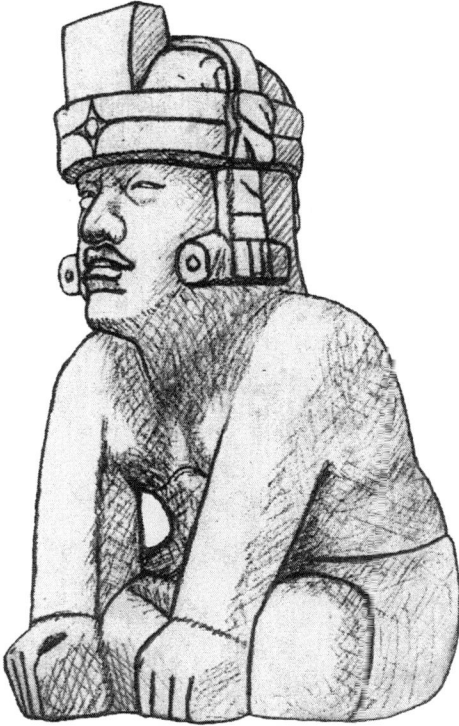

Figure 4.2. Cruz del Milagro Monument 1 (drawing by the author, after author's photographs and Benson and Fuente 1996: 167).

because of these features (see, for example, Drucker 1952: 154–55; Drucker et al. 1959: 25–26); however, large stone sculptures with fleshy, rounded chests and short skirts (figure 4.2) were summarily asserted to be male.

Direct assertions of sex or gender in Olmec imagery often have been based in *argumentum ad ignorantiam*—asserting a conclusion based on the absence of features rather than on the presence of features, which is a recognized logical fallacy (see Follensbee 2000: 9–18). However, even this method was applied in a one-sided manner: the absence of large, rounded breasts and overt female genitalia was assumed to indicate male gender, but the absence of facial hair and any indication of male genitalia was not assumed to imply female gender. Fully ambiguous Olmec images that do not clearly exhibit sexed or gendered characteristics, especially those that express power and leadership, were asserted a priori to be male; the huge, formidable Colossal Heads (figure 4.3), for example, have been designated by many scholars as exclusively male, although no physical characteristics clearly identify them as such (see, for example, Coe 1972: 5; Fuente 1992).

Figure 4.3. La Venta Monument 1 (drawing by the author, after author's photographs and Vela 1996: n.p.).

The pervasive confusion about sex and gender in much Gulf Coast Olmec imagery is understandable, however, as large Olmec stone sculpture is notorious for its sexual ambiguity. Most anthropomorphic figures are androgynous, with thick, blocky, stylized forms; even figures with naturalistic faces often have physically ambiguous bodies. And while clothing tends to be scanty in large Olmec stone sculpture, full nudity is uncommon, and any indication of genitalia is extremely rare (see also Blomster, this volume).

The Ceramic Figurines

Progress in recognizing sex and gender is possible through the study of the small, handmade ceramic figurines, which are generally much more physically naturalistic than Olmec stone sculptures. Early archaeological explorations of the Gulf Coast Olmec sites of San Lorenzo, La Venta, and Tres Zapotes produced a total of 1,550 identifiably human, Formative period figurine fragments (see Coe and Diehl 1980; Drucker 1943, 1952; Drucker et al. 1959; Heizer et al. 1968; Piña Chan 1989; Weiant 1943), and systematic analysis of these figurines has proven very useful in clarifying different aspects of other Olmec sculpture (Follensbee 2000: 26–89).[3]

Although some variation of form exists among figurines of the different sites and time periods, in-depth study reveals that certain body and head features consistently follow clear patterns, regardless of differences in form. These patterns vary little among the three sites and are consistent from the Early Formative (Initial Olmec phase, 1200 BCE) through the Late Formative period (Epi-Olmec phase, 100 CE).[4] Previous classifications of Gulf Coast Olmec ceramic figurines focused heavily on the heads to create primary figurine typologies. Since over 95 percent of the heads are separated from the bodies, however, head-based typologies are inadequate for systematic studies of more-body-specific traits (see Follensbee 2000: 26–89); the figurine bodies are much more helpful in determining gender and age distinctions, and the consistency of body forms on the figurines allows for a useful classification system based first on close analysis of their physical features, then on close analysis of their garments and adornments (table 4.1).

The figurines from these sites all readily fall into three general categories: relatively naturalistic, the somewhat abstracted, and the "grotesque." The relatively naturalistic figurines, which are those closest in form to natural human anatomy, are the most prevalent type, comprising roughly 92 percent of the total sample. As has been justifiably noted by most previous scholars, the majority of these figurine bodies appear to be anatomically consistent with young adult females (see, for example, Drucker 1943: 76–86, 1952: 132–41; Weiant 1943: 93–99). As among other Olmec sculpture, pubic genitalia is extremely rare in ceramic figurines, but the figurines differ from other sculpture in that they plainly exhibit secondary sexual characteristics that appear in consistent combinations. Although secondary characteristics cannot be relied upon individually to reliably reveal sex or gender,[5] consistent combinations of such characteristics, along with other consistently gender-associated features, form clear patterns. When these are considered collectively, they reinforce greatly the probability of accurate identification of sex and gender in the figurines.

The most obviously sexed figurines among the relatively naturalistic images are those with prominent female breasts. Some of these figurine bodies show women of advanced age, with stooped shoulders and flaccid, sagging breasts (figure 4.4a); others, with large distended bellies and especially full breasts, are clearly meant to portray adult, pregnant females. Meanwhile,

Table 4.1. Gender and Age in Gulf Coast Olmec Small Ceramic Figurines

Site[a]	Heads	Bodies	Identifiably human		Male	Female	Juveniles	Adolescents	Dwarfs	Elderly	Clothed	Clothed (belts/aprons)
			Heads	Bodies								
SL	165	433[b]	129	189	32	284	13	19	5	2	47	65
LV	124	327	138	114	12	226	8	9	4	6	13	29
TZ	596	418	562	418	41	887	25	15	3	16	52	167
Total	885	1,178	829	721	85	1,397	46	43	12	24	112	261
Percentage of total identifiably human sample			53.5	46.5	5.5	90	3	3	1	2	7	17

a. LV = La Venta, SL = San Lorenzo, TZ = Tres Zapotes.
b. Coe and Diehl (1980) classified 747 artifacts generally within the category "figurine fragments," but as many as 149 of these consist of small ceramic items that are not human, animal, or supernatural figurine fragments.

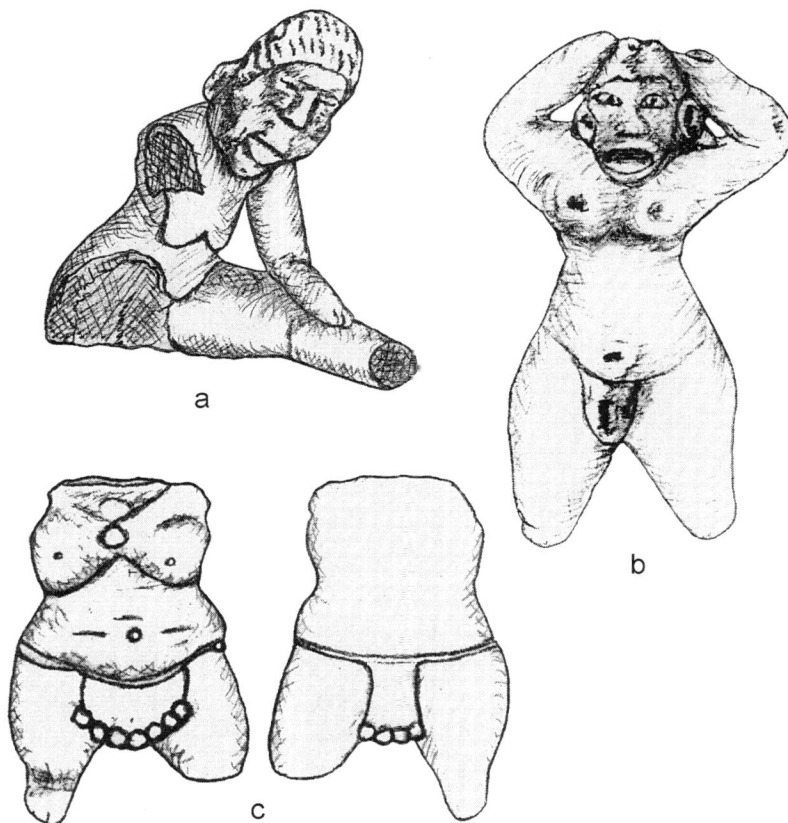

Figure 4.4. La Venta figurines (note: figurines not to scale): *a*, old woman (drawing by the author, after Heizer et al. 1968: pl. 8a); *b*, woman wearing pubic apron (drawing by the author, after Piña Chan 1989: 60); *c*, woman wearing pubic apron with both front and back pendant flaps (drawing by the author).

slender, nonpregnant figurines with similarly pronounced breasts display other consistent physical characteristics, including pinched waists that start just below the breasts, lower torsos that slope out to flaring hips, and wide thighs that taper sharply to the lower legs (figure 4.4a). These figures also often have shapely buttocks with pronounced cleavage, and a clearly indicated Y or a triangular shape at the pubic area—a feature widely recognized by scholars as an almost universal form of female sex indicator, appearing on ancient female ceramic figurines throughout Mesoamerica and around the world.

An interesting aspect revealed by this study is that large breasts are actually an unusual trait among Olmec figurines. As noted by the early excavators, while the figurines are identifiably female because of their other consistent body characteristics, they most often tend to have relatively subtle indications of breasts (Drucker 1943: 76–86, 1952: 132–41; Weiant 1943: 98–99); instead of accentuated breasts, the female chest is indicated by small, pointy protrusions, by a rounded undulation, or simply by an edge or a line in a rounded W shape, under an only slightly modulated chest area (figures 4.4b and 4.4c). That breasts are represented this way on Olmec adult female figurines is hardly unusual, as studies of provenienced Formative period figurines from other Mesoamerican cultural regions such as Central Mexico (for example, Cyphers Guillén 1989; Vaillant and Vaillant 1934), the Oaxaca area (for example, Marcus 1998), the Mazatan region of coastal Chiapas (for example, Lesure 1997), and the Maya area (for example, Joyce 1993) frequently indicated adult female breasts rather minimally on clearly sexed images of women, even completely obscuring any indication of breast features with clothing (see Follensbee 2000: 59–65; see also Joyce 1996: 169). Likewise, rather than accentuated breasts, the aforementioned characteristics—the slender, pinched waist; the sloping torso and flaring hips; the wide, tapering limbs; the pubic Y or triangle; and the rounded W-shaped line underneath the chest—are clearly the traits emphasized by the Olmec as primary indicators of femaleness.

The majority of provenienced Olmec ceramic figurine bodies are nude, although most also have extended limbs that would have facilitated the addition of perishable garments (see Follensbee 2000: 77–85 and 149–51). Only 7 percent of the figurines wear substantial clothing; however, nearly 17 percent wear some type of body garment, if only a simple belt or pubic covering—and many of these garments show strongly gender-associated patterns.

The most common garment on female figures is the loincloth apron, or pubic apron—an article of clothing that appears frequently on Formative figurines throughout Mesoamerica. This simple pubic covering is often overlooked on these figurines, as here it often appears simply as an applied pellet of clay that has been flattened over the pubic area (figure 4.4b). Examples with greater detail reveal that this garment actually consisted of a low-slung, "hip-hugger" belt that may be plain, braided, beaded, or fringed, with a free-hanging flap in the front; sometimes there is also a free-hanging flap in the back (figures 4.4b and 4.4c; also see figure 4.5c).

Another relatively common garment is the skirt (figure 4.5a; see also

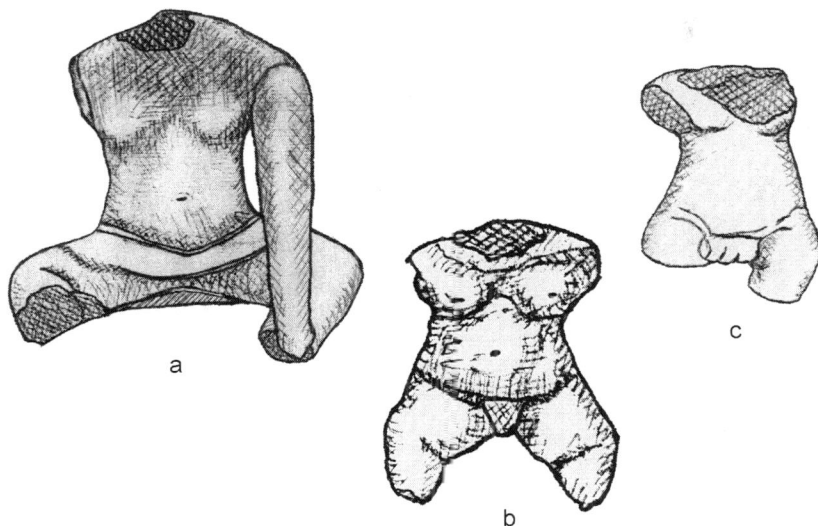

Figure 4.5. Childlike figurines (note: figurines not to scale): *a*, adolescent with slender body and rounded chest area, wearing short, low-slung skirt, from San Lorenzo (drawing by the author); *b*, supine baby with pubic triangle, from La Venta (drawing by the author); *c*, child wearing pubic apron, from La Venta (drawing by the author).

figure 4.7b); however, unlike in many later Mesoamerican cultures, Olmec female figurines wear short skirts as well as long. Like the aprons, the Olmec female skirt is quite low-slung, with the top of the skirt placed where the hips start to flare.[6] Female figures also wear capes, vests, tunics, breast bands, pectoral ornaments, necklaces, low-slung plain or beaded belts, and ear spools or ear ornaments that often have pendant pieces (Follensbee 2000: 42–45).

These identifications of adult physical characteristics and associated garb have also facilitated the identification of figures of youths among this group. Although relatively modest breasts are common on adult female figures, some figures with slightly rounded chest areas also have slender, more generalized bodies and only a slight indication of a pinched waist; these likely represent adolescents (figure 4.5a). Others have tubby bodies with the small, fleshy breasts associated with baby fat and only slight pinching underneath the chest; these likely represent infants and young children (figures 4.5b and 4.5c). These figures also display pubic Ys or triangles and/ or wear gendered garments that clearly identify them as female. Some of

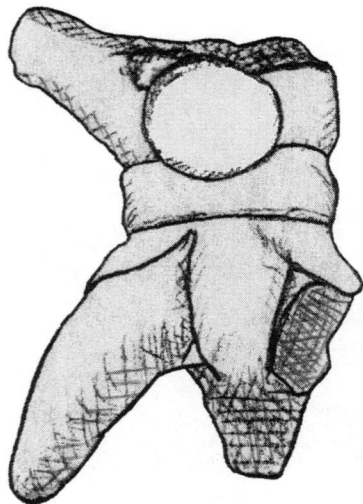

Figure 4.6. San Lorenzo tripod male figurine with lightbulb-shaped body, wearing wrapped loincloth and backflap skirt (drawing by the author, after author's photographs and Coe and Diehl 1980: fig. 305).

these figures could simply represent chunky adults, but most of them almost certainly depict female children. While poses vary widely among Olmec figurines, those that are likely babies frequently lie on their backs with flexed legs, which also helps to support their identification as infants (see also Follensbee 2006: 255 and note 13).

The somewhat abstracted group of Olmec figurines, comprising about 4 percent of the assemblage, contrasts markedly with the relatively naturalistic figurines. The bodies of these figures are much more geometric, taking the form of cylinders or flat rectangles, or, in the case of tripod figures, they have smooth, lightbulb-shaped bodies to accommodate the rear leg support (figure 4.6). Invariably, all of these have completely smooth chests and torsos, with no undulations or demarcations. In addition to significantly different bodies, these figures wear complex garments that are strongly consistent with male-gendered garments of later Mesoamerican cultures, such as the male loincloth and hip cloth. Male loincloths differ clearly from Olmec female loincloth aprons; while they may or may not have a pendant flap in front, they wrap securely underneath the groin and between the legs. Olmec male loincloths are also worn with wide or multilayered belts that are placed high on the waist, which contrasts strongly with the typical female "hip-hugger" apron belt and low-slung skirt. These figures may also wear capes, vests, pectoral ornaments, ear spools, and necklaces or tied fillets around the neck, but given the strong contrasts of the other garments

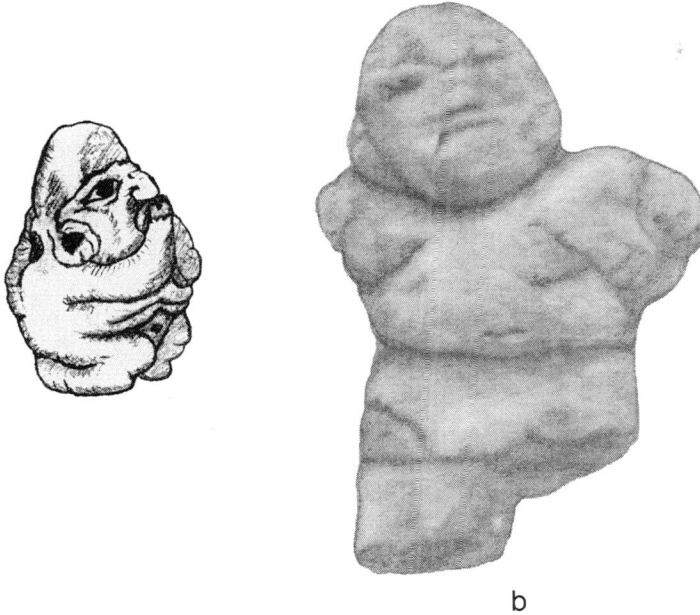

b

Figure 4.7. "Grotesque" figurines (note: figurines not to scale): *a*, baby, from La Venta (drawing by the author); *b*, dwarf, from San Lorenzo (drawing by the author).

and the bodies, the more-abstracted figures likely represent male images. Unfortunately, the strong stylization of their bodies and the heavy clothing obscure distinctions in relative body development, which obstructs identifications of age groups among these male figurines.

The third group of figurines, comprising the remaining 4 percent of the total sample, is the compact-bodied, "grotesque" group. Some of these are heavily abstracted, misshapen, aberrant figures, but upon closer examination others appear to be naturalistic chubby humans (see Follensbee 2006: 255–67). Some of these have arms and legs drawn up to the body in a crouch, and these may represent tubby babies (figure 4.7a). The others, however, have wide, pudgy torsos and stubby limbs, wear skirts or pubic aprons, and display pinched waists, flaring hips, and/or more pronounced breasts, which serve to identify them as adult female dwarfs rather than children (figure 4.7b).

Surprisingly, no poses clearly appear to be gendered among the ceramic figurine bodies. Elderly figurines, identifiable by sagging breasts and stooped shoulders, are usually seated; babies usually lie on their backs with flexed legs or crouch with arms and legs bent and held close to the body. However, the other figurines assume a plethora of different poses. Female figurines even frequently assume a pose that previously has been postulated to signify a position of "male authority"—seated with the legs crossed tailor-fashion (see, for example, Marcus 1998: 177–81).

The ceramic figurine heads clearly show age only in the elderly representations, with a few heads showing sunken cheeks and prominent cheekbones (figure 4.4a); another head shows sunken cheeks as well as emphasized facial hair, which together are commonly used to indicate men of advanced age in Mesoamerican depictions (Weiant 1943: pl. 29, fig. 4). The heads are overall very distinctive, however, in hairstyle or headdress, and the most common hairstyles frame the face with an inverted U shape. The top of these hairstyles is squared or rounded, and the surface is often vertically striated, presumably to show straight hair; central or side buns are frequently added. Other common styles include coils of hair or ornamental headbands wrapped around the head, closely cropped hair, and shaven heads, also often embellished with central or side buns. Because the vast majority of the figurine bodies represent females, one may reasonably surmise that most of the figurine heads and their associated hairstyles belonged to female bodies. This conclusion is confirmed by more-complete figurines, which both sport these representative hairstyles and have female body forms and garments (for example, figures 4.4a, 4.4b, and 4.7b).

A few figurine heads sport beards, thus representing men; the small sample of these heads correlates well with the small sample of male bodies. These heads may also wear large conical hats or crested headdresses that frame the face in a square, which likely represent male-gendered garb. Beyond the above characteristics, however, facial features are similarly stylized for both male and female depictions.

Overall these studies indicate that, as asserted by the early excavators, female images make up the vast majority of provenienced Gulf Coast Olmec ceramic figurines, forming about 90 percent of the assemblage, while male figures comprise only 5.5 percent of the total sample. This high female ratio compares readily with the vast majority of Formative period figurine studies in other parts of Mesoamerica (compare Cheetham, this volume). The majority of figurines appear to represent young adults, but the very young and the elderly are also substantially represented. While these groups are in the minority, the simple fact that children and the elderly are clearly portrayed indicates recognition of these age groups as distinct from adults. The depiction of some of these figures with relatively elaborate garb also suggests that certain personages among them may have held more elite status, regardless of age.

In regard to function and symbolism, these figurines were recovered from nearly all areas of the sites, but as with most collections of Mesoamerican Formative period figurines, they were concentrated in debris from dwelling areas, in secondary deposits of household refuse and fill dirt (Coe and Diehl 1980: 260; Drucker 1943: 10–22; Weiant 1943: 6–15 and 84–116; see also Follensbee 2000: 26–28 and 77). Specific functions for any subcategory of the figurines are thus unclear. Early scholars often summarily categorized all such figurines collectively as "fertility figures" for human reproduction rituals; this has been largely discredited as essentialist (see, for example, Follensbee 2000: 65–88; Nelson 1997: 151–68). Studies of figurines from throughout Mesoamerica do, however, support that ceramic figurine functions were based in ritual.

While small, nearly complete figurines have occasionally been recovered, most Gulf Coast figurines are fragmentary, broken not only at structurally weak points such as the neck and limbs but also often in the middle of the body, where the structure was the strongest. This suggests that purposefully breaking the figurines may have been intrinsic to use, implying a ritual function. While the figurines' ubiquity shows that they may have been used occasionally in public, their concentration in household debris supports that they were used primarily in the home, by or for private individuals. Some evidence exists for use in agricultural ritual, but the strongest evidence supports the use of the figurines in personal home ritual, predominantly for curing and for the prevention of disease (see Follensbee 2000: 65–88). Recent evidence suggests that these rituals may have been accompanied by feasting (Tway 2004).

In addition to the small ceramic figurines, fragments of large, hollow ceramic figures were also recovered in early archaeological explorations of the Gulf Coast (see, for example, Coe and Diehl 1980: figs. 292, 346; Drucker 1952: pls. 33, 36). The survival of nearly complete figures of this type is rare, but a group of five such sculptures from La Venta are displayed in Mexico City's National Museum of Anthropology and History.[7] Not only do the large ceramic figures use precisely the same stylizations as the small figurines, but four of the five large figures display clear genitalia.

Two of the sculptures are seated with thighs spread and hands on the knees (figures 4.8a and 4.8b); they have young adult female hourglass figures, with flaring hips and waists strongly pinched under the chests. One has small but well-rounded, fleshy breasts. Although clearly female, the

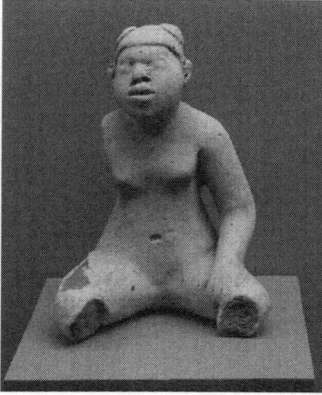

a

b

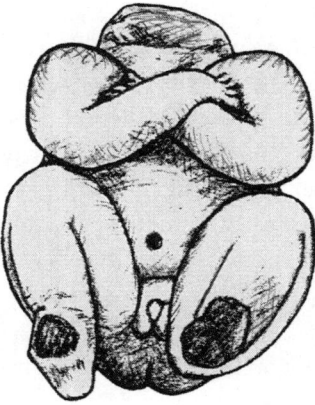
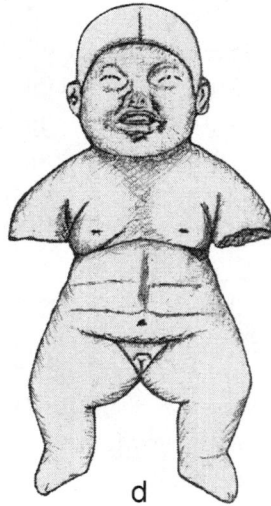

c

d

Figure 4.8. La Venta large, hollow ceramic figures (note: figurines not to scale): *a*, young woman (photograph by the author); *b*, headless young woman (photograph by the author); *c*, headless baby boy (drawing by the author); *d*, toddler girl, one of a pair of twin figures (drawing by the author).

figurine shows only a Y-shaped delineation at the groin; it also wears a very closely cropped, U-shaped hairstyle with a bun on each side of the head. The other figure has only a rounded chest area but defined nipples and a deeply indented line below the chest in a well-rounded W shape. The figure also has a clear pubic triangle and female genitalia.

The other three large, hollow ceramic La Venta figures depict very young children. One takes the form of a male baby, with a smoothly bulb-shaped body and tiny but clear male genitalia; its arms are crossed, and its legs are drawn up in the crouch often assumed by small ceramic baby figurines (figure 4.8c). The remaining two figures are a pair of twinlike female toddler figures in supine poses (figure 4.8d). These sculptures show clear female genitalia at the groin, babylike faces, and simple, rounded hairstyles that frame their faces in a U shape. Their tubby, babylike bodies have fleshy chests, slight pinching at the waist, and flaring hips similar to the features of childlike small ceramic figurines.

Overall, the strong, consistent correlations of the features of these five large, hollow ceramic figures with the features of the small ceramic figurines, combined with the clearly defined sexual features of these large figures, strongly confirms the identifying sex, gender, and age characteristics isolated in this research. These data also provide solid points of comparison useful for identifying the primary sexed features, gendered features, gendered garments and accouterments, and age groups in other forms of Olmec sculpture.

Small Stone Figures

At least forty-two small-scale human images in stone have been collected in archaeological explorations of Gulf Coast Olmec sites (table 4.2; see also Follensbee 2006). While holes at the neck indicate that some of these figures may previously have served as pendants, all of the provenienced images were recovered from ritual deposits in elite graves or caches (see Follensbee 2000: 90–152; Marcus, this volume); in their final deposition, several of the figures were used to create what appear to be historical or ritual scenes.

In contrast to the ceramic figurines, only 17 percent of the small stone figures are naturalistic, and 10 percent take the form of distorted "grotesques." Instead, nearly two-thirds of these figures are strongly stylized, taking the classic form known as the Olmec "baby-face."[8] Not to be conflated with the depiction of an actual baby, a "baby-face" is a formulaic image that most often portrays a young adult (see Follensbee 2006: 249 and 257–58). "Baby-face" figures have shaven or closely cropped, smooth heads; constricted,

Table 4.2. Gender and Age in Gulf Coast Olmec Small-Scale Stone Anthropomorphic Sculptures

Sculpture and context[a]	Type	Gender[b]	Age
LV Off. #3, Figure 2	"Baby-face"	DF, modified to DM	Adult
LV Mound A-2, Figure 2	"Baby-face"	PF	Adult
LV Mound A-2, Figure 3	"Baby-face"	PF, modified to DM	Adult
LV Mound A-2, Figure 4	"Baby-face"	PF	Adult?
LV Mound A-2, Figure 5	"Baby-face"	GA, modified to DM	Adult?
LV North Platform, Figure 6	"Baby-face"?	DM	Adult?
LV Off. 1943-M, Figure 8	"Baby-face"	DF	Child
LV Off. 1943-M, Figure 9	"Baby-face"	DF	Child
LV Off. 1943-M, Figure 12	"Baby-face"	DF	Adult?
LV Off. #4, Figure 7	"Baby-face"	DM	Adult
LV Off. #4, Figure 8	"Baby-face"	GA, modified to DM	Adult
LV Off. #4, Figure 9	"Baby-face"	DF	Adult
LV Off. #4, Figure 10	"Baby-face"	GA, modified to DM	Adult
LV Off. #4, Figure 11	"Baby-face"	GA, modified to DM	Adult
LV Off. #4, Figure 12	"Baby-face"	DM	Adult
LV Off. #4, Figure 13	"Baby-face"	GA, modified to DM	Adult
LV Off. #4, Figure 14	"Baby-face"	DM, modified to more DM	Adult
LV Off. #4, Figure 15	"Baby-face"	DM	Adult
LV Off. #4, Figure 16	"Baby-face"	DM	Adult
LV Off. #4, Figure 17	"Baby-face"	GA, modified to DM	Adult
LV Off. #4, Figure 18	"Baby-face"	PF	Adult
LV Off. #4, Figure 19	"Baby-face"	DM	Adult
LV Off. #4, Figure 20	"Baby-face"	GA, modified to PM	Adult
LV Off. #4, Figure 21	"Baby-face"	GA, modified to PM	Adult
LV Off. #4, Figure 22	"Baby-face"	GA, modified to PM	Adult
LV Str. A-1-E	"Baby-face"?	PF	Adult?
EMa Figure 1	"Baby-face"	GA	Adult
SL Mon. 99	Naturalistic	GA	Child
SL Mon. 130	Naturalistic	PF	Child?
SL Mon. 131	Naturalistic	PF	Adult dwarf
SL Mon. 132	Naturalistic	AR	Child?
LV Mound A-2, Figure 1	Naturalistic	DF	Adult
LV Str. 3, Figure 7	Naturalistic	PF	Adult
LV O 1943-M, Figure 11	Naturalistic	GA	Child
SL Mon. 119	Grotesque	DF	Child?
LV Off. #3, Figure 1	Grotesque	GA	Adult dwarf?
LV Off. 1943-M, Figure 10	Grotesque	GA	Adult dwarf?
LMe Figure 1	Grotesque (figural axe)	GA	Child supernatural?
LV Off. #2, Celt A	Incised figure	PF	Adult?
LV Off. #2, Celt B	Incised figure	DM	Adult
LV Off. #2, Celt E	Incised head	GA	Ambiguous
LV Off. #4, Celts 3 & 4	Incised figure	DM	Adult

a. Site abbreviations: LV = La Venta, EMa = El Manatí, LMe = La Merced, SL = San Lorenzo. Sculpture designation abbreviations: Mon. = Monument, Off. = Offering, Str. = Stratitrench.
b. DF = definitely female, PF = possibly female, DM = definitely male, PM = possibly male, GA = gender-ambiguous, AR = ambiguous, ruined, or unfinished.

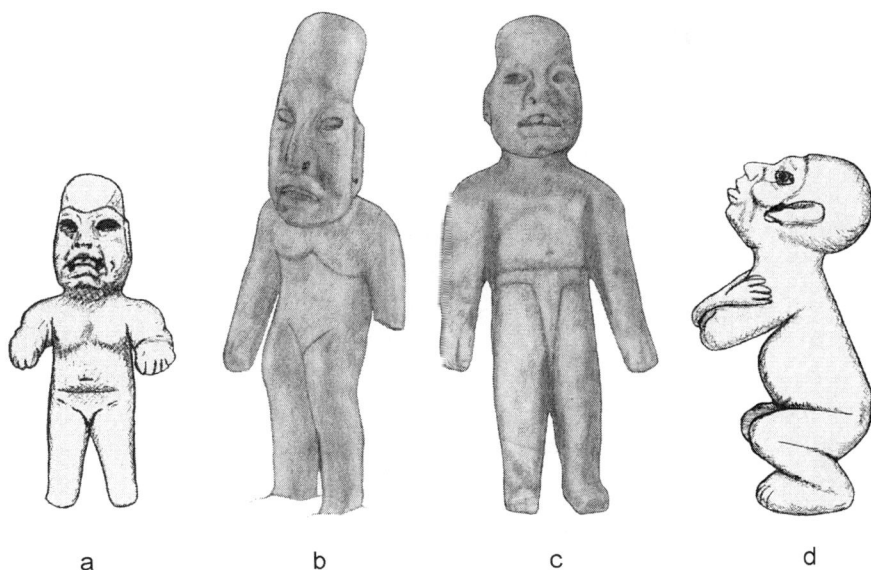

Figure 4.9. La Venta jade figurines (note: figurines not to scale): *a*, Offering 1943-M (drawing by the author, after Drucker 1952: pl. 50a); *b*, Offering #4 Figure 9 (drawing by the author, after Benson and Fuente 1996: 104); *c*, Offering #4 Figure 15 (drawing by the author, after Drucker et al. 1959: pl. 35); *d*, Offering 1943-M Figure 11 (drawing by the author, after Drucker 1952: pl. 51b).

tabular-erect cranial modification; almond-shaped, puffy eyes; and exaggerated, frowning grimaces (figures 4.9a, 4.9b, and 4.9c).

The poses assumed by these "baby-faces" take only a few variations: two of them, one standing and one kneeling, hold their hands to their abdomens; two more, both seated, rest their hands on their thighs; and two others—the only two with clearly childlike proportions—stand and hold their hands up like paws (figure 4.9a). The remaining twenty provenienced "baby-faces" take the most common "baby-face" body form and pose: they have generally flat, slender bodies and adult proportions; they stand with slightly bent knees, legs apart in a V, and feet flat; and they hold their arms stiffly out from their sides, with elbows slightly bent (figures 4.9b and 4.9c).

These strong, consistent stylizations render the "baby-faces" particularly androgynous, and defining the sex of these figures tends to be much more difficult than for other forms of Olmec sculpture. This is further complicated by the fact that many of these figures show evidence of modification subsequent to their original carving, with surface incision added and other areas of the body smoothed. The crudeness of some added incision and surface carving, juxtaposed with the fineness of the original carving, suggests that some "baby-faces" were made initially in an ungendered form, to be engendered later as desired, and that sometimes a figure was changed from one gender to another for reuse.[9]

Close study and comparison with the traits isolated from the ceramic figurines reveals that most of these figures were clearly engendered as male or female in their final form. The primary female gender-identifying imagery used on the "baby-faces" consists of the pubic Y or pubic triangle; chest delineation in the form of a well-rounded W shape; shapely buttocks with strong cleavage; and/or a hairline that frames the face in an inverted U shape (figures 4.9a and 4.9b).[10] The primary male gender-identifying imagery, meanwhile, consists of either a clearly rendered loincloth and belt worn on the natural waist or above, or an underwear-like garment, sometimes along with lightly modeled or incised pectoral delineation that varies from an incised straight line to a wide, shallow, inverted U shape just under the chest area (figure 4.9c). The scant clothing and open poses of most "baby-face" figures suggests that they were adorned with separate, perishable garments and accouterments—a hypothesis strongly supported by the figures' drilled ear holes, which are clearly meant for the addition of ornament, and perhaps by their constricted upper crania, which would facilitate the securing of hairpieces or headdresses (see Follensbee 2000: 77–85 and 149–51). Such garments would serve to further engender the figures, confirming carved gendered imagery or possibly even changing it as needed for the figure's reuse.

Of the few provenienced small stone anthropomorphic figures that do not take the form of "baby-faces," seven are relatively naturalistic, four are "grotesques," and four are incised images on small stone objects. One recently recovered "grotesque" figurine from San Lorenzo, Monument 119, has a heavily recarved head, but its body clearly illustrates a pubic triangle, infantile body proportions and buttocks, and the crouched pose typical of a small ceramic baby figure (Cyphers 2004: 197–99). The remaining "grotesques" tend to be wide-bodied, androgynous dwarfs or gender-ambiguous supernaturals. The naturalistic images and the incised images, meanwhile, tend to follow the gendered conventions of the ceramic figurines even more closely than do the "baby-face" images. The incised images include a standing figure with a pinched waist that suggests it may be female; an ungendered, supernatural face; and two male-gendered figures that wear wide belts, high on the waist, and loincloths (Follensbee 2000: 139–44).

Among the naturalistic small stone images is Monument 131 from San Lorenzo, which strongly resembles La Venta Monument 5, a large stone sculpture of a dwarf. These two images have large heads, wide bodies, and stubby limbs, and they also wear a distinctive bun hairstyle that is a typically female coiffure among the ceramic figurines. Two more figures that are naturalistic are a female-gendered torso from La Venta Stratitrench 3 and the famous La Venta Figure 1 from Mound A-2, a small jade image that is widely accepted as portraying a woman (see, for example, Bernal 1969: 72; Castro-Leal 1996: 216; Drucker 1952: 154–55), which is seated with legs crossed tailor-fashion (see figure 4.1). Although a pinched waist was not emphasized in these two figures, they show other features that correlate well with the female-gendered traits of the ceramic figurines, including small, rounded breasts; slightly flaring hips; and shapely buttocks. In addition, La Venta Figure 1 has an inverted U-shaped coiffure with vertical striations, and she wears a low-slung, short skirt. Although she does not assume an open pose and therefore would not have been adorned with additional garments other than possibly a cape, she wears ear spools that are pierced, perhaps to accommodate additional pendant pieces, and she wears a mirror of specular hematite secured to her chest. These accouterments suggest that this person or character held elite status in Olmec society.

The remaining four naturalistic figures appear to be relatively accurate images of young babies, with corpulent bodies, relatively proportional limbs, and, when present, heads that are large (figure 4.9d). Three of the figures have arms crossed over the chest and legs flexed into a crouch, similar to the poses of large and small ceramic depictions of babies; there are, however, no clear indications of gender on the four stone figures (see Follensbee 2006: 258–59, 2008; see also Tate and Bendersky 1999). In the better-preserved specimens (such as figure 4.9d), the figures have drilled holes in the ears for the addition of ear ornamentation, like the "baby-faces" and the figure from La Venta Mound A-2, and they may represent children of elite status.

Large Stone Images

Of the 234 anthropomorphic stone sculptural images thus far recovered in Gulf Coast Olmec excavations and explorations, the vast majority—192 in all—are large-scale stone sculptures, which appear at virtually all Gulf Coast sites (tables 4.3–4.8). Careful comparison reveals that, as with the small stone sculptures, the gender- and age-defining traits derived from the analyses of the small ceramic figurines have clear correlations with the

Table 4.3. Gender and Age in Gulf Coast Olmec Large-Scale Anthropomorphic
Reliefs: Stelae and Other Flat-Faced Monuments

Monument[a]	Images, Principal[b]	Images, Subordinate[b]	Age
SL Mon. 56	1 PM	1 GA	1 adult, 1 ambiguous
SL Mon. 83	1 PM	0?	1 adult?
SL Mon. 112	1 DM	0	1 adult
LV Stela 1	1 DF	0	1 adult
LV Stela 2	1 GA	6 DM	7 adults
LV Stela 3	1 DF, 1 PM	1 DF, 3DM, 2 AR	5 adults, 1 elderly adult, 2 ambiguous
LV Stela 5	1 DM	2 DF, 1 DM	3 adults, 1 elderly adult
LV Mon. 13	1 DM	0	1 elderly adult
LV Mon. 19	1 GA	0	1 adult
LV Mon. 33	1 PM	0	1 adult?
LV Mon. 38	1 PM	0	1 ambiguous
LV Mon. 42	1 DM	1 DF	1 adult, 1 adolescent?
LV Mon. 61	1 DM	0	1 adult
LV Mon. 63	1 DM	0	1 adult
TZ Stela A	1 PF	1 DF, 1 PF	3 adults
TZ Stela D	1 DF	2 DM	3 adults
Al Stela	1 DM	1 PF	1 adult, 1 adult dwarf
LM Stela[c]	1 GA	0	1 adult
EV Stela	1 GA	1 PM	2 adults

a. Al = Alvarado, EV = El Viejón, LM = La Mojarra, LV = La Venta, SL = San Lorenzo, TZ = Tres Zapotes. Note that Mon. = Monument.
b. DF = definitely female, PF = possibly female, DM = definitely male, PM = possibly male, GA = gender-ambiguous, AR = ambiguous, ruined, or unfinished.
c. Although the argument could be made that this monument may postdate the Gulf Coast Olmec, it is clearly an Olmec-related sculpture that follows Olmec conventions.

traits of the large stone anthropomorphic figures. These correlations are generally consistent from the Early through Late Formative period, as well as throughout the different Olmec centers. A particularly interesting revelation, however, is that the Olmec emphasized different age- and gender-defining traits in the different types of large stone sculpture (see Follensbee 2000: 437–49).

In relief sculpture, the key traits for indicating female personages are a pinched waist that begins high on the torso and widely flaring hips and thighs (figures 4.10, 4.11, and 4.12), which may taper funnel-style into slender ankles (figure 4.11). Female figures also often have wide upper arms

Table 4.4. Gender and Age in Gulf Coast Olmec Large-Scale Anthropomorphic
Reliefs: Thrones (Formerly Called Altars)

Monument[a]	Images, Principal[b]	Images, Subordinate[b]	Age
SL Mon. 14	1 DM	1 DF, 1 AR	2 adults, 1 ambiguous
SL Mon. 15	1 AR	0	1 ambiguous
SL Mon. 18	2 DF	0	2 adult dwarfs
SL Mon. 20	1 AR	1 AR	1 adult? 1 child
LdZ/PN Mon. 2	2 DF	0	2 adult dwarfs
LV Altar 2	1 AR	1 AR	1 adult? 1 child
LV Altar 3	1 DM	1 DF, 2 DM, 1 AR	3 adults, 1 elderly adult? 1 ambiguous
LV Altar 4	1 DM	1 DM, 1 AR	2 adults, 1 ambiguous
LV Altar 5	1 DM	1 DF, 1 PF, 2 DM, 5 GA	5 adults, 5 children
LV Altar 6	1 AR	0	1 adult?
LV Altar 7	1 PF	3 DF, 1 PF, 2 AR	5 adults, 2 ambiguous
LV Mon. 21	1 DF	0	1 adult
LV Mon. 40	1 DM	0	1 adult?
LdC Mon. 5	1 DM	0	1 adult
LdC Mon. 9	1 PF	0	1 ambiguous
LdC Mon. 28	1 PF	0	1 adult
LdC mon. with 2 figures	2 AR	0	2 ambiguous
EM throne	1 PM	0	1 adult

a. EM = El Marquesillo, LdC = Laguna de los Cerros, LdZ = Loma del Zapote, LV = La Venta, PN = Potrero Nuevo, SL = San Lorenzo. Note that Mon. = Monument.
b. DF = definitely female, PF = possibly female, DM = definitely male, PM = possibly male, GA = gender-ambiguous, AR = ambiguous, ruined, or unfinished.

that taper to slender wrists (figures 4.10 and 4.11) and hairstyles that frame
the face with an inverted U, often with locks of hair in front of the ears
(figure 4.10). As on ceramic and small stone sculptures, female breasts are
usually minimized when the figure is nude, defined predominantly by a
well-rounded W shape under the chest (figure 4.10), and breasts are obscured completely when clothing is worn (figure 4.11). A female figure in
profile will often cover her bare chest with her arm in relief depictions,
and in this case the chest will flare out above the arm, creating a marked
discrepancy with the more slender outline of the torso below the arm and
clearly suggesting breasts underneath (figures 4.11 and 4.12). Large-scale
female figures often wear low-slung, short skirts in relief depictions (figures
4.10–4.12), sometimes with a wide "hip- hugger" belt (figures 4.11 and 4.12),
or they may wear low-slung loincloth aprons. They also wear capes, pec-

Table 4.5. Gender and Age in Gulf Coast Olmec Large-Scale Sculptures-in-the-Round: Anthropomorphic Figures

Monument[a]	Images, Principal[b]	Images, Subordinate[b]	Age
SL Mon. 10	1 DM	0	1 supernatural
SL Mon. 11	1 DM	0	1 adult
SL Mon. 12	1 DM	1 AR	1 adult, 1 child
SL Mon. 24	1 AR	0	1 adult?
SL Mon. 25	1 PM	0	1 ambiguous
SL Mon. 26	1 GA	0	1 supernatural?
SL Mon. 34	1 DM	0	1 adult
SL Mon. 41	1 GA	0	1 supernatural
SL Mon. 42	1 GA	0	1 ambiguous
SL Mon. 47	1 DF	0	1 adult
SL Mon. 52	1 GA	0	1 supernatural
SL Mon. 54	1 PF	0	1 adult?
SL Catalogue #13-385	1 PF	1 AR	1 adult, 1 child
SL Mon. 103	1 GA	0	1 supernatural
SL Mon. 104	1 PM	0	1 supernatural
SL Mon. 105	1 AR	0	1 ambiguous
SL Mon. 107	1 GA	1 DM	1 supernatural, 1 adult
SL Mon. 123	1 GA	0	1 ambiguous
SL Mon. 133	1 GA	0	1 supernatural?
Te Mon. 1	1 DM	1 AR	2 adults
Te Mon. 6	1 AR	0	1 ambiguous
LdZ Mon. 3	2 AR	0	1 supernatural, 1 ambiguous
LdZ Mon. 5	1 GA	0	1 adult
LdZ Mon. 8	1 DM	0	1 adolescent
LdZ Mon. 9	1 DM	0	1 adolescent
LdZ Mon. 11	1 PF	0	1 adolescent
LdZ Mon. 12/SL Mon. 6	1 AR	0	1 adult?
CdM Mon. 1	1 DF	0	1 adolescent
Cu Mon. 1	1 DF	0	1 adult
LL Mon. 1	1 DM	1 DM	1 adolescent, 1 child
PN Mon. 1	1 AR	0	1 supernatural
SMP Mon. 1	1 DM	0	1 adult?
LV Mon. 5	1 PF	0	1 adult dwarf
LV Mon. 8	1 AR	0	1 adult
LV Mon. 9	1 DM	0	1 supernatural
LV Mon. 10	1 DM	0	1 supernatural
LV Mon. 11	1 GA	0	1 supernatural
LV Mon. 23	1 DM	0	1 adult
LV Mon. 29	1 AR	0	1 adult?
LV Mon. 30	1 DM	0	1 adult
LV Mon. 31	1 GA	0	1 adolescent?
LV Mon. 39	1 PM	0	1 ambiguous

LV Mon. 44	1 AR	0	1 ambiguous
LV Mon. 52	1 AR	0	1 supernatural
LV Mon. 57	1 PM	0	1 adult?
LV Mon. 65	1 PF	0	1 adult dwarf?
LV Mon. 68	1 AR	1 AR	2 ambiguous
LV Mon. 70	1 PF	0	1 supernatural
LV Mon. 72	1 PF	0	1 adult dwarf
LV Mon. 73	1 DM	0	1 adolescent?
LV Mon. 74	1 GA	0	1 supernatural
LV Mon. 75	1 GA	0	1 supernatural
LV Mon. 77	1 DM	0	1 adult
LV Mon. 78	1 GA	0	1 ambiguous
LV Unnumbered mon.	1 DM	0	1 adult
LS Mon. 1	1 DM	0	1 supernatural
TZ Mon. F[c]	1 GA	0	1 ambiguous
TZ Mon. G[c]	1 GA	0	1 ambiguous
TZ Mon. I	1 PM	0	1 ambiguous
TZ Mon. J	1 AR	0	1 ambiguous
TZ Mon. K	1 AR	0	1 ambiguous
TZ Mon. M	1 PM	0	1 supernatural
AP Mon. 1[c]	1 DM	0	1 elderly adult?
LdC Mon. 3	1 DM	0	1 adolescent?
LdC Mon. 6	1 GA	0	1 elderly adult?
LdC Mon. 8	1 AR	0	1 child?
LdC Mon. 11	1 DM	0	1 adult
LdC Mon. 19	1 DM	0	1 adult
LdC Mon. 20	1 DM	0	1 adult?
LdP Mon. 1	1 PM	0	1 adult
ER Mon. 3	1 DM	1 PF	1 adult, 1 child
ER Mon. 4/LIs Mon. 1	1 PM	0	1 supernatural?
ER Mon. 6	1 PF	0	1 adult
ReC Mon. 1	1 GA	0	1 adult?
LId Mon. 1	1 PM	0	1 adult
LId Mon. 8	1 DM	0	1 adult
LId Mon. 16	1 DF	1 DM	1 elderly adult, 1 child

a. Sculptures that are so fragmentary that their identification as anthropomorphic is tenuous (for example, San Lorenzo Monuments 97 and 128) and sculptures that consist solely of figures that are clearly and predominantly supernatural zoomorphs, with no gendered traits (for example, Loma del Zapote Monuments 1, 7, and 10) have not been included in this compilation. Site abbreviations: AP = Antonio Plaza, CdM = Cruz del Milagro, Cu = Cuautotoloapan, ER = Estero Rabón, LdC = Laguna de los Cerros, LdP = Loma de la Piedra, LdZ = Loma del Zapote, LId = Los Idolos, LIs = La Isla, LL = Las Limas, LS = Los Soldados, LV = La Venta, PN = Potrero Nuevo, ReC = Rancho El Cardonal, SL = San Lorenzo, SMP = San Martín Pajápan, Te = Tenochtitlán, TZ = Tres Zapotes. Note that Mon. = Monument.

b. DF = definitely female, PF = possibly female, DM = definitely male, PM = possibly male, GA = gender-ambiguous, AR = ambiguous, ruined, or unfinished.

c. Although this monument likely postdates the Gulf Coast Olmec, it has traditionally been included in studies of the Olmec, and it is included here in the interest of being as comprehensive as possible.

Table 4.6. Gender and Age in Gulf Coast Olmec Large-Scale Sculptures-in-the-Round: Colossal Heads

Monument[a]	Images, Principal[b]	Images, Subordinate[b]	Age
SL Head 1	GA	0	Elderly adult
SL Head 2	GA	0	Elderly adult
SL Head 3	PF	0	Elderly adult
SL Head 4	GA	0	Elderly adult
SL Head 5	GA	0	Adult
SL Head 6	GA	0	Elderly adult
SL Head 7	GA	0	Elderly adult
SL Head 8	GA	0	Elderly adult
SL Head 9	GA	0	Elderly adult
SL Head 10	GA	0	Adult
LV Mon. 1	PF	0	Adult
LV Mon. 2	GA	0	Elderly adult
LV Mon. 3	GA	0	Elderly adult
LV Mon. 4	PF	0	Elderly adult
TZ Mon. A	GA	0	Elderly adult
TZ Mon. Q	GA	0	Elderly adult
RC Head 1	GA	0	Adult

a. LV = La Venta, RC = Rancho la Cobata, SL = San Lorenzo, TZ = Tres Zapotes. Note that Mon. = Monument.
b. PF = possibly female, GA = gender-ambiguous.

Table 4.7. Gender in Anthropomorphic Olmec Large Stone Sculpture

Image type	Ruined/unfinished	Gender-ambiguous	Male	Female	Total no. of images
Principal images					
Reliefs	5/1	4	13–19	8–12	41
Sculptures-in-the-round	12/3	32	24–33	4–15	95
Total	17/4	36	37–52	12–27	136
Subordinate images					
Reliefs	9/0	6	17–18	11–15	48
Sculptures-in-the-round	4/0	0	3	0–1	8
Total	13/0	6	20–21	11–16	56
Total images	30/4	42	57–73	23–43	192
Percentage of total sample	18%	22%	30%–38%	12%–22%	100%

Table 4.8. Gender and Images of Juveniles and the Elderly in Anthropomorphic Olmec Large Stone Sculpture

	Ruined/ unfinished	Gender-ambiguous	Male	Female	Total no. of images	Percentage of total sample
Children						**6%**
Principal images	0	0	0	0	0	0
Subordinate images	4/1	5	1	0–1	12	6%
Adolescents						**5%**
Principal images	0	1	5	1–2	8	4%
Subordinate images	0	0	0	1	1	0.5%
Elderly adults						**10%**
Principal images	0	12	2–3	1–3	18	9%
Subordinate images	0	0	1	1	2	1%

Figure 4.10. La Venta Stela 1 (drawing on photograph, both by the author).

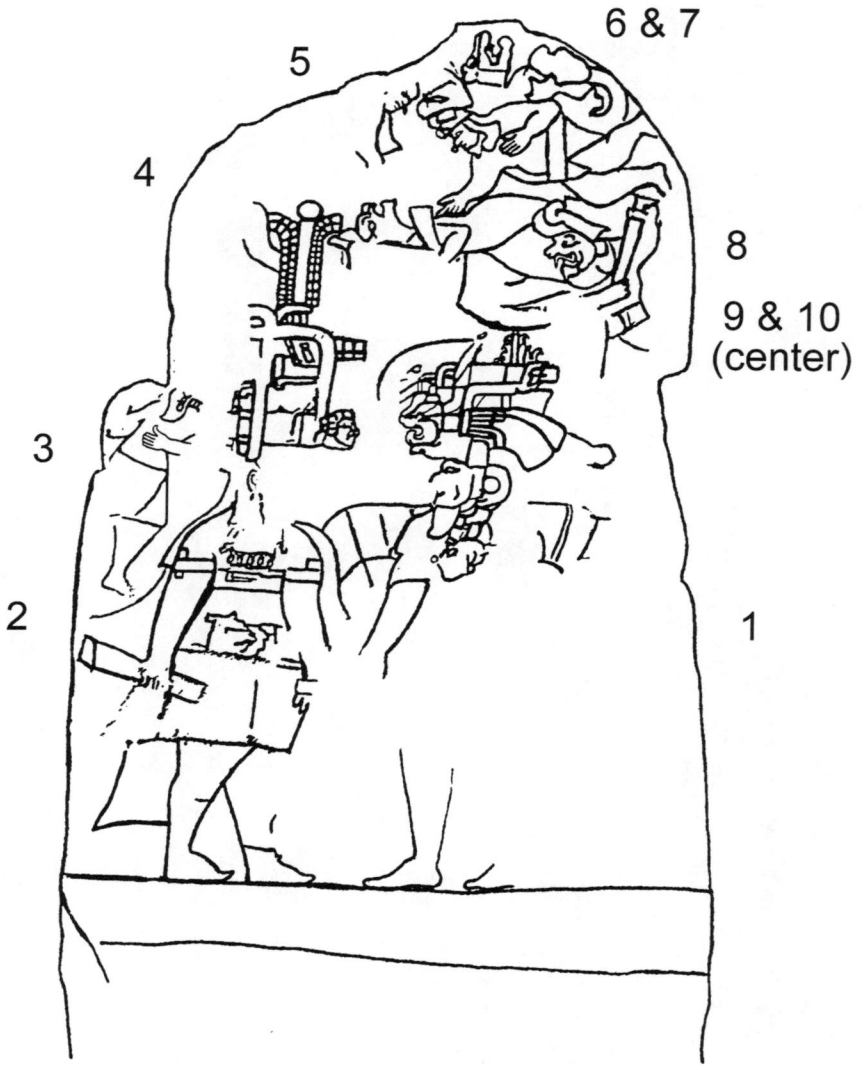

Figure 4.11. La Venta Stela 3: figures 2 and 3 are female; figures 4 and 5 are ambiguous; figures 1, 6, 8, and 9 are male (drawing by the author).

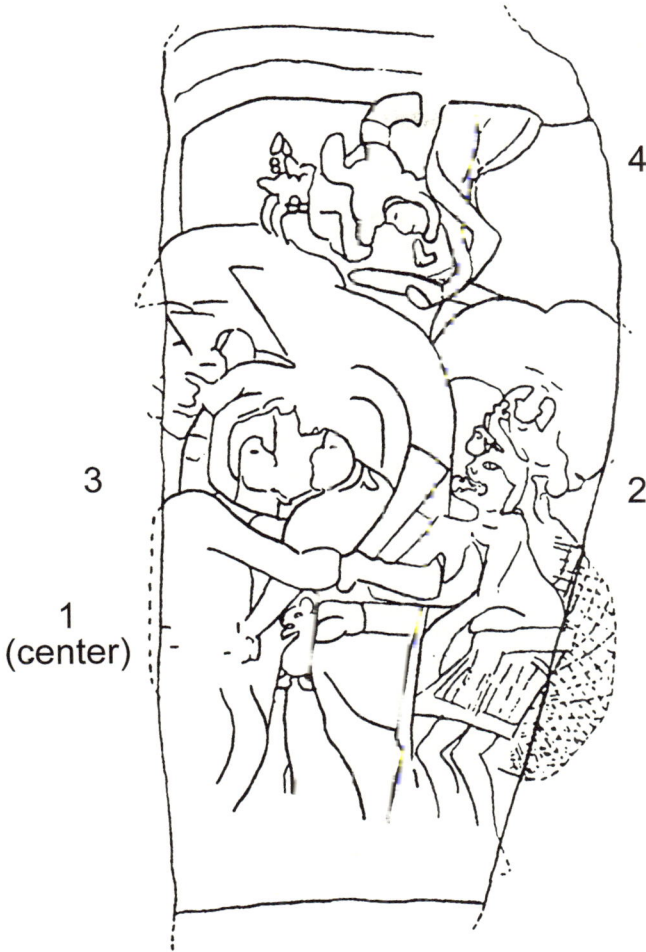

Figure 4.12. La Venta Stela 5: figures 1 and 3 are male; figures 2 and 4 are female (drawing by the author, after author's photographs and González Lauck 1996: 101).

torals, footwear, armbands, wrist bands, breast bands, and/or suspender-like garments (figure 4.11), as well as headdresses that range from a simple helmet to a tall and elaborate structure, lower-face masks, ear spools with or without pendant ornaments, and pendant ornaments on other parts of their bodies (figures 4.10 and 4.11). Women assume many different poses in relief sculpture, but only one pose is possibly female-gendered: seated with one leg crossed in front of the figure and the other leg either bent into a kneeling posture or dangling over the side of a platform.

In contrast to the relief portrayals, Olmec sculptures-in-the-round emphasize different imagery to indicate female gender (see figure 4.2). As on the naturalistic small stone figures, the bodies of these female images are more uniform; they do not emphasize the pinched waist but flare out gently at the hips. Likewise, female breasts are indicated modestly on large-scale stone sculptures as small, rounded forms, sometimes underscored by a clear, incised line in the shape of a well-rounded W. Female figures may have shaven heads, sometimes with central or side buns, or they may have inverted, U-shaped hairstyles. As on other forms of Olmec sculpture, clothing on the sculptures-in-the-round is often minimal, but the garments worn most often by female images are the low-slung, short skirt and/or pubic apron, sometimes along with a belt;[11] they also may wear capes, tunics, neck bands, wrist bands, pectoral ornaments, and helmetlike headdresses.

Likewise, male gender-defining traits are differently emphasized in Olmec large stone relief sculpture and sculpture-in-the-round. As seen on ceramic figurines, male relief figures may wear real or false beards, and they have straight-sided or smoothly pear-shaped bodies; they also usually have uniform or only gently tapering limbs (figure 4.11).[12] Similarly, bare male chests tend to be featureless in the reliefs; only in very rare cases do squared, flat pectorals appear (see Follensbee 2000: 254–59).

Conversely, male sculptures-in-the-round tend to be more gender-identifiable than are male relief images. Like the ceramic figurines, large stone male figures tend to have more geometric, straight-sided bodies; they may be adorned with pectoral ornaments that obscure their chests, and bare areas may appear featureless (see, for example, Follensbee 2000: 292–93, 314–17). However, male sculptures-in-the-round are most frequently portrayed with fleshy but flat pectoral muscles, usually with a straight-bottomed silhouette underneath the chest area (figure 4.13).[13]

In both the large stone reliefs and sculptures-in-the-round, male figures wear garments that correspond to those on the ceramic male figurines. These garments include wide and/or multilayered belts worn at the natural waist or above,[14] wrapped loincloths with or without a pendant flap, and/or hip cloths; the sculptures-in-the-round may also wear underwear-like garments, and their belts may have squared ornaments and/or cloth tassels (figures 4.11–4.15). In addition, large stone male images wear real or false beards, leg bands, pectorals, ear spools, and capes. Male relief figures may also wear sandals or other footwear and headdresses that range from helmets to elaborate superstructures, while male sculptures-in-the-round

Figure 4.13. La Venta
Monument 23
(photograph by the
author).

may also wear neck bands, wrist bands, and headdresses that vary from elaborate headbands to cone-shaped hats.[15]

Male figures in reliefs and sculptures-in-the-round assume many different poses, but a pose that appears to be exclusively male-gendered (perhaps because it reveals the groin) is seated with one knee up and the foot flat on the ground, and the other leg in a kneeling position; a variation of this pose in male sculptures-in-the-round is one knee up and the other leg crossed in front of the figure. These poses appear to be the male counterpart to the one exclusively female-gendered pose described previously.[16]

The extreme naturalism and portrait features of the Colossal Heads make them unique in Olmec anthropomorphic sculpture-in-the-round (figure 4.3 and table 4.6). Contrary to many summary assertions, no Colossal Head displays conclusively sex-defining physical traits that would confirm it to be male; some heads do have strong facial features that suggest masculinity, but other heads actually have softer features that suggest femininity—and depictions of both men and women in other forms of Olmec sculpture have facial features and headgear comparable to those seen on the Colossal Heads (figure 4.10; see also Follensbee 2000: 403–11). In combination with traits associated with other, clearly gendered images, gender identifications may be assigned to a few of the Colossal Heads, but even these are very tentative (table 4.6; see Follensbee 2000: 411–12). In contrast, the age of individuals portrayed as Colossal Heads tends to be more identifiable. Of the

a   b

c

Figure 4.14. La Venta Altar 5: *a*, proper right side; *b*, front; *c*, proper left side (drawings by the author).

seventeen heads, only four appear to portray relatively youthful adults; the other heads depict older individuals, with drooping eyes and lined, sagging faces.

As in the ceramic figurines, in both sculptures-in-the-round and in reliefs, aged figures are identifiable facially by their sunken, lined cheeks and, in male depictions, by emphasized facial hair (figure 4.11). Also as in the ceramic figurines, body features in large-scale sculpture that indicate advanced age include sagging, somewhat flattened breasts and stooped pos-

Figure 4.15. Las Limas Monument 1 (drawing by the author, after author's photographs and Benson and Fuente 1996: 171).

tures, particularly in female depictions (figure 4.12). Overall, a much larger percentage of large-scale stone anthropomorphic sculptures appears to represent elderly individuals than do other forms of Olmec sculpture (table 4.8), and all of these images appear to be of individuals of elite status.

Depictions of children in large-scale stone Gulf Coast Olmec sculpture are more difficult to discern. At least thirty-two images in Olmec relief sculpture are childlike in scale but have adult proportions; in the art of Mesoamerican cultures such as the Maya, depictions of children take the form of such small-scale adults, interacting directly in scenes with full-size, adult personages. In Olmec sculpture, however, specialized contexts clarify that such miniaturized depictions of adults are not children but most likely represent supporting relatives, ancestor spirits, or supernaturals (figures 4.11

and 4.12). These figures are separated from the action of the main scene, appearing in a separate panel or side, where they interact with other figures of the same scale; alternatively, they float above the main scene, sometimes wearing a supernatural mask (see Follensbee 2006: 259–61).

Because of their wide, adult-sized torsos, large heads, and stubby limbs, depictions of adult dwarfs are often readily distinguishable from those of children, as are chunky Olmec supernaturals, which illustrate complex combinations of human, animal, and/or supernatural features.[17] In contrast, human children are depicted in Olmec imagery with large heads but more naturalistic, clearly childlike bodies and proportions. Recent analysis has shown that at least sixteen and as many as twenty-one of the anthropomorphic images on Olmec large stone sculpture represent youths.[18] Of these, seven take the form of a limp baby that lies in the lap of an elite figure, either sculpted in high relief or in-the-round, and four other child images take the form of frantically struggling toddlers, each being restrained by an elite adult on La Venta "Altar" 5 (figures 4.14 and 4.15). The poses and contexts of these images consistently indicate that these scenes are portrayals of young children who have been or are about to be sacrificed, apparently as offerings for accession to power (Follensbee 1998, 2006: 261–63).

The relatively large heads, youthful facial features, and body forms of the remaining five clearly subadult sculptures-in-the-round suggest that they represent adolescents (Follensbee 2006: 263–66). As on the ceramic figurines, their bodies tend to be either unusually slender and less developed than adult bodies, or stocky and firm but only modestly developed. One of these figures is Cruz del Milagro Monument 1 (figure 4.2), often referred to as "the Prince." Close analysis reveals that this figure has a stocky, youthful body, with representations of small, firm, rounded breasts visible on each side of the chest, as well as a well-rounded, W-shaped delineation incised below them; the torso also flares out gently at the hips. In addition, the figure wears a low-slung skirt, a helmetlike headdress, and elite ear ornamentation, all of which are consistent with female adornment. The figure leans forward over her crossed legs in a pose that has been associated with status and even domination (see Follensbee 2000: 321–25). All together, these physical features and garments confirm that this sculpture should be renamed "the Princess," as it clearly represents an autonomous female who has already attained high status as an adolescent (see Follensbee 2000: 321–25).

Another Olmec adolescent portrayal is the well-known Las Limas Monument 1 (figure 4.15), a figure that also presents a child sacrifice. The figure's youthful chest is squared but quite flat, in contrast to the fleshy pectorals typically depicted on Olmec mature male figures. It also wears a male-style, wrapped loincloth, visible on the back. As an image of an autonomous youth who assumes a position—seated and holding a limp child—that is otherwise assumed only by elite images, this adolescent is likely being depicted as acceding to a high level of social status and power.[19]

Conclusions

Close, systematic examination of the physical traits, subtle stylizations, garments, and accouterments of the small ceramic figurines recovered from Gulf Coast Olmec sites has enabled the isolation of numerous sexed and gendered physical features as well as clearly gendered garments and adornments. The identification of these features and accouterments also facilitates the identification of male and female portrayals in small and large Gulf Coast Olmec stone sculpture (Follensbee 2000: 90–464). Further analysis of the ceramic figurines provides a means to understanding representations of distinct age groups in Olmec imagery, clarifying the characteristics that are associated with childhood, adolescence, adulthood, and old age (Follensbee 2006).

Comparisons of the traits isolated from the ceramic figurines with the provenienced small stone Olmec images reveal some surprising results. In contrast to the ceramic figurines, a substantial number of the small stone figurines—17 percent—were apparently made intentionally androgynous, without clearly sexed or gendered features; another 21 percent are only slightly gendered, with only minor male- or female-gendered traits, and 2.5 percent are too ruined to identify. The majority of the small stone figurines are clearly male-gendered, however, at 45 percent of the total assemblage; an additional 2.5 percent have some male-gendered traits and are also possibly male. Nevertheless, 14 percent of these figurines are clearly female, with another 19 percent exhibiting some female-gendered traits.

Although no recognizable images of elderly people are apparent among the small stone sculptures, children do make up a significant portion, forming between 10 and 19 percent of the total assemblage. These portrayals of women and children, while in the minority, nevertheless form a much more significant portion of these images than scholars had previously understood. These figures were adorned with elite ornamentation and likely also were provided with additional garments, and all of the provenienced small stone figurines were incorporated into elite grave deposits and caches, sometimes arranged in re-creations of ritual or historic scenes. Together these factors illustrate that women and children held importance in Olmec ritual imagery, and by extension, there were likely women and children who actively participated in and enjoyed considerable status in Olmec society.

Among large-scale stone anthropomorphic Olmec sculpture, clear correlations of the sexed and gendered imagery isolated from the ceramic figurines reveal that an even larger percentage of these sculptural depictions—22 percent—were apparently made intentionally gender-neutral, with only sexually ambiguous physical traits and gender-ambiguous clothing. As was the practice in many later Mesoamerican cultures, sculptures-in-the-round of this type could have been further engendered through additional, perishable clothing and adornments. Some of these, along with the gender-neutral relief images, however, may have represented a station or an office rather than an individual.

Male figures make up the strong majority of gender-identifiable, large-scale stone images in every category, not only forming the bulk of principal images and most of the main characters but also forming the majority of subordinate or supporting images in the sculpture. Nevertheless, as among the small stone figurines, female images form a much larger percentage of large stone sculpted images than has previously been recognized, with 12 percent of depictions securely identifiable as female and as much as another 10 percent of images showing some female-gendered characteristics. These female images form a substantial number of main characters in relief scenes and in sculptures-in-the-round, as well as a considerable number of the subordinate, supporting figures.

Although such a percentage of female images may initially appear to be unprecedented in comparison to depictions of women in other Mesoamerican cultures, this is not the case. A survey of large stone female depictions at the Classic period Maya site of Palenque, for example, reveals that at least 10 percent of its large stone sculptural images are representations of women (see Robertson 1983). The Classic period Maya site of Yaxchilan shows even more substantial female representation, with fully 21 percent of its large stone images confirmed to represent elite women (see Tate 1992). In Postclassic cultures, images of women likewise figure prominently. In the imagery of the Mixtec, who recorded the histories of their elites in painted codices rather than in sculpture, elite women appear frequently, for example, making up 22 percent of the figures represented in the Codex Nuttall (see Nuttall 1975).[20] As a whole, images of elite, powerful women are a well-documented phenomenon throughout ancient Mesoamerica, and the estimation that a substantial number of Olmec images represent such women is far from implausible.

Likewise, juvenile images make up a substantial portion of large-scale Gulf Coast Olmec anthropomorphic stone images. Small children form about 6 percent of the images; however, all are subordinate characters, and they are largely ungendered and unindividualized.[21] This androgynous homogeneity is likely because these children are consistently portrayed in the role of child sacrifices and thus as anonymous, powerless pawns used to empower an elite hierarchy (Follensbee 2006). Depictions of adolescents, meanwhile, almost always take the form of main characters, and the majority of these images are readily gender-identifiable. While forming only about 5 percent of the assemblage, these images portray strong, autonomous elite individuals, suggesting that some youths in Olmec society could accede to levels of substantial power—some perhaps while too young to have earned this status through personal agency (Follensbee 2006).

Portrayals of elderly persons are also much more strongly represented than was previously realized. Ten percent of the images in large-scale Olmec stone sculpture portray older adults, with eighteen images assuming a principal role and two assuming a secondary role, but all wearing relatively elaborate garb. That older adults were always depicted as holding elite status may reflect the esteem in which the elderly were held.

Overall, the results of these studies indicate that Olmec sculpture incorporates clear cultural signifiers of sex, gender, age, and social status and that Olmec sculpture is much more diverse and specific in its portrayals than scholars previously recognized. Despite its initially overall androgynous and perhaps homogeneous appearance, Olmec stone sculpture reveals, through simple traits, male, female, and also intentionally sexually ambiguous images, as well as clear portrayals of children, adolescents, adults, and the elderly. The findings of this research challenge previous assumptions not only about gender and age in Olmec art but also about Olmec society. The recognition, for example, that the young, women, and the elderly could all hold high positions of status strongly affects our understanding of Olmec political organization, ritual, and social stratification.

When all these facets are taken together, this study illustrates that close and thorough analysis of small ceramic figurines provides many insights into Olmec imagery as a whole. The figurines clearly serve as social metaphors, unaffectedly reflecting the cultures that made and used them and revealing much about the diverse individuals that they portray, from age and gender to social roles and social status. The fuller understanding of

Olmec imagery that the figurines ultimately provide can also be extended to other Olmec material culture, and in this, the figurines have the potential to increase our understanding of all aspects of Gulf Coast Olmec culture.

Acknowledgments

I express my deep gratitude to all of those who generously allowed me access to study their collections of Formative period Gulf Coast ceramic figurines (especially collections that were not yet published), including Director Vince Wilcox and David Rosenthal at the Smithsonian Institution Museum Support Center, Department of Anthropology, in Suitland, Maryland (La Venta and Tres Zapotes figurines); Michael Coe and Director Richard Burger at Yale University (San Lorenzo); and Christopher Pool (Tres Zapotes), Philip Arnold III (La Joya), Robert Kruger (San Carlos), Barbara Stark (La Mixtequilla), Javier Urcid and Tom Killion (the region between Tres Zapotes and Laguna de los Cerros), and Mary Pohl (San Andrés). I also acknowledge Rhonda Taube, Christina Halperin, and Kata Faust for their encouragement and for asking me to participate in the session that led to this publication. I especially thank my husband, Perry John Elkins, for his continued love and support.

Notes

1. This chapter, although revised and updated, is heavily based on my doctoral dissertation research (Follensbee 2000). Some adjustments have been made to these data and conclusions since my dissertation and other previous publications (Follensbee 2000, 2006), as I have incorporated newly discovered sculptures and have continued to refine my analyses.

2. While considerations of a third gender or multiple genders are valid avenues for research (see Blomster, this volume), the lack of any sort of prior systematic study of sex and gender in Olmec imagery necessitates, first and foremost, that male and female sexed and gendered imagery first be identified before one moves on to more subtle identifications.

3. Subsequent to my main dissertation research, several figurine collections recovered from surveys and excavations of Formative period Gulf Coast sites were made available for study (see Follensbee 2000: 58–59; see also Follensbee and Arnold 2001; Tway 2004). These data strongly corroborate rather than contradict the conclusions of the dissertation research.

4. For a cogent discussion of Olmec cultural continuity beyond the Terminal Olmec phase, see Pool 2000: 137–53. This consistency throughout the time span is especially apparent in Philip Drucker's analyses, where he creates very complex categories, only to

acknowledge at the end of his analysis that the figurines were relatively homogenous in their forms and patterns (Drucker 1943: 76–86, 1952: 132–41; see also Follensbee 2000: 26–34; Weiant 1943: 98–99). This is also clearly the case for the figurines excavated by Michael Coe and Richard Diehl at San Lorenzo (see Coe and Diehl 1980: 259–79; Follensbee 2000: 32–33).

5. As is corroborated by Jeffrey Blomster (this volume). In contrast, David Cheetham's study of early San Lorenzo ceramic figurines (this volume) relies solely on evaluation of chests to identify sex and gender, and his conclusions about the ratio of male to female figurines contradict those of this study. The main difficulty with Cheetham's methodology is that, as discussed later in this chapter chests are well recognized as the most ambiguous of the secondary sexed features on Mesoamerican Formative period figurines. Determinations of sex or gender using chest features are therefore only meaningful when taken in the context of the other features present on the figurines and of the consistent patterns among these features. Furthermore, Cheetham's determinations of male versus female chests are contradicted, if not negated, by the clearly sexed Gulf Coast Olmec hollow ceramic figures also discussed and illustrated in this chapter.

6. In rare instances, a female figurine may wear a belt or skirt higher on the waist, although this placement is much more predominant in male garments; apparently this placement was used by women in certain unusual circumstances, and perhaps it might indicate a certain status or even incidence of a third gender. In contrast, low-slung, "hip-hugger" garments appear to be consistently and exclusively female-gendered.

7. These five figures are reported by the museum to have been recovered from La Venta. Piña Chan's excavation report (1989: 48–69) illustrates one of these figures (see figure 4.8a) but offers no further information on context. See also Follensbee 2000: 55–58.

8. Another group of "baby-face" images is the group of thirty-seven wooden busts recovered from El Manatí. While many of these figures are so abbreviated that they are sexually ambiguous, at least four have well-rounded, protruding chests and are immediately identifiable as female—as noted by those who recovered them and gave the figures female monikers (see Ortíz Ceballos and Rodríguez Martínez 1997; Vela 1996: 38–41).

9. That some of these figures were later incised or recarved should not be surprising, as there is widespread acknowledgment among scholars that Olmec small stone and large stone sculptures were modified, recarved, and reused in antiquity (see, for example, Drucker et al. 1959: 161; Porter 1989, 1992); for fuller discussion, see Follensbee 2000: 144–51 and 103–5 for a specific example. In the case of the Gulf Coast "baby-face" figures, most often the modification consisted of the addition of a lightly carved or incised loincloth and belt to engender the figure as male. In some cases, a male figure was clearly originally gendered female, where a crudely incised loincloth contradicts the sensitive original carving of a pubic Y or triangle, and the figure either still retains a rounded, W-shaped line defining the chest or the chest has been smoothed off in irregular planes that contrast with the fine original carving (see, for example, Follensbee 2000: 98–101 and 103–5).

10. The only exception to this rule is La Venta Figure 12 from Offering 1943-G (see

Follensbee 2000: 112–15). The entire front of this figure is flat, and the figure's closed stance and hands on the abdomen do not follow the formulaic imagery of other Olmec "baby-face" figures. While its chest is undefined, the figure has other strongly female-gendered features, including a pinched waist, a pubic triangle, and a female coiffure, and this figure may therefore simply represent a young girl. Strangely, the body of Figure 12 appears to follow the conventions of relief sculpture more than that of small stone "baby-face" figures—perhaps the result of its overall flat front surface.

11. As in other forms of Olmec sculpture, low-slung, "hip-hugger" garments are exclusively female in the large-scale stone sculpture, but in rare instances clearly female figures wear garments higher, as on Los Idolos Monument 16, and this might indicate certain status or a third gender. However, another explanation may be that these are certain types of belts that might be placed differently on certain garments. The likely female adolescent portrayed in Loma del Zapote Monument 11, for example, wears a tunic with a belt cinching it around the waist in the middle of the torso, and this belt acts as a cummerbund, strongly emphasizing the figure's hourglass shape (see Cyphers 2004: 257; see also Follensbee 2006: 265–66). Unlike the male-gendered belts, this belt is composed of ropes and tied in a large knot with dangling rope tassels in front. The only similar belt is that worn by the securely female central figure on Tres Zapotes Stela D.

12. A unique exception to this rule is the central male figure on La Venta Stela 5, which has tapering legs; however, these do not taper funnel-like but exhibit strange, angular, almost animalistic forms. The male figure to his proper right, meanwhile, has uniform limbs.

13. Facial hair is rare on sculptures-in-the-round, but it appears on at least one figure believed to be Olmec (see Follensbee 2000: 381–84).

14. In relief depictions, this belt may sag in front of a rounded midriff (such as in figure 4.11).

15. Depictions of uncovered heads are extremely rare on large stone male images. In one unusual example (figure 4.15), an adolescent male figure has an uncovered head and wears straight hair that is simply parted in the center. This hairstyle may be representative of youth, however, rather than being an exclusively male-gendered hairstyle.

16. All three of these poses are highly suggestive of the poses assumed by royal figures in later Mesoamerican depictions (see Fähmel 1997; Miller 1981: 31–86; Schaffer 1986: 203–16).

17. Six to ten images exhibit the wide, adult-sized torsos, enlarged heads, and chunky, stunted limbs of adult humans with achondroplasia (commonly called dwarfs). Supernaturals are generally gender- and age-ambiguous; they may represent supernatural children, supernatural dwarfs, or anthropomorphic, supernatural animals—or the Olmec may simply have portrayed their supernaturals in this squat form.

18. Six possible figures of children have been added to this list since my last publication (Follensbee 2006).

19. Confirming these interpretations of young individuals who have achieved high status are numerous archaeological finds of burials and offerings uncovered at Gulf Coast sites (see Follensbee 2006: 266–69). For example, discoveries of burned, canni-

balized, and carved children's bones (Coe and Diehl 1980; Cyphers 1997; Ortíz Ceballos and Rodríguez Martínez 1997; Rodríguez Martínez and Ortíz Ceballos 1994) confirm that the Olmec very likely engaged in the practice of child sacrifice. Conversely, several elaborate graves and offerings made in honor of other young individuals suggest that these youths held elite status—some of them while far too young to have earned this status through their own agency.

20. These findings are corroborated by studies of the Codex Nuttall by Sharisse Mc-Cafferty and Geoffrey McCafferty (2001), who also found large ratios of female images in several other Mixtec codices—for example, 16 percent of human images in the Codex Vindobonensis are female; 29 percent in the Codex Bodley are female; and 33 percent in the Codex Selden are female—with an overall average ratio of 76 percent male to 22 percent female (and 2 percent unidentifiable) among seven codices.

21. The only exception is the child held by the primary individual in Las Limas Monument 1, which wears a supernatural mask and a male-indicative wrapped loin-cloth; thus, although gendered, this child is anonymous, taking on the persona of a supernatural (see Follensbee 2000: 327–30).

References Cited

Benson, Elizabeth P., and Beatriz de la Fuente, eds. 1996. *Olmec Art of Ancient Mexico*. National Gallery of Art, Washington, D.C.

Bernal, Ignacio. 1969. *The Olmec World*. University of California Press, Berkeley.

Bruhns, Karen O., and Nancy L. Kelker. 2007. Did the Olmec Know How to Write? *Science* 315: 1365.

Castro-Leal, Marcia. 1996. The Olmec Collections of the National Museum of Anthropology, Mexico City. In *Olmec Art of Ancient Mexico*, ed. E. P. Benson and B. de la Fuente, 139–43. National Gallery of Art, Washington, D.C.

Coe, Michael D. 1972. Olmec Jaguars and Olmec Kings. In *The Cult of the Feline*, ed. E. P. Benson, 1–18. Dumbarton Oaks, Washington, D.C.

Coe, Michael D., and Richard A. Diehl. 1980. *In the Land of the Olmec*, vol. 1, *The Archaeology of San Lorenzo Tenochtitlán*. University of Texas Press, Austin.

Cyphers (Guillén), Ann. 1989. Cultos y cuentos: Reflexiones en torno a las figurillas de Chalcatzingo, Morelos. In *El preclasico o formativo: Avances y perspectivas*, ed. M. Carmona, 207–21. Consejo Nacional Para la Cultura y las Artes, Mexico City.

———, ed. 1997. *Población, subsistencia, y medio ambiente en San Lorenzo Tenochtitlán*. Universidad Nacional Autónoma de México, Instituto de Investigaciones Antropológicas, Mexico City.

———. 2004. *Escultura olmeca de San Lorenzo Tenochtitlán*. Universidad Nacional Autónoma de México, Mexico City.

———. 2007a. Sobre el Bloque Labrado de El Cascajal, Jaltipan, Veracruz. *Arqueología Mexicana* 14 (84): 6–8.

———. 2007b. Mas sobre el Bloque Labrado de El Cascajal, Jaltipan, Veracruz. *Arqueología Mexicana* 14 (85): 6–8.

Drucker, Philip. 1943. *Ceramic Sequences at Tres Zapotes, Veracruz, Mexico.* Smithsonian Institution Bureau of American Ethnology Bulletin 140. U.S. Government Printing Office, Washington, D.C.

———. 1952. *La Venta, Tabasco: A Study of Olmec Ceramics and Art.* Smithsonian Institution Bureau of American Ethnology Bulletin 153. U.S. Government Printing Office, Washington, D.C.

Drucker, Philip, Robert F. Heizer, and Robert Squier. 1959. *Excavations at La Venta, Tabasco, 1955.* Smithsonian Institution Bureau of American Ethnology Bulletin 170. U.S. Government Printing Office, Washington, D.C.

Fähmel, Bernd. 1997. Observaciones sobre la religión e iconografía de San Lorenzo. In *Población, subsistencia, y medio ambiente en San Lorenzo, Tenochtitlán,* ed. A. Cyphers, 243–51. Universidad Nacional Autónoma de México, Instituto de Investigaciones Antropológicas, Mexico City.

Follensbee, Billie J. A. 1998. Slaughter of the Innocents? The Evidence for Infant Human Sacrifice among the Gulf Coast Olmec. Paper presented at the 97th Annual Meeting of the Society for American Archaeology, Seattle.

———. 2000. *Sex and Gender in Olmec Art and Archaeology.* Ph.D. diss., Department of Art History and Archaeology, University of Maryland, College Park.

———. 2006. The Child and the Childlike in Olmec Art and Archaeology. In *The Social Experience of Childhood in Ancient Mesoamerica,* ed. T. Ardren and S. R. Hutson, 249–80. University Press of Colorado, Boulder.

———. 2008. Fiber Technology and Weaving in Formative Period Gulf Coast Cultures. *Ancient Mesoamerica* 19 (1): 87–110.

Follensbee, Billie J. A., and Philip Arnold III. 2001. Gulf Olmec Figurines from La Joya, Veracruz, Mexico. Paper presented at the 66th Annual Meeting of the Society for American Archaeology, New Orleans.

Fuente, Beatriz de la. 1992. *Las cabezas colosales olmecas.* El Colegio Nacional, Mexico City.

González-Lauck, Rebeca. 1996. La antigua ciudad olmeca en La Venta, Tabasco. In *Los Olmecas en Mesoamérica,* ed. J. E. Clark, 93–111. Citibank/México, Mexico City.

Heizer, Robert F., John A. Graham, and Lewis K. Napton. 1968. The 1968 Investigations at La Venta. In *Papers on Mesoamerican Archaeology,* Contributions of the University of California Archaeological Research Facility 5. University of California Department of Anthropology, Berkeley.

Houston, Stephen D. 2004. Writing in Early Mesoamerica. In *The First Writing: Script Invention as History and Process,* ed. S. D. Houston, 274–309. Cambridge University Press, Cambridge.

Joyce, Rosemary A. 1993. Women's Work: Images of Production and Reproduction in Pre-Hispanic Southern Central America. *Current Anthropology* 3 (June): 255–74.

———. 1996. The Construction of Gender in Classic Maya Monuments. In *Gender in Archaeology,* ed. R. P. Wright, 167–95. University of Pennsylvania Press, Philadelphia.

Justeson, John S., and Terrence Kaufman. 1993. A Decipherment of Epi-Olmec Hieroglyphic Writing. *Science* 259: 1703–10.

Lesure, Richard G. 1997. Figurines and Social Identities in Early Sedentary Societies of Coastal Chiapas, Mexico, 1550–800 BC. In *Women in Prehistory: North America and Mesoamerica*, ed. C. Claassen and R. A. Joyce, 227–48. University of Pennsylvania Press, Philadelphia.

Macri, Martha J., and Laura M. Stark. 1993. *A Sign Catalog of the La Mojarra Script*. Pre-Columbian Art Research Institute Monograph 5. San Francisco, Calif.

Marcus, Joyce. 1998. *Women's Ritual in Formative Oaxaca: Figurine-Making, Divination, Death and the Ancestors*. University of Michigan, Ann Arbor.

McCafferty, Sharisse, and Geoffrey G. McCafferty. 2001. Tricky *Traje*: Mixtec Costume as Symbolic Communication. Paper presented at the 66th Annual Meeting of the Society for American Archaeology, New Orleans.

Miller, Virginia Elizabeth. 1981. Pose and Gesture in Classic Maya Monumental Sculpture. Ph.D. diss., University of Texas, Austin.

Nelson, Sarah Milledge. 1997. *Gender in Archaeology: Analyzing Power and Prestige*. AltaMira Press, Walnut Creek, Calif.

Nuttall, Zelia. 1975. *The Codex Nuttall: A Picture Manuscript from Ancient Mexico*. Dover Publications, New York.

Ortíz Ceballos, Ponciano, and María del Carmen Rodríguez Martínez. 1997. *Las investigaciones arqueológicas en el Cerro Sagrado Manatí*. Universidad Veracruzana, Xalapa, Veracruz.

———. 2007. Respuesta. *Arqueología Mexicana* 14 (84): 8.

Piña Chan, Román. 1989. *The Olmec: Mother Culture of Mesoamerica*. Ed. L. Laurencich Minelli. Rizzoli International, New York.

Pohl, Mary E., Kevin O. Pope, and Christopher von Nagy. 2002. Olmec Origins of Mesoamerican Writing. *Science* 298: 1984–87.

Pool, Christopher A. 2000. From Olmec to Epi-Olmec at Tres Zapotes, Veracruz, Mexico. In *Olmec Art and Archaeology in Mesoamerica*, ed. J. E. Clark and M. E. Pye, 137–53. Trustees of the National Gallery of Art, Washington, D.C.

Porter, James B. 1989. Olmec Colossal Heads as Recarved Thrones: "Mutilation," Revolution and Recarving. *RES* 17/18: 22–29.

———. 1992. "Estelas celtiformes": Un nuevo tipo de escultura olmeca y sus implicaciones para los epigrafistas. *Arqueología* 8: 3–7.

Robertson, Merle Greene. c. 1983. *The Sculpture of Palenque*. 3 vols. Princeton University Press, Princeton, N.J.

Rodríguez Martínez, María del Carmen, and Ponciano Ortíz Ceballos. 1994. *El Manatí: Un espacio sagrado olmeca*. Instituto Nacional de Antropología e Historia, Xalapa, Veracruz.

Rodríguez Martínez, María del Carmen, Michael D. Coe, Richard A. Diehl, Stephen D. Houston, Karl A. Taube, and Alfredo Delgado Calderón. 2006. Oldest Writing in the New World. *Science* 313: 1610–14.

———. 2007. Response. *Science* 315: 1365–66.

Schaffer, Anne-Louise. 1986. The Maya Posture of "Royal Ease." In *Sixth Palenque Round Table, 1986*, ed. V. Fields, 203–16. University of Oklahoma Press, Norman.

Tate, Carolyn. 1992. *Yaxchilan: The Design of a Maya Ceremonial City*. University of Texas Press, Austin.

Tate, Carolyn, and Gordon Bendersky. 1999. Olmec Sculptures of the Human Fetus. *Perspectives in Biology and Medicine* 42 (3): 303–32.

Tway, Maria B. Derilo. 2004. Gender, Context, and Figurine Use: Ceramic Images from the Formative Period San Andrés Site, Tabasco, Mexico. Master's thesis, Department of Anthropology, Florida State University, Tallahassee.

Vaillant, Suzannah B., and George C. Vaillant. 1934. *Excavations at Gualupita.* Anthropological Papers of the American Museum of Natural History 35, part 1. New York.

Vela, Enrique, ed. 1996. *Olmecs: Special Edition, Arqueología Mexicana.* Editorial Raices and Instituto Nacional de Antropología e Historia, Mexico City.

Weiant, Clarence Wolsey. 1943. *An Introduction to the Ceramics of Tres Zapotes, Veracruz, Mexico.* Smithsonian Institution Bureau of American Ethnology Bulletin 157. U.S. Government Printing Office, Washington, D.C.

5

Identity, Gender, and Power

Representational Juxtapositions in Early Formative Figurines from Oaxaca, Mexico

JEFFREY P. BLOMSTER

Clay figurines constitute one of the few artifact categories that provide insights into how Early Formative (1500–900/850 BCE) villagers viewed the human body, themselves, and social identities; they illustrate a kind of self-awareness that is very physical and more visual than on other ceramic objects. Figurines not only represent important decisions about body form and its miniaturization but also were objects through which humans reflexively created their understandings of embodiment (Joyce 2006). As Douglass Bailey (1996: 294) notes, they serve as narrative by making relationships understood; figurines are potent ways of expressing relationships between individuals, by "claiming and legitimating one's own identity or for suggesting and realigning the identity of others."

For archaeologists interested in the emergence of social complexity, figurines are particularly of interest because they first appeared in quantity during a time of change in Mesoamerica, as early villages and associated new social roles and identities in everyday life were established and transformed. While figurines may show actual individuals, on at least one level they show idealized or abstracted social categories or identities. The makers and users of figurines expressed ideas about both the human form and identity and how these aspects of individuals related to those of others. Figurines may have materialized attempts to express and negotiate the connection between the self and the relationships of the social world. As some archaeologists have noted, figurines show relations between nascent social divisions and the exercise of power (Lesure 1997). Beginning with the first emerging chiefdoms of the Mokaya in Soconusco, various opportunities arose for the negotiation of status and identity. Figurines may have shown and naturalized these new social relations, but they may also represent efforts to understand, challenge, and question these relationships. In some cases, figurines may express resistance to new statuses (Joyce 1993).

In terms of interpretation, it would be a mistake to ascribe only one role or function to figurines. While there is much debate over the role—or, more realistically, the roles—figurines played in society, they first occurred before the appearance of sociopolitical structures and state-sanctioned religions that came to typify Mesoamerican societies. Figurines signify activities that occurred initially at a nonpublic and household level; such related behaviors and rituals were gradually accepted among groups of households or larger corporate entities. Initially they reflect the individual's exploration of relationships with close associates, both living and dead, as well as his or her role in larger social phenomenon, while through time figurines become more standardized in their imagery (and at least in some parts of Oaxaca, occur less frequently archaeologically). An Early Formative figurine assemblage (still under analysis), which may materialize societal transformations and negotiations, derives from excavations at Etlatongo, in the Nochixtlán Valley of the Mixteca Alta.

Figurines and Gender

While figurines are compelling at least in part because aspects of biological sex are often indicated, the connections between sexual characteristics and social identity and gender roles are complex. Running through the vast majority of figurine analyses is a problematic assumption: biological sexual characteristics—whether primary or secondary—on figurines can be used to infer gender. Such a direct link between sex and gender has been shown to be problematic in living and ancient societies throughout the world (see Gero and Conkey 1991). The binary division between only two genders also limits possibilities; for example, third genders—and more—among numerous Native American groups in North America have been well documented (Holliman 1997). Ethnographic data also caution against static gender categories tied with universal ideas about biological sex. Among the Hua of New Guinea, gender is a lifelong process; all children are born at least partially female and polluted (Gailey 1987). Similar concepts appear within Mesoamerican societies. While Nahuatl age terminology divided preadolescents into several types, specific gender forms were absent until adolescence (López Austin 1988: 1: 285–90). As informed by a praxis perspective (Bourdieu 1977; Giddens 1984), gender is discursively constructed and is context dependent. Gender differences are both constructed and maintained through discourse pertaining to agency and identity (Knapp 1998). In many societies, biological sex may be strongly correlated with gender, but maintaining a critical perspective encourages examination of other, noncorporeal attributes of the figurine—costume, implements held, posture, and so forth. Indeed, some scholars advocate for relying on offerings rather than the actual bones from a burial to determine gender (Claassen 2002: 216). On the basis of numerous weaving-related artifacts and the association between weaving and Postclassic female gender, the main individual in the famous Tomb 7 of Monte Albán (in the Valley of Oaxaca) has been pronounced gender-female, despite analysis of the fragmentary bones that interpreted the individual as biologically male, suggesting either that the earlier osteological analysis was incorrect or that sex and gender differed with this individual (McCafferty and McCafferty 1994). A focus on social identities, in addition to grappling with sex and gender, has provided stimulating new dimensions to figurine studies.

Linking sex and gender is especially problematic in Early Formative figurines from areas such as Oaxaca, where even determining biological sex on these eroded and generally fragmentary objects can be inconclusive. For their creators and users, on many of these figurines it was not necessarily critical to show primary and secondary sexual characteristics, which challenges our assumptions both about the links between sex and gender and about the importance of male-female dichotomies. Clearly, other social roles concerned ancient villagers; indeed, in some cases, figurines may primarily be illustrating identities linked with age differences, not sex or gender (Joyce 2003). At the same time, we also have to be cautious not to overcompensate in the nature of identities and genders that we impose on Early Formative villages. While studies from around the world open the door to a host of intriguing gender possibilities (Gailey 1987), these concepts may be no less applicable to Formative Mesoamerican villagers than male-female dichotomies. Christine Gailey (1987) notes that one of the few gender universals is its basic role in the division of labor in all societies; to this I would add its importance, along with age, in constructing and negotiating social identity.

My examination of Early Formative figurines from Oaxaca for sex and gender relies heavily on primary and secondary sexual characteristics, as distinctive clothing—used by researchers in other parts of Mesoamerica to explore sex and gender (Stark 2001)—is not frequently indicated, except for headgear. Unfortunately, primary external genitalia are rarely shown, and when present are depicted only on females. It may be that showing primary sexual characteristics was not considered important; maleness may have been primarily visually linked not with genitalia but with secondary sexual characteristics. Genitalia may also largely be absent on Formative figurines, as some scholars (Coe and Diehl 1980: 260) have suggested, because of the original presence of perishable costumes covering some figurines. Throughout Mesoamerica, costumes may more consistently designate the wearer's gender rather than sex and may have provided part of the context in which gender was performed.

One clear biological trait that represents femaleness in some figurines is pregnancy, although this is not as common in the Etlatongo figurine assemblage as in those from other regions. Identification of female sex is primarily linked with secondary sexual characteristics, particularly breasts, and long hair that is often wrapped in elaborate hairdos. As secondary sexual characteristics are not involved in biological reproduction, however, they may provide (along with any related paraphernalia depicted) an emic indicator of how ancient villagers constructed gender and social identity that does not essentialize female gender based solely on reproductive roles. The frequent depiction of large thighs on figurines with clear breasts and other female attributes suggests local notions of embodiment and beauty.

Early Formative Figurines from Oaxaca

My focus is on Oaxacan figurines primarily from the later portion of the Early Formative period, approximately 1200–900/850 BCE. This span of time corresponds to two local ceramic chronologies in the best-known regions of Oaxaca: the San José phase in the Valley of Oaxaca, and Cruz B in the Nochixtlán Valley of the Mixteca Alta (figure 5.1). I shall also refer to figurines from the preceding ceramic phases, 1500–1200 BCE—the Tierras Largas phase in the Valley of Oaxaca and the Cruz A phase in the Nochixtlán Valley. Figurines began to appear prior to 1500 BCE, shortly after the emergence of full-time sedentary villages in Oaxaca.

A large corpus of figurines has been excavated at the site of Etlatongo. The site has an extremely limited pre–Cruz B occupation; no primary contexts dating to Cruz A have yet been documented (Blomster 2004; Zárate Morán 1987). During Cruz B, Etlatongo grew to over 26 hectares, while Yucuita, which had previously been the largest site in the Nochixtlán Valley, shrank in size. Etlatongo was probably the center of a small chiefdom in this portion of the Nochixtlán Valley, similar to contemporaneous San José Mogote in the Valley of Oaxaca (Blomster 2004).

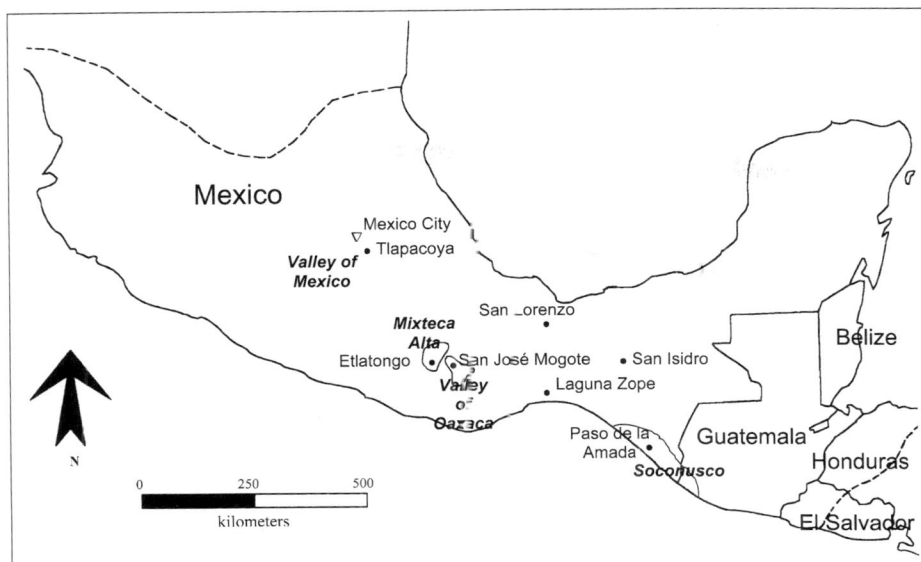

Figure 5.1. Map of Early Formative Mesoamerica.

Figurine Contexts at Etlatongo

With one notable exception, solid figurines primarily come from household refuse. Invariably fragmentary, figurines were excavated in middens, in storage pits, above house surfaces, and in fill, often reutilized to construct platforms for both private and public space (Blomster 2004). There does not seem to be any correlation with higher-status residences and higher figurine frequency at Etlatongo. Some types, especially the hollow Olmec-style figurines discussed below, do appear restricted in their distribution—they were not equally available to all members of society. The contexts of the vast majority of Early Formative solid figurines at Etlatongo reinforce their association with activities on the household level.

One exceptional figurine context comes from the southern edge of the Cruz B occupation of Etlatongo, where Unit 1 produced a disproportionate amount of solid Olmec-style—and other types of—figurines. After an earlier, and somewhat raised, Cruz B floor had ceased to be utilized, it served as a locus for midden deposits that ultimately elevated the surface of this area (interpreted as a possible early public space), prior to the construction of another surface, which was at least one meter higher than the surrounding land (Blomster 2004: fig. 4.3). These Unit 1 midden/platform fill deposits exhibit a remarkable proportional increase in figurine fragments compared with vessel fragments; I calculate figurine frequency from these midden deposits as over ten times greater than anywhere else at Etlatongo. I interpret the high frequency of figurine fragments in these deposits as supportive of their multiple functions, depending on context and audience. While these figurines may have had a variety of uses during their active use life when intact, a disproportionate amount of them ended up in trash that was used to elevate public space. Their level of completeness prior to being deposited here is not clear; it has been possible, even from this spatially limited sample, to join some fragments, suggesting that substantial utilization and/or breakage may have actually occurred in the vicinity of Unit 1. These figurines appear to have formed part of a specialized fill to delimit space within Early Formative Etlatongo. A similar pattern has been documented for a roughly contemporaneous deposit at Puerto Escondido, Honduras (Joyce 2003: 249), where figurines were used in the fill of the early stages of construction of an earthen platform. Many of the illustrated figurines in this chapter come from this context.

Tierras Largas and Cruz A Figurines

Figurines became common items of a household's material culture during the Tierras Largas and Cruz A phases, and they appear to be more frequent in the Valley of Oaxaca (at sites such as Hacienda Blanca, Tierras Largas, and San José Mogote) than in the Mixteca Alta (with examples primarily from Yucuita and Etlatongo). Two general figurine types have been defined for the Valley of Oaxaca (Winter 2005), and both display much naturalism and individuality. Figurines throughout the Early Formative period are generally found discarded in household trash. Unlike Central Mexican sites such as Tlatilco (García Moll et al. 1991), Early Formative figurines in Oaxaca rarely appear in burials—Marcus Winter (2005: table 2) lists a total of four for the Tierras Largas and San José phases in the Valley of Oaxaca. Joyce Marcus (1998) notes that they are never found, at least in primary context, in areas that she and Kent Flannery designate as "public areas."

Winter (2005) and Stacie King (1997; King and Winter 1996) have analyzed Early Formative figurines from the Valley of Oaxaca sites of Hacienda Blanca (599 figurine fragments) and Tierras Largas (1,583 fragments). Only 2 of the figurines from Hacienda Blanca show external female genitalia. Based on secondary sexual characteristics, Winter and King interpret 80 percent of figurines from these sites as clearly female; they do not report any clear male figurines. Many figurines they examined correspond with female roles in the life cycle. During their project at Hacienda Blanca, Winter and Susana Ramírez Urrea encountered an intact female figurine with a fetus inside the body—a dramatic example of the life cycle (Winter 1989: 20). A study of Valley of Oaxaca figurines by Marcus (1998) supports the high female figurine frequencies, although she also identifies select Tierras Largas phase figurines as male—contradicting King and Winter (1996). In contrast to the illustration commissioned by Marcus (1998: fig. 8.7), probably based on a photograph published by Winter (1994: fig. 8.4), none of the figurines from Hacienda Blanca can be clearly identified as male based on primary and secondary sexual characteristics.

While figurines were probably mostly made on a household level throughout Oaxaca, there is the possibility that Early Formative figurine production in the Valley of Oaxaca may have been organized on the village level. Because of the large quantity of figurines at Hacienda Blanca, as well as several possible wasters and small ovens, Winter (2005: 46) suggests that the village may have been a center of figurine production.

Few Cruz A figurines have been found in the Mixteca Alta at Yucuita and Etlatongo (figure 5.2). The disparity in figurine quantities between the Nochixtlán Valley and the Valley of Oaxaca could be attributable to the lack of significant Cruz A deposits at Etlatongo. Extensive excavations and

Figure 5.2. Cruz A figurine head found in redeposited Cruz B midden, Unit 1, Etlatongo.

survey at Yucuita (Plunket 1990; Winter 1984), however, produced abundant examples of Cruz A households and debris but few figurines. Although estimates of its size vary (see Blomster 2004), Yucuita was as large as any contemporaneous Tierras Largas phase village in the Valley of Oaxaca; demographics alone do not account for the different figurine frequencies. Thus, there may be significant underlying social processes at work that could explain this quantitative disparity in figurines. At Yucuita, the few early figurines were found in the well-documented Cruz A portion of the village. These figurines often have a three-punctation hairstyle, sometimes with patterned red paint, and are "finely crafted, realistic and delicate, especially in facial features, and are not as stylized as the later San José phase figurines" (Winter 1984: 187). The few Cruz A figurines encountered at Etlatongo were all redeposited in Cruz B contexts. The less-stylized facial features, however, clearly distinguish the few Cruz A figurines at Etlatongo from Cruz B figurines, as does the more naturalistic modeling of the human body.

San José and Cruz B Figurines

The high frequency of figurines continued into the San José phase in the Valley of Oaxaca; in the Cruz B of the Mixteca Alta, the overall quantity of figurines greatly increased compared with Cruz A. Given the results of the Etlatongo excavations, I suggest that in contrast with Cruz A, Cruz B figurines are as frequent in the Nochixtlán Valley as are San José phase figurines in the Valley of Oaxaca. Cruz B and San José phase figurines continue to be found primarily as discarded household refuse, but in one noteworthy example from San José Mogote, four figurines were arranged in a scene (Marcus and Flannery 1996). While the types of representations increased to at least three in the Valley of Oaxaca (Winter 2005), there is less variety and individuality within these types compared to the preceding phase. The shape of the eyes is especially diagnostic in determining phase. During the San José and Cruz B phases, artisans frequently made eyes with two "plowing" strokes, sometimes over an oval clay appliqué, leaving a raised area in the center.

A dramatic change in the sex depicted on figurines occurs in both the Valley of Oaxaca and Nochixtlán Valley—clear male figurines appeared for the first time in the San José and Cruz B phases. The ways in which sex and gender are inscribed in these figurines challenge easy categorization. Some investigators (Marcus 1998), because of the preponderance of female figurines and in lieu of actual male genitalia, have classified flat-chested figurines as prepubescent females, probably inflating the frequency of female figurines. A graphic from Marcus's (1998: fig. 10.17) well-illustrated figurine monograph supposedly shows the entire spectrum of female age grades, from prepubescent to matronly—but her Specimen 63 cannot be classified as female solely because it has a flat chest, nor should we assume that "female" was even part of the emic classification system for prepubescents, as ethnographic examples from Mesoamerica suggest otherwise (see below). There is a similar problem with the supposed three figurines interpreted as male retainers to the seated chief/leader figurine found arranged in a scene buried under House 16 at San José Mogote (Marcus 1998: 177–78). The identification of the "chief" as male stems from his seated position, which in itself is a dubious proposition, as burials of individuals seated "tailor-style" are not necessarily elite (Blomster 2004). The association between seated position and high-status "chiefs" comes primarily from later Panamanian burial data rather than additional contemporaneous Oaxacan burials (Marcus and Flannery 1996), which also proves problematic. The idea that a leader would have male retainers seems to be the primary determinant of the sex and gender of the three standing figurines that accompany the seated House 16 figurine, as such an attribution ignores the physical characteristics of these three figurines. The two intact standing figurines (see Marcus 1998: fig. 13.13), which have typical San José phase eyes and hairdos, manifest clear breasts (although the breasts are largely obscured by the figurines' folded arms), and have large thighs combined with thin lower legs. I interpret these standing "retainer" figurines as biologically— and probably gendered—female.

The appearance of male figurines reflects broader transformations in social identities during a time of increasing sociopolitical complexity. Primary sexual characteristics, however, are not indicated on male figurines. In Oaxaca, male genitalia were not graphically shown until the creation of the first urban center, Monte Albán, and the Danzantes sculptural program dating from 500 BCE. The infrequency of genitalia in depictions of the male body relates to a larger phenomenon across a vast span of time throughout many parts of Mesoamerica. To show genitalia was to inscribe humiliation. Maya rulers, for example, rarely exhibited their penises in public art, despite their important role in autosacrifice; instead, bound captives were more likely to be shown with exposed penises (Houston et al. 2006). Indeed, at least some of the Danzantes figures that exhibit penises—usually mutilated—are prob-

Figure 5.3. Eroded and damaged Cruz B male figurine head with beard, found in a post–Cruz B mixed context at Etlatongo.

ably captives/sacrificial offerings or represent individuals who engaged in autosacrifice in the founding ceremony commemorated by this sculptural program at Monte Albán.

While male figurines are often identified simply by the lack of female characteristics, figurines characterized as male from Etlatongo have broad chests, either flat or with subtle pectoral muscles, without exaggerated thighs and bellies. At least at Etlatongo, images of fat male elders present at earlier Soconusco chiefly sites, such as Paso de la Amada (Lesure 1997), are not part of the representational system for maleness; other obese images from Soconusco, usually seated on stools, also show females or figures without clearly identifiable sex. Male heads are much harder to sex, especially when not attached to bodies. Male heads are often bald or with limited hair, perhaps obscured by a helmet or some kind of headgear; these characteristics have also been used to determine sex on figurines in the Valley of Oaxaca (Marcus 1998). If hair is shown on males, it is generally confined to the back of the head, where it may emerge from under headgear. The one case in which hair definitively indicates maleness is when it occurs in the form of facial hair, such as the beard on the eroded head in figure

5.3; such examples, however, are rare. Females are often shown with long, flowing hair, with striations clearly indicated, and sometimes with elaborate hairdos or headgear, especially so-called turbans. Both males and females may have incisions on the back of the head. On probable males, these incisions more often form a possible symbol or iconographic element, while on females they tend to detail the hair.

In a sample of thirty relatively complete torsos from Etlatongo, often with at least some limbs attached, twenty-four bodies appear to be clearly or probably female (80 percent) in terms of biological sex, while three bodies are probably male and three are too ambiguous to determine. Females can be identified through secondary sexual characteristics; in addition to breasts and pregnant bellies, legs are produced in a way that is associated with other female traits. In contrast to the relatively naturalistic portrayal of Tierras Largas/Cruz A figurine legs, many Cruz B female figurines are shown with massive thighs and narrow calves. These massive legs are often juxtaposed with a relatively slender waist.

With regard to figurines that do not display clear sexual characteristics, I question the notion that these represent an "ambiguous gender" or that we must force them into either a male or a female category. Instead, I suggest that in most cases, sex or gender was not important in social identity or representation, or gender may have been indicated but in ways not dependent on biological sex—missing costume elements or implements may have signaled gender and/or identity. Sexual organs were not the only—or even major—way in which Mesoamericans inscribed gender differences. Among contemporary Mixtecs, John Monaghan (2001: 289) reports that while male and female genital differences are deeply understood, the focus is not on genitalia but on an anal-genital pollution zone—resulting from the sexual act—that is equally problematic on both males and females. In the Postclassic codices, naked individuals generally appear without genitalia, but associated texts, names/titles, and documents demonstrate that such individuals are not genderless (Monaghan 2001: 291). Additionally, some figurines may represent children or other individuals whose gender may have been a work in progress. In the absence of extra information in the form of costume, implements, and iconography, sex (where clearly indicated) provides one clue to understanding gender.

At Etlatongo, the most common Cruz B figurine is a female with two plowing-stroke eyes, well-defined breasts, a narrow to robust (but usually not plump or pregnant) waist, and ample to large and exaggerated thighs (figures 5.4 and 5.5). Several of these figurines do have incised lines or

Figure 5.4. Typical Cruz B female figurine head with nose ornament and elaborate hairdo, found in redeposited Cruz B midden, Unit 1, Etlatongo.

punctations that appear to represent genitalia—more so than those in the King and Winter (1996) study of Valley of Oaxaca figurines. These female figurines are also the most likely to have vestiges of red pigment on them. Well-preserved examples evince blocks of the red pigment on the left leg and right breast and shoulder region (figure 5.6), and vice versa. These figurines appear to be completely nude, although in a few cases there appears to be a thin garment or G-string below the waist and covering the pubic

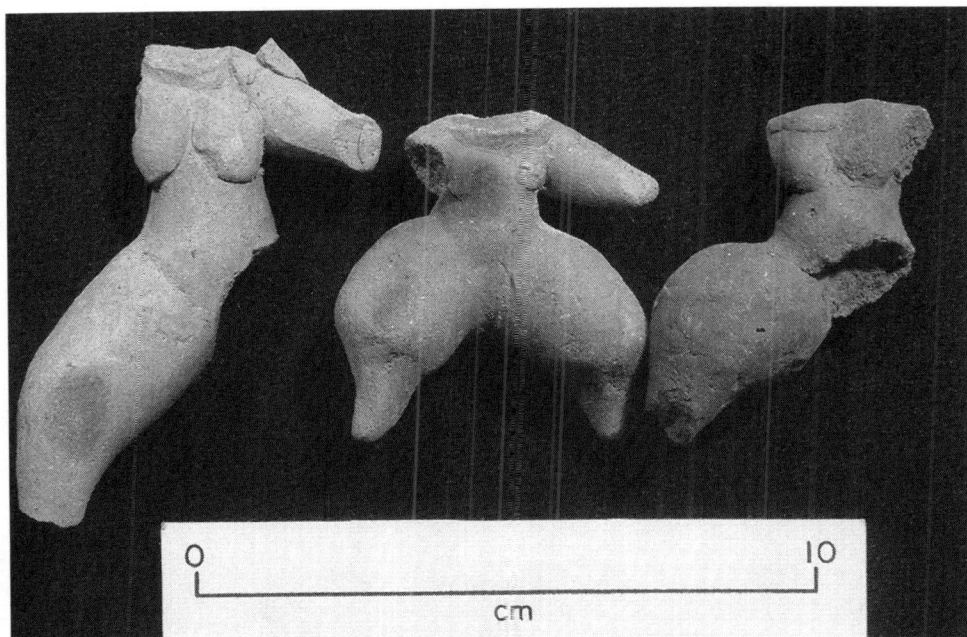

Figure 5.5. Typical Cruz B female figurine bodies, found in redeposited Cruz B midden, Unit 1, Etlatongo.

region. Hair is arranged in braids on either side of the face, often with a cloth or other headgear covering the hair atop the head.

Body position and stance are fairly consistent on Cruz B figurines. Most of the Etlatongo figurines stand, rather statically—arms to the sides, with straight, slightly outleaning legs. In some cases, legs are more outstretched and less parallel, although these have particularly exaggerated thighs that may have forced this arrangement (see center and right figurines in figure 5.5); arms may also be upraised, perpendicular to the body. A few figurines are in seated positions, while others exhibit unusual positions, often not possible to fully reconstruct owing to the small portion of the figurine recovered.

Animal figurines first began to appear during the Cruz B phase at Etlatongo. Bodies of what are probably dogs appear most frequently. Heads, when present on these dog bodies, are roughly modeled and are not naturalistic. In addition to dogs, some figurines may represent animals similar to those in the figurine corpus of the Valley of Oaxaca, such as monkeys (figure 5.7). Such depictions are extremely rare at Etlatongo, which is far from this animal's natural habitat. Several bird heads—which may have been part

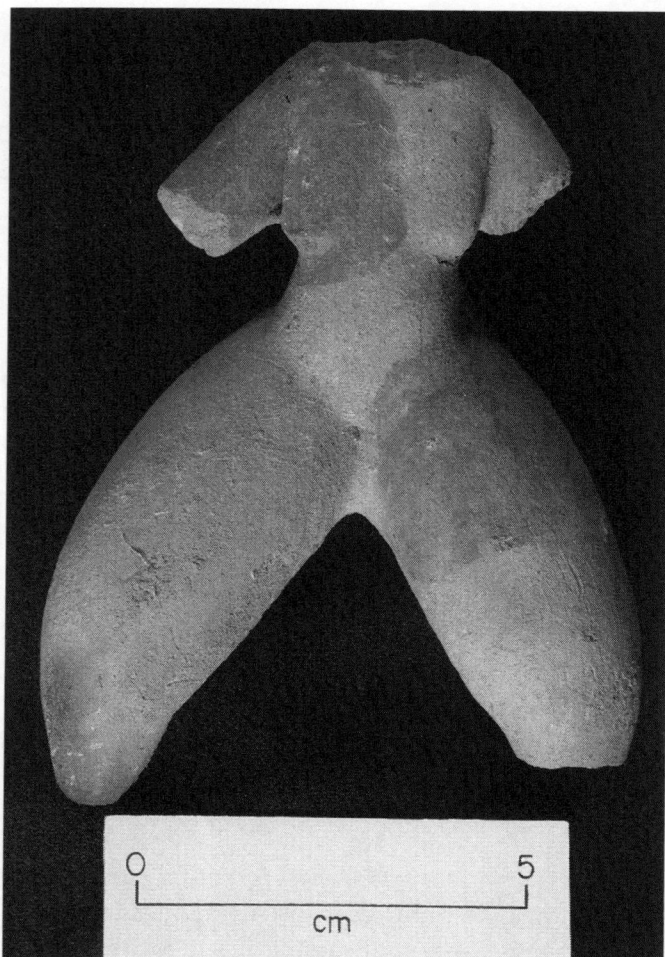

Figure 5.6. Cruz B female figurine body with zones of red pigment, found in redeposited Cruz B midden, Unit 1, Etlatongo.

of either figurines or vessel attachments—also come from Cruz B contexts. In one example (figure 5.8), the plumage is arranged as three balls atop the head of this long-beaked creature.

Olmec-Style Figurines and Style Juxtaposition

Several varieties of figurines coexisted with the most common type at Etlatongo. Most types share similar production techniques, surface finish, and overall aesthetics. One type, however, is in stark juxtaposition stylistically

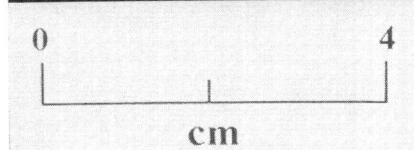

Figure 5.7. Cruz B possible monkey figurine head, found in redeposited midden, Unit 1, Etlatongo.

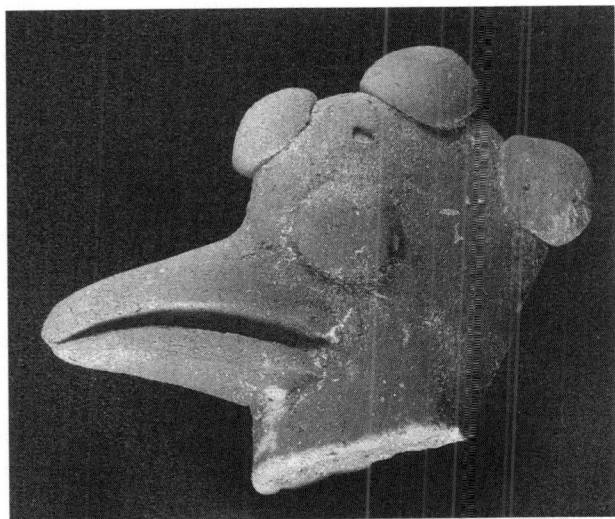

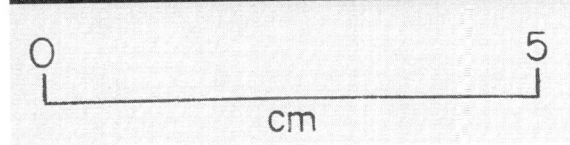

Figure 5.8. Cruz B bird head, found in redeposited midden, Unit 1, Etlatongo.

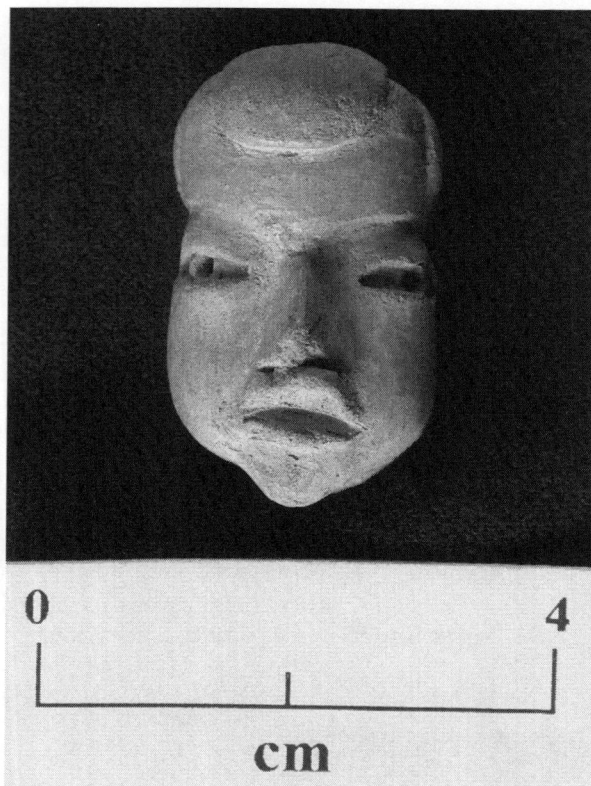

Figure 5.9. White-slipped, burnished Olmec-style figurine head, found in redeposited Cruz B midden, Unit 1, Etlatongo.

with the Etlatongo figurine corpus. Often referred to as Olmec style, these occur at Etlatongo as both solid and hollow figurines (figure 5.9).

I use the term *Olmec style* to refer to imagery that corresponds with Gulf Coast Olmec art from San Lorenzo. The use of the term *Olmec style* does not mean that these objects are necessarily from the Gulf Coast— that is a separate point that must be proved through robust testing such as Instrumental Neutron Activation Analysis (INAA), which has recently determined that certain Olmec-style ceramics were produced by the Gulf Coast Olmec and exported throughout Mesoamerica, including both San José Mogote and Etlatongo (Blomster et al. 2005).

In terms of surface treatment, Olmec-style figurines differ from other solid figurines in having a slip, usually white to cream colored, and have been burnished to achieve a lustrous surface. Some of the pertinent features (see Blomster 2002; Coe 1965) are

Realistic depiction of the body
Elongated head, evincing cranial modification
Fat, puffy cheeks and jowls

Trough or L-shaped eyes, or neatly incised eyes with or without pupils,
    framed by puffy eyelids
Downturned, trapezoidal mouth

Solid figurines

Solid figurines in the Olmec style represent a very small percentage of the
overall figurine corpus at Etlatongo. While fragmentary, the majority of Olmec-style fragments appear to represent males, applying the same criteria
as detailed above for Cruz B figurines and those used by other scholars who
have focused on figurines from San Lorenzo (see Cheetham, this volume).
Some of the body fragments have traces of red paint over the white slip that
may represent clothing or other adornments and designs. While information on body poses is limited, one clear body fragment in the Olmec style
is unusual in that the figure appears to be in a kneeling position, with red
pigment delimiting a probable garment over the groin (figure 5.10).

As noted above, Cruz B figurines occasionally have a symbol or incising
on the back of the head. The Olmec-style figurines are more likely to have

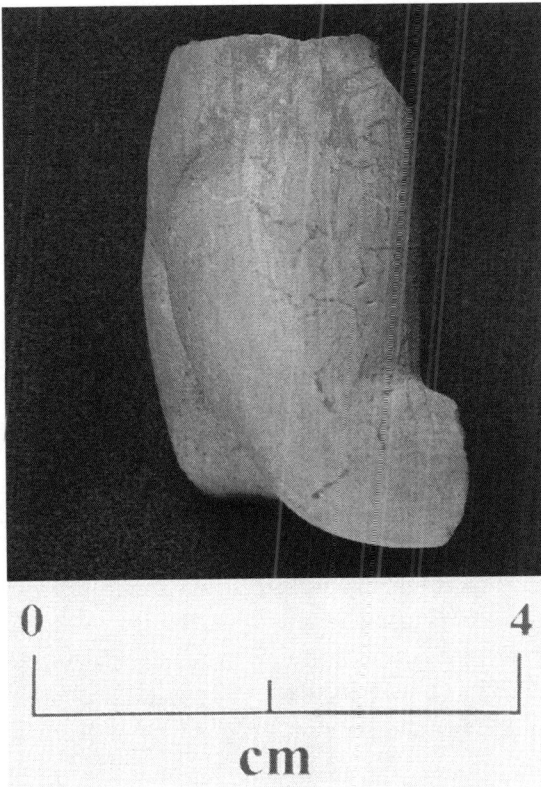

Figure 5.10. Cruz B, white-slipped kneeling body fragment from redeposited Cruz B midden, Unit 1, Etlatongo, with red pigment over the groin.

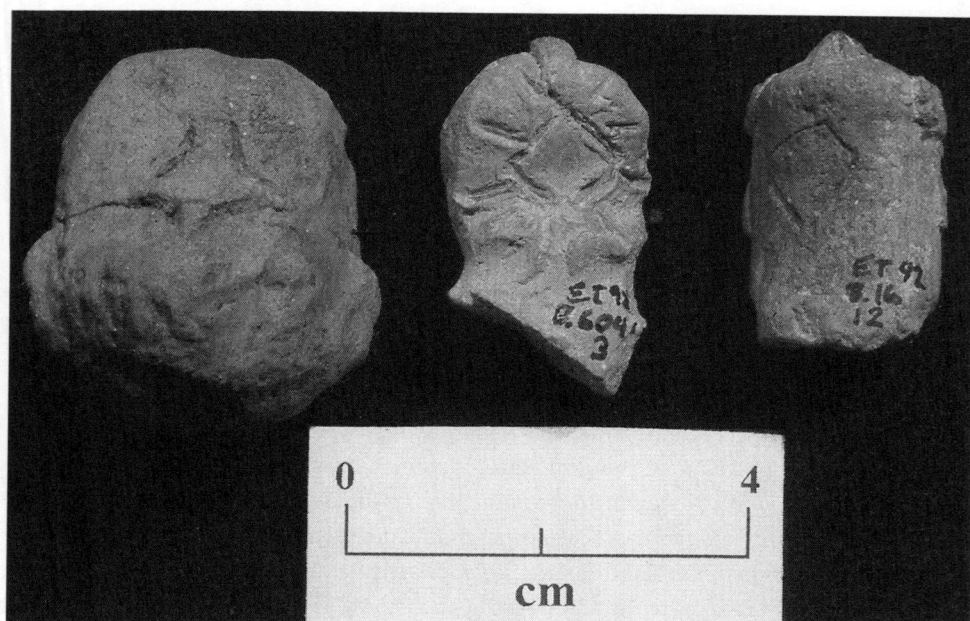

Figure 5.11. Three Cruz B figurines with incisions on the back of their heads, Etlatongo; the one on the left is Olmec style.

this incising, and only rarely does it appear to be actual hair. In addition to the possibility that at least some of these designs represent symbols/iconography, some may also represent scarification, tattooing, and other forms of bodily transformation, beautification, and manipulation. The three designs illustrated in figure 5.11 include what may be a possible Venus sign on the left and two diamond-shaped symbols on the center and right figurines (see also fig. 6.20, this volume). Both the center and right figurines appear to have hair and/or headdresses; whether the "rays" emanating from the symbol on the back of the center head pertain to it or represent hair is unclear. Of the sample analyzed from Etlatongo, incised iconography on the back of the head appears to occur more frequently with probable male figurines on both Olmec- and non-Olmec-style figurines. The identification of these as male heads is based on lack of hair; one could also argue that the absence of any depiction of hair was deliberate, to permit a symbol to be placed on the back of the head. In some cases, there may be "buns" of hair either atop the head or at the back of the neck, creating space for the design. As seen with the Classic Maya, the head, either anatomical or metaphorical, often designates someone as belonging to a particular category of person, with name glyphs often in the headdresses of lords—a practice that may go back to the Olmec (Houston et al. 2006: 62, 68). Among the Postclassic Mixtec, personal names could be placed in the headdress (Smith 1973: 27). Thus, the symbols on the back of some Etlatongo figurines' heads may relate to personal and social identities and, based on their greater frequency on male figurines, may be important aspects of gender identity.

Hollow Figurines

In addition to solid figurines, human images were also depicted as hollow figurines. Just as several different styles of solid figurines were in use at any given time at Etlatongo, so too were there different types or styles of hollow figurines (figure 5.12). Compared to solid figurines, hollow ones in all styles represent an extremely rare artifact category at Valley of Oaxaca sites and at Etlatongo. Data from both Tierras Largas and San José Mogote support the association of hollow figurines of various types with differently ranked households (Marcus 1998).

Figure 5.12. Different styles of hollow figurine head fragments from Cruz B phase Etlatongo: *top,* Group 1 or Olmec style; *bottom,* Group 2.

Although several hollow figurines found at Etlatongo are either completely local or local emulations of the Olmec style (what I have called Group 2—see the bottom three heads in figure 5.12), a small subset of hollow figurines made purely in the Olmec style constitutes part of an object category commonly referred to as "hollow babies" (Group 1 in my terminology; Blomster 1998, 2002). Although hollow babies have been reported from across Mesoamerica, their general context has been incorrectly characterized as Central Mexican because of a focus on complete examples (Flannery and Marcus 1994). Also, many items reported as hollow babies actually belong to Group 2—local emulations or approximations. Only one of the hollow babies purportedly from Central Mexico was actually recovered archaeologically (from later mixed fill); the others were looted and lack any secure provenience (Blomster 1998). If we look at hollow baby fragments instead of intact, but looted, hollow figurines, their characterization as primarily Central Mexican in origin becomes problematic. Fragments of hollow baby heads were recovered archaeologically in greatest frequency at San Lorenzo—the Early Formative Olmec center in Veracruz (Coe and Diehl 1980). Although fragments from sites such as San José Mogote are referred to as "hollow baby dolls" (Marcus 1998), I classify those published from the Valley of Oaxaca as Group 2 (Blomster 2002).

In addition to fragments such as those shown in the top row of figure 5.12, a nearly intact Group 1 figurine was found in a large bell-shaped pit on the eastern edge of the Cruz B occupation at Etlatongo (figure 5.13; Blomster 1998). Located in a deposit close to the base of this pit, secondary refuse filled the remainder of the pit above the hollow figurine. The association of this figurine with a variety of nonutilitarian materials suggests that it may have been part of a cache of damaged or spent ritual paraphernalia. Additionally, the figurine was associated with refuse of a higher-status household relative to other contemporaneous households at Etlatongo. The fact that this relatively intact figurine (the portion of the head above the eyes is missing) was deposited in this pit is indicative of a nonfunerary function; the object had clearly been utilized prior to its deposition in the bell-shaped pit. This hollow figurine displays all the basic features of a "hollow baby" figurine: white slip, highly polished, fat and well-modeled body, slit eyes, wide nose, flabby cheeks, and downturned mouth.

As with other figurine types, Group 1 figurines from across Mesoamerica do not exhibit biological sex. If we consider secondary sexual characteristics, as with solid figurines, these objects generally have pectoral muscles; they are probably more male than female, but sex and gender were probably not

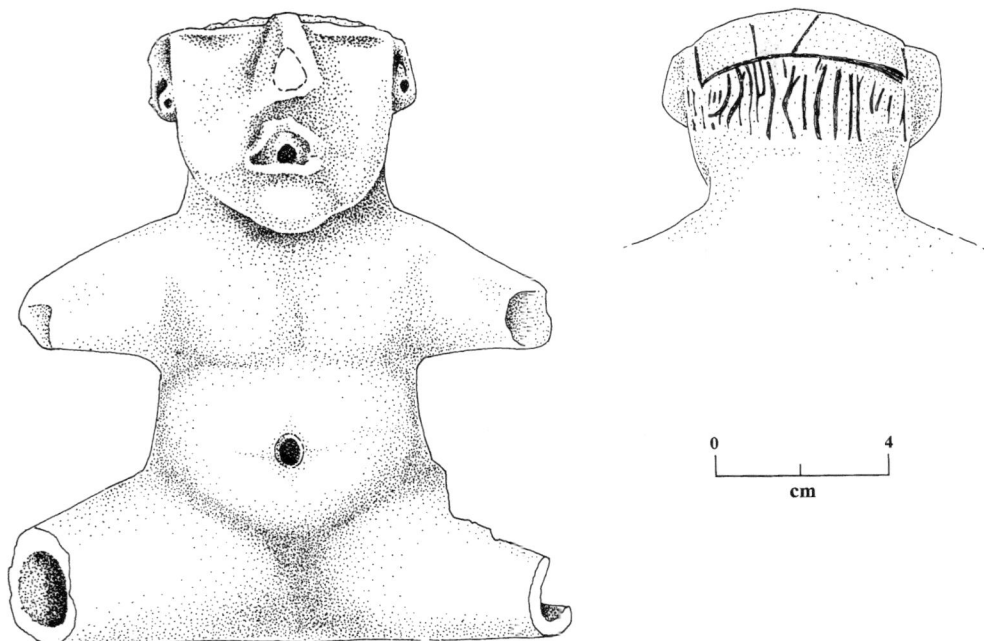

Figure 5.13. Front and back of a nearly intact Group 1 hollow figurine found in a large Cruz B bell-shaped pit at the eastern edge of Etlatongo (drawing by Jason Trout).

the foci of these images. The presence of adult musculature argues against their being children or babies, despite the unfortunate name given to these objects. I interpret these as indicating supernatural creatures in largely human form rather than representing actual human infants or dwarves. They are similar to creatures (referred to as everything from dwarves to were-jaguar babies) shown on monumental Gulf Coast Olmec art and contrast with local Mixtec representational systems at Etlatongo of how the human form and physiognomy should be depicted. I have argued that "hollow babies" depict something that transcends—or transforms—typical social and gender roles (Blomster 1998). On Olmec art at both San Lorenzo (Monuments 12 and 20) and the later La Venta (Altar 5), rulers depicted on basalt sculptures (some of which, although previously known as altars, are actual thrones) hold these dwarflike creatures as they emerge (on thrones) from niches—symbolic caves. In addition to any ritual use, material representations of these creatures served also as powerful manifestations of political strategies in Formative ranked societies.

Gender, Juxtaposition, and Power

Early Formative solid figurines in the Valley of Oaxaca have been inter-preted in a variety of ways, from children's toys (Winter 2005) to depic-tions of ancestors (Marcus 1998). Indeed, Marcus (1998) argues that female figurines were made and used by women, who had spheres of ritual dis-tinct from those of men; women honored recent ancestors, whereas men invoked distant ancestors. While parts of this argument are appealing and may account for the preponderance of female figurines, it does not account for the male figurines, which (for reasons noted above) are probably under-estimated in the San José phase Valley of Oaxaca counts. It also stresses a dichotomy between gender roles that has little support with other lines of evidence in Early Formative Oaxaca.

Figurines may not have served primarily as gender-defining artifacts, al-though physical features were undoubtedly important—which leads to dif-ficult questions. If women made these images during the San José and Cruz B phases, as Marcus (1998) suggests, why would they show themselves—or their ancestors—with massive thighs? Does this tell us something particular about a life stage or identity? Perhaps such physical characteristics were ac-centuated to represent dancing or other physical activities that emphasized active legs. While massive thighs may document Early Formative ideas of beauty, the inconsistent presence of this feature among the figurine assem-blage suggests that other factors were at work. Additionally, social actors sometimes create and use material culture that intentionally misrepresents themselves and others—as witnessed in today's society with the advent of Internet dating and the often disingenuous images employed to lure an un-suspecting mate to a rendezvous. People may also use material culture that was simply never intended to represent themselves on an individual or per-sonal level, serving instead as a cultural aesthetic or idealized social iden-tity within society. Mokaya female figurines from Soconusco, made without arms (or with arms depicted as short stubs), epitomize such an aesthetic; Richard Lesure interprets the lack of arms as indicative of a lack of value in the productive labor of young females (Lesure 1997: 247). Repeated physi-cal characteristics of the figurines do seem to indicate certain underlying conventions of the human body held by at least the producers of these figu-rines.

Even in one place and time, solid figurines served a variety of purposes, responding to temporally divergent interests within societies. At least one use involved household ritual. Ann Cyphers Guillén (1993) argues that Cantera phase figurines from Chalcatzingo were used primarily in female life-cycle rituals related to menstruation, marriage, and childbirth. For various reasons, perhaps including the young age at which people died, neither the figurines from Chalcatzingo nor those from Oaxaca appear to depict elderly individuals, at least not in a way that can be clearly identified. Many societies have more ceremonies that mark different life-cycle stages for females than for males, corresponding with the much greater frequency of female figurines. I would expand on this interpretation to suggest that while they may have served in rituals involving physical life-cycle crises, they may also have been used in passages involving social identity independent of biological changes. These ritual moments may have been opportunities when social identities were negotiated and larger corporate bonds established and recognized.

The relationship between object and maker and/or user proves central to Rosemary Joyce's (2003, 2006) interpretation of figurines from Honduras, which focuses on the recursive relationship between the creation of figurines and production of societal members, evoking the interplay between modifying both living bodies and corpses and fashioning figurines, both solid and hollow—which she sees as composed of layers of clay. In addition to ceremonies marking biological life passages, the figurines may have commemorated stages in one's social life cycle on both an informal household level and increasingly, in the San José and Cruz B phases in Oaxaca, on a larger corporate level. At Etlatongo, the exaggeration during the Cruz B phase of female secondary sexual characteristics—such as the massive thighs and ample breasts on some figurines—may reflect a less egalitarian mentality than had existed several hundred years earlier, as social identities came to reflect increasingly stereotyped gender roles and commoditization. As is often seen in sociopolitically complex societies, in which identities beyond the household become emphasized and reproduction politicized, there may be more-rigid roles in general, especially those associated with women, whose status is generally highest in preindustrial, nonagricultural societies with the least economic and political stratification (Gailey 1987).

While the actual use of the figurine varies in the above interpretations, an underlying theme is that throughout a person's social life, both males and especially females may have deployed figurines. In some cases, these figurines may have represented the user and/or his or her stereotyped identity (or identities). Some figurines probably did serve in curing ceremonies, and they may have been broken during or after the ritual. Although scholars disagree on the issue of intentional breakage of figurines (see Cyphers

Guillén 1993 versus Grove and Gillespie 1984 for contrastive perspectives on the same assemblage), the paucity of not merely whole but also matching fragments from the same contexts at Etlatongo suggests that figurines were actively handled during rituals. While data are limited, I note that of the five comparable female torsos that still have an attached arm, four have left arms.

At least some rituals involving figurines involved active negotiation of status and social identity. While applying ethnographic analogies from around the world to Early Formative Mesoamerica is problematic—what Martin Wobst (1978) has called the "tyranny of the ethnographic record," as it limits possibilities to those societies observed by cultural anthropologists—available case studies may at least provide a window into various possibilities. The ethnographic literature is rich with examples in which figurines, in various media, are created and used. Contemporary Japanese of Kawakura, for example, try to reconstitute family unity and cosmological exchange after the death of an unmarried family member by purchasing a bride doll figurine, to which the deceased is spiritually wed. These dolls serve as vessels that must be activated by being infused with a transformative spirit, similar to the Buddhist rite of eye-opening—when a deity is induced to enter its physical representation in this world (Schattschneider 2001). The idea that figurines could be infused with an animating spirit is particularly appropriate to Oaxaca and Mesoamerica; different figurines could have been channels for different kinds of forces.

The different "types" or "styles" of figurines may correlate with different uses or different representations of social roles beyond simply gender. Although females may have made and used some figurines, female figurines may have been sources of inscription and reflection for both males and females, as proposed for the armless Paqui figurines of Mazatan (see above), where young people were objects of marriage negotiations arranged by elders (Lesure 1997).

Of particular interest to possible changing social identities and gender roles is the introduction during the Cruz B and San José phases of male figurines. This occurred during a time when the archaeological record at Etlatongo documents clear signs of higher-status individuals (although social differentiation remained along a continuum). In the Valley of Oaxaca, such individuals lived in somewhat better houses than the rest of the community, may have organized craft production, and had more access to exotic goods (Marcus and Flannery 1996). Such individuals may also have been represented in clay figurines and as such would have formed an important new ingredient in negotiations of social identity in this time of sociopolitical transformation throughout Oaxaca. As power relations changed in Oaxaca villages, many of the infrequent male figurines in the assemblage began to be depicted in a contrasting style.

Interaction and Style Juxtaposition

The juxtaposition of styles during the Cruz B phase at Etlatongo, particularly the presence of Olmec-style solid and hollow figurines, suggests deployment of different style and imagery in negotiations of social identity and status. As noted above, INAA has demonstrated that vessels bearing Olmec iconography were exported from the Gulf Coast to several parts of Oaxaca; the same technique documents that at least some Olmec-style figurines outside of the Gulf Coast were produced and disseminated by the Olmec (Blomster 2002; Cheetham 2006, this volume). Thus, at least some items fashioned by Gulf Coast Olmec artisans appear to have been imported into parts of Oaxaca.

What is of special interest in this juxtaposition is not necessarily understanding the Olmec, but the use of contrasting styles, with one referencing foreign imagery. In Oaxaca, there is no visual precedent for the conventions of the Olmec style. I see significant meaning created by the juxtaposition of local with exotic styles in a similar medium; art and style often function as bridges—or boundaries—between groups. What Esther Pasztory (1989) calls "ethnic style" serves to mark who is a member of a group and who is not, and ethnic style usually occurs in public contexts. What does it mean, then, when some people in society choose to display human representations in a foreign style? In Oaxaca, certain individuals chose to show a relationship with something that was "other." The use of white slip on both solid and hollow figurines in the Olmec style adds yet another physical layer to the embodied object (Joyce 2003), just as the display of such an item adds another facet to social identity. In Oaxaca, imagery appears in the form of Olmec-style figurines that is both exotic and for the first time shows males. Although the data at this time do not support an interpretation that the first male figurines at Etlatongo were in the Olmec style, such figurines emerged at a critical juncture in the development of social complexity in the Mixteca Alta, and they may represent fundamental transformations in social roles, power, and interaction. An important subset of largely male figurines was intended for public display—hollow figurines.

Hollow figurines—both larger and more restricted than solid figurines—

inscribed both male gender (if sex and gender were even important themes) and a style that emphasized otherness: the Olmec style. The size of these objects, which appear to have been seen from all sides, suggests a different role for these objects in rituals involving several participants. They may have been deployed only by ritual practitioners, who may have had a disproportionate amount of esoteric knowledge. The exotic nature of their appearance may have been a source of power. As Mary Helms (1979) has noted, foreign contact or involvement with people outside the home society may be used to legitimize the origins of ruling houses. These objects were deployed and involved social discourses distinct from those of solid figurines and may have provided dimensions of social power for both local and foreign agents.

The ultimate impact of Olmec influence lies beyond the scope of this chapter. Using Mazatan data over several phases, John Clark and Mary Pye (2000) have shown how contact with the Gulf Coast Olmec fundamentally changed the Mokaya people. Although at places such as Etlatongo such interaction was not as transformative, the imagery and ideology were compelling to a certain stratum of society. Indeed, the discovery of a mask in the Olmec style from a higher-status context at Etlatongo is a striking example of transformation and disguise involving exotic imagery—an example of changing face and identity.

Conclusion

After 1200 BCE in Oaxaca, figurine types increased, but the variety within those types decreased from the preceding phase. The growing homogeneity within these stylistic types may indicate a more rigid structuring of identities in a society witnessing the emergence of higher-status actors and new power relations. These emerging higher-status individuals exercised greater control over exotic items and ritual paraphernalia. Despite these changes, small solid figurines remained in the spectrum of all community members' items of material culture, serving a plethora of uses while new social roles were introduced and negotiated in the community. Indeed, one use may have been reflecting—if not actively promoting—the new social roles within society.

Juxtaposed against this common referent were Olmec-style figurines, in both solid and hollow types, wielded by the same individuals in society who were negotiating enhanced power roles. Although some elements of Olmec style may represent foreign ideology and beliefs, local versions served to incorporate and transform elements of it. Olmec-style figurines do not explicitly depict primary sexual characteristics, nor do most contemporaneous figurines in Oaxaca. Genitalia, however, often are not the focus for gender differentiation in Mesoamerica (Monaghan 2001: 291). The appearance of Olmec-style figurines, generally male, and local representations of male figurines suggests that these objects served to negotiate and reflect important transformations in gender and social roles. The figurine that may best reflect this relationship comes from San José Mogote, where it was found in 1995 by Enrique Fernández (Fernández Dávila and Gómez Serafín 1997: 85). Found redeposited in a later tomb, a solid figurine with a gray slip and highly burnished exterior depicts a female in purely local Early to Middle Formative style suckling what appears to be a baby with a long, cylindrical Olmec-style modified cranium. It graphically represents the creation of connections and relationships among local people and makes the exotic local and the local exotic.

Acknowledgments

The field research that permitted the excavation of the Etlatongo figurine corpus was supported by a Fulbright (IIE) Fellowship and the permits and support of colleagues and dedicated officials in Mexico City, Oaxaca, and Etlatongo. Marcus Winter has been generous with his vast knowledge on Oaxacan figurines. Specific information and comments that improved this manuscript came from Christina Halperin, Byron Hamann, Rosemary Joyce and two anonymous reviewers. I alone remain responsible for the content of this chapter. I also wish to thank Mannetta Braunstein and Aurore Giguet for organizing and supporting the very stimulating conference in Las Vegas at which I presented an earlier draft of this chapter.

References Cited

Bailey, Douglass. 1996. The Interpretation of Figurines: The Emergence of Illusion and New Ways of Seeing. *Cambridge Archaeological Journal* 6 (2): 291–95.

Blomster, Jeffrey P. 1998. Context, Cult, and Early Formative Public Ritual in the Mixteca Alta: Analysis of a Hollow Baby Figurine from Etlatongo, Oaxaca. *Ancient Mesoamerica* 9 (2): 309–26.

———. 2002. What and Where Is Olmec Style? Regional Perspectives on Hollow Figurines in Early Formative Mesoamerica. *Ancient Mesoamerica* 13 (2): 171–95.

———. 2004. *Etlatongo: Social Complexity, Interaction, and Village Life in the Mixteca Alta of Oaxaca, Mexico.* Wadsworth, Belmont, Calif.

Blomster, Jeffrey P., Hector Neff, and Michael D. Glascock. 2005. Olmec Pottery Production and Export in Ancient Mexico Determined through Elemental Analysis. *Science* 307: 1068–72.

Bourdieu, Pierre. 1977. *Outline of a Theory of Practice.* Cambridge University Press, New York.

Cheetham, David. 2006. Early Olmec Figurines from Two Regions: Style as Cultural Imperative. Paper presented at the 1st Annual Braunstein Figurine Symposium, Las Vegas.

Claassen, Cheryl. 2002. Gender and Archaeology. In *Archaeology: Original Readings in Method and Practice,* ed. P. N. Peregrine, C. R. Ember, and M. Ember, 210–24. Prentice Hall, Upper Saddle River, N.J.

Clark, John E., and Mary E. Pye. 2000. The Pacific Coast and the Olmec Question. In *Olmec Art and Archaeology in Mesoamerica,* ed. J. E. Clark and M. E. Pye, 217–51. Studies in the History of Art 58. National Gallery of Art, Washington, D.C.

Coe, Michael D. 1965. The Olmec Style and Its Distribution. In *Handbook of Middle American Indians,* vol. 3, *Archaeology of Southern Mesoamerica,* part 2, ed. R. Wauchope and G. R. Willey, 739–75. University of Texas Press, Austin.

Coe, Michael D., and Richard A. Diehl. 1980. In *Land of the Olmec,* vol. 1, *The Archaeology of San Lorenzo Tenochtitlán.* University of Texas Press, Austin.

Cyphers Guillén, Ann. 1993. Women, Rituals, and Social Dynamics at Ancient Chalcatzingo. *Latin American Antiquity* 4 (3): 209–24.

Fernández Dávila, Enrique, and Susana Gómez Serafín. 1997. Arqueología y arte: Evolución de los Zapotecos de los valles centrales, periodo formativo. In *Historia del arte de Oaxaca,* vol. 1, *Arte prehispánico,* ed. M. Dalton Palomo and V. Loera y Chávez C., 79–105. Instituto Oaxaqueño de las Culturas, Oaxaca, Mexico.

Flannery, Kent V., and Joyce Marcus. 1994. *Early Formative Pottery of the Valley of Oaxaca, Mexico.* Memoir 27. Museum of Anthropology, University of Michigan, Ann Arbor.

Gailey, Christine Ward. 1987. Evolutionary Perspectives on Gender Hierarchy. In *Analyzing Gender: A Handbook of Social Science Research,* ed. B. B. Hess and M. M. Ferree, 32–67. Sage Publications, Beverly Hills, Calif.

García Moll, Roberto, Daniel Juárez Cossío, Carmen Pijoan Aguade, Ma. Elena Salas Cuesta, and Marcela Salas Cuesta. 1991. *Catálogo de entierros de San Luis Tlatilco, México: Temporada IV.* Instituto Nacional de Antropología e Historia, Mexico City.

Gero, Joan, and Margaret Conkey, eds. 1991. *Engendering Archaeology.* Blackwell, Malden, Mass.

Giddens, Anthony. 1984. *The Constitution of Society: Outline of the Theory of Structuration.* University of California Press, Berkeley.

Grove, David C., and Susan D. Gillespie. 1984. Chalcatzingo's Portrait Figurines and the Cult of the Ruler. *Archaeology* 37 (4): 27–33.

Helms, Mary W. 1979. *Ancient Panama: Chiefs in Search of Power.* University of Texas Press, Austin.

Holliman, Sandra 1997. The Third Gender in Native California. In *Women in Prehistory: North America and Mesoamerica,* ed. C. Claassen and R. A. Joyce, 173–88. University of Pennsylvania Press, Philadelphia.

Houston, Stephen D., Karl A. Taube, and David Stuart. 2006. *The Memory of Bones: Body, Being and Experience among the Classic Maya.* University of Texas Press, Austin.

Joyce, Rosemary. 1993. Women's Work: Images of Production and Reproduction in Pre-Hispanic Southern Central America. *Current Anthropology* 34 (3): 255–74.

———. 2003. Making Something of Herself: Embodiment in Life and Death at Playa de los Muertos, Honduras. *Cambridge Archaeological Journal* 13: 248–61.

———. 2006. When the Flesh Is Solid but the Person Is Hollow Inside: Formal Variation in Hand-Modeled Figurines from Formative Mesoamerica. Paper presented at the 71st Annual Meeting of the Society for American Archaeology, San Juan, P.R.

King, Stacie M. 1997. Early and Middle Formative Figurines from the Valley of Oaxaca. Paper presented at the 62nd Annual Meeting of the Society for American Archaeology, Nashville.

King, Stacie M., and Marcus Winter. 1996. Las figurillas antropomórfas pre-Monte Albán del Valle de Oaxaca. Paper presented at the Segunda Conferencia Biannual de Estudios Oaxacaqueños, Welte Institute, Oaxaca, Mexico.

Knapp, A. Bernard. 1998. Boys Will Be Boys: Masculinist Approaches to a Gendered Archaeology. In *Reader in Archaeological Theory: Post-Processual and Cognitive Approaches,* ed. D. S. Whitley, 241–49. Routledge, New York.

Lesure, Richard G. 1997. Figurines and Social Identities in Early Sedentary Societies of Coastal Chiapas, Mexico. In *Women in Prehistory: North America and Mesoamerica,* ed. C. Claassen and R. A. Joyce 227–48. University of Pennsylvania Press, Philadelphia.

López Austin, Alfredo. 1988. *The Human Body and Ideology: Concepts of the Ancient Nahuas.* 2 vols. University of Utah Press, Salt Lake City.

Marcus, Joyce. 1998. *Women's Ritual in Formative Oaxaca: Figurine-Making, Divination, Death and the Ancestors.* Memoir 33. Museum of Anthropology, University of Michigan, Ann Arbor.

Marcus, Joyce, and Kent V. Flannery. 1996. *Zapotec Civilization: How Urban Society Evolved in Mexico's Oaxaca Valley.* Thames and Hudson, New York.

McCafferty, Sharisse D., and Geoffrey G. McCafferty. 1994. Engendering Tomb 7 at Monte Albán: Respinning an Old Yarn. *Current Anthropology* 35 (2): 143–66.

Monaghan, John. 2001. Physiology, Production, and Gendered Differences: The Evidence from Mixtec and Other Mesoamerican Societies. In *Gender in Pre-hispanic America,* ed. C. F. Klein, 285–304. Dumbarton Oaks, Washington, D.C.

Pasztory, Esther. 1989. Identity and Difference: The Uses and Meanings of Ethnic Styles. In *Cultural Differentiation and Cultural Identity in the Visual Arts,* ed. S. J. Barnes and W. S. Melion, 15–38. Studies in the History of Art 27. National Gallery of Art, Washington, D.C.

Plunket, Patricia. 1990. Patrones de asentamiento en el Valle de Nochixtlán y su aportación a la evolución cultural en la Mixteca Alta. In *Lecturas históricas del estado de*

Oaxaca, vol. 1, *Época prehispánica*, ed. M. C. Winter, 349–78. Instituto Nacional de Antropología e Historia, Mexico City.

Schattschneider, Ellen. 2001. "Buy me a bride": Death and Exchange in Northern Japanese Bride-Doll Marriage. *American Ethnologist* 28 (4): 854–80.

Smith, Mary Elizabeth. 1973. *Picture Writing from Ancient Southern Mexico: Mixtec Place Signs and Maps.* University of Oklahoma Press, Norman.

Stark, Barbara. 2001. Figurines and Other Artifacts. In *Classic Period Mixtequilla, Veracruz, Mexico,* ed. B. Stark, 180–210. IMS Monograph 12. Institute for Mesoamerican Studies, State University of New York, Albany.

Winter, Marcus. 1984. Exchange in Formative Highland Oaxaca. In *Trade and Exchange in Early Mesoamerica,* ed. K. G. Hirth, 179–214. University of New Mexico Press, Albuquerque.

———. 1989. *Oaxaca: The Archaeological Record.* Minutiae Mexicana, Mexico City.

———. 1994. Los altos de Oaxaca y los Olmecas. In *Los Olmecas en Mesoamérica,* ed. J. E. Clark, 129–41. El Equilibrista, Mexico City.

———. 2005. Producción y uso de figurillas tempranas en el Valle de Oaxaca. *Acervos* 29: 37–54.

Wobst, H. Martin. 1978. The Archaeo-ethnology of Hunter-Gatherers or the Tyranny of the Ethnographic Record in Archaeology. *American Antiquity* 42 (2): 303–9.

Zárate Morán, Roberto. 1987. *Excavaciones de un sitio preclásico en San Mateo Etlatongo, Nochixtlán, Oaxaca, México.* BAR International Series 322. British Archaeological Reports, Oxford.

6

Early Olmec Figurines from Two Regions

Style as Cultural Imperative

DAVID CHEETHAM

Olmec style—among Mesoamerican archaeologists the mere mention of this phrase can incite heated debate and intense posturing. At stake is its meaning in terms of early Mesoamerican peoples and cultures. After all, as the first widespread art style, it is tied to the birth of Mesoamerica itself. Of this there is little disagreement. But is this distinctive style ultimately attributable to a single archaeological culture, the Gulf Olmec (Clark 1990; Coe 1968a; Piña Chan 1989)? When portable Olmec-style objects such as figurines occur beyond the Gulf Coast, can they be linked to the migration of Gulf Olmecs, local emulation, or both scenarios? Or is the Olmec style, as one distinguished group of Mesoamerican scholars asserts, the product of disparate yet politically equivalent cultures—peer polities—that drew upon a preexisting Mesoamerica-wide belief system for inspiration, resulting in similar-looking objects with no single artistic point of origin (Flannery and Marcus 2000; Grove 1989, 1993)? Most important, can these and other notions be rigorously and objectively tested?

Through stylistic comparison, I aim to demonstrate that Olmec-style figurines—one of the two major classes of Olmec-style portable objects, along with pottery—were a creation of Gulf Olmec peoples and that their appearance in regions beyond the Gulf is in one way or another tied to Gulf Olmecs. In the case I present in detail, these ties appear to be directly related to colonization: a rather extreme case, to be sure, but one that necessarily injects people into the equation and permits an assessment of the thematic elements that were meaningful to the originators of these objects and their descendants. This unusual case also provides a yardstick with which to consider the occurrence of Olmec-style figurines in regions of Mesoamerica where outright colonization is not evident.

San Lorenzo and Cantón Corralito

Cantón Corralito is located about 400 kilometers southeast of San Lorenzo, Veracruz, along the Pacific coast of Chiapas (figure 6.1). The excavated collections I use in this study date between approximately 1150 and 1000 BC[1] in radiocarbon years, an era archaeologists call the "San Lorenzo horizon" or "Early horizon." Throughout this discussion, I call it the "Early Olmec horizon." It is the time frame in which the Olmec style appeared in Mesoamerica.

The site of San Lorenzo is famous for colossal sculpture and other monumental works (Coe 1968b, 1981; Coe and Diehl 1980; Cyphers 1994, 1997; Fuente 1994; Velson and Clark 1975). It is also the geographic and cultural nucleus of all scenarios attributing the Olmec style to Gulf Olmec peoples (for example, Blomster et al. 2005). San Lorenzo was a massive settlement between 1150 and 1000 BC and the likely birthplace of state political structure in the Americas (Clark 1997, 2007; Diehl and Coe 1995). Despite claims to the contrary, current evidence indicates that San Lorenzo had no political rivals in Mesoamerica during its heyday.

Cantón Corralito is located in the heart of Mazatan, a small but incredibly fertile zone where some of the earliest chiefdom societies in Mesoamerica emerged (Blake 1991; Clark 1994; Clark and Blake 1994). The site was first explored in 1997 (Pérez Suárez 2002) after local residents discovered Olmec-style objects while digging wells and trash pits. Test pits subsequently yielded a large number of striking Olmec-style pot sherds and artifacts, prompting John Clark to propose that Mazatan was conquered and subsequently reorganized by Gulf Olmec peoples circa 1150 BC, with Cantón Corralito serving as the administrative hub of this acquired territory (Clark 2007; Clark and Pye 2000). Key to Clark's view is the abandonment of Paso de la Amada, the area's largest and most influential center before 1150 BC.

The Cantón Corralito Project was initiated in 2004 under the auspices of the New World Archaeological Foundation. The immediate objective was to determine the extent of the site, now buried under a thick blanket of river sand, and the distribution of Olmec-style objects within it. Over 6,000 Olmec-style figurine and pottery fragments were recovered from pits and trenches across Cantón Corralito. Based on site size (more than twenty-five hectares) and data from excavations, it is conservatively estimated that Cantón Corralito contains 2–4 million more Olmec-style objects. The second objective and ultimate goal of the project was to test the identity

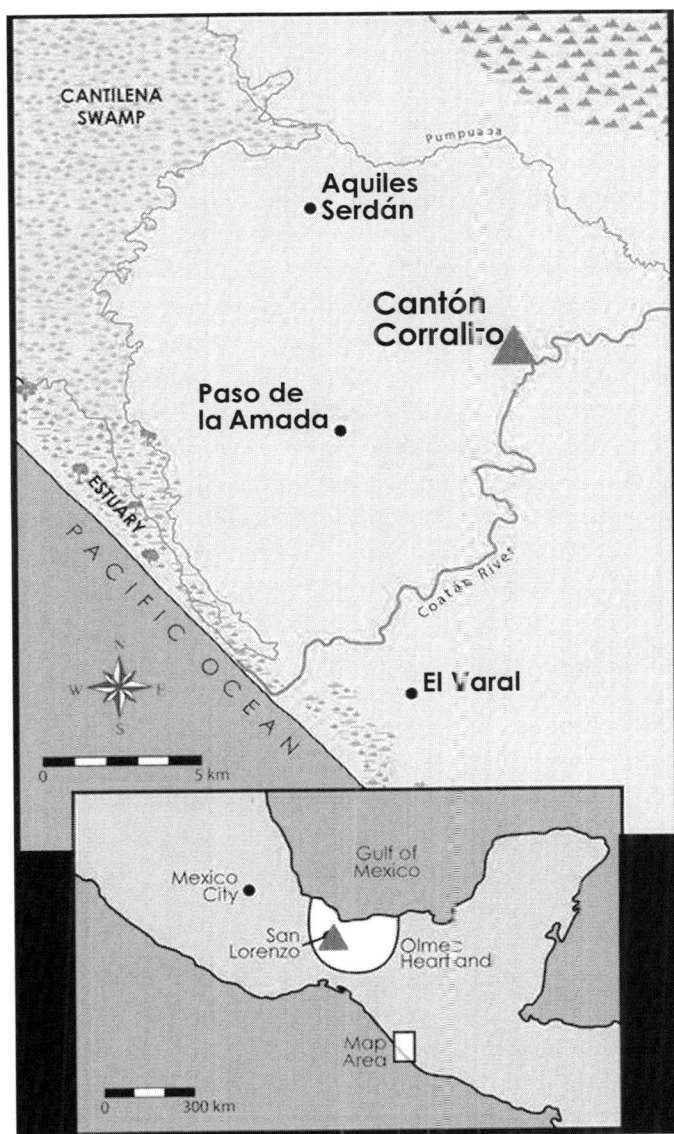

Figure 6.1. Map of Mazatan and the Olmec heartland (inset).

or cultural affiliation of the site's ancient inhabitants by comparing excavated materials with similar objects from San Lorenzo (Cheetham 2006a; Cheetham and Clark 2006).

Figurines represent only one class of Olmec-style object discovered in large quantities at Cantón Corralito. Other kinds of objects are also being compared with materials from San Lorenzo, including decorated ceramic pots (Cheetham 2006b). More important for the present discussion is the fact that all Olmec-style figurine heads from Cantón Corralito and most specimens from San Lorenzo have been chemically tested to determine their origin of manufacture. The results, currently in preparation for publication, indicate that figurines were regularly taken to Cantón Corralito from San Lorenzo, although most were made locally. I mention this in advance to assure you that I do not compare objects made at the same site.

Because much of what we know about Olmec-style figurines comes from unprovenienced objects, some mention of context is necessary. At Cantón Corralito, figurine fragments were found in domestic trash pits, on or below floors, and in architectural fill. This is also the case at San Lorenzo and other sites in the Olmec heartland. No figurines were deposited in special locations or arrangements. Rather, after use and possibly intentional breakage, they seem to have been unceremoniously tossed into garbage heaps along with other domestic trash, including broken pieces of Olmec-style pots. In addition, and unlike sites in the Central Highlands (such as Tlatilco), complete figurines were not found at either site.

Comparative Figurine Data

The figurine collections from San Lorenzo and Cantón Corralito are roughly the same size and consist of similar fragments (table 6.1). Each category listed in table 6.1 includes solid and hollow specimens, although hollow fragments are relatively rare, representing only 13 percent of the collection at San Lorenzo and 8 percent at Cantón Corralito.

Figurine Bodies

Torsos and torso fragments from San Lorenzo and Cantón Corralito (figure 6.2) share numerous traits. There is an authoritative rigidity about the overall composition, as if the persons depicted are in the midst of very im-

Table 6.1. Enumeration of Figurine Fragments, 1150-1000 BC

Body part	San Lorenzo	Cantón Corralito
Head	122	91
Torso	131	153
Arm/hand	55	43
Leg/foot	101	134
Arm or leg	125	412
Unidentified	44	7
Total	578	840

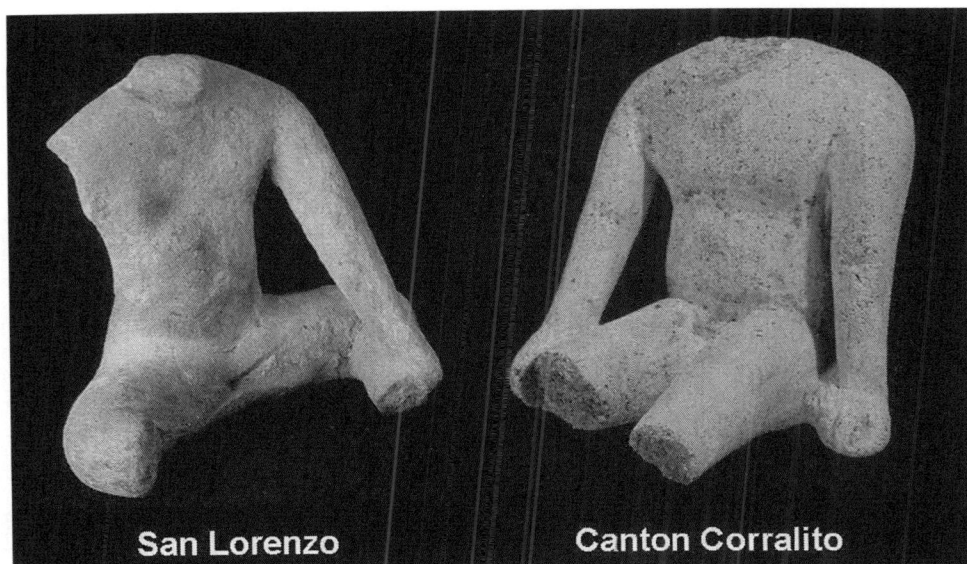

Figure 6.2. Figurine torsos.

portant acts that command the respect and attention of an audience or the viewer. Bodies tend to be naturalistic and well proportioned, with the trunk either vertical or leaning slightly forward, again, as if the individual depicted is absorbed in some pressing affair involving an audience. The composition recalls the pose assumed by figures seated within niches in the stone altars of San Lorenzo and other major Gulf Olmec sites, which also tend to lean forward (see Coe and Diehl 1980: fig. 439).

There is a remarkable consistency in basic body positions (table 6.2), with seated figures dominating the collections from both sites. Closer scrutiny of these specimens reveals numerous shared postures, a few of which are included in figure 6.3. Figures with legs crossed "tailor-style" are common (figure 6.3a), the majority with one or both hands resting on the knee or thigh (figure 6.3b). Other variants of the seated position include figures

Table 6.2. Body Positions, Based on Torsos

Position	San Lorenzo	Cantón Corralito
Seated	85%	90%
Standing	15%	7%
Other	--	3%

Note: San Lorenzo, n=101; Cantón Corralito, n=116.

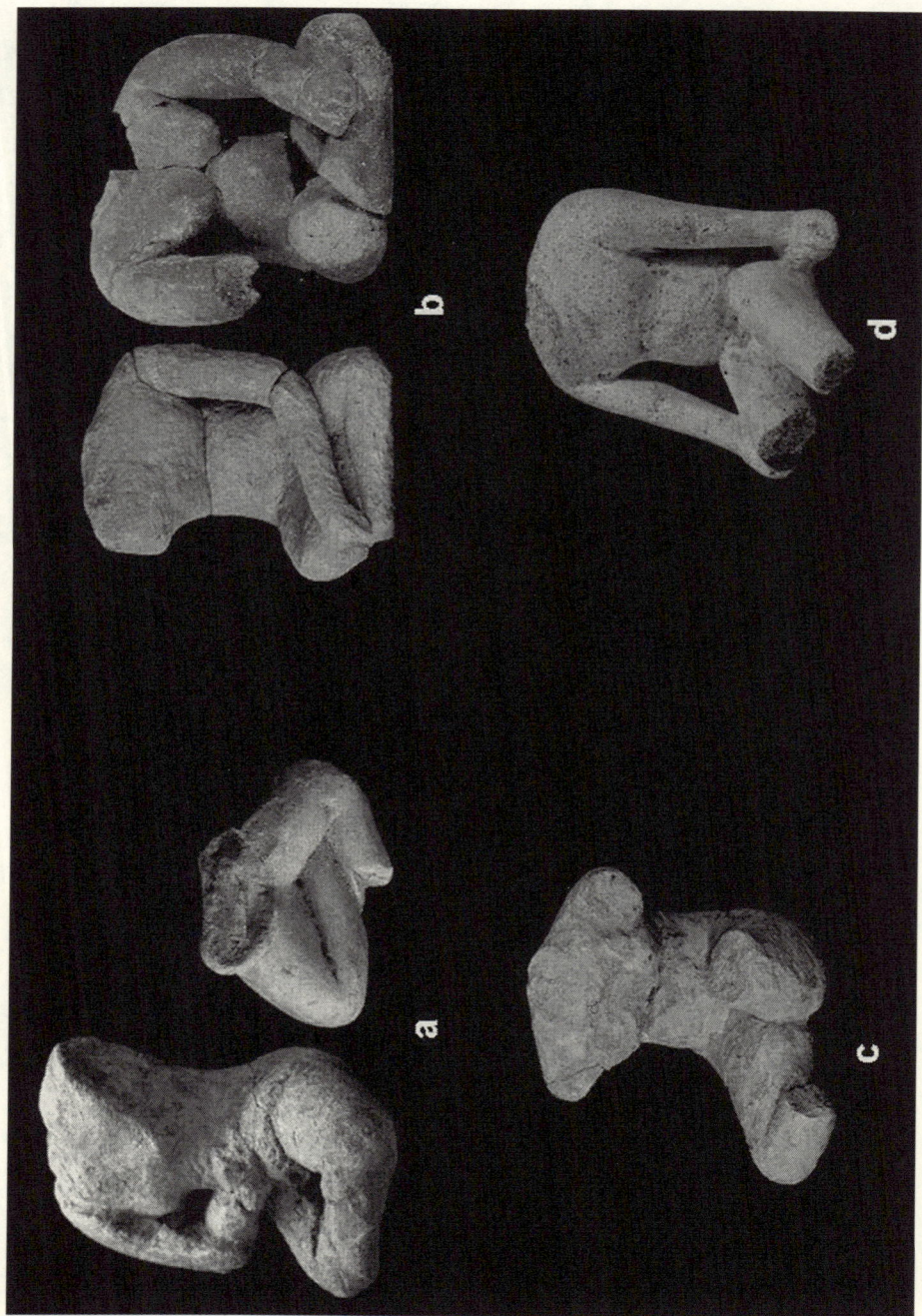

Figure 6.3. Body positions: *a*, legs crossed; *b*, legs crossed, hand(s) on leg; *c*, one leg crossed, one raised/bent; *d*, legs extended.

Table 6.3. Applied Clothing and Jewelry, Excluding Headgear and Ballplayers

Item	San Lorenzo	Cantón Corralito
Medium-length skirt	1.0%	0.1%
Short skirt	0.3%	0.5%
Bikini strap	0.5%	0.2%
Belt (waist)	0.3%	--
Scarf/sash (neck to crotch)	0.2%	--
Necklace	0.2%	--
Medallion/mirror	0.2%	--
Unidentified pectoral object	0.2%	0.1%
Cape	0.2%	--
Spotted (reed-impressed) clothes	--	0.7%
Incised skin (tattoo? scarification?)	--	0.2%

Note: Percentages based on entire collection: San Lorenzo, N=578; Cantón Corralito, N=840.

with one leg crossed wile the other is raised up and bent at the knee (figure 6.3c). Still other figures have legs that extend straight out (figure 6.3d).

Clothing

Aside from ballplayer figurines, which I address below, clothing and ornamentation (table 6.3) are rare in both collections, applied to only 3 percent of the San Lorenzo torsos (compare Follensbee, this volume) and 2 percent of the Cantón Corralito figures. Although a greater variety of clothing elements occurs at San Lorenzo, skirts (the most common kind of clothing) occur at both sites and are remarkably similar (figure 6.4). Two types are evident. Short skirts encircle the waist between the hips and the crotch, and

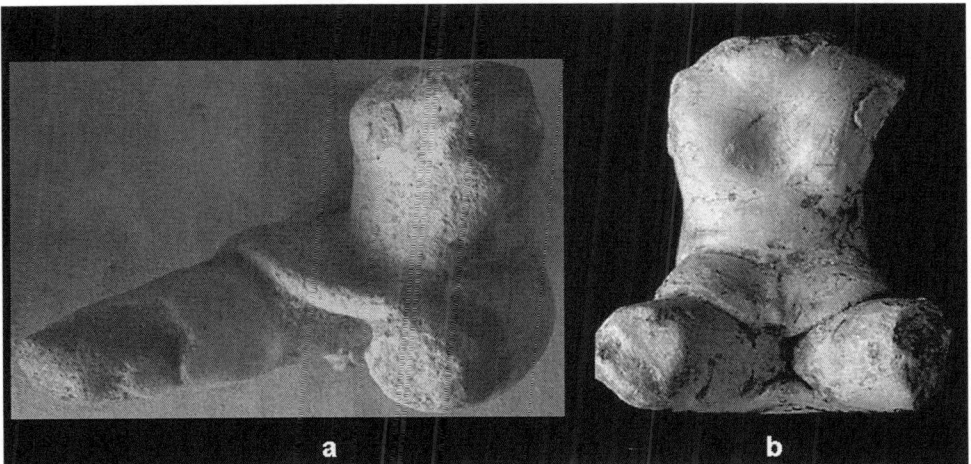

Figure 6.4. Skirts: *a*, medium length; *b*, short (wrap).

medium-length skirts reach to midthigh or the knee. These garments, likely made of cotton, appear to have been worn exclusively by women, although their rarity suggests that only certain women wore them or that they were used only on special occasions. One type of garment that is not shown here—spotted coats and leggings most likely made of jaguar skins—occurs only at Cantón Corralito.

Torso Dimensions

The dimensions of torsos suggest a shared, habitual manner of manufacture among the figurine makers at San Lorenzo and Cantón Corralito. The size of finished products is incredibly similar. In my opinion, this reflects a discrete technical style that could only have resulted from a shared tradition and learning (see Lechtman 1977; Lemonnier 1986, 1992; Stark 1998). The most informative measurements are width of the waist and height from the buttocks of seated figures to the shoulder (figure 6.5). The tabulated results (tables 6.4–6.5) are startling. For example, the average height of seated specimens differs by only one millimeter, as does the standard deviation (table 6.4). The complete range of height is nearly identical as well. Torso width is similarly uniform, with a difference of only one millimeter in the

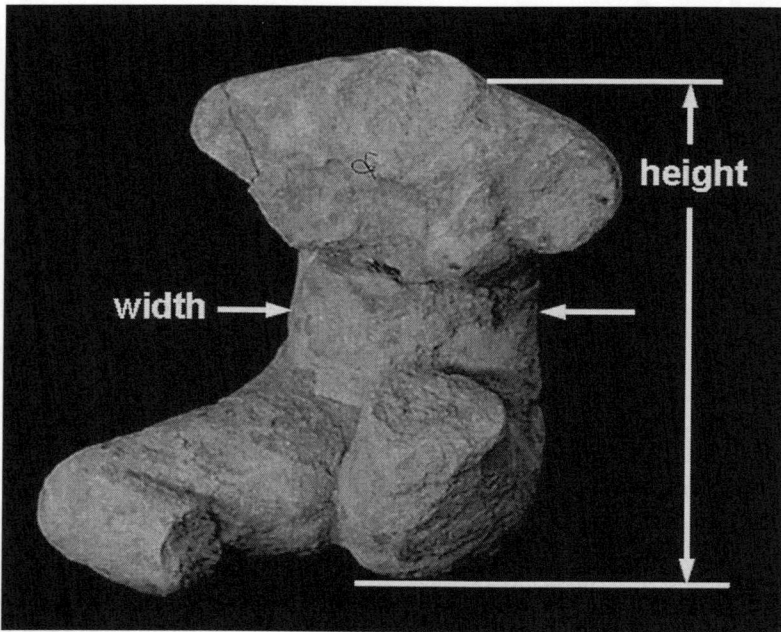

Figure 6.5. Technical style indices for torsos.

Table 6.4. Torso Height, Excluding Ballplayers

Position	Site	Mean (mm)	SD (mm)	Range (mm)
Seated	San Lorenzo	58	18	33-100
	Cantón Corralito	57	19	30-91
Standing	San Lorenzo	59	--	
	Cantón Corralito	37	--	-

Table 6.5. Torso Width, Excluding Ballplayers

Position	Site	Mean (mm)	SD (mm)	Range (mm)
Seated	San Lorenzo	31	8	18-55
	Cantón Corralito	32	9	20-54
Standing	San Lorenzo	28	--	--
	Cantón Corralito	24	9	15-36
Indeterminate	San Lorenzo	29	8	16-60
	Cantón Corralito	33	12	17-64

average and standard deviation of seated specimens (table 6.5). The width of the indeterminate class (table 6.5) includes torsos with the bottom part broken away. Most of these specimens probably come from seated figures. In any case, the dimensions of these objects are quite similar at both sites.

Gender

One area in which torsos differ between collections is the percentage of male and female specimens (figure 6.6). Admittedly, designating torsos as male or female is a difficult and somewhat subjective task in any figurine collection. In my analysis, I interpret the presence of breasts to indicate female figures, while defined pectoral muscles or a flat chest implies a male. Male figures occur almost twice as frequently at San Lorenzo than at Cantón Corralito, where female figures are more prevalent than males (figure 6.6). Androgynous features are visible on 6 percent of the specimens from San Lorenzo and 13 percent at Cantón Corralito, with a much smaller percentage of specimens defined as infantile or baby in appearance.

The high percentage of male figurines at San Lorenzo completely contradicts Billie Follensbee's (2006; see also chapter 4, this volume) conclusion that the majority of Formative period Gulf Olmec figurines are female. I suspect that this finding is determined in part by her temporal and spatial scope and her classification of what I consider to represent pectoral muscles (or incisions defining pectoral muscles) as female breasts. Also noteworthy is that the comparatively high percentage of female figurines at Cantón

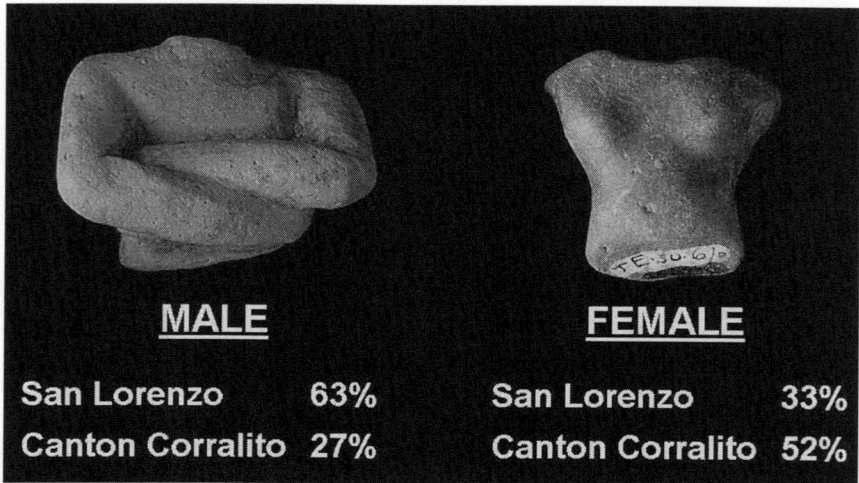

Figure 6.6. Percentages of male and female figurines at San Lorenzo and Cantón Corralito as indicated by torsos.

Corralito contradicts Clark's (1993) observation that seated male figurines completely replaced an earlier tradition of standing females in Mazatan beginning around 1200 BC.

Ballplayer torsos, all of which appear to be male, are unique given their protective waist, groin, neck, arm, and leg padding as well as other decorative elements such as large mirror pectorals (figure 6.7). Although relatively few ballplayer torsos were found at Cantón Corralito, the ones found are very similar to specimens from San Lorenzo. Most figures are depicted in action: stretching, crouching, or otherwise performing athletic maneuvers. Another shared trait is the rear support prong, shown on the lower left specimen in figure 6.7. A few ballplayers at both sites appear to carry animal carcasses on their backs.

Figurine Heads

The best measure of Olmec-style figurines is the portrayal of heads and head fragments. The proportion of Olmec-style heads at San Lorenzo and Cantón Corralito is almost identical (figure 6.8). As described by Michael Coe and Richard Diehl (1980: 264) using heads from San Lorenzo, Olmec-style figurines are bald or partly bald, with slit eyes, arched "Oriental" eyebrows, thick frowning lips (the upper one generally more pronounced), and triangular flat noses. In classifying the specimens at both sites, I employed this strict definition and excluded all specimens that were not 100 percent

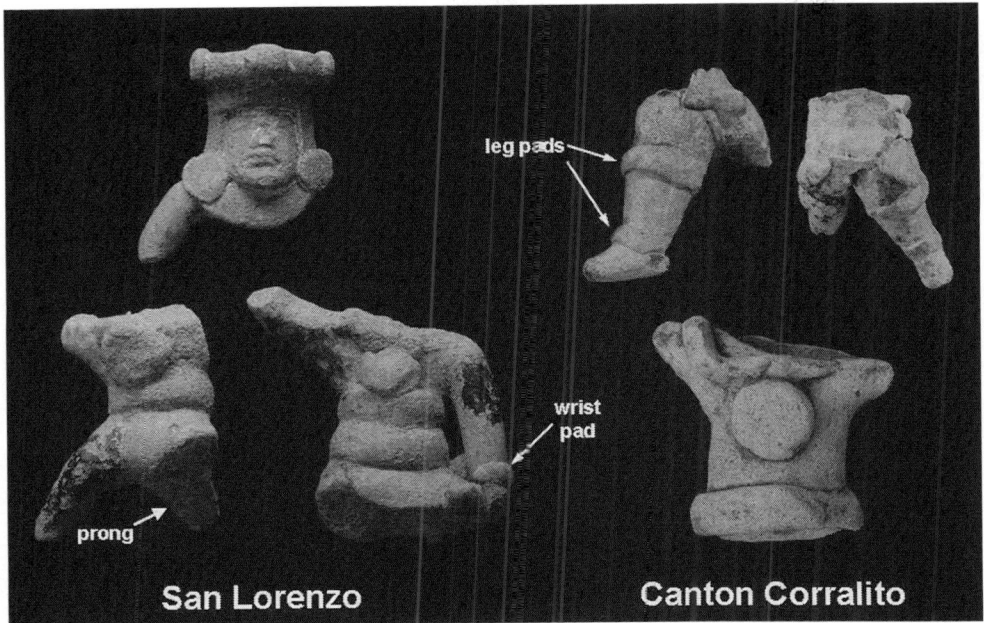

Figure 6.7. Ballplayer figurine fragments showing appliqué equipment and other paraphernalia.

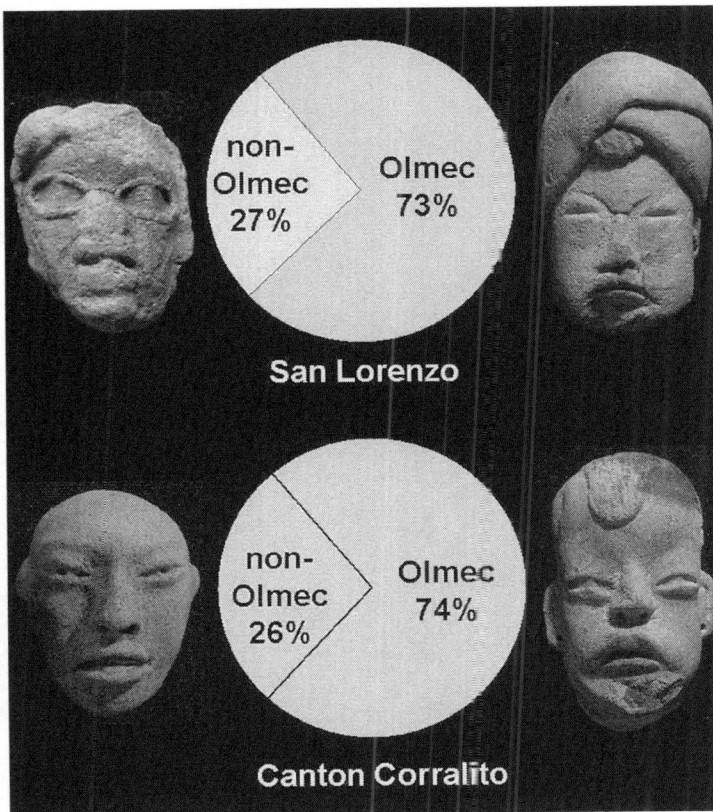

Figure 6.8. Early Olmec (1150–1000 BC) figurine styles and corresponding frequencies.

Olmec. In addition to the aforementioned traits, there are several other defining characteristics of Olmec-style figurine heads fashioned at San Lorenzo and Cantón Corralito.

Cranial Deformation

About three-quarters of Olmec-style heads at both sites depict cranial deformation from eye level up (figure 6.9). Two other shared traits are evident in figure 6.9. Necks are angled forward or craned. If this interpretation of orientation is incorrect and the necks were positioned vertically, then the figures would have looked upward. Whichever is the case, they are exactly alike at both sites. Also noteworthy is the addition of clay at the nape of the neck on many specimens, creating an elongated bulge.

I have diagrammed these traits on a head from Cantón Corralito (figure 6.10). The neck orientation forms a roughly 45-degree angle with the vertical axis of the head, and the skull is deformed at or just above eye level, forming an elongated, bulbous crown. This kind of head deformation

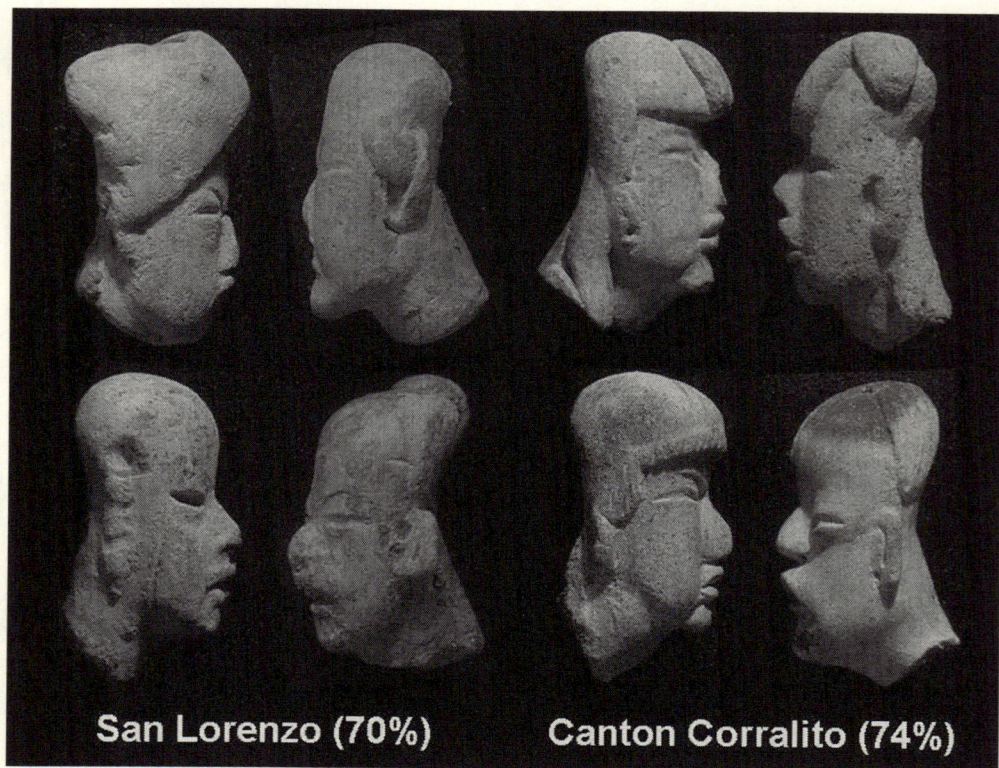

Figure 6.9. Cranial deformation and corresponding frequencies.

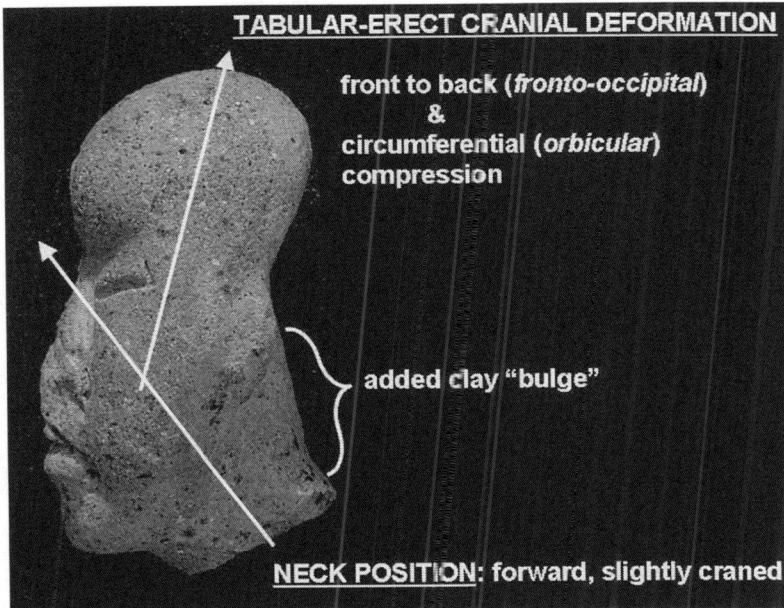

Figure 6.10. Anatomy of a typical Early Olmec–style figurine head.

involves compression from front to back and from side to side, the latter achieved by the application of tight bands encircling the skull. The accuracy of such depictions suggests that these are portraits of actual people who underwent the process of cranial deformation during infancy. The frequency of this trait suggests that the practice was common, at least among the folks who were portrayed in clay figures

Eyes

Distinctive eye styles occur in both collections (figure 6.11). Among the most common are slit and puffy eyes, both of which are usually framed by arched eyebrows or brow ridges that extend from the bridge of the nose. Slit eyes are depicted in two manners: narrow single slits executed with a single slash of the instrument; and double slits, which are more deeply impressed into the clay and are formed by two opposing slits moving out from the center, or would-be iris, to the interior and exterior edges. In both cases, a single line was created, having either a horizontal or a slightly arched aspect.

Puffy eyes, shown at the bottom of figure 6.11, consist of slit eyes embedded in a raised circular area, the lower portion of which creates pronounced bags. This trait also occurs on colossal stone sculptures at San Lorenzo. The

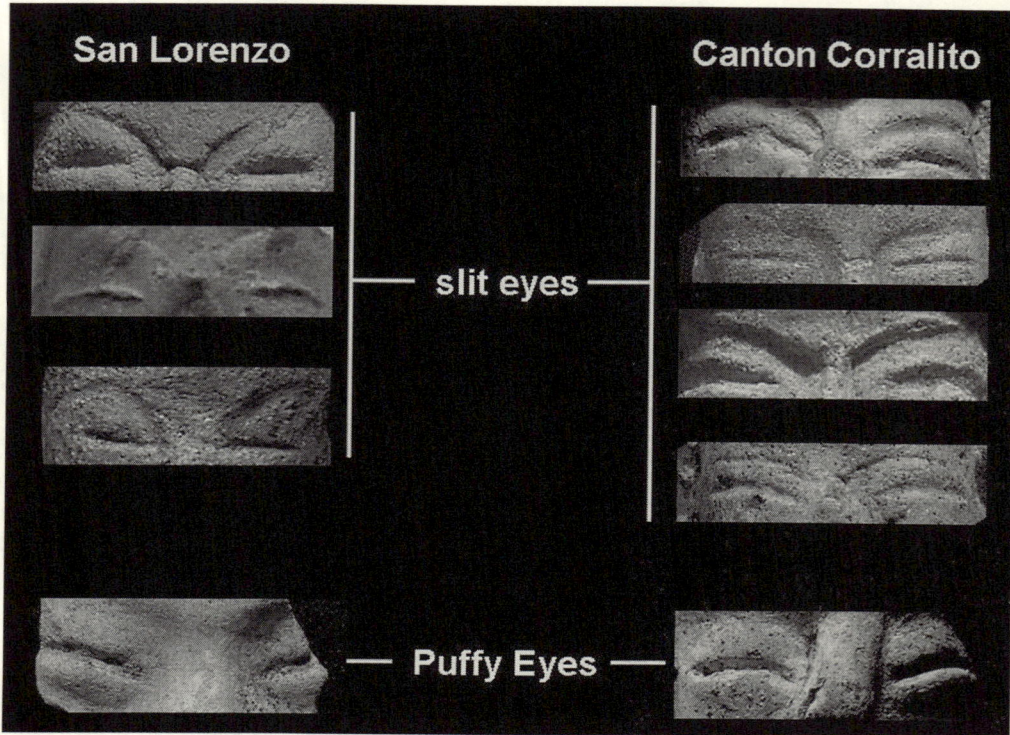

Figure 6.11. Dominant eye modes of Early Olmec–style figurines.

most notable example is Monument 6 (figure 6.12), probably the largest sculpture at the site, which depicts a head broken from a complete seated figure. Coe and Diehl (1980: 310) believe this was a portrait of a bald Olmec ruler wearing a square headband. The morphology closely resembles Olmec-style figurine heads from San Lorenzo and Cantón Corralito.

The most striking manner of figurine eye treatment at both sites is one in which they are not shown at all (figure 6.13). These figures may be portraits of sleeping or dead individuals. Regardless of meaning, the similarities are striking, particularly the head from San Lorenzo and the Cantón Corralito specimen on the far right of the bottom row.

Hair and Ornamentation

Approximately 30 percent of Olmec-style specimens at both sites are bald (figure 6.14). These presumably represent individuals who completely shaved their heads, perhaps with obsidian blades. As with most Olmec-style heads, the majority seem to portray adults, probably of both sexes.

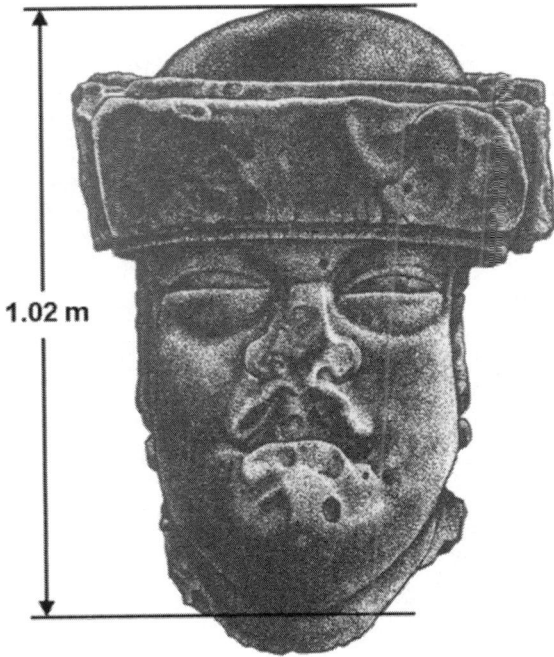

Figure 6.12. A colossal figure: San Lorenzo Monument 6. Estimated height of complete monument is 2.3 meters (after Coe and Diehl 1980: fig. 429).

San Lorenzo

Canton Corralito

Figure 6.13. Eyeless Early Olmec–style figures. These heads may represent sleeping or deceased individuals.

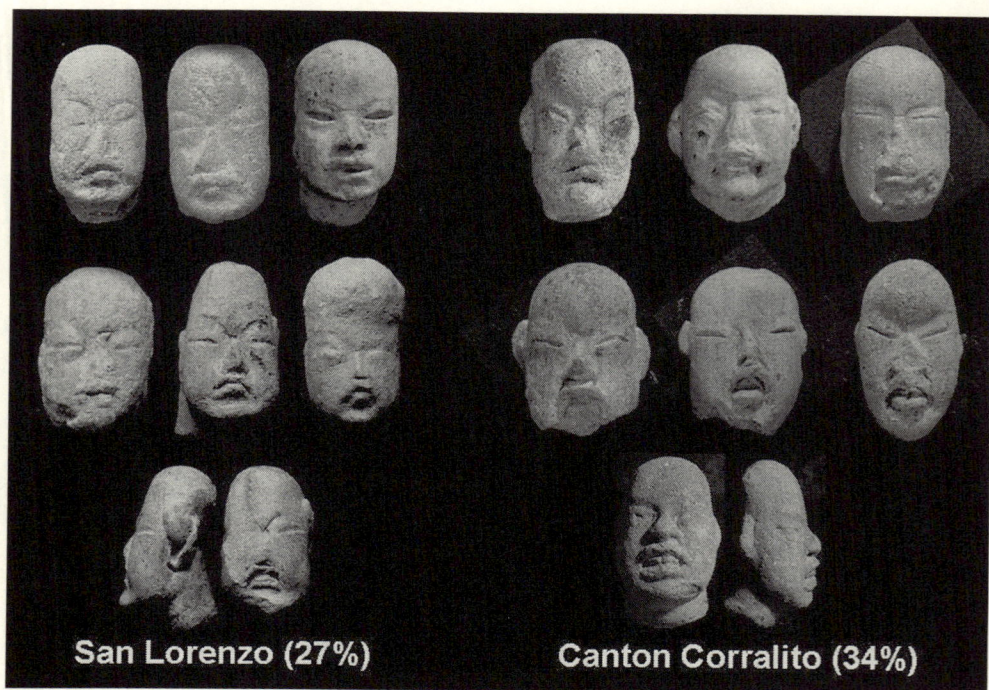

Figure 6.14. Bald Early Olmec–style figures and corresponding frequencies.

There are, however, a few specimens that may represent infants. For example, note the head in the second row of figure 6.14, second from the right. This Cantón Corralito specimen has widely spaced puffy eyes and a round fleshy face, characteristics that may qualify it as a baby portrait.

Several specimens are depicted with headgear (figure 6.15). One example from Cantón Corralito, at the top of figure 6.15, wears a cap or helmet with a frontal projecting circular ornament. The similarity between this specimen and a weathered head from San Lorenzo, to its immediate left, is so pronounced that they seem to portray the same person. In these examples, a cape or possibly hair extends from the cap and drapes down the back. Sometimes the cap or helmet lacks the frontal adorno, as shown in the center specimens of figure 6.15. The cap is formed in the same way at both sites. It projects from the forehead, and a small tab extension covers the temple, much like the helmets of American football players. Turbans, shown at the bottom of figure 6.15, are frontally crossed, representing one flat, thick piece of cloth that was wrapped around the bald head and fastened at the back.

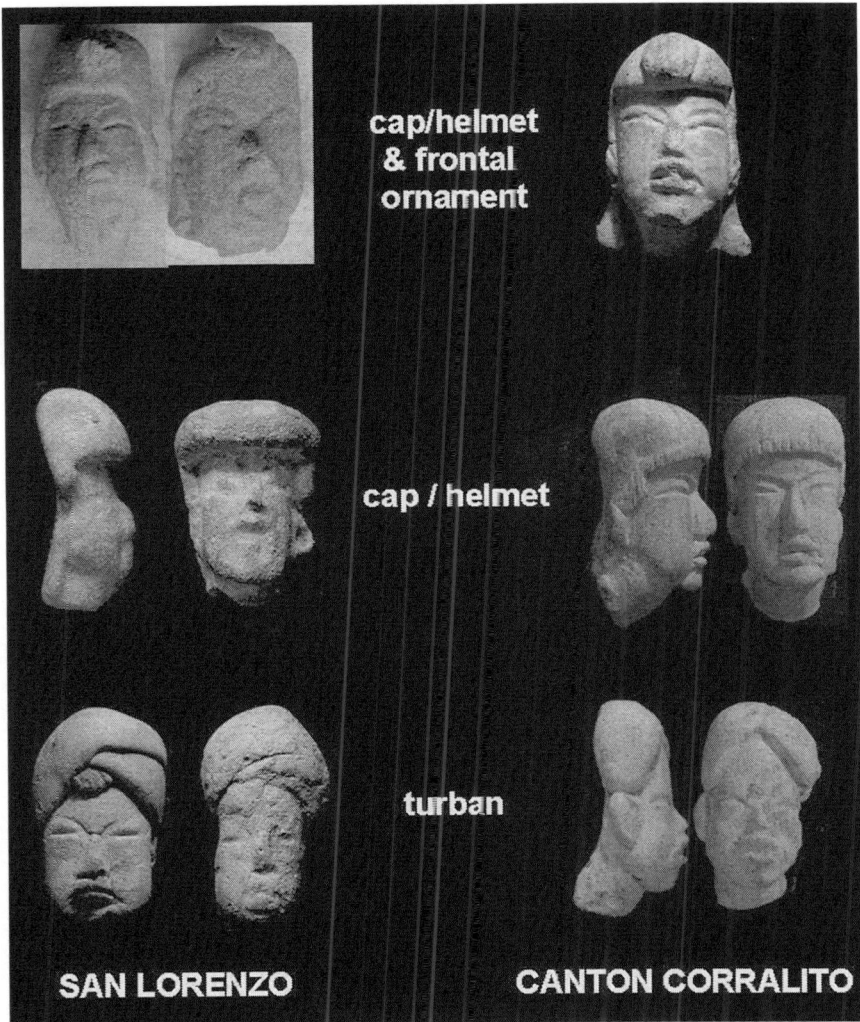

Figure 6.15. Headgear similarities, Early Olmec style.

Other specimens represent individuals with heads that are only partially shaved or not shaved at all (figure 6.16). Several of these (at the top of figure 6.16) have what appears to be an elongated lock of hair over the forehead, which alternatively may reference some kind of protective headgear. Other figures have part of the upper forehead shaved, accentuating and forming a center part. Still others have a well-defined center part and incised hair that is neatly tied in the back, forming a small projecting bun. Other portraits

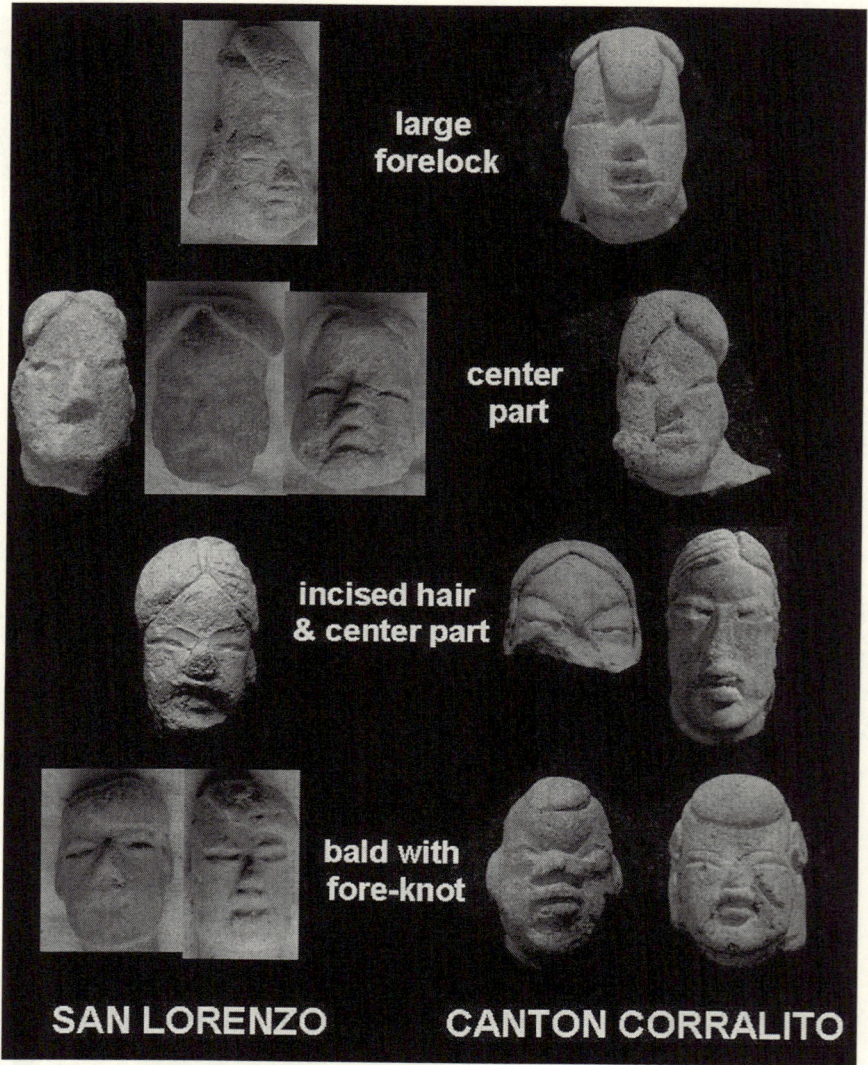

Figure 6.16. Hairdo similarities, Early Olmec style.

(figure 6.16, bottom row) have a circular frontal patch of hair, while the rest of the head is shaved.

Head Dimensions

All of the figurine heads were measured to facilitate a determination of the extent of correspondence between collections. Like the torsos, the heads disclose a shared, habitual manner of manufacture. The sizes of finished

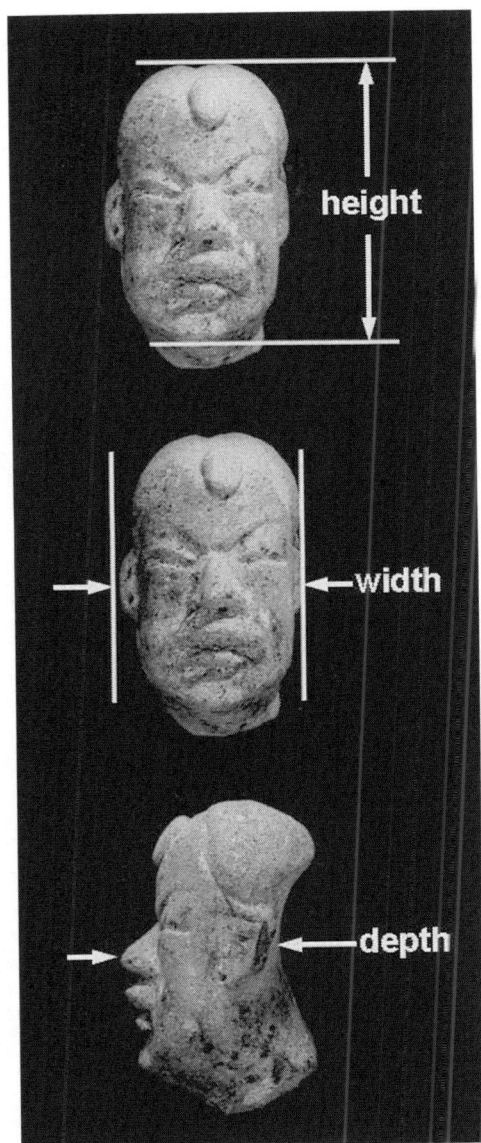

Figure 6.17. Technical style indices, Early Olmec–style heads.

products are very similar and are attributable to a shared technical style. As shown on a head from Cantón Corralito (figure 6.17), the three key measurements are height, width, and depth. The tabulated results of the Olmec-style head measurements reveal a difference of five to eight millimeters for average height, width, and depth (table 6.6). At least half of this difference is due to the eroded condition (outer surface) of the heads from San Lorenzo.

Table 6.6. Descriptive Statistics of Early Olmec–Style Heads

Dimension	Site	Mean (mm)	SD (mm)	Range (mm)
Height	San Lorenzo	41	9	27–66
	Cantón Corralito	49	14	22–73
Width	San Lorenzo	25	6	14–43
	Cantón Corralito	33	10	15–61
Depth	San Lorenzo	20	5	13–39
	Cantón Corralito	25	8	12–48

Table 6.7. Dimension Ratios of Early Olmec–Style Heads

Ratio	Site	Mean (mm)	SD (mm)	Range (mm)
Height/width	San Lorenzo	1.7	0.2	1.2–2.6
	Cantón Corralito	1.5	0.2	0.6–2.0
Height/depth	San Lorenzo	2.1	0.3	1.6–2.9
	Cantón Corralito	1.9	0.2	1.0–2.5
Width/depth	San Lorenzo	1.2	0.2	0.9–1.7
	Cantón Corralito	1.3	0.1	0.9–1.8

Thus, on average, the Cantón Corralito heads appear to be a few millimeters larger than their counterparts at San Lorenzo. In terms of technical style, this difference is insignificant.

Because of the eroded condition of the San Lorenzo specimens, ratios were also calculated (table 6.7). Ratios of height to width, height to depth, and width to depth are nearly identical for Olmec-style heads at both sites, again indicating a single technical style.

Hollow Figures

Although rare in comparison with the solid specimens, hollow Olmec-style figurines occur at both sites (figure 6.18). Most are at least twice as large as their solid counterparts and seem to represent adults. A few, such as the San Lorenzo specimens shown at the bottom left of figure 18, have small mouths and pudgy cheeks that may qualify them as babies. The rarity of baby figurines at these sites is no surprise. As Jeffrey Blomster (2002) has noted, most hollow figurines classified as babies are really adults. Babies are rare wherever Olmec figurines are found, including the Central Highlands of Mexico, which, contrary to many claims (for example, Flannery and Marcus 1994), did not have a monopoly on this kind of portraiture.

The naturalistic quality of some hollow specimens is remarkable (see top row of figure 6.18), as is the identical manner in which hollow limbs were fashioned at both sites. Detailed fingers and toes are standard, and some

San Lorenzo   **Canton Corralito**

Figure 6.18. Hollow Early Olmec–style figurine head fragments.

hands were modeled so that they could hold a bar or a similar cylindrical object.

Eccentric Figures and Features

Dwarfs represent one of the more unusual types of Olmec-style portraiture at both sites (figure 6.19). Although eroded, Olmec-style facial features are discernable on these specimens, which are nearly identical. At both San Lorenzo and Cantón Corralito, dwarfs have stooped, deformed backs, lack necks, and are fat and bald. They are also the same size.

Star or diamond symbols were carved into the back of Olmec-style heads at both sites (figure 6.20) (see also fig. 5.11, this volume). On one head from Cantón Corralito, additional symbols continue over the top of the head and onto the forehead in a sequence highly suggestive of writing (Lee and Cheetham forthcoming). If so, this would be the earliest example of script in the Americas, predating the recently discovered Cascajal block (Rodríguez Martínez et al. 2006) by a century or more.

Figure 6.19. Dwarfs.

Figure 6.20. Rear view of Early Olmec–style heads with carved symbols.

Figure 6.21. "One-Eyed God" figurine heads. Note conical projection from top, incised eyelashes, and other shared grotesque features.

One of the more bizarre correspondences is the so-called One-Eyed God (figure 6.21). These grotesque froglike portraits have one empty eye socket, while the other eye is covered by a thick eyelid with vertically incised eyelashes. The mouth is open and disproportionately large. The nose is triangular, and a conical projection rises up from the top of the head. Coe and Diehl (1980: 270) suggest that these were attached to the bodies of ballplayer figurines.

Although not expressly figurines, masquettes that are too small to cover a human face were made at both sites (figure 6.22). Aged individuals—probably old women, or "hags," to use Peter Joralemon's (1981) term—represent one shared theme. Rather than representing a mask, one example from San Lorenzo (figure 6.22, lower left) may have been part of a hollow figurine. These effigies have wrinkled cheeks, a swollen lower lip, and sunken eyes framed by a raised appliqué strip of clay. Several unprovenienced examples of old hag figurines and aged person masquettes are reported for Veracruz (Joralemon 1981: fig. 8) and the Central Highlands of Mexico (Coe 1965: figs. 161, 163, 200; Joralemon 1981: fig. 2). Another masquette theme at Cantón Corralito consists of morbid but remarkably realistic skulls with

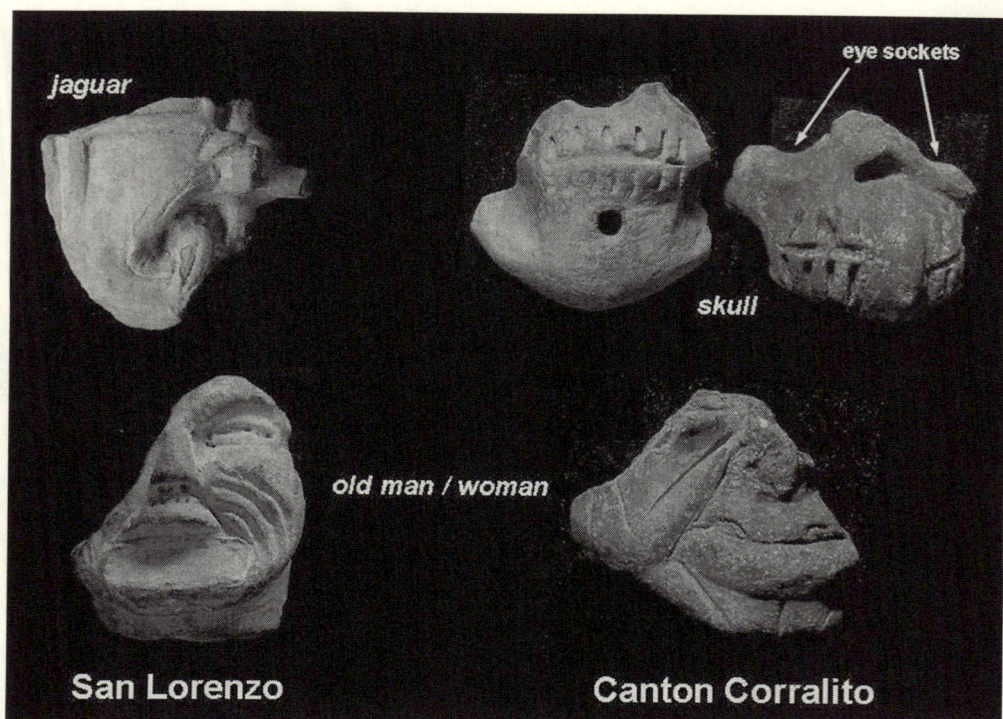

Figure 6.22. Small masquettes.

incised teeth. On one example (figure 6.22, upper right), a ring clamps the mandible shut. No counterparts occur at San Lorenzo, but a few similar fragments are known from the highlands of Mexico (*Arqueología Mexicana* 2005: 78; Viesca 2005: 40).

Style, Meaning, and Thematic Content

The subtitle of this chapter, "Style as Cultural Imperative," was chosen to stress the following premise: Olmec-style figurines made at Cantón Corralito were fashioned by the hands of Gulf Olmec people and their descendants. It is also probable that some Gulf Olmec immigrants intermarried with local peoples in the Mazatan region, who then became "Olmecized" as a result. The persistence of exact replication suggests that these figurines are not merely "good copies" made by indigenous folks who embraced the style as a result of chance or even planned encounters with Gulf Olmecs. Neither is it possible that they are similar by virtue of a pan-Mesoamerican belief system predating the Early Olmec horizon. Large-scale migration of

Olmec peoples from the Gulf Coast is the only rational explanation for this phenomenon. If we consider the wide distribution of figurines and other Olmec-style objects at Cantón Corralito (Cheetham 2006a), then the site is best classified as a settlement enclave.

While the precise meaning of Early Olmec horizon figurines may never be known, the fact that these objects at San Lorenzo and Cantón Corralito mirror each other on so many levels suggests that, in this instance, the style was indeed a cultural imperative. Despite the great distance between these two sites and 150 years or more of continuous production, the Cantón Corralito figurine makers remained faithful to the stylistic canons of San Lorenzo. This implies a rigid set of figurine meanings and practices integral to Gulf Olmec identity. It may further imply that these objects were somehow involved with the enculturation of the young members of society. Although we are left with only tangible remains, thematic content provides insight into what was meaningful to the people who made these objects and, perhaps, what some of these meanings and practices were.

The recurrent and detailed features of the effigies suggest that they represent real people. The majority seem to assert authority through their very posture and gaze, compelling the onlooker to accept something. There is a determined, fierce quality that is somehow instructional in nature and was probably accompanied by oration. As mentioned earlier, the composition recalls the figures seated within the niche of massive stone "altars"—actually thrones—at the great Gulf Olmec centers, including San Lorenzo. If apt, this analogy hints that some of the figurines made by Gulf Olmecs were closely associated with, or even represented, portraits of elite individuals who held political or religious office.

What of the fact that the percentages of male and female effigies are inversely related, with males dominant at San Lorenzo and females at Cantón Corralito? As the only conspicuous thematic divergence in the collections, this is indeed puzzling. I suspect that the circumstances of colonization were somehow involved. The peoples of Mazatan had long enjoyed a tradition of female figurine production (Clark 1993, 1994; Lesure 1997). Very likely, this tradition was retained and subtly blended with the Olmec style. This would imply that rather than representing an insulated trading enclave of Gulf Olmec peoples, Cantón Corralito was a place where social intercourse and intermarriage with locals was common.

One additional point regarding female figurines is noteworthy. In both collections, there is a uniform depiction of the stomach. Only a few of the figurines have swollen bellies that may represent the late stage of pregnancy.

The majority are flat or nearly flat, suggesting that a fertility fetish interpretation is unsuitable, at least for all the specimens.

Ballplayer figurines represent one unmistakable theme. These effigies may have been used to recall great sporting events or conversely may have served some function in preparation for such events. Whatever the case, ballplayer figurines are more common at San Lorenzo than at Cantón Corralito. This echoes a parallel trend at several San Lorenzo satellite sites, including those explored by archaeologists Ponciano Ortíz and Carmen Rodríguez (personal observations 2005). The uniformity of this disparity suggests that epicentral San Lorenzo was especially involved with the ballgame. The costumes of the ballplayer figurines at San Lorenzo were very elaborate, involving animal masks, towering headdresses, and other nonprotective paraphernalia, including what may be identified as animal carcasses draped over the back of players. One very specific entity that may be associated with the ballgame is the One-Eyed God. On the whole, the costume and associated regalia suggest that each ballgame involved the recreation of an animistic origin myth.

Concluding Observations

While the preceding discussion may come as no surprise to those who are familiar with Olmec-style figurines, the extent of thematic uniformity between San Lorenzo and Cantón Corralito should. If I am correct in stating that Olmec-style objects were made by Gulf Olmecs at Cantón Corralito—or a mix of Gulf Olmecs and local people who adopted a Gulf Olmec identity—this can help us to model early Gulf Olmec interaction with other regions of Mesoamerica.

A detailed discussion of this observation is beyond the scope of the present text, but at sites in the Central Highlands of Mexico where Olmec-style figurines are present, they occur alongside a local figurine style, which is more frequently represented. Moreover, some of the "Olmec" pieces from this area are not quite true to the style elaborated within the Olmec heartland. To the best of my knowledge, there is no Central Mexican equivalent of Cantón Corralito, although the site of Las Bocas in Puebla is one candidate sorely in need of investigation. There is no doubt that contact between Gulf Olmecs and highland groups took place, but the nature of this interaction seems to have been very different from that which characterizes Mazatan (see Blomster, this volume). Contact with some Central Mexican highland groups was certainly less pervasive and seems to have been lacking prior

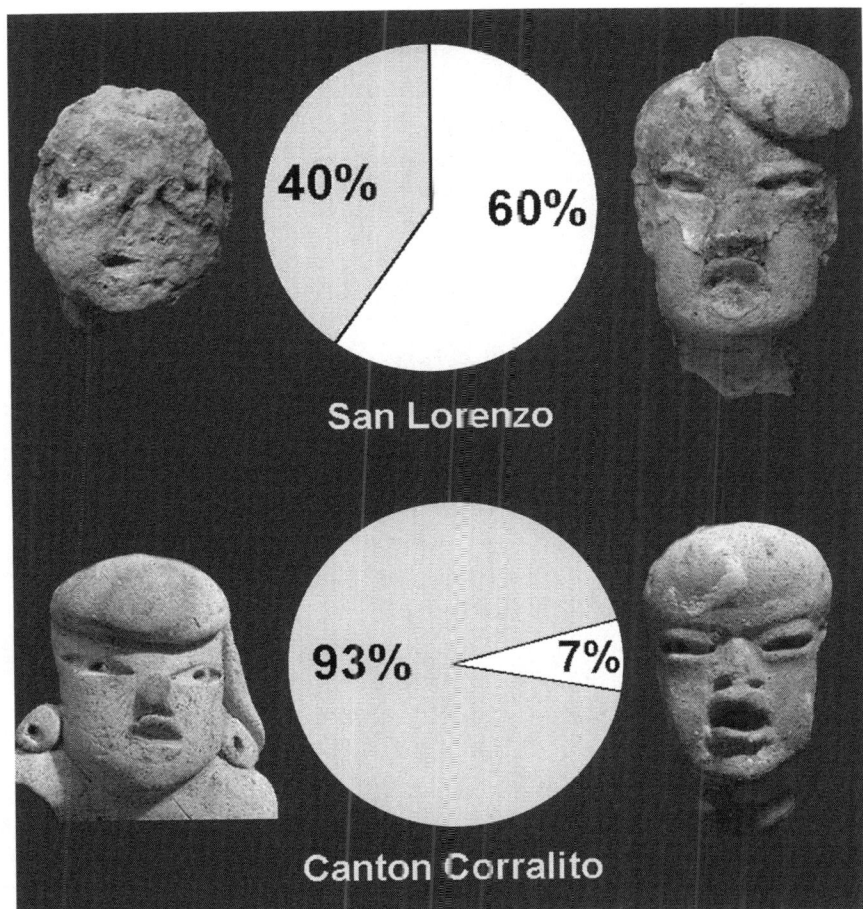

Figure 6.23. Initial Olmec–era (1250–1150 BC) figurine styles and corresponding frequencies.

to 1150 BC, a time during which it is evident between the Gulf Coast and Mazatan regions (figure 6.23).

During the century spanning 1250 and 1150 BC, ceramics and other objects began to be imported from San Lorenzo to several Mazatan centers, including Cantón Corralito. At least one figurine style was shared, as indicated by the Olmec-looking effigies depicted on the right side of figure 6.23. Although these "Initial Olmec"-era figures at Cantón Corralito were made locally, several very high-quality, fine-paste (kaolin and orange) imports occur at the nearby sites of Paso de la Amada and Aquiles Serdán. Neither site has locally made versions, suggesting that these objects were gifts received directly from San Lorenzo or though an intermediary—perhaps even Cantón Corralito. Whatever the case, there clearly is a deep history of Gulf Olmec contact with the peoples of Mazatan that does not, on the basis of current evidence, appear to have been shared with the Central Mexican Highlands or any other region of Mesoamerica.

Acknowledgments

Funding for this study and related Cantón Corralito Project research was obtained through generous grants from the New World Archaeological Foundation, the Reinhart Foundation, the Foundation for the Advancement of Mesoamerican Studies, the National Science Foundation, the School of Human Evolution and Social Change at Arizona State University, the Graduate and Professional Student Association of Arizona State University, and the University of Missouri Research Reactor Center (MURR). I thank Manetta Braunstein and Aurore Giguet for involving me in the 2006 figurine conference at the University of Nevada–Las Vegas. The keen editorial eye of Katherine Ann Faust (of the University of California–Riverside) greatly improved this paper. The cooperation of two institutions was fundamental to this study: Mexico's Instituto Nacional de Antropología e Historia (Joaquín García Bárcena and Roberto García Moll, directors) and the anthropology collections division (Roger Colten and Maureen DaRos) at the Peabody Museum of Natural History, Yale University. John Hodgson accompanied me to Yale on two occasions and was helpful and fun in and out of the lab. Special thanks are due to Michael Coe, who enabled this and other aspects of my work to move forward and provided great conversation and advice while I was at Yale, and to John Clark, who has assisted immeasurably with all things Cantón Corralito–related.

Notes

1. All dates in this paper are reported in uncalibrated radiocarbon years bc.

References Cited

Arqueología Mexicana. 2005. El esplendor del barro: Ayer y hoy. Special issue.

Blake, Michael. 1991. An Emerging Early Formative Chiefdom at Paso de la Amada, Chiapas, Mexico. In *The Formation of Complex Society in Southeastern Mesoamerica*, ed. W. R. Fowler Jr., 27–46. CRC Press, Boca Raton, Fla.

Blomster, Jeffrey P. 2002. What and Where Is Olmec Style? Regional Perspectives on

Early Formative Hollow Figurines from Mesoamerica. *Ancient Mesoamerica* 13 (2): 171–95.

Blomster, Jeffrey P., Hector Neff, and Michael D. Glascock. 2005. Olmec Pottery Production and Export in Ancient Mexico Determined through Elemental Analysis. *Science* 307: 1068–72.

Cheetham, David. 2006a. The Americas' First Colony? *Archaeology* 59 (1): 42–46.

———. 2006b. Style as Cultural Imperative (II): Early Olmec Pottery from Cantón Corralito and San Lorenzo. Paper presented at the 71st Annual Meeting of the Society for American Archaeology, San Juan, P.R.

Cheetham, David, and John E. Clark. 2006. Investigaciones recientes en Cantón Corralito: Un posible enclave olmeca en la costa pacífica de Chiapas, México. In *XIX Simposio de Investigaciones Arqueológicas en Guatemala*, ed. J. P. Laporte, B. Arroyo, and H. E. Mejía, 3–8. Museo Nacional de Arqueología y Etnografía, Guatemala City.

Clark, John E. 1990. Olmecas, olmequismo y olmequización en Mesoamérica. *Arqueología* 3: 49–55.

———. 1993. Competing Representations of Reproductive Power in Early Mesoamerica. Paper presented at the 92nd Annual Meeting of the American Anthropological Association, Washington, D.C.

———. 1994. The Development of Early Formative Rank Societies in the Soconusco, Chiapas, Mexico. Ph.D. diss., Department of Anthropology, University of Michigan, Ann Arbor.

———. 1997. The Arts of Government in Early Mesoamerica. *Annual Review of Anthropology* 26: 211–34.

———. 2007. Mesoamerica's First State. In *The Political Economy of Ancient Mesoamerica: Transformations during the Formative and Classic Periods*, ed. V. Scarborough and J. E. Clark, 11–46. University of New Mexico Press, Albuquerque.

Clark, John E., and Michael Blake. 1994. The Power of Prestige: Competitive Generosity and the Emergence of Rank Societies in Lowland Mesoamerica. In *Factional Competition and Political Development in the New World*, ed. E. M. Brumfiel and J. W. Fox, 17–30. Cambridge University Press, Cambridge.

Clark, John E., and Mary E. Pye. 2000. The Pacific Coast and the Olmec Question. In *Olmec Art and Archaeology in Mesoamerica*, ed. J. E. Clark and M. E. Pye, 217–51. National Gallery of Art, Washington, D.C.

Coe, Michael D. 1965. *The Jaguar's Children: Preclassic Central Mexico*. Museum of Primitive Art, New York.

———. 1968a. *America's First Civilization*. American Heritage, New York.

———. 1968b. San Lorenzo and the Olmec Civilization. In *Dumbarton Oaks Conference on the Olmec*, ed. E. P. Benson, 41–71. Dumbarton Oaks, Washington, D.C.

———. 1981. San Lorenzo Tenochtitlán. In *Supplement to the Handbook of Middle American Indians: Archaeology*, ed. J. A. Sabloff, 117–46. University of Texas Press, Austin.

Coe, Michael D., and Richard A. Diehl. 1980. *In the Land of the Olmec*, vol. 1, *The Archaeology of San Lorenzo Tenochtitlán*. University of Texas Press, Austin.

Cyphers, Ann. 1994. San Lorenzo Tenochtitlán. In *Los Olmecas en Mesoamérica,* ed. J. E. Clark, 43–67. El Equilibrista, Mexico City.

———. 1997. Olmec Architecture at San Lorenzo. In *Olmec to Aztec: Settlement Patterns in the Ancient Gulf Lowlands,* ed. B. L. Stark and P. J. Arnold III, 96–114. University of Arizona Press, Tucson.

Diehl, Richard A., and Michael D. Coe. 1995. Olmec Archaeology. In *The Olmec World: Ritual and Rulership,* 11–25. Art Museum, Princeton University, Princeton, N.J.

Flannery, Kent V., and Joyce Marcus. 1994. *Early Formative Pottery of the Valley of Oaxaca.* Memoir 27. Museum of Anthropology, University of Michigan, Ann Arbor.

———. 2000. Formative Mexican Chiefdoms and the Myth of the "Mother Culture." *Journal of Anthropological Archaeology* 19 (1): 1–37.

Follensbee, Billie J. A. 2006. The Gift that Keeps on Giving: Formative Period Gulf Coast Ceramic Figurines. Paper presented at the 71st Annual Meeting of the Society for American Archaeology, San Juan, P.R.

Fuente, Beatriz de la. 1994. Arte monumental olmeca. In *Los Olmecas en Mesoamérica,* ed. J. E. Clark, 203–21. El Equilibrista, Mexico City.

Grove, David C. 1989. Olmec: What's in a Name? In *Regional Perspectives on the Olmec,* ed. R. J. Sharer and D. C. Grove, 8–14. Cambridge University Press, Cambridge.

———. 1993. "Olmec" Horizons in Formative Period Mesoamerica: Diffusion or Social Evolution? In *Latin American Horizons,* ed. D. S. Rice, 83–111. Dumbarton Oaks, Washington, D.C.

Joralemon, Peter D. 1981. The Old Woman and the Child: Themes in the Iconography of Preclassic Mesoamerica. In *The Olmec and Their Neighbors: Essays in Memory of Matthew W. Stirling,* ed. E. P. Benson, 163–80. Dumbarton Oaks, Washington, D.C.

Lechtman, Heather. 1977. Style in Technology—Some Early Thoughts. In *Material Culture: Style, Organization, and Dynamics of Technology,* ed. H. Lechtman and R. S. Merrill, 3–20. West Publishing, New York.

Lee W., Thomas A., and David Cheetham. Forthcoming. Lengua y escritura olmeca. In *Mesa Redonda Olmeca: Balances y perspectivas.* Instituto Nacional de Antropología e Historia and Universidad Nacional Autónoma de México, Mexico City.

Lemonnier, Pierre. 1986. The Study of Material Culture Today: Towards an Anthropology of Technical Systems. *Journal of Anthropological Archaeology* 5: 147–86.

———. 1992. *Elements for an Anthropology of Technology.* Anthropological Papers 88. Museum of Anthropology, University of Michigan, Ann Arbor.

Lesure, Richard G. 1997. Figurines and Social Identities in Early Sedentary Societies of Coastal Chiapas, Mexico, 1550–800 BC. In *Women in Prehistory: North America and Mesoamerica,* ed. C. Claassen and R. A. Joyce, 227–48. University of Pennsylvania Press, Philadelphia.

Pérez Suárez, T. 2002. Cantón Corralito: Un sitio olmeca en el litoral Chiapaneco. In *Arqueología mexicana, historia y esencia,* ed. J. Nava Rivero, 71–92. Instituto Nacional de Antropología e Historia, Mexico City.

Piña Chan, Román 1989. *The Olmec: Mother Culture of Mesoamerica*, ed. L. Laurencich Minelli. Rizzoli Publications, New York.

Rodríguez Martínez, Ma. del Carmen, Ponciano Ortíz Ceballos, Michael D. Coe, Richard A. Diehl, Stephen D. Houston, Karl A. Taube, and Alfredo Delgado Calderón. 2006. Oldest Writing in the New World. *Science* 313 (5793): 1610–14.

Stark, Miriam T. 1998. Technical Choices and Social Boundaries in Material Culture Patterning: An Introduction. In *The Archaeology of Social Boundaries*, ed. M. T. Stark, 1–11. Smithsonian Institution Press, Washington, D.C.

Velson, Joseph S., and Thomas C. Clark. 1975. Transport of Stone Monuments to the La Venta and San Lorenzo Sites. *Contributions to the University of California Archaeological Research Facility* 24: 1–39.

Viesca, Carlos. 2005. Las enfermedades en Mesoamérica. *Arqueología Mexicana* 13 (74): 38–41.

Part III

Cultural Aesthetics

7

Crafting the Body Beautiful

Performing Social Identity at Santa Isabel, Nicaragua

GEOFFREY G. MCCAFFERTY AND SHARISSE D. MCCAFFERTY

The recent theoretical trend toward agency-based archaeology includes greater interest in the human body as an arena for the expression and negotiation of social identity. As such, it further advances the utility of archaeological evidence as a means for inferring anthropologically relevant information with a diachronic perspective. One application of such an approach has yielded a valuable discussion of aspects of body image from the material culture of the Early Postclassic Sapoá phase site of Santa Isabel, Nicaragua.

In a recent review article, Erica Reisher and Kathryn Koo (2004) discuss the dual roles of the human body as both symbol and agent. A symbolic body serves as a "conduit of social meaning." Following Mary Douglas, a symbolic body is a "text upon which social meanings are inscribed" with a "common symbol set needed to decipher those meanings" (Reisher and Koo 2004: 300). In contrast, the agentic body is an active participant in the construction of the social world, or, more specifically, functions as the agency of the person. Both of these concepts act in unison to communicate externally and internally, to the society at large as well as to reinforce concepts of self.

Tied to these characteristics of the body is the idealized form that Reisher and Koo describe as the "body beautiful," which they identify as the primary site for the construction and performance of gender. While they specifically focus on femininity, the "body beautiful" is by no means the exclusive domain of women; as anthropologists, we should be aware of the multiple gender identities that exist in the present and certainly existed in the past. The various performances of the "body beautiful" may provide important clues that enable us to better understand the social identities present in the past.

An example of this type of analysis has been presented by Marlys Pearson and Paul Mullins (1999) in their article "Domesticating Barbie: An Archaeology of Barbie Material Culture and Domestic Ideology." By taking a diachronic perspective to the original "material girl," Pearson and Mullins interpret changes in body proportion, hairstyle, and costume as these aspects relate to changing social perceptions of the "body beautiful" in late-twentieth-century America, along with the possible roles of material culture in shaping gender ideologies.

In her review of the archaeology of the body, Rosemary Joyce (2005) looks at how archaeologists use material culture from the past, as well as actual skeletal remains, to explore this research direction. Joyce echoes the dual dimensions suggested earlier, of human bodies that were both the scene of display and embodied agency. She identifies several areas in which archaeologists might identify aspects of the "body beautiful": within the skeletal remains of deceased individuals; in elements of dress and adornment; and in representational art such as murals, sculpture, and figurines. Joyce operationalizes these ideas in her analyses of embodiment from Playa de los Muertos, Honduras, particularly in the polychrome ceramic figurines (see also Joyce 1993).

Cultural Context

With these ideas in mind, we have considered the archaeological assemblage recovered between 2000 and 2005 at the site of Santa Isabel, Nicaragua. Santa Isabel is located on the shore of Lake Nicaragua, just north of modern San Jorge in the Rivas district (figure 7.1). Rivas is among the best-known archaeological regions of Nicaragua because of the excavations of Gordon Willey and Albert Norweb in the early 1960s that were analyzed and published by Paul Healy (1980) and through the regional survey of Karen Niemel (2003). Nevertheless, Nicaragua as a whole has experienced limited archaeological investigation, and the Santa Isabel project was the most intensive research project ever conducted in the region. Consequently, little comparative data is presently available for detailed interpretations, apart from museum and private collections of objects lacking secure provenience.

The Santa Isabel project was conceived as a test of ethnohistorical accounts of Mesoamerican ethnicity in the Greater Nicoya region of Pacific Nicaragua and northwestern Costa Rica. According to sixteenth-century accounts (Motolinía 1951; Oviedo y Valdés 1976; Torquemada 1975–83),

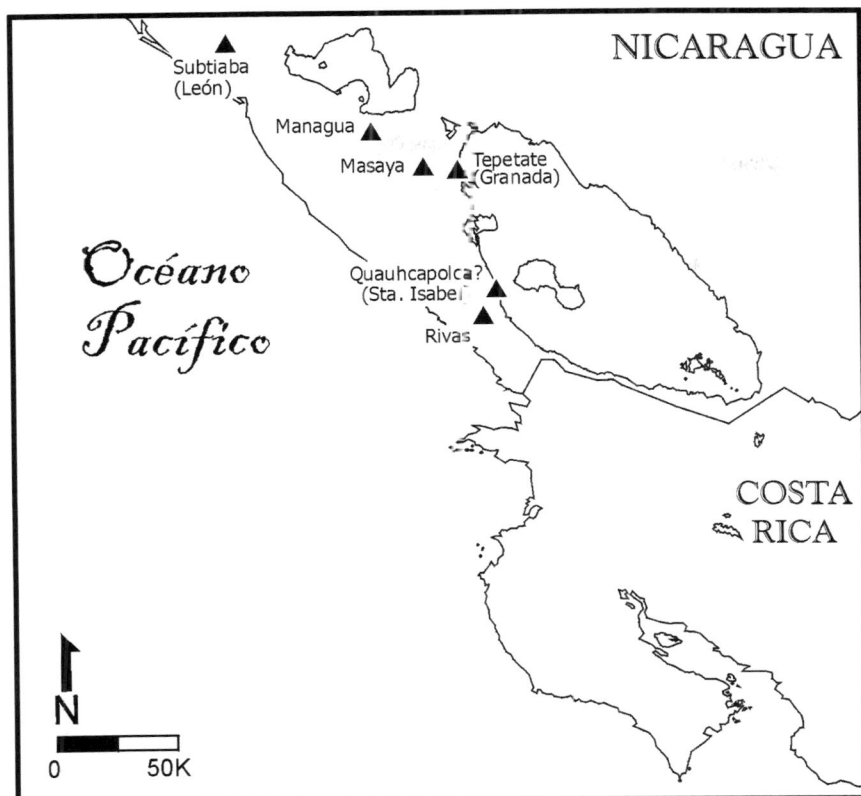

Figure 7.1. Map of Greater Nicoya, indicating location of Santa Isabel site.

migrants from Central Mexico, specifically Cholula, moved first into the Soconusco region of Chiapas and eventually to Central America, beginning in the Early Postclassic period: circa 800 CE. Two major groups were the Oto-Manguean-speaking Chorotega and the Nahuatl-speaking Nicarao, with the Nicarao arriving in the Late Postclassic period (circa 1300 CE). The Nicarao settled in the Isthmus of Rivas, where their capital city was ruled by the cacique Nicaragua in 1522 when Spanish conquistador Gil González Dávila first encountered the group. The Chorotega are generally believed to have occupied the region prior to the arrival of the Nicarao, and a native population, perhaps of Chibchan stock, is believed to have lived in the region prior to the Postclassic migrations (Ibarra Rojas 2001: 46).

Santa Isabel, identified as the largest Postclassic site in the region (Niemel 2003), was initially believed to have been a likely candidate for ancient Quauhcapolca, capital city of the cacique Nicaragua at the time of the

Spanish conquest. Investigators for the Santa Isabel project surveyed and then excavated residential contexts from the final occupation of the site. After recovering a suite of seventeen radiocarbon dates ranging between 800 CE and 1250 CE (calibrated; G. McCafferty 2008; G. McCafferty and Steinbrenner 2005a), we have concluded that Santa Isabel was not the Late Postclassic capital of the Nahua Nicarao and therefore was possibly occupied by the preceding Chorotega culture. It may have been abandoned at the time of the arrival of the Nicarao, but additional investigation will be required to support or refute this premise.

Santa Isabel consists of about forty low residential mounds spread over 270 hectares (Niemel 2003) along the shore of Lake Nicaragua. This is a semitropical environment known for its high agricultural productivity and for the abundance of fish and other animals in the lacustrine environment. Intensive investigations of the domestic practices at Santa Isabel, however, are challenging the ethnohistorically derived assumptions about Chorotega ethnicity (G. McCafferty 2008). For example, manioc was probably preferred over maize as the staple, and no evidence for *comales* or incense burners has been found to support Mesoamerican cultural practices. However, the presence of decorated pottery that features Mixteca-Puebla-style decoration (Day 1994), including representations of the deities Tlaloc and Ehecatl, suggests that social identity may have been contested between native and "Mexican" factors (G. McCafferty and Steinbrenner 2005b). A detailed evaluation of the material culture is ongoing and will be used to characterize the cultural practices of Santa Isabel as a baseline for future comparisons. An interpretation of perceptions of the "body beautiful" has potential to reveal emic concepts of self for comparison with Mesoamerican ideals versus preceding styles from the Greater Nicoyan region.

To date, portions of ten residential mounds have been sampled with systematic shovel testing, and cumulatively, 113 square meters have been excavated at five of the mounds (figure 7.2). The excellent preservation of organic materials and minimal postdepositional disturbance have helped to make Santa Isabel a particularly rich site for the recovery of material remains, including those that can relate to body decoration. This will be discussed in reference to actual skeletal remains, to objects of adornment, and to ceramic figurines and representations on polychrome pottery. Discussion of the archaeological remains is supplemented, when appropriate, with ethnohistorical descriptions of contact-period practices and information from related archaeological collections.

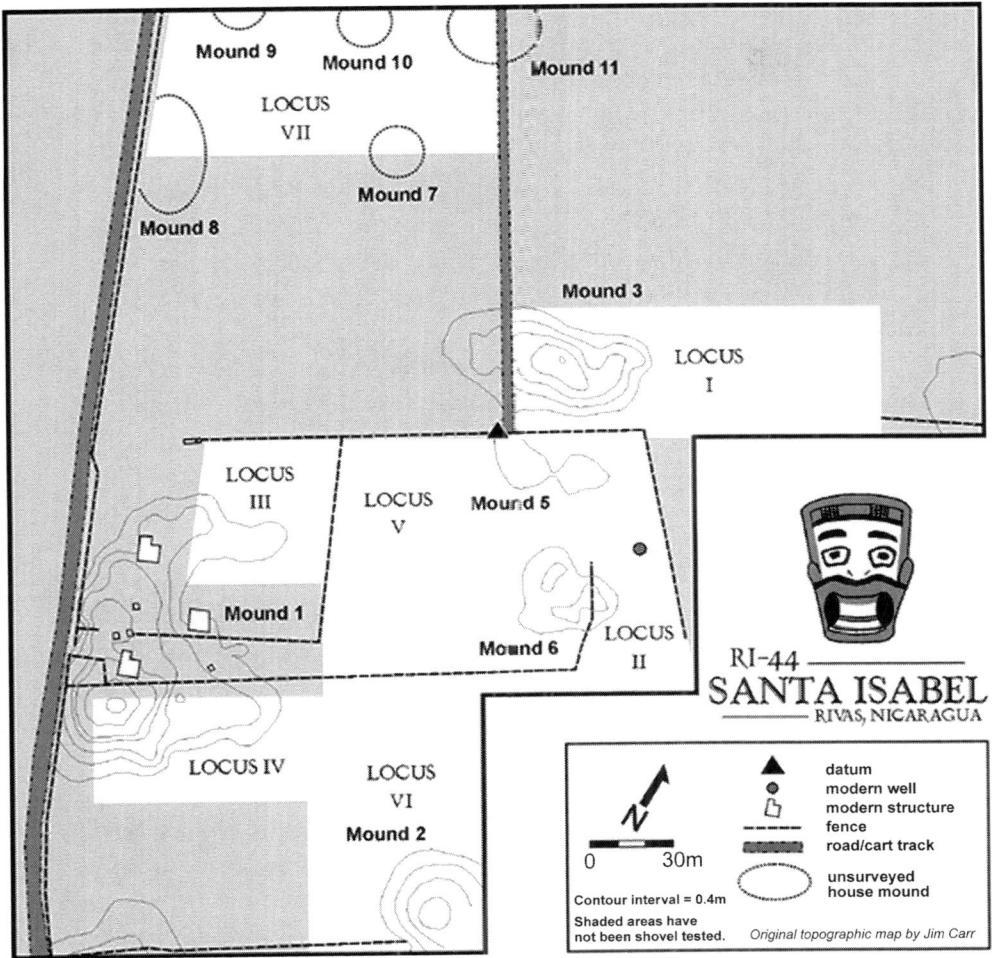

Figure 7.2. Map of central zone of Santa Isabel, indicating mounds and area covered by Santa Isabel project.

Skeletal Remains

Skeletal remains of eleven individuals were recovered from the site (Chilcote and McCafferty 2005). These were primarily the skeletons of infants interred in large Sacasa-type shoe-shaped urns. One adult male and two children were found as primary burials, but the compressed nature of the skeletons (owing to postdepositional factors such as plowing with heavy machinery) prevented investigators from ascertaining possible skeletal modifications.

One isolated tooth was found with evidence of filing into an A2 pattern, a scalloped pattern with two notches in the occlusal surface.

The preponderance of infant burials is in contrast to known cemetery sites from the period, which were more commonly the burial sites of adults (Briggs 1994; Haberland 1992; G. McCafferty 2008: 73–74). On nearby Ometepe Island, for example, a minimum of fifty adult burials were found in an extended position. Many of these exhibited evidence of cranial flattening, and some had dental modifications. The ethnic group with which these individuals were affiliated is unclear, but they are generally assumed to have been Nicarao.

Supporting evidence for specific body modifications can be found in the ethnohistorical sources from the region dating to the early Colonial period. For example, Gonzalo Fernando de Oviedo y Valdés, a chronicler who lived in Nicaragua in the 1530s, reported cranial modification among the Nahua Nicarao: "When our children are young, their heads are tender, and are then molded into the shape which you see in us, by means of two pieces of wood, hollowed in the middle. Our gods instructed our ancestors that, by so doing, we should have a noble air, and the head be better fitted to bear burdens" (Oviedo y Valdés 1851: 2: 345). Regarding hairstyles, Oviedo y Valdés reported that they "frequently shaved the head, leaving only a circle of hair extending along the edge of the forehead, from ear to ear. They all had a custom of cleaving the underpart of the tongue, and of piercing their ears for the introduction of ornaments." Specifically in reference to the Chorotega, he noted the piercing of the lower lip to place a bone or occasionally a gold plug. And he observed that "both sexes pierce their ears and make drawings on their bodies with stone knives, which are made black and permanent, by a kind of coal called *tile*" (Oviedo y Valdés 1851: 2: 341). The principal cacique had his nostrils pierced after a year of penitence and prayer in the temple.

The sources are frustratingly vague about which groups practiced particular forms of body modifications, instead generalizing that indigenous groups shared some of these practices. Additionally, these descriptions refer to the early 1500s rather than the earlier period reflected in the Santa Isabel interments. Nevertheless, they allow a glimpse of how Europeans perceived the invasive body modifications of the native population at the time of first contact.

Costume and Adornment

The Santa Isabel site featured many objects of personal adornment, including beads, pendants, and ear spools. These were made of a variety of materials, such as ceramic, shell, bone, greenstone, and other semiprecious stones. There was evidence of production of ornaments on-site, so investigators could not ascertain how many of the objects were designed for use by the Santa Isabel residents and whether some were produced for trade or tribute outside of the community.

Most beads were ceramic. The majority were simple perforated reddish brown spheres (figure 7.3a). Others, however, were segmented or zoomorphic in form, including a small ceramic frog. A large bead, roughly two centimeters in diameter, was sculpted with the face of the Mexican storm god Tlaloc, suggesting the presence of a Mesoamerican religious ideology at the site (figure 7.3b).

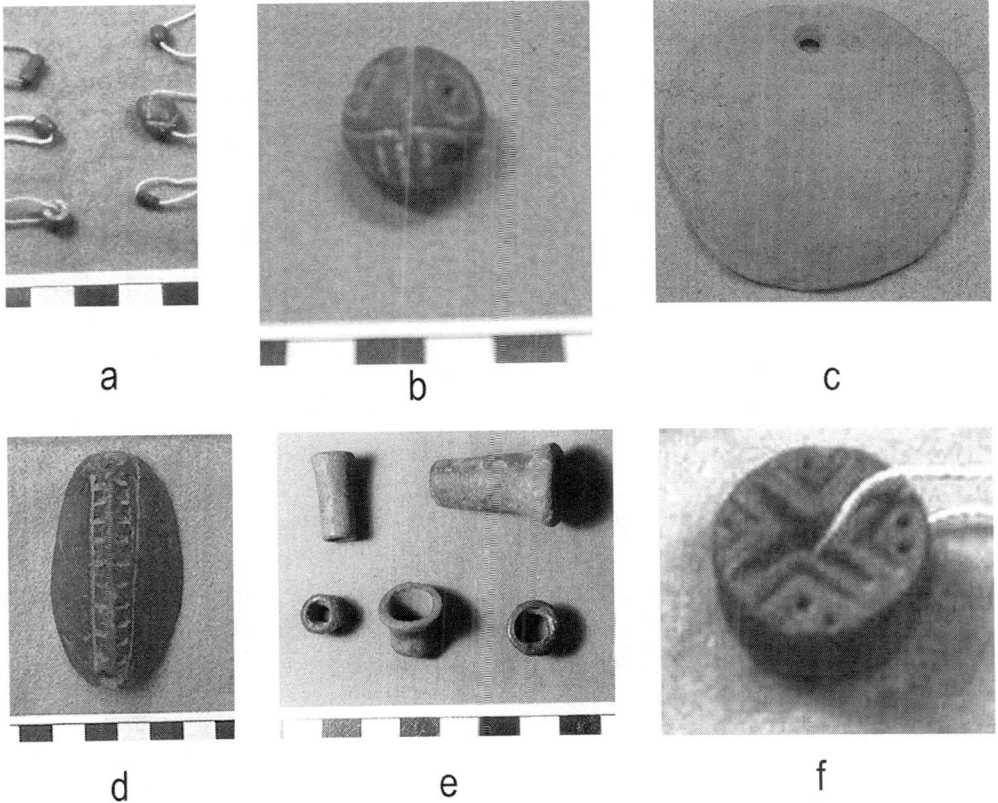

Figure 7.3. Adornment: *a,* ceramic beads; *b,* Tlaloc bead; *c,* reworked sherd pendant; *d,* cacao-pod pendant; *e,* ceramic ear spools; *f,* decorated ear spool.

A very common class of pendant consisted of large sections of reworked potsherds (figure 7.3c). These were ground to an even edge, usually in a rounded or oval form, and with one or two drilled perforations for suspension. Some of the ceramic pendants were made from polychrome sherds, but these were often eroded and no attempt was made to isolate particular patterns for display, so decoration does not seem to have been important in the selection of raw materials. One ceramic pendant was molded into an oval shape, then folded to create a ridge lengthwise down the center (figure 7.3d). The center ridge featured perpendicular scoring, and the pendant was perforated at either end. Whereas our initial impression was that this looked like a football, we now see cacao pod elements. An identical object was illustrated by Carl Bovallius (1886) from Ometepe Island in the late nineteenth century.

Clay was also used to make ear spools in various forms (figure 7.3e). The most common are slightly hourglass-shaped cylinders that are hollow in the center. These come in several sizes, from half a centimeter to about two centimeters in diameter. One reasonable speculation is that these could relate to status distinctions or perhaps age grades. On one pair of solid ear spools, the central field was decorated with incising in a cross pattern (figure 7.3f). Several longer ceramic tubes may have been worn in the ear or lip or may have had some other unidentified function.

Ornaments made of polished greenstone were also found, including beads and pendants (figure 7.4). Since evidence of greenstone production was also found, the extent to which the finished products had been used by the residents of Santa Isabel (or whether they had been involved solely in the manufacture for trade or tribute) remains unclear. The adult male individual buried at Locus 5 had several small chips of prepared but unfinished greenstone associated with his skeleton, including one in his mouth, and a fine chert drill that had possibly served as a lapidary tool (figure 7.4a). A highly polished, rectangular pendant is nearly identical in form to an unfinished preform, indicating possible on-site production (figure 7.4c). And a finished greenstone bead is similar to another that may have been discarded because the drill holes did not meet up in the center. Nevertheless, because several finished pieces of greenstone jewelry were found, it is at least plausible that some were used by the inhabitants of Santa Isabel.

Shell jewelry was also manufactured at Santa Isabel, and again there is the question as to whether it was for local use or exchange. Whereas freshwater shell was fairly abundant at the site as evidence for consumption, marine shell was consistently found with cut marks or as discard after use-

a

b

c

d

Figure 7.4. Greenstone objects.

ful segments had been removed. Spondylus, or thorny oyster, was the most common marine shell used; it was likely obtained from the nearby Pacific coast. Shell jewelry was generally made from simple cut pieces, perforated at one end for suspension (figure 7.5). One large triangular piece features two holes at the top edge (figure 7.5b). A perforated olive shell resembles an ankle tinkler worn by Mesoamerican warriors and dancers (figure 7.5c). More pieces of worked and discarded shell debitage were found than actual finished pieces, so at least some of the shell jewelry is likely to have been produced for foreign consumption.

Some of the most elaborate jewelry in terms of craftsmanship was made of carved bone. Again, there is some evidence of production at the site, and bone weaving tools and fishhooks were also produced on-site. Nevertheless, use-wear on a carved pectoral indicates that it was worn at least briefly

Figure 7.5. Shell objects.

before being discarded or lost at Mound 3. It is a piece of hollow bird bone, with twin perforations on either side of a worn area that may have held a leather or cloth strap (figure 7.6a). On either end of the bone are carved eagle and serpent heads, in a style reminiscent of the Mixteca-Puebla tradition of Central Mexico. A similarly shaped but uncarved bone was found at the same mound, perhaps serving as evidence of an unfinished piece discarded during production.

Another carved bone piece may have been used as jewelry or perhaps as part of a headdress. It likely represents the mandible of a caiman, with rounded teeth above an area decorated with a band of triangles (figure 7.6b). Within the band are two holes that may have been hollows for inset stones. Several "jewels" were found at the site, including raw amber, cut obsidian, and an unidentified round stone that resembles a pearl; these may have served as decorations in such an ornament.

Finally, a turtle carapace features drilled perforations (figure 7.6c), suggesting that it too was used as costume adornment, probably as a pendant or perhaps part of a headdress. A nearly identical piece excavated at the site of Malacatoya, north of Granada (Espinoza et al. 1999: photo 25), was associated with ceramics that suggest contemporaneity with the Santa Isabel occupation.

Additionally, four human teeth were found that had been perforated for suspension, probably on a necklace or bracelet (figure 7.6d–e). These are

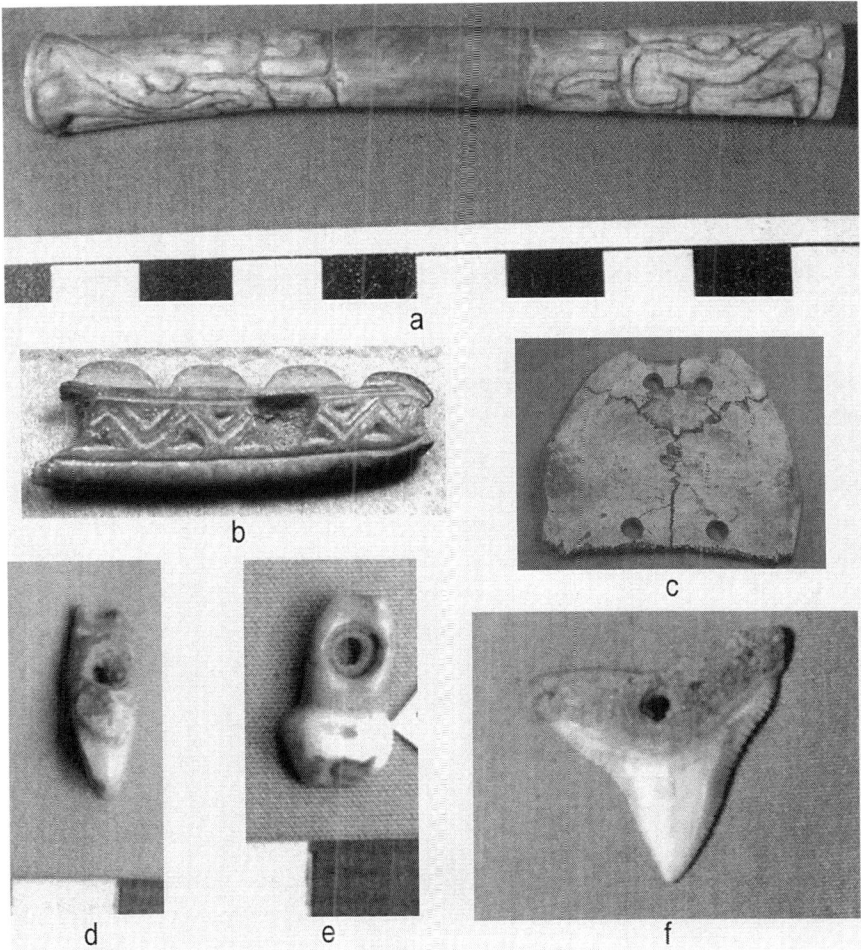

Figure 7.6. Bone and tooth objects.

adult teeth, perforated through the root to hang down from a cord. Among modern indigenous populations, a child's first deciduous tooth is worn suspended on a chain around the neck of his or her mother. Additional perforated tooth pendants include shark and peccary (figure 7.6f).

Because of the tropical climate, no remains of actual textiles were found, though numerous spindle whorls and bone weaving and embroidery tools suggest that textile production was a prominent activity of domestic practice (S. McCafferty and G. McCafferty 2008). Oviedo y Valdés (1851: 2: 346–47) describes local costume from the early sixteenth century:

The men wore a sort of doublet without sleeves, and a belt, which after passing around the body, was carried between the legs, and fastened behind. The women had a *nagua* hanging from the girdle as low as the knees. Those of the better orders had them falling as low as the ankle, and also wore a handkerchief covering their breasts. Both sexes wore sandals made of deer skins, and called *cutares,* which were fastened by a cotton cord, passing between the toes and around the heel.

The warriors wore "quilted jackets and short breeches covering the thighs, made of cotton" (Oviedo y Valdés 1851: 2: 347).

Healy (1980) described some of these objects from previous investigations in the Rivas region. Perhaps because of the less rigorous collection strategies employed by Willey and Norweb in the early 1960s, smaller objects such as beads were not encountered, but Healy described seventeen ear spools and three lip plugs (1980: 271). He also described "perforated potsherd discs" that probably correspond to the reworked sherd pendants found in abundance at Santa Isabel (Healy 1980: 266–68). Although these objects of adornment have not been reported from Malacatoya (Espinoza et al. 1999), investigators there did recover numerous beads of greenstone, and three of *tumbaga* gold (an alloy of gold and copper), from burial contexts.

Figurines

The third material category that can provide an emic perspective on the "body beautiful" is in the actual self-imaging found in the artwork of Santa Isabel. Polychrome figurines are the best artifact class for identifying such self-imaging. No complete figurines were found at Santa Isabel, but many of the 375 fragments were decorated with painted patterns that represent textile clothing and possible body paint or tattooing. Some additional human imagery is found on the painted pottery, particularly as tripod supports.

Polychrome figurines correspond to the Papagayo ceramic type that was introduced as a diagnostic of the Sapoá phase and continued into the subsequent Ometepe phase. Papagayo is characterized by a white slip over which geometric and more-complex designs are painted in black, red, and orange (Bonilla et al. 1990; Healy 1980). The Papagayo figurines are mold-made and are represented either standing or seated with bulbous legs splayed out to the sides (figure 7.7). Arms are usually on the hips with elbows jutting out to create a hollow beneath the armpit, with hands on the lap and elbows

a
b

Figure 7.7. Complete Papagayo figurines showing posture (courtesy of Mi Museo, Granada, Nicaragua).

tucked in (if seated), or with arms hanging straight beside the body. Figurines generally have an abnormal head-to-body ratio, with proportionally larger and more detailed faces and headdresses. Most represent females, as identified by small breasts and diagnostic costume elements.

The faces of the Papagayo figurines have low relief features and painted decoration (figure 7.8a–b). Eyes are most commonly tear-drop shaped with an upward slant or rectangular; their shape is outlined in black paint with a solid pupil. Eyebrows are also indicated by black painted lines. The mouth is generally outlined in reddish orange paint that extends to the ear. Teeth are occasionally depicted with possible evidence of dental modification (figure 7.8c–d), but most figurines lack details of the teeth. Ears are often depicted with multiple lobes, as if they had been mutilated through autosacrifice, and often include round ear spools. The chin is not well defined, and the heads tend to run into the body without a neck.

Headbands are depicted as woven textiles most often wrapped around the forehead and crown, obscuring the hair. A plaited twill motif is the most common pattern (figure 7.8e), but less frequently net motifs, bars and crosses, and more-complex patterns (including animals) were used (figure 7.8f–g). The plaited twill pattern consists of groups of parallel lines that meet on either an angle or a perpendicular; similar patterns are used as spindle whorl and vessel decorations, and similar woven patterns are used to represent textiles on the carved stone "metate" thrones common in Greater Nicoya. The same pattern is a symbolic representation of textiles in the Mixteca-Puebla stylistic tradition of Mesoamerica, also designating "culture over nature" and political authority (S. McCafferty and G. McCafferty 2006).

One figurine wears a possible turban or has the hair woven into a turban-like style. Some figurines exhibit specific hairstyles, such as the tonsured style in which the crown is shaven, leaving a tuft at the top where the hair is brought to a peak, with strands hanging past the front of the ear. One example depicts a shaven crown but with a ring of evenly separated hanks of hair, like dreadlocks (figure 7.8h). Another individual's head has been shaven from forehead to neck, leaving two conical buns, like horns, on either side (figure 7.8i). Two interesting examples depict a textile pattern on the back of the head. One displays the plaited twill motif on the back of the head (figure 7.8j), as if the hair was woven into cornrows or the individual was wearing a textile head-covering with a peak at the top. The second is more elaborate, with vertical and horizontal banding filled with minor patterns.

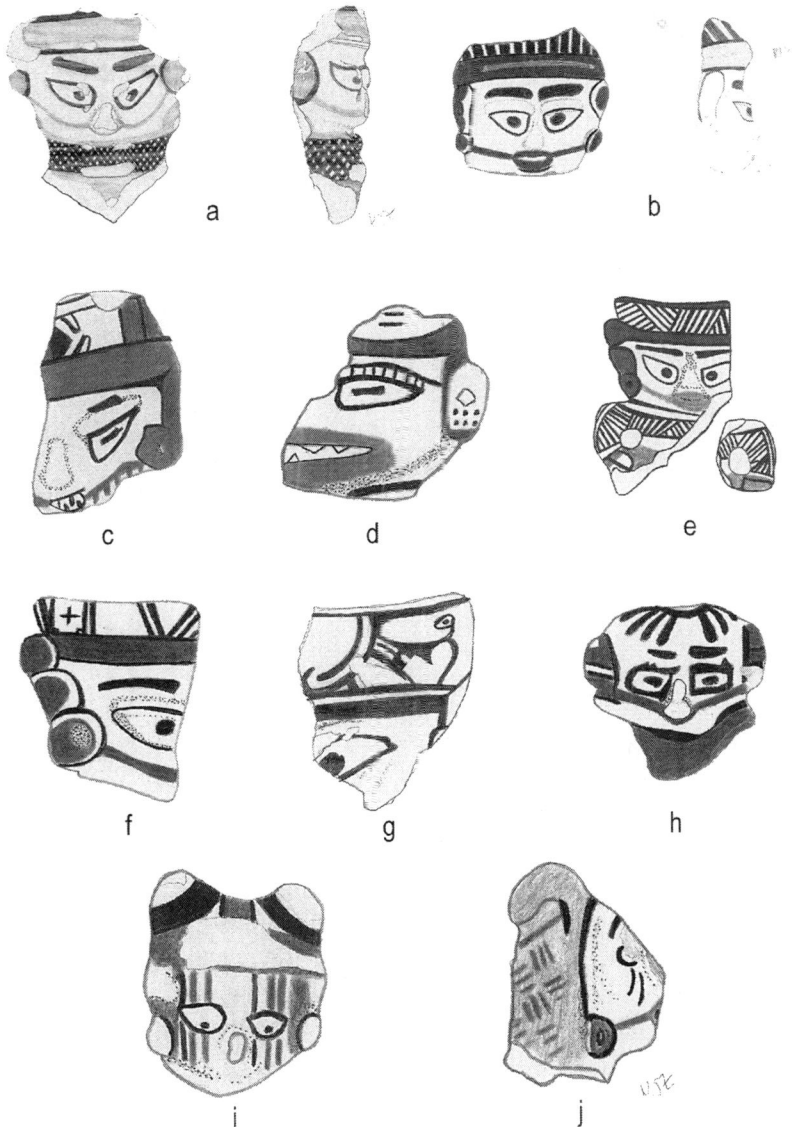

Figure 7.8. Details of figurine heads: *a*, Papagayo head and torso; *b*, Papagayo face with paint; *c–d*, dental modification; *e*, figurine with plaited twill headband; *f–g*, complex headbands; *h*, tonsure hairstyle; *i*, hair in twin horns; *j*, plaited twill hairstyle.

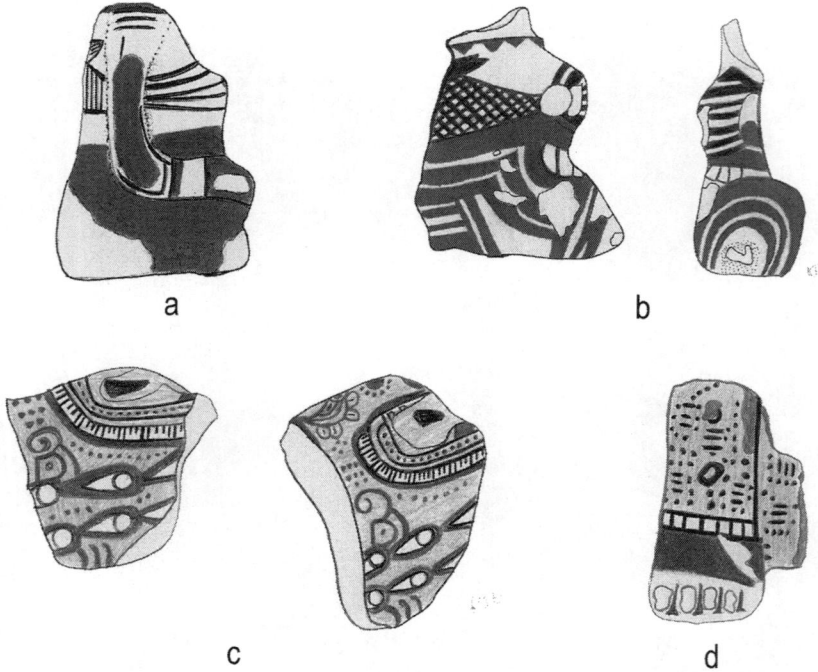

Figure 7.9. Papagayo clothing and body decoration.

Clothing is represented by painted designs, and observers may sometimes have difficulty distinguishing textiles from body decoration, such as paint or tattooing (figure 7.9a–b). Women's upper body garments generally appear to be long loosely woven textiles that bind the breasts, with the ends looped over the shoulders and tucked into the back beneath the arm. Net and plaited twill patterns are most common. Skirts may be banded or solid and occasionally depict a border. Two fragments with more elaborate textile patterns were found: one with multiple motifs that include dots, teardrops, feathers, and abstract shapes (figure 7.9c). The neck opening exhibits a fringed effect. Another uses horizontal banding filled with triangles. Two figurines depict costuming of possible jaguar skin; one is a full-body tunic, while the other preserves the pattern on a human leg (figure 7.9d).

In addition to the Papagayo polychrome figures, there were monochrome or occasional bichrome figurines. They are a medium to dark gray-brown in color, but the bichromes feature a reddish brown slip over the natural surface and occasional painted highlights. Most of the monochrome bodies are nude with well-defined features, including rounded bellies, full breasts and

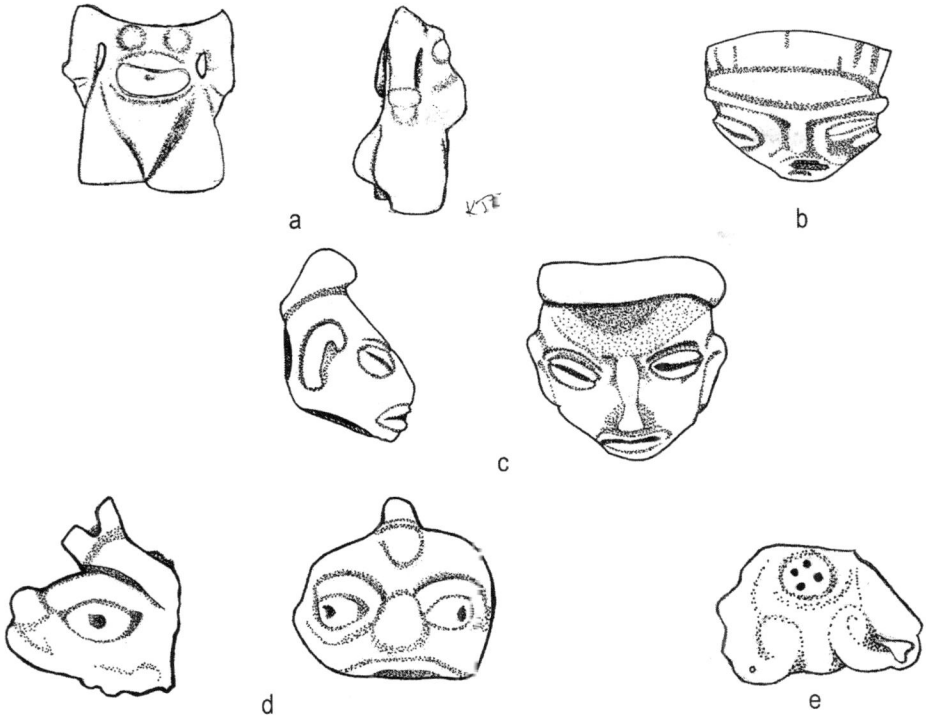

Figure 7.10. Monochrome figurines.

buttocks, and a pronounced pubic mound (figure 7.10). The monochrome heads often represent well-defined facial features, such as coffee-bean eyes that are more diagnostic of the preceding Bagaces phase (300–800 CE), brow ridges and nose, and mouth with teeth. The heads occasionally feature simple head bands of either hair or cloth. One has braided bands, together with an ear spool, while another has a possible diadem protruding from the band. A monochrome torso features a circular pendant with punctates, while another fragment features a similar ornament (though the body portion is ambiguous).

The other major class of anthropomorphic figurine probably represents the Mesoamerican wind god, Ehecatl. This commonly shows up as vessel supports on Papagayo Cervantes, Fonseca, and Mandador varieties and on Pataky polychrome. It is depicted as a human face but with an elongated reddish beak (figure 7.11a), similar to the spoonbill bird beak that is a diagnostic of Ehecatl. A figurine head may also depict Ehecatl in his characteristic conical cap and with an accentuated mouth/beak (figure 7.11b).

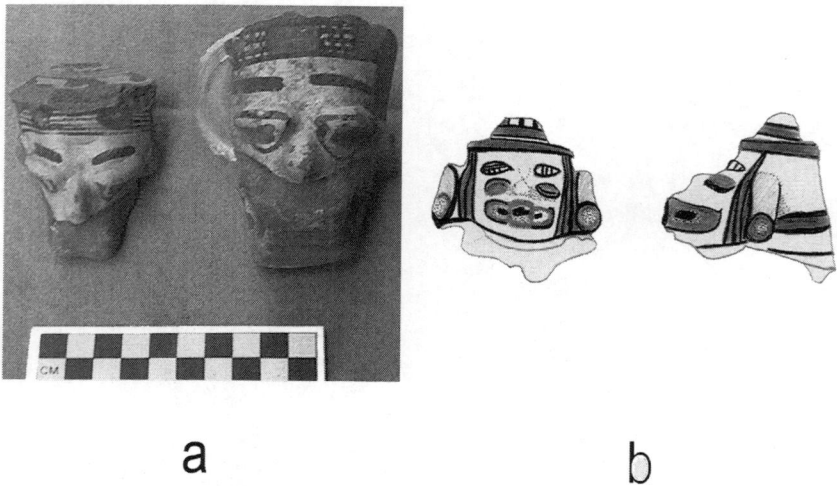

a   b

Figure 7.11. Ehecatl figures: *a*, vessel supports; *b*, figurine.

A Papagayo Cervantes variety bowl also depicts a human head with decorative elements, including a prominent feather headdress (figure 7.12a–b). A diagnostic characteristic on Papagayo Mandador variety polychromes is a horizontal human head with a distinctively triangular face and stylized headdress (figure 7.12c–d).

A final anthropomorphic representation is a small metal figurine, probably of native copper, that was found at Mound 3. Although corroded, this figure appears as a standing figure that may have had wings similar to "bird men" found in lower Central America that have been interpreted as shamans.

The most complete discussion of Nicaraguan figurines is again by Healy (1980: 257–66), based on 68 fragments from excavated contexts from the Rivas region. Over half (*n*=38) were hollow, mold-made figurines that he classified as Papagayo polychrome, many assigned to the Mandador variety based on similarities between the bulbous legs and vessel supports. He distinguished between open- and closed-head figurines depending on whether the top of the head has an opening. He also describes the painted facial characteristics and woven pattern as possible clothing.

An extensive treatment of the figurines of the Greater Nicoya region is being prepared by Laura (Brannen) Wingfield for her Ph.D. dissertation in art history at Emory University, based on museum and private collections of complete figurines. Brannen (2006) interprets the many female figurines as possible rulers or shamanesses, reifying identities of living humans in-

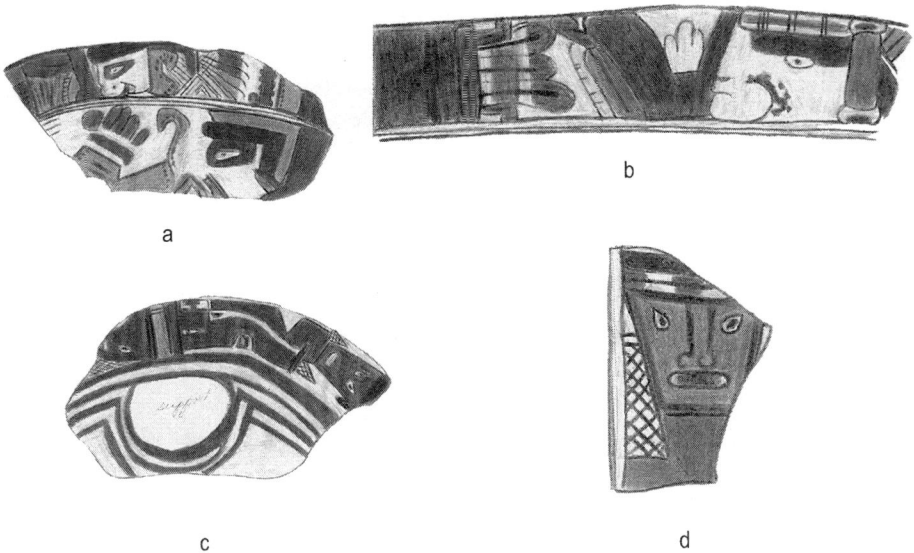

Figure 7.12. Human faces on Papagayo pottery.

tertwined with supernatural roles. In contrast, the male figurines are often hunchbacks who may have been ritual assistants.

Conclusion

The Santa Isabel site has produced a rich variety of material culture useful for inferring concepts of the "body beautiful" among its ancient inhabitants. In the case of the modified dentition and the ear spools, as well as the possible tattooing, this beautification was actually inscribed onto the body. In other cases, the adornment was probably draped on the body as if it were a canvas for symbolic communication. To the extent that the messaging was systematic, it likely related to qualities of social identity, including gender, age, status, and ethnicity. Through the regular performance of these identities, selectively chosen to conform to contextual practices, individuals acted as agents within their community or on a more restricted level within their household. The performance even served to reify perceptions of self on the most personal level, allowing for minor variations to reflect the negotiations of identity toward the society at large.

Spatial analysis of material culture patterning is ongoing, but some preliminary observations can be made. The majority of the small, ceramic beads were found at Mound 6. Some of the more "valuable" objects (such as greenstone pendants, the carved bone pendant, and the copper figurine) were found at Mound 3, which was likely the highest-status residence gauging by labor investment in house construction (G. McCafferty 2008). These data, among others, suggest a degree of social variation across the community. However, figurines were ubiquitous among the excavated mounds, and no distinctions have been found to suggest ethnic differences. The use of both the Papagayo polychrome and the monochrome figurines may relate to different functions for the objects (for example, ritual objects versus children's toys), may indicate the presence of heirlooms from an earlier time period, or may reveal the cultural blending of a multiethnic community.

No strong correlation exists between the material objects of costume and adornment and the figurine decorations. Ear spools are found archaeologically and are commonly represented on the figurines. But pendants, the most common object of adornment archaeologically, are present only in one case from the figurines recovered from Santa Isabel. The pendant on the monochrome figurine is round, like the reworked sherd pendants, but is depicted as decorated with pitting, unlike the sherd pendants. No beads or other pendants are represented on the excavated figurines, though they have been occasionally observed on figurines in museum collections.

Because of the limited database available from Nicaragua at present, the interpretations are limited. We hope that as more sites are excavated and the material culture is reported, Santa Isabel can serve as a model for further comparison toward more robust conclusions. Because one of the research goals of the Nicaragua project is specifically the inference of cultural identities, particularly relating to ethnicity, concepts of the body and aesthetic principles of beauty and identity are key issues that will continue as the scope of investigation is expanded in future research.

Acknowledgments

The Santa Isabel Archaeological Project was supported with grants from the Social Sciences and Humanities Research Council of Canada and from the University of Calgary and was conducted under permit from the Department of Cultural Patrimony, Managua, Nicaragua. Many people have assisted in the research, and we are particularly grateful to Larry Steinbrenner and Denise Gibson, who helped with supervised initial artifact analyses related to this research. Silvia Salgado (of the University of Costa Rica) has advised on all phases of the investigation, and we appreciate her generosity and profound knowledge of Nicaraguan archaeology. Laura (Brannen) Wingfield (of Emory University) has kindly shared her extensive wisdom on Greater Nicoyan figurines, including elements from her dissertation on the subject and image archive. Her comments on earlier drafts of this paper have been particularly helpful. We are also grateful to Peder Kolind and the staff of Mi Museo (Granada, Nicaragua) for providing us with an additional collection of figurine images, two of which are used with permission.

References Cited

Bonilla, Leidy, Marlin Calvo, Juan Guerrero, Silvia Salgado, and Frederick Lange. 1990. La cerámica de la Gran Nicoya. *Vinculos: Revista de Antropología del Museo Nacional de Costa Rica* 13 (1–2): 1–327.

Bovallius, Carl. 1886. Nicaraguan Antiquities. Serie Arqueologica 1. Swedish Society of Anthropology and Geography. Stockholm, Sweden.

Briggs, Peter S. 1994. Fatal Attractions: Interpretation of Prehistoric Mortuary Remains from Lower Central America. In *Reinterpreting Prehistory of Central America*, ed. M. Miller Graham. University Press of Colorado, Niwot.

Chilcote, Celise, and Geoffrey G. McCafferty. 2005. Tooth and Consequences: Mortuary Analysis from Santa Isabel, Nicaragua. Paper presented at the 38th Meeting of the Chacmool Conference, Calgary, Alberta.

Day, Jane Stevenson. 1994. Central Mexican Imagery in Greater Nicoya. In *Mixteca-Puebla: Discoveries and Research in Mesoamerican Art and Archaeology*, ed. H. B. Nicholson and E. Quiñones Keber, 235–48. Labyrinthos Press, Culver City, Calif.

Espinoza P., Edgar, Ramiro García V., and Fumiyo Suganuma. 1999. *Rescate arqueológico en el sitio San Pedro, Malacatoya, Granada, Nicaragua*. Instituto Nicaraguense de Cultura, Museo Nacional de Nicaragua, Managua, Nicaragua.

Haberland, Wolfgang. 1992. The Culture History of Ometepe Island: Preliminary Sketch (Survey and Excavations, 1962–1963). In *The Archaeology of Pacific Nicaragua*, ed. F. W. Lange, P. D. Sheets, A. Martinez, and S. Abel-Vidor, 63–118. University of New Mexico Press, Albuquerque.

Healy, Paul F. 1980. *Archaeology of the Rivas Region, Nicaragua*. Wilfred Laurier University Press, Waterloo, Ont.

Ibarra Rojas, Eugenia. 2001. *Fronteras etnicas en la conquista de Nicaragua y Nicoya: Entre la solidaridad y el conflicto de 800 d.C.–1544*. Editorial de la Universidad de Costa Rica, San Jose.

Joyce, Rosemary A. 1993. Women's Work: Images of Production and Reproduction in Pre-Hispanic Southern Central America. *Current Anthropology* 34 (3): 255–74.

———. 2005. Archaeology of the Body. *Annual Review of Anthropology* 34: 139–58.

McCafferty, Geoffrey G. 2008. Domestic Practice in Postclassic Santa Isabel, Nicaragua. *Latin American Antiquity* 19 (1): 64-82.

McCafferty, Geoffrey G., and Larry Steinbrenner. 2005a. Chronological Implications for Greater Nicoya from the Santa Isabel Project, Nicaragua. *Ancient Mesoamerica* 16 (1): 131–46.

———. 2005b. The Meaning of the Mixteca-Puebla Stylistic Tradition on the Southern Periphery of Mesoamerica: The View from Nicaragua. In *Art for Archaeology's Sake: Material Culture and Style across the Disciplines,* ed. A. Waters-Rist, C. Cluny, C. McNamee, and L. Steinbrenner, 282–92. Proceedings of the 33rd Annual Chacmool Conference. Archaeological Association of the University of Calgary, Alberta.

McCafferty, Sharisse D., and Geoffrey G. McCafferty. 2006. Weaving Space: Textile Imagery and Landscape in the Mixtec Codices. In *Space and Spatial Analysis in Archaeology,* ed. E. C. Robertson, J. D. Seibert, D. C. Fernandez, and M. U. Zender. Proceedings of the 34th Annual Chacmool Conference. University of Calgary Press, Calgary, Alta.

———. 2008. Spinning and Weaving Tools from Santa Isabel, Nicaragua. *Ancient Mesoamerica* 19 (1): 143–56.

Motolinía, Fray Toribio de Benavente. 1951. *History of the Indians of New Spain.* Trans. F. B. Steck. Academy of American Franciscan History, Washington, D.C. Originally written in 1540.

Niemel, Karen Stephanie. 2003. *Social Change and Migration in the Rivas Region, Pacific Nicaragua (1000 BC–AD 1522).* Ph.D. diss., Department of Anthropology, State University of New York, Buffalo.

Oviedo y Valdés, Gonzalo Fernando de. [ca. 1560] 1976. *Nicaragua en las Crónicas de Indias: Oviedo.* Trans. E. Squier. Banco de America, Fondo de Promoción Cultural, Serie Cronistas 3. Managua, Nicaragua.

Pearson, Marlys, and Paul R. Mullins. 1999. Domesticating Barbie: An Archaeology of Barbie Material Culture and Domestic Ideology. *International Journal of Historical Archaeology* 3: 225–59.

Reischer, Erica, and Kathryn S. Koo. 2004. The Body Beautiful: Symbolism and Agency in the Social World. *Annual Review of Anthropology* 33: 297–317.

Torquemada, Fray Juan de. 1975–83. *Monarquía Indiana.* 7 vols. Coordinated by M. León-Portilla. Instituto de Investigaciones Historicas, Universidad Nacional Autonoma de México, Mexico City. Originally written in 1615.

8

New Fire Figurines and the Iconography
of Penitence in Huastec Art

KATHERINE A. FAUST

Any tattoo—indeed—a mark of any kind—on the skin, is a registration of the
causal factors which produced it, and hence a symbolic residue of the totality of
causal factors, events, social obligations, individual and collective relationships
impinging on the social person. Thus a tattoo . . . is always a registration of an
external social milieu, because it is only in relation to that milieu that the tattoo
has meaning.

Gell 1993: 36–37

Iconography adorning anthropomorphic figurines, sculptures, and vessels speaks to the vigorous manner in which the Huastec inhabitants of the northeastern Gulf Coast region of Mesoamerica marked and branded their bodies, thereby creating a unique aesthetic of self. While scholars generally agree that pre-Columbian Huastec art reflects social identity alongside religious and cosmological concerns (see Castro-Leal 1979; Fuente 1980; Trejo 2004; Zaragoza Ocaña 1999), the specific symbols that comprise this ideology written upon the body are poorly understood.

Iconographic, ethnohistoric, and ethnographic analyses of a rare set of figurines (reportedly from the Tampico-Pánuco region of the Huasteca) in the collection of the Museo de Antropología, Xalapa, Veracruz, demonstrate that motifs depicted on these small clay bodies collectively reference concepts pertaining to primordial creation, particularly the drilling of fire (producing flame by rapidly rotating a vertical wooden stick upon a horizontal one) and ritual blood sacrifice. More specifically, the symbols on these figurines are representations of divinatory regalia and the tools of penitence, including shining mirrors, fire drills, maguey thorns, and sharp obsidian blades. By permanently marking the body with images of the instruments used to periodically inflict and bleed the body, the aesthetic ideal of penitence and the ritual potency of penitential acts is memorialized in the Huastec self and in material representations of the Huastec body. As portrayals of small bodies inscribed with a limited range of "essentialized" imagery, the figures from the Tampico-Pánuco region, referred to here as "New Fire" figurines, are instrumental to understanding the significance and placement of similar motifs on other examples of Huastec art.[1]

Huastec Iconography and the Tampico-Pánuco New Fire Figurines

The Middle and Late Postclassic (circa 1150–1521 CE) Huastec produced one of the most unique art styles in ancient Mesoamerica, inspiring scholarly interest since the turn of the nineteenth century (for example, Beyer 1934; Fewkes 1906; Meade 1942: 53–67; Nuttall 1888; Saville 1900). Composed primarily through the repetition of highly stylized motifs, Huastec iconography adorning anthropomorphic sculptures, vessels, and figurines emphasizes an aesthetic of self that involved temporarily marking or permanently tattooing the body to create a "social skin," using the terminology of Terrence Turner (1980).

Ethnohistorical sources similarly imply that painting, tattooing, piercing, tooth filing, and other modificatory practices were central to Huastec identity, social status, and military status (see Durán 1964: ch. 14, 105–8; Sahagún 1950–69: bk. 10: 185). In addition to recording adornmental practices, analyses of Huastec art have emphasized that bodily iconography reflects religious and cosmological content, particularly as pertains to agricultural fertility and the cyclical regeneration of life through death (Castro Leal 1989; Trejo 1989). Appreciating the long (albeit turbulent) history of indigenous presence in the Huasteca, scholars have also productively incorporated ethnographic data into their interpretations of ancient art (see Ochoa 1991; Ochoa and Gutiérrez 1996–99). A more recent trend is to examine Huastec iconography within the historical and sociopolitical contexts of its production (see Richter 2004). This represents an important turn, as meaning is dependent on the circumscribing social milieu (Gell 1993: 36; see also Koontz 1994).

Some of the symbols inscribed in the Tampico-Pánuco figurines also adorn the most elaborate examples of Huastec sculptures and are likewise prevalent in the ceramic types known as Huastec Black-on-White and Tancol Bi- and Polychrome. These materials first appeared in the Huasteca around 1000 CE, during the middle part of the cultural phases known as Las Flores or Panuco V in the Ekholm chronology (1944), Isla B in the Wilkerson chronology (1972), and Tamul in the Merino Carrión and García Cook chronology and continue to characterize the ritual ceramic tradition of the Huasteca throughout the Middle and Late Postclassic periods (Merino Carrión and García Cook 1987: 62–65; Zaragoza Ocaña 2003a). The predominance of Huastec Black-on-White and Tancol Bi- and Polychrome wares corresponds with a decline in the manufacture, skillful production, and variety of figurines made in the Huasteca, which first appeared around 1400 BCE (Merino Carrión and García Cook 1987: 38, 62). While determining the precise antiquity of the figurines in question is difficult, stylistic and thematic parallels suggest that they too were produced sometime during this time frame, not predating 1000 CE.[2]

The Principle of Compression

As some of the most elaborate examples of Huastec art, certain sculptures including the Huastec Youth, also known as El Adolescente (Fuente and Gutierrez Solana 1980: pl. CCLVII), and one of the Huilocintla stelae are among the objects most frequently analyzed. One of the challenges to understanding the imagery adorning these sculptures is that Huastec motifs are highly stylized and frequently merge together. This tendency effectively creates a sense of bodily *horror vacui*, in which exposed arms, legs, and torsos can be so completely filled with standardized designs that ascertaining where one symbol ends and another begins becomes difficult. In this respect, much of Huastec art (including sculptures and vessels alike) exhibits a quality akin to what Alfred Gell (1998: 79–90) has described as complex, apotropaic, and snarelike patterns, which reel in viewers (or, alternately, malevolent spirits) only to lose them within the "intricacy," "multiplicity," and "interminability" of convoluted design (figure 8.1).

Whereas the large surface area of sculpture has abundant space for inscription, figurines, in contrast, are small, representational objects. Diminutive size clearly constrains the quantity of graphic information that can be written on the palm-sized bodies. Douglass Bailey (2005: 32) has recently referred to this condition as the "principle of compression." In miniature objects, details are reduced and strategically selected to ensure retention of meaning. Bailey's concept is useful in considering the iconography adorning Huastec figurines because upon their more limited surface area, the visual cacophony of imagery adorning larger examples of art is reduced to the minimal meaningful units. Furthermore, as small anthropomorphic representations, these figurines can tell us a great deal about the relationship between essential symbol sets and the Huastec ideology of the human body.

Figure 8.1. Stela from Huilocintla, Veracruz. Relief-carved stone monument depicting a figure engaged in autosacrifice. Middle to Late Postclassic period (circa 1150–1521 CE). Museo Nacional de Antropología, México.

Characteristics of New Fire Figurines

Huastec figurines pertaining to several classificatory types and periods were often ornamented with painted, tattoolike markings. Less frequently, however, they were gouged and incised with designs like those appearing on sculptures and vessels. The objects analyzed here represent one such set of uniquely inscribed figurines and are of particular interest for this reason (figure 8.2). Although their stratigraphic provenience is unknown, these artifacts were all reportedly found in the Tampico or Pánuco region of the Huasteca. The figurine fragments range from two and one-half inches to slightly over four inches in height. With one exception (figure 8.2b), all are made of fine-grained, light-colored clay. Gender is clearly indicated in each of the examples. Seven of the eight figures are female, identifiable by the presence of rounded breasts and a vaginal cleft. Only one male is represented, called to the observer's attention by a small phallic protrusion (figure 8.2g). While several examples are rather squat, truncated bodily forms, four are torsos of articulated figurines. Their pelvic and scapular areas are clearly pierced with small holes through which limbs can be secured (figure 8.2e–h). In the two instances in which the head remains attached, facial detail is limited. On one figure, a small, punched pellet of clay applied atop a slit forms the eye, and two slight holes suggest nostrils. The mouth is the most remarkable feature: the lips are tightly pursed, as if whistling, blowing, or exhaling (figure 8.2e; see also figure 8.3a). The head of the second figurine is formed from a flat disk of clay. The eye construction is the same; the nose is made from a small clay pellet; and there is no indication of a mouth (figure 8.2b).

Iconographic detail varies from one figure to the next, but there seems to be a basic schema of representation. The frontal aspect of several examples is marked with a series of vertical lines, creating a corsetlike binding about the waist. These lines often terminate in a series of punctured semicircles, which stretch across the hip area. When present, the lower body is inscribed with scrolls or other dropletlike forms. The backsides of the figurines are frequently decorated with a disc from which swirling volutes emerge. Although the sticklike corset may reference bundles of reeds, the circular back ornaments likely allude to smoking mirrors and the fiery contexts associated with these devices in Mesoamerican art and thought. The imagery on the single male figurine is particularly compelling because it explicitly references body piercing or the drilling of fire. If these interpretations are accurate, then this group of figurines is evocative of the creation of fire, sacrifice, air and breath, and even penitential bloodletting.[3]

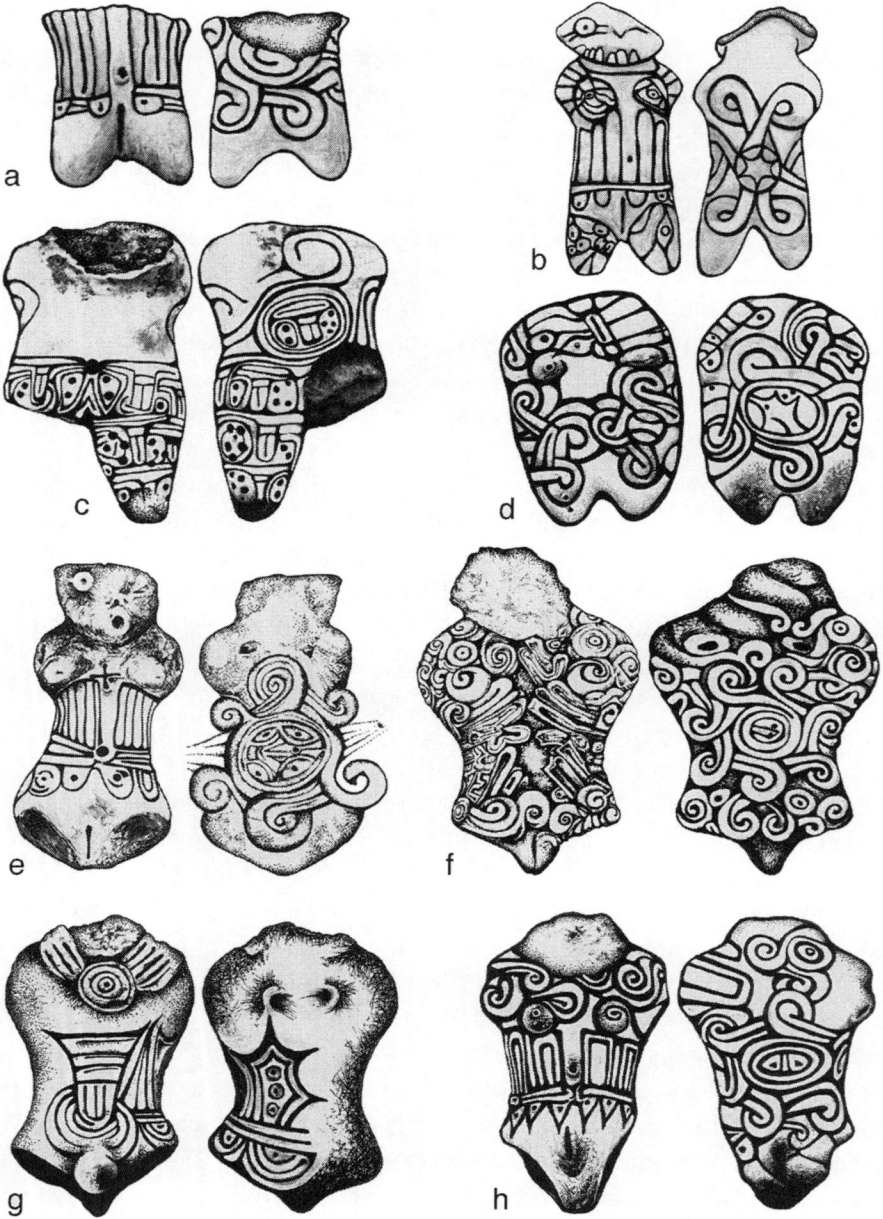

Figure 8.2. "New Fire" figurines from the Tampico-Pánuco region of the Huasteca. Ceramic, inscribed with designs pertaining to fire drilling and sacrifice. Middle to Late Postclassic period (circa 1150–1521 CE). Museo de Antropología, Xalapa, Veracruz.

Previous Descriptions

Gordon Ekholm, whose excavations at Tampico and Pánuco resulted in the first chronology for the Huasteca, found very few figurines that are stylistically similar to the ones herein examined (Ekholm 1944: 450, fig. 39b–d,g,k). As this figurine type represented an anomaly compared with other ceramic materials, Ekholm commented only briefly on the comparatively rough appearance of the figurines and noted that they cannot be temporally anchored, as they were either purchased or represent parts of surface collections made at the sites of Las Flores, Pavón, and San Cristóbal (in the present-day city of Tampico). In his comparative study of the figurines of the Huasteca and the Valley of Mexico Wilfredo Du Solier (1950: 24–25) similarly remarked on the unrefined quality of a few figurines exhibiting morphology similar to those examined here, and he postulated that they represent a chronologically more recent (versus archaic) tradition.

Of these figurines documented by both Ekholm and Du Solier, only one is decorated with designs. Ekholm compared the imagery on one roughly carved figurine (1944: 453, fig. 39k) to a set of incised Huastec figures illustrated in a 1916 publication by Caecilie Seler. Eduard and Caecilie Seler collected no less than five of these figurines in Pánuco, twenty-eight years prior to the date of publication, during their travels in the Huasteca in 1888 (C. Seler 1916: 98). These objects are identical in style to the figurines examined in this text (figure 8.3). The materials assembled by the Selers on their journey, now located in the Berlin Museum für Völkerkunde, represent one of the most important collections of Huastec art.

Huastec Fire Drill Motif

Eduard Seler ([1902–23] 1990: vi: 239–40) first suggested that the inverted triangular (alternatively, rectangular) elements that frequently appear on Huastec vessels represent a fire drill. On one example from Tanquian that he analyzed, smoky volutes are depicted emanating from the drill (figure 8.4a). From among these swirls, a tripointed figure inset with several painted spots emerges. Along with the drill, this pointed element (of which there are many variations) represents one of the most ubiquitous motifs in Huastec art. In contemporary scholarship, this enigmatic form has been consistently referred to as the "alma de maíz" (the soul or spirit of maize) since the renowned Huastec historian Joaquín Meade (1942: 103–5) first suggested that these motifs refer to corn. Meade noted that the arms and

Figure 8.3. Clay figurines from Pánuco, Veracruz. Middle to Late Postclassic period (circa 1150–1521 CE). Museum für Völkerkunde, Berlin (redrawn from C. Seler 1916: 120–22, figs. 37–41).

especially the right leg of the famous Huastec Youth sculpture were literally covered with this emblem (figure 8.4c), recalling a passage from the Popol Vuh of the Quiché Maya in which the creator gods of the four directions formed the bodies of humans from cornmeal dough: "Formaron sus carnes del producto de las mazorcas amarillas y blancas, como alimento de los brazos y de las piernas de la gente" (Villacorta and Rodas 1927: ch. 7, bk. 10).

Figure 8.4. Huastec fire drill and Teotihuacan butterfly imagery: *a*, drill, smoke, and flame as detail on Black-on-White style vessel from Tanquian, San Luis Potosí (redrawn from C. Seler 1916: 108, fig. 14c); *b*, detail of drill and flame motif encircling waist of figure 8.2g; *c*, detail of a so-called Huastec maize emblem adorning the Huastec Youth sculpture (redrawn after Meade 1982: pl. 14); *d*, polychrome butterfly on earthenware vessel fragment from Teotihuacan (redrawn from E. Seler [1902–23] 1990: 6: 240, fig. 179a); *e*, butterfly wing *adorno* from Teotihuacan (drawing by Ilona Faust after Sugiyama 2002: fig. PN14-32); *f*, drill and flame detail on Black-on-White style vessel from Tanquian (redrawn from C. Seler 1916: 108, fig. 13c) *g*, digital image of Huastec ceramic stamp (digital image in Museum of Huastec Culture, Tampico); *h*, drill, starlike flame, and year bundle from Chichén Itzá (redrawn from Taube 2000: 293, fig. 10.14e).

In a more detailed analysis of the same sculpture, Meade (1982: pl. 14) called this pointy form "el signo del maíz huasteco" (the Huastec sign for maize) and compared it with the Maya glyph for *tamale,* which is also thought to represent a grain of corn (see Montgomery 2002: 261).

For Eduard Seler ([1902–23] 1990: vi: 239–40), who had an encyclopedic knowledge of Mesoamerican iconography, these *alma* or maize emblems (as they later came to be called) closely resembled butterfly imagery in the artistic conventions of Classic period Teotihuacan and were particularly similar to representations of butterfly wing *adornos* decorating *incensarios,* produced in large quantities at this metropolis (figure 8.4d–e). The presence of butterflies on the fiery censers prompted Seler to suggest that the pointy Huastec symbol metaphorically referenced a winglike spark or flame, as did the Late Postclassic Central Mexican convention of literally representing flames as butterflies (E. Seler [1902–23] 1990: vi: 713–14).

Fire Drill Figurine

The complex of fire drill imagery adorning the Huastec vessel described by Seler is present on the articulated male figurine (figures 8.4b, 8.2g). The drill pierces the navel, and the concentric circles into which the drill is thrust likely allude to the action of boring. A line emerges from the focal drill motif, accentuating the curve of the hip. A series of partial discs is visible below this line, likely referencing *chalchihuitl* symbols. Denoting preciousness, jade, or turquoise and emblematic of water and blood, these discs simultaneously represent a series of drilled holes. The symbols depicted along the upper border of the waistline are more difficult to interpret, but the final motif is clearly a depiction of the fiery butterfly wing. In other Huastec vessels and stamps, the drill and flame are not separated by intervening elements but are instead bound together (figure 8.4f–g). Schematically, these examples are remarkably similar to a carved image of a pump drill and emergent starlike flame (in the company of a year bundle) at the Early Postclassic site of Chichén Itzá (figure 8.4h).

Fire Drilling and Creation

To better appreciate the meaning of the fire drill portrayed on this figurine, we should briefly consider the manifestations of fire drills and drilling events on a broader, pan-Mesoamerican scale. The action of drilling is first and foremost one of creation, resulting in an anticipated event, whether physiological, sociopolitical, or temporal in nature. But drilling also marks completion and termination and is thus a key symbol of transformation.[4]

The *Historia de los Mexicanos por sus pinturas* describes how the god Tezcatlipoca (Smoking Mirror)—in the guise of Mixcoatl (Cloud Serpent)— first drilled fire (García Icazbalceta 1941: 234), lifting the heavens from the earth with the rising cloud of smoke. The drilling of fire, especially on the supine body of human and supernatural beings, is envisioned as a fundamental symbol of primordial creation in Mesoamerican thought. Drilling is commonly represented in Central Mexican and Maya almanacs, and the action was featured in calendric rites of which the Aztec New Fire ceremony is likely the most famous. Performed once every fifty-two years to mark the complete cycling of the 365-day solar and the 260-day ritual calendars, this dramatic ceremony simultaneously initiated the new Calendar Round.

An essential component of this ritual involved human sacrifice. At a specific moment, a group of priests extracted the beating heart from the chest of a sacrificial victim. In this cavity, the New Fire was drilled, and the flame was spread throughout the city of Tenochtitlan. Successful kindling of fire ensured the resurrection of the sun and signified that the new fifty-two-year cycle had successfully been set into motion (Berdan 1982: 119).

As indices of initiation, fire-drilling rituals were important in marking the foundations of places and dynasties and are particularly well represented in the Mixteca-Puebla (Ringle 2004: 187) and Aztec traditions.[5] One scene of investiture occurs in the Codex Borgia illustrating fire being drilled on the body of a sacrificial victim (figure 8.5d). One of the most explicit examples of drilling in Huastec-style art occurs on a round shell-disk facing of an ear plug (figure 8.5b). According to Hermann Beyer (1934: 173–74), Mixcoatl drills the primordial flame on this fine adornment.

Indices of drilling are present even in the absence of a drill-wielding protagonist. The fundamental symbol for drilling is composed of a two-part device: the drill shaft, and the resultant disklike hole (or horizontal stick) in which the drill is twirled. Even when a drill is not represented in conjunction with the hole, the disc may appear on the body, especially the navel area or backside of serpentine, crocodilian, or other earth-associated creatures, suggesting that they have received treatment from the drill (figure 8.5a). This chalchihuitl marking may thus be considered as a species of tattoo—a permanent mark or scar of the birthing action that took place. The same is true in examples of Huastec art. On one zoomorphic vessel in particular, the black-painted navel flanked by the winglike flame motifs arguably implies piercing (figure 8.5c).

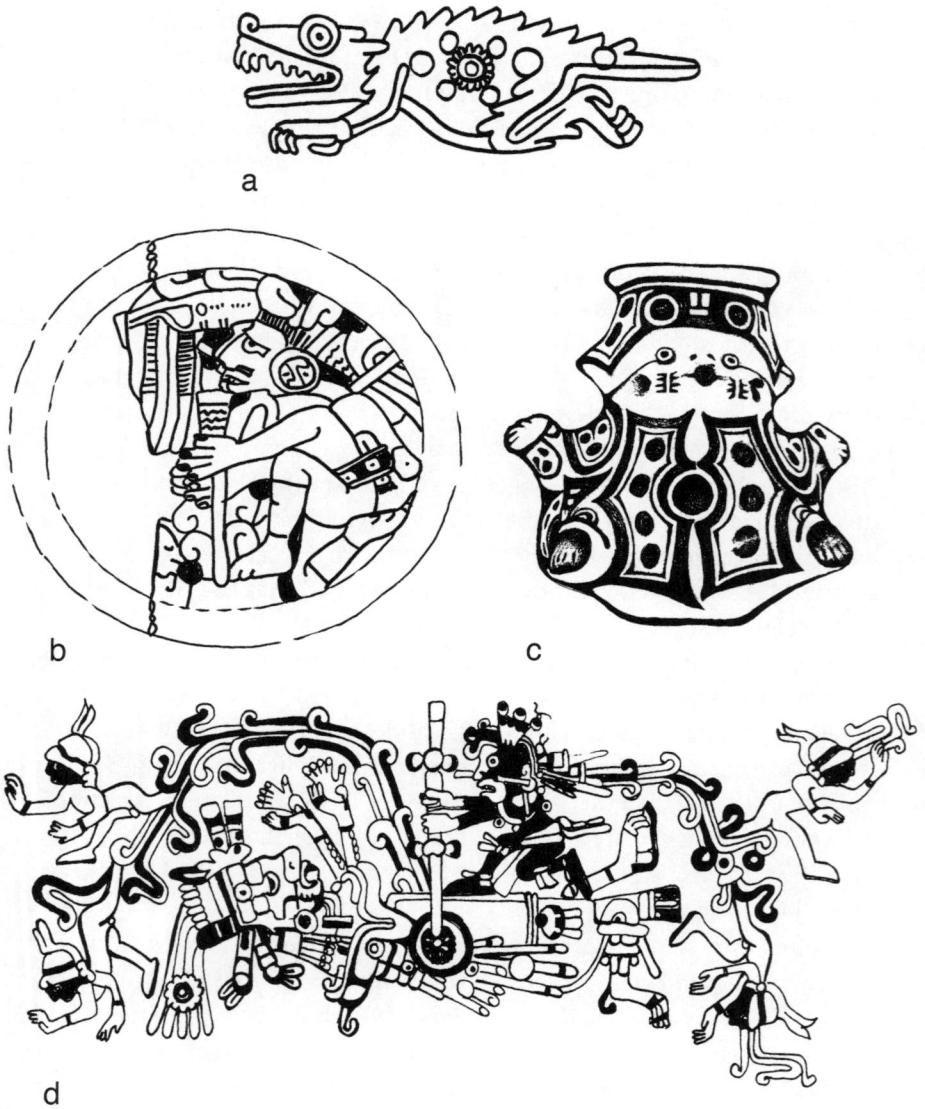

Figure 8.5. Fire drilling in Central Mexican and Huastec Art: *a,* saurian creature with drilled *chalchihuitl* marking, depicted in the Codex Laud, p. 2 (drawing by Ilona Faust); *b,* carved shell ear ornament depicting Mixcoatl drilling fire (drawing by Ilona Faust from Beyer 1934: 173–74); *c,* Huastec Black-on-White-style *soplador* vessel, Museo de la Cultura Huasteca, Tampico; *d,* fire drilling on the body of a sacrificed victim during investiture sequence in the Codex Borgia, p. 46 (drawing by Ilona Faust).

In a detailed study pertaining to mirror imagery at Teotihuacan, Karl Taube (1992: 184–87) has demonstrated that this drilled-hole motif is synonymous with shining or smoking mirrors in Central Mexican iconography. The relationship between the action of drilling and the smoking mirror is most explicitly represented in the persona of Tezcatlipoca, who is identifiable by his smoking mirror headdress and foot. Significantly, in the *Historia de los Mexicanos por sus pinturas* (Garibay 1973), Tezcatlipoca drilled fire directly on the body of the Earth Monster. This creature tore from Tezcatlipoca his foot, which the glinting mirror then replaced. The smoking mirror headdress of this god is often represented with a protruding flame or drill, possibly memorializing this act.

Smoking Mirror as Burning Hearth

As places of emergence and birth, mirrors conceptually overlap with the drilled hole in Mesoamerican thought, and the bright shining surface of these devices—associated with smoke and fire—is likewise emblematic of burning hearths and censers (Taube 1992: 184–85). On the backsides of ten of the figurines (figures 8.6a, 8.2a–f, 8.2h, 8.3b–d), swirling volutes emanate from circular disks, suggesting that they are indeed representations of smoking mirrors. This pattern is frequently repeated on Postclassic Huastec vessels as well (figures 8.6b–c).

Depicted as they are on the backside of the figurines, the disks are smoking representations of the *tezcacuitlapilli* back mirror, a common item of military and political regalia in ancient Mesoamerica. At the Postclassic Huastec site of El Consuelo (also known as Tamohi), a procession of finely attired figures is depicted on the side of the polychrome altar located in the central plaza. Several individuals wear the tezcacuitlapilli as part of a belt assemblage from which featherlike ornaments trail (Zaragoza Ocaña 2003b: figs. 10, 19). Variations of the mirror and drill-hole motif similarly adorn the backsides of anthropomorphic and zoomorphic Huastec containers, as well as nonrepresentational forms (figures 8.6d, 8.6f). Frequently appearing with segmented borders, the mirror motifs on many of the Huastec examples are particularly similar to the turquoise hearth in the Codex Borgia (figure 8.6g). Taube (1992: 187) has demonstrated that this device is synonymous with actual mosaic mirrors found in offertory contexts (figure 8.6e), which in turn, he notes, are examples of the tezcacuitlapilli carved on the backsides of the Atlantean warrior columns at Tula. Radiating from the face of the tezcacuitlapilli, the four Xiuhcoatl images represent emergent smoke and flame (Taube 1992: 172, 186).

Figure 8.6. Smoking mirror, *tezcacuitlapilli,* and burning hearth in Huastec and Aztec art: *a,* detail of smoking mirror on backside of figure 8.2e; *b,* bottom view of Huastec Black-on-White-style vessel from Pánuco (redrawn from C. Seler 1916: 110, fig. 20b); *c,* detail of smoking mirror on Huastec Black-on-White-style vessel, Museo de la Cultura Huasteca; *d,* polychrome stucco Huastec vessel, Museo de Antropología, Xalapa; *e,* schematic drawing of turquoise mirror from Temple of Chac Mool, Museo Nacional de Anthropología, Mexico City; *f,* front and back view of Huastec Black-on-White-style anthropomorphic vessel with *tezcacuitlapilli*-like fire drill emblem depicted on the back, Museo de Antropología, Xalapa (drawing by Ilona Faust); *g,* burning hearth, depicted in the Codex Borgia, p. 46 (drawing by Ilona Faust).

Figure 8.7. Representations of blades in Huastec art: *a,* bladelike motif in smoking mirror on backside of figure 8.2d; *b,* blade emerging from nasal cavity of a skeletal headdress (shell pectoral detail, drawing by Ilona Faust from Beyer 1934: 161, pl. 1); *c,* Huilocintla stela detail of *xiuhcoatl*-like creature with bladelike motifs as fiery scales.

The faces of the smoking mirrors depicted on the figurines differ from one another. While some are more difficult to make out, two are particularly compelling as representations of chalchihuitl emblems (figures 8.2d front view and 8.3d), while others resemble shell-, star-, or bladelike formations (figures 8.2b, 8.2d, 8.3b). If they are portrayals of the spiraling cross-section of conch, the *ehecacozcatl,* that is, the "spiral twisted wind jewel" of Quetzalcoatl Ehecatl (E. Seler [1902–23] 1990: iii: 284), these etchings imbue the design with sentiments of breeze and air while reinforcing the smoky context. On another figurine (figure 8.2c), the mirror is inscribed with a T-shaped design that recalls the glyph for the Maya term *ik,* meaning "wind," "air," or "breath," as does the Nahuatl term *ehecatl.* Surrounded by numerous punctured holes, this T-shaped motif in the center of the mirror may equally represent a drill or piercing device. The union of breath and drilling in acts of creation is apparent in the words of the Aztec midwife to the newborn infant when she says, "You were breathed into, you were drilled into" (López Austin 1988: 1: 208).

The serrated motif depicted on the backside of one of these examples (figures 8.2d, 8.7a) may likewise represent a sacrificial knife, as it closely recalls other Huastec depictions of blades, such as the projectile point emerging from the nasal cavity of the skeletal headdress engraved on a Huastec shell pectoral (figure 8.7b). The motif also resembles the bladelike flames or scales of the Xiuhcoatl-like figure depicted on the Huilocintla Monument (figure 8.7c). The profiles of these Huastec representations of blades are strikingly similar to the fire-butterfly wing motifs identified by Eduard Seler, the absence of inset disks being the primary distinction. The reference to blades on the backside of these small figurines may indicate the medium from which the mirror was hewn, possibly suggesting that it was conceptualized as obsidian or some other finely polished stone. Indeed, several of the mirror designs seem to emulate the mosaic-work of actual tezcacuitlapilli mirrors (figures 8.2e, 8.3c, 8.3e). However, if these motifs are intended to be read as blades inserted within the smoking mirrors, they may equally be indicative of fire or may imply that these little clay bodies are pierced and stabbed, thus underscoring the concept of sacrifice.

Fire Bundles

While the backsides are emblazoned with the smoking mirror, the frontal aspect of several of the figurines is adorned with a series of vertical lines that terminate in a band encircling the waist, below which circular droplet or disclike forms are discernable (figures 8.8a, 8.2a–b, 8.2e, 8.3b–e), recalling the drilled chalchihuitl design on the male fire drill figurine (figure 8.2g). These vertical markings, which seem to tightly bind the figurine bodies, may evoke the mortuary practice of bundling the deceased (figure 8.8b). But they can also be interpreted as bundles of sticks or reeds.

Like the drilling of fire, reed bundles were similarly important accouterments in calendric ceremonies and rites of investiture and as offerings in other ceremonial contexts. In Aztec New Fire ceremonies, reed bundles known as *xiuhmohpilli,* comprising fifty-two sticks to symbolize each of the fifty-two years of the cycle that had come to a close, were ceremonially burned (figure 8.8c). Crowned with butterfly-like flames, the bundles regurgitated from the flexed maws of the fire serpent on the Bilimek Pulque Vessel (figure 8.8d) recall the corsetlike motif on the figurines, which may thus be interpreted as personified parallels of the Late Postclassic Aztec xiuhmohpilli. The burning mirror emblems depicted on the backsides of the figurines reinforce the identification of sticks or bundles meant for burning, whereby they schematically resemble a sacrificial victim laid atop a kindling-filled brazier on Late Classic Piedras Negras Stela 11 (figure 8.8e).

On two of the figurines, the bundles terminate in arrowlike points (figures

a   b   c

 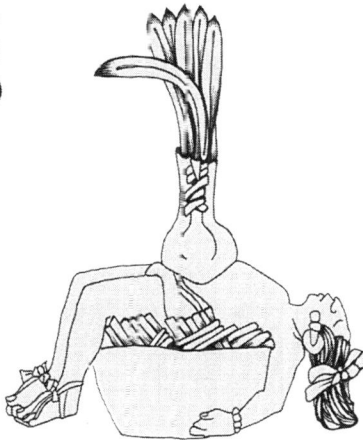 

d   e   f

Figure 8.8. Tampico-Pánuco figurines as mortuary and personified reed bundles: *a,* front view of articulated female figurine (figure 8.2e); *b,* body bundle, depicted in the Codex Madrid, p. 101; *c,* Aztec priest with *xiuhmonpilli* bundle during New Fire ceremony, depicted in the Codex Borbonicus, p. 34 (drawing by Ilona Faust); *d,* Xiuhcoatl depicted on the Bilimek Pulque Vessel (redrawn from E. Seler [1902–23] 1990: 4: 108, fig. 7a); *e,* sacrificial victim laid atop kindling-filled vessel, detail from Piedras Negras Stela 11 (redrawn from Schele and Miller 1986: 112, fig. 11.4); *f,* Huastec personage carrying reeds in Ochpaniztli *trecena* procession, depicted in the Codex Borbonicus, p. 30 (drawing by Ilona Faust).

8.2d, 8.2h). On figure 8.2d, the bundle folds across the left shoulder rather than the midsection. These reeds may reference arrows or darts, evoking an image of conflict, warfare, or autosacrifice. This convention also recalls the emblem for *malinalli* (grass or reeds), often associated with sacrifice and penitence. In the Codex Borbonicus, this concept of reeds and penitential bloodletting is implied in the depiction of the Ochpaniztli harvest festival in which Huastec impersonators with artificial phalli dance in procession while holding bundles of reeds (figure 8.8f), arguably intended for use in the staging of phallic blood sacrifice (Taube 1998: 4).

On the most intricately carved figurine from the set, smoke scrolls engulf what appear to be bundles of sticks jutting from the hips and rib cage. A symbol suggestive of a splash of water wraps from behind the right hip (figure 8.2f). Combining burning sticks and watery scrolls, the imagery on this figure is suggestive of the Aztec concept *atl-tlachinoli,* or warfare.

Obsidian Patterns and Personified Sacrificial Blades

As mentioned above, the Huastec symbol interpreted thus far as a wing-like flame can simultaneously be viewed as a sharp obsidian blade, another premier tool of sacrifice and penitence. In another study pertaining to the iconography of Huastec identity, Taube (1998: 3) has highlighted the Aztec tendency to depict the Huastec with obsidian designs on their bodies. He notes that as a prefix, the Nahuatl term *itztli-* describes obsidian-patterned objects and is often represented in Late Postclassic Central Mexican art as a series of triangles forming a serrated device (figure 8.9a). Although this identification may have been based on actual Huastec body-art designs in the form of the triangular itztli bands, Taube notes that the comparison may be based on Aztec interpretation of the butterfly wing–flame motif (figure 8.4c)—persistently depicted on Huastec anthropomorphic art—as indicative of obsidian. This interpretation builds upon, rather than refutes, the identification made by Eduard Seler, since butterfly wings, fire, and obsidian blades are conceptually related in Mesoamerican thought. As volcanic glass that is often smoky or black in color, obsidian is literally fire in its solidified state. Furthermore, flakes and blades made from this material are thought to be remnants of stars or comets in both historical and ethnographic references (Taube 2000: 299), and thus imbued with the essence of fire.

The unification of obsidian blades and butterflies is most plainly embodied in the Aztec deity Itzpapalotl, the Obsidian Butterfly. Another important obsidian-related deity of Late Postclassic Central Mexico often depicted in conjunction with the serrated itztli pattern is Itzlacoliuhqui-Ixquimilli (fig-

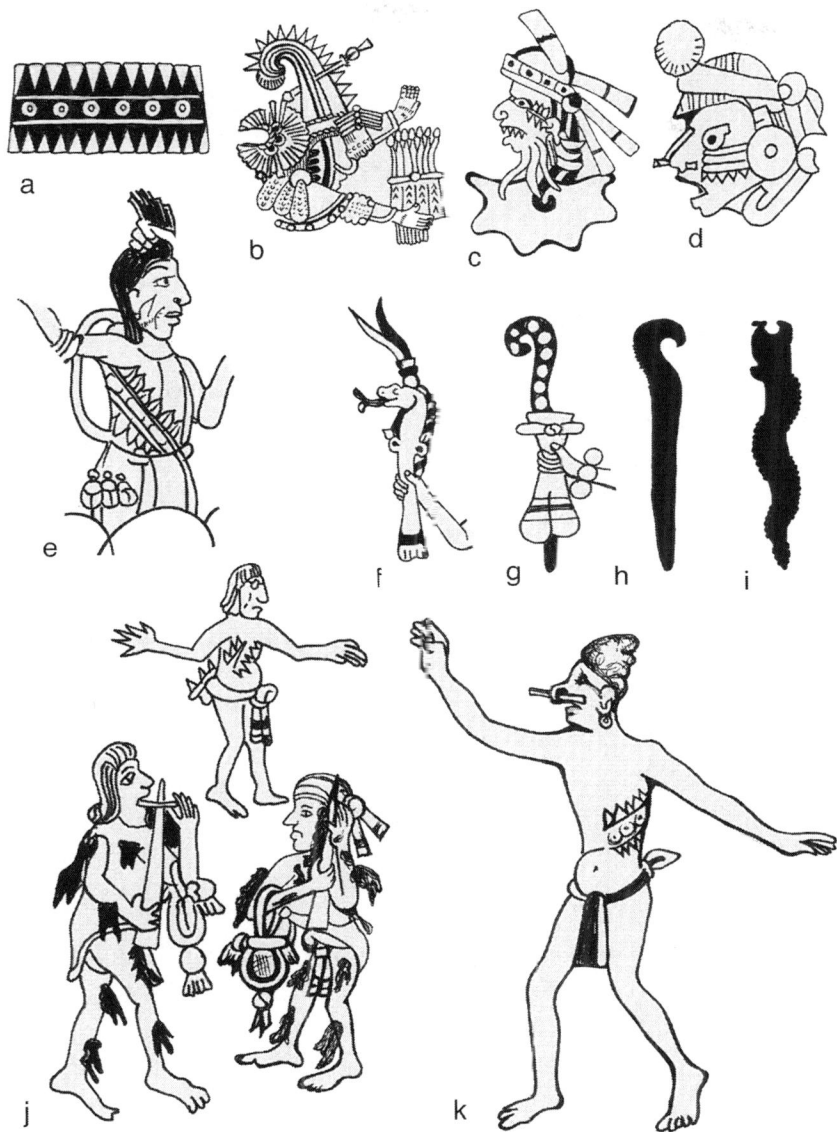

Figure 8.9. Obsidian patterns and the Huastec body: *a,* obsidian mat, depicted in the Codex Borgia, p. 45; *b,* Itzlacoliuhqui-Ixquimilli, depicted in the Codex Borbonicus, p. 12; *c,* gold ornament in the image of Huastec Quetzalcoatl, Codex Tepeucila (redrawn from Herrera Meza and Ruíz Medrano 1997: 21); *d,* detail of Huastec shell pectoral depicting warrior with obsidian-patterned cheek band (redrawn from Whittington 2001: 219); *e,* Huastec warrior, depicted in the Codex of Xicotepec, Section 10 (redrawn from Stresser-Péan 1995: 89); *f,* Xiuhcoatl weapon, depicted in the Codex Magliabechiano; *g,* curving blade weapon, depicted in the Codex Magliabechiano; *h,* curving obsidian scepter, Museo del Templo Mayor, Mexico City; *i,* obsidian blade in the form of a serpent, Museo del Templo Mayor, Mexico City; *j,* bloodletting and penitence scene, Codex Magliabechiano; *k,* dancing Huastec figure, depicted in the Florentine Codex, bk. 9: 50 (all drawings by Ilona Faust).

ure 8.9b). One of the diagnostic traits of this being is a curved headdress, often edged with obsidian spikes. Literally perceived as a personification of obsidian blades, Itzlacoliuhqui was closely related to warrior festivities and penitential bloodletting (Miller and Taube 1993: 100). Furthermore, this deity is consistently depicted with emblems associated with Huastec identity as perceived by the Aztec. These include the *yacameztli* lunar nose ornament, characteristic facial painting, and cotton garments (Taube 1998: 4). In the Codex Borbonicus, Itzlacoliuhqui is depicted holding a bundle of reeds, as are the Huastec personages engaged in the dramatization of phallic autosacrifice. The Borbonicus portrayal of Huastec with tall pointed caps may indicate that they were performing as personified blades (Taube 1998: 3).

Like deities, mythological creatures are also depicted as zoomorphic representations of blades. The Xiuhcoatl is a Late Postclassic serpentine creature of fire frequently appearing in contexts of sacrifice and warfare. In Aztec codices, deities are often depicted wielding a turquoise serpent weapon, similarly referred to as Xiuhcoatl (figure 8.9f). Another variation of this weapon appears as a curving black blade—perhaps of obsidian—with glistening facets rendered as shining stars (figure 8.9g). Curving obsidian blades that recall these devices were cached in large quantities at the Aztec Templo Mayor, as were eccentric blades hewn into serpentine forms (figures 8.9h–i). Sometimes these obsidian serpent blades are so slender and delicate, the most plausible use is careful sacrificial bloodletting.

Obsidian Serpent Blades on the Huastec Body

In the Florentine Codex, Bernardino de Sahagún (1950–69: bk. 9: 73) writes about the craft specialists who fashioned molds for casting metals. An image of a "dancing" Huastec (figure 8.9k) with a prominent tattoo across his side is paired with the following text: "[If] a good likeness of an animal, was started, [the core] was carved to correspond to the likeness, the form in nature [that] it imitated, so that from it would issue [in metal] whatsoever it was desired to make—perhaps a Huaxtec, perhaps a stranger, one with a pierced, perforated nose, an arrow across the face, painted [tattooed] upon the body with obsidian serpents."

The tattoolike path on the hip of the articulated male figurine (figure 8.2g) is reminiscent of the *itztli* obsidian serpent pattern on the waist of the dancing Huastec in the Florentine Codex and across the chest of the captive Huastec warrior depicted in the Codex of Xicotepec (figure 8.9e). The same pattern appears on a portrayal of Quetzalcoatl—rendered as a

Huastec being—in the Codex Tepeucila (figure 8.9c) (Taube 1998: 4). In the Tepeucila image, the serrated band stretches from the outer edge of the eye to the top of the ear, likely representing scarification. A similar eye slash (albeit without the serrated edge) is present on the Florentine Huastec figure and is common on Huastec sculptures and effigy vessels. The serrated slash marks may equally reference the scar as well as the object and practice that created it. If the "obsidian serpents" mentioned by Sahagún are literally envisioned as blades, then the motif, as represented on the body, may refer to the "path" or "bite" of the obsidian serpent—that is, to laceration as penitential offering. In a graphically depicted bloodletting scene in the Codex Magliabechiano, a figure with this telltale serrated mark on his chest is depicted in the company of two other blood-drenched individuals who pierce their tongues and ears with sharp maguey thorns (figure 8.9j). Conspicuously free of blood, the figure standing with open arms displaying the itztli pattern on his chest may bear the scars of past penitential rites.

In addition to the Aztec association of itztli patterns with Huastec identity, at least some members of Huastec society may have had a similar idea, as renditions of the itztli obsidian serpent motif appear in Huastec art. For example, the serrated pattern marks the cheek of a Huastec warrior depicted on a shell pectoral (figure 8.9d). Although the style of the pectoral suggests that it dates to the Postclassic period, *chapopote* designs on many Classic period figurines recall the itztli bands, possibly implying that this manner of personal adornment was indeed Huastec in origin, regardless of whether it embodied the same symbolic meaning among the Huastec as it did among the Aztec.

Heart Sacrifice and Body Partition

A small cross-shaped incision is depicted on several of the figurines, possibly indicating heart extraction (figures 8.2e, 8.3c, 8.3e). Noting the presence of this pattern on many of the vessels and pottery fragments collected in the Huasteca, and in light of the fire drilling symbolism identified by Eduard Seler, Caecilie Seler (1916: 112) suggested that this design may reference crossed fire-drilling sticks. But the emblem may also represent the Kan cross, indexing fire, heat, centrality (Taube 2000: 313), and more precisely the sun as the recipient of sacrificed hearts.

While the limbs of several figurines terminate in abbreviated stubs—some marked with scratches possibly indicating fingers—the other four are torsos of articulated figures. Such figurines are relatively rare in Mesoamerica, and the significance of articulation is poorly understood. One obvious feature of articulation is that it allows for manipulation, movement, and performance; thus, figurines with moveable appendages are frequently interpreted as toys. However, given the facility with which articulated limbs can be repeatedly separated from and reattached to the balance of the body, the extremities may have been meant to be "ceremonially severed" or detached.

The Aztec Coyolxauhqui monument represents an incident of sacrifice and body partition writ large in Late Postclassic Mesoamerican art (figure 8.10a). Although on a much grander scale, the dismembered body of Coyolxauhqui is strikingly similar in manner of depiction and content to the Huastec figurines. The ragged flesh where Coyolxauhqui's arms and thighs are torn can be compared with the truncated bodies and especially to the droplets and incised lines—possibly blood scrolls—depicted on the extremities of one figurine (figure 8.2b). On two examples in the Berlin collection, the area below the waist is repeatedly marked with smoking swirls, implying that drilling or sacrifice has taken place all over these small bodies (figures 8.3b, 8.3d, 8.2g). This idea is even more graphically depicted on one of the Tampico-Pánuco New Fire figurines (figure 8.2c). On this object, T-shaped piercing devices cover the lower body alongside the punctured holes. In the Nahuatl language, *nepoztecya* signifies "joints" or "moving places" of the body, as well as "our breaking places" (López Austin 1996: 176). The limbs are termed *nepalehuiya,* meaning "our helping places" (López Austin 1996: 175). An individual's extremities are indices of personal ability and effectiveness to move and accomplish things. In this sense, partition alludes to the deletion of agency. But because sacrifice and death are inextricably linked with creation, partition may simultaneously embody spreading and regeneration of agency.

As mentioned before, almost all of the heads have been broken from the figurine bodies. In the few instances in which they remain intact, faces are stylized, and pursed lips (or a pinhole mouth) are the predominant feature. This characteristic expression frequently appears on zoomorphic or anthropomorphic Huastec vessels referred to as *sopladores* (blowers), which are often associated with the wind deity Ehecatl. The handle and spout on one example are modeled to suggest upturned arms, whereby the figure assumes the hocker position, a fetal pose simultaneously signifying the body birthing and as bound in death (figure 8.6f). On the figurines, this facial pose seems to equate the exhalation of breath with the onset of death, recalling the countenance of the suspended trophy heads depicted, for ex-

a

b

Figure 8.10. Sacrifice and body partition in Aztec art: *a*, Coyolxauhqui monument, Museo del Templo Mayor, Mexico City; *b*, sacrificial piercing of the joints of Yohualtecuhtli, depicted in the Codex Borgia, p. 40 (drawing by Ilona Faust from Séjourné 1962: 117, fig. 140).

ample, on Yaxchilan Lintel 9.[6] As a final index of sacrifice and death, one of the figures (figure 8.2h) was rubbed with red pigment (possibly cinnabar or hematite) in emulation of the practice of dusting the deceased human body with such substances in preparation for interment.

In summation, the figurines are inscribed with symbols rich in metaphorical value pertaining to primordial creation, calendric ceremonies, and even rites of passage in Mesoamerican art. At all of these events, blood sacrifice and fire rituals were integral to instating new chapters of cosmological, social, and personal histories. But what is the meaning of marking the body with such motifs, and how might the figurines have been used, in light of ethnohistorical and ethnographic data?

The Aesthetic of the Penitent Body

The manner in which the physical being is adorned and presented in society is central to the reproduction of social identity. Similarly, depictions of the idealized aesthetic body affirm cultural understandings of self. Personal modifications and artistic representations of such treatments are intimately connected to the indigenous theory of the external and internal body. In this schema, the inflictive technique of modification is culturally meaningful, and the placement of motifs is an important factor in understanding significance (Gell 1993: 18, 35).

As the boundary between the external world and the inner being, the skin is the container of one's essential self. By breaching the skin, the "procreative" act of tattooing exteriorizes the interior while simultaneously interiorizing the exterior (Gell 1993: 29–39). In other words, tattooing or scarification expels blood and results in the internalization of a motif as a registration of the event. Given the emphasis on bloodletting and autosacrifice in the Huasteca and throughout Mesoamerica in general, a tattooed or otherwise branded body would memorialize the incidence of such sacrificial acts. At the same time, markings made on the body can also communicate cultural ideas regarding the internal state to the external world. In many tattooing societies, muscles, organs, bones, and other physiologically and culturally significant, spiritual interior parts are represented on the skin via specific motifs and the manner in which they are arranged on the external body (Gell 1993).

Tools of Sacrifice and the Meaning of Location

Jesse Walter Fewkes (1906: 636–37) wrote the following about the symbols adorning the body of the central figure depicted on the Huilocintla Stela (figure 8.1):

> [C]oncerning the decorations on the legs and arms of the priest. It is not clear . . . whether these ornamentations should be regarded as body painting or tattooing, but they are probably intended for one or the other rather than for clothing. The designs represented are not especially noteworthy, but it is interesting to observe that circular figures and dots appear at the joints and elbow, and that these are repeated at the waist, knees, and ankles as well as the wrists. In other words, wherever there are joints, circles are represented. This may be a symbolic way of depicting the articulations at these places.

The disks on the ankles, knees, and wrists of the Huilocintla actor that Fewkes comments on are clearly representations of the chalchihuitl, or mirrorlike drill hole (accompanied by the drill itself), and of the winglike flame or blade motif. The image of the drill similarly resembles depictions of maguey thorns—other preferred bloodletting tools—thus symbolically linking the sacrificial actions of drilling and blood sacrifice, which create and release heat, vitality, and soul from the body as an offering to the gods.

The symbolism on the Huilocintla figure is even more meaningful in consideration of ancient and contemporary Mesoamerican beliefs that the soul resides within the joints of the body. For example, Guido Münch Galindo (1983: 201) notes that the Veracruz Nahua from the community of Mecayapan consider the pulse felt at the joints to be the "hearts of the spirit" (Furst 1995: 130). This belief explains, in part, the complex systems of "pulsing" employed by native healers to gauge health and illness of their patients. The strength or weakness of the pulse is measured at the hands, wrists, arms, temples, neck, chest, and waist (Furst 1995: 129–30). A pulse felt at the elbow (but not the wrist) indicates that a patient is very sick. In this circumstance, the Potosino Teenek informants of Janice Alcorn (1984: 230) emphasize, "The soul is not present at the wrist." Furthermore, colonial sources tell us that sorcerers would often focus supernatural attacks on the joints of intended victims for the aforementioned reasons (López Austin 1988: 1: 132).

Sacrificial piercing is commonly centered on the joints of deities in Post-classic Mesoamerican art. In the Codex Borgia, for example, the splayed image of Yohualtecuhtli is assaulted at these vital points, from which small, personified hearts (as manifestations of the soul) are extracted (figure 8.10b). The body ideology disclosed in this imagery is reflected in language. The Nahuatl term *tilahua*, for example, refers to the thickness or thinness of flesh and is often used to reference places where the skin is thin, comparable to paper or a tortilla. Examples include the earlobe and tongue but also the areas where bones lie close to the surface of the body, including the wrists, ankles, and knees (López Austin 1996: 85). As pulse points and areas where the skin is thin and veins plainly visible, the regions around the joints are indeed ideal locations for bloodletting.

On the tattooed individual depicted on the Huilocintla Stela, frequently identified as a Quetzalcoatl priest (Fewkes 1906: 638–39; E. Seler [1902–1923] 1993: iv: 284), the positioning of the designs implies that sacrifice occurs all over the body, in a manner recalling the bleeding penitents depicted in the Codex Magliabechiano (figure 8.9j), who likewise perforate their tongues. Furthermore, as symbols that reference fire drills and other piercing implements, the statement being made is that the skin is drilled or otherwise breached at the location of the joints—the loci of movement— where the soul is most concentrated. Although many examples of Huastec art (such as the Tampico-Pánuco figurines) lack accompanying narrative frames (the Huilocintla Stela being a notable exception), the events, conditions, and contexts periodically surrounding the body are made implicit via the cutting and piercing implements. As tattoos or other corporeal modifications, tools of sacrifice and creation manifest directly on the canvas of the skin—literally pervade it—thus implying a perpetual penitential mode and a permanent visual record of the Huastec ontology of the body and soul.

Discussion

One of the aims of the present volume is to explore the myriad ways in which figurines are instrumental to our understandings of society, ideology, and identity in the pre-Columbian world. This chapter represents one case study wherein a basic quality of figurines, namely their small size, is key in the concomitant agenda to make some propositions regarding the semiotic meanings conveyed in Huastec iconography. As anthropomorphic representations inscribed with "essential" symbols, the New Fire figurines are central to understanding the relationships between iconographic motifs and the human body as understood by the Late Postclassic Huastec.

On the living human body, as on figurines, vessels, and sculptures, visually poetic metaphors abound regarding the treatment of the body and other meritorious media. For example, on a previously mentioned ear ornament, primordial creation is indexed by the fire-drilling Mixcoatl (figure 8.5b). This image is inscribed on an object similarly created through the act of drilling and meant for display in a perforated, plied earlobe.

As points of penetration, fiery drill holes can equally be conceived as precious blood and shining mirrors; fiery butterfly wings, as animate obsidian blades. These and other allegorical motifs including drills, thorns, and reed bundles, bound as they were to the body and its representations, underscore an ideology in which the environment pervades the body just as people inhabit their environment. More than simple designs, location-specific body motifs likely serve as ever-present reminders of the aesthetic and creative value of penitence and sacrifice in ancient Huastec society, central to transformation and the continuity of time, cosmos, and social life. Thus, while the style of Late Postclassic Huastec art is highly distinctive, thematic content echoes religious and ideological beliefs shared on a pan-Mesoamerican scale during and prior to this time.

Acknowledgments

This research was made possible by funding provided by the Foundation for the Advancement of Mesoamerican Studies, Inc. (FAMSI), Research Grant No. 06087 and by the University of California–Riverside. Special thanks are due to these institutions and to the Faust and Erickson families, without whose support this study would not have been possible. The Instituto Nacional de Antropología e Historia (INAH) kindly granted permission to work with archaeological materials in Mexico. I am grateful to this institution, as I am to Sara Ladrón de Guevara, director of the Museo de Antropología, Xalapa; Alejandrina Elias Ortíz, director of the Museo de la Cultura Huasteca, Tampico; and their staff, who generously facilitated my review of Huastec materials in these fine museums. I am indebted to Karl Taube and Wendy Ashmore for their critical insights, guidance, and support in my investigations of Huastec art and society and for their feedback on the research presented herein. Karl Taube generously shared with me unpublished material pertaining to Huastec iconography and ethnicity, for which I am very grateful. I also wish to thank Christina Halperin, Chelsea Blackmore, Kim Richter, Sophie Marchegay, Manetta Braunstein, Andy Faust III, Elizabath Faust, Joel Palka, and an anonymous reviewer for their constructive comments pertaining to this study. All errors and oversights are my own.

Notes

1. Used in historical and ethnographic literature to refer to a cultural group as well as a geographical area, the term "Huastec" also denotes a very distinctive style of art that emerged in this northeastern Gulf Coast region during the Postclassic period (Merino Carrión and García Cook 1987: 62–65). In this chapter, I use the term "Huastec" to simultaneously reference this artistic style and the ancient people (most likely of Tenek ethnicity) who were responsible for its development. For a brief discussion of the confusion that can arise as a result of the vague definition of the term "Huastec" in historical scholarship, see Alcorn 1984: 10–12.

2. Iconography adorning Huastec Black-on-White and Tancol Polychrome ceramic wares manifested rather suddenly as a seemingly unprecedented yet fully developed artistic tradition (Ekholm 1944: 364). To date, the origin and developmental trajectory of the characteristic Huastec iconographic style is still to be accounted for, although scholars suggest an immediately southerly or southwesterly possibility (see, for example, Merino Carrión and García Cook 1987: 61).

3. While a full exploration of the relationship between the inscribed figurines examined herein and other Huastec clay figures lies beyond the scope of this chapter, these examples share similar body morphology, facial features, and diacritic ornamentations such as necklaces and chest incisions with other Huastec figurines I investigated in the Museo de Antropología, Xalapa, in the Museo de la Cultura Huasteca, Tampico, and in the Museo Regional, Ciudad Valles.

4. The metaphorical value of fire drilling and the sexual act of procreation is a common belief among indigenous peoples of Mexico and includes the drilling of the earth for sowing seed. For more on the metaphorical value of drilling and creation, see Furst 1995: 64–66 and Taube 2000.

5. According to William Ringle (2004: 197), political rites of investiture and the foundations of new centers and dynasties in Epiclassic and Postclassic Mesoamerica were intimately linked with an ideology of rulership founded on the authority of Quetzalcoatl. Kim Richter (2004) has convincingly argued that centers in the Huasteca participated in this cult as well and specifically highlights the role of body modification in this paradigm.

6. I am thankful to Christina Halperin for calling to my attention the similar pursed-lip quality shared by the Huastec vessels and figures and Maya depictions of decapitated trophy heads.

References Cited

Alcorn, Janice. 1984. *Huastec Mayan Ethnobotany.* University of Texas Press, Austin.

Bailey, Douglass W. 2005. *Prehistoric Figurines: Representation and Corporeality in the Neolithic.* New York, Routledge.

Berdan, Frances F. 1982. *The Aztecs of Central Mexico: An Imperial Society.* Holt, Rinehart and Winston, New York.

Beyer, Hermann. 1934. *Shell Ornament Sets from the Huasteca, Mexico.* Middle American Research Institute, New Orleans.

Castro-Leal, Marcia. 1979. La colección huaxteca de esculturas de piedra del Museo Nacional de Antropología de México: Un ensayo de interpretación. In *Actes du XLIIe Congres,* vol. 9b, 57–66. Société des Américanistes, Paris.

———. 1989. La Lapida de Tepetzintla, Veracruz: Un ejemplo de iconografía en la escultura huaxteca. In *Enquêtes sur l'Amérique moyenne: Mélanges offerts à Guy Stresser-Péan,* vol. 16, ed. D. Michelet, 69–80. Etudes Mésoaméricaines, Mexico City.

Codex Borbonicus. 1974. Facsimile, ed. K. A. Nowotny and J. de Durand-Forest. Akademische Druck- und Verlagsanstalt, Graz.

Codex Borgia. 1976. Facsimile, ed. K. A. Nowotny and J. de Durand-Forest. Akademische Druck- und Verlagsanstalt, Graz.

Codex Laud. 1966. Facsimile, ed. C. A. Burland. Akademische Druck- und Verlagsanstalt, Graz.

Codex Magliabechiano. 1983. Facsimile, ed. Z. Nuttall. University of California, Berkeley.

Durán, Diego. 1964. *The Aztecs: A History of the Indies of New Spain.* Ed. D. Heyden and F. Horcasitas. Orion Press, New York.

Du Solier, Wilfrido. 1950. *La plástica en las cabecitas arcaicas del Valle de México y la Huaxteca.* Ediciones Mexicanas, Mexico City.

Ekholm, Gordon F. 1944. *Excavations at Tampico and Panuco in the Huasteca, Mexico.* Anthropological Papers of the American Museum of Natural History, vol. 37, no. 5, 319–512. New York.

Fewkes, Walter J. 1906. An Ancient Megalith in Jalapa, Veracruz. *American Anthropologist* 8 (4): 633–39.

Fuente, Beatriz de la. 1980. Main Subjects in Huastec Sculpture. In *Fourth Palenque Round Table,* ed. E. P. Benson, 303–12. Pre-Columbian Art Research Institute, San Francisco.

Fuente, Beatriz de la, and Nelly Gutierrez Solana. 1980. Escultura huasteca en piedra: Catalogo. Cuadernos del Historia del Arte 9. Instituto de Investigaciones Estéticas, Universidad Nacional Autónoma de México, Mexico City.

Furst, Jill Leslie M. 1995. *The Natural History of the Soul in Ancient Mesoamerica.* Yale University Press, New Haven, Conn.

García Icazbalceta, Joaquín. 1941. *La historia de los Mexicanos por sus pinturas.* Nueva Colección de Documentos para la Historia de México, vol. 3. Chávez Hayhoe, Mexico City.

Garibay, Ángel María K. 1973. *Teogonía e historia de los Mexicanos: Tres opúsculos del siglo XVI.* Editorial Porrúa, Mexico City.

Gell, Alfred. 1993. *Wrapping in Images: Tattooing in Polynesia.* Oxford University Press, Oxford.

———. 1998. *Art and Agency: An Anthropological Theory.* Oxford, Oxford University Press.

Herrera Meza, María del Carmen, and Ethelia Ruiz Medrano. 1997. *El Códice de Tepeucila: El entintado mundo de la fijeza imaginaria.* Instituto Nacional de Antropología e Historia, Mexico City.

Koontz, Rex Ashley. 1994. *The Iconography of El Tajín, Veracruz, Mexico.* Ph.D. diss., Department of Art History, University of Texas, Austin. University Microfilms International, Ann Arbor, Mich.

López Austin, Alfredo. 1988. *The Human Body and Ideology: Concepts of the Ancient Nahuas.* 2 vols. University of Utah Press, Salt Lake City.

———. 1996. *Cuerpo humano e ideología: Las concepciones de los antiguos Nahuas, México,* vol. 2. Universidad Nacional Autónoma de México, Mexico City.

Meade, Joaquín. 1942. *La Huasteca, época antigua.* Editorial Cossio, Mexico City.

———. 1982. *El Adolescente: Escultura huasteca—una interpretación.* Universidad Autónoma de Tamaulipas, Ciudad Victoria.

Merino Carrión, B. Leonor, and Ángel García Cook. 1987. Proyecto Arqueológico Huaxteca. *Arqueología* 1: 31–72.

Miller, Mary, and Karl Taube. 1993. *An Illustrated Dictionary of the Gods and Symbols of Ancient Mexico and the Maya.* Thames and Hudson, London.

Montgomery, John. 2002. *Dictionary of Maya Hieroglyphs.* Hippocrene Books, New York.

Münch Galindo, Guido. 1983. *Etnología del Istmo Veracruzano.* Serie Antropológica 50. Universidad Nacional Autónoma de México, Mexico City.

Nuttall, Zelia. 1888. *Penitential Rite of the Ancient Mexicans.* Peabody Museum of American Archaeology and Ethnology, vol. 1, no. 1, 439–62. Harvard University Press, Cambridge.

Ochoa, Lorenzo. 1991. Tres esculturas postclásicas del sur de la Huaxteca. *Anales de Antropología* 28: 205–40.

Ochoa, Lorenzo, and Gerardo Gutiérrez. 1996–99. Notas en torno a la cosmovisión y religión de los Huaxtecos. *Anales de Antropología* 33: 91–163.

Richter, Kim Nicole. 2004. The Meaning and Function of Incised Skin Motifs on Epiclassic/Early Postclassic Huastec Sculpture. M.A. thesis, Department of Art History, University of California, Los Angeles.

Ringle, William M. 2004. On the Political Organization of Chichén Itzá. *Ancient Mesoamerica* 15: 167–218.

Sahagún, Fray Bernardino de. 1959 and 1961. *General History of the Things of New Spain: Florentine Codex. Book 9—The Merchants,* and *Book 10—The People.* Ed. A. J. O. Anderson and C. E. Dibble. School of American Research, Santa Fe, N.Mex.; University of Utah Press, Salt Late City.

Saville, Marshall H. 1900. A Shell Gorget from the Huasteca. *Bulletin of the American Museum of Natural History* 13: 99–103.

Schele, Linda, and Mary Ellen Miller. 1986. *The Blood of Kings: Dynasty and Ritual in Maya Art.* Kimbell Art Museum, Fort Worth, Texas; G. Braziller, New York.

Séjourné, Laurette. 1962. El universo de Quetzalcóatl. Fondo de Cultura Económica, Mexico City.

Seler, Caecilie. 1916. *Die Huaxteca-Sammlung: Des KGL Museums für Völkerkunde zu Berlin.* Druck- und Verlag von B. G. Teubner, Leipzig.

Seler, Eduard. [1902–23] 1990–98. *Collected Works in Mesoamerican Linguistics and Archaeology.* 6 vols. Ed. J. E. S. Thompson and F. B. Richardson. Labyrinthos Press, Culver City, Calif.

Sugiyama, Saburo. 2002. Censer Symbolism and the State Polity in Teotihuacán. Foundation for the Advancement of Mesoamerican Studies, http://famsi.org/reports/97050.

Taube, Karl. 1992. The Iconography of Mirrors at Teotihuacán. In *Art, Ideology, and the City of Teotihuacán,* ed. J. C. Berlo, 169–204. Dumbarton Oaks, Washington, D.C.

———. 1998. Unpublished manuscript on theme of Maya and Central Mexican penitential blood sacrifice. In possession of author.

———. 2000. The Turquoise Hearth: Fire, Self Sacrifice, and the Central Mexican Cult of War. In *Mesoamerica's Classic Heritage: From Teotihuacán to the Aztecs,* ed. D. Carrasco, L. Jones, and S. Sessions, 269–340. University Press of Colorado, Boulder.

Trejo, Silvia. 1989. *Escultura huaxteca de Río Tamuín: Figuras masculinas.* Universidad Nacional Autónoma de México, Mexico City.

———. 2004. El Adolescente huaxteca de Río Tamuin. *Arqueología Mexicana* 12 (67): 62–65.

Turner, Terrence. 1980. The Social Skin. In *Not Work Alone: A Cross-Cultural View of Activities Superfluous to Survival,* ed. J. Cherfas and R. Lewin, 112–40. Temple Smith, Beverly Hills, Calif.

Villacorta C., J. Antonio, and Flavio N. Rodas. 1927. *Manuscrito de Chichicastenango (Popol Buj).* Sánchez and de Guise, Guatemala.

Whittington, Michael E. 2001. *The Sport of Life and Death: The Mesoamerican Ballgame.* Thames and Hudson, Charlotte, N.C.

Wilkerson, S. Jeffrey K. 1972. Ethnogenesis of the Huastecs and the Totonacs: Early Cultures of North-Central Veracruz at Santa Luisa, Mexico. Ph.D. diss., Department of Anthropology, Tulane University. University Microfilms, Ann Arbor, Mich.

Zaragoza Ocaña, Diana. 1999. Un excéntrico pectoral de concha de la huasteca potosina. *Arqueología* 21: 137–44.

———. 2003a. Algunas consideraciones sobre la cerámica huasteca negro sobre blanco. *Arqueología* 29: 125–40.

———. 2003b. *Tamohi: Su pintura mural.* Gobierno del Estado de Tamaulipas, Mexico City.

9

The Beautiful, the Bad, and the Ugly

Aesthetics and Morality in Maya Figurines

RHONDA TAUBE AND KARL TAUBE

Beautiful and ugly depend on principles of taste. For European philoso-
phers, such as Immanuel Kant, aesthetics—the philosophy of the beautiful—denotes a branch of metaphysics, which contains the laws of refined
taste as perceived through the visual. This appraisal of things visually pleasing has a striking parallel in Classic period Maya notions of the beautiful in
art. The Maya concept of aesthetics bears a great deal of relevance for the
interpretation of ancient Maya figurines. Employing a visual paradigm, one
that involves gazing at small-scale works of art, is a particularly apt method
for exploring Maya notions of representation. In K'iche', the verb "to look"
or "to see," *ilik*, also carries the significance "to enjoy" or "to like." In K'iche',
it is assumed that if you like something you look at it, and looking implies
pleasure. Evon Vogt (1976: 205) discusses a similar concept among the
Tzotzil Maya of Zinacantan. To look at something implies a whole range of
associated meanings and ideas of understanding. For the Zinacantecos, the
act of looking is a validating act. There is striking evidence that these types
of concepts are not only widespread but also very ancient. Stephen Houston
and Karl Taube (2000: 261, 281–89) discuss sight as a tangible phenomenon
among the Pre-Classic Maya. Through an investigation of monumental art
and hieroglyphics, they demonstrate the procreative aspects of the eye: "It
not only receives images from the outer world, but positively affects and
changes that world through the power of sight" (Houston and Taube 2000:
281). The Maya "gaze" was, and remains today, a concrete experience.

Maya aesthetics implies not only looking but also viewing pleasing imagery. Among the Classic Maya, the corporeal being of the ruler was the most
notable expression of the physical ideal. Perfect comportment of nobility
was expressed in flawless beauty, as well as youthfulness, physical vigor, fit-
ness, elegant gestures, and control. Although texts frequently indicate that

kings are old, kings are invariably portrayed as still youthful, in their prime, as in the art of ancient Egypt. The deities of life, wealth, and sustenance, such as the Maize God and the comely god of breath and wind reflect these same qualities (K. Taube 1985, 2004a). Courtly codes of conduct reflect these very divine traits, as seen in numerous works of monumental art and public performances. Monuments commemorating specific performative events in the lives of the rulers show them in a relatively static position of dance, often indicated by no more than a raised foot or lifted arm. In addition, laughter, folly, jest, and the comic are opposed to the gravitas of the ruler and nobility. However, joking and humorous play constitute a performative genre that often depends on nonverbal modes of behavior, which includes many ritual forms, such as clowning, jesting, and parody.

We follow Linda Hutcheon's (2000) distinction of the differences between parody and satire. Parody is not simply intended to ridicule but is also a form of imitation. Parody implies critical distance and ironic commentary often situating itself within recognized intertextualities. Parody is not satire. Societies rationally direct satire toward amelioration of social vices and folly. Codes of parody do not function merely as an isolated hermeneutic device but are mediated by the society's entire discursive practices. For Hutcheon, parody is a way to claim continuity with the past and stand at ironical distance from it, even while societies use parody to restructure their communal identity. As Hutcheon (2000: 2) notes, a study of parody can indicate how subjects interact with their own society with both cultural and ideological implications.

Because of the extensive distribution of figurines, they constitute one art form that intersects between the royalty and "commoners." Whereas monumental art and accompanying hieroglyphic inscriptions mark the public sphere, figurines extend beyond this realm to the private household, visually separating two divisions that differ widely from one another (Joyce 1992). Monumental art expresses the nature of political and religious life; figurines capture the daily concerns of wider society. Unlike large-scale sculpture, figurines are portable, small objects that one can hold and view from all angles. In addition, they portray aspects of ancient Maya life rarely seen in monumental art, such as genre scenes and ritual clowning (Joyce 1992, 1993; K. Taube 1989). Aside from such physical traits as agedness and zoomorphic features, Classic Maya ritual clowns are often dancers and hold accouterments of dance and performance, such as rattles or fans (figure 9.1). Because of the many themes absent from elite monuments, figurines can be viewed as a "mass" media and are demonstrative of an active popu-

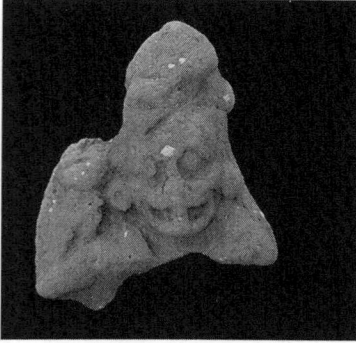

a   b

c

Figure 9.1. Late Classic Maya figurine portrayals of ritual clowns: *a,* aged clown holding dance rattle from Piedras Negras (photo by Rhonda Taube, reproduced courtesy of Piedras Negras Archaeological Project, directed by Stephen Houston and Hector Escobedo); *b,* seated female figurine holding dance fan (photo by Rhonda Taube, reproduced courtesy of Piedras Negras Archaeological Project, directed by Stephen Houston and Hector Escobedo); *c,* dancing corpulent clown (courtesy of the Marjorie Barrick Museum of Natural History, University of Nevada, Las Vegas).

lar culture among the ancient Maya. They are, in several ways, similar to sixteenth-century Netherlandish prints that circulated widely among commoner households and featured a minging of mythological, religious, and secular scenarios: "Compared to the elitism of more traditional forms of art, the print medium offered a portable format that was not only accessible to wider audiences, but gave the freedom to illustrate everyday anxieties and fears" (Nurse 1998: 42). Although many were fashioned after the masters, many others featured portraits of locally celebrated individuals and themes that did not usually make their way into monumental art forms, such as Gonnella, the sixteenth-century domestic jester of the Duke of Ferrara.

Exceptionally popular were satires portraying episodes of folly, such as ill-matched lovers, one of which captures a young beauty contrasted with a grotesque and elderly man who fondles her breast (figure 9.2). Throughout Germany and other areas of the Northern Renaissance, a well-liked and often portrayed theme was the woman as femme fatale, either a temptress or a harridan. Appearing in many comic episodes, she openly misbehaves and tarnishes her counterpart's reputation One spirited example is the story of

a

b

Figure 9.2. The unequal lover scenes in northern European Renaissance art: *a, The Dissimilar Couple,* by Israhel van Meckenem, c. 1495–1503 (courtesy of the National Gallery of Art, Rosenwald Collection 1943.3.154); *b, Ill-Matched Lovers,* by Quentin Massys, c. 1520–25 (courtesy of the National Gallery of Art, Alisa Mellon Bruce Fund 1971.55.1).

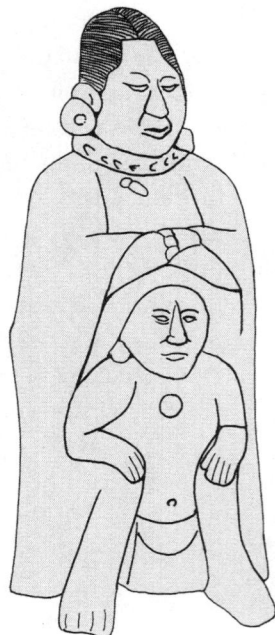

a   b

Figure 9.3. Women dominating men, gender role reversal in Maya and European art: *a, Phyllis Riding Aristotle,* by Master MZ or the "Housebook Master" (courtesy of the Boston Museum of Fine Arts, William A. Sargent and Stephen Bullard Memorial Fund); *b,* Jaina-style figurine of a seated man in the folds of a woman's dress (from Schele 1997: 52).

Phyllis and Aristotle—after he warns off her next conquest, Alexander the Great, she decides to seduce the famous philosopher in retaliation. Once he is smitten, she demands that he prove his passion by allowing her to publicly ride atop him. Although not appearing in any history recorded by Plutarch or Diogenes, this was an incredibly popular Germanic tale reproduced and disseminated in printed form (figure 9.3a). These fictional anecdotes were both cautionary and humorous, and they provide a striking parallel for our interpretation of ancient Maya figurines. A Maya example, known not only from numerous figurines but also carried over to painted polychrome vases, is the theme of a nubile woman dancing or embracing a haggard and hoary-looking male (figure 9.4; see K. Taube 1989). His declining looks in sharp contrast with her youthful, becoming appearance bears an astonishing affinity to the German ill-matched lovers. Quite frequently, the aged male bears bestial traits, again reinforcing his repugnant and

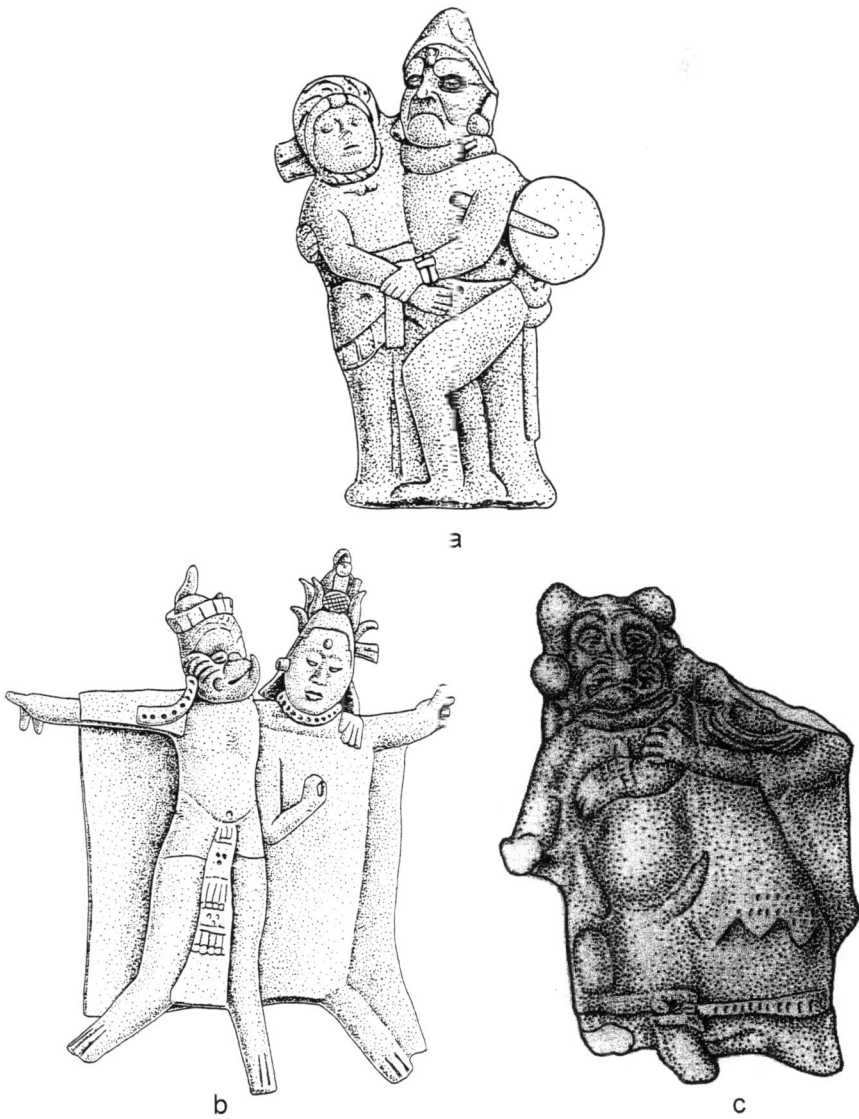

Figure 9.4. Late Classic Maya figurines portraying old bestial clowns dancing with nubile women: *a*, figurine of couple in sexual embrace from Usumacinta region—note dance fan (drawing by Karl Taube from Taube 1989: fig. 24-12c); *b*, couple in dance pose (drawing by Karl Taube from Taube 1989: fig. 24-13c); *c*, dance couple from Aguateca *grieta* (courtesy of Reiko Ishihara and Takeshi Inomata of the Aguateca Archaeological Project).

antisocial nature (figure 9.4b). Reiko Ishihara (2007) excavated one such figurine in the *grieta* at Aguateca (figure 9.4c). A Jaina-style figurine in the American Museum of Natural History provides another striking and direct comparison to Renaissance prints (figure 9.3b). It features a stately looking female standing over and enshrouding a middle-aged, somewhat corpulent man who squats under her skirts. Clearly not meant as a portrayal of royal dignity, this figurine captures an instance of Maya popular culture.

We follow the definition of popular culture as "both 'folk' or 'popular' beliefs, practices, and objects rooted in local traditions as well as 'mass' beliefs, practices, and objects generated from political and commercial centers" (Mukerji and Schudson 1986: 48). The quotidian contact, requirements, and wishes of the everyday lives of the ordinary populations determine the content of popular culture. These items usually appeal to a broad spectrum of society and allow people the opportunity to define themselves in relation to everyone else, building identity through a sense of belonging. Often manifesting in vernacular language, comical folk or ritual humor celebrates the masses and frequently lampoons the upper stratum of society or socially inappropriate behavior (Bakhtin 1968). For ritual humor to function in this vein, it requires the audience-participants to be "in on" the jokes performed and portrayed, implying forms of communication and a steady flow of information. For comedies and farces, or folk culture, to be successful, they require preexisting stereotypical characters. This helps to explain the similarity of figurine types throughout varying archaeological sites. Moreover, objects of popular culture are created by a continuing interaction between the meaning-makers and consumers, although they do not always reflect singularly imposed concepts or beliefs.

The contact period Aztecs are known to have ascribed a sacred and profound meaning to the ballgame, while at the same time male members of society played it as a recreational sport, creating an overlap of sacred and profane. Likewise, Maya public performances and characters of mythology may have also crossed over from the numinous into the popular realm. Certain characters of Maya mythology—such as the Maize God and God N—appear with some frequency in figurines. Analyzing these objects as a reflection of popular taste provides insight into the daily life of the general populace. The plasticity of clay allowed artists a great deal of choice in rendering expressive facial characteristics and what appear to be individualized features on many figurines. In addition, molds allowed for the mass production of images, much like the advent of the printing press in Renaissance Europe (Halperin 2006; this volume, chapter 13). Many figurines also functioned as whistles, with an empty body cavity serving as the resonating chamber, or as rattles with several clay balls inserted into a hollow, closed compartment, indicating that they were used in music making or public performances.

Maya figurines represent rulers, market women, warriors, entertainers, dancers, ballplayers, boxers, an assortment of animals, and a host of mythic characters that exhibit incredibly lifelike qualities. As mentioned, for figurines to be successful as types, either real or fictitious, they have to relate to well-known genres from everyday Maya life, religion, or lore. This would also explain the fundamental continuity of certain subject matters and designs from one ancient Maya city to another over a long time. Early Classic figurines are quite rare, and high-quality examples occur in only several known archaeological contexts, such as at Río Azul (Rands and Rands 1965). In contrast to contemporaneous Teotihuacan, they are hand-modeled rather than mold-made, indicating that they were not intended to be viewed by many individuals. Late Classic figurines are virtually ubiquitous at Maya sites and fit in with other traditions of Classic period Maya art, yet they do exhibit several unique local attributes.

In many state-level societies, human social conventions are satirized by animals behaving as people, a situation clearly regarded as humorous. This could well derive from the strict mores of etiquette of complex societies, in which every move and act is watched and appraised. Animals are beyond these parameters, and they are "safe," with no immediate social or political repercussions, as they are not people. For ancient Sumer, a lyre—clearly an instrument for entertainment—portrays animals serving a banquet, including a standing fox holding a large platter of food (figure 9.5a). In the upper scene, a lion bearing a drink walks behind his likely mate, who is shown with a knife and butchered game, quite possibly the opposite roles of husband and wife in public feasts. Below, an ass brays to a lyre held by a clearly top-heavy bear bracing the instrument in an entirely unnecessary and clearly precarious effort.

In papyrus scenes of New Kingdom Egypt, animals also engage in human acts, such as cats serving a mouse mistress and foxes tending to animals in their pen (see Terrace and Fischer 1970: 150–51). In this case, the roles between animals are inverted, with cats subservient to mice and the denizens of the barnyard as the caring keepers (figure 9.5b). In the papyrus of Turin, a pharaonic mouse rides a chariot to destroy a fort "manned" by cats (see Terrace and Fischer 1970: 152). A twelfth-century Japanese scroll portrays monkeys and other creatures engaged in otherwise solemn acts, including

Figure 9.5. Animals as humans in ancient art: *a*, scene from Sumerian lyre excavated in the Royal Graves at Ur, early second millennium BC (after Frankfort 1996: fig. 78); *b*, New Kingdom Egyptian portrayal of cats serving mice, detail of papyrus from Twentieth Dynasty (after Terrace and Fisher 1970: No. 34); *c*, Japanese scene of simian monk before probable Buddha appearing as a toad, detail from Choju Giga scrolls dating to early twelfth century AD (from Houston et al. 2006: fig. 4.1).

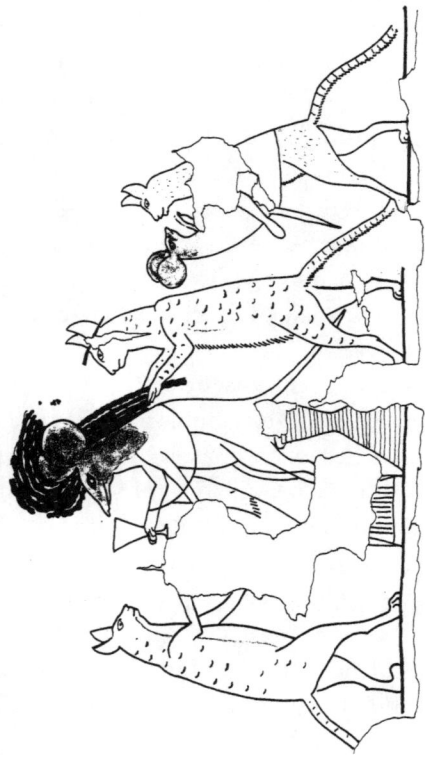

Figure 9.6. Detail of Late Classic Chama vessel scene of animals playing music and dancing (drawn after photo by Justin Kerr [K3332]).

well-dressed monkey monks worshipping a probable Buddha sculpted as a corpulent toad or frog (figure 9.5c).

Classic Maya art is filled with scenes of animals acting as people. Of course, not all should be regarded as humorous. The sinister *way* spirits of the forest appear frequently in the form of jaguars, monkeys, and deer, but their bestial bodies portray them as their soul essence, without any immediate reference to humor (for the relation of way spirits to the forest wilds, see K. Taube 2003, 2004). In addition, certain gods have animal aspects, such as the Principal Bird Deity as the avian avatar of Itzamnaaj. Nonetheless, there are very clear scenes of animals as musicians and entertainers, recalling the lyre from the Royal Graves of Ur (figure 9.6). Such scenes appear frequently in Late Classic Nebaj-style vases, with a cadre of jaguars, deer, rabbits, armadillos, and other creatures earnestly beating, blowing, and shaking away to tunes long lost (M. Miller 1988). In this context, the animals quite probably are intended to be amusing. However, among the Classic Maya there is a whole other genre of animal beings who are both bestial and old. Although anthropomorphic, they bear aged faces displaying both human and animal traits. From Classic times to the present, one of the most popular themes of Maya ritual humor is agedness (Bricker 1973; K. Taube 1989). Although this may seem antithetical to Maya conceptions of elders as embodiments of knowledge, dignity, and respect, this genre appears for precisely this reason. It provides a disturbing view of inappropriate behavior with the individuals most esteemed for their civility, dignity, and grace.

Although many researchers have commented on the aggressive Koshare and playful Koyemshi ritual clowns of the Hopi, these are only part of a far larger Hopi clowning complex, which also includes such genres as Old People, Navajo, and White Girl (Wright 1994). Still today, a very common theme in Maya dance humor is that of "outsiders," whether they be "Lacon-dones" in Zinacantan or "Mexicanos" in Momostenango (Bricker 1973; R. Taube 2006a). In this light, we may usefully consider Classic Maya portray-als of foreign dance characters. At the Late Classic Puuc site of Oxkintok, Yucatan, one structure features a potbellied "Fat God" holding a fan, in-dicating that he is a performer (see Pollock 1980: fig. 303; Proskouriakoff 1950: fig. 97a). An aged clown, probably another example of the Fat God, wears a very similar suit while dancing (figure 9.1b). The Oxkintok structure portrays another monumental figure wearing a version of the triple-knotted headdress known for Teotihuacan elites (Pollock 1980; Proskouriakoff 1950). In addition, he wears gaiters with dangling elements commonly found with Late Classic Maya portrayals of Teotihuacanos, including examples from Structure 10L-26 at Copán (see Fash 2001: fig. 9.1c). Although by the time of the Puuc florescence Teotihuacan was already in historical memory, this structure appears to portray an actor dressed as a foreign emissary from this distant place.

Aside from animals and aged people, another popular topic in Classic Maya humor is dwarfism (figures 9.7, 9.8). As in many parts of the world, dwarfs were regarded as very special and "rare" beings who were clearly prized members of royal courts. In Classic Maya vessel scenes, dwarfs com-monly are close to the royal throne, a theme that can be traced to the Early Formative Olmec. At San Lorenzo, several thrones depict dwarfs, including Potrero Nuevo Monument 2, which portrays a pair of dwarfs supporting the celestial seat of the king (see Coe and Diehl 1980: fig. 496). Among the Classic Maya, images of dwarfs also ornament royal thrones (see Miller and Martin 2004: pls. 7–8). For the Early Formative Olmec, dwarfs were also mirror bearers. The Dallas Museum of Art has two figurines of hunch-backed dwarfs attributed to Las Bocas. Whereas one displays a mirror, the other holds a tablet, quite possibly a version of the recently reported ser-pentine block from Cascajal bearing Olmec writing (Rodriguez Martínez et al. 2006).

Although dwarf scribes will be subsequently discussed for the Classic Maya, the mirror bearer also relates to Classic Maya conventions. In addi-tion, among the Classic Maya, one important office of dwarfs was to serve as the mirror bearer to the ruler, thus contrasting their appearance to that of the royal body. In one palace scene featuring a hunchback and a guzzling dwarf, there is also a far smaller dwarf holding a mirror (Miller and Martin 2004: pl. 14). As Stephen Houston (personal communication 2005) notes, this diminutive figure is actually an object, a sculpture serving as a mir-

Figure 9.7. Portrayal of Maya dwarfs as ballplayers from Piedras Negras (photo by Rhonda Taube, reproduced courtesy of Piedras Negras Archaeological Project, directed by Stephen Houston and Hector Escobedo).

a

b

Figure 9.8. Portrayal of dwarfs in Maya and European art: *a*, aged Maya dwarf with deer headdress from Jaina (from Schele 1997: 152); *b*, Antonis Mor's *Cardinal Granvelle's Dwarf* (1570), a portrait of a European court jester-dwarf dressed in royal garb (photo: Alinari/Art Resources).

ror holder. Remarkably, several Classic period wooden mirror bearers have survived (see Ekholm 1964; Reents-Budet 1994: fig. 3.17b). The magnificent Early Classic example at the Metropolitan Museum of Art displays the facial features of an achondroplastic dwarf (Ekholm 1964; see also Easby and Scott 1970: no. 182). In the vessel scene, the rotund lord looking on is clearly bemused and wears a rabbit headdress, a creature widely identified with humor and drunkenness in ancient Mesoamerica (Burkhart 1986). Such an explicit portrayal of amusement in ancient Maya art is quite rare and indicates the importance of dwarfs, humor, and alcohol in Classic Maya courtly thought.

Rather than being portrayed as static, passive beings, dwarfs played an important and dynamic part of courtly life, and in many scenes they dance in the company of kings. The well-known Holmul Dancer scenes of Late Classic Maya pottery feature dwarfs with maize gods, once again contrasting the regal and beautiful with conceptions of the strange and grotesque. In addition, dwarfs frequently appear as ripened and grizzled, with pronounced wrinkles and facial hair (figure 9.8a), a basic trait of agedness of both men and women in Classic Maya canons (Houston et al. 2006). However, aside from serving as courtly assistants and entertainers, dwarfs were probably also important repositories of regal life and history. Although widely regarded as a monkey, the well-known scribe sculpture from Structure 9N-82 at Copan is an old dwarf holding his pen and inkpot (see Schele and Miller 1986: 151). As has been mentioned, the scribal office of dwarfs probably has its roots in the Early Formative Olmec.

Achondroplastic dwarfs constitute a major genre of Late Classic Maya figurines; in the case of Piedras Negras, many were pendants and meant to be suspended or worn. Easily recognizable by their squat bodies and frequently large occipital forehead protrusion, they are one of the most popular Classic Maya figurine characters and are invariably male. For the roughly 1,500 identifiable figurine types from the recent excavations directed by Stephen Houston and Hector Escobedo at Piedras Negras, slightly over 10 percent are dwarfs (R. Taube 2006b). Dwarfs commonly appear in Maya vessel scenes holding mirrors or attending ballplayers (V. Miller 1985). At the time of Spanish contact, large groups of dwarfs were kept at court to provide entertainment for the Aztec *tlatoani,* and they may have performed this function for Maya royalty as well (Sahagún 1950–82: bk. 8: 29–30). Clearly, dwarfs held prominent positions, easily shifting from royal sculpture (such as the Copan scribe) to popular small-scale objects, including painted polychrome vessels and figurines. However, their popularity does

not seem to transfer over to other media, as there are few explicit representations of dwarfs in major monumental art.

Although dwarfs remain primarily confined to clay figurines, ceramic
jewelry, and painted ceramic vessels, they highlight a common means of
reworking and producing the male image through visual codes. The visual code of the ruler relies on images that portray his strength, virility,
and vitality, especially in the role of warrior. Depictions of the ruler's body
foreground physical characteristics equated with a moral code. Dwarfs are
rarely in a position to pose a power threat to the ruler, and they not only
provided amusement but also emphasized male identity in opposition to
their own physical traits. The set of visual codes established by the body of
the ruler is enhanced through a confrontation with their absence, namely,
with the body of the dwarf. Thus, the dynamics of self-definition through
visual codes imply relations of inequality, created by the superposition of
political, economic, and the physical. The unequal character of the Maya
male versus Maya dwarf implies that identity construction can be seen as
ideological in establishing social interests and power relations (Robyns
1994).

European monarchs often made use of a similar type of comparison, between the body of the king and that of his dwarf-jester. Several Renaissance
portraits capture the royal dwarf in the same costume and posture as that of
the king, emphasizing the physical schism between the two and bolstering
the valorousness and exalted quality of the ruler that much more. Antonis
Mor's 1570 portrait *Cardinal Granvelle's Dwarf* in comparison with Titian's
portrait *Charles V,* painted forty years earlier, is a case in point. The dwarf is
dressed as a warrior-knight, replete with his regular-sized sword. He wears
all of the trimmings and paraphernalia of a regal personage, placing him
in his appropriate station in life. He carries in his right hand the jester's
bauble (*Narrenzepter*), equating him with the king (Otto 2001: 49). The cultural codes portrayed offer the dwarf the "armor of an alienating identity"
(Berger 1994: 113), linking and transposing him with the ruler. The costume,
the scepter, and the hand easily resting on the back of the dog's neck are all
borrowed from Titian's famous *Charles V.* The contrast, however, is what is
crucial in this comparison: the direct imitation of royal portraiture, emphasizing the absurd role of the dwarf and the physical perfection of the king.

These sixteenth-century European works of art are different from portrayals of Classic period Maya kings and dwarfs, but they provide a parallel
that allows us to think about Maya works of art differently. The popularity of dwarfs in Renaissance art is a reflection of their widespread appeal

in popular society as well. Certain dwarfs achieved such a high level of prominence that they became household names; the ephemeral art form of the print publicized and immortalized their antics throughout society (Otto 2001; Swain 1932; Welsford 1935). Likewise, Maya figurines serve as a similar type of mass media circulating widely throughout society (Halperin 2006; see also this volume, chapter 13). This suggests that several works of Maya art featuring dwarfs may also be portraits of specific individuals, for example, the so-called Monkey Scribe from Copan Sepulturas. If he is a dwarf—and we believe he is—then this is a life-sized portrait, most likely of a well-known and important individual.

A Late Classic vessel in the collection of Dumbarton Oaks features several men before a seated king leaning heavily over on one arm, a gesture of power that appears not only on Piedras Negras Panel 3 but also (and earlier) among the Middle Formative Olmec (K. Taube 2004b: 101). In contrast to the handsome lord, the two kneeling figures before the throne are decidedly not handsome: one exhibits a potbelly and the other, a huge, bulbous nose (see Coe 1975: no. 13). The large-nosed figure also sports a toad headdress, hardly an animal figure to aspire to. In fact, one of the unflattering nicknames *(pat k'aaba)* in modern Yukatek is *much*, meaning "toad," and it commonly refers to people with broad facial features (K. Taube 1989).

One of the common supernatural brunts of Classic Maya ritual humor is God N, commonly known as Pawahtun, although currently epigraphers debate this reading. He consistently appears as an old, fat man without the elaborate headdresses and gear generally found on stelae and other public monuments portraying the weighty deeds of kings. He is generally seminude and wears the simple netted headdress also found with scribes, including the aforementioned Copan sculpture. Such relatively casual costume indicates that he is someone of the working court, that is, the day-to-day affairs of law, finance, and taxation (in other words, someone wholly repugnant to much of the greater world). In one Copan sculpture, he is the personification of senility and a life badly lived (figure 9.9). A vessel recently excavated at Aguateca similarly portrays him as an open-mouthed, bleary individual, hardly the paragon of power that his mythic office presents him as (see Inomata 2003: 117).

Late Classic Maya figurines provide a wonderful corpus of genres concerning ritual clowning. In contrast to the stone and stucco sculpture of elite public architecture, both figurines and vases depict far more intimate and anecdotal scenes of courtly life (K. Taube 1989). It is therefore important to note that certain beings appearing as figurines are also in vessel

Figure 9.9. God N appearing with senile features, Late Classic Copan (drawing by Karl Taube).

scenes. One of the most striking examples is an old opossum dancer with an extended belly playing a gourd rasp (see K. Taube 1989). Such a change in media indicates that these are not simply the works of one eccentric artist at one locale but were widely known and recognized genres, such as, in contemporary American humor, the mother-in-law, the farmer's daughter, the absent-minded professor, and so on. In terms of Maya figurines, there are themes that appear to be so specific as to be even from the same mold, but close inspection often reveals that they were made at separate, distinct times. For example, one figurine group in the Museo Nacional de Antropología in Guatemala City features two youthful singing men surrounded by a group of five toadlike musicians who stand in obvious contrast to the pair, perhaps denoting the difference between animal sounds and human speech and song (figure 9.10b). Another figurine group features a nearly identical ensemble, although a careful view quickly reveals that this piece was created from an entirely different mold (figure 9.10a).

Another repetitive theme is an old duck musician, probably a ritual clown, holding a turtle-shell drum (figure 9.11). Although in one example he is seated, another figurine portrays him standing. The similarities shared between these two figurines are striking, including the pair of circular head-

a

b

Figure 9.10. Late Classic figurines portraying complex scenes of musicians: *a,* figurine group of musicians with pair of human singers, Museo Nacional de Antropología e Historia, Guatemala City (drawing by Karl Taube); *b,* figurine group of rotund bestial musicians and two probable human singers—note bicephalic serpent sky band across center of composition (drawing by Karl Taube from photo by Justin Kerr [K6753]).

Figure 9.11. Late Classic Maya portrayals of duck musicians with turtle carapace drum: *a,* seated duck figure holding drum in lap (drawing by Karl Taube from photograph by Justin Kerr [K3550]; *b,* standing duck performer with turtle drum and antler-tine drumstick (drawing by Karl Taube from Schele 1997: 132).

dress elements with strips of pendant cloth or paper. Aside from the duck musician, there are also figurines portraying the "monkey grandmother," an old spider monkey woman with pendant breasts and a human or simian infant in her lap (figure 9.12). Although two of the cited examples have no archaeological context, an excellent example was recently discovered at Aguateca (figure 9.12a). The monkey grandmother theme may well relate to the common figurine genre of women at market, as children are often in the laps of the vendors, a probable necessity when women vendors were away from home for hours or even days (figure 9.13). One Late Classic figurine portrays a merchant dog woman with her vessel of food or drink (figure 9.13b). As in the case of the "monkey grandmother," this figurine was probably a means of satirizing the social roles of women.

a

b

c

Figure 9.12. The monkey grandmother theme in Late Classic Maya figurines:
a, Aguateca figurine of corpulent simian figure holding human child (drawing
by Karl Taube from photograph courtesy of Takeshi Inomata and the Aguateca
Archaeological Project); *b,* monkey woman holding monkey infant on lap (from
Sotheby's 1983: No. 185); *c,* monkey woman holding infant (drawing by Karl Taube
from photograph by Justin Kerr [K6727]).

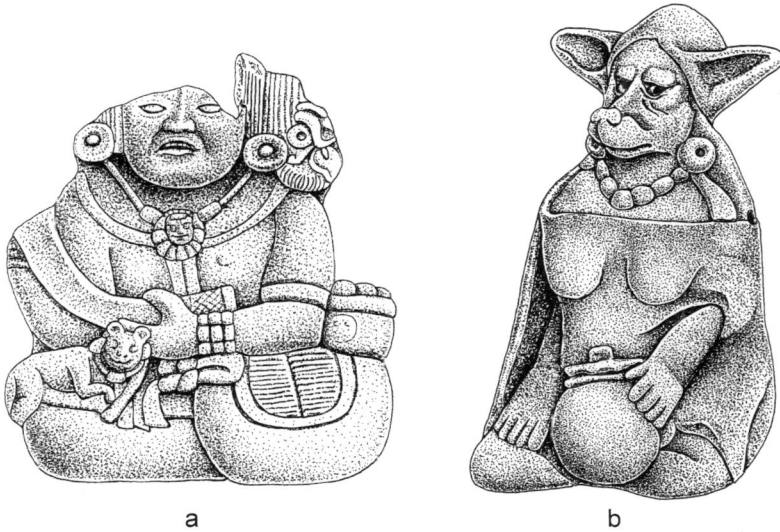

Figure 9.13. Women at market: *a*, woman with dog, tamales, and tortillas (from Houston et al. 2006: fig. 3.4); *b*, dog lady with vessel (drawing by Karl Taube from photograph by Justin Kerr [K7202]).

Maya figurines represent a set of practices, or a process, in the production of social significance that influenced conduct. As jocoserious objects of everyday life, they provided meaning and insight from a popular perspective, lending value or significance that is apart from monumental art and strictly official ideas. They traversed the line between refined taste and comedic ridicule and functioned as part of a dialogic process that suspended, however casually or briefly, the distinctions among different levels of society by combining targets of scorn and mockery (Bakhtin 1968). For the ancient Maya, viewing and looking—at monumental art as well as farcical performances and objects—were powerful occasions. Lost to us are the various farces and parodies in their performed or prosaic forms. We might easily consider, however, that these existed and expressed concerns in a written counterpart similar to Menippean satire that captured and lampooned the human condition as perceived through recognizable types, such as the old lecherous man, the market woman, the dwarf, and the young, nubile temptress. These characters portrayed in clay expressed the visual codes that reflected the norms by which social life was ordered. In this manner, Maya Classic period figurines functioned much like Native North American Hopi *tihu katsina* dolls: the images of holy beings that are didactic and at the same time, are owned by most members of society. In addition to functioning in religious ceremonies, they are also children's playthings that cross the barrier of the sacred and profane and serve as mementos of *katsina* characters who appeared at specific holy performances.

References Cited

Bakhtin, Mikhail. 1968. *Rabelais and His World*. Trans. H. Iswolsky. MIT Press, Cambridge, Mass.

Berger, Harry, Jr. 1994. Fictions of the Pose: Facing the Gaze of Early Modern Portraiture. *Representations* 46 (Spring): 87–120.

Bricker, Victoria Reifler. 1973. *Ritual Humor in Highland Chiapas*. University of Texas Press, Austin.

Burkhart, Louise. 1986. Moral Deviance in Sixteenth-Century Nahua and Christian Thought: The Rabbit and the Deer. *Journal of Latin American Lore* 12 (2): 107–39.

Coe, Michael D. 1975. *Classic Maya Pottery at Dumbarton Oaks*. Dumbarton Oaks, Washington, D.C.

Coe, Michael D., and Richard A. Diehl. 1980. *In the Land of the Olmec*, vol. 1, *The Archaeology of San Lorenzo Tenochtitlán*. University of Texas Press, Austin.

Easby, Elizabeth Kennedy, and John F. Scott. 1970. *Before Cortés: Sculpture of Middle America*. Metropolitan Museum of Art, New York.

Ekholm, Gordon. 1964. *A Maya Sculpture in Wood*. The Museum of Primitive Art Studies 4. New York.

Fash, William L., rev. ed. 2001. *Scribes, Warriors and Kings: The City of Copan and the Ancient Maya*. Thames and Hudson, New York.

Frankfort, Henri. 1996. *The Art and Architecture of the Ancient Orient*. 5th ed. Yale University Press, New Haven, Conn.

Halperin, Christina. 2006. What Does Politics Have to Do with It? Figurines as Bearers of and Burdens in Late Classic Maya State Politics. Paper presented at the 71st Annual Meeting of the Society for American Archaeology, San Juan, P.R.

Houston, Stephen D., David Stuart, and Karl A. Taube. 2006. *The Memory of Bones: Body, Being, and Experience among the Classic Maya*. University of Texas Press, Austin.

Houston, Stephen D., and Karl Taube. 2000. An Archaeology of the Senses: Perception and Cultural Expression in Ancient Mesoamerica. *Cambridge Archaeological Journal* 10 (2): 261–94.

Hutcheon, Linda. 2000. *A Theory of Parody: The Teachings of Twentieth-Century Art Forms*. University of Illinois Press, Urbana.

Inomata, Takeshi. 2003. Aguateca: New Revelations of the Maya Elite. *National Geographic* (May): 110–19.

Ishihara, Reiko. 2007. Bridging the Chasm between Religion and Politics: Archaeological Investigations of the Grietas at the Late Classic Maya Site of Aguateca, Peten, Guatemala. Ph.D. diss., Department of Anthropology, University of California, Riverside.

Joyce, Rosemary A. 1992. Images of Gender and Labor Organization in Classic Maya Society. In *Exploring Gender through Archaeology: Selected Papers from the Boone Conference*, ed. C. Claassen, 63–70. Monographs of World Archaeology 2. Prehistory Press, Madison, Wis.

———. 1993. Women's Work: Images of Production and Reproduction in Pre-Hispanic Southern Central America. *Current Anthropology* 34 (3): 255–74.

Miller, Mary E. 1988. The Boys in the Bonampak Band. In *Maya Iconography*, ed. E. P. Benson and G. Griffin, 318–30. Princeton University Press, Princeton, N.J.

Miller, Mary E., and Simon Martin. 2004. *Courtly Art of the Ancient Maya.* Thames and Hudson, New York.

Miller, Virginia E. 1985. The Dwarf Motif in Classic Maya Art. In *The Fourth Palenque Round Table, 1980*, ed. E. P. Benson, 141–53. Pre-Columbian Art Research Institute, San Francisco.

Mukerji, Chandra, and Michael Schudson. 1986. Popular Culture. *Annual Review of Sociology* 12: 47–66.

Nurse, Julia. 1998. She-Devils, Harlots and Harridans in Northern Renaissance Prints. *History Today* 18 (7): 41–48.

Otto, Beatrice K. 2001. *Fools Are Everywhere: The Court Jester around the World.* University of Chicago Press, Chicago.

Pollock, H. E. D. 1980. *The Puuc: An Architectural Survey of the Hill Country of Yucatan and Northern Campeche, Mexico.* Peabody Museum of Archaeology and Ethnology, Harvard University, Cambridge, Mass.

Proskouriakoff, Tatiana. 1950. *A Study of Classic Maya Sculpture.* Carnegie Institution of Washington, Washington, D.C.

Rands, R. L., and B. C. Rands. 1965. Pottery Figurines of the Maya Lowlands. In *Handbook of Middle American Indians*, vol. 2, ed. G. R. Willey, 535–60. University of Texas Press, Austin.

Reents-Budet, Dorie. 1994. *Painting the Maya Universe: Royal Ceramics of the Classic Period.* Duke University Press, Durham, N.C.

Robyns, Clem. 1994. Translation and Discursive Identity. *Poetics Today* 15 (3): 405–28.

Rodriguez Martínez, Ma. del Carmen, Ponciano Ortíz Ceballos, Michael D. Coe, Richard A. Diehl, Stephen D. Houston, Karl A. Taube, and Alfredo Delgado Calderón. 2006. Oldest Writing in the New World. *Science* 313: 1610–14.

Sahagún, Fray Bernardino de. 1950–82. *General History of the Things of New Spain: Florentine Codex.* Ed. and trans. A. J. O. Anderson and C. E. Dibble. School of American Research, Santa Fe, N.Mex.

Schele, Linda. 1997. *Hidden Faces of the Maya.* Impetus Comunicación, Mexico City.

Schele, Linda, and Mary Ellen Miller. 1986. *The Blood of Kings: Dynasty and Ritual in Maya Art.* Kimbell Art Museum, Fort Worth, Texas; George Braziller, New York.

Sotheby's. 1983. *Important Pre-Columbian Art, Sale 5034.* Sotheby Parke Bernet, New York.

Swain, Barbara. 1932. *Fools and Folly during the Middle Ages and Renaissance.* Columbia University Press, New York.

Taube, Karl A. 1985. The Classic Maya Maize God: A Reappraisal. In *The Fifth Palenque Round Table, 1983,* ed. V. M. Fields, 171–81. Pre-Columbian Art Research Institute, San Francisco.

———. 1989. Ritual Humor in Classic Maya Religion. In *Word and Image in Maya Culture,* ed. W. F. Hanks and D. S. Rice, pp. 351–82. University of Utah Press, Salt Lake City.

———. 2003. Ancient and Contemporary Maya Conceptions about Field and Forest. In *The Lowland Maya Area: Three Millennia at the Human-Wildland Interface,* ed. A. Gomez-Pompa, M. Allen, S. Fedick, and J. Jimenez-Osornio, 461–92. Haworth Press, New York.

———. 2004a. Flower Mountain: Concepts of Life, Beauty, and Paradise among the Classic Maya. *RES* 45: 69–98.

———. 2004b. *Olmec Art at Dumbarton Oaks.* Dumbarton Oaks, Washington, D.C.

Taube, Rhonda. 2006a. Pageantry and Parody in Contemporary Maya Performance: Repetition and Revision in Momostenango, Guatemala. Paper presented at the College Art Association, Boston.

———. 2006b. The Figurines of Piedras Negras: An Iconographical Analysis. Paper presented at the Society for American Archaeology, San Juan, P.R.

Terrace, Edward L. B., and Henry G. Fischer. 1970. *Treasures of Egyptian Art from the Cairo Museum.* Thames and Hudson, New York.

Vogt, Evon Zartman. 1976. *Tortillas for the Gods: A Symbolic Analysis of Zinacanteco Rituals.* Harvard University Press, Cambridge, Mass.

Welsford, Enid. 1935. *The Fool: His Social and Literary History.* Faber and Faber, London.

Wright, Barton. 1994. *Clowns of the Hopi: Tradition Keepers and Delight Makers.* Northland, Flagstaff, Ariz.

Part IV

Embodiment

10

The Weeping Baby and the Nahua Corn Spirit

The Human Body as Key Symbol
in the Huasteca Veracruzana, Mexico

ALAN R. SANDSTROM

Many North American anthropologists continue to be fascinated by symbols, meaning systems, and the emic realm in their studies of culture. The aim of their research strategy is *interpreting,* or giving an account of people's behavior. The focus on meaning, however, is often accomplished at the expense of important economic, ecological, political, or social variables that in themselves can go a long way toward *explaining* human behavior. Exclusive reliance on meaning-based analysis will, I argue, always be inadequate to the task of explaining behavior, owing to the fundamentally flexible nature of cultural symbols. Shared symbols do not constrain behavior in the same way that economic and ecological factors do. Individuals are more likely to vary their interpretation of cultural symbols in response to pragmatic concerns than the reverse.

In this chapter, I examine how contemporary Nahua incorporate ideas about the human body into their religious thought and symbolism. Nahua concepts of the corn spirit in particular indicate that the human body is a key symbol in Nahua religious ideology. Nevertheless, although the concept of key symbol can be helpful in analyzing esoteric symbolic systems, it needs to be used with caution in light of the Nahua data. Understanding the role of the body in Nahua symbolism is necessary but not sufficient to explain why individual Nahua respond in specific ways to this important element of their culture. Finally, I will suggest that genuine progress in improving our understanding of Mesoamerican religion can best be achieved through cooperative archaeological, ethnohistorical, and ethnographic investigation rather than reliance on one analytical approach.

The publication in 1980 of Alfredo López Austin's monumental *Cuerpo humano e ideología: Las concepciones de los antiguos nahuas* (see López

Austin 1988 for the English translation) established the central symbolic importance of the human body in pre-Hispanic Mesoamerican thought and stimulated numerous ethnographers to apply his insights to the analysis of contemporary Native American religious systems.[1] On the place of the human body in ancient Nahua culture, López Austin writes, "As an ideological system, concepts of the human body [occupy] the center of the world view since [they respond] as much to the yearnings, needs, worries, and drive for understanding that is innate in man as [they do] to the universality of all that exists in a world that was conceived as anthropomorphic" (1988: 1: 419, corrections in the translation mine). I have discovered that contemporary Nahua also have elaborated conceptions of the body that are fundamental to their cosmology and worldview. Similar concepts are shared by many indigenous groups throughout Mesoamerica and beyond, indicating that these ideas form a system of great antiquity (see, for example, Classen 1993).[2]

Ethnographers have written extensively about religion in contemporary Mesoamerica, yet advances in techniques for analyzing and explaining field data have been slow and sporadic. Two major factors have slowed theoretical progress. First, Mesoamerica is composed of a mosaic of indigenous groups, each of which, despite fundamental similarities, has developed its unique blend of pre-Hispanic traditions and Spanish Catholicism. This situation is further complicated by the intrusion of North American Protestantism in recent years. The sheer complexity of this syncretic process and the varying influences of pre-Hispanic and Euro-American factors make it difficult for investigators to generalize about the nature of indigenous religion (Beals 1967: 450; Madsen 1967). The second factor is even more problematic. Recording systematic and in-depth information on indigenous religious beliefs and practices has proven extraordinarily difficult even for a single ethnic group. Anthropologists have found that certain factors (discussed below) often make field research focused on religion in indigenous communities a protracted and frustrating experience. Although the situation has changed in recent years, the greatest obstacle to progress in understanding contemporary Mesoamerican religion remains the scarcity of in-depth, holistic descriptions and analyses of specific religious systems.[3]

López Austin's analysis of the ancient Nahua worldview suggests one avenue of inquiry that promises to lead literally and figuratively to the very heart of contemporary Native American religion. However, methodological problems of collecting empirical information on abstract conceptions of the human body continue to hinder progress. As a prime example, much research has been conducted over the years on indigenous medical practices (for a recent overview, see Huber and Sandstrom 2001). Healing is an area in which the body is of central concern not only to the patient but also to the larger kin group and community, and to the medical practitioner as well. Yet in the extensive professional literature on the topic, the body often remains in the background, dimly perceived or even neglected by the researcher. This oversight is not always the fault of the investigator, as I explain below.

Religion, Symbolic Systems, and Studies of the Body

Religion, as a conceptual aspect of culture, may be defined as a system of shared symbols that people create to interact more effectively with their world (Geertz 1968: 406; 1973: 90). Religious rituals in particular are highly symbolic and are often usefully viewed by anthropologists as systems of communication (Leach 1968, 1976). In Clifford Geertz's well-known formulation, religious symbols simultaneously provide a people with models *of* reality and models *for* reality (Geertz 1973: 91–94). Symbols are models that help people understand the structure and nature of the cosmos, but they are also blueprints for behavior that provide the means for people to act reasonably in a coherent universe. Some symbols, however, are more important than others because they serve as focal points that organize additional, lesser symbols. Sherry Ortner (1973) calls these organizing elements "key symbols."

Ortner distinguishes two basic types of key symbols: summarizing and elaborating. Summarizing symbols "are those symbols which are seen as summing up, expressing, representing for participants in an emotionally powerful and relatively undifferentiated way, what the system means to them. This category is essentially the category of sacred symbols" (Ortner 1973: 1339–40). Examples include the cross for Christians and the flag of a country for patriots. Elaborating symbols "work in the opposite direction, providing vehicles for sorting out complex and undifferentiated feelings and ideas" and have the "capacity to order experience; they are essentially analytic" (Ortner 1973: 1340). She classes some elaborating symbols as "root metaphors" when they provide categories for understanding many aspects of experience. These approximate Geertz's "models *of* reality." Other elaborating symbols act as "key scenarios" that provide "clear-cut modes of action appropriate to correct and successful living in the culture" (Ortner 1973: 1341). These approximate Geertz's "models *for* reality."

If we apply these definitions, then we can see that the human body was a key symbol for the ancient Nahua and that it continues to play that role among their contemporary descendants. Anthropologists have long been interested in cultural formulations of the body, but there has been a resurgence of research in this area in the last several years.[4] Mary Douglas (1973) has used the almost universal importance of the body in cultural systems as a basis for a theory of "natural symbols." Douglas writes that humans exist within a physical body and a social body and states that "there is continual exchange of meanings between the two kinds of bodily experience so that each reinforces the categories of the other" (1973: 93). She adds, "The physical body is a microcosm of society, facing the center of power, contracting and expanding its claims in direct accordance with the increase and relaxation of social pressures" (1973: 101). Victor Turner (1967: 90) argues that the body and its experiences are the source and origin of all cultural systems of classification. These and other works (for example, Blacking 1977; Needham 1973) place the human body at the center of cultural meaning and typology.[5] Although body symbolism is a universal aspect of the world's cultures, very little has been written about the contemporary Nahua use of body symbolism.

Contemporary Nahua of the Huasteca Veracruzana

The Nahua of the Huasteca Veracruzana on the Gulf Coast of Mexico generally live in small remote villages and support themselves through slash-and-burn horticulture and periodic wage labor.[6] Despite increasing bilingualism, Nahuatl is the language of choice for daily interaction. Beginning in the early 1980s, Nahua and other local indigenous peoples began to convert in large numbers to various Protestant sects. In the mid-1980s, however, when much of the data for this study were collected, most Nahua continued to participate in the round of ritual offerings they call *costumbres,* which are based largely on pre-Hispanic traditions. Elements of Spanish Catholicism, such as observance of saints' days and the Christian cross, have been incorporated into local beliefs and practices, but they have generally been interpreted according to the Nahua frame of reference.[7] In addition to the Nahua, four other indigenous groups—the Otomí, Tepehua, Huastec (Teenek), and Totonac—inhabit the Huasteca Veracruzana and surrounding region. These groups have been the subject of several ethnographic studies, most of which focus on religious beliefs and rituals.[8]

The diversity of ethnic groups and languages in this region rests on a foundation of common beliefs and ritual techniques. A noteworthy illustration of this commonality is the practice whereby shamans (or ritual specialists) from each of the various groups cut sacred figures from paper for use in rituals and sorcery. Use of the term *shaman* to describe Mesoamerican religious practitioners is controversial (see Jolly 2005; Kehoe 2000; Klein et al. 2002; Lewis-Williams 2004), but I continue to use *shaman* and *ritual specialist* interchangeably while acknowledging the ongoing debate. The fact that contemporary Nahua shamans (men and women alike) receive their power from dreams or callings from the spirit world and draw on special relationships with animals and inanimate objects to cure, divine, and mobilize spiritual powers to the benefit (or sometimes, destruction) of human beings argues in favor of the terminology.

Paper cutting was an important religious practice throughout pre-Hispanic Mesoamerica, and the Huasteca is one of the few places where extensive ritual use of paper has continued to the present day. For this reason, it is not surprising that so many researchers have focused their efforts on documenting this intriguing survival (Christensen 1942; Lenz 1973 [1948], 1984; Sandstrom and Sandstrom 1986; also see Barrera Rivera et al. 2001 for a report of the remarkable discovery of a cache of pre-Hispanic paper in a ritual context at the Templo Mayor site in Mexico City). Little progress has been made, however, in deepening our understanding of the key symbols lying behind the ritual practices and beliefs of the paper cult religion (for exceptions see Dow 1986; Galinier 1990).

Most of my own research has been carried out in the pseudonymous village of Amatlán in the *municipio* of Ixhuatlán de Madero.[9] An early explorer in the Huasteca Veracruzana, Hans Lenz, noted that "it is dangerous to penetrate the sierra de Ixhuatlán beyond a certain point. This is particularly true if the object of the trip is to gather information on the pagano-Christian customs of the Indians who live there or to collect samples of papers they cut for their offerings or witchcraft" (Lenz 1973 [1948]: 139, translation mine; compare Sandstrom and Sandstrom 1986: 70). Danger aside, rarely are religious specialists or nonspecialists alike articulate about religious matters. This fact reflects a characteristic reticence shared among Native Americans of the region by which detailed explanation of beliefs or practices is avoided in normal conversation. This scarcity of explication also results from the way in which people living in small, close-knit villages are socialized. Indigenous religion in this area is characterized by a high level of ritual activity and a relatively low level of theological elaboration. Children learn the beliefs of their parents by hearing myths recited and by attending rituals in which they pick up information through observation with a minimum of explication. The fieldworker does not generally share this extensive experience, and villagers thus have no systematic procedure for introducing the naive outsider to the intricacies of ritual symbolism and underlying ideology. The most effective way to gain information on indigenous beliefs and practices is for ethnographers to spend extended periods of time in the field, repeatedly observing ritual occasions and recording what native exegeses they can.

Recent trends in ethnographic reporting emphasize that researchers relate the type and quality of information they produce to their particular fieldwork experiences. Accordingly, I recount the story of a weeping baby and how it led to my discovery of the importance of body symbolism among contemporary Nahua. By relating the weeping baby story and its links to the corn spirit, I hope the reader will better be able to evaluate its significance and meaning as it unfolds.

The Weeping Baby

In the spring of 1990, on the twentieth anniversary of my first fieldwork in the region, my family and I traveled to northern Veracruz to record myths and oral narratives told by the Nahua who live there. Most Nahua of the region are well aware that, despite some superficial similarities, their religious beliefs and practices differ fundamentally from that of mestizos and urban Mexicans. I have argued elsewhere (Sandstrom 1991: 323–77; see also Hernández Cuellar 1982: 140) that Nahua have used their religion as a tool or even a weapon through which to resist domination by mestizo elites, and it is therefore an important element in defining their ethnic identity. For this reason, local villagers have been strongly motivated to retain and perpetuate their customs. In the mid-1980s, beliefs and practices deriving from Native American traditions continued to have deep meaning for many villagers who grow corn and other crops by techniques little changed from those of their pre-Hispanic antecedents (Sandstrom 1991: 119–27). The recent turn to Protestantism by people in the region signals that the colonial social arrangements are breaking down in response to profound economic and political changes originating at the national and international levels, causing fundamental shifts in religious orientation. Interestingly, villagers are embracing Protestantism, a religion that acts to separate them from local mestizo elites who continue to identify with dominant Catholicism.

Field research among the Nahua requires considerable patience. Life in a small village lacks the sense of urgency that permeates most urban settings. In general, people there reveal information about themselves and their culture in a slow and measured way, sometimes subtly elaborating a point over the course of many years. When I first began research as a graduate student in 1970, villagers were understandably reticent to share information with a stranger and an obvious foreigner. But by 1990, my wife and I, along with our son, had been living in the village of Amatlán on and off for years, and we knew many people from the time they were children. We had become ritual kin to many of the villagers, and village authorities had relied upon us on several occasions to handle important community business in the state capital. The difficulty I experienced in eliciting consistent interpretations from villagers is a problem other researchers have reported from other indigenous communities in Mesoamerica (Lipp 1991: 24; Vogt 1976: 1–7). As mentioned, these difficulties are due as much to cultural factors influencing how people disseminate information as to the perennial problem of communicating esoteric and abstract information across a considerable cultural barrier.

Nahua expect both children and anthropologists to learn in an unhurried way through observation, supplemented by little or no formal instruction. For example, over the years I had recorded in painstaking detail the dozens of rituals I was privileged to witness in hopes that patterns would emerge that could then be used to elicit explanatory statements from participants. These types of explanations, however, have virtually no place in Nahua society. What analyses I was able to coax from villagers always seemed incomplete and cursory. Despite my numerous and probably tiresome questions, some people seemed unable to formulate explanations that I could understand. Others assumed that I already knew the answers and would therefore not be interested in their knowledge.

Some of the best information, therefore, came through serendipity in unexpected and spontaneous comments that people made from time to time. I responded to these statements with eager follow-up questions; the speakers, after expressing wonder at my ignorance of basic facts, were often glad to talk at length about even esoteric aspects of the religion. If I pressed anyone for answers under other circumstances, I usually received gentle evasions, but if people brought up the subject themselves they felt free to answer my questions and even elaborate. Thus, I learned after several years in the field that by waiting for the right moment to present itself, many of my burning questions would eventually be addressed.

In the spring of 1990, I had been trying to learn more about the nature of the corn spirit, particularly how and why members of households decide to sponsor a costly ritual offering to this important member of the spirit pantheon. Nahua from northern Veracruz conceive of the corn spirit as a male-female pair of twin children—a boy called in Nahuatl Chicomexochitl (Seven-Flower) and a girl Macuilxochitl (Five-Flower). Villagers described the pair as having flaxen hair that resembles the golden silk emerging from the top of each ear of corn. The names of these divine children have pre-Hispanic origins (see Berdan 1982: 135; Mönnich 1976: 143; and Read 1986: 129; these scholars also note the symbolic link between children and corn among the classical Aztecs). However, when asked about these spirits, villagers offered what appeared to be a folk etymology. They stated that the name Seven-Flower comes from a miraculous corn plant bearing seven ears of corn. No one I spoke to was able to explain the origin of the appellation Five-Flower.

Ritual specialists portray the corn spirit by cutting anthropomorphic paper images with hands upraised by the sides of the head (see figure 10.1; see also Sandstrom and Sandstrom 1986 for a larger sample of Nahua seed spirits [pp. 114–23] and discussion of the role of ritual specialists as paper cutters [pp. 72–74] and the problematic concepts of "spirit" and "soul" [p. 253]). Women helpers dress the paper image of Seven-Flower as a young boy in a tiny pair of cloth pants and a shirt, sometimes adding a diminutive hat and shoes or sandals (figure 10.1b). They dress the paper image of Five-Flower in a doll-sized cloth dress identical to the style worn by village girls and adorn the figure with tiny earrings and a necklace (figure 10.1c). Thomas Grigsby and Carmen Cook de Leonard (1992: 113–15) report that in the Nahua town of Tepoztlán in the state of Morelos, people make doll figures directly out of ears of corn.[10]

Over the months and years, I documented many seed rituals and recorded what interpretive statements I could elicit from villagers (see Hernández Cristóbal et al. 1982; Ixmatlahua Montalvo et al. 1982 for descriptions of corn rituals in neighboring Nahua villages). Still, I was always left with the sense that something was missing, some element that could tie together the complex relationship between the Nahua and their corn spirit. Then one evening a long-time friend stopped by for a chat. He is a man in his mid forties, respected by his neighbors for his honesty and sense of fairness, who had already served in most of the leadership positions of the village. We had become close friends and ritual kinsmen over the years, and I had taken him for his first real excursion to a city. It was always a pleasure when he came to visit, and I pulled a low bench close to his so that we could talk.

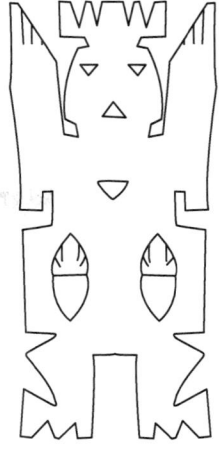

1a   1b   1c   1d

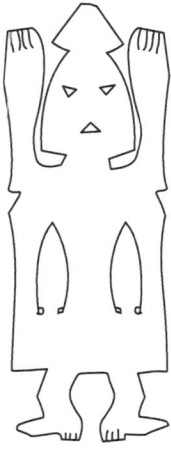

1e

Figure 10.1. Representations of corn spirits. *a, Pilsintsi,* "little corn." White paper, original 18 × 6 cm. This image is a typical anthropomorphic portrayal of the corn spirit as an infant. The headdress represents a ripening tassel, the leg cuts are roots, and developing ears of corn have been cut from the body. The central V-cut represents the heart or life force of the spirit. *b, Sintli,* "corn." White paper, white cloth outfit, original 29 × 7.5 cm (see Sandstrom and Sandstrom 1986: 120, fig. 46). This portrayal of Seven-Flower is dressed in clothing based on styles worn by Nahua men and boys. The headdress is a maturing ear of corn. The image of Seven-Flower represents corn in general, hence the name given by the shaman. Figures like this and other seed spirits are kept in a sacred box and are the subject of ritual offerings. *c, Sintli,* "corn." White paper, pink, blue, and white cloth dress, original 29 × 7.5 cm (see Sandstrom and Sandstrom 1986: 119, fig. 45). The crown in this portrayal of Five-Flower is a maturing ear of corn. As the female aspect of Seven-Flower, this figure is used by the shaman to represent corn in general. *d, Chicomexochitl,* "Seven-Flower." Manila paper, original 21 × 9 cm (see Sandstrom 1991: 264, fig. 5). Here is another example of the image of Seven-Flower, the youthful manifestation of the fertile corn spirit. Ripening ears of corn have been cut from the body. *e, Sintli,* "corn." White paper, original 20.5 × 6.5 cm (see Sandstrom and Sandstrom 1986: 116, fig. 40). Fully grown ears of corn have been cut from the body of this image of the mature maize spirit.

As we sipped from a bottle of the powerful *aguardiente* favored by village men, he told me that he would have to spend hours the next day in his milpa. I asked why, since I knew he had completed an arduous weeding of his fields only a few days before. He replied that he had "the dream" the night before and that he was very worried. I inquired what dream this was and he looked at me with a quizzical expression and replied something to the effect, "Don't you even know about the dream?" What followed was one of those sought-after moments of revelation as he explained about his dream, about the corn spirit, and about a major reason why people decide to hold seed rituals when they do. He not only answered my questions willingly but also invited me to his milpa on the following day to illustrate his points.

My friend had dreamed of a baby weeping, and because he had just finished tending to his field, he interpreted the dream as a sign that the corn plants in the milpa were under stress. He informed me that the cause could be an impending windstorm or the presence of an animal or flock of birds eating the crop. The weeping baby is the ear of corn, still wrapped in its green leaves, communicating its fear to the farmer through the medium of dreaming. I interjected that I understood the corn spirit to be in fact two children, and he replied that this is true when the plant matures a bit more. He added that the corn spirit can also be thought of as an old man and old woman when the shucks become brown and the cob dries. In other words, following the pre-Hispanic pattern, the stages of maturity of the plant mirror the human life cycle. The corn spirit appears in both male and female aspects: as a baby in the guise of *Pilsintsi* (little corn) (figure 10.1a), as the children Seven-Flower (figures 10.1b, 10.1d), and Five-Flower (figure 10.1c), and as the mature person, *Sintli* (corn) (figure 10.1e).[11]

In the milpa the next day, my friend pointed out the corn plant's roots, stalk, and tassel, which correspond to its feet, body, and head. In her arms, the corn mother holds the precious baby with the golden hair. Pollen released from the tassel down upon the plant is said to be milk that nourishes the baby. Further questioning revealed that human beings indeed owe their physical form to corn, the staple of the Nahua diet, and that its structure (roots, stalk, and tassel) is the primordial blueprint for the human body.[12] While chanting, shamans rarely refer to men or women directly, calling them instead *tlalchamantli* (earth sprouts) to link them to corn. In a phrase that sums up the Nahua perspective on the relationship between humans and their beloved grain, villagers say, *Sintli ne toeso* (Corn is our blood).

Whenever a baby weeps too long for no apparent reason, the parents engage the services of a shaman and sponsor a curing ritual. Similarly, my friend's dream of a baby weeping drove him to act to benefit his corn crop. The way he chose to accomplish this was by conscientiously checking his milpa for insects, searching for animal burrow or tracks, damming up eroded gullies, mounding dirt around the base of each plant, repairing the fence, taking precautions against possible storm damage, and finally, by holding a ritual offering to the corn spirit. But I learned that the dream may have multiple meanings depending on the circumstances. Besides threats to the milpa, the dream may convey information that weevils have infested the corn stored in a person's house, that a thief may be stealing property, that a mestizo rancher or the political authorities may be planning to usurp villagers' lands, or that disease, injury, or death may be waiting. The corn spirit intrudes upon a person's dreams for a wide range of reasons.[13]

Once I clearly understood the Nahua idea that corn is anthropomorphic and that humans take their bodily form from corn, much of my confusion vanished about certain symbolic objects used in seed rituals. I realized that sacred items are often symbolic body parts. For example, a forklike implement made from bamboo called a *xochimapili* (little flower hand) occupies a prominent place on altars. Marigolds, planted in the milpa and closely associated with corn, are skewered on the fork's long tines, and shamans informed me that the object represents the hand of the corn child (see figure 10.2). It is placed on the altar to help the villagers increase crop yields and meet their needs. A sacred bundle of three ears of corn used in rituals is found on a special altar in each person's house; it represents the baby corn spirit. One ear represents the backbone, and the other two comprise the spirit's face. These adornments are called *eloconemej* (corn children) (see figure 10.3). The term includes the word stem *elo-*, from *elotl,* signifying the sweet-kerneled immature ear of corn at the stage before its kernels harden.

Two additional adornments play an important role in seed rituals. These are made from a special palm leaf to which is tied freshly picked marigolds or other flowers available seasonally. One of these wandlike adornments is fashioned from seven rows of blossoms and the other from five. When made of orange marigold blossoms, these objects strongly resemble ears of corn, and they evoke the reproductive power of Seven-Flower and Five-Flower, male and female aspects of the corn spirit. In effect, they represent the physical bodies of the corn spirits with all of their intrinsic powers. The villagers place these objects on the altar or, more significantly, in the carrying basket loaded with corn seed before it is taken to the milpa and planted.

Above: Figure 10.2. Three sacred corn bundles representing Seven-Flower and Five-Flower. The bundles, here placed on a palm sleeping mat (*petate*), are formed from ears of corn wrapped in new bandanas. To the right and the left of the candle at the top of each bundle is a *xochimapili* ("little flower hand"), with marigold blossoms impaled on the tines of each implement.

Left: Figure 10.3. A close-up of a corn bundle decorated with palm leaves. This example of a bundle has a Seven-Flower wand leaning against it.

In this way, the reproductive potency of the corn spirit is conveyed to the seeds about to be planted (see figures 10.4–10.6; for additional information on Nahua altar design, see Sandstrom 2003).

The striking symbolic connection between corn and a child's body was brought home one afternoon when our *comadre* approached our dwelling carrying a colorful bundle. It was early in the spring, when the corn was still sweet and tender and could be eaten right off the cob. The villagers were enjoying a special kind of tamale called *xamitl* (literally, "adobe"), which is made from the ground kernels of the new corn. With some ceremony, our comadre presented us with the package, neatly wrapped in an embroidered cloth. We opened it and found an enormous tamale the size of a newborn infant, steaming hot and wrapped in banana leaves. This special dish epito-

Figure 10.4. Altar to the corn spirit constructed the evening before planting a milpa. The seed corn is in the carrying basket in the foreground. The tall broomlike object on the right side of the altar table is the flower of a coyol palm. The coyol flower and other offerings are to promote vigorous growth of the corn.

Above: Figure 10.5. The ritual specialist Encarnación Téllez Hernández chants before the altar. A boy (*left*) places candles on the altar as a woman (*right*) brings in a sacrificial chicken. The altar and offerings dedicated to the corn spirit are to ensure success of the crop.

Left: Figure 10.6. Close-up of the basket of seed corn with palm-leaf decorations. The taller flower-covered wand (*center*) represents Seven-Flower, the male aspect of corn, and the shorter flower-covered wand (*right*) represents Five-Flower, his twin sister and the female aspect of corn. The red and white flowers are substitutes for marigolds, which are not available in sufficient numbers during this time of the year.

mizes the season, and our friend called it a *xamconetl*, or "*xamitl* child." We were privileged to partake of the corn baby in a celebration of the fecundity and life-giving significance of the corn plant. Consuming the flesh of the corn spirit is analogous to the Christian Eucharist in which the flesh of God is eaten to celebrate wholehearted acceptance of the spirit.

The Human Body and the Cosmos

Additional symbolic uses of the human body in contemporary Nahua thought could be cataloged indefinitely, but I will limit myself to three examples that depict key pragmatic concerns. The Nahua of Amatlán conceive of the celestial realm, called *ilhuicactli* as a gigantic curved mirror (*tescatl*) reflecting the brilliance of the sun and stars. This mirror takes the form of a human body with its feet in the east and head in the west. This gigantic human being enfolds all of the cosmos within its arch and encompasses all the individuals and events that constitute our current age. Another example, on a smaller scale, is the earth (*tlali*), an important sacred presence with numerous spiritual manifestations in Nahua religious thought. The earth also exists in human form, with its head corresponding to the mountains, its body the bulk of the earth's mass, and feet corresponding to the underworld (see figure 10.7 for paper representations of earth spirits). Villagers state that the soil is the earth's flesh, the water its blood, and the rocks its bones. When shamans go to the top of a mountain to make an offering, they travel to the earth's head, wherein lies the magnificent power of earthly fertility as well as the power of death. As a final example, Nahua ritual specialists study the structure and workings of the cosmos by peering into quartz crystals. These they sometimes call "mirrors," and in the smoky interior of these crystals, the trained eye is able to divine causes of misfortune and foretell events. These windows on the spiritual world also assume the form of a human body. The pointed tip of the crystal corresponds to the head, the faceted shaft the body, and the rough, unfaceted base the feet.

The day's fortuitous conversation opened a whole new avenue of fruitful research. I spent several months checking my friend's statements against the beliefs of others and found that most villagers viewed what he said to be self-evident. I was eventually able to record myths surrounding the corn spirit that have proven to be rich sources of additional information about how Nahua employ the human body as a metaphor. For example, I found that the seeds are regarded as the children of the mother deity, *Tonantsij* (our sacred mother), who lives in a cave atop the sacred hill *Postectli* (for

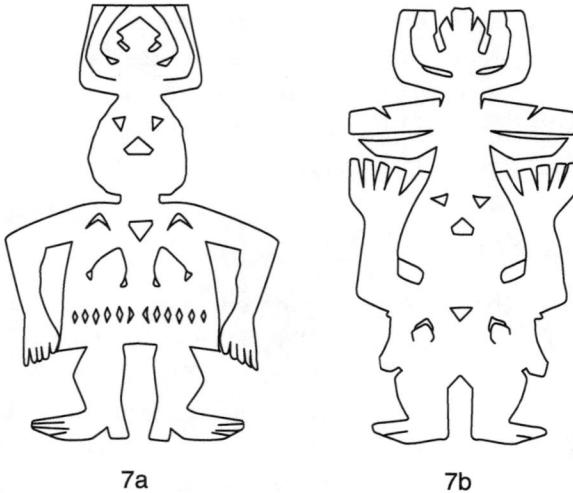

7a   7b

Figure 10.7. Representations of earth spirits. *a, Tlaltepactli,* "earth's surface." White paper, original 24.5 × 13.5 cm (see Sandstrom 1991: 262, fig. 1). The Nahua earth spirit has countless manifestations. This image portrays the surface of the earth where human beings live. The motif of downward-pointing arms is often found in earth-related spirits and is sometimes associated with death. *b, Tepetl,* "hill." White paper, original 18 × 9 cm (see Sandstrom 1991: 262, fig. 2). Features of the sacred earth such as this hill spirit are also portrayed using the human form.

a description of a pilgrimage to the cave, see Sandstrom 2001). Villagers associate Tonantsij with the moon, earth, water, and fertility, and her most important manifestation is the Virgin of Guadalupe. In ancient times, the seed spirits were lured from the interior of a mountain by the shamans, and they are now maintained in the sacred boxes containing the paper images. The seed children agree to stay in the village so long as they are treated with respect and receive periodic offerings, and the community remains a pleasant place free from fighting and discord. Should the seed spirits ever leave the village to return to their mountain home, the crops would fail and people would starve.

One myth tells about the birth of Seven-Flower. The corn spirit's mother was kept in a large earthen pot by her fearful parents to prevent her from meeting a man, marrying, and leaving home. One day, while filling her water pot at a spring, she saw a beautiful crystal ("mirror") in the water and kept it in her mouth so that no one would discover it. She accidentally swallowed the crystal and shortly afterwards found herself pregnant with Seven-Flower. The grandmother of Seven-Flower was a *tsitsimitl,* a kind of sorceress (see Klein 2000), and one day while attending her grandchild she decided to kill him. The old woman repeatedly threw the child in the water or buried him in the earth but found, much to her consternation, that he soon reappeared. After several such thwarted attempts, she placed the child in the sweat bath and lit a huge fire. He again emerged unhurt; using guile, he convinced his grandmother to step into the sweat bath in his place. She immediately expired and was reduced to ashes, whereupon Seven-Flower gathered up the ashes, placed them in a box, and gave the box to a toad to cast into the sea. Curiosity got the better of the toad, and against explicit instructions he opened the box and inadvertently released all of the world's poisonous and stinging insects. Today, the toad's descendants retain the bumpy skin caused by insect bites, the consequence of their ancestor's disobedience.

Shortly after this incident, Seven-Flower escaped from the world by sequestering himself inside a sacred mountain. The mountain identified in the story as Postectitla or Postectli (Broken Place) is a giant basaltic core jutting from the earth several kilometers north of the village. The shape of its peak gives the impression that the mountain has been broken off at the top. With Seven-Flower gone, the milpas failed and hunger threatened the village. One day, the villagers saw red ants carrying grains of corn from a cave on the mountainside, and they went to investigate.[14] They persuaded the water spirit, who lives in the sea and controls thunder and lightning, to break open the mountain. Flames engulfed the mountain, threatening the seeds. Thunder spirits, conceived by the Nahua as dwarflike old men carrying staffs, retrieved water from Tonantsij's cave and extinguished the fire with raindrops. Some corn escaped the flames entirely, and this comes down to us as white corn. Yellow corn descends from seeds that were slightly scorched, and red corn descends from seeds that were severely burned. Black (or purple) corn comes from the grains that were almost destroyed by the fire. Here we have the Nahua explanation for the origin of different varieties of corn (see Sandstrom and Gómez Martínez 2004 for a chant recounting the myth of the corn spirit).

These myths, and many similar ones that I have recorded, are composed of episodes linked to each other in Nahua thought through the key symbol of the human body. Tonantsij, seen as an earth mother and manifestation of fertility, lives in a cave on a mountain peak corresponding to the earth's head. Water, regarded as the earth's blood, is retrieved from her cave by the rain dwarfs and sprinkled on the growing fields of corn. The mother of Seven-Flower is collecting precious spring water from the earth when she finds a crystal with its tiny head, body, and feet. The fertilizing crystal causes her to give birth to the corn spirit, who in turn lends his form to the human race that he will later nourish and sustain. Bent on his destruction, Seven-Flower's grandmother tries to bury him in the earth, but like the seed in the fertile field, he returns anew after a short absence. The grandmother's body is reduced to ashes, and she is carried to the seashore, a liminal place where the earth's blood and flesh meet. The poisonous and malevolent components of her body are revealed in the stinging insects unleashed by the foolish toad. Eventually, Seven-Flower hides out in the interior of a mountain, where his ensuing rescue by the water spirit burns his body, giving us the varieties of corn grown by people to this day.

The culture hero Seven-Flower, through his superior wit and special powers, defeats his murderous grandmother and sacrifices his body so that people may live. Mythic episodes usually involve only Seven-Flower, but as I have explained, the corn spirit exists in multiple aspects that may be old/young or male/female simultaneously. Shamans cut separate paper figures (see figure 10.1) of each manifestation of the corn spirit, and each has a distinct role in seed rituals. Nahua identify Seven-Flower with their ethnicity in their belief that the corn spirit favors the more respectful Native Americans over and above mestizos. Most important, the corn spirit's body represents the fruitful conjunction of earth, water, and sunlight that nourishes humans and gives the gift of life.

Human beings live by consuming the flesh of the corn, but, as we have seen, the link between corn and humans is far more intimate and complex than this subsistence relationship implies. For the Nahua, the essence of the human body is corn. In Nahua thought, our physical body is what links us to the sacred powers of the universe, and the cosmic forces residing in the body are what make us alive. López Austin called these forces "animistic entities" and their physical locations in the body "animistic centers" (López Austin 1988: 1: 181–201, 204–36). The animistic entities are the closest approximation to the Western concept of soul. In ancient Nahua thought, according to López Austin, each human being possessed three major souls: *ihiyotl, teyolia,* and *tonali.* Among contemporary Nahua, one of these—the ihiyotl, "breath soul"—has been lost or, more likely, transformed into literally disembodied wind spirits that cause disease (see figure 10.8). The disembodiment of the soul from its human host, especially souls of relatives who experienced unfortunate deaths, is what makes the winds unpredictable and dangerous. However, most Nahua continue to hold a belief in versions of the other two souls. The first they call the *yolotl,* "heart," and

Figure 10.8. Representations of wind spirits. *a, Ejecatl,* "wind." Manila paper, original 23 × 8.5 cm. Wind spirits cause disease in Nahua belief, and they too are portrayed in human form. These dangerous spirits are the *yolotl* ("heart") souls of people who died violent deaths. *b,* Another example of a malevolent wind spirit. Manila paper, original 23.5 × 8 cm.

8a   8b

it corresponds to the ancient teyolia. Like the older concept, this soul is a kind of impersonal life force found in animals and some objects in addition to humans. The second soul is the tonali, which modern Nahua conceive as a segmented personal soul associated with the sun's heat, body heat, fate, destiny, and the individual personality. We know what these souls look like because shamans portray them in cut-paper images. Not surprisingly, like the corn that supplies the sacred animating power of human life, these souls take the form of tiny human beings (see figure 10.9; see McKeever Furst 1995 for a general treatment of soul beliefs and an extensive analysis of ancient Nahua concepts).

The etymology of the terms for these two soul concepts provides an insight into their nature. *Yoloti* derives from the Nahuatl *olin,* meaning "movement" (León-Portilla 1963: 5). The yolotl soul is the animating principle, that which makes something or someone alive. *Tonali* derives from *tona,* meaning "heat" or "to be warm." The word for the physical sun, *tonatij,* also is formed from this root. In Nahua thought, the sun provides the energy (*chicahualistli*) that animates the beings and objects in the universe; this is the source of the soul concepts yolotl and tonali. The sun, called *Totiotsij* (our sacred deity) in its spiritual aspect, rises in the morning at the celestial mirror's feet, traverses its body, and sets each evening at its head. As it marks its passage along the length of the cosmic body, it supplies the universe with energy and enters our own bodies when we consume the sacred corn (figure 10.10d represents the sun in the form of the spirit of the cross).

9a   9b

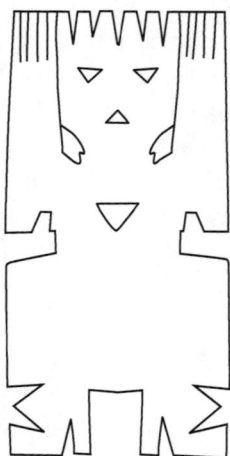

9c

Figure 10.9. Representations of human souls. *a, Tonali,* "soul." Manila paper, original 19.5 × 17 cm. The tonali ("heat") soul of a human being is portrayed in this paired anthropomorphic figure. *b, Tonali,* "soul." Manila paper, original 21 × 18.5 cm (see Sandstrom 1991: 276, fig. 30). This double figure portrays a female soul on the left along with her male companion. Nahua shamans use this image in magical rituals to make people fall in love. *c, Tonali conetsi,* "child's soul." Manila paper, original 21 × 10 cm. The souls of children as well as adults are visualized by the Nahua as having human form.

The paper-cutting tradition allows us to witness directly the power of the human form in Nahua thought. Shamans can portray and manipulate the spiritual essence of people, animals, inanimate objects, and natural phenomena by cutting the images of their yolotl and/or tonali souls from paper and submitting these to appropriate ritual treatment. With the exception of a few theriomorphic forms and some rare leafy images representing plants, these cuttings are invariably anthropomorphic. A ritual may require cutting hundreds or even thousands of paper images representing many different

10a

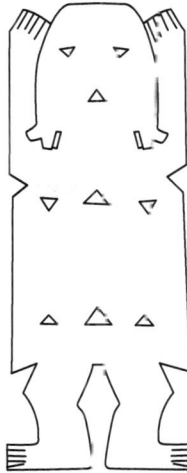

10b

10c

10d

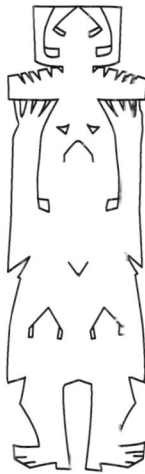

10e

10f

Figure 10.10. Representations of spirits of plants, natural phenomena, and guardians. *a, Chili,* "chile." Manila paper, original 17.5 × 5.5 cm. This image represents the spirit of the chile. Directly above the images of chile peppers is a triangle representing the spirit's heart. *b, Tlixihuantsij,* "sacred fire." Manila paper, original 17.5 × 6.5 cm (see Sandstrom 1991: 265, fig. 7). Anthropomorphic portrayal of the fire spirit. *c, Sitlalij,* "star." Manila paper, original 17.5 × 5.5 cm (see Sandstrom 1991: 264, fig. 6). Stars are guardian spirits in Nahua belief, and they are portrayed by shamans in the form of the human body. *d, Carus,* "cross." Manila paper, original 17 × 6 cm. The spirit of the cross, generally associated with the sun in Nahua thought, is portrayed as a human figure. *e, Tlamocuitlahuijquetl,* "witness or guardian." White paper, original 24 × 6.5 cm. In Nahua belief, many guardian spirits such as this example inhabit the cosmos. *f, Miquilistli,* "death." Manila paper, original 21.5 × 14 cm. Even death takes an anthropomorphic form in Nahua religious belief.

spirit entities, as illustrated by the small sample in figures 10.1 and figures 10.7–10.10. The basic feature of each cutting is a relatively undifferentiated human form. This form represents the animating force (the tonali, yolotl, or combination of tonali and yolotl) of whatever entity the shaman wishes to represent; figure 10.10 underscores the point that crops, guardian spirits, and even death are similarly depicted as human bodies. The ritual specialist cuts symbolic or iconographic markers either within the body or as outcroppings emerging from the body to establish a particular spirit's identity. The core human form is what links the paper image with the spiritual essence and the spiritual essence, in turn, with all that is sacred in the cosmos. Elsewhere, my coauthor and I have argued that the human form in the paper figures represents the principle of animation and that it is this common element in the paper figures that reveals the pantheistic quality of the paper cult religions (Sandstrom and Sandstrom 1986: 275–77; see also León-Portilla 1992: 21). The cosmos is the human body writ large, and like a body it is suffused with the sacred and animating power of life.

Conclusion

By describing aspects of contemporary Nahua religion in terms of concepts deriving from the pre-Hispanic era, I am not implying that the Nahua have remained unchanged over the past half millennium. Since the conquest, the Native American inhabitants of Mesoamerica have experienced some of the most catastrophic events of any people on earth, and they have met these challenges by adapting their culture to the changing circumstances of their existence. Yet many of their ancient cultural patterns remain undeniably intact. López Austin illustrated the importance of the human body in the religious ideology of ancient Nahua, and the body continues to play a crucial role in the beliefs and practices of many of their descendants. There is an ever-present danger in comparisons of this sort that cultural elements can be taken out of context and mixed and matched unsystematically, resulting in spurious correlations and false continuities. Nevertheless, culture is far from ephemeral or arbitrary. My friend's dream of the weeping baby and his statement—surprising to me—was so deeply a part of his worldview that he could not imagine that I did not possess such fundamental knowledge.

Emic perspectives can be based on models or structures that fall outside of the awareness of the people using them (Harris 1979: 37). The metaphor of the human body is so fundamental to the contemporary Nahua worldview that it lies beyond the direct consciousness of most villagers with whom I talked and consulted. Its symbolism is revealed to the outsider partially and incompletely in unexpected circumstances such as myth episodes, ritual objects that represent body parts, offhand comments by informants, and giant tamales swaddled like babies. For this reason, key symbols often lie in an epistemological no-man's-land, difficult to approach through the analysis of either emic data collected among informants or etic observations recorded by field researchers. Once one understands that the concept of the human body is of such central importance, however, one can more easily witness how pervasive it is in Nahua life.[15]

Ortner offers no specific technique for identifying key symbols in cultural analysis but states that they may be "discovered by virtue of a number of reliable indicators which point to a cultural focus of interest" (Ortner 1973: 1344). In other words, there is no methodology by which to distinguish key symbols from less-important symbols, but researchers are likely to recognize them when they appear. However, a symbol deeply embedded in the cosmology is by no means easy to isolate and identify, and Ortner overstates the facility with which key symbols may be identified. As important as the human body is in Nahua thought, no religious specialist or nonspecialist has ever volunteered that the human body is central to their religious symbolism. They only confirmed the idea after I presented it to them in the appropriate context.

The amorphous and unformulated character of such central ideas should make investigators cautious when using symbols as the basis of their attempts to understand similarities and differences among cultures. Although the body is a symbol of unequaled importance for Nahua and easily fits a key symbol category as it has been defined, there is no way of knowing that it is *the* key symbol. Other symbolic elements such as colors, directions, ethnic identifiers, and distinctions of center/periphery and purity/pollution also serve important organizing and orienting functions for the Nahua. Each of these could also qualify as a key to understand Nahua symbolic thought. In fact, depending on context, almost any set of symbols can take on characteristics of the key symbol as defined by Ortner. Built-in flexibility—the polysemic or polyvocal quality of symbols—is probably a necessary attribute of symbols (key or otherwise) if they are to play an active role in social and cultural systems. But this flexibility or malleability in how symbols are understood and manipulated by people undermines the ability of the key symbol concept to provide verifiable measures of cultural difference and culture change.

Although the human body is certainly an orienting symbolic principle for the Nahua, I am not convinced that its functions can be as neatly analyzed as Geertz and Ortner have suggested. Anthropologists and others have developed numerous schemes for determining how symbols do their work in a culture (see Kelly and Kaplan 1990: 120). Many of these spring from semiotics and take as their model the analysis of language (Leach 1968: 524). These analysts isolate characteristics of individual symbols, distinguish different functions for various types of symbols, show how symbols are combined, or illustrate how the same symbol can serve different functions in different contexts. When we examine how the Nahua use the symbol of the human body, however, many of these logical distinctions seem artificial and far removed from real life.

For the contemporary Nahua, the human body is more than a summarizing or elaborating symbol, more than a model *of* or *for* reality; it is instead the sum and substance of the cosmos itself. Sky, earth, corn, ritual objects, and divinatory crystals are literally human bodies, whether large or small. As we have seen, the sacred paper images, representing both harmful and salutary spirits, are cut into bodily forms by shamans. And the animating principles of yolotl and tonali are conceived of by the Nahua as anthropomorphic in nature. The form, substance, and internal dynamics of the human body are identical to the structure and forces that power the universe. In short, the body in Nahua conception appears simultaneously to serve several of the distinct functions outlined by Geertz and Ortner. It acts as a model of reality and a model for reality at the same time (functioning both to elaborate and to summarize)—a property Geertz (1973: 93) calls "intertransposability" that he claims is characteristic of many cultural symbols. Thus, while breaking symbols down into component functions for an etic analysis of Nahua mental life may be fruitful, doing so will not go far in helping us to understand how people act or think in relation to their important symbols. The problem is that there are few constraints on the ways in which people respond to the key symbols in their cultures. Thus, the very nature of cultural symbols means that symbolic analysis alone will always be incomplete. This problem can be resolved only by research that focuses on how individuals use cultural symbols as guideposts in the universe of meaning that the symbols themselves partially create, as well as how individuals manipulate these symbols to produce and sustain a more satisfying life.

To illustrate this point, let me briefly review the weeping baby phenomenon. The connections that Nahua draw between an ear of corn and a baby are not obvious to the outside observer: they are symbolic and understandable only in the context of Nahua culture. The link is the product of a long chain of associations deriving from a fundamental view that the cosmos is anthropomorphic. The corn baby is thus a model *of* a wider reality. But the corn plant gives humans their physical form, and so the corn baby is a model *for* reality at the same time. It is also the model for the production of sacred objects such as paper images, "flower hands," baby-sized tamales, and the bundle of cobs representing the corn child's face. The symbolic image of the corn child is clearly summarizing, in Ortner's (1973: 1340) formulation, in that it is an emotionally charged sacred symbol but serves simultaneously as an elaborating symbol in that it orders experience. It is a root metaphor because it allows villagers to visualize their relationship to the wider cosmos (in particular, the energy-producing sun) and to their fields. Finally, the corn baby provides a key scenario, in Ortner's terms, in that it channels actions of the individual farmer, motivating him to hold ritual observances, exercise greater care for his fields, and take steps to ensure the perpetuation of his universe.

Thus, the corn baby (as an extension of the more fundamental key symbol of the human body) itself becomes a key symbol in Nahua thought. Like the body, it can play a variety of roles and serve a number of ends at the same time. My friend interpreted his dream of the weeping baby as a key scenario and reacted accordingly. But one cannot predict precisely how a person will react to such a dream. Another man, experiencing a similar dream, will be led to search for threats to his relationship with the sacred sun, to create fresh sacred images for his house altar, to meditate upon the ephemeral nature of life, to guard his field against a thief or sorcerer, to check for pests in his stockpile of corn, and ultimately to feel satisfied that he is a *masehuali*—a Native American farmer—and not a disrespectful *coyotl*. In short, although the appearance of the weeping baby in his dream caused my friend to return to his cornfields, he could have responded in many other ways, each of which would be consistent with the meaning of this key symbol. Employing key symbols to understand why people behave the way they do will always be of limited use because a given symbol is a cultural tool that people can choose to wield in various ways at a number of levels depending on their circumstances. People respond to symbols, just as this one villager did, but we cannot fully appreciate why people behave the way they do until we also take into account the ecological, economic, political, or other pragmatic factors that lead them to select from a variety of possible meanings and interpret a given symbol in a certain way.

The human body qualifies as a key symbol in Nahua culture, and its recognition as such allows the anthropologist to detect a hidden order in the bewildering diversity of myths, beliefs, ritual acts, statements, sacred objects, interactions, and behaviors that constitute Nahua daily existence. But that order is only partly and inconsistently determined by the symbolic substratum of the culture. The degree to which symbols account for observed behavior must be determined by the investigator for each given instance under study. In some cases, key symbols may account for much of what is observed, but moments later, people may respond primarily to pragmatic factors and apparently contradict their own symbolic understandings. Additionally, one can often explain a great deal of behavior without regard to the symbol system at all.

In conclusion, the myths, symbols, and behaviors that contribute to the Nahua conception of corn can be clarified by referring to the key symbol of the human body. But because human beings are active agents in the creation and maintenance of culture, this symbol-making power (and the conceptualization of the corn spirit that it gives rise to it) is complex and flexible. People interpret symbols variously depending on their pragmatic circumstances. This variability is so great that it has become almost invisible in village life; even extensive field research by numerous ethnographers has failed to illuminate this important key symbol. Among New World peoples, the Nahua are unique because of the extensive ethnohistorical record of their culture that begins before European contact. In analyzing this record, López Austin revealed that concepts of the human body in multiple elaborations lie near the heart of Nahua culture. Cultures with a less-complete record would be far more difficult to analyze in terms of key symbols. Although such symbols are important in helping us organize and comprehend the complexity of social life, they cannot lead to comprehensive or even very satisfactory explanations of socially shared behavior patterns. This is because symbols, and especially key symbols, deliberately allow for variable interpretations on the part of members of the society under study.[16]

Acknowledgments

I thank the following people for their helpful comments on earlier drafts: Norm Bradley, James W. Dow, Katherine A. Faust, Brad R. Huber, John A. Mead, Pamela Effrein Sandstrom, and James M. Taggart. I would like especially to thank Professor Jesús Ruvalcaba Mercado of the Centro de Investigaciones y Estudios Superiores en Antropología Social (CIESAS) for giving permission to publish an updated English version of an earlier contribution that originally appeared as Sandstrom 1993.

Notes

1. Recent ethnographic work that builds on López Austin 1988 includes Aramoni 1990; Galinier 1990; Sandstrom 1991; and Signorini and Lupo 1989. For recent ethnohistorical analyses of the interaction between Spaniards and Native Americans during the colonial period, see also Burkhart 1989; Klor de Alva 1982; Lockhart 1991, 1992. This research promises to uncover historical processes linking pre-Hispanic with contemporary indigenous religious beliefs and practices.

2. It is significant that López Austin's interpretations of the crucial symbolic role played by the human body in Nahua culture have proven so useful to investigators of contemporary Native American culture. Most of the documents upon which he bases his work date from the colonial period, and more than four hundred years of often-turbulent history separate these records from the modern Native Americans. López Austin himself recognized continuities between past and present indigenous cultures, and he even used ethnographic data to supplement his analysis of the ethnohistorical sources (López Austin 1988: 1: 24–28). The parallels between ancient and modern systems of belief are evidence of the remarkable persistence of pre-Hispanic religious concepts. This fact contradicts the opinions of scholars who conclude that Spanish missionary efforts overcame Native American religion in all but the most inaccessible areas of Mesoamerica (for example, Friedlander 1975; Ricard 1966 [1933]: 276–82). In addition to uncovering the roots of contemporary beliefs, López Austin also affirms the remarkable unity of religion throughout Mesoamerica (see Hunt 1977: 46 on the shared symbolic systems among cultures of the region; see also Gossen 1986). Insights derived from a study of contemporary Nahua religion can be applied fruitfully to other groups, both ancient and modern.

3. A sample of recent ethnographic studies reflecting improved data gathering and analysis includes Dow 1974, 1986; Galinier 1987, 1990; Gossen 1974; Lipp 1991; Nutini 1993; Signorini and Lupo 1989; and Taggart 1975, 1983.

4. For a summary of developments in this area, see Bell 1992: ch. 5. Earlier in the century, Robert Hertz (1973 [1909]) and Marcell Mauss (1973 [1936]) wrote now-classic essays placing the body in its social context.

5. For a discussion of cultural universals with reference to body symbolism and adornment, facial expression, and handedness, see also Brown 1991.

6. The 2000 census reveals that the ninety-four municipios constituting the Huasteca region (of which the Huasteca Veracruzana is a significant component) are inhabited by 460,736 Nahuatl speakers ages five and older (INEGI 2006; Sandstrom 1995: 184).

7. Few smaller villages have a resident priest or permanent church building. However, in recent years, North American Protestant missionaries have moved into the area and have succeeded in making converts even among people living in remote hamlets. Their successes can be linked in part to the changing economic circumstances in Mex-

ico and the breakdown of the social order that traces to colonial times. For an analysis of this process, see Dow and Sandstrom 2001; Sandstrom 1991: ch. 7.

8. Studies of the Nahua include Chamoux 1981; Huber 1990a, 1990b; Montoya Briones 1964; Reyes García 1960; Reyes García and Christensen 1976; Sandstrom 1991; Sandstrom and Sandstrom 1986; Taggart 1975, 1983; and Williams García 1957. On the Otomí, see Boilès 1971; Dow 1974, 1986; Galinier 1987, 1990; and Lenz 1973 [1948]; on the Tepehua, see Gessain 1938; and Williams García 1963, 1972; on the Totonac, see Garma Navarro 1986, 1987; Ichon 1969; and Masferrer Kan 1986a, 1986b; on the Huastec (Teenek), see Alcorn 1984; Ariel de Vidas 2004; and Ruvalcaba Mercado 1987, 1992. Recent general works on the Huasteca region, of which northern Veracruz is a part, include Gortari Krauss and Ruvalcaba Mercado 1990; Michelet 1989; Sandstrom 1995, 2000; Sandstrom and García Valencia 2005; and Stresser-Péan 1979.

9. I have conducted research in this village for various periods totaling more than forty-eight months beginning in 1970. Amatlán is inhabited by about six hundred people who support themselves through slash-and-burn horticulture. The village is quite remote, far from tertiary roads and more than a three-hour walk from the *cabecera* of Ixhuatlán de Madero. My research has been supported by several funding agencies, including Fulbright-Hayes, the Organization of American States, Indiana University–Bloomington, Indiana University–Purdue University Fort Wayne (IPFW), American Council of Learned Societies, American Philosophical Society, and Foundation for the Advancement of Mesoamerican Studies, Inc. (FAMSI). In Mexico, the research has been sponsored by the Instituto de Antropología, Universidad Veracruzana, and the Centro de Investigaciones y Estudios Superiores en Antropología Social (CIESAS).

10. Ever since I began conducting research in this region of Mexico, I have been intrigued by the shamanic art of portraying important spirits in cut paper (see also Sandstrom and Sandstrom 2002). My curiosity grew when I learned that shamans carefully store these fully dressed images of the corn spirit in a sacred box that they preserve on a special altar along with images of the spirits of other crops. The ritual specialists and their assistants place beeswax candles, miniature house furnishings, spare clothing, and other items in the box with the seed images, along with lists they maintain of people who had donated money and offerings so that the seed spirits would remember whom to bless with increased crop yields. Throughout the year, individuals place offerings before the box, and occasionally a particular household may elect to sponsor an elaborate ritual dedicated to the seeds. Corn is used by the Nahua to represent all of the crops they grow, and thus images of the corn spirit in the guise of the golden twin children are always at the center of crop-increase rituals.

11. One would think that a spirit of such importance would find its origin in pre-Hispanic belief systems, and indeed we have records of numerous deities among the Aztecs that are directly or indirectly associated with corn. The Aztec Chicomecoatl (Seven Serpent), also called Chicomolotzin (Seven Ears of Corn), was the goddess of general vegetation and sustenance and was sometimes portrayed holding double ears of corn. Centeotl was the god of corn in a general manifestation, Xilonen (Corn Baby) the

tender or immature ear of corn, and Llamatecuhtli (Lady Old Woman) the dry, mature ear, according to Bernardino de Sahagún (1970 [1575–80?]: bk. 1: 13) and Alfonso Caso (1970 [1958]: 45–47). Caso also points out that the number seven in Aztec thought was associated with seeds and often appeared in the names of crop deities.

12. López Austin (1988: 1: 162) notes the link between corn and the human body among ancient Nahua, and this same relationship has been reported among contemporary Nahua (Signorini and Lupo 1989: 48). For a remarkable description of the congruence of the Nahua and scientific understanding of corn fertility, see Pollan 2006: 28–29: the pollen splits into two twin nuclei to penetrate the silk, enter the flower, and create the germ of the kernel.

13. The Nahua tell a story that illustrates the relationship between corn and people: Once a coyotl (coyote, the general term for a non–Native American) was loading corn and he let some grains drop on the ground. A masehuali (Native American farmer) passing by heard a child crying, and when he approached, he saw the abandoned kernels weeping at the lack of respect shown them by the coyotl. The man carefully collected each kernel, and from that time on corn has supported the Native Americans. In fact, on many occasions I have noticed that villagers take great care to gather up any stray kernels of corn that may have been scattered in shelling or grinding.

14. Note the similarity of this account to the myth told among the classical Aztecs found in Taggart 1983: 88–89.

15. That such a deeply held conception of the world permeates so many areas of Nahua life suggests that it must be firmly rooted in Mesoamerican culture. Although people in all societies make some use of the human body as a metaphor, the indigenous people of this region have elaborated the practice to the extreme. Archaeologists may make use of this propensity when they interpret religious concepts from past civilizations. For example, the Olmec civilization left sculptures of giant heads, babies, anthropomorphic celts, and numerous figurines. Although it is not yet possible to demonstrate a direct connection between the extant and ancient ideologies, the human body is very likely the key symbol that links the mysterious artifacts of Olmec and other ancient cultures with contemporary Native American symbolic systems. Numerous recent works point to the growing interest among archaeologists in pre-Hispanic figurines and the human body, particularly Bachand et al. 2003; Bradley 2006; Brumfiel 2005; Grove 2000; Lesure 1999, 2002, 2005; Marcus 1998; and Palka 2002. See especially Joyce 2005 for an extensive review of the literature available to archaeologists and other scholars.

16. Figures 10.1b, 10.1c, and 10.1e are reproduced from Sandstrom and Sandstrom 1986: figs. 46, 45, and 40, respectively and figures 10.1d, 10.7a, 10.7b, 10.9b, 10.10b, 10.10c are from Sandstrom 1991: figs. 5, 1, 2, 30, 7, and 6, respectively. The other figures were first published in Sandstrom 1998. All of the paper cuttings were created by Nahua ritual specialists from Amatlán (a pseudonym), in Ixhuatlán de Madero, northern Veracruz, Mexico. The line drawings were done by Pamela Effrein Sandstrom and Michael A. Sandstrom and digitized by James Whitcraft of IPFW's Learning Resource Center.

References Cited

Alcorn, Janice. 1984. *Huastec Mayan Ethnobotany.* University of Texas Press, Austin.

Aramoni, Ma. Elena. 1990. *Talokan tata, talokan nana; nuestras raíces: Hierofanías y testimonios de un mundo indígena.* Consejo Nacional para la Cultura y las Artes, Mexico City.

Ariel de Vidas, Anath. 2004. *Thunder Doesn't Live Here Anymore: The Culture of Marginality among the Teeneks of Tantoyuca.* University Press of Colorado, Boulder.

Bachand, H., R. Joyce, and J. A. Hendon. 2003. Bodies Moving in Space: Ancient Mesoamerican Human Sculpture and Embodiment. *Cambridge Archaeological Journal* 13 (2): 238–47.

Barrera Rivera, J. A., M. de L. Gallardo Parrodi, and A. Montúfor López. 2001. La ofrenda 102 del Templo Mayor. *Arqueología Mexicana* 8 (48): 70–77.

Beals, Ralph L. 1967. Acculturation. In *Social Anthropology,* ed. M. Nash, 449–68. University of Texas Press, Austin.

Bell, Catherine. 1992. *Ritual Theory, Ritual Practice.* University of Oxford Press, Oxford.

Berdan, Frances. 1982. *The Aztecs of Central Mexico: An Imperial Society.* Holt, Rinehart, and Winston, New York.

Blacking, John, ed. 1977. *Anthropology of the Body.* Academic Press, London.

Boilès, Charles L. 1971. Síntesis y sincretismo en el carnaval otomí. *América Indígena* 31 (3): 555–63.

Bradley, Douglas E. 2006. Painted Souls of Ancient Mesoamerica. Paper presented at the 1st Annual Braunstein Symposium, University of Nevada–Las Vegas, Marjorie Barrick Museum of Natural History, Las Vegas.

Brown, Donald E. 1991. *Human Universals.* McGraw-Hill, New York.

Brumfiel, Elizabeth M., ed. 2005. *La producción local y el poder en el Xaltocan Postclasico* [Production and Power at Postclassic Xaltocan]. Instituto Nacional de Antropología e Historia, Mexico City.

Burkhart, Louise. 1989. *The Slippery Earth: Nahua-Christian Moral Dialogue in Sixteenth-Century Mexico.* University of Arizona Press, Tucson.

Caso, Alfonso. 1970 [1958]. *The Aztecs: People of the Sun.* Trans. L. Dunham. Civilization of the American Indian Series 50. Reprint, University of Oklahoma Press, Norman.

Chamoux, Marie Nöelle. 1981. *Indiens de la sierra: La communauté paysanne au mexique.* Editions L'Harmattan, Paris.

Christensen, Bodil. 1942. Notas sobre la fabricación del papel indígena y su empleo para "brujerías" en la Sierra Norte de Puebla, México. *Revista Mexicana de Estudios Antropológicos* 6 (1–2): 109–24.

Classen, Constance. 1993. *Inca Cosmology and the Human Body.* University of Utah Press, Salt Lake City.

Douglas, Mary. 1973. *Natural Symbols: Explorations in Cosmology.* 2nd ed. Barrie and Jenkins, London.

Dow, James W. 1974. *Santos y supervivencias: Funciones de la religión en una comuni-*

dad otomí, México. Colección SEP-INI 33. Instituto Nacional Indigenista y Secretaría de Educación Pública, Mexico City.

———. 1986. *The Shaman's Touch: Otomí Indian Symbolic Healing.* University of Utah Press, Salt Lake City.

Dow, James W., and Alan R. Sandstrom, eds 2001. *Holy Saints and Fiery Preachers: The Anthropology of Protestantism in Mexico and Central America.* Praeger, Westport, Conn.

Friedlander, Judith. 1975. *Being Indian in Hueyapan: A Study of Forced Identity in Contemporary Mexico.* St. Martin's, New York.

Galinier, Jacques. 1987. *Pueblos de la Sierra Madre: Etnografía de la comunidad otomí.* Instituto Nacional Indigenista, Mexico City.

———. 1990. *La mitad del mundo: Cuerpo y cosmos en los rituales otomies.* Universidad Nacional Autónoma de México; Centro de Estudios Mexicanos y Centroamericanos; and Instituto Nacional Indigenista, Mexico City.

Garma Navarro, Carlos. 1986. El protestantismo en una comunidad totonaca: Un estudio político. In *Religíon popular: Hegemonía y resistencia,* ed. E. Boege and E. Masferrer K., 97–116. Cuaderno de Trabajo 6. Instituto Nacional de Antropología e Historia, Mexico City.

———. 1987. *Protestantismo en una comunidad totonaca de Puebla, México.* Serie de Antropología Social, Colección 76. Instituto Nacional Indigenista, Mexico City.

Geertz, Clifford. 1968. "Religion." In *International Encyclopedia of the Social Sciences,* vol. 13, ed. D. Sills, 398–406. Macmillan and Free Press, New York.

———. 1973. Religion as a Cultural System. In *The Interpretation of Cultures,* ed. C. Geertz, 87–125. Basic Books, New York.

Gessain, Robert. 1938. Contribution a l'étude des cultes et des cérémonies indigènes de la région de Huehuetla (Hidalgo). *Journal de la Société des Américanistes* n.s. 30: 343–71.

Gortari Krauss, Ludka de, and Jesús Ruvalcaba Mercado eds. 1990. *La huasteca: Vida y milagro.* Cuadernos de la Casa Chata 173. Centro de Investigaciones y Estudios Superiores en Antropología Social, Mexico City.

Gossen, Gary H. 1974. *Chamulas in the World of the Sun: Time and Space in a Maya Oral Tradition.* Harvard University Press, Cambridge, Mass.

———. 1986. Mesoamerican Ideas as a Foundation for Regional Synthesis. In *Symbol and Meaning beyond the Closed Community: Essays in Mesoamerican Ideas,* ed. G. Gossen, 1–8. Institute for Mesoamerican Studies, State University of New York, Albany.

Grigsby, Thomas L., and Carmen Cook de Leonard. 1992. Xilonen in Tepoztlán: A Comparison of Tepoztecan and Aztec Agrarian Ritual Schedules. *Ethnohistory* 39 (2): 108–47.

Grove, David C. 2000. Faces of the Earth at Chalcatzingo, Mexico: Serpents, Caves, and Mountains in Middle Formative Period Iconography. *Studies in the History of Art* 58: 276–95.

Harris, Marvin. 1979. *Cultural Materialism: The Struggle for a Science of Culture.* Random House, New York.

Hernández Cristóbal, Amalia, Rogelio Xocua Cuicahuac, Aurora Tequihuactle Jiménez, and Benito Chimalhua Cosme. 1982. Las ceremonias del cerro Xochipapatla, Huitzitzilco, Ixhuatlán de Madero, Veracruz. In *Nuestra maíz: Treinta monografías populares*, vol. 2, ed. M. E. Hope and L. Pereyra, 45–66. Museo Nacional de Culturas Populares, Mexico City.

Hernández Cuellar, Rosendo. 1982. *La religion nahua en Texoloc, municipio de Xochiatipan, Hgo.* Cuadernos de Información y Divulgación para Maestros Bilingües, Etnolingüística, 51. Instituto Nacional Indigenista y Secretaría de Educación Pública, Programa de Formación Profesional de Etnolingüistas, Mexico City.

Hertz, Robert. 1973 [1909]. The Pre-eminence of the Right Hand: A Study in Religious Polarity. In *Right and Left: Essays on Dual Symbolic Classification*, ed. R. Needham, 3–31. University of Chicago Press, Chicago.

Huber, Brad R. 1990a. The Recruitment of Nahua Curers: Role Conflict and Gender. *Ethnology* 29: 159–76.

———. 1990b. Curers, Illness, and Healing in San Andrés Hueyapan, a Nahuat-Speaking Community of the Sierra Norte de Puebla, Mexico. *Notas Mesoamericanas* 12: 51–66.

Huber, Brad R., and Alan R. Sandstrom, eds. 2001. *Mesoamerican Healers.* University of Texas Press, Austin.

Hunt, Eva. 1977. *The Transformation of the Hummingbird: Cultural Roots of a Zinacanteco Mythical Poem.* Cornell University Press, Ithaca, N.Y.

Ichon, Alain. 1969. *La religion de totonaques de la Sierra.* Etudes et documents de l'Institut d'ethnologie. Editions du Centre National de la Recherche Scientifique, Paris.

INEGI. 2006. Población de 5 años y más que habla alguna lengua indígena por municipio y lengua indígena según condición de habla española y sexo. *II Conteo de población y vivienda, 2005: Resultados definitivos; Tabulados básicos.* Instituto Nacional de Estadística Geográfica e Informática, Aguascalientes. http://www.inegi.gob.mx/est/contenidos/espanol/sistemas/conteo2005/Default.asp (posted May 2006).

Ixmatlahua Montalvo, Isabel, María Martínez Gertrudes, Manuel Orea Méndez, Benito Martínez Hernández, and Juan Antonio Martínez Aldrete. 1982. El cultivo del maíz y tres rituales asociados a su producción: Cacahuatengo, Ixhuatlán de Madero, Veracruz. In *Nuestra maíz: Treinta monografías populares*, vol. 2, ed. M. E. Hope and L. Pereyra, 67–101. Museo Nacional de Culturas Populares, Mexico City.

Jolly, Pieter. 2005. On the Definition of Shamanism. *Current Anthropology* 46 (1): 127–28.

Joyce, Rosemary. 2005. Archaeology of the Body. *Annual Review of Anthropology* 34: 139–58.

Kehoe, Alice Beck. 2000. *Shamans and Religion: An Anthropological Exploration in Critical Thinking.* Waveland Press, Prospect Heights, Ill.

Kelly, John D., and Martha Kaplan. 1990. History, Structure, and Ritual. *Annual Review of Anthropology* 19: 119–50.

Klein, Cecelia F. 2000. The Devil and the Skirt: An Iconographic Inquiry into the Pre-Hispanic Nature of the *Tzitzimime. Ancient Mesoamerica* 11: 1–26.

Klein, Cecelia F., Eulogio Guzmán, Elisa C. Mandell, and Maya Stanfield-Mazzi. 2002. The Role of Shamanism in Mesoamerican Art: A Reassessment. *Current Anthropology* 43 (3): 383–419.

Klor de Alva, Jorge. 1982. Spiritual Conflict and Accommodation in New Spain: Toward a Typology of Aztec Responses to Christianity. In *The Inca and Aztec States, 1400–1800: Anthropology and History*. ed. G. A. Collier, R. I. Rosaldo, and J. D. Wirth, 345–66. Academic Press, New York.

Leach, Edmund. 1968. Ritual. In *International Encyclopedia of the Social Sciences,* vol. 13, ed. D. Sills, 520–26. Macmillan and Free Press, New York.

———. 1976. *Culture and Communication: The Logic by which Symbols Are Connected.* Cambridge University Press, Cambridge.

Lenz, Hans. 1973 [1948]. *El papel indígera mexicano.* SepSetentas 65. Secretaría de Educación Pública, Mexico City.

———. 1984. *Cosas del papel en Mesoamérica.* Editorial Libros de México, Mexico City.

León-Portilla, Miguel. 1963. *Aztec Thought and Culture: A Study of the Ancient Nahuatl Mind.* University of Oklahoma Press, Norman.

———. 1992. *The Aztec Image of Self and Society: An Introduction to Nahua Culture.* University of Utah Press, Salt Lake City.

Lesure, Richard G. 1999. Figurines as Representations and Products at Paso de la Amada, Mexico. *Cambridge Archaeology Journal* 9 (2): 209–20.

———. 2002. The Goddess Diffracted: Thinking about the Figurines of Early Villages. *Current Anthropology* 43 (4): 587–610.

———. 2005. Linking Theory and Evidence in an Archaeology of Human Agency: Iconography, Style, and Theories of Embodiment. *Journal of Archaeological Method and Theory* 12 (3): 237–55.

Lewis-Williams, J. David. 2004. On Sharpness and Scholarship in the Debate on "Shamanism." *Current Anthropology* 45 (3): 404–5.

Lipp, Frank J. 1991. *The Mixe of Oaxaca: Religion, Ritual, and Healing.* University of Texas Press, Austin.

Lockhart, James. 1991. *Nahuas and Spaniards: Postconquest Central Mexican History and Philology.* Nahuatl Studies Series 3. Stanford University Press, Stanford, Calif.

———. 1992. *The Nahuas after the Conquest: A Social and Cultural History of the Indians of Central Mexico, Sixteenth through Eighteenth Centuries.* Stanford University Press, Stanford, Calif.

López Austin, Alfredo. 1988. *The Human Body and Ideology: Concepts of the Ancient Nahuas,* vol. 1. Trans. T. Ortiz de Montellano and B. Ortiz de Montellano. University of Utah Press, Salt Lake City. Originally published in 1980 as *Cuerpo humano e ideología: Las concepciones de los antiguos nahuas,* 2 vols. Universidad Nacional Autónoma de México, Mexico City.

Madsen, William. 1967. Religious Syncretism. In *Social Anthropology,* ed. M. Nash, 369–91. University of Texas Press, Austin.

Marcus, Joyce. 1998. *Women's Ritual in Formative Oaxaca: Figurine-Making, Divination, Death, and the Ancestors.* University of Michigan Museum of Anthropology, Ann Arbor.

Masferrer Kan, Elio. 1986a. Simbolismo y ritual en la Semana Santa de Santiago Nana-catlán (Totonacas de la Sierra Norte de Puebla). In *Religíon popular: Hegemonía y resistencia*, ed. E. Boege and E. Masferrer Kan, 15–33. Cuaderno de Trabajo 6. Instituto Nacional de Antropología e Historia, Mexico City.

———. 1986b. Religión y política en la Sierra Norte de Puebla. *América Indígena* 46 (3): 531–44.

Mauss, Marcel. 1973 [1936]. Techniques of the Body. Trans. Ben Brewster. *Economy and Society* 2: 70–88.

McKeever Furst, J. L. 1995. *The Natural History of the Soul in Ancient Mesoamerica.* Yale University Press, New Haven, Conn.

Michelet, Dominique, ed. 1989. *Enquêtes sur l'Amérique moyenne: Mélanges offerts á Guy Stresser-Péan.* Etudes Mésoaméricaines 16. Instituto Nacional de Antropología e Historía; Consejo Nacional para la Cultura y las Artes; and Centre d'Etudes Mexicaines et Centroaméricaines, Mexico City.

Mönnich, Anneliese. 1976. La supervivencia de antiguas representaciones indígenas en la región popular de los Nawas de Veracruz y Puebla. In *Das Ring aus Tlalocan: Mythen und Gabete, Lieder und Erzahlungen der heutigen Nahua in Veracruz und Puebla, Mexiko [El Anillo de Tlalocan: Mitos, oraciones, cantos y cuentos de los Nawas actuales de los Estados de Veracruz y Puebla, México]*, ed. L. Reyes García and D. Christensen, 139–43. Quellenwerke zur alten Geschichte Amerikas aufgeze-ichnet in den Sprachen der Eingeborenen 12. Gebr. Mann, Berlin.

Montoya Briones, José de Jesús. 1964. *Atla: Etnografía de un pueblo náhuatl.* Departa-mento de Investigaciones Antropológicos, Publicaciones 14. Instituto Nacional de Antropología e Historia, Mexico City.

Needham, Rodney, ed. 1973. *Right and Left: Essays on Dual Symbolic Classification.* University of Chicago Press, Chicago.

Nutini, Hugo. 1993. *Bloodsucking Witchcraft: An Epistemological Study of Anthropo-morphic Supernaturalism in Rural Tlaxcala.* University of Arizona Press, Tucson.

Ortner, Sherry. 1973. On Key Symbols. *American Anthropologist* 75 (5): 1338–46.

Palka, Joel. 2002. Left/Right Symbolism and the Body in Ancient Maya Iconography and Culture. *Latin American Antiquity* 13 (4): 419–43.

Pollan, Michael. 2006. *The Omnivore's Dilemma: A Natural History of Four Meals.* Penguin Press, New York.

Read, Kay. 1986. The Fleeting Moment: Cosmogony, Eschatology, and Ethics in Aztec Religion and Society. *Journal of Religious Ethics* 14: 113–38.

Reyes García, Luis. 1960. *Pasión y muerte del Cristo sol: Carnaval y cuaresma en Ich-catepec.* Universidad Veracruzana, Xalapa, Veracruz.

Reyes García, Luis, and Dieter Christensen, eds. 1976. *Das Ring aus Tlalocan: Mythen und Gabete, Lieder und Erzahlungen der heutigen Nahua in Veracruz und Pueb-la, Mexiko [El Anillo de Tlalocan: Mitos, oraciones, cantos y cuentos de los Nawas actuales de los Estados de Veracruz y Puebla, México].* Quellenwerke zur alten Geschichte Amerikas aufgezeichnet in den Sprachen der Eingeborenen 12. Gebr. Mann, Berlin.

Ricard, Robert. 1966 [1933]. *The Spiritual Conquest of Mexico: An Essay on the Apostate and the Evangelizing Methods of the Mendicant Orders in New Spain, 1523–1572.* Trans. L. B. Simpson. University of California Press, Berkeley. (Originally published in 1933 as *La 'conquête spirituelle' du Mexique.* Institut d'Ethnologie, Paris.)

Ruvalcaba Mercado, Jesús. 1987. *Vida cotidiana y consumo de maíz en la Huasteca veracruzana.* Cuadernos de la Casa Chata 134. Centro de Investigaciones y Estudios Superiores en Antropología Social, Mexico City.

———. 1992. *Tecnología agrícola y trabajo familiar: Una etnografía agrícola de la Huasteca veracruzana.* Ediciones de la Casa Chata. Centro de Investigaciones y Estudios Superiores en Antropología Social. Mexico City.

Sahagún, Bernardino de. 1970 [1575–80?]. *General History of the Things of New Spain: Florentine Codex, Book 1, The Gods,* ed. and trans. C. E. Dibble and A. J. O. Anderson. Monographs of the School of American Research, no. 14, parts 1–13. School of American Research, Santa Fe, N.M.; University of Utah, Salt Lake City.

Sandstrom, Alan R. 1991. *Corn Is Our Blood: Culture and Ethnic Identity in a Contemporary Aztec Indian Village.* Civilization of the American Indian 206. University of Oklahoma Press, Norman.

———. 1995. Nahuas of the Huasteca. In *Middle America and the Caribbean,* ed. J. W. Dow and R. V. Kemper, 184–87. *Encyclopedia of World Cultures,* vol. 8. G. K. Hall; Human Relations Area Files, Boston.

———. 1998. El nene lloroso y el espíritu nahua del maíz: El cuerpo humano como símbolo clave en la Huasteca veracruzana. In *Nuevos aportes al conocimiento de la Huasteca,* ed. J. Ruvalcaba Mercado, 59–94. Selección de trabajos pertenecientes al VIII Encuentro de Investigadores de la Huasteca, Tlalpan, México, November 1995. CIESAS, Mexico City.

———. 2000. Contemporary Cultures of the Gulf Coast. In *Ethnology,* ed. J. D. Monaghan, 83–119. *Supplement to the Handbook of Middle American Indians,* vol. 6, gen. ed. V. R. Bricker. University of Texas Press, Austin.

———. 2001. Nahua Blood Sacrifice and Pilgrimage to the Sacred Mountain Postectli, June 2001. Foundation for the Advancement of Mesoamerican Studies, Inc. (FAMSI) Contingency Grant award #01001 final report. Available at http://www.famsi.org/reports/01001/index.html.

———. 2003. Sacred Mountains and Miniature Worlds: Altar Design among the Nahua of Northern Veracruz, Mexico. In *Mesas and Cosmologies in Mesoamerica,* ed. D. Sharon, 51–70. San Diego Museum of Man, San Diego, Calif.

Sandstrom, Alan R., and E. Hugo García Valencia, eds. 2005. *Native Peoples of the Gulf Coast of Mexico.* Native Peoples of the Americas. University of Arizona Press, Tucson.

Sandstrom, Alan R., and Arturo Gómez Martínez. 2004. Petición a Chicomexóchitl: Un canto al espíritu del maíz por la chamana nahua Silveria Hernández Hernández. In *La Huasteca, un recorrido por su diversidad,* ed. J. Ruvalcaba Mercado, J. Manuel Pérez Zevallos, and O. Herrera, 343–67. CIESAS, Mexico City.

Sandstrom, Alan R., and Pamela Effrein Sandstrom. 1986. *Traditional Papermaking and Paper Cult Figures of Mexico.* University of Oklahoma Press, Norman.

———. 2002. The Shaman's Art. In *Personal Encounters: A Reader in Cultural Anthropology,* ed. L. Walbridge and A. K. Sievert, 163–70. McGraw-Hill, New York.

Signorini, Italo, and Alessandro Lupo. 1989. *Los tres ejes de la vida: Almas, cuerpo, enfermedad entre los nahuas de la Sierra de Puebla.* Universidad Veracruzana, Xalapa, Veracruz.

Stresser-Péan, Guy, ed. 1979. La Huasteca et la frontière nord-est de la Mesoamérique. *Actes de XLIIe Congrès International des Américanistes, Paris, 1976* 9B: 1–157.

Taggart, James M. 1975. *Estructura de los grupos domésticos de una comunidad nahuat de Puebla.* Instituto Nacional Indigenista y Secretaría de Educación Pública, Mexico City.

———. 1983. *Nahuat Myth and Social Structure.* University of Texas Press, Austin.

Turner, Victor. 1967. *The Forest of Symbols: Aspects of Ndembu Ritual.* Cornell University Press, Ithaca, N.Y.

Vogt, Evon Z. 1976. *Tortillas for the Gods: A Symbolic Analysis of Zinacanteco Rituals.* Harvard University Press, Cambridge, Mass.

Williams García, Roberto. 1957. Ichcacuatitla. *La palabra y el hombre* 3: 51–63.

———. 1963. *Los tepehuas.* Universidad Veracruzana, Xalapa, Veracruz.

———. 1972. *Mitos tepehuas.* SepSetentas 27. Secretaría de Educación Pública, Mexico City.

11

Alien Bodies, Everyday People, and Hollow Spaces

Embodiment, Figurines, and Social Discourse in Postclassic Mexico

ELIZABETH M. BRUMFIEL AND LISA OVERHOLTZER

At Xaltocan, a Postclassic site in the northern Basin of Mexico, figurines come in many forms (Brumfiel 1995a, 2005; Rivera 2003). These include figurine heads that predate the occupation of the site; minimally human "mud men" (some of which are clearly "mud women"); freestanding, mold-made, flat-backed figurines, which are the most common figurine type at the site; large hand-molded figures attached to braziers; hollow rattle-figurines; human and animal heads attached to flutes; and animal heads and feet attached to jars. These figurine types are so different from one another in manufacture, form, and function that they must constitute separate genres. Together, they challenge the archaeological practice of grouping all figurines together as if they were a single, homogeneous artifact category.

What purposes did this extravaganza of figurine types serve, and what social realities did these figurines address? These questions are not easily answered. As is generally the case in Mesoamerica, Xaltocan's figurines are not found in use contexts, they are almost always broken, and the ethnohistoric record concerning the uses and meanings of ceramic figurines is scanty, at best. But recent thinking about embodiment, how bodily sensations and experience shape identity, provides some assistance in our efforts to understand these artifacts.[1]

Figurines naturally enter into discussions of embodiment. As miniaturized human forms, figurines provoke discussions about appearance, substance, sameness, and difference that define social categories and shape social relations (Bailey 2005). To reconstruct bodily-based ideologies in ancient contexts, archaeologists have considered the size, detail, and decoration of different body parts, the body's pose, its placement with other figures in scenes, and the archaeological context within which bodily representations appear. These variables suggest the goals of the ancient ideologies of the body (asserting gender, class, or ethnic difference; establishing criteria of beauty and value, and so on), which can then be related to actors' social strategies (Bailey 2005; Cyphers 1993; Joyce 2000, 2001b, 2003, 2005; Lesure 1997). Figurines can also be compared to human representations in other media such as stone sculpture, murals, and manuscript painting. Representational differences among these various media expose some of the tensions generated by the negotiation of social categories and social relations, especially when the different media are controlled by different groups (Brumfiel 1996b; Cohodas 2002; Joyce 1993; Lesure 1999).[2]

But the potential of embodiment as an analytical tool has not been fully exploited. In the following analysis, we demonstrate two ways in which the consideration of the body and bodily experience contributes to archaeological analysis. First, embodiment encourages consideration of the relationship between material culture and human sensory faculties, and this can provide clues to figurine use and meaning. Figurine attributes such as shape and finish are chosen to suit the human body, and the choices will differ according to whether the figurine was intended to be held, heard, or displayed. The sensory consequences of figurine attributes are consistent with some figurine functions and meanings and incompatible with others. Second, embodiment encourages us to consider the kinds of bodies represented in figurine assemblages, and this directs us to the range of social issues that the different bodies might address. To date, archaeologists have assigned an important role to figurines in defining and naturalizing difference within a social system. Archaeologists have suggested that figurines serve as exemplary bodies: they prescribe the roles and appearance of social categories as defined by gender or status (Joyce 2001a; Sørensen 2000). But bodies might also be important in representing "Others" who live outside of society, or bodies might express cosmological principles that locate humans within broader frameworks of understanding. We suggest that prehistoric people endowed figurines with bodily attributes that focus attention on these different issues and that archaeologists who are attentive to figurine bodies can hope to grasp the conceptual frameworks that structured social negotiations in ancient times.

Embodiment has proven particularly helpful in understanding figurines from Xaltocan because the site yields a variety of figurine types that cannot be explained by temporal difference or ethnic heterogeneity. Although typology is a popular approach to figurine analysis, few archaeologists have considered why two or more figurine types sometimes occur in a single occupation (but see Lesure 1997). We argue that the people of Xaltocan used different figurine types to present the body through different series of contrasts. The contrasts addressed different dimensions of social identity, including community membership, male/female, and commoner/noble/divinity. Specifically, we suggest that figurines with radically alien and underdefined bodies helped to establish local community identity and promoted community relations of mutual respect and reciprocity. Figurines representing the familiar bodies of everyday people supported a discourse about differences within the household and the community based on gender and quality of lineage, which were regarded as physiologically based. Figurines emphasizing the interiority of human and animal bodies explored the transformative capacities of earthly bodies and their linkage to divine processes of cosmic generation.

Postclassic Xaltocan

Xaltocan is a low island rising 5–6 meters above the bed of Lake Xaltocan in the northern Basin of Mexico (figure 11.1). It is roughly oval, with an east–west length of 800 meters and a north–south width of 400 meters. The pre-Hispanic site lies under the modern town and in some places extends beyond its borders to cover an area of 68 hectares. The site's surface is marked by concentrations of pottery, lithic debris, and large, low, irregular mounds that contain stratified deposits of household refuse. In pre-Hispanic times, Xaltocan was surrounded by a shallow, brackish lake and marsh; at the time of Spanish conquest, a causeway linked the island to the western shore (Díaz del Castillo 1956: 356).

The political history of Xaltocan is outlined in native narratives recorded shortly after Spanish conquest. According to native history, Xaltocan was settled in the mid-eleventh century CE, shortly after the fall of Tollan (Alva Ixtlilxóchitl 1975–77: 1: 293; Velázquez 1945: 14). During the twelfth and thirteenth centuries, Xaltocan was an important regional center, the capital of Otomí-speaking peoples in southern Hidalgo and the northern Basin of Mexico (Alva Ixtlilxóchitl 1975–77: 1: 423, 2: 299; see Carrasco 1950). During this time, Xaltocan interacted with other important settlements in the Basin of Mexico including Tollan, Azcapotzalco, Tenayuca, Huexotla,

Figure 11.1. The Basin of Mexico, showing the location of Xaltocan and other important Aztec-period sites.

Culhuacan, and Chalco (Carrasco 1950: 260–61; see also Alva Ixtlilxóchitl 1975–77: 2: 17, 18, 51; Davies 1980: 144–45; Nazareo 1940; Toscano et al. 1948: 28).

In 1395, Xaltocan lost a war to the neighboring town of Cuauhtitlan, which was aided by Tepanec allies from Azcapotzalco. In the wake of Xaltocan's defeat, the town was deserted and lay empty for more than thirty years (Velázquez 1945: 50). In 1428, it fell under the rule of the Aztec Triple

Alliance, and the rulers of Tenochtitlan and Tlatelolco resettled the town with tribute payers (Hicks 1994). Xaltocan was governed by a military ruler (*cuauhtlatoani*) sent from Tenochtitlan (Nazareo 1940: 120) until 1521, when the town was attacked and burned by Hernán Cortés (Cortés 1970: 118). However, Xaltocan persisted into the colonial era, and it continues to flourish today.

Archaeological research at Xaltocan began in 1987 with the mapping and the systematic surface collection of most of the site. This was followed by the excavation of twenty-four 2×2-meter test pits, three of which were expanded into broader excavations of Aztec I houses (Brumfiel 2005) (figure 11.2). Ceramics from these excavations provided the basis for a four-phase chronology, anchored by absolute dates.[3] Figurines recovered from surface collections and excavations can be dated by their associated ceramics.

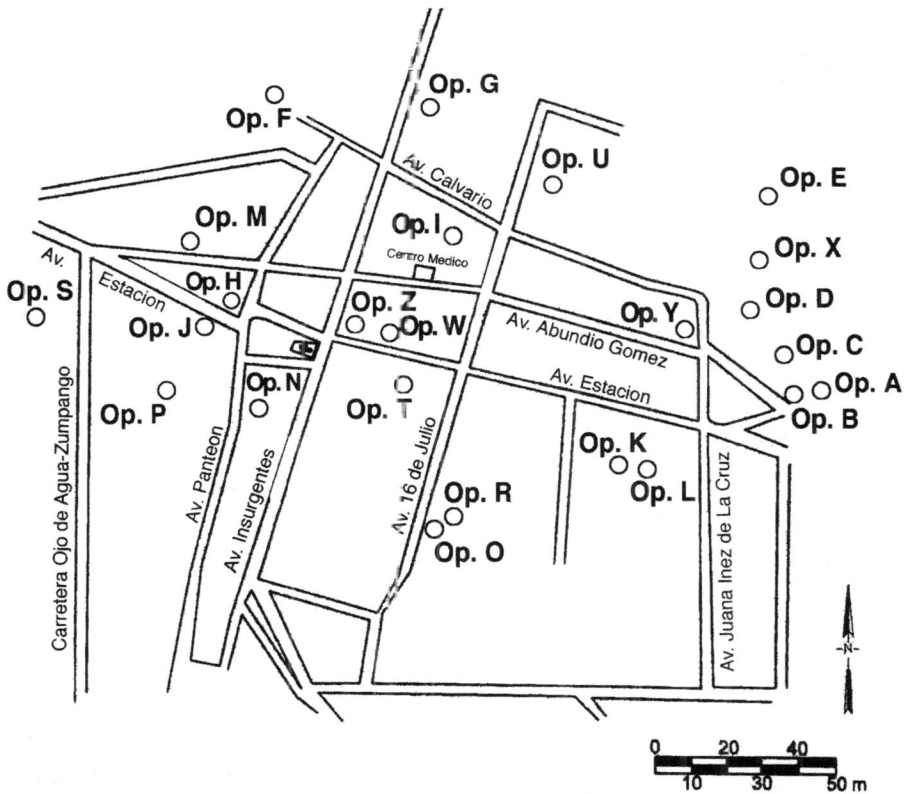

Figure 11.2. Xaltocan, showing the locations of excavated test pits.

Table 11.1. Figurine Types at Xaltocan, Mexico

Type	Count	Percentage
Curated	50	13.4
Mud men/women	28	7.5
Attached to braziers	12	3.2
Flat-backed	220	59.1
Rattles	11	3.0
Flutes	4	1.1
Animals	43	11.6
Other	4	1.1
Total	372	100.0

Table 11.2. Figurine Types by Phase at Xaltocan, Mexico

Phase	Curated	Mud men/women	Braziers	Flat-backed	Rattles	Flutes	Animals	Other	Total
1	5	11	2	30	0	2	8	1	59
1,2[a]	3	0	1	8	0	0	1	0	13
2	12	4	3	21	0	0	4	0	44
3	15	5	1	90	6	1	16	2	136
3,4[b]	4	0	0	7	1	0	0	0	12
4	1	3	1	21	4	0	4	1	35
Total	40	23	8	177	11	3	33	4	299

Note: Counts for types are lower in table 11.2 than in table 11.1 because some figurines were found in mixed contexts or contexts that could not be securely dated.
a. Contexts of mixed phase 1 and 2 deposits.
b. Contexts of mixed phase 3 and 4 deposits.

At Xaltocan, as elsewhere in Postclassic Central Mexico, figurines are found on house floors, in middens, and occasionally associated with burials. These are disposal contexts rather than use contexts, but they do suggest that figurines were involved in practices and performances carried out at the household level. Figurines of all the different types occur in household contexts; we have been unable to define distinct patterns of use for any of the types. Below, we describe the types, how their bodies are defined, and the issues that these bodies might address (see table 1 for the frequencies of each type and table 2 for their temporal distributions).

Alien Beings: Curated Figurines and Mud Men and Women

About 13 percent of the figurines at Xaltocan predate the Postclassic occupation of the site (figure 11.3). Their styles indicate that they were manufactured at various times during the Early Formative through the Late Classic periods, but they are present in undisturbed layers of Postclassic occupa-

Figure 11.3. Curated figurines from Xaltocan (drawing by Edward J. Rohn).

tion. Evidently, they were collected and curated by the Postclassic inhabitants of the site. The figurines' widespread distribution over the site suggests that many different commoner households engaged in figurine collecting. We argue that this practice parallels, although it antedates by four centuries, a pattern of activity that has been identified for Aztec rulers: collecting and reusing objects from the past (Umberger 1987).

Byron Hamann (2002: 354) suggests that Aztec rulers used the remains of ancient cultures to substantiate narratives of cosmic creation and destruction. He argues that these narratives were an important element of elite ideology: they reminded commoners that the continued existence of the present world depended on elite-organized warfare and human sacrifice to compensate the gods for their act of creation. Hamann suggests that Aztec *elites* used jades and statues from earlier civilizations to substantiate the accounts of cyclical creation. But in Xaltocan, *commoners* may have verified similar narratives using ancient figurines.[4]

The forms of the ancient figurines are well suited to this purpose. Almost always, the broken heads of figurines were the portion collected; thus, the nature of their bodies was open to speculation. Like the European Neolithic figurines studied by Douglass Bailey (2005), many of the curated heads at Xaltocan are really weird. They are distorted, underdefined, and ambiguous. This is particularly true of Tzacualli figurines (100–150 CE), which are overrepresented at Xaltocan, constituting about half of the ancient figurines (the others represent Early Formative to Late Classic types, 1250 BCE–600 CE). The source of the Tzacualli figurines at Xaltocan is something of a mystery; we do not know of any Tzacualli sites in the immediate area. A small Epi-Classic site, ET or Michpilco, lies just one kilometer north of Xaltocan, and this site yielded many mold-made figurines in the later Metepec style (mostly to looters). Yet this nearby source of ancient figurines was bypassed in preference to Tzacualli figurines from some more distant locale. We suggest that weirder was better for representing humans of a time before the current social order.

The commoners who used these ancient figurines to contemplate earlier creations might have been concerned with these figurines' implications for their own social relations rather than the legitimacy of political elites. Today, narratives of earlier worlds in the Mixtec community of Nuyoo underscore the contrast between villagers as cultural and social beings who engage in relations of mutual respect and exchange and the presocial beings of earlier creations whose asocial natures doomed them to lives of hunger and misery (Monaghan 1995: 32). These narratives of earlier worlds equate contemporary social relations with the very definition of humanness. Similarly, we argue that in Postclassic Xaltocan, contemplation of ancient figurines was linked to narratives of alien, earlier worlds that, by contrast to the present, validated community norms as a part of residents' human identity.

"Mud-men" figurines are a second variety of distinctly alien beings. (Female figurines are included in the term "mud men.") These figurines are only minimally human: often, their humanity is established only by three holes, placed so as to suggest two eyes and a mouth (figure 11.4). Details such as noses, breasts, necklaces, and hands are added only occasionally and then in a rudimentary way. The surfaces of these figurines are rough, unburnished and unpainted, exposing rather than concealing their clay substance. They are so crude that they appear to be the spontaneous creations of unskilled children, but this suggestion is countered by the fact that they were a widespread conventionalized form, appearing in Chalco and Morelos as well as the northern Basin of Mexico during the Early, Middle,

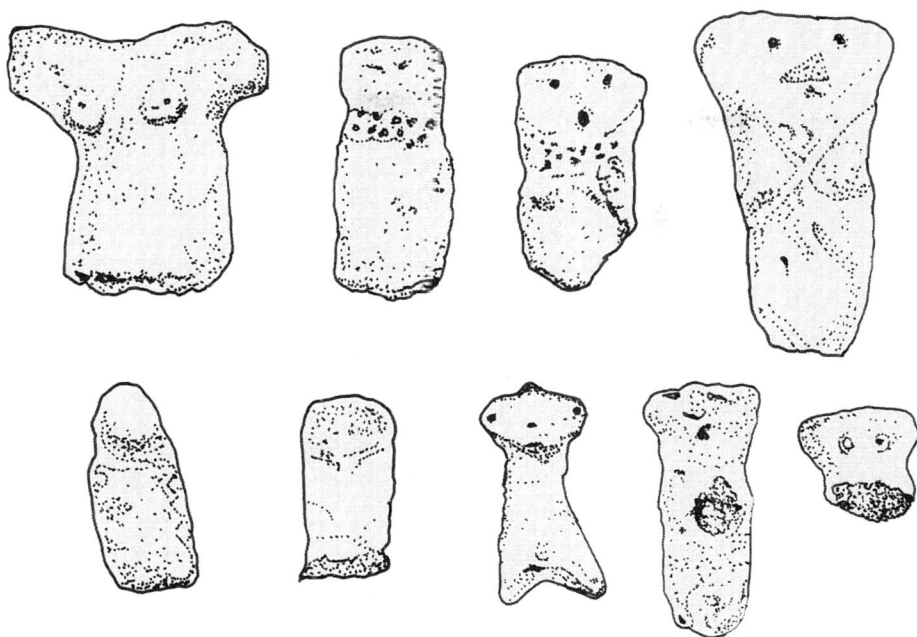

Figure 11.4. Mud-men figurines from Xaltocan (drawing by Tom Quinn).

and Late Postclassic periods (Montoya 1996; Norr 1987; Smith 2002).[5] Mud men account for eight percent of Xaltocan's figurine assemblage.

The distribution of mud men at Xaltocan overlaps with the distribution of curated figurines; thus, mud men may have simply augmented the supply of ancient and alien beings. But it is also possible that mud men and curated figurines represent different kinds of presocial beings. They might represent different stages of creation: for example, the Maya Popol Vuh records that the gods engaged with several failed experiments in making people first from earth, then wood, before settling on humans made of corn dough (Tedlock 1985). However, Enrique Florescano (1994: 10) finds no such evolutionary scenario among the Aztec creation narratives. Alternatively, curated figurines might represent the past while mud men represent presocial beings still in existence for example, the immature souls of infants and young children (Joyce 2000; López Austin 1988). Or mud men might represent earth beings.

Today, people in many areas of Mexico postulate the existence of earth beings. For example, the Mixtecs of Nuyoo believe that these beings live below the surface of the earth, residing in fields, forests, swamps, rivers, hearths, ovens, or sweatbaths (Monaghan 1995: 99–104). They control the size of maize harvests, and when offended, they can cause illness or even death by seizing a person's soul. Nahuas in Veracruz have a similar idea: "Every hill, valley, spring, lake, stream, section of river, boulder, plain, grove, gorge, and cave has its . . . associated spirit" (Sandstrom 1991: 241; see also chapter 10, this volume). Earth beings can take various shapes: for Mixtecs, old women and old men with beards, one or two feet tall, and giant snakes; for Nahuas, old bearded men. Mixtecs also believe that earth spirits can also take the form of unusually shaped rocks and even pre-Hispanic figurines, which they occasionally find in the earth.

Among the Mixtecs, humans and earth beings are linked by a moral economy. Ideally, the earth beings care for humans, and humans offer the earth beings respect and gifts, including candles, incense, pulque, liquor, flowers, and corn (Monaghan 1995: 211–26). Nahuas similarly adhere to a policy of respect toward the earth, offering it gifts, ritual cleansing, and drops of pulque (Sandstrom 1991: 240–41). Today, these beliefs and offerings represent a level of religious observance below the pantheon of Catholic saints. The relationship between humans and earth beings is so intensely local that it short-circuits efforts at intervention or control by larger-scale, higher-order governmental or religious institutions. Analogously, if the mud men of Xaltocan were endowed with similar properties, they might index a sanctified link between the community and its land.

The existence of earth beings was not recognized by Nahua speakers in twentieth-century Central Mexico (Ingham 1986; Madsen 1960; Redfield 1930), although in Xaltocan, tales of small, earth-dwelling *duendes* persist in local gossip (usually accompanied by stories of visits from extraterrestrials). It would not be surprising if beliefs regarding earth beings were abandoned during five centuries of contact with mestizo culture and the Catholic Church. But these ideas may have started to change even before European contact, during the era of Aztec dominance. At least, this is consistent with the nearly complete absence of both curated figurines and mud men in excavated assemblages representing Period 4 at Xaltocan (1430–1521 CE), coinciding with the arrival of newly settled Aztec tribute payers.

These colonists were probably organized in collective *calpolli* or *tlaxi-lacalli* units, parts of a top-down Aztec administrative structure, and they may not have had the strong sense of commitment to a wider community or direct ownership of the land that earlier residents enjoyed. The frequency of mud-men figurines also declined sharply in other regions during the Aztec period, for example, rural Morelos, even without population discontinuity (Smith 2002). This may reflect the at-least-partial success of the Aztecs and allied provincial elites in imposing imperial bureaucratic structures on subject populations in the imperial heartland, disrupting community-wide social relations, and subverting the idea that access to the land was mediated by earth beings rather than conquering nobles. Perhaps this was part of the process through which commoners were reduced to the status of tribute-paying subjects (*macehualtin*) during the Postclassic period, as described by Frederic Hicks (1986: 46).

Everyday People: Figurines on Braziers and Solid, Mold-Made Figurines

As morphologically nonhuman beings, the curated figurines and mud men at Xaltocan contrast with two other figurine types: figurines on braziers and freestanding mold-made figurines. Unlike the curated figurines and mud men, these two types reproduce the dress and posture of a range of people from everyday life as they are depicted in Aztec manuscripts such as the Codex Mendoza and the Codex Magliabechiano. They must represent persons of the contemporary social order.

At Xaltocan, large figurines were sometimes attached to braziers (figure 11.5). The braziers are thick, tan, biconical vessels, between 18 and 20 centimeters tall. The braziers are finished with rough surfaces that support thick white paint, which is overlain with painted designs. The anthropomorphic figures attached to the front of the braziers are also covered by thick white paint, with details added in black and blue paint. Although they resemble the *xantiles* of Cholula, Coxcatlan, and elsewhere in Central Mexico (McCafferty 2001: 27), the local manufacture of these vessels in Xaltocan is suggested by the recovery of a mold for a large figurine head, of the appropriate size for an effigy vessel, from an adobe-walled Aztec I house in Operation G7 at Xaltocan.

Three complete figures on braziers have been recovered from Xaltocan, and each is unique. One figure is standing. It wears a loincloth and a short-sleeved tunic (probably quilted cotton armor) and carries a shield. The second figure also stands. Its bare legs suggest that the lower part of its body was covered by a loincloth or kilt rather than a skirt. This figure also carries a shield and wears an animal-head headdress. A human face is suspended around its neck, possibly a war trophy or a figurine. The third figure kneels. A short cape covers its chest; neither a shield nor a loincloth is visible. It wears large ear plugs and a tall headdress. The clothing and pose of these

Figure 11.5. Human figure on a brazier from Xaltocan, Operation Z.

three figures suggest that the first two are men and the third figure is a woman.[6]

The elaborate dress of the figures and their presence on braziers, used for making offerings (Sahagún 1997: 70), suggests that these individuals were ritually important. But none bears the conventional insignia of a Postclassic deity. The faces of these figures are large in proportion to their bodies, representing 50 percent of total body length on the first figure, 40 percent on the second figure, and 55 percent on the third figure. The large faces could indicate that the individual identities of these figures were important. The only effigy vessel recovered in context at the site lay face down on the earth floor of an Aztec I house in Operation Z, implying that effigy vessels were used in rituals to address beings relevant to that particular house, such as honored ancestors, lineage founders, and culture heroes from historical narratives. We suggest that these figurines provided symbols of unity and authority for groupings of households based on common ancestry and shared history (Gillespie 2000).

Fragments of large figurines that would have been attached to braziers are most common in the Aztec I occupation at Xaltocan (Phases 1 and 2).

Figure 11.6. Solid, flat-backed female figurines from Xaltocan (drawing by Tom Quinn).

Over time, figurines attached to braziers may have been replaced by free-standing, flat-backed, mold-made figurines.

Freestanding, flat-backed, mold-made figurines are by far the most common type of figurine at Xaltocan, accounting for 59 percent of the sample (figures 11.6, 11.7). They are thin and flat, with smooth but unburnished surfaces. Details of costume are molded in low relief. The remains of a white paint undercoat appear on many figurines, suggesting that their surfaces were enhanced with painted designs, probably highlighting the molded detail. Molded elements of dress include headdresses, earrings, pendants, necklaces, clothing edges, implements, and sometimes textile designs. We have included in this category Mazapan-style figurines because they are technologically similar to other flat-backed, mold-made figurines at Xaltocan, and they were probably used in similar ways.[7]

Observing the flatness and fugitive painted surfaces of mold-made figurines, Overholtzer (2005: 45) concludes that they were meant to be viewed, not handled. She characterizes these figurines as essentially two-

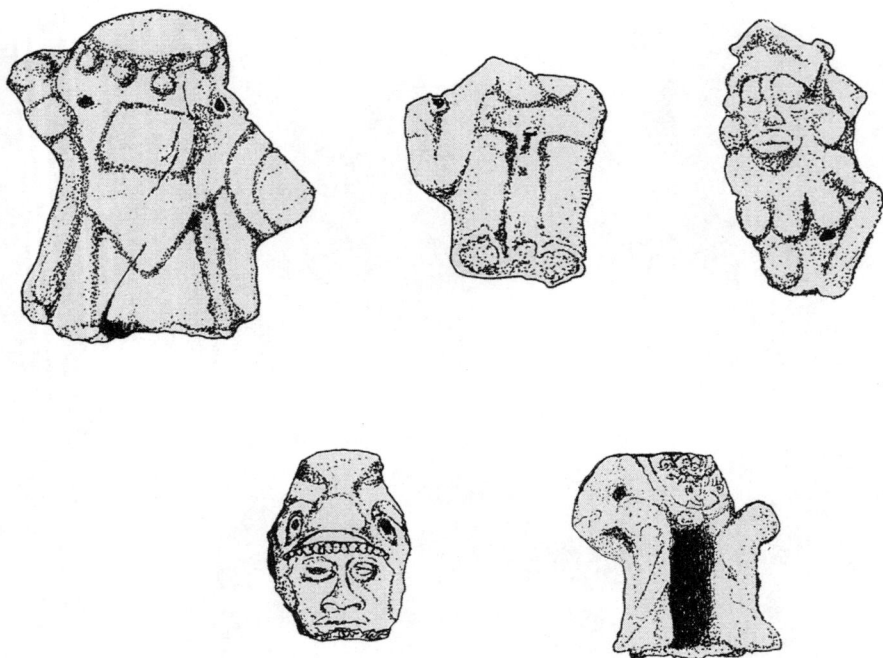

Figure 11.7. Solid, flat-backed male figurines from Xaltocan (drawing by Tom Quinn).

dimensional: "flat, thin, and plaque-like," with large bases that enabled them to stand. Overholtzer suggests that these figurines appeared on household altars, "their undecorated backs to the wall." Bernardino de Sahagún (1997: 70) indicates that incense for household gods was thrown in braziers or offered in censers; hence, an altar-with-standing-figurines-and-a-censer might be the functional equivalent of the earlier effigy brazier.

With their molded and painted elements of body and dress, these figurines seem designed to define and communicate messages of social difference and identity. The figurines emphasize two axes of difference: gender and quality, both equated with physiological differences/processes in Aztec Mexico (López Austin 1988).

The clearest differences among figures are by gender. Women can be identified by their breasts and their clothing, which consists of a skirt below and sometimes a long overblouse (*huipilli*) or triangular cape (*quechquemitl*) above. Women either stand, with their hands resting on their skirts (67 percent), or they kneel (33 percent). Some hold small children or dogs on

Table 11.3. Male and Female Figurines by Phase at Xaltocan, Mexico

	Early (Phases 1 and 2)	Late (Phases 3 and 4)	Total
Male	14	19	33
Female	11	49	60
Total	25	68	93

their hips or in front of them. Men wear loincloths (*maxtli*). They stand (70 percent), sit with their hands on their knees (26 percent), or occasionally kneel on one knee (4 percent). They sometimes carry accessories such as shields or drums. Of the 115 figurines that can be distinguished by gender in their fragmentary states, 65 percent are female and 35 percent are male.

The relative percentages of female and male figurines change markedly over time. In Phases 1 and 2, male figurines are in the majority, accounting for 56 percent of the flat-backed, mold-made figurines, but in Phases 3 and 4, female figurines become more common, constituting 72 percent of the figurines (table 11.3). We regard this as a signal of commoner resistance to the state's glorification of male warriors in the Middle and Late Postclassic Basin of Mexico, resistance born of increasing popular concern with household well-being as the state increased its extraction of tribute goods and labor from household units (see Brumfiel 1991, 1996b).

The second axis of difference is marked by the elaboration of costume. Some figurines show simple headdresses and plain chests (61 percent); others display elaborate headdresses and chests adorned with fancy capes or necklaces (39 percent). Some of these fancy images bear the distinctive insignia of Aztec deities, as recorded in sixteenth-century codices, but even the fancy figurines that are not deity images manage to convey superiority of person through superiority of dress. This may be related to Postclassic ideologies of class difference.

Aztec nobles claimed that they, like deities, were endowed with greater vitality (*tonalli*) than common people, the result of their noble lineage, carefully guarded against the debilitating effects of pollution and sin and enhanced by rigorous moral education in temple schools (López Austin 1988). The vitality of noble lineage was demonstrated by wearing craft goods that radiated light: costume accessories made from burnished metal, polished jade, and shimmering quetzal feathers; and textiles embroidered with shiny rabbit-hair thread (Brumfiel 2000; Houston and Taube 2000). Thus, the elaborate and plain costumes on Xaltocan's figurines may have presented social class as a matter of deeply ingrained physiological difference.

Table 11.4. Plain and Fancy Figurines by Gender at Xaltocan, Mexico

	Plain	Fancy	Total
Male	10	13	23
Female	42	13	55
Total	52	26	78

Elaborate costuming appears on 57 percent of male figurines but only 24 percent of the female figurines (table 11.4). We think that the lower percentage of fancy female figurines is due to the role played by figurines representing ordinary women in rituals promoting reproductive success. These figurines were particularly popular in Phases 3 and 4 (see below).

Hollow Spaces: Hollow Rattle-Figurines, Flutes, and Effigy Vessels

The final group of figurine types is defined by their hollow bodies. They include hollow rattle-figurines, flutes, and effigy vessels. We suggest that these figurines referred in different ways to the transformative capacity of bodies as containers for divine processes of creation and transformation.

Hollow rattle-figurines depict standing women with highly conventional looped hairdos, bare breasts, and skirts (figure 11.8); they sometimes bear a child on one hip. In hairstyle, dress, and pose, these figurines resemble many of the solid mold-made figurines at Xaltocan, but they are hollow with small clay pellets inside, making them effective rattles. Hollow rattle-figurines account for 3 percent of Xaltocan's figurine assemblage. Both their appearance and their hollowness seem to associate these figurines with female reproduction.

Examining a large sample of hollow female figurines from the Basin of Mexico, Overholtzer (2005: 51) calls attention to the sensual, embodied properties of these figurines. She points out that these figurines were meant to be held: they are rounded and three-dimensional, "so that the hand would have wrapped comfortably around the figurine, with no sharp edges." They have burnished surfaces that are smooth to the touch. Overholtzer (2005) observes that these figures represent three stages in a woman's reproductive cycle: not pregnant, pregnant, and postpartum (holding a child). Citing archaeological and ethnohistoric data, Overholtzer suggests that these figurines were used in female reproduction and healing rituals (see also Klein and Victoria Lona, this volume, chapter twelve). In terms of archaeological context, rattle-figurines have been found only in habitation rooms and sweat-bath areas at Cihuatecpan, a provincial palace in the Teotihuacan

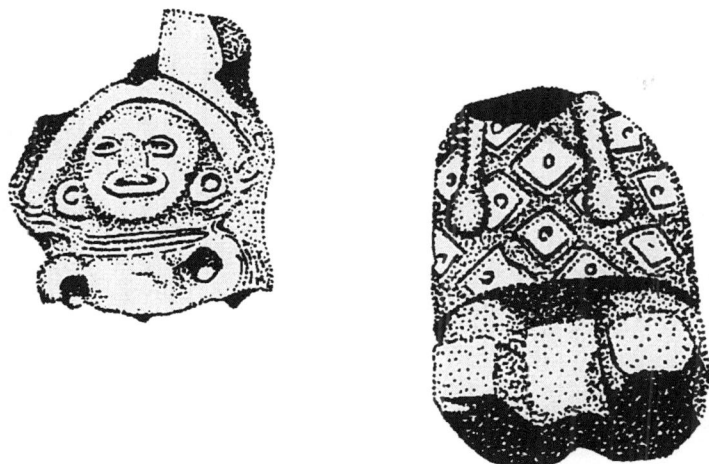

Figure 11.8. Hollow rattle-figurines from Xaltocan (drawing by Edward J. Rohn).

Valley (Evans 1990). Although both Aztec men and women visited sweat baths to cure disease, sweat baths were places where women received regular treatments before and after childbirth to ensure reproductive success (Boone and Nuttall 1983: 77r; Sahagún 1950–82: bk. 1: 70; bk. 6: 155; bk. 8: 48; see Houston 1996). In this context, the hollow rattle-figurines might have been used to avert or draw off dryness and sterility from women's bodies: according to Sahagún (1950–82: bk. 6: 157), pregnant Aztec women took precautions "so that the baby not be formed like a pottery rattle, so that it not [dry out] as a gourd rattle, so that it not sicken."

These rattle-figurines and the reproductive concerns that they addressed are related to the many fecund cavities that were regarded as sources of creation and transformation in Mesoamerica. Wombs, jars, earth ovens, kilns, sweat baths, and caves were containers that produced such essential and varied products as children, tamales, salt, thickened maguey syrup, medicinal oil, roasted meat and maguey hearts, ceramic pots, charcoal, slaked lime, good health, and ancestors (Monaghan 2001; Sahagún 1950–82: bk. 1: 29; Sullivan 1966). Bodies, containers, and other hollow objects enabled the Aztecs to reflect upon the conditions that determined the success or failure of production efforts

Hollow rattle-figurines at Xaltocan occur only in Phase 3 and 4 deposits, a time of warfare and militarism in the community and domination by a military government. As warfare took its toll in human lives and as the state's demand for tribute intensified physical labor and made pregnancy

Figure 11.9. Flute with figurine head from Xaltocan (drawing by Edward J. Rohn).

and childbirth more difficult, the people of Xaltocan may have experienced growing concern over effective human reproduction, accounting for the popularity of hollow rattle-figurines and the plain female figurines discussed above.

The people of Xaltocan also contemplated hollow bodies in other forms. Four ceramic flutes from Xaltocan have human heads attached to their ends (figure 11.9). Flute music may have been regarded as flowing from the mouths of the human heads, with the flute constituting a human body reduced to a mechanism for moving columns of air and sound. This, then, is another view of the human body as a productive container, able to transform air into song.[8]

Finally, forty-three animal figurines have been recovered at Xaltocan, including seventeen dog heads; animal figurines represent 12 percent of the figurine sample (figure 11.10). However, few bodies have been found to go with the more numerous heads. An explanation for this anomaly is suggested by a complete dog effigy vessel found at Xaltocan (figure 11.11). This vessel was a plain jar with a dog's head attached to its basket handle and stubby dog legs attached to its rounded body. This jar was recovered during construction activity at Xaltocan, and thus its use context is uncertain, but its undamaged condition suggests that it accompanied a burial. In Aztec Mexico, dogs were killed and cremated with the deceased so that they could carry the dead on their backs across the river that lay deep in the earth on the path to Mictlan, the Land of the Dead (Sahagún 1950–82: bk. 3: 43–44).

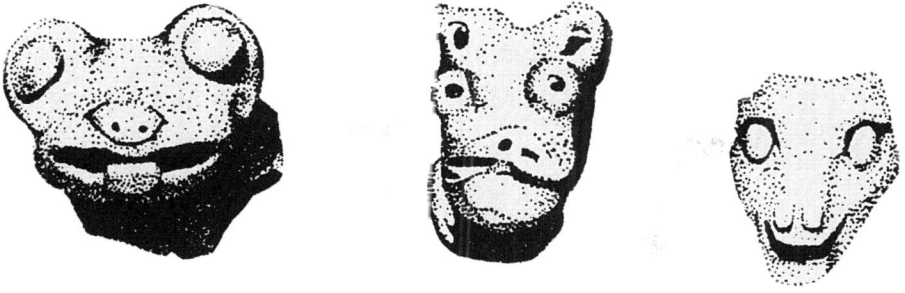

Figure 11.10. Animal-head figurines from Xaltocan (drawing by Edward J. Rohn).

Figure 11.11. A dog effigy vessel from Xaltocan.

Dog effigy vessels may have supplemented or replaced actual dogs in burials.[9] At Xaltocan, a second dog's-head figurine was clearly attached to a handle, although it had broken off from the handle. The other dog heads may also have been attached to effigy jars. These jars may have represented dog bodies as protected interior spaces, such as the earth itself, where the transformation from life to death was carried to completion.

Discussion

We return to our initial question: what purposes did the variety of figurine types serve, and what realities did the figurines address? We suggest that many figurine types occur because for the Early and Middle Postclassic people of Xaltocan, as for the Late Postclassic Aztecs, the body provided a microcosm of the universe: the physiology of living things provided instances of larger cosmic processes (López Austin 1988: 3). The metabolic energy of the human body and other living beings constituted one phase in the circulation of sacred energy/cosmic energy. Emanating from a divine source, this energy provided heat, light, and movement to the sun. It imparted growth and reproduction to plants and animals and lent them nutritive value. It ignited the fires that burned in hearths, kilns, and sweatbaths, endowing them with transformative powers. Through acts of sacrifice, this energy returned to its divine source and renewed its vigor.

Sharing a common essence, each manifestation of divine energy could stand for any of the others. But perhaps because of the immediacy of embodied sensual experience, the human body provided the most common metaphor for understanding moving things and transformative processes. Bodies were regarded as the creative instruments of the gods. Thus, for the Aztecs, the sun was the body of Nanahuatl, who flung himself on a divine brazier to provide the world with light, and the moon was the body of Tecuciztecatl, who cast himself into the same brazier after it had burned to an afterglow (Sahagún 1950–82: bk. 7: 6). The earth and sky were halves of the body of the Earth Monster Tlaltecuhtli, torn apart by the creator gods Tezcatlipoca and Quetzalcoatl (Historia de México 1965: 108).[10] Maguey sprang from the bones of the goddess Mayahuel, and other crops constituted the body of the Cinteotl (Historia de México 1965: 107, 110). The body even provided a metaphor for the passage of time: according to Eduard Seler (1963), the twenty days of the divinatory calendar could be read as body parts.

As well as expressing the shared essence of all forms of divine energy, bodies could distinguish its variable outcomes. Different results were produced by different conjunctions of cosmic forces at critical phases of production and by different forms of nurture provided during growth (López Austin 1988: 296–99, 388–400; Monaghan 1988, 2001; Sahagún 1950–82: bk. 4). Differences in nature and nurture resulted in products with distinct constitutions and varying capacities for action. Many of these differences of character and power were instantiated as bodily differences (Hunt 1977: 95–115).

Given the polysemic importance of bodies in Central Mexico as representations of divine energy, creative process, and cultivated difference, it is not surprising that many topics were addressed through the imagery of figurines. At Xaltocan, community unity was invoked through figurines that represented the exotic bodies of alien life forms. Divisions of gender and quality of lineage were represented by cultivated differences in the dress and pose of figurines that were conventionally human. And creative processes and transformations of divine energy were both represented by and implemented through clay bodies that actively participated in human performances as ritual rattles, festive flutes, and burial containers. Because the body was a key metaphor for the people of Xaltocan and other Mesoamerican people, issues of embodiment ranged far beyond those that we might imagine from our own, Western-based definition of the body and bodily domains (see also Meskell and Joyce 2003; Weismantel 2004). Thinking explicitly about the body, especially at Xaltocan, where many kinds of bodies are present within the figurine assemblage, helps us to imagine the various realms of social discourse that these figurines addressed.

Acknowledgments

Christina Halperin, John Millhauser, Cynthia Robin, Enrique Rodríguez-Alegría, and Mary Weismantel very kindly read earlier drafts of this chapter and provided many suggestions for revision. We are grateful for their efforts.

Notes

1. In archaeology, discussions of embodiment represent the confluence of several streams of earlier work: considerations of material culture as an active agent in social life (DeMarrais et al. 1996; Hodder 1986; Sørensen 2006); analyses of how social control, socialization, and performance shape identity (Butler 1990, 1993; Foucault 1977; Joyce 1998, 2001a, 2001b, 2004; Meskell 2002; Perry and Joyce 2001; Sørensen 2000); curiosity about how the past was experienced (Gilchrist 1994, 2000; Kus 1982, 1992; Merleau-Ponty 1962; Thomas 1990); and a concern with how sexuality was (and is) socially constructed (Foucault 1978; Gilchrist 1999; Meskell 2002; Meskell and Joyce 2003; Schmidt and Voss 2000; Weismantel 2004). As Rosemary Joyce (2005) observes, as interest in embodiment has grown, earlier views of the body and its ornaments as

media for communicating social status and identity have been supplemented or replaced by discussion of how the body through its sensual experience shapes identity: an earlier outward orientation has shifted to an inward orientation. For summary statements on embodiment in archaeology, see Hamilakis et al. 2002; Joyce 2005; Meskell 1996.

2. Fruitful comparisons can also be made between figurines and burials and between figurines and architecture, since burials and movement in architectural space present further opportunities for representing social categories and social relations (Joyce 2001a; Marcus 1998).

3. Carbon-14 dates suggest that Xaltocan was settled at the beginning of the tenth century CE, instead of in the mid-eleventh century, as recorded in the ethnohistoric documents.

4. Because interest in ancient figurines at Xaltocan predates the archaisms of the Aztec Great Temple by four centuries or so, Aztec rulers may have appropriated this commoner tradition of collecting and reusing objects from the past to substantiate their own very different moral economy: one that claimed that the persistence of the present world depended on state-organized warfare and human sacrifice (see Kus and Raharijaona 2000).

5. Beyond Central Mexico, seven cached figurines from Dzibilchaltun resemble Xaltocan's mud men in their rough hand-modeling and unburnished surfaces (Taschek 1994: 204, fig. 49). They differ, however, in having hand-modeled arms and legs. These figurines date to the Decadent period at Dzibilchaltun, after 1200 CE, and are therefore roughly contemporaneous with Phase 2 deposits at Xaltocan.

6. Kneeling is considered the conventional "Aztec women's pose" (Baird 1993: 127; Caso 1960: 14; Robertson 1966: 302).

7. Representing roughly 5 percent of the figurines in Phases 1, 2, and 3, Mazapan figurines appear to have continued to be used at Xaltocan much longer than previous research has suggested for this type. Research on Mazapan pottery has defined a temporal distribution of AD 950–1150 (Scott 1993; Stocker 1983), whereas at Xaltocan, Mazapan figurines continued through Phase 3, roughly 1300–1425 CE.

8. These flutes may represent a broader pattern of activity among Mesoamerican peoples: the effort to make invisible or transitory sensations more visible and concrete. Stephen Houston and Karl Taube (2000) argue that ancient Mesoamerican people used an array of graphic conventions to visually express the immaterial. For example, they rendered sound as speech scrolls or song scrolls emanating from speakers' mouths. The figurine heads attached to the ends of flutes may have enhanced the sensual experience of music by making it a visual as well as an auditory experience and thereby may have made the music more enduring.

9. A plumbate dog effigy vessel containing ashes and partially burned human bones was recovered from the Great Temple in Mexico City (Matos 1988: 160).

10. In an extended meditation upon the body, the "Historia de México" (1965: 108) reports that the Earth Monster's hair sprouted trees, flowers, and herbs; her skin supported grass and tiny flowers; her eyes were transformed into wells, springs, and small caverns; her mouth became the source of rivers and large caves; her nose was transformed into mountain valleys; and her shoulders became mountains.

References Cited

Alva Ixtlilxóchitl, Fernando de. [1600–4C] 1975–77. *Obras históricas*. 2 vols. Ed. E. O'Gorman. Universidad Nacional Autónoma de México, Mexico City.

Bailey, Douglass W. 2005. *Prehistoric Figurines: Representation and Corporeality in the Neolithic*. Routledge, London.

Baird, Ellen T. 1993. *The Drawings of Sahagún's "Primeros Memoriales."* University of Oklahoma Press, Norman.

Boone, Elizabeth H., and Zelia Nuttall, eds. 1983. *Codex Magliabechiano*. 2 vols. University of California Press, Berkeley.

Brumfiel, Elizabeth M. 1991. Weaving and Cooking: Women's Production in Aztec Mexico. In *Engendering Archaeology: Women and Prehistory*, ed. J. M. Gero and M. W. Conkey, 224–51. Basil Blackwell, London.

———. 1996a. Figurines at Xaltocan, Mexico. Paper presented at the 61st Meeting of the Society for American Archaeology, New Orleans.

———. 1996b. Figurines and the Aztec State: Testing the Effectiveness of Ideological Domination. In *Gender in Archaeology: Essays in Research and Practice*, ed. R. P. Wright, 143–66. University of Pennsylvania Press, Philadelphia.

———. 2000. The Politics of High Culture. In *Order, Legitimacy, and Wealth in Ancient States*, ed. J. Richards and M. Van Buren, 131–39. Cambridge University Press, Cambridge.

———, ed. 2005. *Production and Power at Postclassic Xaltocan*. Instituto Nacional de Antropología e Historia, Mexico City, and University of Pittsburgh, Pittsburgh.

Butler, Judith. 1990. *Gender Trouble*. Routledge, London.

———. 1993. *Bodies That Matter*. Routledge, London.

Carrasco, Pedro. 1950. *Los Otomíes: Culture e historia prehispánica de los pueblos mesoamericanos de habla Otomiana*. Biblioteca Enciclopédica del Estado de México, Mexico City.

Caso, Alfonso. 1960. *Interpretation of the Codex Bodley 2858*. Sociedad Mexicana de Antropología, Mexico City.

Cohodas, Marvin. 2002. Multiplicity and Discourse in Maya Gender Relations. In *Ancient Maya Gender Identity and Relations*, ed. L. S. Gustafson and A. M. Trevelyan, 11–53. Bergin and Garvey, Westport, Conn.

Cortés, Hernán. [1519–26] 1970. *Cartas de relación*. Porrúa, Mexico City.

Cyphers Guillén, Ann. 1993. Women, Rituals, and Social Dynamics at Ancient Chalcatzingo. *Latin American Antiquity* 4: 209–24.

Davies, Nigel. 1980. *Toltec Heritage: From the Fall of Tula to the Rise of Tenochtitlan*. University of Oklahoma Press, Norman.

DeMarrais, Elizabeth, Luis Jaime Castillo, and Timothy Earle. 1996. Ideology, Materialization, and Power Strategies. *Current Anthropology* 37: 15–31.

Díaz del Castillo, Bernal. [1568] 1955. *The Discovery and Conquest of Mexico*. Trans. A. P. Maudslay. Noonday Press, New York.

Evans, Susan T. 1990. Household Ritual in Aztec Life. Paper presented at the 55th Annual Meeting of the Society for American Archaeology, Las Vegas.

Florescano, Enrique. 1994. *Memory, Myth and Time in Mexico.* University of Texas Press, Austin.

Foucault, Michel. 1977. *Discipline and Punish.* Penguin, London.

———. 1978. *The History of Sexuality.* Penguin, Harmondsworth, U.K.

Gilchrist, Roberta. 1994. *Gender and Material Culture.* Routledge, London.

———. 1999. *Gender and Archaeology.* Routledge, London.

———. 2000. Unsexing the Body: The Interior Sexuality of Medieval Religious Women. In *Archaeologies of Sexuality,* ed. R. A. Schmidt and B. L. Voss, 89–103. Routledge, London.

Gillespie, Susan. 2000. Beyond Kinship: An Introduction. In *Beyond Kinship: Social and Material Reproduction in House Societies,* ed. R. Joyce and S. Gillespie, 1–21. University of Pennsylvania Press, Philadelphia.

Hamann, Byron. 2002. The Social Life of Pre-Sunrise Things. *Current Anthropology* 43: 351–82.

Hamilakis, Yannis, Mark Pluciennik, and Sarah Tarlow. 2002. Introduction: Thinking Through the Body. In *Thinking Through the Body,* ed. Y. Hamilakis, M. Pluciennik, and S. Tarlow, 1–21. Kluwer Academic/Plenum, New York.

Hicks, Frederic. 1986. Prehispanic Background of Colonial Political and Economic Organization in Central Mexico. In *Supplement* to *The Handbook of Middle American Indians,* vol. 4, *Ethnohistory,* ed. R. Spores, 35–54. University of Texas Press, Austin.

———. 1994. Xaltocan under Mexica Domination, 1435–1520. In *Caciques and Their People: A Volume in Honor of Ronald Spores,* ed. J. Marcus and J. F. Zeitlin, 67–85. Museum of Anthropology, Anthropological Papers 89. University of Michigan, Ann Arbor.

Historia de México. [c. 1543] 1965. In *Trogonía e historia de los Mexicanos,* ed. A. Ma. Garibay, 91–120. Porrúa, Mexico City.

Hodder, Ian. 1986. *Reading the Past.* Cambridge University Press, Cambridge.

Houston, Stephen D. 1996. Symbolic Sweatbaths of the Maya: Architectural Meaning in the Cross Group at Palenque, Mexico. *Latin American Antiquity* 7: 132–51.

Houston, Stephen D., and Karl Taube. 2000. An Archaeology of the Senses: Perception and Cultural Expression in Ancient Mesoamerica. *Cambridge Archaeological Journal* 10: 261–94.

Hunt, Eva. 1977. *The Transformation of the Hummingbird.* Cornell University Press, Ithaca, N.Y.

Ingham, John M. 1986. *Mary, Michael, and Lucifer: Folk Catholicism in Central Mexico.* University of Texas Press, Austin.

Joyce, Rosemary A. 1993. Women's Work: Images of Production and Reproduction in Pre-Hispanic Southern Central America. *Current Anthropology* 34: 255–74.

———. 1998. Performing the Body in Prehispanic Central America. *RES* 33: 147–65.

———. 2000. Girling the Girl and Boying the Boy: The Production of Adulthood in Ancient Mesoamerica. *World Archaeology* 31: 473–83.

———. 2001a. *Gender and Power in Prehispanic Mesoamerica.* University of Texas Press, Austin.

———. 2001b. Negotiating Sex and Gender in Classic Maya Society. In *Gender in Pre-Hispanic America*, ed. C. Klein, 109–41. Dumbarton Oaks, Washington, D.C.

———. 2003. Making Something of Herself: Embodiment in Life and Death at Playa de los Muertos, Honduras. *Cambridge Archaeological Journal* 13: 248–61.

———. 2004. Embodied Subjectivity: Gender, Femininity, Masculinity, Sexuality. In *A Companion to Social Archaeology*, ed. L. Meskell and R. W. Preucel, 82–95. Blackwell, Oxford, U.K.

———. 2005. Archaeology of the Body. *Annual Review of Anthropology* 34: 139–58.

Kus, Susan. 1982. Matters Material and Ideal. In *Symbolic and Structural Archaeology*, ed. I. Hodder, 47–62. Cambridge University Press, Cambridge.

———. 1992. Toward an Archaeology of Body and Soul. In *Representations in Archaeology*, ed. C. Peebles and J. C. Gardin, 168–77. Indiana University Press, Bloomington.

Kus, Susan, and V. Raharijaona. 2000. House to Palace, Village to State: Scaling Up Architecture and Ideology. *American Anthropologist* 102: 98–113.

Lesure, Richard G. 1997. Figurines and Social Identities in Early Sedentary Societies of Coastal Chiapas, Mexico, 1550–800 BC. In *Women in Prehistory: North America and Mesoamerica*, ed. C. Claassen and R. A. Joyce, 227–48. University of Pennsylvania Press, Philadelphia.

———. 1999. Figurines as Representations and Products at Paso de la Amada, Mexico. *Cambridge Archaeological Journal* 9: 209–20.

López Austin, Alfredo. 1988. *The Human Body and Ideology*. Trans. T. Ortiz de Montellano and B. Ortiz de Montellano. University of Utah Press, Salt Lake City.

Madsen, William. 1960. *The Virgin's Children*. University of Texas Press, Austin.

Marcus, Joyce. 1998. *Women's Ritual in Formative Oaxaca: Figurine-Making, Divination, Death and the Ancestors*. Memoir 33. Museum of Anthropology, University of Michigan, Ann Arbor.

Matos Moctezuma, Eduardo. 1988. *The Great Temple of the Aztecs*. Thames and Hudson, London.

McCafferty, Geoffrey G. 2001. *Ceramics of Postclassic Cholula, Mexico*. Monograph 43. Cotsen Institute of Archaeology. Los Angeles.

Merleau-Ponty, M. 1962. *The Phenomenology of Perception*. Trans. C. Smith. Routledge, London.

Meskell, Lynn M. 1996. The Somatization of Archaeology: Institutions, Discourses, Corporeality. *Norwegian Archaeological Review* 29: 1–16.

———. 2002. Intersections of Identity and Politics in Archaeology. *Annual Review of Anthropology* 31: 279–301.

Meskell, Lynn M., and Rosemary A. Joyce. 2003. *Embodied Lives*. Routledge, London.

Monaghan, John. 1988. The Person, Destiny, and the Construction of Difference in Mesoamerica. *RES* 33: 137–46.

———. 1995. *The Covenants with Earth and Rain: Exchange, Sacrifice, and Revelation in Mixtec Sociality*. University of Oklahoma Press, Norman.

———. 2001. Physiology, Production, and Gendered Difference: The Evidence from Mixtec and Other Mesoamerican Societies. In *Gender in Pre-Hispanic America*, ed. C. F. Klein, 285–304. Dumbarton Oaks, Washington, D.C.

Montoya, Janet. 1996. Clay Figurines from Mound 65 at Chalco. Paper presented at the Annual Meeting of the Society for American Archaeology, New Orleans.

Nazareo de Xaltocan, Don Pablo. [1566] 1940. *Carta al Rey Don Felipe II*. In *Epistolario de Nueva España*, vol. 10, ed. F. del Paso y Troncoso, 109–29. Antigua Librería Robredo, Mexico City.

Norr, Lynette. 1987. Postclassic Artifacts from Tetla. In *Ancient Chalcatzingo*, ed. D. C. Grove, 525–46. University of Texas Press, Austin.

Overholtzer, Lisa Marie. 2005. The Kneeling Mexica Woman: Evidence for Male Domination or Gender Complementarity? Senior honor thesis, Department of Anthropology, University of California, Berkeley.

Perry, E. M., and Rosemary A. Joyce. 2001. Providing a Past for Bodies that Matter: Judith Butler's Impact on the Archaeology of Gender. *International Journal of Sex and Gender Studies* 6: 63–76.

Redfield, Robert. 1930. *Teopotzlan*. University of Chicago Press, Chicago.

Rivera, Alex. 2003. Study of the Break Patterns in Aztec Figurines at the Site of Xaltocan and Their Relation to Functionality. Paper on file, Northwestern University.

Robertson, Donald. 1966. The Mixtec Religious Manuscripts. In *Ancient Oaxaca*, ed. J. Paddock, 298–312. Stanford University Press, Stanford, Calif.

Sahagún, Bernardino de. [1561–65] 1950–82. *Florentine Codex*. Trans. A. J. O. Anderson and C. E. Dibble. School of American Research, Santa Fe, N.Mex., and University of Utah, Salt Lake City.

———. [1559–61] 1997. *Primeros Memoriales*. Trans. T. Sullivan with additions by H. B. Nicholson, A. J. O. Anderson, C. E. Dibble, E. Quiñones Keber, and W. Ruwet. University of Oklahoma Press, Norman.

Sandstrom, Alan R. 1991. *Corn Is Our Blood*. University of Oklahoma Press, Norman.

Schmidt, Robert A., and Barbara L. Voss, eds. 2000. *Archaeologies of Sexuality*. Routledge, London.

Scott, Sue. 1993. *Teotihuacan Mazapan Figurines and the Xipe Totec Statue: A Link between the Basin of Mexico and the Valley of Oaxaca*. Vanderbilt University, Nashville, Tenn.

Seler, Eduard. 1963. *Comentarios al Códice Borgia*. Fondo de Cultural Económica, Mexico City.

Smith, Michael E. 2002. Domestic Ritual at Aztec Provincial Sites in Morelos. In *Domestic Ritual in Ancient Mesoamerica*, ed. P. Plunket, 93–114. Cotsen Institute of Archaeology, Los Angeles.

Sørensen, Marie Louise Stig. 2000. *Gender Archaeology*. Polity Press, Cambridge, U.K.

———. 2006. Gender, Things, and Material Culture. In *Handbook of Gender in Archaeology*, ed. S. M. Nelson, 105–35. AltaMira Press, Lanham, Md.

Stocker, Terry. 1983. Clay Figurines from Tula, Hidalgo, Mexico. Ph.D. diss., Department of Anthropology, University of Illinois, Urbana.

Sullivan, Thelma. 1966. Pregnancy, Childbirth and the Deification of the Women Who Died in Childbirth. *Estudios de Cultura Náhuatl* 6: 63–96.

Taschek, Jennifer T. 1994. *The Artifacts of Dzibilchaltun, Yucatan, Mexico.* Middle American Research Institute, Publication 50. Tulane University, New Orleans.

Tedlock, Dennis. 1985. *Popol Vuh: The Mayan Book of the Dawn of Life.* Simon and Schuster, New York.

Thomas, Julian. 1990. Monuments from the Inside. *World Archaeology* 22: 168–78.

Toscano, Salvador, Heinrich Berlin, and Robert H. Barlow, eds. [c. 1528–31] 1948. *Anales de Tlatelolco.* Antigua Librería de José Porrúa e Hijos, Mexico City.

Umberger, Emily. 1987. Antiques, Revivals, and References to the Past in Aztec Art. *RES* 13: 62–105.

Velázquez, Primo Feliciano, trans. [1570] 1945. Anales de Cuauhtitlan. In *Códice Chimalpopoca,* 1–118. Universidad Nacional Autónoma de México, Mexico City.

Weismantel, Mary. 2004. Moche Sex Pots: Reproduction and Temporality in Ancient South America. *American Anthropologist* 106: 495–505.

Part V

State and Household Relations

12

Sex in the City

A Comparison of Aztec Ceramic Figurines to Copal Figurines from the Templo Mayor

CECELIA F. KLEIN AND NAOLI VICTORIA LONA

Scholars have often noted that of the thousands upon thousands of cached artifacts unearthed at the Aztec Templo Mayor, or "Great Temple," the largest and most important temple-pyramid in the Aztec imperial capital, Tenochtitlan, none is a ceramic figurine.[1] This is surprising because thousands of Aztec ceramic figurines exist in museum and archaeological site collections. Averaging between 3 and 15 centimeters in height and generally entirely or partially mold-made, these ceramic figurines were both widely available and easily transportable. Regardless, they are usually recovered, broken and fragmented, from household debris, often in towns and peasant villages located outside the largest urban centers. Michael Smith (1997: 79) has uncovered evidence that some of the Postclassic period (AD 950–1521) ceramic figurines excavated at the Nahuatl-speaking villages of Yautepec, Cuexcomate, and Capilco in Morelos were kept in wall niches inside the home, recalling the sixteenth-century Dominican Diego Durán's (1967: 1: 248; 1971: 235) report that the Aztecs placed "idols" in their household shrines.[2] In the Teotihuacan Valley, Susan Evans (1990) found Late Post-classic (AD 1340–1500) ceramic figurines not only inside Aztec houses but also nearby at *temascales,* or sweat baths. Other ceramic figurines in Central Mexico had been buried in fields and, rarely, graves, as well as found at the bottom of ancient canals, springs, rivers, lakes, and in temples and palaces (Elson 1999; Kaplan 1958: 175; Millian 1981: 21, 46; Porcayo 1998: 248, 258–59, 263).

But if ceramic figurines played such an important role in the daily lives of ordinary Aztec householders and farmers, why were they absent from the Templo Mayor offerings? The Templo Mayor offerings are known to contain numerous objects obtained, whether by gift or by tribute, from regions outside the capital. Many of these are relatively small and assume a human or animal form, yet none are of clay. Some reasons for the absence of clay figurines in these offerings are suggested by analysis of a genre of figurines that are represented in the Templo Mayor offerings: those made of copal. Copal, as Naoli Victoria Lona (2004a, 2004b) has pointed out, comes from the resin of several trees, primarily those of the species *Bursera bipinnata*.[3] When burned, this resin emits a white, pleasant-smelling smoke still believed by many Mesoamericans to nourish and delight the gods. The presence of figurines made of copal where ceramic figurines are absent begs for an understanding of the historical and iconographic relationship of the two genres.

Several aspects of this relationship are salient, including subject matter, standardization, and gender. The subject matter of the copal figurines is greatly limited in comparison with that of ceramic figurines, and their style and iconography are far more standardized. The female figurines made of copal have numerous counterparts among the ceramic figurines, whereas the copal males do not. Moreover, the latter seem to relate to a single ceramic male type that is extremely rare. For some reason, the copal males do not resemble a popular type of ceramic figurine.

Any explanation of this situation must take into account the identities of the personages represented in both clay and copal. Since the beginning of the twentieth century, scholars have traditionally identified many Aztec ceramic figurine types with deities in the Aztec state pantheon. They have, moreover, usually assumed that the iconography of the clay figurines reflects the influence of the expanding state's official religion. However, there is little persuasive evidence for identifying the vast majority of the ceramic figurines with the official gods and goddesses portrayed in and near the capital. In making this point, we follow the lead taken by Alva Millian, who, in her Columbia University master's thesis in art history (1981: 476), declined to label any of her figurine groups with the name of a deity. Millian believed that "there is reasonable evidence to support the contention that some Aztec figurines [*sic*] types previously labeled as deities are, instead, humans—perhaps petitioners or deity impersonators" (see also Millian 1981: 3, 113–15). This may be so, but there is also support for Michael Smith's (2002: 102–5; 2005) suggestion that many ceramic figurines represent not a specific personage per se but rather the spiritual essence or collective life force of an entity in the natural or built environment (see also Brumfiel and Overholtzer, this volume; Sandstrom, this volume).

In addition, most of the clay figurine types that have been associated by scholars with a state deity were in existence before the Aztec government at Tenochtitlan formed and codified its pantheon. They appear in the archaeological and artistic record prior to the peak of imperial expansion. Moreover, they bear little resemblance to the manuscript paintings and written descriptions of those deities that were produced in the aftermath of the 1521 Spanish conquest, which tell us only about the physical appearances of Aztec deities as they were portrayed after the state had reached its imperial apogee. This does not necessarily mean that all of the ceramic figurines in some way resembling Aztec deities were made before the state had consolidated its power or that none represent the spread and influence of the state religion. What it does mean is that the entities represented in these figurine types had been playing a role in local belief systems beyond the reach of the urban government before the state appropriated, elaborated on, codified, and incorporated them into its official pantheon. This finding supports Smith's (2002: 102) contention that "when we free [ceramic] figurines from the interpretive constraints of official Aztec religion, it becomes clear that they functioned in the context of a distinctive domestic religion only distantly related to the public great tradition religion of Tenochtitlan."

The Ceramic Figurines

The copal figurines found at the Templo Mayor have been thoroughly analyzed by Victoria Lona (2004a, 2004b; compare López Luján 2006; López Luján and Fauvet-Berthelot 2005). The study of Aztec ceramic figurines, however, is still far from complete; to date there is no comprehensive study of Aztec figurines made of clay.[4] Because Millian's (1981: 47) sample, which she divided into "groups" rather than "types," is the largest to date, we have chosen her typology to structure our analysis of the ceramic figurines. Moreover, like Millian, we focus on figurines in human form, in particular those that have been argued to share stylistic and iconographic elements with Aztec deities. In so doing, we must necessarily ignore not only the vast majority of humanoid figurines, which lack any recognizable characteristics of Aztec deities, but also the numerous clay miniatures that take the form of an animal or a building. This neglect calls out for future redress.[5] Nonetheless, the fact that the Aztec ceramic figurine corpus is so diverse in style and iconography supports our contention that the majority of the ceramic figurines were unrelated to members of the official Aztec pantheon.

"Group I" Ceramic Female Figurines

Most scholars who have worked with Aztec ceramic figurines have distinguished between those that are hollow and those that are solid. The former
are typically larger than the latter, are often rattles, were frequently made
to stand upright, and were usually made of a reddish orange clay using two
molds, one for the front and one for the back. Millian (1981: 54–55) placed
these figurines in her "Group I." The majority represent a standing, bare-
breasted, long-skirted female human with a hairdo in which either a single
"rope" of twisted hair is wrapped around the head, a style known as *tlacoyal,* or the hair is parted in the middle, the two sides looped up on each
side of the head to terminate in a vertical tuft (figure 12.1). Although the
loops sometimes seem excessively large and awkwardly placed because of
the thinness of these figurines, this hairdo is usually compared favorably
with that of the typical married Aztec woman, whose hair on each side
of the head was brought to the top and fastened, with the end projecting
upward in what the Spaniards described as a "horn." Female figurines that
likewise sport either the twisted "rope" hairdo or a two-horned hairdo also
occur in solid form, albeit usually smaller than their hollow counterparts
and sometimes made of a lighter colored clay or slip. Some solid Group I
figurines are jointed as well (González Rul 1988: 70, pl. 51; Parsons 1972:
88). Like the hollow rattles, the solid Group I females exhibit minor variations in size, dress, pose, and attributes; some appear to be pregnant, for
example, while others are deformed. Many hold one or two small "babies"
or human figurines, or a small animal, in their arm(s) or over their chests
(Millian 1981: 75).

Because the highly standardized Group I female figurines were widely
distributed throughout the Basin of Mexico, Cynthia Otis-Charlton (1991:
40; 1994: 206–8) concluded that the female hollow rattles found at Otumba
had been traded in from the Basin of Mexico via a regional market system,
a conclusion reiterated by Smith (2005: 45–46, fig. 2) regarding figurines
of this type that he found in Morelos.[6] This, together with the technique
and materials employed in the manufacturing process of the hollow female
figurines—especially the use of two molds, a fine paste, high firing tempera-
tures, and a high burnish—all seem to point to a common locus of origin "in
or near the Triple Alliance cities," according to Otis-Charlton (1994: 207).

The popularity of these figurines over a large area, together with their
standardized form and apparent origin in or near the Aztec capital, has
encouraged the assumption that they represent a widely recognized deity
in the government-sponsored pantheon. There is, however, little persuasive

a   b

Figure 12.1. Group I hollow female with child. Clay, 21 cm. Lukas Vischer Collection, Museum der Kulturen (formerly the Ethnographic Museum), Basel. *a*, Front view (from Baer 1996: pl. IVb, no. 533); *b*, side view (from Baer 1996: pl. IVb, no. 533).

iconographic evidence that these figurines represent a specific goddess. For example, Robert Barlow and Herbert Lehmann's (1956: 167) identification of the Group I figurines as Xochiquetzal, "Precious Flower," a popular Aztec fertility goddess, was based on a misunderstanding: they misread the two "horns" of hair in the figurines as the two plumes of headdress feathers that are diagnostic of Xochiquetzal in Central Mexican manuscript paintings (figure 12.2a).

Flora Kaplan (1958: 13, 13–19), who compiled the first systematic typology of Aztec ceramic figurines for her anthropology master's thesis at Columbia University, was followed by Mary Hrones Parsons (1972: 83, 85) in identifying these figurines as Coatlicue, "Snakes-Her-Skirt," the legend-

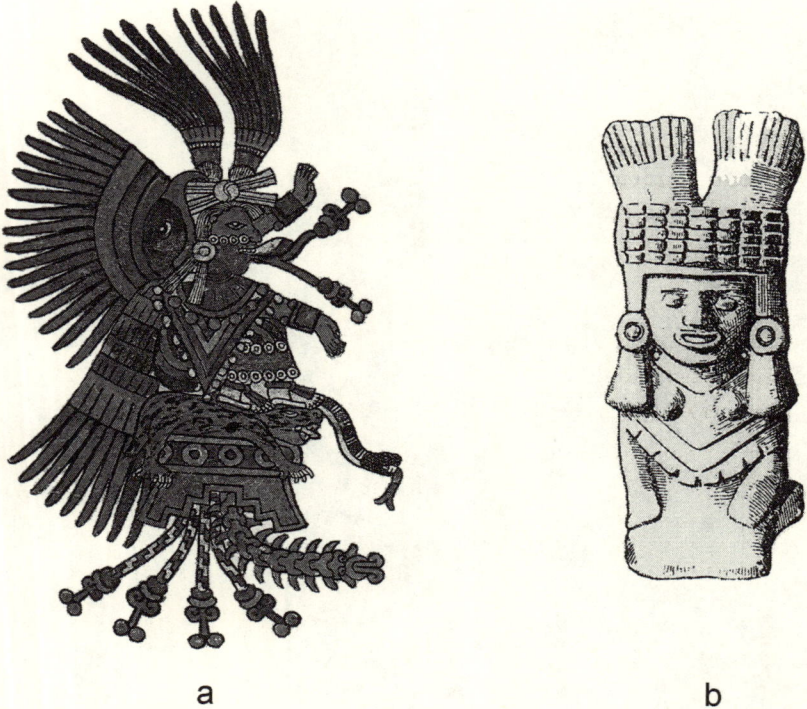

a   b

Figure 12.2. Xochiquetzal and Group II figurine. *a,* Xochiquetzal, depicted in the
Codex Borbonicus, pl. 19 (courtesy of Akademische Druck- u. Verlagsanstalt, Graz;
from Nowotny 1974). *b,* Group II female with double-plumed headdress. Clay. Uhde
Collection, Ethnographic Museum, Berlin (from Noguera 1946: 482).

ary mother of the Aztec national patron deity Huitzilopochtli, "Humming-
bird-Left," another reading for which there is no plausible evidence. Kaplan
(1958: 16) argued that the long skirt decorated with a diamond pattern that
is frequently seen on Group I figurines is a "simplification" of the interlaced
serpents that form Coatlicue's skirt (and serve as an ideograph of her name)
in official Aztec imagery.[7] However, as Millian (1981: 58–59) pointed out,
skirts decorated with a diamond pattern appear on other Aztec goddesses
and/or their impersonators, as well as on the conventional sign for mountain and the body of the earth alligator Cipactli.[8] They are particularly common on maize and fertility goddesses, which led Millian (1981: 64–65), who
also noted that most urban Aztec women did not go about bare breasted,
to propose that these figurines were simply "part of the [generalized] earth/
fertility complex."[9] In the Codex Borbonicus (pls. 29, 30), priest-impersonators of goddesses carrying double ears of corn, an attribute of vegetation

goddesses, are clad in flayed female skins with bare breasts and skirts decorated with a diamond pattern.[10]

Eduard Seler (1990–2000: 2: 166, figs. 29a,b) may have come closest to the mark when he wrote that it was "quite probable" that the figurines represent the Aztec goddess of parturient mothers and midwives, Cihuacoatl (Snake Woman). This identification was later accepted by Lewis Spence (1923: 181) and Carmen Cook de Leonard (1950: 96).[11] Seler (1990–2000: 2: 166) based his attribution on an unidentified passage from Bernardino de Sahagún, presumably Sahagún's *Historia general de las cosas de Nueva España* (1977: 1: 46–47), in which the Franciscan describes Cihuacoatl's hair as arranged with "some little horns crossed over the front [of the head]" and says that she carried a cradle like that which normally contains a child.[12]

Except for the two-horned hairdo and the occasional presence of smaller figures possibly representing children, however, Group I figurines bear little in common with Aztec depictions of Chuacoatl. In the same passage cited above, for example, Sahagún added that the upper half of the goddess's face was painted red, the lower half black, and that she wore "a headdress of [eagle] feathers" and "a triangular shoulder shawl." All of these elements, along with a white circle on the cheek, appear in his native illustrators' depictions of Cihuacoatl in both the Florentine Codex (Sahagún 1979: 1: prologue page 10v) and his earlier manuscript, the *Primeros memoriales* (Sahagún 1993: fol. 264r). The text and images in both the *Primeros memoriales* and the Florentine Codex also show that Cihuacoatl carried both a shield decorated with eagle feathers and a weaving batten (see also Sahagún 1950–82: bk. 1: 11) (figure 12.3a), as she does in the cognate codices Magliabechiano (fol. 45r), Tudela (fol. 26r), and Ixtlilxochitl (fol. 102v), in which she also sports a skeletal nose and jaw (figure 12.3b). The red and black face paint, skeletal features, circles on the cheeks, eagle plumes in the hair, shield, batten, and cradle or knife: none of these elements appear on the ceramic females in this category.

There are, however, two bare-breasted female figures in relief on the famous Tizoc Stone, as well as on its predecessor, now known as the Archbishop's Stone, that may link the Group I females to Cihuacoatl (Alcina Franch et al. 1992: 199–200, 208–9, pls. XLIa–d, XLIIa–d). On both monuments, the figures appear among several others being taken captive by an Aztec warrior. One of these captives has been suggested to represent the patron deity of Xochimilco, the other that of Colhuacan, both towns on the mainland that were militarily brought, early in the state's history, under Tenochtitlan's control (Wicke 1976) (figure 12.3c). Cihuacoatl was the

coaH , quilaztli

a

b

c

Figure 12.3. Cihuacoatl. *a,* Depicted in the *Primeros memoriales,* fol. 264r (copyright Patrimonio Nacional, Madrid) (from Sahagún 1993). *b,* Depicted in the Codex Magliabechiano, fol. 45r (from Nuttall 1978). *c,* Cihuacoatl as Colhuacan's patron deity, Archbishop's Stone, 1440–81 (from Solís 1992: pl. XLI).

patron deity of both of these towns. On the Archbishop's Stone, the figure representing Colhuacan holds a weaving batten in one hand, whereas that of Xochimilco does not; the situation is reversed on the Tizoc Stone. Because the Archbishop's Stone may have been carved as early as 1440, before the state had formalized its official pantheon, Cihuacoatl may originally have been envisioned as a relatively ordinary, bare-breasted woman whose appearance in the urban centers gradually changed over time at the hands of the imperial government to become, by the time of the conquest, much more complex and macabre.[13]

As the archetypal parturient, moreover, Cihuacoatl was the leader of the collective shades, or spirits, of those unfortunate women who had died in childbirth. The Aztecs referred to these unhappy spirits as the Cihuateteo (singular form, Cihuateotl), "Divine Women," or the Cihuapipiltin (singular form, Cihuapipilli), "Noble Women." Millian (1981: 65) pointed out a possible relationship between the Group I figurines and a genre of three-dimensional Aztec stone sculptures representing kneeling, often bare-breasted females who have been interpreted as members of the Cihuapipiltin (for example, see Nicholson and Keber 1983: 68). Some of these statues have bared teeth and appear to grimace, implying anger and unhappiness, while others have clawed hands and skeletal faces (figure 12.4a).[14] Two of the latter have carved on their heads the date 1 Cuauhtli (1 Eagle), which was one of the days on which the Cihuapipiltin, it was feared, would descend to earth from their home in the western sky to harm pregnant women, their fetuses, and their children.[15] At these times, the Aztecs set up statues of the Cihuapipiltin at crossroads to receive offerings from anxious mothers seeking to appease them. Like the Cihuapipilli depicted in Sahagún's *Primeros memoriales*, these statues are depicted in his Florentine Codex as ordinary women wearing the "two-horn" hairdo (Sahagún 1979: 1: bk. 4, fol. 62v, center and bottom) (figure 12.4b).[16] Although Sahagún's artists always depicted the Cihuapipiltin as fully clothed, two manuscripts painted before the conquest—the Codices Borgia (pls. 47–48) and Vaticanus B (pls. 77–79)—present them as naked from the waist up (figure 12.4c).[17] The wrinkled abdomens of these figures identify them as having given birth, while their missing eyes and, in one case (Codex Vaticanus B, pl. 79), deformed feet tell us that the outcome of their labor was unfortunate.

Thus, the Group I ceramic figurines, like Cihuacoatl and the stone statues of Cihuapipiltin in the capital, may have embodied women's hopes and fears regarding conception, childbirth, and the survival and good health of their offspring (Klein 1998, 2000; see also Brumfiel and Overholtzer, this

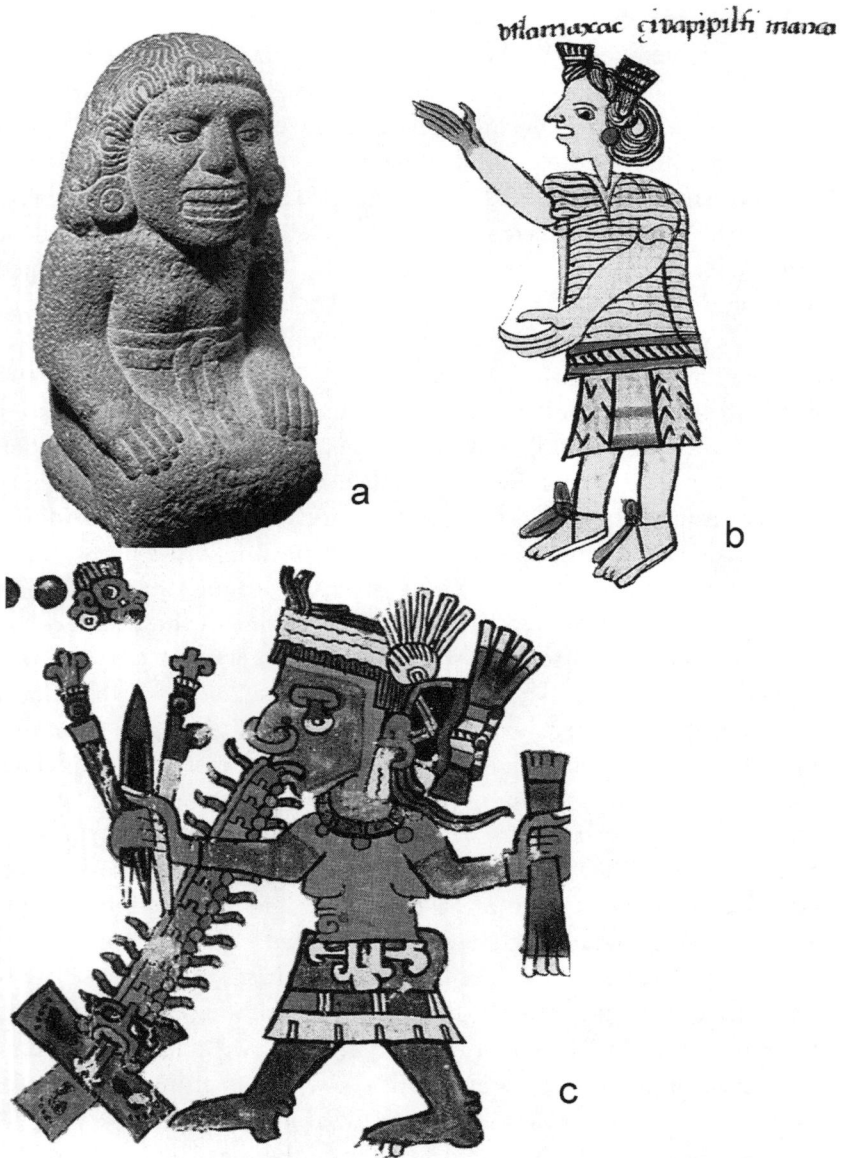

Figure 12.4. Figures of mothers dead in childbirth. *a*, Kneeling woman (a Cihuapipilli?). Greenstone, 64.7 cm (courtesy of the National Museum of the American Indian, Smithsonian Institution; from *Glanz und Untergang* 1986: 2: fig. 218). *b*, A Cihuapipilli (Cihuateotl), depicted in Sahagún's *Primeros memoriales*, fol. 266r (copyright Patrimonio Nacional, Madrid). *c*, A Cihuapipilli (Cihuateotl), depicted in the Codex Borgia, pl. 47 (courtesy of Akademische Druck- u. Verlagsanstalt, Graz; from Nowotny 1976).

volume). This reading resonates with previous identifications of a group of female figurines found in a large *olla* in front of the Temple of Ehecatl at Tlatelolco as representing Cihuapipiltin. Eduardo Corona S. (1972: fig. 9) identified a Group I female figurine found at that site, which has the two-horned coiffure and a series of vertical cuts on its chest and shoulders, as a Cihuapipilli. Because Sahagún (1950–82: bk. 1: 19) described the faces of Aztec statues of the Cihuapipiltin as having been "whitened with chalk," Salvador Guilliem Arroyo (1997: 114–16, 118, 133) later proposed that at least some of these figurines, which had been painted white, represent those goddesses. The figurines depict women with their hair styled in either the feminine two-horned coiffure or the twisted tlacoyal. Some are hollow; others, which are of a type that Guilliem Arroyo (1997: 118) called *galleta,* have rigid bodies, upturned eyes, snarling mouths with bared teeth, and arms crossed over their chests. This suggested to Guilliem Arroyo that these apparently unhappy women are dead. Although some have a painted blouse covering their upper torsos, others are naked from the waist up. The latter, like many of the Group I female figurines, hold a small child.

The Tlatelolco figurines therefore seem to represent an iconographic bridge between the Group I clay figurines, most of which look like an ordinary woman or mother and some of which are pregnant or deformed, and the deformed, grimacing, and/or skeletal Cihuapipiltin seen in manuscript paintings and stone statues. If this is correct, then the Group I figurines do not represent specific women and probably were never individually addressed by name. Instead, they embodied the generalized essence, or spirit, of human reproduction and motherhood, the spiritual guide of all women engaged in, or dead from, childbirth—a notion that would have held importance for any married couple. Sahagún (1950–82: bk. 4: 93) said that each Aztec midwife made offerings to the Cihuapipiltin "in her own home." Klein suggests that these domestic offerings, as well as those made by women hoping to conceive and those seeking the easy delivery of a healthy child, were made to Group I clay figurines.

If so, this concept was surely ancient and widespread, as small, generic figurines of women holding a child dominate the pre-Aztec, Mazapan-style ceramic corpus of the Toltec during the Early Postclassic period (AD 950–1150) (Stocker 1983: 160). Elizabeth Boone (2003: 215–16) has noted that throughout the Late Postclassic, the Cihuapipiltin formed part of an international symbol set spread over a wide area ranging from Oaxaca to Puebla and Tlaxcala.[18] She and Smith (2003: 192) noted that this symbol set, as manifested in the codices and other media, was already "well established by the start of the Late Postclassic period." The portrayal of the Cihuapipiltin as bare-breasted women thus predated the fifteenth-century rise of the imperial government headquartered at Tenochtitlan. This means that if the Group I female figurines represent the Cihuapipiltin and/or their leader Cihuacoatl, the figurines portray these entities in their earlier, pre-imperial guise.

Solid Figurines in Groups II–V

A similar argument can be made for many of the other solid figurines, which seem to represent generic beings that had been widely known throughout much of Mexico before the imperial pantheon was formed. These figurines are much more diverse in style and subject matter than the Group I figurines discussed above, and they tend to be smaller; many are made of lighter colored clay (Kaplan 1958; Millian 1981; Parsons 1972). Although the vast majority of the solid figurines possess no discernible features associated with deities in the Aztec pantheon, the question that we are addressing in this chapter requires that we focus on those that do.

Most of the solid female figurines fall into Millian's Groups II and III.[19] They usually wear a *quechquemitl*, a triangular woman's garment worn over the upper torso, over which a medallion or *chalchihuitl* (greenstone roundel) hangs from a beaded necklace or cord (Millian 1981: 66–68). The women in both groups either stand or adopt the kneeling position exclusive to Aztec women, and both wear elaborate headdresses topped by one or two plumes of feathers (Millian 1981: 66, 71). Like other scholars before her, Millian (1981: 66) distinguished females whose headdress bands are decorated with either horizontal rows of beads or a single row of flowers from those whose headdress bands are bordered at the top and bottom with a row of beads. In addition, some female figurines wear a headdress band decorated with flowers. Millian placed the figurines wearing either a flowered headdress or one decorated with horizontal rows of "beads" in her Group II. These headdresses often sport two vertical plumes rising from the top (figure 12.2b). In contrast, figurines with the headdress band bordered by a row of "beads" at top and bottom, which make up Millian's Group III, more often have a single plume or no plume at all (figure 12.5a). The figurines in Group III also typically wear the pleated bark-paper fan called *amacuexpalli*, which in real life was attached to the back of the wearer's head or neck. As Millian (1981: 66, 69–70) noted, however, many of the Group III headdress attributes, including the pleated neck fan, are shared with the figurines in Group II, just as elements of the latter appear among

a   b

Figure 12.5. Female figures with pleated fan headdress. *a*, Group III solid female figurine. Clay, 15.3 cm. Lukas Vischer Collection, Ethnographic Museum Basel (from Baer 1996: fig. IVb, no. 475). *b*, Chalchiuhtlicue, depicted in the Codex Magliabechiano, fol. 31r (from Nuttall 1978).

figurines in the former. This supports our suspicion that we are not always, if ever, looking at distinctive personages with individual names, but are instead seeing various aspects of a generalized collectivity.

There is additional iconographic support for this assertion. Prior to Millian's study, headdresses with a flowered band had been taken as evidence that the wearer is Xochiquetzal, because that goddess's name includes the word for flower (for example, Kaplan 1958: 95; Noguera 1946; Stocker 1983: 160–61). To our knowledge, however, Xochiquetzal's headdress is never described as decorated with flowers in colonial texts and painted manuscripts. Moreover, although Xochiquetzal's headdress often sports two vertical plumes of feathers in colonial manuscripts (figure 12.2a), double and single plumes, as Millian (1981: 68) pointed out, are also sometimes seen in those same manuscripts in the headdresses of other fertility deities, including the goddesses Cihuacoatl and Coatlicue. For that reason, Millian (1981: 69–70) declined to identify Group II figurines as Xochiquetzal, concluding instead that "it is probably prudent to recognize traits that associate these images with fertility" and to generally classify them "as a 'fertility theme' group." We concur with this opinion. In the Codex Borgia (pls. 20, 53, 58–60), a row of flowers appears in the hair of several women who, while they may represent the "flower" of youthful sexuality, are not, in all likelihood, goddesses.

The figurines in Group III, in turn, have been traditionally identified as the Aztec water goddess Chalchiuhtlicue, "Jade [or Precious] Skirt," who consistently appears in painted manuscripts wearing a headband bordered at the top and bottom with a row of beads and backed by an amacuexpalli (for example, Codex Borbonicus, pl. 5) (figure 12.5b). Millian (1981: 71) again demurred, however, pointing out that in Aztec imperial stone sculpture, the pleated neck fan is seen on other Aztec water and fertility deities as well. We are likewise unconvinced that the Group III figurines should be interpreted as exclusive representations of that—or any—goddess in the Aztec pantheon. Instead, like the Group II females, they probably represent one aspect of a collective but multifaceted notion of female fertility.

There are also some solid ceramic female figurines that hold, carry on their back, or wear around their neck one or more ears of corn. Although Millian's (1981: 75) sample revealed scant evidence of agricultural symbols, maize ears appear on clay figurines more often than has been usually recognized. The presence of corn on these figurines suggests that they were used, at least in part, to assuage concerns about crop fertility. Theodore Preuss (1901: figs. 10, 12–13, 15) published drawings of four of these figurines, all of which are in the Uhde Collection in the Ethnographic Museum in Berlin, identifying them as the Aztec maize goddess Chicomecoatl, "Seven Snake" (figure 12.6a). In postconquest manuscript paintings, Chicomecoatl is depicted holding a pair of corn ears in each hand (figure 12.6b). The Uhde Collection figurines are not anomalous: Parsons (1972: 98) reported six figurines from the Teotihuacan Valley that wear a necklace of corn ears, an ornament also seen on a figurine in the British Museum (Pasztory 1983: pl. 302). Five of the figurines reported by Parsons were pot attachments. There are also two figurines with a corn necklace in the Lukas Vischer Collection in Basel (Baer 1996: 123, figs. 451, 446), as well as a figurine attached to a small pot that holds in each hand the container with two maize ears known as a *cemmaitl* (figure 12.6c). Other figurines hold a container with maize ears in one hand and a rattle staff, or *chicahuaztli,* in the other hand (Preuss 1901: fig. 12).[20] Nonetheless, the headdresses of ceramic figurines with maize attributes vary, in some cases replicating headdresses seen in Groups II and III. This pattern is also seen in painted manuscripts of Chalchiuhtlicue, Chicomecoatl, and Xilonen, who likewise often share various

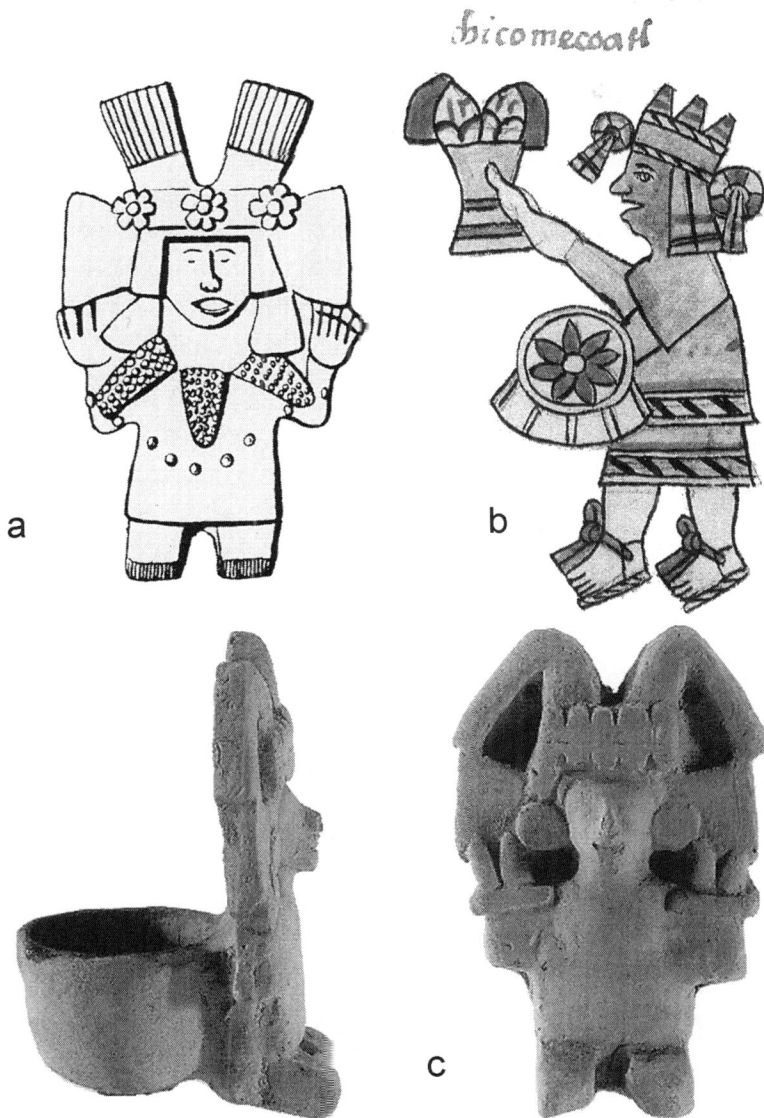

chicomecoatl

a

b

c

Figure 12.6. Female figures with corn a, Solid female figurine with corn-ear necklace. Clay. Uhde Collection, Ethnographic Museum, Berlin (from Preuss 1901: fig. 10). b, Chicomecoatl, depicted in Sahagún's *Primeros memoriales*, fol. 262r (copyright Patrimonio Nacional, Madrid). c, Pot with attached effigy of female(?) holding two *cemmaitli*, 2 views. Clay, 8 cm. Lukas Vischer Collection, Ethnographic Museum Basel (from Baer 1996: fig. IVb, no. 1030).

headdress elements (see, for example, Codex Borbonicus, pl. 7; Codex Magliabechiano, fol. 36).[21] The interchangeability of attributes among all of the Groups II and III female figurines strongly implies that their roles may have overlapped, with figurines used on behalf of reproductive fertility having also been used to enhance crop fertility.

Further evidence that some of the solid ceramic female figurines were tied to local agricultural concerns comes from one of Preuss's (1901: fig. 13) examples of a clay female holding a cemmaitl in each hand. This figurine wears a large rectangular headband with what appears to be a projecting molding around its four sides. Inside the rectangle is a row of four large roundels. This figurine type appears elsewhere; one example is now in the Lukas Vischer Collection in Basel (figure 12.7a). Parsons (1972: 97–98, fig. 18) described fragments of two figurines with this kind of headband, both of which had been attached to pots. Although previous scholars (for example, Millian 1981: 69) have not associated its presence with ceramic figurines, Klein thinks that these roundels were part of the headdress called *amacalli*, "paper house," which is often seen on Aztec stone sculptures of women holding ears of maize. Esther Pasztory and her students (*Aztec Stone Sculpture* 1976: 13) referred to this headdress as "the Temple Headdress" because of its resemblance to the façade of a building, its doorway framing the wearer's head (for example, *Aztecs* 2002: figs. 109, 234, 458) (figure 12.7b). In manuscript paintings and stone sculptures, a rosette appears at either two or four of the upper corners of these headdresses. Like several other statues with the Temple Headdress, that worn by a stone carved female now in the Musée du quai Branly has a row of concentric roundels running across its front (López Luján and Fauvet-Berthelot 2005: pl. 3).[22]

At the time of the conquest, Temple Headdresses like those seen in stone were worn by priest-impersonators of the maize goddess Chicomecoatl and the Mother of the Gods, Teteoinnan, during the events leading up to and during the harvest festival Ochpaniztli. In the Codex Borbonicus (pl. 30), which depicts events immediately preceding Ochpaniztli, the costume of the priest wearing the flayed skin of the sacrificed Chicomecoatl impersonator includes an enormous, highly elaborate Temple Headdress. This headdress has four rosettes, a year sign, two gigantic ears of corn (one red, one yellow), and paper streamers hanging to the ground on either side (figure 12.7c). Sahagún (1950–82: bk. 2: 121) describes a similar headdress that was worn by the priest who donned the skin and costume of the sacrificed woman who impersonated Teteoinnan shortly afterward.[23] Aztec stone sculptures of a man carrying, on his back, a smaller person wearing a Temple Headdress

Figure 12.7. Female figures with Temple Headdress. *a*, Female figurine with Temple Headdress(?). Clay, 11.6 cm. Lukas Vischer Collection, Ethnographic Museum Basel (from Baer 1996: fig. IVb, no. 1043). *b*, Woman with Temple Headdress. Stone, 68 cm. Ethnological Museum, Berlin, #IV Ca 46167 (courtesy of Bildarchiv Preussischer Kulturbesitz/Art Resources; from *Aztecs* 2002: pl. 109). *c*, Priest-impersonator of Chicomecoatl or Teteoinnan wearing Temple Headdress, depicted in the Codex Borbonicus, pl. 30 (courtesy of Akademische Druck- u. Verlagsanstalt, Graz; from Nowotny 1974).

recalls Sahagún's (1950–82: bk. 2: 19) and Durán's (1971: 233) reports that the young woman impersonating Teteoinnan during Ochpaniztli was carried to the place of her decapitation on the back of a priest (*Aztec Empire* 2004: pl. 108). The woman was positioned with "her face upward," according to Durán. The headdresses worn by the smaller figures have a framed rectangular headband containing four large roundels exactly like those seen in some ceramic figurines. The row of crenellations at the top of the figure's headband reappears not only in other Temple Headdresses (*Dioses del México antigua* 1995: 131, figs. 134–35) but also in manuscript depictions of Chicomecoatl (Codex Borbonicus, pl. 29) (figure 12.6b). Thus, although there is no reason to assume that the ceramic figurines wearing ears of corn and Temple Headdresses actually represent Aztec goddesses, many of them clearly reflect a concern for agricultural fertility.

Hollow and Solid Male Ceramic Figurines

Like Group I female figurines, many of the male figurines, including the hollow males in Millian's Groups C and D, display no known attributes of deities in the state pantheon (Millian 1981: 37). Of Millian's thirteen groups of male figurines, only three groups bear attributes that appear consistently in images of Aztec deities whose cults were administered by the state. There is archaeological and iconographic evidence, moreover, that all three of these groups existed over a wide area well before the Aztec government had established its hegemony and formulated an official religion (Boone 2003: 211–13). Rather than read the figurines in these two groups as rural versions of gods honored in the capital during the Late Postclassic period, we should consider the possibility that some, if not most, of them were actually precursors of those deities.

The three groups of male figurines that have a demonstrable iconographic relation to an Aztec god are Millian's (1981: 76–77) Group A ("conical cap and buccal mask"), Group G ("flayed figures"), and Group F ("headgear with two vertical projections bearing four circles"). Group A figurines, which are always solid, may stand or sit; some sit on the platform of a miniature stepped pyramid (Baer 1996: fig. 345) (figure 12.8a). The distinguishing features are a tall, conical, sometimes phallic-looking hat and a projecting, beaklike buccal mask. The distinctive earrings (*epcololli*) are either hooked or vertically split in the center, and there is often a cut-shell ornament (*ehecacozcatl*) on the chest (Millian 1981: 78–80; see also Baer 1996: p. 90, figs. 345, 457, 497, 498, 500, 908; p. 101, figs. 511–13, 148, 886).

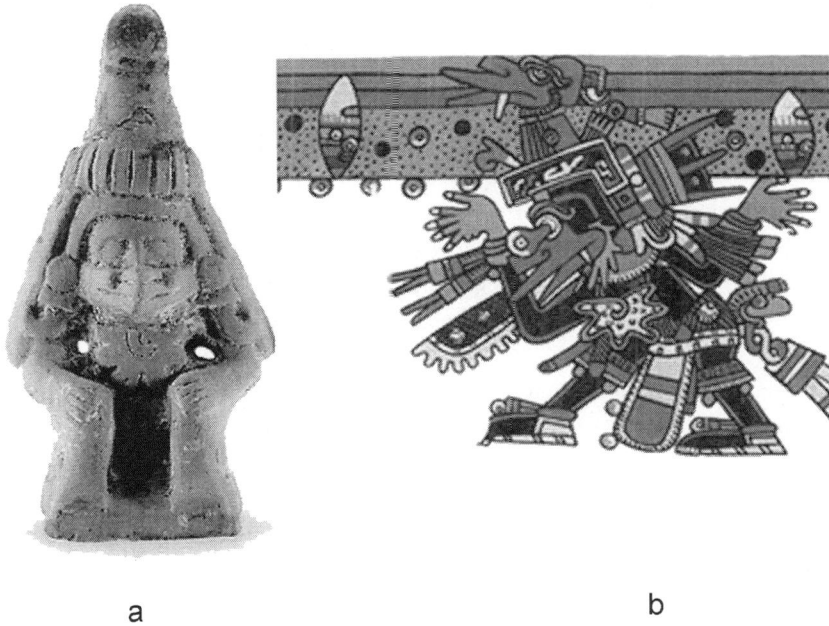

a   b

Figure 12.8. Male figure with buccal mask and Ehecatl. *a*, Group A (conical cap and buccal mask) male figurine. Clay, 13.2 cm Lukas Vischer Collection, Ethnographic Museum Basel (from Baer 1996: fig. IVb, no. 500). *b*, Ehecatl, depicted in the Codex Borgia, pl. 56 (courtesy of Akademische Druck- u. Verlagsanstalt, Graz; from Nowotny 1976).

Beginning with Seler (1990–2000: vol. 2: fig. 32 on p. 167; vol. 4: 238–39, figs. 3, 4 on p. 238; vol. 5: 71, figs. 86, 87 on p. 70), these figurines have been identified with the Aztec creator god Quetzalcoatl, "Precious/Quetzal Snake," in his manifestation as the wind god Ehecatl (from *eecatl*, "wind"). Ehecatl consistently appears in Aztec painted manuscripts and stone sculpture with a beaklike buccal mask, a conical hat, hooked shell earrings, and a large, cross-sectioned conch shell on his chest. Some or all of the same attributes appear in preconquest painted manuscripts from Puebla and the Mixteca—in the latter case, however, dating back several centuries before the conquest (figure 12.8b). The features that distinguish Ehecatl in Aztec art were therefore in place before the emergence of the Aztec polity.

The same can be said of the second figurine type that has been compared to a specific Aztec god: Millian's (1981: 77) Group G. These figurines wear a flayed human skin over their torso, typically have a large feathered headdress, and hold a staff in the right hand and a shield in the left (Millian 1981: 92) (figure 12.9a). These attributes are so consistently seen in painted manuscript versions of the Aztec deity Xipe Totec (Flayer Lord) that scholars, beginning with Preuss (1901: 88, figs. 22–29) and Seler (1990–2000: 2: 167–68, fig. 34), have identified these figurines as Xipe Totec (figure 12.9b). In Aztec state ceremonies, Xipe Totec was associated primarily with warfare. Not only were war captives presented and sacrificed during the month festival Tlacaxipehualiztli, which was dedicated to Xipe Totec, but the Aztec ruler Moteuczoma II owned a Xipe costume that, as seen in manuscript paintings, he wore into the battle with Toluca (Codex Vaticanus 3738 [Ríos]: fol. 85v; Codex Cozcatzin, fols. 14v, 15r; Codex en Cruz: fol. 2b[F]). William Barnes (2005) thought that the Group G ceramic figurines represent a ruler in his Xipe Totec war dress, but as we will see, the god's significance to the man-in-the-street was probably different. Barnes does show, however, that Xipe Totec had been imported into Central Mexico from Oaxaca well before the rise of the Aztec state.

The rest of the male figurines in Millian's sample bear little or no resemblance to gods in the Aztec pantheon.[24] Scholars, starting with Preuss (1901: 89–90) and Seler (1990–2000: 2: fig. 35), have tended to identify the figurines in Millian's Group F, "headgear with two vertical projections bearing four circles," with the closely related Aztec gods Macuilxochitl (Five Flower) and Xochipilli (Flower Prince). These deities were patrons of the nobility, sexual and recreational pleasure, games, and music. The principal basis of the identification has been the presence of earrings and necklace ornaments in the form of framed ovals known as *oyoualli*. In painted manuscripts, these ornaments are characteristic of Macuilxochitl-Xochipilli, although they appear on other deities as well (Codex Magliabechiano, fol. 60r). Although some male figurines wear a headdress with a single vertical projection at the top like that seen on wood and stone statues believed to represent Macuilxochitl (*Aztecs* 2002: pl. 321), Millian did not discuss this headdress, and no one, to our knowledge, has linked it to that god.

The headdress used by Millian to connect Group F with Macuilxochitl-Xochipilli has two vertical projections bearing roundels usually identified as *tonallo*, symbols of solar warmth and daytime (Millian 1981: 90–91; see also Baer 1996: 109, figs. 455–56). In painted manuscripts, however, tonallo appear not in the god's headdress but rather on his shield or in proximity to him (see, for example, Codex Magliabechiano, fol. 60r). Millian (1981: 109–10) also identified some of the figures who appear on miniature ceramic stepped pyramids as Macuilxochitl-Xochipilli on the basis of their

a

c

b

Figure 12.9. Flayed male figures and Xipe Totec. *a,* Group G ("flayed figures") male figurine. Clay. Uhde Collection, Ethnological Museum, Berlin, #IV-Ca-2870 (photo courtesy of Bildarchiv Preussischer Kulturbesitz/Art Resources). *b,* Xipe Totec, depicted in the Codex Borbonicus, pl. 14 (courtesy of Akademische Druck- u. Verlagsanstalt, Graz; from Nowotny 1974). *c,* Male figurine in flayed human skin, with mask. Clay, 12 cm. Museo Nacional de Antropología e Historia, Mexico City (courtesy of the Instituto Nacional de Antropología e Historia, CONACULTA-INAH, #10-116778 2/2; from *Aztecs* 2002: fig. 96).

ovoid earrings and cut-shell pendants. Some of these, like other figurines often identified as Macuilxochitl-Xochipilli, have curly hair or a curly wig, which scholars, beginning with Kaplan (1958: 30, 153), have associated with those gods. Sahagún's descriptions of Macuilxochitl-Xochipilli, however, say nothing about his hair being curly, claiming instead that he had quetzal feathers at the top of his head, and the friar's artists depicted neither Macuilxochitl nor Xochipilli with hair of this kind (Sahagún 1950–82: bk. 1: 32; 1979: 1, prologue page 11v; 1993: fols. 265v, 266r; 1997: 109, 111).

Moreover, except for the oyoualli and the (misplaced) tonallo, the diagnostic attributes of these two gods as they appear in painted manuscripts never appear on ceramic figurines. For example, the white hand on Macuilxochitl's lower jaw that is often seen in manuscript paintings and sculptures is missing among the ceramic figurines. Because the white hand-on-jaw does appear on five male beings in the preconquest codices Borgia (pls. 47–48), Vaticanus B (Anders 1972: pls. 77–79), and Aubin Manuscript no. 20, that feature was probably in existence prior to the rise of the Aztec state. These figures, usually identified as the Macuiltonalque or Macuilxochitls (for example, Boone 2003: 215), are paired there with five Cihuapipiltin, or Cihuateteo, and, like them, probably represented a collective notion rather than an individual deity. A single representative of this collective may have emerged later, under the name Macuilxochitl, to serve as a divine patron of the Aztec elite.

One important aspect of this discussion is that Aztec ceramic figurines bearing the distinctive features of the imperial Aztec god of water and vegetation known as Tlaloc are extremely rare. Tlaloc typically appears in Aztec imagery with large rings, or "goggles," around his eyes; a thick, moustache-like upper lip; and large upper teeth or "tusks" (figure 12.10a). His nose and eyebrows are sometimes formed of a twisted, two-headed serpent. Although Parsons (1972: 102, pls. 31d,e) reported four head fragments from the Teotihuacan Valley that have one or two of these features, neither Kaplan nor Millian encountered examples in the collections they studied. Nor has Klein observed any in the Aztec figurine collections she viewed. This is puzzling, because Classic (AD 300–950) and Early Postclassic (AD 950–1150) clay figurines of Tlaloc are common (for example, Kaplan 1958: 31, fig. 25; Porcayo 1998: 266–67, 288–89, Fig. 29 and Fotos 41, 58). Below, we propose an explanation for their absence. For the moment, however, it is worth noting that, like those of the male deities discussed above, Tlaloc's diagnostic features appear in artworks produced prior to the rise of the Aztec state—in his case, centuries, if not millennia, earlier (Carballo 2007).

a

b

Figure 12.10. Figures of Tlaloc and male water priest. *a,* Tlaloc, depicted in the Codex Magliabechiano, fol. 34r (from Nuttall 1978). *b,* Male figurine, front and side views. Clay, 12.1 cm. Lukas Vischer Collection, Ethnographic Museum Basel (from Baer 1996: fig. IVb, no. 432).

There is, however, one additional type of male ceramic figurine that, although examples are extremely rare, does share a possible relation to Tlaloc. These figurines represent a man wearing a headdress very similar to that of many of the Group III females, whose costume, as we have seen, contains elements seen on the Aztec water goddess Chalchiuhtlicue. At the top of these male figurines' headdress is a wide spray of what appear to be feathers, and to each side is the "wing" of a large pleated fan, or amacuexpalli. An example in the Lukas Vischer Collection in Basel sits with its knees drawn up, supporting its crossed arms (figure 12.10b). Parsons (1972: pl. 22c) illustrates a head fragment of an apparently male figurine that also seems to wear this headdress. To our knowledge, no one has ever commented on these figurines.

The Function of Aztec Ceramic Figurines

We argue above that many of the attributes of those Aztec deities who have been traditionally identified among ceramic figurines appeared in the material record prior to their appearance in early colonial Aztec manuscript paintings. But were they already deities? Smith (2002: 112) has suggested that the beliefs and practices that underwrote Aztec ceramic figurines can be productively compared to those documented for rural Nahuatl speakers living today in eastern Mexico. There, attention is paid not to deities per se but to spirits, or animate essences, of the natural, supernatural, and architectural forces and objects that played important roles in determining the quality of peoples' daily lives. For example, Nahuas studied by Alan Sandstrom (1991: 242, 240–45) believe in a class of spirits called *xinaxtli* (*xinachtli*), meaning "seed." For them, as for farmers everywhere, a successful harvest is vital to subsistence. Among the eastern Nahuas observed by Sandstrom, the most important crop is corn, whose xinaxtli has both a male and a female aspect. The female aspect is called Macuilxochitl, "Five Flower," a name shared by the Aztec god of sexual and recreational pleasure whose oyoualli ornament appears on some Aztec ceramic figurines. The male aspect, in turn, is called Chicomexochitl, "Seven Flower." Seler (1990–2000: 1: 126) believed that Chicomexochitl was a male counterpart of the goddess Xochiquetzal. Other kinds of spirits have been reported by Sandstrom (1991) as well, including those responsible for curing illnesses and protecting the local water supply. Smith (2002: 112) has suggested that Aztec ceramic figurines, like these entities, were perceived not as deities with individual personalities but as "more generalized spirits that are invoked for specific purposes, such as curing illnesses and protecting the local water supply."

In northern Veracruz, as in parts of Hidalgo, these spirits are materialized in the form of cut-paper figurines, which Smith (2002: 112) suggests may derive from preconquest clay figurines. Sandstrom (1986: 67–68; 1991: 244) attended a spring ritual in which the local religious practitioner placed cut-paper figures representing seed spirits on an altar, where they received sacrificial offerings. Twelve days later, these paper figurines were dressed in tiny clothes made of real cloth and were given miniature chairs and grinding stones. The practice recalls the Aztec practice of dressing figurines, including statues of the Cihuapipiltin in miniature paper and cloth garments (Durán 1971: 416, 419; Motolinía 1950: 55; Sahagún 1950–82: bk. 1: 47, 49; bk. 2: 37).

Today, the spirits of natural phenomena are often seen as influencing multiple aspects of human well-being, including both crop fertility and the health and reproductive success of the people. These multiple roles parallel the tendency for deity insignia in ceramic figurines to be mixed and shared. In the rural Nahua village in Veracruz studied by Alan Sandstrom, there is today a class of spirits called *ejecatl* (plural form, *ejecamej*), who are clearly descendants of the Aztec wind god Quetzalcoatl-Ehecatl. Sandstrom (1991: 252) translated their name as "gusts of wind" and said that they are believed not only to spread disease but also to cause crop failure and illness and to inflict infertility. Similar beings have been documented for other present-day rural Nahua communities (Knab 2004: 107, 112, 123; Ortiz de Montellano 1990: 211–12). Nahuas say that the ejecamej are the unhappy souls of "people who had died bad deaths or . . . been forgotten by their kinsmen" (Sandstrom 1991: 252). This recalls Guilliem Arroyo's (1997: 133) identification of the ceramic female figurines found in an olla at Tlatelolco as the unhappy spirits of mothers who had died in childbirth. Smith (2002: 106) has suggested that Aztec ceramic figurines with attributes of the wind god Ehecatl are precursors of the modern cut-paper figures of these multifaceted ejecamej, a proposal supported by the fact that the practice of using cut-paper figurines in rituals is documented for the sixteenth century (Stresser-Péan 2005: 187).

Millian drew attention to the considerable evidence that nearly all of the supernaturals whose attributes appear in the human figurines were believed to both cause and cure physical deformities and illnesses and to influence human conception and childbirth. A "notable proportion" of her sample, both male and female, she observed, "display [sic] abnormal physical conditions" (Millian 1981: 12–13). Other scholars have found this to be true as well. Evans (1990), for example, noted that some of the figurines she found at Cihuatecpan in the Teotihuacan Valley have protruding chests—a symptom of rickets—and, possibly, dementia. Durán (1971: 420, but see 269) said that Aztec children under twelve years of age were rewarded for ritual fasting and bloodletting with objects tied to a cord that they could wear around their necks and wrists. "With this," he explained, "they were made to believe that they could avoid illness and that no evil would befall them." The objects suspended from these cords, as others have noted, may well have included ceramic figurines.

Although the Aztec goddess Chalchiuhtlicue, who controlled the local streams, lakes, and rivers, is usually perceived as an agricultural deity, she also played a vital role in peoples' health. This is seen in a passage from Hernando Ruíz de Alarcón (1984: 213), who wrote that if people felt they had become sick near a stream or a river, their doctor had them make offerings at the site to "the goddess of waters, whom they call Matlalcueyeque [sic] or Chalchihuitl Icue." Durán's (1971: 269) remark that "clay dolls" were among the items thrown into streams and springs by "new mothers who had given birth, and also the sick" takes this practice back another hundred years. This would explain the presence of an infant or child in the arms of some of the figurines with attributes of Chalchiuhtlicue (figure 12.11a). Infants also appear with some of the figurines wearing the double-plumed headdress diagnostic of the goddess Xochiquetzal, as well as figurines whose attributes resemble those of the maize goddesses Chicomecoatl and Xilonen (Preuss 1901: figs. 1, 3) (figure 12.11b). Xochiquetzal's roles included presiding over the sex lives of Aztec women; her reproductive fertility was evidenced by her close association with twins. Chicomecoatl was, in the seventeenth century, still receiving sacrifices from those who were sick or had a sick child (Ruíz de Alarcón 1984: 213).

The male deities whose traits appear on some ceramic figurines were also directly linked to concerns with health and fertility. Although the reproductive and curative powers of Quetzalcoatl-Ehecatl, Xipe Totec, and Macuilxochitl-Xochipilli may not have been the virtues of greatest interest to the Aztec state, the sources make it clear that these gods' ability to affect human health and fertility must have been very much on the minds of the average Aztec citizen. Quetzalcoatl-Ehecatl, for example, was reported to have controlled diseases such as coughs and colds, rheumatism, and eye ailments, as well as tumors and female sterility, and images of the god were petitioned for relief (Durán 1971: 135; Millian 1981: 78–79). In Tepoztlan,

a   b

Figure 12.11. Female figures with child. *a,* Group III female figurine with child. Clay, 7 cm. Lukas Vischer Collection, Ethnographic Museum Basel (from Baer 1996: fig. IVb, no. 1027). *b,* Group II female figurine with double plumes and child. Clay. Uhde Collection, Ethnological Museum, Berlin (from Preuss 1901: fig. 1).

Morelos, the statue of Quetzalcoatl-Ehecatl's counterpart, Tepuztecatl, received offerings of infant umbilical cords wrapped in bundles (Maldonado Jiménez 2000: 96–97). The urns buried in the platform fronting the Temple of Ehecatl at Tlatelolco contained mostly children and women in a fetal position who were accompanied by miniature garments and, as we have seen, clay figurines. Michel Graulich (1992a), citing Sahagún (1950–82: bk. 6: 181, 202), has shown that Quetzalcoatl-Ehecatl was perceived as a "bringer of life" and was invoked in matters of human conception, a role that may explain not only figurines in which Ehecatl's conical hat appears phallic in shape but also stone sculptures showing him with an enlarged penis and testicles (Franco 1961: figs. 3, 4; Kelly 1955). Graulich (1992a: 34–35) cites the chronicler Juan de Torquemada (1975: 2: 52), who wrote that "barren [Aztec] women made offerings and sacrifices to Quetzalcoatl-Ehecatl in order to become pregnant."

Quetzalcoatl-Ehecatl, like Macuilxochitl-Xochipilli, was closely associated with the monkey and the opossum, both of which were linked to concerns for human fertility (Aguilera 1985; Espinosa Pineda 2001: 261–65; Munn 1984). Figurines in Millian's Group D, some of which are hollow, have the head of a monkey and an enlarged abdomen implying pregnancy. Millian (1981: 86) linked them to the Aztec god Macuilxochitl on the basis of the oval-shaped earrings seen on one example, and, following Barlow and Lehmann's example (1956: 172), to Quetzalcoatl in the case of a figurine formerly in the Musée de l'Homme in Paris that wears a cut-shell pectoral (*Aztecs* 2002: pl. 61). Aztec stone sculptures of animals wearing these gods' ornaments are fairly common (Nicholson and Quiñones Keber 1983: fig. 48). The Museo Nacional de Antropología possesses a stone statue of a dancing, anthropomorphized simian with a bulging (pregnant?) abdomen and the buccal mask of Ehecatl (*Aztecs* 2002: pl. 102).

The importance of monkeys and opossums to prospective and new parents is implied by the discovery of numerous animal figurines of monkeys and opossums at the foot of the Temple of Ehecatl at Tlatelolco. One of the urns found there contained a beautifully preserved, painted ceramic rattle representing an opossum with its offspring on its back (Graulich 1992a: 36; Guilliem Arroyo 1997: 126). Smith (2002: 107) reported that the opossum was the most common animal found among the ceramic figurines he uncovered in Morelos. Like the monkey, the opossum was closely associated with pregnant women; a medicine made of its hair, combined with the ground-up bones and hair of a monkey, was used to facilitate a woman's labor (Ortiz de Montellano 1990: 186, 191).[25] Its tail was also used to increase a mother's milk and to clean the digestive, pulmonary, and urinary tracts (Aguilera 1985: 43–44). On the face of this evidence, ceramic figurines identifiable as monkeys or opossums are likely to have been used primarily for medicinal purposes.

In the same vein, although Xipe Totec is primarily known to Aztec scholars as a god of war, flayed war prisoners, and the collection of tribute, the population at large was probably more concerned with his control of certain health issues. Xipe Totec was blamed for blisters, pimples, and other skin diseases (including smallpox after the conquest), as well as multiple eye ailments, including cataracts (Ortiz de Montellano 1990: 131–32). Sahagún's (1950–82: bk. 1: 39) informants said, "When sickness befell one of us men, he made a vow to him, he pledged him that he would put on the skin [of the god]; he would don it when the feast day Tlacaxipehualiztli was celebrated." The passage provides the motives of those individuals who voluntarily wore, for twenty days, the surely odorous flayed skins of war captives sacrificed during the month festival Tlacaxipehualiztli. The ceramic figurines of men wearing a flayed skin in Millian's Group G therefore may relate to personal vows of this kind. We know that the dough figurines known as the Tepictoton, who represented local mountains, were created in fulfillment of a vow. Sahagún (1950–82: bk. 1: 49) said that some Tepictoton figurines were made for Aztec "winemakers" (that is, makers of pulque) as they attempted to avoid having "their mouth become twisted to one side, become lame in one foot, or begin to tremble." It stands to reason that figurines of men wearing a flayed skin may have been used for similar purposes. Guilliem Arroyo (1997: 130) discussed two exceptionally well executed ceramic figurines of a man wearing a flayed skin, one with a detachable mask, that were found at Tlatelolco; both had been deposited in a container holding the remains of an infant (see figure 12.9c).[26]

Finally, the Aztecs attributed to Macuilxochitl-Xochipilli such delicate annoyances as "piles, hemorrhoids, suppurating genitals, [and] disease[s] of the groin"; vows were made to him to "quiet, remove, [and] abate the sickness" (Sahagún 1950–82: bk. 1: 31). Offerings made to this god during his festival included "dolls" made of amaranth dough. Ceramic figurines bearing the oyoualli may have served a similar purpose. Thus, as both Millian (1981: 47) and Smith (2002: 108–9) have previously proposed, the primary function of nearly all of the ceramic figurines bearing traits of Aztec deities was very likely apotropaic; the figurines functioned to protect people from illness and harm. None of these figurines, however, should be assumed to represent a deity of the kind being honored at the time of the conquest in state-sponsored ceremonies. Instead, they should be regarded as possible embodiments of generalized essences of natural phenomena such as wind and water or as embodied states of being such as motherhood. As such, they served to materialize, for a time, the needs and desires of individuals and small groups living the simple life of a peasant or commoner, most often outside the city limits of the Aztec capital.

The Copal Figurines

Victoria Lona (2004a, 2004b) has analyzed eighty copal figurines that have been scientifically excavated to date from the Templo Mayor. Although five of these figurines are 30 centimeters or more high, the corpus as a whole averages 16 to 22 centimeters in height. They are thus substantially larger than the ceramic figurines. The copal figurines from the Templo Mayor closely match over a half dozen other copal figurines now in museum collections in Mexico City and Paris (Victoria Lona 2004a, 2004b). Although the museum specimens were not retrieved under scientific conditions, at least some of them may have also come from the Templo Mayor.

In contrast to the ceramic figurines, which include representations of animals and buildings, the copal figurines are all human effigies (figure 12.12). Like the ceramic figurines, however, the copal figurines were made with molds, the details having been added by hand. A copal, or mixed copal and stucco, nucleus was usually covered with a layer of stucco, followed by paint, usually red (Victoria Lona 2004a, 2004b). The recent excavation of Offering 102 at the Templo Mayor, where four copal figurines were found in an exceptionally well preserved condition, shows that some, if not all, of these figurines had also been painted, dressed in miniature paper garments, and given miniature instruments, such as wooden staves and jars, before deposit.

Figure 12.12. Male copal figurine from the Templo Mayor. Museo Templo Mayor, Mexico City (from Victoria Lona 2004b: 71; courtesy of the Instituto Nacional de Antropología e Historia, CONACULTA-INAH).

Male figurine attributes

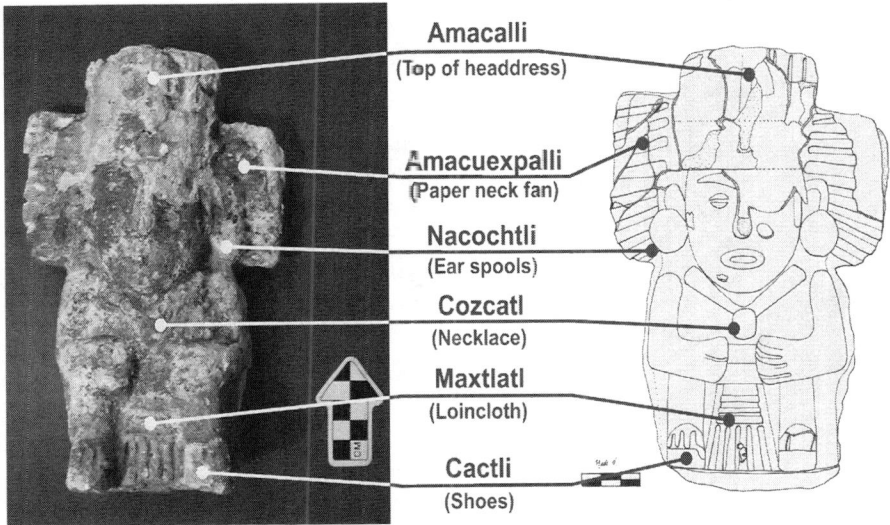

Amacalli
(Top of headdress)

Amacuexpalli
(Paper neck fan)

Nacochtli
(Ear spools)

Cozcatl
(Necklace)

Maxtlatl
(Loincloth)

Cactli
(Shoes)

Figure 12.13. Diagram of costume elements of male copal figurines from the Templo Mayor (courtesy of Naoli Victoria Lona).

When the copal figurines assume a seated pose, their legs are pulled up in front of them and bent at the knees, a pose exclusive to males in Aztec stone sculpture. Many of the seated figurines are also wearing a *maxtlatl*, or male loincloth, confirming that they are male (figure 12.13). Females, in contrast, can be so identified on the basis of their *quechquemitl*, the triangular garment covering their upper torso. Over this garment they wear a modeled three-strand necklace similar to those worn by some of the male figurines. Some of the female figurines assume the kneeling pose exclusive to Aztec women as well. One or two upright plumes spring from the top of their headdress (Victoria Lona 2004a: 153; 2004b) (figure 12.14).

The differences in pose and dress between these two groups demonstrate that, in sharp contrast to the ceramic figurines, the great majority of the copal figurines are male (Victoria Lona 2004a, 2004b). Discounting eight copal figurines that, because of deterioration, could not be distinguished as male or female, the Templo Mayor to date has yielded fifty-three male figurines as opposed to only nineteen females (Victoria Lona 2004a: 252–53). Of the four copal figurines that Leonardo López Luján (2006: 1: 208–9; 2:

Female figurine attributes

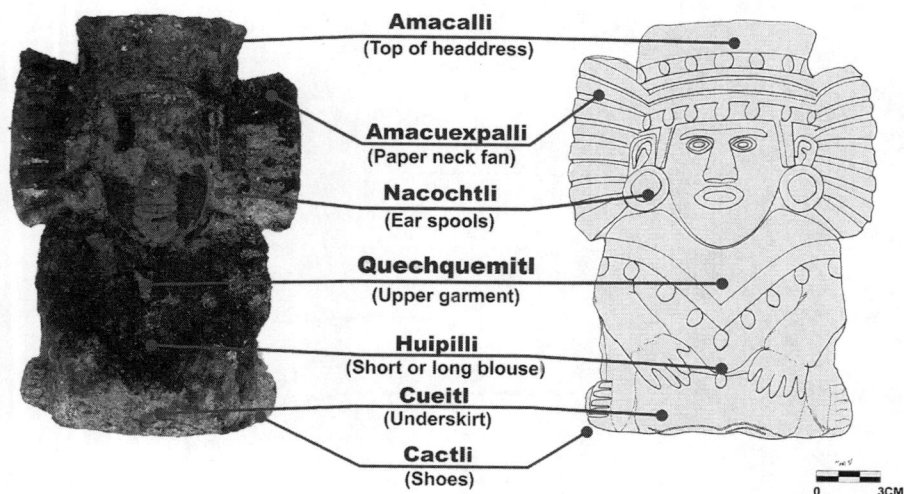

Amacalli
(Top of headdress)

Amacuexpalli
(Paper neck fan)

Nacochtli
(Ear spools)

Quechquemitl
(Upper garment)

Huipilli
(Short or long blouse)

Cueitl
(Underskirt)

Cactli
(Shoes)

0   3CM

Figure 12.14. Diagram of costume elements of female copal figurines from the Templo Mayor (courtesy of Naoli Victoria Lona).

figs. 312–13) excavated at the Temple of the Eagles, located just to the north of the Templo Mayor, only one was female. Similarly, the majority of the copal figurines unearthed in 1901 by Leopold Batres (1990: 134, 152) appear from his photographs to be male, as does the badly deteriorated copal figurine found in the Lake of the Moon at the top of Mt. Xinantecatl, an extinct volcano also known as El Nevado de Toluca (Guzmán Peredo 1972: 61, 82–84; Luna Erreguerena 2000).[27]

Victoria Lona's (2004a, 2004b) study of the copal figurines revealed that the headdresses of both females and males are highly standardized. These headdresses consist of a headband, sometimes decorated at top and bottom with a row of small beads, which has a large pleated neck fan, or amacuexpalli, attached at the back (figures 12.13, 12.14). The similarity of these headdresses to those of the female ceramic figurines in Millian's Group III is evident. As we have seen, Millian related Group III figurines to the Aztec water goddess Chalchiuhtlicue, although she declined to identify them as the goddess. However, as Victoria Lona (2004a, 2004b) pointed out, what appears to be a pair of vertical black stripes on the face of the female copal figurine in the Musée du quai Branly suggests a relationship to the maize

Figure 12.15. Female figurine. Copal, wood, and sand, 34.1 cm. Musée du quai Branly, Paris (©Photo SCALA, Florence, 2007).

goddess Chicomecoatl, since two vertical stripes of black paint appear on the cheeks of the woman carrying ears of maize in plate 7 of the Codex Borbonicus (figure 12.15).[28] Victoria Lona (2004a, 2004b) therefore identified the copal female figurines as representations of Chalchiuhtlicue and/or Chicomecoatl. Similarly, López Luján (2006: 1: 209) identifies the female copal figurine unearthed at the Temple of the Eagles, located to the north of the Templo Mayor, as a combination of Chalchiuhtlicue and Chicomecoatl. The fusion of diagnostic traits of these two goddesses in the copal female figurines parallels the shared attributes of many ceramic female figurines.

Although the copal females from the Templo Mayor closely resemble the ceramic females in Millian's Group III, the male figurines of copal are another matter. In sharp contrast to the ceramic corpus, none of the copal male figurines resemble any of the male gods traditionally believed to be represented in ceramic figurines. Copal figurines of Quetzalcoatl-Ehecatl, Xipe Totec, and Macuilxochitl-Xochipilli do not exist. Instead, the head-dresses of the male copal figurines found at the Templo Mayor, like those of the three male copal figurines recently excavated by López Luján at the Temple of the Eagles and most of the copal figurines excavated by Batres (1990: 134, 152), closely resemble that of the water and vegetation god Tlaloc, who is seldom seen among clay figurines. For that reason, and be-cause she doubts that any being other than a deity would be represented in the offerings at the most important building in the empire, Victoria Lona (2004a, 2004b) thinks that the copal versions represent either Tlaloc or his assistants, the Tlaloque, who are known to have resembled Tlaloc in appearance. This is supported by the presence on the male copal figurines of costume attributes usually associated with the water gods: the rectangu-lar headdress with vertical projections that can be interpreted as plumes, the paper amacuexpalli at the back of the neck, and the miniature wood banners painted red and white, which are commonly seen in the painted manuscripts on Tlaloc or his divine assistants (figure 12.13).

Klein is skeptical of this interpretation, however, because the copal males found in the capital all lack Tlaloc's distinctive eye rings, thick upper lip, heavy eyebrows, and long upper teeth (figure 12.10a). That copal artisans knew how to render those features is evident from a copal figurine, one of two found in a cave at Mt. Iztaccihuatl on the mainland, which, with its goggled eyes, thick upper lip, and large teeth, unequivocally represents Tlaloc (*Aztecs* 2002: fig. 241; Navarrete 1968). Klein suggests instead that the copal male figurines found at the Templo Mayor represent high-ranking priests who served the cult of Tlaloc, rather than representing the god him-self. We know from sixteenth-century texts that some of Tlaloc's priests dressed like the god (Sahagún 1950–82: bk. 2: 87; see also Klein 1984; 1986: 148; 1988; 2001: 36). Klein proposes that one of the artists illustrating Sa-hagún's (1993: fol. 262v) *Primeros memoriales* based his figure of Tlaloc, which lacks the god's facial features, on these priests (figure 12.16a). She has argued elsewhere (Klein 1984, 1988) that at least one other figure labeled as an Aztec deity in that manuscript represents a priest rather than a deity.[29] The *Primeros memoriales* figure closely resembles a figure in the Codex Borbonicus (pl. 32) that is likewise a priest. Similarly, paintings in the cog-nate codices Magliabechiano (fol. 29r), Tudela (fol. 11r), and Ixtlilxochitl (fol. 94r) that refer to the month Atlacahualo (Xilomanaliztli), dedicated to Tlaloc, depict a man whose face is entirely human wearing a Tlaloc costume (figure 12.16b). José Tudela de la Orden (1980: 266) identified the object

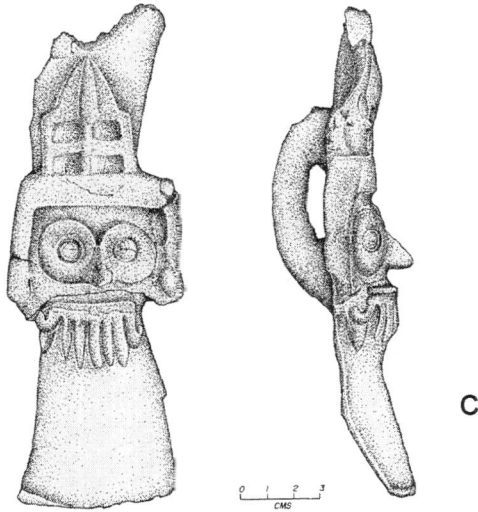

Figure 12.16. Tlaloc priests. *a,* Tlaloc priest(?) holding ritual object, depicted in the Codex Magliabechiano, fol. 29r (from Nuttall 1978). *b,* Tlaloc priest(?), depicted in the *Primeros memoriales,* fol. 261v (copyright Patrimonio Nacional, Madrid) (from Sahagún 1993). *c,* Ritual object with effigy of Tlaloc, from Cholula, front and side views. Clay, approx. 21 cm. (courtesy Society for American Archaeology) (from Uruñuela et al. 1997: fig. 4).

held by the figure as the god's mask, since it bears the god's effigy. Klein, however, agrees with Gabriela Uruñuela and colleagues (1997: 68) that it represents a Late Postclassic ceramic ritual object of the kind frequently found in the Puebla-Tlaxcala area, including Cholula (figure 12.16c). These objects, which Eduardo Noguera (1954: 207, 274–75) was the first to illustrate, not only have a conical base sporting Tlaloc's diagnostic features but also, like the object held by the figures in the codices Magliabechiano and Tudela, have a handle at the back as well.[30] In the Codex Borgia (pls. 27, 28, 37, 75), Tlaloc holds such an object. Uruñuela and colleagues (1997: 68) suggested that these objects were used by priests during water and vegetation rituals. If these priests were impersonating the rain god, that might explain the near-total absence of ceramic figurines representing him: Tlaloc was seldom depicted in clay because in rituals he was represented in the flesh by one of his priests.

Further evidence that at least some of the copal figurines found at the Templo Mayor represent high-ranking priests comes from their placement near a larger object as if to attend upon or guard it. The spectacular Offering 102, which dates to Phase VI, contained a large "Two-Tufted" figure that was flanked on either side by a copal figurine (Barrera Rivera et al. 2001; Guzmán Acevedo 2004, 2005). Although the identity of the "Two-Tufted" figures is controversial, most scholars agree that it represents a divinity (López Luján 2005; Nagao 1985; compare Guzmán Acevedo 2004, 2005). Another copal figurine in the same offering sat in front of a large olla bearing the face of Tlaloc (Barrera Rivera et al. 2001). Victoria Lona (2004a, 2004b) reported that most of the copal figurines in Offering 102 were painted red and dressed with paper headdresses as well as pieces of cloth and that they originally held paper flags or plain sticks. A life-size wooden mask of Tlaloc, together with a headdress, was included, as was a necklace, a bracelet, bags with painted faces on them containing seeds and raw copal, and a well-preserved *xicolli*, or man's shirt, that had been hand painted with a complex design (Barrera Rivera et al. 2001: 73–74; López Luján, personal communication, 2006). This suggests that the water god was represented in Offering 102 by his costume, a costume most likely once worn by a priest-impersonator. If the copal male figurines at the Templo Mayor did represent, in permanent form, high-ranking priests rather than the god, then the preponderance of males among the copal figurines could be explained by the fact that the majority of the priests in Tenochtitlan were men.[31]

What the Copal Figurines Tell Us

But what might explain the complete absence of ceramic figurines at the Templo Mayor? We have already seen that ceramic figurines of Group I females possibly representing the spirits of women dead in childbirth, as well as those of males wearing flayed skins like Xipe Totec, were found in offerings and burials in front of the Temple of Ehecatl at Tlatelolco. Why were none buried at the main precinct in Tenochtitlan? The explanation may lie in part with the increased availability of copal in the government center. That Tenochtitlan, by the time of the conquest, was importing large quantities of copal from conquered regions in the form of tribute is well documented in the Codex Mendoza (fols. 36r, 37r, 51r) (Victoria Lona 2004a, 2004b). Part of the explanation may also rest with the fact that— in addition to its practical uses, such as an adhesive in the manufacture of mosaics—copal was widely believed to have intrinsic magical properties (Victoria Lona 2004a, 2004b). Victoria Lona (2004a) classified many Templo Mayor copal objects as bars, balls, and other abstract shapes, some of which are geometric, as well as knife bases, figurines of indeterminate gender, and miscellaneous fragments. Archaeologists often find copal in the form of simple balls, cones, and amorphous clumps in cached offerings and large bodies of water, both within and outside of the capital; some of these items date back to the Early Postclassic (Coggins and Shane 1984: 129–32; Guzmán Peredo 1972: 52–57). Ruíz de Alarcón (1984: 108, 171–73, 182–83) reported that seventeenth-century Nahua farmers were using copal offerings to protect their fields, as well as employing copal in the treatment of eye problems, earaches, and bleeding mouth sores. Its uses for other medical reasons have also been documented: as a plaster for fractures; as a cure for diarrhea, fever, toothache, venereal disease, and poisonous animal bites; and in the treatment of illnesses caused by cold and dampness, of tumors caused by illicit love relationships, of female hemorrhage during childbirth, and of "strangulation" of the uterus (Heyden 1997: 244, 264–65; Victoria Lona 2004a, 2004b). When mixed with rubber and *chapopotli* (*chapopote*), a kind of pitch much like asphalt, copal could be applied to the body as a protection against illness and evil forces (Sahagún 1977: 3: 339). Copal was so effective against illness and injury that Aztec children carried little balls of copal to protect them from disease (Aguilera 1985: 127).

Copal therefore must have been regarded as an extremely powerful material, which may explain why, according to Durán (1967: 1: 82), the large statue of Tlaloc at the Templo Mayor always had a leather bag full of copal in its left hand. An Aztec prayer to Tlaloc refers to him as the "Lord of Copal" (Sahagún 1950–82: bk. 4: 35), which might further explain why, in the Templo Mayor offerings, his priestly attendants were rendered in that material.

As far as Klein has been able to determine, the Aztecs attributed no such spiritual or curative powers to clay. Colonial sources are silent on the matter. Clay appears to have been synonymous with the soil of the earth, however; as such, it would have been perceived as the skin or flesh of the zoomorphic earth deity Tlaltecuhtli, "Earth Lord." People living today in eastern Mexico often consider soft, sandy, or clayish soil to be the earth's flesh, just as they perceive rocks and stones to be its bones (Stresser-Péan 2005: 404). Guy Stresser-Péan (2005: 404) has pointed out that because clay is used to make containers for liquids and food, it represents for people today the means to a "civilized" life, a life that was created for them by the maize god. Clay, however, in marked contrast to copal, does not appear to have been regarded as a sacred and an intrinsically powerful substance. Accordingly, it may have been regarded as unworthy of the greatest building in the empire.

Another part of the answer may be chronological. Because of the high water table beneath and frequent enlargements of the Templo Mayor, the earlier levels of construction are unfortunately less well known than the later phases. Perhaps for that reason, none of the copal figurines pulled from the Templo Mayor predate 1440.[32] This means, however, that all currently datable copal figurines fall in the later phase, Phase B, of Smith's (2003: 30) chronology for the Late Postclassic, which he dated to 1430–1520. Indeed, the largest number of excavated copal figurines (twenty-nine) currently corresponds to the temple's construction Phase IVb, which Eduardo Matos Moctezuma (1981: 17–50) has dated to the reign of Axayacatl, 1469–81 (Victoria Lona 2004a, 2004b). Although the numbers of copal figurines deposited in the later phases will never be known, because of their near-total destruction at the hands of the Spaniards, the four copal figurines excavated by López Luján (2006) at the nearby Temple of the Eagles are even later in date. They date to Phase 4 of that building, which corresponds to the Templo Mayor's Phase VI, 1486 to 1502 (López Luján, personal communication, 2006).[33]

This does not mean, of course, that copal figurines were not used elsewhere as offerings at an earlier date. According to Clemency Coggins and Orrin Shane (1984: 132), a copal effigy and other copal offerings found at the bottom of the Maya Cenote of Sacrifice at Chichén Itzá in Yucatán may date as early as the Middle Postclassic (AD 1150–1350). Miguel Guzmán Peredo (1972: 59) has suggested that the copal offerings found in the Lake of the Moon at the summit of Mt. Xinantecatl, which included the human figurine discussed above, were deposited even earlier.

However, copal figurines found closer to the Aztec capital appear to be late. The copal figurine representing Tlaloc that was found at Mt. Iztaccihuatl has been recently dated by Felipe Solís to circa AD 1500 (*Aztecs* 2002: 295, fig. 241). Certainly, by the time of the conquest, the Aztecs were making ceremonial use of copal figurines. Sahagún (1950–82: bk. 2: 89) said that during the month festival Etzalcualiztli, which was dedicated to Tlaloc, Aztec priests used to carry "incense pieces which look like men" to the whirlpool in Lake Texcoco known as Pantitlan, where they tossed in the incense, or copal, pieces. Writing after the conquest, Pedro Ponce de León (1973: 122) reported seeing "idols" in the area that were made of copal. At present, however, there is no firm evidence that copal figurines were popular items in Tenochtitlan prior to the middle of the Late Postclassic period.

What the Ceramic Figurines Tell Us

In contrast, archaeologists have found Aztec ceramic figurines that date back to the Middle Postclassic. Kaplan (1958: 173), referring to George Vaillant's unpublished field notes for Chiconautla, reported that he dated some of the Aztec-style figurines from that site to as early as AD 1299, and Elizabeth Brumfiel (1996: 151) found ceramic figurines at Huexotla, Xico, and Xaltocan that are likewise Middle Postclassic in date. Similarly, Parsons (1972: 116) speculated that the solid figurines from the Teotihuacan Valley (her Type III) "were probably first made in Early Aztec times," which would place them in the Middle Postclassic as well (Smith 2003: 29). Although Parsons added that the hollow and jointed figurines (her Types I and II) "may have been made during orly late Aztec times" and Otis-Charlton (1991: 37) found most of her specimens in Late Aztec or Early Colonial contexts, Smith (2005: 53) reported that all of the figurine types that he found at Yautepec were present in the earliest period of habitation at that site, which he dated to AD 1100–1300.[34] Thus, although we still lack stratigraphy sufficient to date the vast majority of ceramic figurine types, the constellations of attributes that have been used to link some of them to imperial state deities appear to have been in place outside the Aztec capital well before the copal figurines had become important items in the Templo Mayor offerings.

Similarly, most of the stone sculptures and large ceramic effigy urns that represented state deities inside the capital were almost certainly created late in that city's history (Umberger and Klein 1993: 316). Doris Heyden (1987: 110) proposed that the explanation for the absence of ceramic figurines at the Templo Mayor lay with the state's growing political and economic prosperity, which made it possible "to bring the finest stone works from all corners of the empire." However, the figural sculptures found in association with the earliest building phases at the Templo Mayor, such as the Phase II Chacmool and the nine so-called standard bearers found leaning against the stairs of the Phase III pyramid, are blocky and slablike, with largely plain surfaces; in the case of the Chacmool, details had been rendered in paint. Even the large disk carved in relief with an image of the treacherous Coyolxauhqui, which dates no later than Phase IVb, is planar, the forms stiff, reflecting little interest in registering the bone structure and musculature of the mutilated woman's face and body. The same may be said of the Archbishop's Stone discussed above, which may have been carved as late as the 1470s. Not until the 1490s, as seen in the Tizoc Stone, was there a marked turn toward the more rounded edges, polished surfaces, and greater detail normally associated with the imperial art style. Most of the stone sculptures from the Aztec capital and its environs referred to in this chapter were executed in that mature carving style. Thus, like the painted manuscripts from Central Mexico that are often used in attempts to identify ceramic figurines with Aztec deities, the imperial stone carvings of those deities appear too late in the record to account for the appearances of the figurines.

The same may be said of the large ceramic votive jars and urns that have been found in and near the capital. Many of these have a large effigy, modeled and/or painted, on their outer surface that bears attributes seen on some Group II or III female clay figurines. Although the scale is much larger, and the workmanship finer, these jars seem to represent later, urban versions of the ceramic figurines attached to little pots that are discussed above. For example, a jar representing Chalchiuhtlicue was found in Chamber II at the Templo Mayor, which López Luján (2005: 244) dated to Phase IVb, corresponding to the reign of Axayacatl, from 1469 to 1481 (see also Ahuja 1982). Two jars found in Chamber III at the Templo Mayor, which dates to Phase IVa (1440–69), have a modeled and painted effigy of either Xilonen or Chicomecoatl on one side and an image of Tlaloc or a Tlaloc priest on the other (*Aztecs* 2000: fig. 284; López Luján 2005: 247). These goddesses wear the crenellated Temple Headdress and hold the paired maize ears (cemmaitl) in one hand that we have seen on some ceramic female figurines. The detail that is rendered in paint, however, exceeds anything seen on clay figurines of this kind, and the late date of these deposits suggests that their complex forms evolved from the clay figurines rather than having inspired them.

This does not mean, of course, that the attributes of some ceramic figurines owed nothing to the official religion. Smith (2002: 95) rightly warned that "the situation can be quite complex, with domestic and state rituals each influencing the other through systems of interpenetrating knowledge." He suggests that the Aztec government, having appropriated and reshaped selected ancient customs and beliefs, may have "turned around and tried to impose the imperial version of the ceremony on their subjects." It stands to reason that this may have been the case for figural imagery as well. However, as Brumfiel (1996: 155–60) has pointed out, there are no stone statues from the capital depicting women that hold a child and no clay statues that represent mutilated females or androgynous women. Except for a pre-Aztec example found at Colhuacan, there are no ceramic Chacmools as well (Séjourné 1970: 43, fig. following p. 36).

Given that the Aztecs are well known for their appropriation of architectural and stone sculptural forms, as well as the patron deities of older, conquered communities, evidence that artists working for the Aztec state drew upon an iconographic repertoire already in existence among clay figurines should not come as a total surprise. The eclectic nature of the state pantheon, when taken together with the late appearance of the imperial art style, has been well documented (Umberger 1996: 88–94). The ceramic figurines, however, otherwise had little or no importance to the Aztec state. The diversity of their forms and subjects (together with the absence of most of the attributes associated with deities in the imperial pantheon) indicates that their popularity remained with the peasants and commoners living in the older, more rural towns and villages outside the capital, where concern for the health, reproductive fertility, and nourishment of families and communities continued to shape the vast majority of their religious beliefs.

Acknowledgments

Research for this project was funded by a 2006–7 UCLA Council on Research Faculty Grant. We have benefited enormously from the wise counsel and assistance of many people Leonardo López Luján, Alva Millian, Michael Smith, Susan Haskell of the Peabody Museum of Archaeology, Christina Elson and Ananda Cohen at the American Museum of Natural History,

Nancy Fullerton at the San Antonio Museum of Art, Wendy Teeter at the University of California–Los Angeles Fowler Museum of Cultural History, Carmen Aguilera, William Barnes, Eulogio Guzman Acevedo, Janet Stephens, Kim Richter, and Christina Halperin. Special thanks go to Jennifer Gulley and Eva Sobolevski for their invaluable assistance with the illustrations.

Notes

1. López Luján 2005 and personal communication. Similarly, only one fragment of a pre-Hispanic clay figurine was found at the House of the Eagles (López Luján 2006: 1: 146; 2: fig. 233).

2. The dates used in this chapter for the Postclassic period and its Early, Middle, and Late phases are taken from Smith 2003: 30.

3. Some of the resins used in manufacturing were apparently taken from pine trees (Stacey et al. 2006).

4. The most comprehensive publication of a single museum collection of Aztec ceramic figurines is Gerhard Baer's (1996) study of the Lukas Vischer Collection in the Ethnographic Museum, Basel, Switzerland.

5. A hint of what still remains to be done with Aztec ceramic figurines is provided by Christine Chen's incomplete chart of the types of headdresses seen on the human figurines found by Vaillant at Chiconautla and Nonoalco now in the American Museum of Natural History. Of the forty-two different headdress types recorded by Chen, only a few have been acknowledged in the literature. Klein is extremely grateful to Christina Elson and Ananda Cohen, of the Anthropology Department of the American Museum of Natural History, for making available Chen's chart. For further information on the clay figurines found at Chiconautla and/or Nonoalco, see Cohen and Elson n.d.; Elson 1999; and Vaillant 1962: 160–61.

6. The figurines in Millian's Group I are Group 2 in Smith's classification.

7. *Aztec Empire* 2004: fig. 2; Boone 1999; Klein 2008; Pasztory 1983: pls. 110–13. The larger of these two statues is thought to have once stood in the main ceremonial precinct; the other was recovered from southern Puebla (*Aztec Empire* 2004: fig. 2; Pasztory 1983: pls. 110–13). In Sahagún's Florentine Codex (1979: 1: bk. 3, fol. 3v), Coatlicue is again depicted with a skirt of interlaced serpents.

8. See, for example, *Aztec Empire* 2004: figs. 14, 17.

9. For that reason, Millian (1981: 61) declined to assign a deity's name to that group. In so doing, she echoed the opinion of Preuss (1901: 88) who, eighty years earlier, had concluded that these figurines represent an ordinary Aztec woman. More recently, Smith (2005: 46) has declined to express any opinion regarding their identity.

10. Most scholars identify the principal figures in these scenes as priest-impersonators of the goddess known as Toci (Grandmother), but Toci appears off to the side in the final scene in the Codex Borbonicus (pl. 30) as a mere onlooker. Moreover, the figures wearing flayed skins in the Codex Borbonicus (pls. 29, 30) are not dressed in

Toci's costume. Durán (1971: 229) said that because Toci's feast "fell immediately after the Feast of Chicomecoatl," the two feasts were celebrated together, the first women sacrificed representing the goddess of lepers, Atlatonan, and the corn goddess Chicomecoatl. A diamond-patterned skirt can be seen on a stone statue, now in the Museo Nacional de Antropología, of a woman whose forearms have been broken off but whose headdress is almost identical to that of a second, intact stone statue of a woman who holds twin ears of maize in each hand (*Aztec Empire* 2004: figs. 14, 17). In the Maya Codex Dresden, the diamond pattern represents the word for skirt, *pik,* which has suggested to Karen Bassie-Sweet (2002: 120) that it represents "the quintessential skirt."

11. Parsons (1972: 82–83), in her study of figurines collected by the Teotihuacan Valley Project, chose to compromise by labeling the hollow rattle females as "Type I-A Coatlicue-Cihuacoatl earth goddess."

12. The version in Sahagún's Florentine Codex (1950–82: bk. 1: 11) states that "her womanly hairdress rose up."

13. Most scholars have placed the Archbishop's Stone in the reign of Moteuczoma I, who took office in 1440 and died in 1469 (Pérez-Castro Lira et al. 1989; but see Graulich 1992b). The Tizoc Stone is generally agreed to have been commissioned by the Aztec ruler Tizoc, who reigned from 1481 until his untimely death in 1486 (Wicke 1976).

14. For photographs of carved-stone, kneeling, bare-breasted women who seem to grimace, see *Glanz und Untergang* 1986: 2: fig. 218; and *Aztec Empire* 2004: fig. 110.

15. See Sahagún 1950–82: bk. 2: 36–38; bk. 4: 41, 45, 81–82, 107–9. These two statues, along with two others, form a set found together in 1907. The other two bear the dates 1 Mazatl (1 Deer) and 1 Ozomatl (1 Monkey), respectively; these are also days on which the Cihuapipiltin were believed to descend (Nicholson and Keber 1983: 67–68, pl. 16). For other examples of skull-faced versions, see *Aztecs* 2002: figs. 143–45.

16. Neither the stone statues with human faces nor those with skeletal features wear the two-horned hairdo, however, and the loose hair of the latter is tousled.

17. Florentine Codex depictions of the Cihuapipiltin appear in Sahagún 1950–82: bk. 1: 19; 1979: 1: prologue page 11r; 1979: 1: bk. 4, fols. 28v, 62r; 1993: fol. 266r.

18. Boone (2003: 215) notes that in these manuscripts, as well as Aubin Manuscript no. 20, the Cihuapipiltin/Cihuateteo are paired with five males that she calls "Macuilxochitls." There was a god named Macuilxochitl in the Aztec pantheon, and some ceramic figurines bear his attributes.

19. Millian's (1981) Group IV figurines were distinguished by a headdress with "butterfly" earflaps; those in Group V, by an animal held to the chin. Neither of these groups appears to relate to the copal figurines found at the Templo Mayor.

20. This figurine was also identified as Chicomecoatl by Seler (1990–2000: 2: fig. 31b) and Spence (1923: opp. p. 170).

21. The Codex Magliabechiano commentator identified the figure in folio 36r of the Codex Magliabechiano as Xilonen (Nuttall (1978: fol. 35v), whereas the Codex Tudela commentator specified Chicomecoatl for the cognate painting (Tudela de la Orden 1980: fol. 18r).

22. Sometimes there are two, at other times four or five, of these roundels; see, for example, Baquedano 1984: figs. 9, 10, 15, 16.

23. A Temple Headdress also appears on a woman in folio 75r of the Codex Magliabechiano; she is identified on folio 74v as a pulque goddess named Atlacoaya. Because there is no other known association of a pulque goddess with the Temple Headdress, Klein suggests that the artist confused her name with that of the goddess Atlatonan, whose impersonator was decapitated and flayed during the days leading up to Ochpaniztli (Durán 1971: 223; Sahagún 1950–82: bk. 2: 191).

24. Seler (1900–2000: 2: 167–68, fig. 33a,b) identified the dog-headed figurines in Millian's Group B as Quetzalcoatl's twin brother Xolotl, "Twin," who appears in painted manuscripts as an anthropomorphized canine (for example, Codex Borbonicus, pl. 16). Except for those figurines wearing a fringed or scalloped collar like that seen on Xolotl in manuscript paintings, however, none bear Xolotl's other insignia. In fact, it is not always clear that the animal referenced by the figurines is a dog.

25. For more on the curative properties of opossums and monkeys, see López Austin 1993; Ruíz de Alarcón 1984: 221, 283; and Sahagún 1950–82: bk. 3: 156.

26. The three Xipe Totec figurines from Tlatelolco were first reported by Lorenzo Flores García (1970).

27. Guzmán Peredo (1972: 61) identified this figurine as Tlaloc, but it lacks any evidence of that god's distinctive facial figures. It does, however, assume the pose and bear the amacuexpalli seen on the male copal figurines found at the Templo Mayor, which likewise lack the god's facial features.

28. The Musée du quai Branly piece was identified by Henri Lehmann (1948) as Chicomecoatl, but López Luján (2005: 60) has recently identified it as Chalchiuhtlicue.

29. The figure in question is labeled "Chachalmeca." The Chachalmeca were high-ranking sacrificial priests.

30. Noguera thought that these ritual objects were fairly old, dating to the beginnings of the Choluteca culture, but recent excavations have indicated otherwise (Uruñuela et al. 1997: 69).

31. Two of the four copal figurines in Offering 102 at the Templo Mayor had been placed next to a large stone vase bearing Tlaloc's visage, arranged as though they were his guardians or attendants. This would have been an appropriate arrangement had the copal figurines represented Tlaloc's priests rather than Tlaloc himself.

32. To date, only four copal figurines have come from the foundations of Phase IVa, which corresponds to the reign of Mocteuczoma I, who took office in 1440 (Victoria Lona 2004a, 2004b). We are using here the chronology constructed by Matos Moctezuma (1981: 50); a slightly different dating has been proposed by Emily Umberger (1987). For a discussion and comparison of these, see López Luján 2005: 52–54.

33. For the reign of Tizoc, which corresponds to Phase V, only sixteen copal figurines have been found. Phase VI, which correlates with the reign of Ahuitzotl, from 1486 to 1502, has produced the four examples found in Offering 102, while Phase VII, the last phase corresponding to the fateful reign of Moteuczoma II, has yielded seventeen (Victoria Lona 2004a, 2004b).

34. Otis-Charlton (1991: 37) found the ceramics associated with the ceramic figurines to be stylistically Late Aztec III and Aztec IV, which would "probably" date them to 1500–40.

References Cited

Aguilera, Carmen. 1985. *Flora y fauna mexicana: Mitología y tradiciones.* Everest Mexicana, Mexico City.

Ahuja O., Guillermo. 1982. La cerámica prehispánica en el Templo Mayor. In *El Templo Mayor: Excavaciones y estudios,* ed. E. Matos Moctezuma, 245–52. Instituto Nacional de Antropología e Historia, Mexico City.

Alcina Franch, José, Miguel León-Portilla, and Eduardo Matos. 1992. *Azteca/Mexica: Las culturas del México antiguo.* Sociedad Estatal Quinto Centenario/Lunwerg Editores, Madrid.

Anders, Ferdinand, ed. 1972. *Codex Vaticanus 3773 (Codex Vaticanus B), Biblioteca Apostolica Vaticana.* Akademische Druck- u. Verlagsanstalt, Graz.

Aubin Manuscript no. 20. See Caso 1965.

Aztec Empire, The: Catalogue of the Exhibition. 2004. Curated by Felipe Solís. Guggenheim Museum Publications, New York.

Aztecs. 2002. Curated by Eduardo Matos Moctezuma and Felipe Solís Olguin. Royal Academy of Arts, London.

Aztec Stone Sculpture. 1976. Introduction by Esther Pasztory. Center for Inter-American Relations, New York.

Baer, Gerhard, ed. 1996. *Ancient Mexican Ceramics from the Lukas Vischer Collection, Ethnographic Museum, Basel.* Corpus Americanensium Antiquatum. Friedrich Reinhardt, Basel.

Baquedano, Elizabeth. 1984. *Aztec Sculpture.* British Museum Publications, London.

Barlow, Robert H., and Henri Lehmann. 1956. Statuettes-Grelots Azteques de la Valle de Mexico. *Tribus* 4–5: 157–76.

———. 1990. Figurillas sonajas aztecas del Valle de México. In *Obras de Robert H. Barlow,* vol. 3, ed. J. Monjaras-Ruiz, E. Limón, and M. de la Cruz Pailles, 257–98. Instituto Nacional de Antropología e Historia, Mexico City; Universidad de las Américas, Puebla.

Barnes, William. 2005. Icons of Empire: Royal Presentation and the Conception of Rule in Aztec Mexico. Report submitted to FAMSI (Foundation for the Advancement of Mesoamerican Studies). http://www.famsi.org/reports/0027/index.html.

Barrera Rivera, José Álvaro, María de Lourdes Gallardo Parrodi, and Aurora Montufar López. 2001. La Ofrenda 102 del Templo Mayor. *Arqueología Mexicana* 8 (48): 70–77.

Bassie-Sweet, Karen. 2002. Corn Deities and the Complementary Male/Female Principle. In *La organización social entre los Mayas prehispánicos, coloniales y modernos: Memoria de la Tercera Mesa Redonda de Palenque,* ed. V. Tiesler Blos, R. Cobos, and M. Greene Robertson, 106–25. Consejo Nacional para la Cultura y las Artes, Instituto Nacional de Antropología e Historia, Mexico City; Universidad Autónoma de Yucatán, Mérida, Yucatán.

Batres, Leopoldo. 1990. Exploraciones en las calles de las Escalerillas. In *Trabajos arqueológicos en el centro de México,* ed. E. Matos Moctezuma, 109–67. Instituto Nacional de Antropología e Historia, Mexico City. (Orig. pub. 1902.)

Berdan, Frances F., and Patricia Rieff Anawalt. 1992. *The Codex Mendoza*. 4 vols. University of California Press, Berkeley.

Boone, Elizabeth H. 1999. The "Coatlicues" at the Templo Mayor. *Ancient Mesoamerica* 10: 189–206.

———. 2003. A Web of Understanding: Pictorial Codices and the Shared Intellectual Culture of Late Postclassic Mesoamerica. In *The Postclassic Mesoamerican World*, ed. M. E. Smith and F. F. Berdan, 207–21. University of Utah Press, Salt Lake City.

Brumfiel, Elizabeth M. 1996. Figurines and the Aztec State: Testing the Effectiveness of Ideological Domination. In *Gender and Archaeology*, ed. R. P. Wright, 143–66. University of Pennsylvania Press, Philadelphia.

Carballo, David. 2007. Effigy Vessels, Religious Integration, and the Origins of the Central Mexican Pantheon. *Ancient Mesoamerica* 18 (1): 53–67.

Caso, Alfonso. 1966. El culto al sol: Notas a la interpretación de W. Lehmann. [On Aubin Manuscript no. 20.] *Traducciones Mesoamericanistas* 1: 117–90.

Codex Borbonicus. See Nowotny 1974.

Codex Borgia. See Nowotny 1976.

Codex Cozcatzin. See Valero 1994.

Codex en Crux. See Dibble 1981.

Codex Ixtlilxochitl: Bibliothèque Nationale, Paris (Ms. Mex. 65–71). 1976. Akademische Druck- u. Verlagsanstalt, Graz.

Codex Magliabechiano. See Nuttall 1978.

Codex Mendoza. See Berdan and Anawalt 1992.

Codex Telleriano-Remensis. See Quiñones Keber 1995.

Codex Tudela. See Tudela de la Orden 1980.

Codex Vaticanus B. See Anders 1972.

Codex Vaticanus 3738 ("Cod. Vat. A," "Cod. Ríos") der Biblioteca Apostolica Vaticana. 1979. Akademische Druck- u. Verlagsanstalt, Graz.

Coggins, Clemency Chase, and Orrin C. Shane III, eds. 1984. *Cenote of Sacrifice: Maya Treasures from the Sacred Well at Chichén Itzá*. University of Texas Press, Austin.

Cohen, Ananda, and Christina M. Elson. n.d. The Aztec Occupation of Chiconautla, Mexico. http://anthro.amnh.org/anthropology/research/aztec.htm.

Cook de Leonard, Carmen. 1950. Figurillas de barro de Santiago Tlatelolco. In *Tlatelolco a través de los tiempos*, vol. 11, no. 1, pp. 93–100. Memorias de la Academia de la Historia 9, no. 1. Mexico City.

Corona S., Eduardo. 1972. Los dioses mexicas en la cerámica. In *Religión en Mesoamérica: 12th Mesa Redonda*, Sociedad Mexicana de Antropología, ed. J. Litvak King and N. Castillo, 91–100. Sociedad Mexicana de Antropología, Mexico City.

Dibble, Charles E. 1981. *Codex en Cruz*. 2 vols. University of Utah Press, Salt Lake City.

Dioses del México antiguo. 1995. Antiguo Colegio de San Ildefonso, Mexico City.

Durán, Diego. 1967. *Historia de las Indias de Nueva España e islas de la Tierra Firme*. 2 vols. Ed. A. Ma. Garibay. Editorial Porrúa, Mexico City. (Written c. 1579–81.)

———. 1971. *Book of the Gods and Rites and the Ancient Calendar*. Trans. and ed. F.

Horcasitas and D. Heyden. University of Oklahoma Press, Norman. (Written c. 1579–81.)

Elson, Christina M. 1999. An Aztec Palace at Chiconautla. *Latin American Antiquity* 10: 151–67.

Espinosa Pineda, Gabriel. 2001. La faura de Ehécatl: Propuesta de una taxonomía a partir de las deidades, o la función de la fauna en el orden cósmico. In *Animales y plantas en la cosmovisión mesoamericana*, ed. Y. González Torres, 255–303. Consejo Nacional para la Cultura y las Artes and Instituto Nacional de Antropología e Historia, Mexico City.

Evans, Susan T. 1990. Household Ritual in Aztec Life. Paper presented at the 55th Annual Meeting of the Society for American Archaeology, Las Vegas.

Flores García, Lorenzo. 1970. Tres figurillas vestidas con piel de desollados. *Boletín del Instituto Nacional de Antropología* 42: 43–46.

Franco, José Luis. 1961. Tres representaciones fálicas de Ehecatl-Quetzalcoatl. *Boletín del Centro de Investigaciones Antropológicas de México* 12: 5–8.

Glanz und Untergang des alten Mexiko: Die Azteken und ihre Vorläufer. 1986. 2 vols. Roemer- und Pelizaeus-Museum und Verlag Philipp von Zabern, Hildesheim and Mainz.

González Rul, Francisco. 1988. *La cerámica en Tlatelolco.* Colección Científica 172, Serie Arqueología. Instituto Nacional de Antropología e Historia, Mexico City.

Graulich, Michel. 1992a. Quetzalcoatl-Ehecatl, the Bringer of Life. In *Ancient America: Contributions to New World Archaeology*, ed. N. J. Saunders, 33–38. Oxford University Press, Oxford.

———. 1992b. On the So-Called "Cuauhxicalli of Motecuhzoma Ilhuicamina." *Mexicon* 14 (1): 5–10.

Guilliem Arroyo, Salvador. 1997. Figurillas de Tlatelolco. *Arqueología, n.s.*, 17: 111–38.

Guzmán Acevedo, Eulogio. 2004. Sculpting Imperialism? The Diverse Expression of Local Cults and Corporate Identity in the "Two-Tufted" Figure at the Templo Mayor. Ph.D. diss., Department of Art History, University of California, Los Angeles.

———. 2005. Mexica Portable Sculpture: Symbols of Imperial Power and Cultural Integration. In *Archaeology without Limits: Papers in Honor of Clement W. Meighan*, ed. B. D. Dillon and M. A. Boxt, 325–44. Labyrinthos, Lancaster, Calif.

Guzmán Peredo, Miguel. 1972. Arqueología subacuática. *Artes de México* 152 (19): 75–79.

Heyden, Doris. 1987. Symbolism of Ceramics from the Templo Mayor. In *The Aztec Templo Mayor: A Symposium at Dumbarton Oaks 8th and 9th October 1983*, ed. E. Hill Boone, 109–30. Dumbarton Oaks, Washington, D.C.

———. 1997. La sangre del árbol: El copal y las resinas en el ritual mexicano. In *Códices y documentos sobre México: Segundo simposio*, vol. 2, ed. S. Rueda Smithers, C. Vega Sosa, and R. Martínez Baracs, 243–70. Consejo Nacional para la Cultura y las Artes and Instituto Nacional de Antropología e Historia, Mexico City.

Kaplan, Flora. 1958. The Post-Classic Figurines of Central Mexico. M.A. thesis, Department of Anthropology, Columbia University, New York.

Kelly, David H. 1955. Quetzalcoatl and His Coyote Origins. *El México Antiguo* 8: 399–413.

Klein, Cecelia F. 1984. ¿Dioses de la lluvia o sacerdotes ofrendadores del fuego? Un studio socio-político de algunas representaciones mexicas del dios Tlaloc. *Estudios de Cultura Nahuatl* 17: 33–50.

———. 1986. Masking Empire: The Material Effects of Masks in Aztec Mexico. *Art History* 9 (2): 135–67.

———. 1988. Rethinking Cihuacoatl: Aztec Political Imagery of the Conquered Woman. In *Smoke and Mist: Mesoamerican Studies in Memory of Thelma D. Sullivan,* ed. J. K. Josserand and K. Dakin, 237–77. BAR Press, Oxford, U.K.

———. 2000. The Devil and the Skirt: An Iconographic Inquiry into the Prehispanic Nature of the Tzitzimime. *Ancient Mesoamerica* 11: 1–26.

———. 2001. Impersonation of Deities. In *Oxford Encyclopedia of Mesoamerican Cultures,* ed. D. Carrasco, 33–37. Oxford University Press, New York.

———. 2008. A New Interpretation of the Aztec Statue Known as Coatlicue, "Snakes-Her-Skirt." *Ethnohistory* 55 (2): 229–50.

Knab, Timothy J. 2004. *The Dialogue of Earth and Sky: Dreams, Souls, Curing, and the Modern Aztec Underworld.* University of Arizona Press, Tucson.

Lehmann, Henri. 1948. Une statue aztèque en résine. *Journal de la Société des Américanistes* 37: 269–73.

López Austin, Alfredo. 1993. *The Myths of the Possum: Pathways of Mesoamerican Mythology.* Trans. B. R. Ortiz de Montellano and T. Ortiz Montellano. University of New Mexico Press, Albuquerque.

López Luján, Leonardo. 2005. *The Offerings of the Templo Mayor of Tenochtitlan.* Trans. B. R. Ortiz de Montellano and T. Ortiz de Montellano. University of New Mexico Press, Albuquerque.

———. 2006. *La Casa de las Águilas: Un ejemplo de la arquitectura religiosa de Tenochtitlan.* 2 vols. Fondo de Cultura Económica and Instituto Nacional de Antropología e Historia, Mexico City; Moses Mesoamerican Archive, Harvard University, Cambridge, Mass.

López Luján, Leonardo, and Marie-France Fauvet-Berthelot. 2005. *Aztèques: La collection de sculptures du Musée du quai Branly.* Musée du quai Branly, Paris.

Luna Erreguerena, Pilar. 2000. El Nevado de Toluca: Sitio de veneración prehispanica. *Arqueología Mexicana* 8 (43): 47–49.

Maldonado Jimenez, Druzo. 2000. *Deidades y espacio ritual en Cuauhnáhuac y Huaxtepec: Tlalhuicas y Xochilmilcas de Morelos (siglos XII–XV).* Universidad Nacional Autónoma de México and Institución de Investigación Antropológicas, Mexico City.

Matos Moctezuma, Eduardo. 1981. *Una visita al Templo Mayor.* Instituto Nacional de Antropología e Historia, Mexico City.

Millian, Alva Clarke. 1981. The Iconography of Aztec Ceramic Figurines. M.A. thesis, Department of Art History, Columbia University, New York.

Motolinía, Toribio de Benevente de. 1950. *Motolinía's History of the Indians of New*

Spain. Trans. and ed. E. A. Foster. Greenwood Press, Westport, Conn. (Written c. 1536–43.)

Munn, Henry. 1984. The Opossum in Mesoamerican Mythology. *Journal of Latin American Lore* 10 (1): 23–62.

Nagao, Debra. 1985. *Mexica Buried Offerings: A Historical and Contextual Analysis.* BAR International Series 235. British Archaeological Reports, Oxford.

Navarrete, Carlos. 1968. Dos deidades de las aguas modeladas en resina de árbol. *Boletín del Instituto Nacional de Antropología e Historia* 33: 39–42.

Nicholson, H. B., with Eloise Quiñones Keber. 1983. *Art of Aztec Mexico: Treasures of Tenochtitlan.* National Gallery of Art, Washington, D.C.

Noguera, Eduardo. 1946. Xochiquetzal. In *México prehispánico: Culturas, deidades, y monumentos,* ed. J. A. Vivó, 481–84. Editorial Emma Hurtado, Mexico City.

———. 1954. *La cerámica arqueológica de Cholula.* Editorial Guarania, Mexico City.

Nowotny, Karl Anton, commentator. 1974. *Codex Borbonicus, Bibliothèque de l'Assemblee Nationale, Paris (Y120).* Akademische Druck- u. Verlagsanstalt, Graz.

———. 1976. *Codex Borgia: Biblioteca Apostolica Vaticana.* Akademische Druck- u. Verlagsanstalt, Graz.

Nuttall, Zelia, ed. 1978. *The Book of the Life of the Ancient Mexicans Containing an Account of Their Rites and Superstitions.* University of California Press, Berkeley. (Reprint of 1903 facsimile.)

Ortiz de Montellano, Bernard R. 1990. *Aztec Medicine, Health, and Nutrition.* Rutgers University Press, New Brunswick, N J.

Otis-Charlton, Cynthia L. 1991. Hollow Rattle Figurines of the Otumba Area, Mexico. In *The New World Figurine Project,* ed. T. Stocker and C. Otis-Charlton, 25–53. Research Press, Brigham Young University, Provo.

———. 1994. Plebeians and Patricians: Contrasting Patterns of Production and Distribution in the Aztec Figurine and Lapidary Industries. In *Economies and Polities in the Aztec Realm,* ed. M. G. Hodge and M. E. Smith, 195–219. State University of New York at Albany.

Parsons, Mary Hrones. 1972. Aztec Finds from the Teotihuacan Valley, Mexico. In *Miscellaneous Studies in Mexican Prehistory,* ed. M. W. Spence, J. R. Parsons, and M. H. Parsons, 81–170. University of Michigan Museum of Anthropology Anthropological Papers. Ann Arbor.

Pasztory, Esther. 1983. *Aztec Art.* Harry N. Abrams, New York.

Pérez-Castro Lira, Pedro Feo. Sánchez Nava, Ma. Estefán, Judith Padilla y Yedra, and Antonio Gudiño Garfias. 1989. El Cuauhxicalli de Moctezuma. *Arqueología* 5: 131–51.

Ponce de León, Pedro. 1973. Tratado de los dioses y ritos de la gentilidad (Breve relación de los dioses y ritos de la gentilidad). In *Teogonía e historia de los Mexicanos: Tres opúsculos del siglo XVI,* ed. A. Ma. Garibay K., 121–32. Editorial Porrúa, Mexico City. (Written late 16th c.)

Porcayo Michelini, Antonio. 1998. Las figurillas de cerámicas y la escultura en piedra del postclásico temprano y tardío en el sur de la Cuenca de México. Tesis de licenciatura en arqueología, Escuela Nacional de Antropología e Historia. Instituto Nacional de Antropología e Historia, Mexico City.

Preuss, K[onrad] Theodore. 1901. Mexikanische thonfiguren. *Globus* 79 (6): 87–91.

Quiñones Keber, Eloise. 1995. *Codex Telleriano-Remensis: Ritual, Divination, and History in a Pictorial Aztec Manuscript.* University of Texas Press, Austin.

Ruíz de Alarcón, Hernando. 1984. *Treatise on the Heathen Superstitions That Today Live among the Indians Native to This New Spain, 1629.* Trans. and ed. J. R. Andrews and R. Hassig. University of Oklahoma Press, Norman. (Written c. 1629.)

Sahagún, Bernardino de. 1950–82. *Florentine Codex: General History of the Things of New Spain.* Trans. A. J. O. Anderson and C. E. Dibble. 13 vols. School of American Research, Santa Fe, N.Mex. (Written 1575–77.)

———. 1977. *Historia general de las cosas de Nueva España.* 3rd ed. 4 vols. Editorial Porrúa, Mexico City. (Written 1575–77.)

———. 1979. *Códice Florentino, manuscrito 218–220 de la Colección Palatina de la Biblioteca Medicca Laurenziana.* 3 vols. Secretaría de Gobernación and Archivo General de la Nación, Mexico City. (Completed 1575–77.)

———. 1993. *Primeros memoriales.* Facsimile ed., with photography by Ferdinand Anders. University of Oklahoma Press, Norman.

———. 1997. *Primeros memoriales.* Paleography of Nahuatl text and English translation by Thelma D. Sullivan. Completed and revised, with additions by H. B. Nicholson, A. J. O. Anderson, C. E. Dibble, E. Quiñones Keber, and W. Ruwet. University of Oklahoma Press, Norman. (Written 1559–61.)

Sandstrom, Alan R. 1986. Paper Spirits of Mexico. *Natural History* 95 (1): 66–73.

———. 1991. *Corn Is Our Blood: Culture and Ethnic Identity in a Contemporary Aztec Indian Village.* University of Oklahoma Press, Norman.

Séjourné, Laurette, with Josefina Oliva. 1970. *Arqueología del Valle de México.* Instituto Nacional de Antropología e Historia, Mexico City.

Seler, Eduard. 1990–2000. *Collected Works in Mesoamerican Linguistics and Archaeology: English Translations of German Papers from Gesammelte Abhandlungen zur Amerikanischen sprach- und alterhumskunde.* 2nd ed. Labyrinthos, Lancaster, Calif.

Smith, Michael E. 1997. Life in the Provinces of the Aztec Empire. *Scientific American* 277 (3): 76–83.

———. 2002. Domestic Ritual at Aztec Provincial Sites in Morelos. In *Domestic Ritual in Ancient Mesoamerica,* ed. P. Plunket, 93–114. Cotsen Institute of Archaeology, Los Angeles.

———. 2003. *The Aztecs.* 2nd ed. Blackwell, Malden, Mass.

———. 2005. Aztec-Style Ceramic Figurines from Yautepec, Morelos. *Mexicon* 27 (2/3): 45–55.

Spence, Lewis. 1923. *The Gods of Mexico.* T. Fisher Unwin, London.

Stacey, R. J., C. R. Cartwright, and C. McEwan. 2006. Chemical Characterization of Ancient Mesoamerican "Copal" Resins: Preliminary Results. *Archaeometry* 48 (2): 323–40.

Stocker, Terrence Lynn. 1983. Figurines from Tula, Hidalgo, Mexico. Ph.D. diss., Department of Anthropology, University of Illinois, Urbana-Champaign.

Stresser-Péan, Guy. 2005. *Le soleil-dieu et la Christ: La christianisation des Indiens du Mexique vue de la Sierra de Puebla.* L'Harmattan, Paris.

Torquemada, Juan de. 1975. *Monarquia Indiana.* 5th ed. 3 vols. Editorial Porrúa, Mexico City. (Written 1596–1613.)

Tudela de la Orden, José, ed. 1980. *Códice Tudela.* Prologue by D. Robertson; epilogue by W. Jiménez Moreno. Ediciones Cultura Hispánica del Instituto de Cooperación Iberoamericana, Madrid.

Umberger, Emily. 1987. Events Commemorated by Date Plaques at the Templo Mayor: Further Thoughts on the Solar Metaphor. In *The Aztec Templo Mayor,* ed. E. Hill Boone, 411–50. Dumbarton Oaks, Washington, D.C.

———. 1996. Art and Imperial Strategy in Tenochtitlan. In *Aztec Imperial Strategies,* by Frances F. Berdan et al., 85–106. Dumbarton Oaks, Washington, D.C.

Umberger, Emily, and Cecelia F. Klein. 1993. Aztec Art and Economic Expansion. In *Latin American Horizons,* ed. D. S. Rice and Janet Berlo, 295–336. Dumbarton Oaks, Washington, D.C.

Uruñuela, Gabriela, Patricia Plunket, Gilda Hernández, and Juan Albaitero. 1997. Biconical God Figurines from Cholula and the Codex Borgia. *Latin American Antiquity* 8 (1): 63–70.

Vaillant, George. 1962. *The Aztecs of Mexico.* 2nd ed., rev. S. B. Vaillant. Doubleday, New York.

Valero, Ana Rita. 1994. *Códice Cozcatzin.* Paleography and trans. Rafael Tena. Instituto Nacional de Antropología e Historia, Mexico City; Benemérita Universidad de Puebla.

Victoria Lona, Naoli. 2004a. El copal en las ofrendas del Templo Mayor de Tenochtitlan. Tesis de licenciatura en arqueología, Escuela Nacional de Antropología e Historia. Instituto Nacional de Antropología e Historia and Secretaría de Educación Pública, Mexico City.

———. 2004b. El copal en las ofrendas del Templo Mayor. *Arqueología Mexicana* 12 (67): 66–71.

Wicke, Charles R. 1976. Once More around the Tizoc Stone: A Reconsideration. *Actas del Congreso Internacional de Americanistas, México, 2–7 Septiembre 1974,* vol. 2, 209–22. Instituto Nacional de Antropología e Historia, Mexico City.

13

Figurines as Bearers of and Burdens in Late Classic Maya State Politics

CHRISTINA T. HALPERIN

Mesoamerican scholars often portray clay figurines as resisting (Brumfiel 1996) or unrelated to politics and the affairs of the state (Borhegyi 1956; Gossen and Leventhal 1993: 211; M. Smith 2002). Such conceptions arise from (1) the domestic recovery contexts of figurines, (2) their depictions of humans and supernatural beings that are rarely portrayed in monumental media, and (3) the Western analytical separation of purported public and private domains and by extension domestic and political realms. Alternatively, others argue that iconography and art are inherently political (Adorno [1967] 1991; Adorno and Horkheimer [1944] 1972; Ridless 1984) and that the domestic context of use need not signify an apolitical expression or statement (Bowser 2000). Thus, the question I ask here is not whether Mesoamerican and, more specifically, Late Classic period (AD 600-900) Maya figurines represented or reflected political decisions or dispositions. Rather, the question is this: In what way did figurines either promote Maya state relations and symbols of rulership or represent alternative values and perspectives to the Maya state system and the political elite who sat at the top of such a system? To address these questions, I draw on a theoretical framework of mass media studies to consider archaeologically recovered figurines from the site of Motul de San José, Petén, Guatemala, and its satellite centers (Halperin 2007).

Maya figurines provide an important gauge for understanding the reach of the state to household contexts and among common peoples. During the Late Classic period, state symbols and meanings similar to those found on monuments were disseminated widely through molded figurines. The mechanical nature of figurine production aided in the diffusion of state symbols out of the administrative and sacred realms of the urban centers and into the homes and domestic compounds of elite and common peoples alike. At the same time, figurines also manifested more popular concerns or ideologies expressed by representations of common peoples, trickster figures, and unusual supernatural characters. The relatively decentralized use of figurines may have also allowed a substantial flexibility in the interpretation of their social and political meanings.

Theoretical Background

To sketch out the background to the relation of Maya figurines and politics, I examine the theoretical underpinnings of the Frankfurt School and its ideas relating to mass culture and mechanical reproduction. Although the Frankfurt School scholars were reacting to and writing in the context of capitalism, modernism, and political movements of the early twentieth century, some of their theoretical contributions can be applied to Mesoamerican art in general and Classic Maya figurines in particular. Some of its contributors—namely, Walter Benjamin ([1936] 1969), Theodor Adorno ([1967] 1991; Adorno and Horkheimer [1944] 1972), Max Horkheimer (1972), and Herbert Marcuse (1964)—conceived of art as active, inherently political, and capable of influencing the thoughts and attitudes of the populace at large (Ridless 1984: 95). They believed that changes in its material, technological, and aesthetic form affect the way we perceive and experience reality.

Benjamin ([1936] 1969), for example, argued that mechanical reproduction of art, as seen in photography, film, and printmaking, represents an innovative and altogether different art form than that of classical art. Its mass reproduction and distribution nullifies a piece's uniqueness, individuality, authenticity, and "aura." While recognizing the passive effects that mass media has on its viewers, he also argued that it has the ability to bring to light multiple perspectives and penetrate into contexts that would be out of the original's reach. He stated ([1936] 1969: 236),

> As compared with painting, filmed behavior lends itself more readily to analysis because of its incomparably more precise statements of the situation. In comparison with the stage scene, the filmed behavior item lends itself more readily to analysis because it can be isolated more easily. . . . By close-ups of the things around us, by focusing on hidden details of familiar objects, by exploring commonplace milieus under the ingenious guidance of the camera, the film . . . extends our comprehension of the necessities which rule our lives.

Because of this, he believed that mass media help the members of the common populace to see themselves differently, critique the power relations of which they are a part, and, potentially, mobilize against their current social and economic conditions. In this sense, he highlighted the revolutionary potential of mass-produced art forms.

In contrast, Adorno, Horkheimer, and Marcuse viewed mass-produced and mass-consumed art as inhibiting political and personal action (Adorno [1967] 1991; Adorno and Horkheimer [1944] 1972; Marcuse 1964; Ridless 1984). They argued that instead of creating multiple perspectives, as Benjamin suggested, mechanical reproduction creates a standardized work that destroys the seriousness and efficacy of high art while also eradicating resistive qualities of low art (also known as popular art). Although mass culture—or what they later referred to as the "culture industry"—may serve as a leveling mechanism, allowing all realms of society access to it, they suggested that such a leveling process merely creates an illusion of equality layered over economic and social differences. For example, Adorno stated,

> The concepts of order which it [the culture industry] hammers into human beings are always those of the status quo. They remain unquestioned, unanalyzed and undialectically presupposed, even if they no longer have any substance for those who accept them. In contrast to the Kantian, the categorical imperative of the culture industry no longer has anything in common with freedom. It proclaims: you shall conform, without instruction as to what; conform to that which exists anyway, and to that which everyone thinks anyway as a reflex of its power and omnipresence.

In this sense, instead of sharpening perception, mechanical reproduction dulls it, producing a consenting public. The meanings and ideas associated with mass media become naturalized, stereotyped, and hegemonic through the repetition of a set pattern. The concern that mass media creates a homogenized, passive effect is echoed and then subsequently critiqued by scholars of globalization (Hall 1993; Kearney 1995; Tomlinson 1991).

Although the Frankfurt School authors were reacting to the commercialization of art, a phenomenon specific to capitalist cultures, they draw attention to the ways in which the production, circulation, and consumption of different forms of media alter perceptions of their meanings. One perspective is that mass media may have a subversive quality, inspire new ideas, and contradict dominant ideologies. From an opposing vantage point, such imagery promotes conformity, indifference, and acceptance of the current social order. With respect to Mesoamerican archaeology and iconography, I ask the following questions: What distinctions in the different forms of media existed, and what were the political implications of these distinctions? Can Classic Maya figurines be seen as a type of mass media, albeit on a much smaller scale than that referred to by Frankfurt School scholars?

Mesoamerican Figurines and Mechanical Reproduction

Many Classic and Postclassic period figurines in Mesoamerica are distinct from other forms of imagery in their capacity for mechanical reproduction through mold technology (Allen 1980). Molds were used to produce figurines in Mesoamerica beginning in the Early Classic period and became especially prominent among the Maya during the Late Classic period (Goldstein 1979; Rands and Rands 1965; Willey 1972). In a manner similar to that of Benjamin's photographs, molds allowed a single image to be reproduced many times over. Additional molds may also have been reproduced from previously existing figurines (Causey 1985). Because of the easy accessibility of clay as the principal material in its production and because of figurines' small size, a single figurine image had the potential not only to be produced en masse but also to have been widely distributed and consumed.

Recent research at Motul de San José, the medium-sized capital of a Classic-period polity in Petén, Guatemala, and three of its satellite centers reveals that figurine production and distribution allowed for popular consumption of figurine imagery within the region (figures 13.1, 13.2). Figurines from the area were recovered from archaeological investigations conducted by the Proyecto Arqueológico Motul de San José, directed by Antonia Foias of Williams College, between 1998 and 2005. To date, 2,800 figurines (of which 445 still possess heads) have been recovered from test-pitting and horizontal excavations. Over 98 percent of the sample dates to the Late and Terminal Classic periods, based on figurine style, associated ceramics, and radiocarbon dating. In a pattern similar to that identified at other Maya sites, the figurines were found primarily in household midden and construction fill contexts. At least eighteen sets of figurine matches, that is, identical figurines that were presumably made from the same mold or mold replicas, were recovered (figure 13.3, table 13.1). These matches, which range from two to six duplicates per set, were recovered from palace-type and elite residences within the Motul de San José site core; households in its northern, eastern, and southern peripheries; and its satellite centers, Trinidad de Nosotros, Chachaklum, and Chäkokot. Their widespread dis-

Figure 13.1. Map of the Maya area with selected sites mentioned in the text.

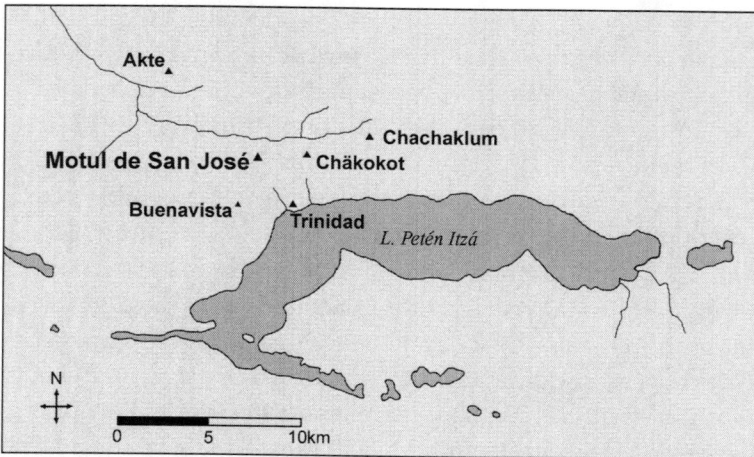

Figure 13.2. Regional map of Motul de San José and its satellite centers.

Table 13.1. Matching Figurine Sets from Motul de San José and Its Satellite Centers

Site[a]	Provenience	Notes on provenience	Image	Match[b]
MSJ	2A-2-7-1	Site core	Dwarf	m01
MSJ	2A-40-3-1	Site core	Dwarf	m01
MSJ	10A-3-7/8-1	Site core	Flat face	m02
MSJ	15A-12-2-5	Site core	Flat face	m02
MSJ	17D-9-1-2	Site core	Flat face	m02
TRI	12A-6-3-5	Satellite site	Woman	m03
TRI	13E-5-3-2	Satellite site	Woman	m03
MSJ	2A-40-3-1	Site core	Woman	m03
MSJ	39G-7-2-1	Northern periphery	Woman	m03
MSJ	36F-2-2-3	Northern periphery	Fat God	m04
MSJ	42H-5-2-1	Northern periphery	Fat God	m04
MSJ	46A-6-3-2	Site core	Fat God	m04
MSJ	2A-3-9-1	Site core	Fat God	m05
MSJ	2B-1-5-1	Site core	Fat God	m05
MSJ	33D-12-1-1	Site core	Fat God	m05
MSJ	12B-23-1-1	Site core	Grotesque	m06
MSJ	15A-50-3-4	Site core	Grotesque	m06
MSJ	2A-3-14-1	Site core	Dwarf or Fat God	m07
MSJ	Trans.Sur.Grp.1B	Southern periphery	Dwarf or Fat God	m07
MSJ	2A-40-5-2	Site core	Ruler	m08
MSJ	4A-1-2-1	Site core	Ruler	m08
MSJ	15A-26-1-1	Site core	Monkey	m09
CHA	1A-1-1-2	Satellite site	Monkey	m09
TRI	12B-1-1-1	Satellite site	Dog	m10
MSJ	42D-7-2-2	Northern periphery	Dog	m10
TRI	4A-2-2-3	Satellite site	Dog	m10
MSJ	2A-3-14-1	Site core	Woman	m11
MSJ	2A-5-6-15	Site core	Woman	m11
MSJ	15A-12-1-1	Site core	Anthropomorph	m12
MSJ	2A-5-6-17	Site core	Anthropomorph	m12
MSJ	2A-1-7-1	Site core	Ruler	m13
CHT	44E-14-3-1	Satellite site	Ruler	m13
MSJ	29D-1-1-1	Site core	Woman	m14
MSJ	29G-13-2-2	Site core	Woman	m14
MSJ	19A-3-1-0	Site core	Woman	m15
MSJ	30A-11-1-1	Site core	Woman	m15
MSJ	17D-6-1-2	Site core	Warrior	m16
MSJ	2A-3-14-1	Site core	Warrior	m16
MSJ	2A-40-4-2	Site core	Warrior	m16
MSJ	3A-3-12-1	Site core	Warrior	m16
TRI	3C-4-3-3	Satellite site	Warrior	m16
MSJ	41F-0-0-0	Eastern periphery	Warrior	m16
MSJ	15A-26-2-1	Site core	Ruler	m17
MSJ	42F-2-1-2	Northern periphery	Ruler	m17
MSJ	29C-1-1-1	Site core	Woman	m18
MSJ	2B-1-4-1	Site core	Woman	m18
TRI	19B-4-3-1	Satellite site	Ballplayer	m19
MSJ	2A-40-4-1	Site core	Ballplayer	m19

a. MSJ = Motul de San José, TRI = Trinidad de Nosotros, CHT = Chäkokot, CHA = Chachaklum.

b. All matching figurines appear to belong to Type 1 figurines (figurine-ocarinas produced from one-sided press molds) in the Motul de San José classification system, with the exception of m02, which may represent molded heads that were likely appliquéd to effigy flutes.

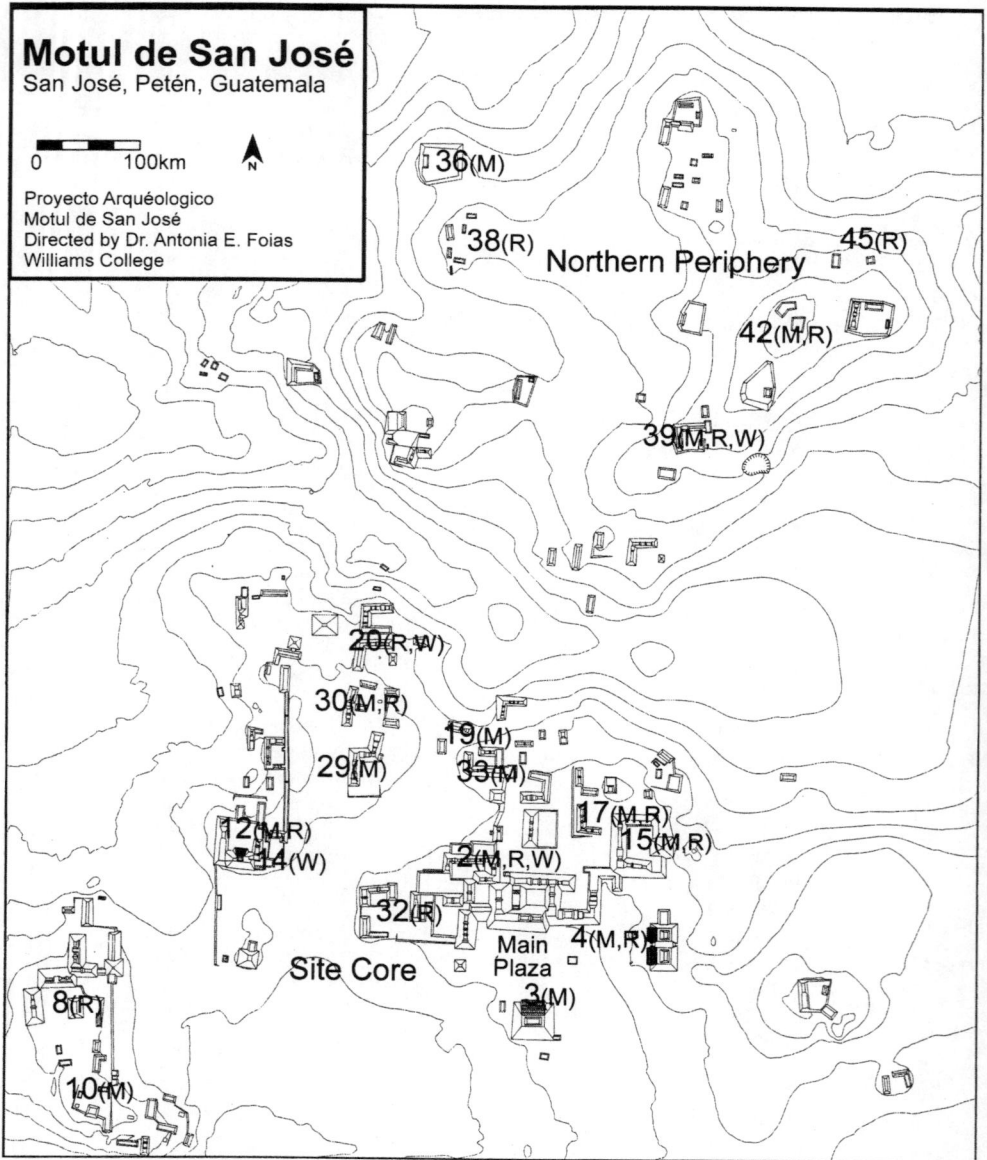

Figure 13.3. Map of Motul de San José with operation numbers labeled where matching figurines (M), ruler figurines (R), and women with dish figurines (W) were recovered.

tribution indicates that identical forms of iconography were present in the households of common peoples in addition to royal and elite households (also compare figurine matches found at Teotihuacan: Allen 1980; Barbour 1975). In this sense, figurines did seem to represent a type of mass media.

Other Late Classic period Maya figurine collections have yielded identical figurines. Some figurines excavated from the island of Jaina share match mates with several figurines from museum collections (Schele 1997: pls. 8, 9). At the site of Lagartero, many of the figurines excavated from a large ceremonial refuse deposit also possessed match mates (Ekholm 1979: 174, 185). Among the figurines depicting women, for example, the most common type was a seated woman with hands on her knees. Susanna Ekholm identified forty examples of this type, of which at least twelve appeared to have been made from the same mold (Ekholm 1979: 175). Although these duplicate figurines tell us little about their distribution, they reveal that some were indeed produced en masse.

Instrumental Neutron Activation Analyses (INAA) conducted on Late Classic Maya figurines indicate that they were often exchanged across sites and regions. Sixteen percent of the Motul de San José region figurines sampled for INAA were produced from nonlocal clays, most likely deriving from in or around Tikal (Halperin 2007: 114–16, tables 8.7, 8.8).[1] This find is not surprising, because epigraphic evidence indicates that Motul de San José was politically subordinate to Tikal during at least part of the Late Classic period (Foias 2000, 2003; Martin and Grube 2000: 45–46). Erin Sears and colleagues' investigations at Cancuen reveal that figurines excavated from the site possessed chemical paste profiles characteristic of Cancuen pastes as well as those from Raxruha Viejo, located less than 20 kilometers south of Cancuen, and Salinas de los Nueve Cerros in Alta Verapaz (Sears 2007; Sears et al. 2004). Marilyn Goldstein's (1979, 1980) documentation of figurine styles and chemical profiles from the western zone of the Maya area indicate that XAC figurines (molded figurines with imagery that includes dynastic themes, warriors, supernatural beings, and ballplayers) were "mass-produced and widely traded" along the lower Usumacinta and Grijalva rivers, all along the Campeche coast, and inland at sites such as Comalcalco and Tortuguero (Goldstein 1980: 95). These molded figurines were the most chemically diverse of the different stylistic groups she assigned to the region. The three figurines that provide evidence for the longest trading distance within the sample (between Jaina and Comalcalco and between Jaina and Palenque) also belonged to the XAC figurine group (Goldstein 1979: 121–22; 1980: 94–95).

The productive and distributional properties of figurines contrast with monumental art, which comprised one-of-a kind objects located primarily in major site centers and in public, centralized spaces. Producers of the latter were often full-time specialists who were either patronized by elites or, more likely, elites themselves (Inomata 2001). The messages and symbolism portrayed on such large-scale media promoted the ruling dynasty, state ideologies of politics and religion, and the elite class in general. Rosemary Joyce (1993, 1996, 2000), for example, notes that large-scale media depict different types, spatial arrangements, and frequencies of males and females than occur on small-scale media, such as painted vases and figurines. She argues that these different forms of media inscribed varying gender ideologies based on social class and other differences. Karl Taube (1989) also finds contrasts in the iconography of large- and small-scale media. He notices that clowning, trickster, and abnormal or grotesquely featured figures are often depicted in figurines and polychrome pottery but rarely occur in large, monumental works. He suggests that this corpus of characters provided a source of social commentary of rulers and elite society in general (see also Mock 2003; Taube and Taube, this volume).

Mold-made figurines,[2] among small-scale media, may also contrast with other forms, such as finely modeled or partly modeled figurines[3] (for examples, see Jaina Group B–F and Jaina Modeled Misc. figurines in Corson 1976) and polychrome pottery with hieroglyphs and figural scenes, in their capacity for mechanical reproduction of iconography. The latter represent unique pieces created by highly specialized craftspeople. The vessels' symbolism, the skill and intensive labor apparent in them, and the prestigious identity of their painters added to their aura and value (Reents-Budet 1994, 1998). In this manner, they often represented inalienable prestige goods that enhanced and legitimized social standing. From a materialist standpoint, mold-made figurines are clearly distinct because they were not unique items; even if a single figurine was made from a single mold, the figurine could have easily been reproduced again through the creation of another mold from the original figurine (Causey 1985). Ethnographic accounts of contemporary potters indicate that molded production (not including the manufacture of the actual mold) required relatively less skill and labor investment than those requiring elaborate modeled techniques (Arnold 1985: 205–7; 1999: 64; Reina and Hill 1978: 262; Torres Quintero and Rodríguez Lazcano 1996). The frequent occurrence of mold-made figurines in commoner residences (Halperin 2007; Ivic de Monterroso 1999; Moholy-Nagy

2003; Willey 1972) further suggests that these were not prestige items in the same fashion as polychrome pottery with hieroglyphics and figural scenes. In this sense, they were unlikely candidates as prestige items that were exclusively used to promote royal and elite political status (Halperin 2007: 272–73, 346–68).

Classic Maya Figurine Imagery: Two Case Examples

To address the question of whether Classic Maya figurines as representations of "mass culture" potentially supported state politics or resisted it, let us now turn to figurine imagery and the distribution of figurine images across the social landscape. Although figurines depict a multitude of different supernatural, human, and animal forms (and a holistic analysis requires examining all such imagery), I restrict my discussion here primarily to images of rulers and of women holding containers of food.

Rulers and Ruling Elites

Molded ruler figurines are found in relatively large frequencies from widely dispersed sites that were the seats of varying degrees of political power: Aguateca (Triadan 2007; Valdés et al. 2001), Altar de Sacrificios (Willey 1972), Comalcalco (Gallegos Gómora 2003), Ixlu (personal observation), Jaina (Corson 1976; Goldstein 1979, 1980, 1994; Piña Chan 1968, 1996), Jonuta (Alvarez and Casasola 1985), Lubaantun (T. Joyce 1933; Wears 1977), several centers in southeastern Petén (including Calzada Mopan, Ixkun, Ixtonton, and Sacul [Laporte et al. 2004]), Palenque (Flores Jiménez 2000, 2002), Piedras Negras (Schlosser 1978; R. Taube 2006), Seibal (Willey 1978), Quirigua (Ashmore n.d.). Tikal (personal observation, 2006), Tonina (Becquelin and Baudez 1982: figs. 256g, 262b,d,e), Topoxté (Hermes 2000: fig. 62-1), Uaxactun (personal observation, 2004), Xunantunich (LeCount 1996: fig. E.35), and sites in the Yucatán (Butler 1935: figs. 1h, 3g), to name a few. Ruler figures are identified by fan-shaped feather headdresses that typically include a zoomorphic or supernatural head perched just above the individual's face. Their identification as rulers or members of the ruling elite is based on the depiction of similar headdresses on named rulers from stelae and other monumental imagery (Cohodas 1994) (figure 13.4). Although these headdresses are usually worn by royal males—as determined by epigraphic evidence, the absence of breasts, and the presence of loincloths—they are also occasionally worn by royal females in both small- and large-

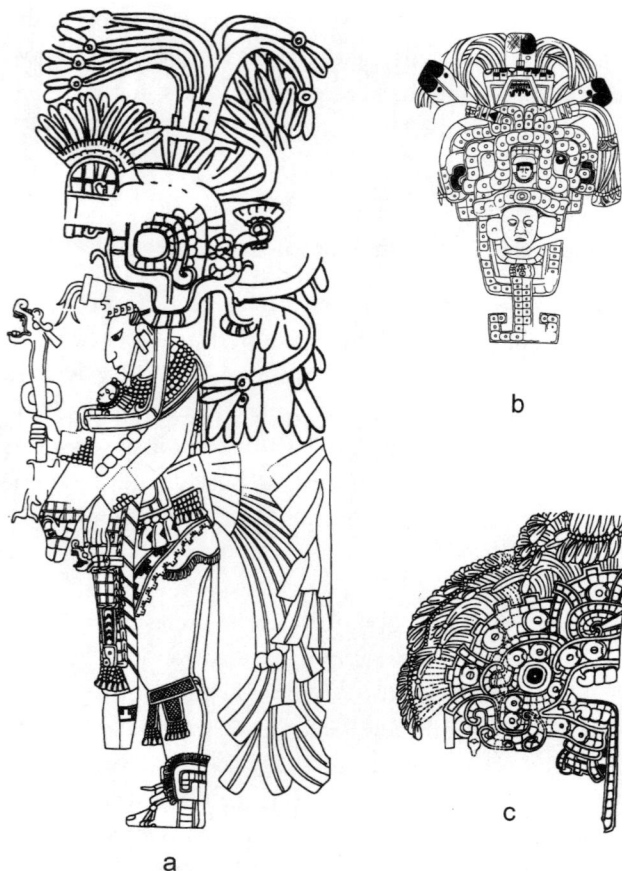

Figure 13.4. Depictions of rulers and War Serpents on Maya monuments: *a,*
headdress from Bonampak Stela 3 (after Mathews 1980: fig. 4); *b,* headdress
from Piedras Negras Stela 7 (after Stuart and Graham 2003: 39); *c,* detail from
Tikal Temple 1, Lintel 2 (after Coe et al. 1961: fig. 12d).

scale media (Josserand 2002: figs. 8.2, 8.5, 8.7, 8.14, 8.15, and 8.16; Martin
and Grube 2000: 149; Schele 1997: pl. 18; Triadan 2007: fig. 10a; Valdés et
al. 2001: fig. 8).

At Motul de San José, ruler figurines ($n=39$) comprise one of the most
common anthropomorphic figurine types, second in frequency only to
women with broad-brimmed hats ($n=50$). Some of the headdresses include
a bird with a mat motif. The most common type of fan-shaped feather
headdresses among the collection, however, is the War Serpent headdress
($n=21$). It closely parallels the War Serpent headdresses on stone monu-

ments in depicting a serpent head with platelet skin similar to cut-shell armor, upturned snout, large reptilian eyes, and fan-shaped feather plumage extending from behind the serpentine head (Halperin 2004; Schele 1997; K. Taube 1992, 2000). Ruler figures with the War Serpent headdress, in both monumental and figurine versions, often carry emblems of war (such as axes, spears or spear-throwers, and shields) or are seated on thrones or palanquins. Karl Taube suggests that War Serpent headdresses in the Maya area derived from symbols of rulership at Teotihuacan. He documents their presence on the heads of rulers portrayed on monuments and other large-scale media from Tikal, Piedras Negras, Lamanai, Bonampak, Copan, and Palenque.

What is most interesting about the Motul de San José data, however, is that a widespread occurrence of ruler figurines exists among both high- and low-status residences as well as at site core and periphery settlement loci. Some of these contexts share matching sets (*n*=3) of identical War Serpent–headdress figurines (figures 13.5, 13.6). For example, a figurine from a commoner farming household from the small periphery site of Chäkokot (CHT44E-14-3-1) shares a match mate with one from an excavation unit located at the edge of the Main Acropolis from Motul de San José's site center (MSJ2A-1-7-1). Another War Serpent–headdress figurine, recovered from a royal household in central Motul de San José (MSJ15A-26-2-1), shares a match mate from a small household group in the northern periphery of the site (MSJ42F-2-1-2). These finds indicate that ruler symbolism was not only inscribed permanently on the monuments in the public procession and ceremonial spaces of site centers but was also found in the form of figurines from the houses and domestic spaces of the commoner populace.

Women Holding Basket or Dish

Another theme in Classic period Maya figurine iconography is a woman holding a dish or basket filled with food, most likely tamales. Molded figurines depicting women holding such containers occur at sites such as Altar de Sacrificios (Willey 1972: fig. 34b), Lubaantun (T. Joyce 1933: pls. IV-3, IV-4, and IV-8), and Xunantunich (LeCount 1996: fig. E.36b). Stephen Houston and colleagues (2006: 110, fig. 3.4) interpret a figurine from Alta Verapaz that depicts a seated woman with a dog, a tumpline, and a container of tamales as a woman vendor selling food. The more limited appearance of these figurines in Maya sites draws a contrast to the ruler figurines, which are common throughout the Maya area (see also Cohodas 2002: 40–41 for a discussion of the widespread exposure of woman

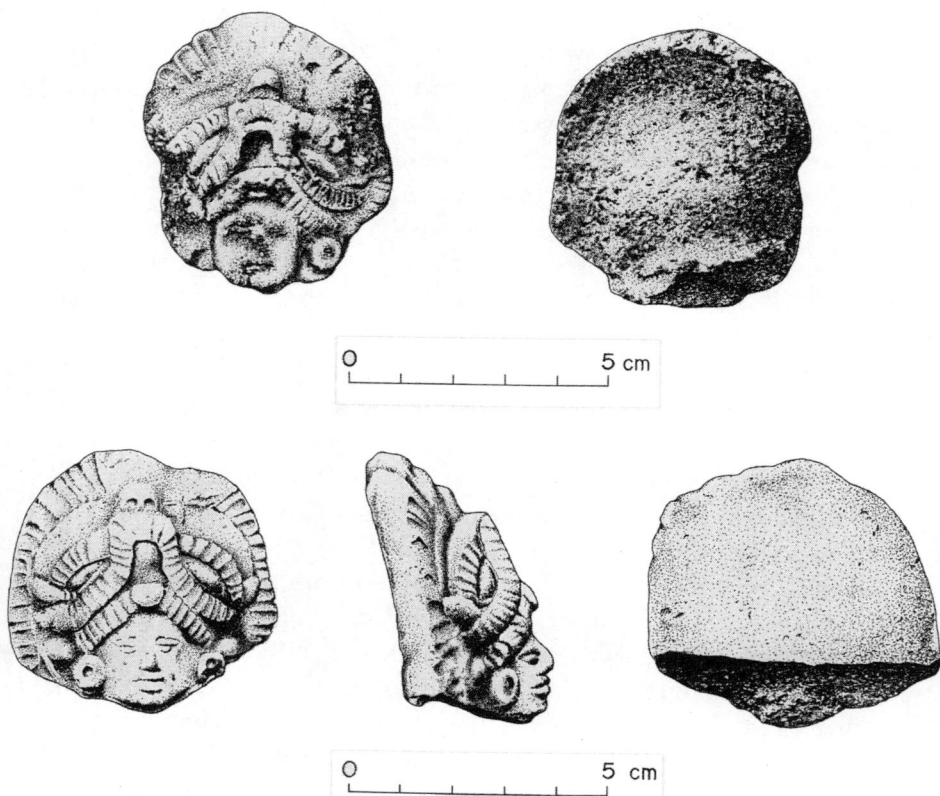

Figure 13.5. Matching set (m13) of ruler figurines with War Serpent headdresses from Motul de San José and Chäkokot (illustration by Luis F. Luin).

weaver figurines in publications despite their restrictive archaeological distribution). The women with containers are not, however, the only types of figurines depicting women, as they are also seen with children or animals, holding fans, embracing with older men or supernatural figures, dancing (primarily found in Western Maya sites), standing, sitting, and donning a diversity of headdresses, ornamentation, and garments. The women with a basket or bowl are singled out here because they make particular reference to women as laborers.

The theme of women as laborers possesses an underlying political significance in that women's labor was valuable both for state and for household reproduction. Rosemary Joyce (1993: 261) highlights both of these roles in discussing representations of women's work. She finds that representations

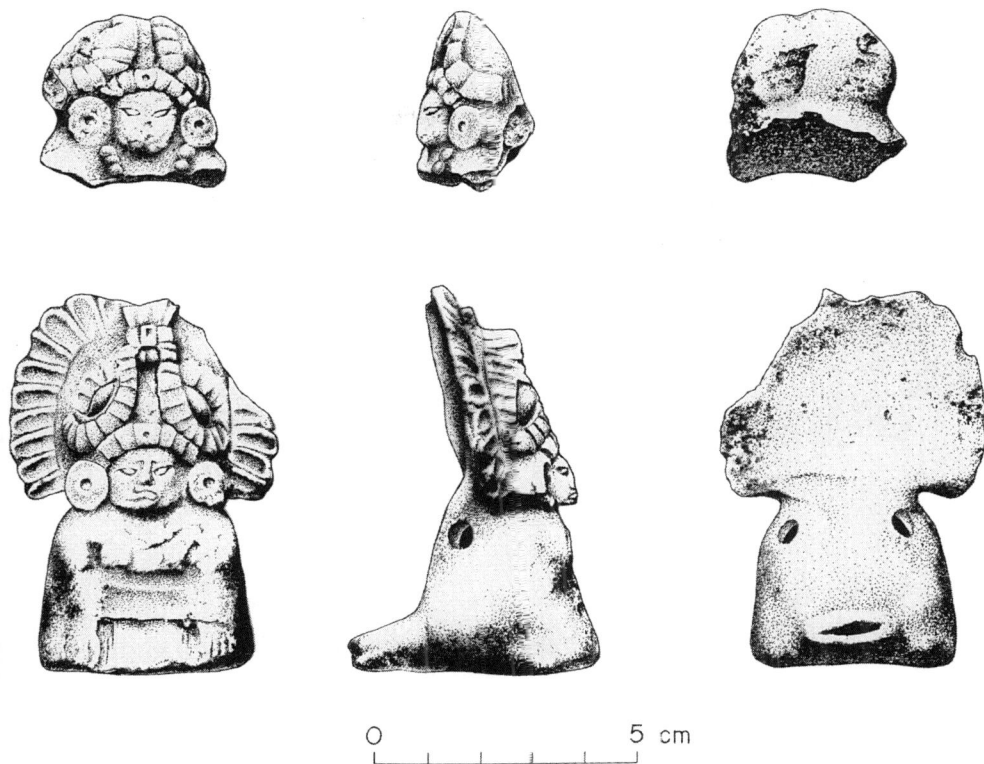

Figure 13.6. Matching set (m8) of ruler figurines with War Serpent headdresses from Motul de San José (illustration by Luis F. Luin).

of women as laborers (particularly commoner women depicted on figurines but not monuments) highlight the political significance of women's production in the maintenance of the state. At the same time, the role of women as laborers may have been celebrated within commoner or noble households, despite the appropriation of their labor by groups outside the household (Joyce 1993: 263; 2000: 88–89).

At Motul de San José, this theme ($n=9$) is manifested by a woman with stepped-cut hair, which is sometimes held in place by a decorated band of cloth (figures 13.7, 13.8). She wears a simple wraparound, off-the-shoulder dress and relatively little adornment. While the heads and bodies are clearly mold-made, the arms holding the bowl or basket were appliquéd onto the molded body of the figurine-ocarina. The placement of the dish or basket on the shoulder implies that the woman is engaged in serving or carrying food rather than offering an item, as depicted with royal women on monu-

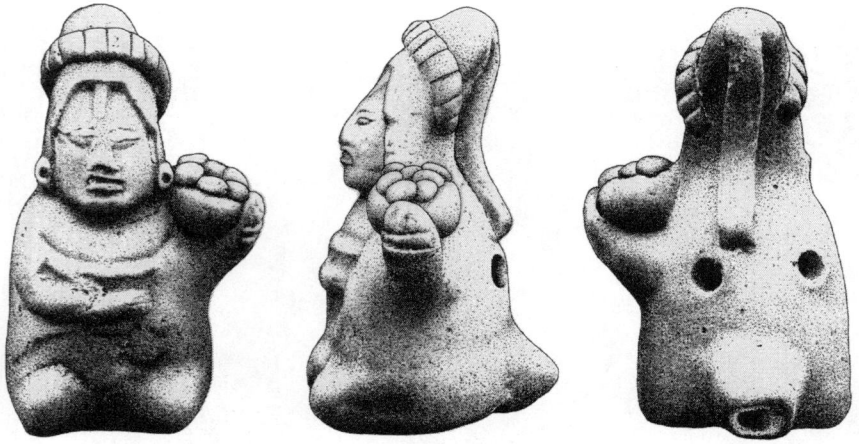

Figure 13.7. Figurine of woman with dish of tamales from Motul de San José (illustration by Luis F. Luin).

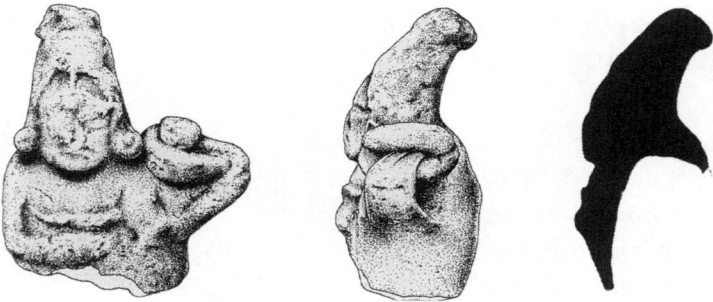

Figure 13.8. Figurine of woman with dish and tamale(?) from Motul de San José (illustration by Luis F. Luin).

ments where the woman holds the bowl in front of her torso. In addition, the lack of a decorated *huipil* or elaborate headdress contrasts with monumental depictions of royal women holding baskets or ceramics filled with ritual objects. Thus, figurine versions may represent women of noble or commoner status.

Most of the aforementioned figurines (*n*=8, 89 percent) were recovered from royal and elite contexts in the site core of Motul de San José and its neighboring center, Trinidad. The only other context where this type of figurine was recovered was a household in the northern periphery of Motul de San José whose buildings possessed vaulted masonry roofs. No identical versions or "matches" have been recovered that possess both the head and body (which would show the bowl/basket). If these figurines do represent common women's labor, it is surprising that they are not as commonly found in small and medium-sized households as are the ruler figurines.

Discussion

Late Classic Maya figurines are similar to what the Frankfurt School scholars referred to as mass media in their easily reducible quality, widespread distribution, and relatively homogenous consumption. These figurines, like more-restrictive forms of media, communicated political values and state ideologies. The most evident manner in which this task was accomplished is in their depictions of the heads of state, the rulers and the ruling elite. They are remarkably similar to their monumental counterparts in style and costume detail. Molded figurines of state dignitaries depicting symbols of political power are not unique to the Maya area. At Monte Albán, for example, the production of a Oaxacan version of War Serpent headdress figurines occurred (Martínez López and Winter 1994). During the Early Classic period, Teotihuacanos, the first cultural group in Mesoamerica to use mold technology to manufacture large quantities of figurines, produced figurines of state officials and prominent political figures in the form of enthroned individuals, elites or officials with large butterfly headdresses, and warriors (Barbour 1975; Goldsmith 2000; Séjourné 1966; von Winning 1987). In addition, there may be some indication that the Teotihuacan state undertook the production and distribution of some of these figurines, as investigations at the urban center uncovered a workshop attached to the Ciudadela that manufactured "portrait" or warrior figurines in addition to large ceramic censers (Munera Bermundez 1985: 38).

The replication of rulers and other state imagery within the medium of figurines, however, is not inherent in all state systems. During the Postclassic period in the northern Maya lowlands, there was more emphasis on small modeled figurines representing mythological and sacrificial scenes than there was on molded figurines, especially those depicting any type of known rulership for that time period (for example, drum major's headdress, woven mat necklace) (Chase 1985; Rands 1965; Rands and Rands 1965; A. L. Smith 1971). An "official" state-centered figurine tradition continued, however, in the form of large modeled effigy censers depicting deities. Among the Aztec, molded figurines were common. However, they rarely depicted state officials or state-sponsored deities and appear to have represented more of a counterculture to imperial state rule (Brumfiel 1996; Olson 2007; Parsons 1972; Smith 2002; see also chapter 12, this volume).

In addition, the presence of mold technology may not always signify standardized production and homogeneity of representation. For example, Jeanne Lopiparo (2003, 2006) and Julia Hendon's (see chapter 3, this volume) research in the Ulúa Valley, Honduras, provides an example of decentralized figurine mold production during the Terminal Classic period. Lopiparo and Hendon document a diversity of figurine imagery between households, particularly in headdress styles, and argue that figurines were not produced en masse. Rather, production and use held particular significance as reproducing household social identities.

Nonetheless, a great deal of homogeneity in figurine imagery does occur across the Maya area during the Late Classic period. This homogeneity includes ruler figurine types, many of which have the same detailed headdresses (such as the War Serpent type). In addition, the widespread distribution of this imagery within a polity as we see at Motul de San José may indicate that state ideologies penetrated into the homes of commoners and relatively more provincial populations. Following Adorno's argument, I suggest that the omnipresence of these ruler figurines may indicate that states used figurines to strengthen or naturalize their authority and help socialize the populace in shaping and accepting their social roles and obligations. Thus, no longer were symbols of rulership restricted to the actual living rulers who inhabited the site's urban centers and to commemorations of their rule found in stelae, towering architectural programs, and other monumental displays. Instead, these images were readily accessible to all realms of the populace, including children (Halperin 2007; Lopiparo 2006; Ruscheinsky 2003). The mass consumption of certain figurine types was undoubtedly facilitated by mechanical reproduction, which enabled craftspeople to easily produce a single image many times over.

If we return to the contradiction outlined by Frankfurt School scholars, Benjamin's point was that mechanical reproduction alters the populace's perception of the object's meaning. In the Maya area and beyond, the media of molded figurines may have allowed for subversive or alternative interpretations and perceptions than could be taken from monuments and other large-scale media, even if some of the iconography was overlapping. The recovery of Maya figurines in royal, elite, and commoner households throughout the Maya area not only signifies that several different social groups had access to figurines but also points to the performative roles of figurines within the confines of these contexts. These performances likely included the production of music, as most of the molded figurines doubled as ocarinas. The production of meaning through these practices could have manifested on the terms of a household or localized community group. In this sense, the small-scale, mobile nature of ruler figurines could have allowed them to be disentangled from their regal aura and reflected upon in new and perhaps critical ways that were not possible within the confines of ceremonial and administrative proceedings at the heart of polity capitals.

On another level, Mesoamerican figurines did not exclusively depict rulers, warriors, and dignitaries and thus may have provided alternative modes of expression to the values and ideologies of the state. For example, Elizabeth Brumfiel's analysis of figurines from the Postclassic Aztec sites of Huexotla, Xico, and Xaltocan reveals that female figurines did not decline in frequency after the Aztec state gained dominance in these areas. She interpreted the persistence of the female figurines and the fact that they appeared to depict women in positive rather than negative roles as a form of resistance to gender ideologies promulgated by the Aztec state.

For the Maya area, as mentioned earlier, Rosemary Joyce (1993, 2000) and Karl Taube (1989) have argued that some of the figurines may either celebrate values and roles of common peoples, such as laboring women, or ridicule state officials in the form of trickster and clowning figures. At Motul de San José, both tricksters (for example, dwarves, grotesques, and clowns) and laboring women figurines have been recovered. Thus, in terms of a politics of representation, figurines challenge the traditional image repertoires of large-scale media. The contexts in which these figurines may have been used, however, are crucial in generating an understanding of how the political implications of the figurines may have manifested. Distribution analysis of figurines of women with bowls or baskets at Motul de San José reveals that they were predominantly found in royal and elite residential contexts. Their relatively lower frequency and distribution indicate that they possessed less exposure among the people they presumably represent. Thus, a closer examination of other women figurines and other alternative modes of expression, their diversity, and their inter- and intraregional contexts are clearly warranted in future analyses.

Conclusion

In sum, the analysis of figurines in terms of mechanical reproduction and mass media bring attention to alternative political discourses than those typically held in the heart of site centers. Previous scholarly attention to figurines has undervalued the roles of these small-scale figural objects in information exchange and conveying cultural and social ideals across community and social boundaries. During the Late Classic period, figurines aided in the dissemination of state symbols and ideologies. Ruler figurines are pervasive throughout the Maya area during the Late Classic period. And in the case of Motul de San José, they are also present in a range of different households throughout the polity. These data suggest that ceramic figurines do not exclusively fall into the realm of isolated household concerns and ritual practices but could have been tied to social and political processes that reinforced centralized authority figures and the roles of the state. Nonetheless, these same figurine qualities (their small scale, their relative ease of manufacture, and their often-widespread dissemination) and their pluralism in representations also point to their potential for culture creation, expression, and the interpretation of meaning outside the realm of the dominant political-religious order. Thus, their potential roles for both making and accepting political statements allowed them to be active at the junctures of competing political strategies and standpoints.

Acknowledgments

This research would not have been possible without the financial assistance from Fulbright IIE, a National Science Foundation Dissertation Improvement Grant (No. 0524955), a Foundation for the Advancement of Mesoamerican Studies, Inc. (FAMSI) Research Grant (No. 05045), a Sigma Xi Grant-in-Aid of Research, and funding from the University of California, Riverside. I am grateful to the Institute of Anthropology and History (IDAEH) for their permission to work at Motul de San José and its satellite sites, as well as to project director Antonia Foias. I thank Jeanette Castellanos, Gerson Martinez Salguero, Crorey Lawton, Guicho Luin, Melanie

Kingsley, Matt Moriarty, Elly Spensley, Erin Thorton, and the Hernandez Gonzalez family for their support and assistance in the field. I would like to thank José Sanchez for allowing me to look at the Tikal collections from the bodega in the Parque Nacional Tikal as well as Tim Pugh and Prudence Rice for allowing me to examine the Ixlu collection. I am also indebted to Wendy Ashmore, Chelsea Blackmore, Kata Faust, Antonia Foias, Joel Palka, Tom Patterson, and Christina Schwenkel for providing advice and commentary on this chapter or its earlier manifestations. All errors are the sole responsibility of the author.

Notes

1. This calculation (13 nonlocal pastes of 82 samples) excludes 22 INAA samples that are identified as "unknown" and currently do not fall under either the inferred local or nonlocal paste groups. Their status as unknown may change with the inclusion of greater sample sizes. INAA analysis was conducted by Ronald Bishop, M. James Blackman, and Erin Sears at the Department of Anthropology, National Museum of Natural History, Smithsonian Institution, Washington, D.C.

2. These figurines were produced with a one-sided press mold. Simple, iconography-free backs and bases of the figurines were modeled onto the molded front, creating a hollow center. This manufacturing type is called Type 1 in the Motul de San José classification system (Halperin 2007), and all of the figurines produced in this way appear to have functioned as ocarinas with the mouthpiece and airholes on the modeled back. Some have minor appliqué elements on the headdress, as ornamentation, or as an appendage or appendages.

3. These include Type 3 and 4 figurines in the Motul de San José classification system (Halperin 2007).

References Cited

Adorno, Theodor W. [1967] 1991. *Culture Industry: Selected Essays on Mass Culture.* 2nd ed. Routledge, London. (1st ed. pub. 1967.)

Adorno, Theodor W., and Max Horkheimer. [1944] 1972. *Dialectic of Enlightenment.* Reprint, Seabury, New York.

Allen, Lawrence P. 1980. Intra-urban Exchange at Teotihuacan: Evidence from Mold-Made Figurines. In *Models and Methods in Regional Exchange,* ed. R. E. Fry, 83–94. SAA Papers 1. Society for American Archaeology, Washington, D.C.

Alvarez, Carlos, and Luis Casasola. 1985. *Las figurillas de Jonuta, Tabasco.* Universidad Nacional Autónoma de México, Mexico City.

Arnold, Dean E. 1985. *Ceramic Theory and Cultural Process.* New Studies in Archaeology. Cambridge University Press, Cambridge.

———. 1999. Advantages and Disadvantages of Vertical-Half Molding Technology: Implications for Production Organization. In *Pottery and People: A Dynamic Interaction*, ed. J. M. Skibo and G. M. Feinman, 81–98. University of Utah Press, Salt Lake City.

Ashmore, Wendy. n.d. Appendix: Quiriguá Artifacts in the Middle American Research Institute. In *Quiriguá Reports*, vol. 5, *Artifacts and Conclusions*. Museum Monographs. University of Pennsylvania Museum, Philadelphia.

Barbour, Warren D. T. 1975. *The Figurines and Figurine Chronology of Ancient Teotihuacán, Mexico*. Ph.D. diss., Department of Anthropology, University of Rochester, Rochester, N.Y.

Becquelin, Pierre, and Claude-Francois Baudez. 1982. *Tonina, une cité Maya du Chiapas*, vol. 3. Editions Recherche sur les Civilisations, Paris.

Benjamin, Walter. [1936] 1969. The Work of Art in the Age of Mechanical Reproduction. In *Illuminations*, by W. Benjamin, 217–51. Schocken, New York.

Borhegyi, Stephen F. 1956. The Development of Folk and Complex Cultures in the Southern Maya Area. *American Antiquity* 21 (4): 343–56.

Bowser, Brenda J. 2000. From Pottery to Politics: An Ethnoarchaeological Study of Political Factionalism, Ethnicity, and Domestic Pottery Style in the Ecuadorian Amazon. *Journal of Archaeological Method and Theory* 7 (3): 219–48.

Brumfiel, Elizabeth M. 1996. Figurines and the Aztec State: Testing the Effectiveness of Ideological Domination. In *Gender and Archaeology*, ed. R. P. Wright, 143–66. University of Pennsylvania Press, Philadelphia.

Butler, Mary. 1935. A Study of Maya Mould-Made Figurines. *American Anthropologist* 37: 636–72.

Causey, Charles Andrew. 1985. Manufacturing Methods of Molded Figurines from Mesoamerica. Master's thesis, Department of Anthropology, University of Texas, Austin.

Chase, Diane Z. 1985. Between Earth and Sky: Idols, Images, and Postclassic Cosmology. In *Fifth Palenque Round Table, 1983*, ed. M. G. Robertson and V. M. Fields, 223–33. Pre-Columbian Art Research Institute, San Francisco.

Coe, William R., Edwin M. Shook, and Linton Satterthwaite. 1961. The Carved Wooden Lintels of Tikal. In *Tikal Reports Numbers 5–10*, 15–112. University Museum, University of Pennsylvania, Philadelphia.

Cohodas, Marvin. 1994. Rulers Are Made to Be Broken: Non-normative Imagery on Late Classic Maya Stela Sculpture. In *Seventh Palenque Round Table, 1989*, ed. M. G. Robertson and V. M. Fields, 157–67. Pre-Columbian Art Research Institute, San Francisco.

———. 2002. Multiplicity and Discourse in Maya Gender Relations. In *Ancient Maya Gender Identity and Relations*, ed. L. S. Gustafson and A. M. Trevelyan, 11–54. Bergin and Garvey, Westport, Conn.

Corson, Christopher. 1976. *Maya Anthropomorphic Figurines from Jaina Island, Campeche*. Ballena Press Studies in Mesoamerican Art, Archaeology and Ethnohistory 1. Ballena Press, Ramona, Calif.

Ekholm, Susanna M. 1979. The Lagartero Figurines. In *Maya Archaeology and Eth-*

nohistory, ed. N. Hammond and G. R. Willey, 172–86. University of Texas Press, Austin.

Flores Jiménez, María de los Angeles. 2000. Las figurillas antropomorfas de Palenque. *Arqueología Mexicana* 8 (45): 44–49.

———. 2002. La organización social de los Mayas palencanos a través de las figurillas. In *La organización social entre los Mayas prehispánicos, coloniales, y modernos*, ed. V. T. Blos, R. Cobos, and M. G. Robertson, 427–39. Instituto Nacional de Antropología e Historia, Mexico City.

Foias, Antonia E. 2000. History, Politics and Economics at Motul de San José. Paper presented at the Maya Hieroglyphic Meetings at Texas, Austin.

———. 2003. Perspectivas teóricas en las dinámicas del estado Clásico Maya: Resultados preliminares del Proyecto Eco-arqueológico Motul de San José. *Mayab* 16: 15–32.

Gallegos Gómora, Miriam Judith. 2003. Mujeres y hombres de barro: Figurillas de Comalcalco. *Arqueología Mexicana* 11 (61): 48–51.

Goldsmith, Kim Cynthia. 2000. Forgotten Images: A Study of the Ceramic Figurines from Teotihuacan, Mexico. Ph.D. diss., Department of Anthropology, University of California, Riverside.

Goldstein, Marilyn M. 1979. Maya Figurines from Campeche, Mexico: Classification on the Basis of Clay Chemistry, Style and Iconography. Ph.D. diss., Department of Anthropology, Columbia University, New York.

———. 1980. Relationships between the Figurines of Jaina and Palenque. In *The Third Palenque Round Table, 1978, Part 2*, ed. M. G. Robertson, 91–98. University of Texas Press, Austin.

———. 1994. Late Classic Maya-Veracruz Figurines: A Consideration of the Significance of Some Traits Rejected in the Cultural Exchange. In *Seventh Palenque Round Table, 1989*, ed. M. G. Robertson and V. M. Fields, 169–75. University of Texas Press, Austin.

Gossen, Gary H., and Richard M. Leventhal. 1993. The Topography of Ancient Maya Religious Pluralism: A Dialogue with the Present. In *Lowland Maya Civilization in the Eighth Century A.D.*, ed. J. A. Sabloff and J. S. Henderson, 185–218. Dumbarton Oaks, Washington, D.C.

Hall, Stuart. 1993. Encoding, Decoding. In *The Cultural Studies Reader*, ed. S. During, 507–17. Routledge, New York.

Halperin, Christina T. 2004. Realeza maya y figurillas con tocados de la Serpiente de Guerra de Motul de San José, Guatemala. *Mayab* 17: 45–60.

———. 2007. Materiality, Bodies, and Practice: The Political Economy of Late Classic Figurines from Motul de San José, Petén, Guatemala. Ph.D. diss., Department of Anthropology, University of California, Riverside.

Hermes, Bernard. 2000. Ofrendas. In *El Sitio Maya de Topoxte: Investigaciones en una isla del lago Yaxhá, Petén, Guatemala*, ed. W. W. Wurster, 77–91. Philipp Von Zabern, Mainz Am Rhein, Germany.

Horkheimer, Max. 1972. *Critical Theory: Selected Essays.* Trans. M. J. O'Connell. Herder and Herder, New York.

Houston, Stephen, David Stuart, and Karl Taube. 2006. *The Memory of Bones: Body, Being, and Experience among the Classic Maya*. University of Texas, Austin.

Inomata, Takeshi. 2001. The Power and Ideology of Artistic Creation. *Current Anthropology* 42 (3): 321–48.

Ivic de Monterroso, Matilde. 1999. Las Figurillas de Piedras Negras: Un análisis preliminar. In *Proyecto Arqueológico Piedras Negras: Informe preliminar no. 3, tercera temporada, 1999*, ed. H. L. Escobedo and S. Houston, 359–73. Report submitted to the Instituto de Antropología e Historia, Guatemala City.

Josserand, J. Kathryn. 2002. Women in Classic Maya Hieroglyphic Texts. In *Ancient Maya Women*, ed. T. Ardren, 114–51. AltaMira Press, Walnut Creek, Calif.

Joyce, Rosemary A. 1993. Women's Work: Images of Production and Reproduction in Pre-Hispanic Southern Central America. *Current Anthropology* 34 (3): 255–74.

———. 1996. The Construction of Gender in Classic Maya Monuments. In *Gender in Archaeology*, ed. R. P. Wright, 167–95. University of Pennsylvania Press, Philadelphia.

———. 2000. *Gender and Power in Prehispanic Mesoamerica*. University of Texas Press, Austin.

Joyce, T. A. 1933. The Pottery-Whistle Figurines of Lubaantun. *Journal of the Royal Anthropological Institute of Great Britain and Ireland* 63: xv–xxv.

Kearney, Michael. 1995. The Local and the Global: The Anthropology of Globalization and Transnationalism. *Annual Review of Anthropology* 24: 547–65.

Laporte, Juan Pedro, Mara A. Reyes, and Jorge E. Chocon. 2004. Catálogo de figurillas y silbatos de barro del Atlas Arqueológico de Guatemala. In *Reconocimiento y excavaciones arqueológicas en los municipios de La Libertad y Dolores y Poptun, Peten*, ed. J. P. Laporte and H. Mejía, 295–344. Atlas Arqueológico de Guatemala y Área de Arqueología, Guatemala City.

LeCount, Lisa J. 1996. Pottery and Power: Feasting, Gifting, and Displaying Wealth among Late and Terminal Classic Lowland Maya. Ph.D. diss., Department of Anthropology, University of California, Los Angeles.

Lopiparo, Jeanne Lynn. 2003. Household Ceramic Production and the Crafting of Society in the Terminal Classic Ulúa Valley, Honduras. Ph.D. diss., Department of Anthropology, University of California, Berkeley.

———. 2006. Crafting Children: Materiality, Social Memory, and Reproduction of Terminal Classic House Societies in the Ulúa Valley, Honduras. In *The Social Experience of Childhood in Ancient Mesoamerica*, ed. T. Ardren and S. R. Hutson, 133–68. University Press of Colorado, Boulder.

Marcuse, Herbert. 1964. *One-Dimensional Man: Studies in the Ideology of Advanced Industrial Society*. Beacon Press, Boston.

Martin, Simon, and Nikolai Grube. 2000. *Chronicle of the Maya Kings and Queens: Deciphering the Dynasties of the Ancient Maya*. Thames and Hudson, London.

Martínez López, Cira, and Marcus Winter. 1994. *Figurillas y silbatos de ceramica de Monte Alban*. Contribución No. 5 del Proyecto Especial Monte Albán, 1991–1994. Instituto Nacional de Antropología e Historia, Oaxaca City.

Mathews, Peter. 1980. Notes on the Dynastic Sequence of Bonampak, Part 1. In *Third*

Palenque Round Table, 1978, ed. M. G. Robertson, 60–73. University of Texas Press, Austin.

Mock, Shirley Boteler. 2003. A Macabre Sense of Humor: Dramas of Conflict and War in Mesoamerica. In *Ancient Mesoamerican Warfare,* ed. M. K. Brown and T. W. Stanton, 245–61. AltaMira Press, Walnut Creek, Calif.

Moholy-Nagy, Hattula. 2003. Beyond the Catalog: The Chronology and Contexts of Tikal Artifacts. In *Tikal: Dynasties, Foreigners, and Affairs of State,* ed. J. A. Sabloff, 3–110. School of American Research Advanced Seminar Series. Santa Fe, N.Mex.

Munera Bermundez, Luis Carlos. 1985. *Un taller de cerámica ritual en la Ciudadela Teotihuacan.* Tesis de licenciado, Escuela Nacional de Antropología e Historia, Mexico City.

Olson, Jan. 2007. A Socioeconomic Interpretation of Figurine Assemblages from Late Postclassic Morelos, Mexico. In *Commoner Ritual and Ideology in Ancient Mesoamerica,* ed. N. Gonlin and J. C. Lohse, 251–79. University Press of Colorado, Boulder.

Parsons, Mary H. 1972. Aztec Figurines from the Teotihuacan Valley, Mexico. In *Miscellaneous Studies in Mexican Prehistory,* ed. M. W. Spence, J. R. Parsons, and M. H. Parsons, 81–117. Anthropological Papers 45. Museum of Anthropology, University of Michigan, Ann Arbor.

Piña Chan, Román. 1968. *Jaina: La casa en el agua.* Instituto Nacional de Antropología e Historia, Mexico City.

———. 1996. Las figurillas de Jaina. *Arqueología Mexicana* 3 (18): 52–59.

Rands, Robert L. 1965. Classic and Postclassic Pottery Figurines of the Guatemalan Highlands. In *Handbook of Middle American Indians,* vol. 2, ed. G. R. Willey, 535–60. University of Texas Press, Austin.

Rands, Robert L., and Barbara C. Rands. 1965. Pottery Figurines of the Maya Lowlands. In *The Handbook of Middle American Indians,* ed. R. Wauchope, 535–60. Middle American Research Institute, Tulane University, New Orleans.

Reents-Budet, Dorie, ed. 1994. *Painting the Maya Universe: Royal Ceramics of the Classic Period.* Duke University Press, Durham, N.C.

———. 1998. Elite Maya Pottery and Artisans as Social Indicators. In *Craft and Social Identity,* ed. C. L. Costin and R. P. Wright, 71–89. Archaeological Papers of the American Anthropological Association. Washington, D.C.

Reina, Ruben E., and Robert M. Hill. 1978. *The Traditional Pottery of Guatemala.* University of Texas Press, Austin.

Rice, Prudence M. 1996. Postclassic Censers around Lake Peten Itza, Guatemala. In *Arqueología Mesoamericana: Homenaje a William T. Sanders II,* ed. A. G. Mastache, J. R. Parsons, R. S. Santley, and M. C. S. Puche, 23–135. Instituto Nacional de Antropología e Historia, Mexico City.

———. 1999. Rethinking Classic Lowland Maya Pottery Censers. *Ancient Mesoamerica* 10: 25–50.

Ridless, Robin. 1984. *Ideology and Art: Theories of Mass Culture from Walter Benjamin to Umberto Eco.* Peter Lang, New York.

Ruscheinsky, Lynn Marie. 2003. The Social Reproduction of Gender Identity through the Production and Reception of Lowland Maya Figurines. Ph.D. diss. Department of Art History, University of British Columbia, Vancouver.

Schele, Linda. 1997. *Hidden Faces of the Maya.* ALTI Publishing, San Diego.

Schlosser, Ann L. 1978. Ceramic Maya Lowland Figurine Development with Special Reference to Piedras Negras, Guatemala. Ph.D. diss., Department of Anthropology, Southern Illinois University, Carbondale.

Sears, Erin L. 2007. Along the Rivers and through the Woods: Cancuén's Figural Contacts. Paper presented at the 2nd Annual Braunstein Symposium, University of Nevada, Las Vegas.

Sears, Erin L., Ronald L. Bishop, and M. James Blackman. 2004. Las figurillas de Cancuen: El surgimiento de una perspectiva regional. Paper presented at the XVIII Simposio de Investigaciones Arqueológicas en Guatemala, Guatemala City.

Séjourné, Laurette. 1966. *El lenguaje de las formas en Teotihuacan.* Siglo XXI, Mexico City.

Smith, A. Ledyard. 1971. *The Pottery of Mayapan: Including Studies of Ceramic Material from Uxmal, Kabah, and Chichen Itza 66.* Papers of the Peabody Museum of Archaeology and Ethnology. Harvard University, Cambridge, Mass.

Smith, Michael E. 2002. Domestic Ritual at Aztec Provincial Sites in Morelos. In *Domestic Ritual in Ancient Mesoamerica,* ed. P. Plunket, 93–114. Costen Institute of Archaeology, Los Angeles.

Stuart, David, and Ian Graham. 2003. *Corpus of Maya Hieroglyphic Inscriptions,* vol. 9, part 1, *Piedras Negras.* Peabody Museum of Archaeology and Ethnology, Harvard University, Cambridge, Mass.

Taube, Karl A. 1989. Ritual Humor in Classic Maya Religion. In *Word and Image in Maya Culture: Explorations in Language, Writing and Representation,* ed. W. F. Hanks and D. S. Rice, 351–82. University of Utah Press, Salt Lake City.

———. 1992. The Temple of Quetzalcoatl and the Cult of the Sacred War at Teotihuacan. *RES* 21: 53–87.

———. 2000. The Turquoise Hearth: Fire, Self Sacrifice, and the Central Mexican Cult of War. In *Mesoamerica's Classic Heritage: From Teotihuacan to the Aztecs,* ed. D. Carrasco, L. Jones, and S. Sessions, 269–340. University Press of Colorado, Boulder.

Taube, Rhonda. 2006. The Figurines of Piedras Negras: An Iconographic Analysis. Paper presented at the 71st Annual Meeting of the Society for American Archaeology, San Juan, P.R.

Thompson, J. Eric S. 1957. *Deities Portrayed on Censers at Mayapan.* Current Reports 40. Carnegie Institution of Washington, Washington, D.C.

Tomlinson, John. 1991. *Cultural Imperialism: A Critical Introduction.* John Hopkins University Press, Baltimore, Md.

Torres Quintero, Sergio, and Catalina Rodríguez Lazcano. 1996. *La alfarería maya de Tierras Bajas.* Instituto Nacional de Antropología e Historia, Mexico City.

Triadan, Daniela. 2007. Warriors, Nobles, Commoners and Beasts: Figurines from Elite Buildings at Aguateca, Guatemala. *Latin American Antiquity* 18 (3): 269–93.

Valdés, Juan Antonio, Mónica Urquizú, Horacio Martínez Paiz, and Carolina Díaz-

Samayoa. 2001. Lo que expresan las figurillas de Aguateca acerca del hombre y los animales. In *XIV Simposio de Investigaciones Arqueologicas en Guatemala, 2000*, ed. J. P. Laporte, A. C. d. Suasnávar, and B. Arroyo, 761–86. Museo Nacional de Arqueología y Etnologia, Guatemala City.

von Winning, Hasso. 1987. *La iconografía de Teotihuacan: Los dioses y los signos*. Universidad Nacional Autónoma de México, Mexico City.

Walker, John A. 1994. *Art in the Age of Mass Media*. Westview Press, Boulder, Colo.

Wears, Priscilla. 1977. A Typological Study of Some Mayan Figurines from Lubaantun, Belize. Master's thesis, University of Bradford, Bradford, U.K.

Willey, Gordon R. 1972. *The Artifacts of Altar de Sacrificios*. Papers of the Peabody Museum of Archaeology and Ethnology 64. Harvard University, Cambridge, Mass.

———. 1978. Artifacts. In *Excavations at Seibal, Department of Peten, Guatemala*, ed. G. R. Willey, 1–189. Peabody Museum of Archaeology and Ethnology, Harvard University, Cambridge, Mass.

Part VI

Discussion

14

Making a World of Their Own

Mesoamerican Figurines
and Mesoamerican Figurine Analysis

ROSEMARY A. JOYCE

The chapters included in this volume raise three interlocking questions. First, is there a viable project we could call Mesoamerican figurine studies? If so, what are its necessary components, and do we each need to supply all of them, or can this be made a corporate project? Finally, if we can have a common project called "Mesoamerican figurine studies," can it encompass the variability seen in different approaches and even allow for contradiction? The answers emerging should be of interest to art historians and archaeologists working in other areas of the world and to scholars in Mesoamerican studies whose work deals with other materials. To achieve the goal of engaging these broader audiences, scholars working in this area need to think carefully about what their subject of study should be and how differences in interpretation will be handled. I develop below an argument for contextual analyses of the life histories of miniaturized representational objects that takes into account the different media, scale, representational content, and forms of semiosis that are merged under the heading "Mesoamerican figurines." Paradoxically, one of the end products of such an analysis will inevitably be the fragmentation of figurine studies and the recognition of extensive connections between these objects and other products of diverse practices that will invite future analysts to group them in very different ways, blurring the boundaries that might otherwise be defined. It is thus worthwhile to begin by considering whether, in fact, there is a subject of study that can easily be labeled "Mesoamerican figurines."

Figural Materialities

To answer this first question, we need to define our subject, which turns out to be complicated. First of all, we know but too often skip over the fact that small-scale iconic images can be made from materials other than fired clay, the material medium so common that unqualified references to "figurines" inherently imply "ceramic." The fact that there are abundant ceramic figurines but relatively few figurines in other media that have survived from pre-Hispanic societies in Central America needs to be taken into critical consideration. Have we lost an equally abundant body of works in shell, bone, wood, resin, paper, basketry, cloth, and other materials, such as the dough images described for the sixteenth-century Mexica? Or were figurines originally, and normally, products of ceramic workshops, imitated in smaller numbers in other media at specific historic times and places? The one study included in this volume that addresses this question directly, Cecelia Klein and Naoli Victoria Lona's (chapter 12) discussion of copal resin figurines recovered from the Mexica Templo Mayor, demonstrates a historical sequence in which ceramic figurines precede and prefigure the rarer analogues.

The cut-paper images made ethnographically, studied by Alan Sandstrom (chapter 10), provide a tantalizing hint of the potential importance of images in other perishable media. Sandstrom emphasizes the active processes of cutting paper as forms of ritual action rather than acts of symbolic representation. The cut-paper figures produced do not represent the corn spirit in a literal fashion; instead, they are a material site for the spirit to come to rest. Although the Nahua people Sandstrom worked with use paper for these images, he notes the use by other Nahua people of ears of corn for the same purpose. Paper is not simply a substitute for ears of corn, which might be thought to be inherently related to corn spirits. The paper cut by the ritual specialists with whom he worked could also be a vehicle for other seed spirits. Nor was the use of perishable materials limited to paper. Marigolds and bamboo were used as other materials for the creation of effigies of the body of the corn spirit or its hands.

Klein and Victoria Lona (chapter 12) brilliantly illustrate how consideration of alternative figural materialities, such as copal resin, can illuminate the contribution of specific materials to the meaning and use of figurines. They explore the social and ritual values of copal, whose medicinal properties may have been substantively appropriate for the particular figurines deposited at the Templo Mayor. Their discussion raises the question of whether the materials Sandstrom documents as used for contemporary Nahua seed spirits—all derived from vegetal sources—might matter as much as the anthropomorphic form they mimic. In a broader framework, we might consider whether copal figures were appropriate for curing, plant-fiber figurines for rituals of the fields, and still other materials for different purposes.

We thus probably need to ask not simply why copal or why paper but why fired clay? The quantitative abundance of fired clay figurines has led us to submerge the material in the definition of the class of object, but we need to ask why this material, rather than any other, was employed so often. In their discussion of "mud-men" figurines at Late Postclassic Xaltocan, Elizabeth Brumfiel and Lisa Overholtzer (chapter 11) note that these fired clay figurines are manufactured so as to foreground the materiality of clay itself.

Two characteristics of clay are generally considered central to understanding the adoption of ceramic technologies: plasticity, and the ability of clay to be irreversibly altered and fixed in shape through firing. Thus, in discussions of the earliest known fired clay figurines in the world, from the central European site of Dolní Věstonice, the performative dimension of firing the hand-modeled images of animals and humans (including a fair proportion that likely exploded during firing) is understood to have been a kind of material instantiation of transformation that was probably of ritual significance (Soffer et al. 1993; Vandiver et al. 1989, 1990). It is worth considering the ways in which the use of clay for figurines in Mesoamerica may have differentially exploited these (and perhaps other) material properties.

When we consider the earliest evidence of figurines from Mesoamerica, we routinely cite a single fired clay figurine from Zohapilco, in the Basin of Mexico, that Christine Niederberger (1976, 1987, 2000) recovered near a Late Archaic hearth dated 2300 ± 100 b.c. (cited as calibrated 2920 BC). A considerable temporal gap follows this single figurine; the next evidence of figural representation in this area is dated to the Early Formative Nevada phase (1400–1250 BC). By this time, fired clay was in widespread, if not universal, use from Mexico to Honduras and El Salvador, for vessels and figurines alike. The question is, can we interpret the Late Archaic Zohapilco figurine as a precocious experiment with deliberately firing clay? Or should we at least consider the possibility that the people who shaped this early figural image exploited the plasticity of wet clay but were not concerned with using fire to permanently and irreversibly fix the shape that they achieved?

There are Archaic period precedents in northern Mexico for traditions of production of unfired clay figural images contemporary with the Zohapilco figurine. In the lower Pecos River region on the Texas-Mexico border, Harry Shafer (1975) described unfired clay figurines in Archaic caves and rock shelters. Two examples were fired—Shafer suggests that this most likely occurred accidentally. Like the Zohapilco figurine, the lower Pecos figurines represent very simple schematic anthropomorphic forms. Some have no indication of a head, and most have no facial features; the most complete head is represented by a long ridge of clay for a nose, punctate eyes, and a small hole below the nose. Shafer (1975: 150) states that normally the torso is the focus of elaboration on these figurines, with some having applied conical "breasts" and linear painted patterns. An associated ^{14}C date at one of the sites yielding these figurines was 1460 ± 160 b.c. The associated lithics suggest a maximal range of 2000–1200 BC for these lower Pecos Archaic figurines. The contexts of examples recovered in excavation include occupation midden as well as cache deposits interpreted as evidence of ritual (Shafer 1975: 152). Related designs were painted on pebbles found in the same sites and contexts (Shafer 1975: 150; Turpin 1990: 266).

These clay figurines, and the painted pebbles that may have been equivalents to them, are a material culture specific to caves and rockshelters in the Archaic Pecos region. This contextual association suggests that we should connect the figurines to specific rituals thought to have been practiced in these sites. Drawing on analysis of plant remains in caves of the Pecos River culture, Carolyn Boyd and J. Philip Dering (1996) suggest that the Pecos River–style rock paintings, Accelerator Mass Spectrometry (AMS) dated to circa 2250–1000 BC (Boyd 1996), depict visionary rituals involving the use of hallucinogenic plants (datura, peyote, and mescal). Anthropomorphic imagery linked the walls of the caves, individual pebbles, and unfired clay objects that analysts identify today as figurines.

If we take this tradition, contemporary with Late Archaic Zohapilco, as a model, then we might consider the possibility that the one figurine recovered in the Basin of Mexico was fired by chance and that other related unfired clay figurines have been lost to us (Joyce 2007). Early figurines made of unfired clay may have mattered first and foremost as objects created of one of the most malleable materials available, similar in this way to the much later copal resin figurines discussed by Klein and Victoria Lona. Unlike later fired clay figurines, unfired clay examples could have been dissolved in water, reformed, or remade. The permanency that firing clay granted to later Formative figurines changed the material register of these things: later ceramic figurines have a stable form that can only be changed by breakage. In this, they have more in common with the monumental stone images whose creation was likewise initiated during the Formative period than with the first modeled clay figurine preserved for us at Zohapilco.

Miniaturization

We might accordingly want to consider figurines not as normatively fired clay artifacts but as a class of things that have recognizable similarities while being heterogeneous in their material properties. Perhaps we should define figurines as characteristically small in scale—that is, miniatures—independent of material. In his studies of figurines, Douglass Bailey (2005) has usefully documented the effects of miniaturization on human experience and cognition. Bailey (2005: 26–35) makes an initial distinction between miniatures and models: models, in his use of the term, strive for reproduction at a smaller scale of a larger prototype, whereas miniatures are neither complete nor accurate. Through their incompletion, they forcibly engage people manipulating or viewing them in making inferences that go beyond what is literally present. The figurines that archaeologists deal with are in Bailey's terms miniatures, not models: always leaving out some details as others are selected for representation.

Miniaturization goes beyond this general effect, which in some degree is part of all representation. Citing psychological experiments, Bailey (2005) describes how miniaturization changes the perception of the passage of time experienced by people manipulating miniatures. The kinds of multi-figure scenes described by Joyce Marcus (chapter 2) reproduce some of the features of these modern experiments. Such scenes raise the possibility that the early Mesoamerican people who composed and recomposed them were engaged in practices that effectively changed their experience of space and time. The boxes that Sandstrom (chapter 10) describes, composed by modern Nahua ritual specialists to contain cut-paper seed spirits and furnished with miniatures of everyday objects, create analogous miniature worlds. Miniatures might be thought of as media of an altered state of consciousness, one in which everyday temporality is shifted.

Taking miniaturization as a defining feature, the significant differences in scale among Mesoamerican figurines from region to region, and even within regions, become issues worthy of consideration. Formative figurines, discussed in this volume by Billie Follensbee (chapter 4), David Cheetham (chapter 6), and Jeffrey Blomster (chapter 5), are among the best materials to permit a consideration of how relative scale works as a dimension of variation in the same time and place. Blomster, discussing the diversity of figurines from Oaxaca, calls attention to the larger size of the hollow figurines with white slip that he identifies as iconographically linked to Gulf Coast Olmec sites. Proposing their use in ritual by specialists, he also suggests that rituals using them may have engaged more participants.

While his central argument is that the smaller solid figurines in styles with local antecedents represent an ethnic identity distinct from the foreign one of the larger, hollow figurine, in this brief mention of relative scale, Blomster opens a field of very productive inquiry. Follensbee (chapter 4), in her study of figurines from the Gulf Coast site of La Venta, identifies the same division of scale, with a small group of larger hollow figurines and a majority of solid figurines of smaller size. Here, in the heartland of the Gulf Coast Olmec, there can be no question of the contrast in scale being primarily a contrast between a local Olmec ethnicity and an intrusive foreign Olmec identity. Follensbee in fact identifies the visual representations at both scales as conforming to the same set of representational features. The smaller figurines are ubiquitous, and Follensbee argues for their use in household-based rituals, including curing ceremonies. The context of the larger figurines from La Venta is unfortunately unknown.

David Cheetham (chapter 6) compares figurines from Cantón Corralito on the Pacific coast of Chiapas to figurines from San Lorenzo on the Gulf Coast. He describes both sites as having figurines in a single Olmec style. In detailed records, he notes that the size and body proportions in both samples are consistent to within mere millimeters. This leads him to suggest that the makers of the Cantón Corralito figurines shared a technical style with the makers of San Lorenzo's figurines, the result of shared learning. Hollow figurines, rare at both sites, are twice the size of the smaller solid figurines that predominate. As at the other sites discussed, the archaeological associations of all the figurines, regardless of scale, were with household contexts, where they were primarily recovered broken and discarded.

In my own work on Honduran Formative figurines, I have noted the same pattern of a small number of hollow figurines (and in this case, figural vessels) that are substantially larger than the more numerous solid figurines in the Playa de los Muertos style (Joyce 2003, 2008). The smaller Playa de los Muertos figurines include a minority that are even smaller. In early assemblages of mixed sizes, dating between 900 and 400 BC, the smallest figurine size range includes all examples of animal subjects. Many of both the human and animal subjects are pierced through the neck, allowing them to be suspended. In the latest assemblages, very small figurines come to predominate. By this time, after 200 BC, there is little or no evidence of their suspension.

The varying scales represented in these Honduran samples led me to consider how their relative scale would have affected the ways that people in the communities where they were made and used engaged with them. Blomster's data from Oaxaca indicate that in at least one case, a larger figurine was part of the refuse from a wealthier household. The same cannot, unfortunately, be said about the larger figurines in the other cases. But what can be said of all these sites is that both larger and smaller (and in the Honduran sites, even smaller) figurines were used and disposed of in household settings within villages.

Through detailed contextual analyses, I have suggested that the residues of feasts following specific ceremonies in the life cycle of villagers formed at least some of the sites of disposal of figurines in Formative Honduras (Joyce et al. forthcoming). In gatherings to commemorate death and burial or to celebrate transitions to adulthood, birth, or other marked points during life, different groups and likely different numbers of people would have been involved. Figurines at a variety of scales established different spatial contexts of potential engagement. The very small figurines that were suspended, perhaps around the neck of individual adults or children, would have been visually available only to those close to the person holding or wearing them. The somewhat larger solid figurines that are the dominant size range in Honduras, as they are in other Formative sites, would have been more easily visible for a group of people, but details would not have been evident from any great distance. Even the least distinguished of solid Formative figurines have specific traits, bodily postures, gestures, indications of jewelry and clothing, hairstyle, and facial features. These figurines would have required an intimacy of contact for their greater legibility.

Larger Formative figurines (and the even larger stone sculptures to which they should be linked, as Follensbee has done in her discussion) differ most radically in this regard from the smaller-scale figurines they resemble in representational details. They potentially would have supported viewing by larger groups of people at greater distances without loss of access to the details that make each of these hand-modeled objects unique. Miniaturization absorbs people into a smaller world. Scaling up expands the scope of that separate dimension of experience.

A provocative analogue to these differences in scale is provided by the carved balsa-wood curing figures of the San Blas Kuna, famously an inspiration for Michael Taussig's exploration of the human urge to mimic others in bodily form (Taussig 1993). The curers who use these images identify with the "vegetal spirit" of the balsa tree that is an effective agent in curing, thereby purging their patients of the animal spirits understood as agents of illness (Severi 2002: 35–36; see also Sherzer 1983). When used for individual healing, the Kuna figure, a container for spirits invoked in chants, is scaled about the same size as the larger hollow Formative figurines of Mesoamerica. When a ceremony is carried out not for an individual but for the benefit of the village as a whole, the figures carved are much larger, still less than life-size but easily visible for the wider group of people involved in these more extensive ceremonies. Klein and Victoria Lona's discussion of the copal figurines from the Templo Mayor (chapter 12) notes a similar relationship in scale: a larger size range for the figurines deposited in this site of state ceremony, compared to the smaller size that is normal for fired clay figurines typical of residential sites. Relative scale may be one way to reinstate some sense of the social and experiential scale of the events in which figurines were present and in action.

Subject Matter

Once we include relative scale as a dimension of variation among figurines, we cannot easily separate certain smaller three-dimensional objects from the continuous range of things extending to include life-size or near-life-size figures in a wide range of materials. Many contributors have found it imperative to relate the subject matter of smaller figurines to that of larger-scale anthropomorphic sculpture. Forms represented at smaller scales may be unique, excluded from the monumental record, as in the parodic figurines described by Rhonda Taube and Karl Taube (chapter 9). Alternatively, figurines may overlap with representations executed at a larger scale and in other media. Any understanding of figurines inevitably will involve links to larger subjects.

Perhaps, then, figurines are better defined as simply an alternative representational medium. The discussions by Katherine Faust (chapter 8), Klein and Victoria Lona (chapter 12), and Christina Halperin (chapter 13) linking figurines to stone sculpture would be models of this approach, taking representational features in different media and at different scales as material for a unified discussion that links figurines to many other products of human action. The tension here arises from attempting not to lose the specificity of the materialities used, and the scales that distinguish figurines from larger sculptures, while engaging in an analysis that extends outward from the small to the large. Granted that some figurines and sculptures in other media at other scales share visual attributes that allow them to be identified as figurations of the same images, there still remains a core of difference introduced by their specific materials and their smaller scale. Faust (chapter 8) dwells on the way in which the relatively restricted surface area provided by the small figurines from the Huasteca results in the elimination of patterning that is found on larger-scale stone sculpture from the same area. She argues that this is an example of what Bailey (2005) calls "compression" achieved by miniaturization. An implication of her analysis is that a different level of attention is invoked by the smaller-scale figurines; as a result, different understandings were facilitated by them. While much of her discussion concerns detailed explication of the rich iconography of these figurines, the most generalizable aspect of her study is this demonstration of the way in which these figurines made meaning.

To pursue the broader question of meaning-making, we might follow the suggestion made by Jeanne Lopiparo and Julia Hendon in chapter 3 and think of figurines not just as objects made of particular materials, at particular physical scales, representing particular topics, but as active and biographically distinctive material subjects that formed part of the networks of relations among human and other nonhumans in the past. From this perspective, the things we examine in the present day are the materializations of histories of practices. As the "object-fication" of practices, the ways these things were made, used, and disposed of, by whom, how often, and with what histories of production and use, matter.

Lopiparo and Hendon (chapter 3) argue for a relational approach to the engagements of human beings with figurines. Such an approach requires the kind of excellent contextual information that is one of the major strengths of contemporary Mesoamerican figurine studies. Lopiparo and Hendon draw on diverse lines of evidence—including identification of firing facilities, use of molds, compositional studies, and iconographic analyses—to document the production of figurines on a household scale and their distribution, largely within individual villages. This biographical approach requires Lopiparo and Hendon to attend to differences in the relative frequencies of figurines and other materials, such as ceramic serving vessels, in sites of different sizes and degrees of stratification. The biographical approach they employ also foregrounds the importance of fragmentary figurines both because these are the products of specific kinds of practices and because the fragmentary figurines facilitated still other practices distinct from those possible with complete objects. Geoffrey McCafferty and Sharisse McCafferty (chapter 7) likewise draw extensively on contextual information to provide object biographies for the Nicaraguan figurines they analyze. Drawing on another well-documented excavated figurine assemblage, they are able to relate the figurines to body practices implied by other forms of artifacts, such as body ornaments, and features, such as burials.

Lopiparo and Hendon use fine-grained excavation data to associate whole artifacts with the beginnings of construction sequences, and fragments with episodes of renewal of such buildings in the Honduran sites they study. The visual imagery of these figurines is closely related to the kinds of contexts in which they were engaged. Figurines that represent apparently naturalistic human beings, with headdresses that vary in frequency from one site to another and may be badges of localized families, were in widespread use in household contexts. They typified the actions of men and women in their poses and gestures. A smaller number of figurines depicted subjects that might be considered associated with cosmology, such as selected animals and an aged human. These images were concentrated in structured deposits that marked episodes of house renewal. The associations noted by Lopiparo and Hendon recall those sketched out for freestanding, flat-backed figurines at Late Postclassic Xaltocan by Brumfiel and Overholtzer (chapter 11).

Lopiparo and Hendon do not ignore representational subject matter, but their analysis takes this as itself informed by the engagements of figurines in action, including the breaking and burial of figurines and fragments. They suggest that the material engagements of people with figurines are primary in the effectiveness of figurines in creating enduring social networks, networks that are partly created by the destruction of the visual integrity of the figurines themselves.

Brumfiel and Overholtzer (chapter 11) likewise trace the biographies of figurines, including the recirculation of parts of figurines from previous societies, as evidence of the way in which figurines work to create social relations, not simply represent them. The pattern of curation described by Brumfiel and Overholtzer is also evident in the figurine collections I am analyzing from the lower Ulúa valley in Honduras. There, figurines made in the Middle Formative period were reused, incorporated in construction of stone platforms built as much as a thousand years later by successor societies (for example, at Travesía; Stone 1941: fig. 68, fig. 74). In the Ulúa Valley, a break in the production of figurines that lasted for several centuries between the Late Formative and Late Classic periods makes the older curated figurines an effective medium for the deliberate construction of links with a deeper past, in the absence of continuities of practice.

Brumfiel and Overholtzer note that the curated figurines at Xaltocan are primarily unusual, striking heads. The curated figurines in the lower Ulúa valley, in contrast, include complete bodies with attached heads, heads, and separate bodies. But the kind of physical and visual engagement that Brumfiel and Overholtzer describe, in which those handling ancient figurines were motivated to contemplate their difference from earlier peoples, is equally relevant. Several chapters in this volume call attention to this property of visual reflexivity inherent in the anthropomorphic subject matter of many figurines. Taube and Taube (chapter 9) emphasize the way that this highly visual medium created an aesthetics of the human form in Maya Classic societies. McCafferty and McCafferty (chapter 7) make the same point for the Nicaraguan figurines they study. Sandstrom (chapter 10), working with ethnographic materials, emphasizes the dual position of anthropomorphic figurines, as modeled on and models for human beings.

Yet not all figurines are anthropomorphic; notable examples from many Mesoamerican traditions depict objects, such as temples, and nonhuman animals are important in many such assemblages. Lopiparo and Hendon (chapter 3), Blomster (chapter 5), Cheetham (chapter 6), Taube and Taube (chapter 9), Brumfiel and Overholtzer (chapter 11), Klein and Victoria Lona (chapter 12), and Halperin (chapter 13) explicitly mention nonhuman animal subjects. Other assemblages are likely to include animal subjects as well. Anthropomorphic figurines are commonly treated separately from zoomorphic ones. If the full range of human and animal subjects could be analyzed together, what (if anything) would change in our understandings of such subjects as political ideology and subjectivity? One hint of the productivity of such an approach is provided by Taube and Taube's identification of animal subjects as a safe representational arena for social commentary in Classic Maya figurines. In Lopiparo and Hendon's work, there are specific hints that animal subjects were different from most human subjects. Animal figurines were found with stylized human images, likely deities, in assemblages used in structured deposits that marked periodic renewal.

Each study must establish independently whether, and how, animal and human subjects were linked or differentiated. That such efforts can be very productive is clear in the pioneering study of figural imagery at Paso de la Amada by Richard Lesure (2000), in which he systematically examines evidence that animals and humans were parts of distinct graphic systems.

The perspectives above help sketch out a field of material phenomena defining a Mesoamerican figurine studies with considerable unity. To pursue its development, we need to operationalize our assumptions and make clearer what might be the significant features at specific times and places of the materialized practices that are figurines. This brings me to answers to my second question: What are the necessary components of figurine studies—and do we all need to do everything?

Elements of Figurine Studies: A First Approximation

I think that there *are* necessary components for figurine studies. For me, these would include engagement with relative scale; consideration of contexts and processes of production; and attention to the consumption and disposal of figurines. The chapters in this volume have all these considerations in play. While ideally we would each be able to encompass all of these in every study, this is not always possible. We can build this field as a cohort, as long as we productively relate individual, contingent contributions to a shared, larger project.

Scale

One component of figurine studies must be explicit identification of scalar ratios of miniaturized images. Ideally, we might consider size with reference to a constant such as the living human body. As anyone knows who has for the first time seen figurines previously encountered only in illustrations, scale is often surprising: figurines may be either smaller or larger than expected.

Such a beginning point allows us to systematically link our smaller subjects to the larger ones with which so many of us assume they are connected. Brumfiel and Overholtzer (chapter 11) describe how figurine features are materially adapted to be experienced by the body that holds and uses them. Figurine scale helps frame such performative experience. From a similar phenomenological perspective, different relations of the maker's body to the produced body would necessarily be a beginning for different experiences both of the figurine and of the person's embodied self. How intimate a viewing experience do different figurines support or require? Nor are the possible questions we can address by considering relative size limited to the use of figurines. Scale (in particular, the bodily measures of scale in production) may also be part of the way in which particular technical styles were produced and reproduced.

Production Processes

As the last observation suggests, a second component of figurine studies must be reflection on production and what factors structured distinct production processes. Compositional work like that reported by Lopiparo and Hendon (chapter 3) is one significant part of the picture, giving us a basis to argue for localized and, in this case, household-based production. But compositional analysis alone is not enough: we have to pursue multiple lines of evidence that allow us to understand whether figurines are made in many distinct workshops, as these authors document for most of the sites they describe, or in one centrally controlled workshop, as is the case at one site in their sample, Cerro Palenque.

Figurine studies have, of course, long used molds as a sign of local production, indeed, of mass production. As examples from both highly centralized and decentralized sites reported here demonstrate, however, we need to resist automatically interpreting reproductive technologies as evidence of mass production. The use of molds in the small scale of production in the lower Ulúa valley, discussed by Lopiparo and Hendon in chapter 3, may better be explained as a technique to allow participation in reproduction of valued images by social group members regardless of skill levels. In the Valley of Oaxaca, Gary Feinman (1999) has also noted the presence in household production contexts of molds that are not easily understood as evidence of mass production.

Even when we emphasize the repeated production of identical products, we may want to rethink which frame of reference we want to use for "mass" production. Halperin (chapter 13), discussing the use of molds in the stratified Maya state center of Motul de San José and in its neighbors, relates this production approach to contemporary studies of mass media and its effects rather than to economic models based in efficiency. She suggests that in this area, the "mechanical reproduction" facilitated by molds allowed a uniform visual culture to move out of the center and into the house compounds. On the basis of her analysis of the imagery of figurines, she sees participation in production as carrying state ideologies into these intimate confines. Klein and Victoria Lona's description of the use of molds for the production of the fewer than one hundred copal figurines recovered at the Templo Mayor (chapter 12) suggests a similar concern, not with efficiencies of scale in mass production but with maintaining visual form. While the social and political scales and degrees of centralization vary, we can trace here a distinctive Mesoamerican concern with the reproduction of imagery, a concern whose social significance may well have varied from the recognition of self and community to the assimilation of state-level ideologies at an intimate scale.

Taking production as a critical part of figurine studies, we have an opportunity to reconstruct technical styles, features of production, and production processes conditioned by intended use. Thus, Brumfiel and Overholtzer (chapter 11) argue that figurines they call "mud men/women" were deliberately produced with features to mark them as ancient or precultural beings. Overholtzer's study of Aztec figurines of kneeling subjects is an example of careful attention to processes of production employed to produce particular effects during the use of figurines, in this case, the slipping and burnishing of figurines intended to be handled (Overholtzer 2005). As these examples all show, production is intimately related to expected use and helps us understand how figurines were employed and discarded.

Contexts of Use and Disposal

So a third necessary component of contemporary figurine studies is contextual analysis of consumption and disposal. The sheer number of figurine fragments in Mesoamerican sites, combined with older methods of excavation, long blocked exploration of what people actually were doing with these things. Thus, we have had to deal with categorical proposals of uses—as dolls, idols, or medical artifacts, for example—based primarily on features of the figurines rather than on their contexts (compare chapter 2). This is changing rapidly. The excellent site-specific data cited by Lopiparo and Hendon (chapter 3), McCafferty and McCafferty (chapter 7), and Halperin (chapter 13) let us see internal distributions that highlight very fine-grained differences both within sites and between sites at a small regional scale.

An obvious tension among advocates of contextual analyses is the relative value of complete or fragmentary objects for our understanding of figurine use. Lopiparo and Hendon (chapter 3) make an explicit argument that breakage and structured deposition of figurines in pieces should be viewed as highly significant. Their argument draws on the influential work of John Chapman (2000), who suggests that the circulation of fragments of wholes was an important process through which social ties were generated and maintained in southeastern Europe. Lopiparo and Hendon argue that the relations created between people, over space and time, through the use and breakage of figurines should be viewed as evidence of the creation of social memory or "hidden" knowledge, as much as the preservation of intact figurines and scenes discussed by Joyce Marcus in chapter 2. Their discussion raises a critical point pertinent to many studies of whole figurines, usually recovered from burials or buried caches. As invisible objects, to what extent were buried, intact figurines effectively different from fragmented ones? Both require active effort for recomposition in memory, in oral tradition, and in practices of curation. In many archaeological settings, as at Xaltocan and in the lower Ulúa Valley, generations-long curation practices are not limited to intact figurines.

If we take Bailey's (2005) arguments for the incomplete nature of figurines as miniatures seriously, then even complete figurines arranged in scenes are incomplete, effectively created as already "broken," requiring effort for their interpretive recomposition. This is a much-needed reminder that figurines, in fragments or complete, singly or in groups, were and thus are open to many different interpretations. Indeed, the debates evident in different chapters about the meanings of the same figurines from Oaxaca (compare chapter 2 and chapter 5) and about visually similar figurines from Gulf Coast Olmec sites (compare chapters 4, 5, and 6) make it clear that even contextually rich analyses of figurines will not necessarily ensure the same conclusions.

Explanatory Variation: Should Mesoamerican Figurines Mean the Same Thing?

This leads me to my third question: can we have a common project that can encompass variability, even contradiction? Many of the authors in this volume have tacked back and forth between their own data and other data sets, noting discontinuities in ways that suggest unease about the contingency of each explanation. What works in one place as a characterization is contradicted by another, equally strong set of data somewhere else.

I think perhaps we should expect precisely such diversity in our understandings of figurines if our analyses actually do capture their original circumstances of manufacture, use, and disposal. If, as these and other studies suggest, figurines—especially the fired clay figurines that are what we normally think of when we hear the word—were products of somewhat decentralized, domestic production, then the intentionalities that are sedimented in them will be as variable as the households within the societies that produced them. In Mesoamerica, even if we sometimes talk as if there were only two relevant social groups, elites and commoners, we actually know there was a range of cross-cutting social segments. These are complex societies, and clay is a highly plastic medium allowing a great deal of variability; we have no reason to assume that the production of fired clay figurines was an occupational specialty controlled by a small number of people, and so we should expect to see malleable products of fluid and active processes of social organization.

What will be problematic in the long run is if we believe that we can test findings in one spatiotemporal context against data from another place and time. Thus, I do not find the more common presence of figurines showing women's work in elite contexts than nonelite contexts at Motul de San José, reported by Halperin (chapter 13), to be problematic for my previously published arguments that figurines showing women working may have been produced in nonroyal households (Joyce 1993). What we presumably have here are differences reflecting localized, historical, segmental differences between social classes and factions in specific communities. It is a singular achievement of contemporary analyses that they are now studies of assemblages from places with unique histories, not just models based on generalizations from wider regions.

Figurines and Representation

Readers who have persisted this long may be wondering why, in my outline of a new figurine studies for Mesoamerica, I have placed little emphasis on the core representational questions about what is being shown. It is not because these are unimportant questions: these concerns are both central to and productive in contemporary figurine studies in Mesoamerica. But I do want to suggest that it is here, in subject matter, that figurine studies is not simply most likely to dissolve into the study of broader representational practices but may actually demand such a broadening, transforming the subject from figurines to visual culture. Taube and Taube's description of figurines as popular culture (chapter 9) and Halperin's use of concepts of "mass media" (chapter 13) are examples of the productivity of seeing figurines as part of a broader visual culture.

From this perspective, what the authors in this volume have done is participate in a fiction, since figurines per se do not form a basis for a coherent interregional study, divorced from other materialities and representational media. But the projects described—reflecting extraordinary new data sets with strong archaeological context, compositional data, and production models—show that this is a useful fiction and foreground what is central to a domain of figurine studies.

The contributors begin to explore how different Mesoamerican agents materialized iconic images that reflected back idealized schema of society and person and thus, as I have argued elsewhere, recursively shaped individual subjectivities and social relations (Joyce 2003). The works presented here amply illustrate that the combination of studies of the experiential interaction between living bodies and manufactured bodies with analyses of production models and depositional patterns that illuminate why specific Mesoamerican images were produced in their times and places can prove especially fruitful. Continuing work with these data sets guarantees the emergence of a new Mesoamerican figurine studies. If the trail laid out in this volume is followed, this will be a richly contextualized field of analysis that interrogates material, scale, production, use, and disposal even as it avoids the arbitrary separation of one set of practices from others.

Acknowledgments

This chapter began as commentary on the 2006 session at the Society for American Archaeology organized by the editors of this volume. It has been informed as well by my participation at the 2006 conference on Mesoamerican figurines at the University of Nevada–Las Vegas, where I presented a revision of a paper originally developed for a conference at the McDonald Institute, Cambridge University, in 2005, on the worldwide origins of human representation. I would like to thank the sponsors of these two conferences for including me in their programs and also thank the other participants in those conferences who are not part of the present volume for the stimulus provided by their work.

References Cited

Bailey, Douglass W. 2005. *Prehistoric Figurines: Representation and Corporeality in the Neolithic*. Routledge, London.

Boyd, Carolyn E. 1996. Shamanic Journeys into the Otherworld of the Archaic Chichimec. *Latin American Antiquity* 7: 152–64.

Boyd, Carolyn E., and J. Philip Dering. 1996. Medicinal and Hallucinogenic Plants Identified in the Sediments and Pictographs of the Lower Pecos, Texas Archaic. *Antiquity* 70: 256–76.

Chapman, John. 2000. *Fragmentation in Archaeology: People, Places and Broken Objects in the Prehistory of South Eastern Europe*. Routledge, London.

Feinman, Gary M. 1999. Rethinking Our Assumptions: Economic Specialization at the Household Scale in Ancient Ejutla, Oaxaca, Mexico. In *Pottery and People*, ed. J. Skibo and G. Feinman, 81–98. University of Utah Press, Salt Lake City.

Joyce, Rosemary A. 1993. Women's Work: Images of Production and Reproduction in Pre-Hispanic Southern Central America. *Current Anthropology* 34: 255–74.

———. 2003. Making Something of Herself: Embodiment in Life and Death at Playa de los Muertos, Honduras. *Cambridge Archaeological Journal* 13: 248–61.

———. 2007. Figurines, Meaning, and Meaning-Making in Early Mesoamerica. In *Material Beginnings: A Global Prehistory of Figurative Representation*, ed. C. Renfrew and I. Morley, 107–16. McDonald Institute for Archaeological Research, Cambridge University, Cambridge.

———. 2008. When the Flesh Is Solid but the Person Is Hollow Inside: Formal Variation in Hand-Modeled Figurines from Formative Mesoamerica. In *Past Bodies*, ed. J. Robb and D. Boric. Oxbow Books, Oxford. Forthcoming.

Joyce, Rosemary A., Julia A. Hendon, and Russell N. Sheptak. Forthcoming. Rethinking Playa de los Muertos: Exploring the Middle Formative Period in Honduras. In *Ideología política y sociedad en el período Formativo*, ed. A. Cyphers Guillen and K. Hirth. Universidad Nacional Autónoma de México, Mexico City.

Lesure, Richard G. 2000. Animal Imagery, Cultural Unities, and Ideologies of Inequality in Early Formative Mesoamerica. In *Olmec Art and Archaeology in Mesoamerica*, ed. J. E. Clark and M. E. Pye, 193–215. Studies in the History of Art 58. Center for Advanced Study in the Visual Arts Symposium Papers 35. National Gallery of Art, Washington, D.C.

Niederberger, Christine. 1976. *Zohapilco: Cinco milenios de ocupacion humana en la Cuenca de Mexico.* Colección Científica, Arqueología 11. Instituto Nacional de Antropología e Historia, Mexico City.

———. 1987. *Paleopaysages et archeologie pre-urbaine du Bassin de Mexico (Mexique).* Etudes Mesoamericaines 11. Centre d'Etudes Mexicaines et Centramericaines, Mexico City.

———. 2000. Ranked Societies, Iconographic Complexity, and Economic Wealth in the Basin of Mexico toward 1200 BC. In *Olmec Art and Archaeology in Mesoamerica*, ed. J. E. Clark and M. E. Pye, 169–92. Studies in the History of Art 58. Center for Advanced Study in the Visual Arts Symposium Papers 35. National Gallery of Art, Washington, D.C.

Overholtzer, Lisa Marie. 2005. The Kneeling Mexica Woman: Evidence for Male Domination or Gender Complementarity? Senior honors thesis, Department of Anthropology, University of California, Berkeley.

Severi, Carlo. 2002. Memory, Reflexivity, and Belief: Reflections on the Ritual Use of Language. *Social Anthropology* 10: 23–40.

Shafer, Harry J. 1975. Clay Figurines from the Lower Pecos Region, Texas. *American Antiquity* 40: 148–58.

Sherzer, Joel. 1983. *Kuna Ways of Speaking: An Ethnographic Perspective.* University of Texas Press, Austin.

Soffer, Olga, Pamela Vandiver, Bohuslav Klima, and Jiri Svoboda. 1993. The Pyrotech-
    nology of Performance Art: Moravian Venuses and Wolverines. In *Before Lascaux:
    The Complex Record of the Early Upper Paleolithic,* ed. H. Knecht, A. Pike-Tay, and
    R. White, 259–76. CRC Press, Boca Raton, Fla.

Stone, Doris Z. 1941. *Archaeology of the North Coast of Honduras.* Memoirs of the Pea-
    body Museum of Archaeology and Ethnology, Harvard University, 9 (1). Peabody
    Museum, Cambridge, Mass.

Taussig, Michael. 1993. *Mimesis and Alterity.* Routledge, New York.

Turpin, Solveig A. 1990. Rock Art and Hunter-Gatherer Archaeology: A Case Study
    from SW Texas and Northern Mexico. *Journal of Field Archaeology* 17: 263–81.

Vandiver, Pamela, Olga Soffer, Bohuslav Klima, and Jiri Svoboda. 1989. The Origins of
    Ceramic Technology at Dolní Vĕstonice, Czechoslovakia. *Science* 246: 1002–8.

———. 1990. Venuses and Wolverines: The Origins of Ceramic Technology at Dolní
    Vĕstonice ca. 26,000 B.P. In *Ceramics and Civilization,* vol. 5, ed. W. D. Kingery,
    13–81. American Ceramics Society, Westville, Ohio.

Contributors

Jeffrey P. Blomster
George Washington University

Elizabeth M. Brumfiel
Northwestern University

David Cheetham
New World Archeological Foundation (Brigham Young University) Arizona
State University

Katherine A. Faust
University of California, Riverside

Billie J. A. Follensbee
Missouri State University

Aurore Giguet
Marjorie Barrick Museum, University of Nevada, Las Vegas

Christina T. Halperin
University of Illinois, Urbana-Champaign

Julia A. Hendon
Gettysburg College

Rosemary A. Joyce
University of California, Berkeley

Cecelia F. Klein
University of California, Los Angeles

Jeanne Lopiparo
University of California, Berkeley

Joyce Marcus
University of Michigan

Geoffrey G. McCafferty
University of Calgary

Sharisse D. McCafferty
University of Calgary

Lisa Overholtzer
Northwestern University

Alan R. Sandstrom
Indiana University–Purdue University Fort Wayne

Karl Taube
University of California, Riverside

Rhonda Taube
University of California, Riverside City College

Naoli Victoria Lona
Instituto Nacional de Antropología e Historia (INAH)

Index

Page numbers in italics refer to illustrations.